Emmins on Sentencing

Third Edition

Martin Wasik, LLB, MA

of Gray's Inn, Barrister
Professor of Law, Manchester University

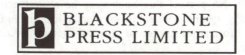
BLACKSTONE PRESS LIMITED

First published in Great Britain 1993 by Blackstone Press Limited,
Aldine Place, London W12 8AA. Telephone 0181-740 2277

ISBN: 1 85431 681 8

Previously published under the title *A Practical Approach to Sentencing*

British Library Cataloguing in Publication Data
A CIP catalogue record for this book is available from the British Library

Typeset by Style Photosetting Ltd, Mayfield, East Sussex
Printed by Ashford Colour Press, Gosport, Hants

Contents

Emmins on
Sentencing

13 Appeals, Rehabilitation and Pardon   377

13.1 Appeal against sentence passed by a magistrates' court   13.2 Appeal by offender against sentence passed by the Crown Court   13.3 Reference by Attorney-General in respect of sentence passed by the Crown Court   13.4 Appeal to House of Lords against sentence   13.5 Disqualifications upon conviction   13.6 Rehabilitation of offenders 13.7 Pardon and release on compassionate grounds

Preface

In the five years since the second edition of this book there have been considerable changes to the law on sentencing. The main statutory changes are summarised at pp. 50–51 below. There are now nearly 250 appellate decisions reported annually in the *Criminal Appeal Reports (Sentencing)*, not to mention others reported in the *Criminal Law Review* and elsewhere. Suffice it to say that every part of the book has required substantial revision. At the time of writing, the Crime (Sentences) Act 1997, which was brought into effect at the end of 1997 and the beginning of 1998, is beginning to have an effect on sentencing practice. The Crime and Disorder Bill currently before Parliament will bring in further substantial changes to sentencing. I have included reference to the main provisions in the Bill where appropriate. The latest version of the Bill available to me was the version ordered by the House of Commons, to be printed 1 April 1998.

There has been much pressure recently for consolidation of sentencing legislation. This has come both from the senior judiciary (see, for example, the comments of Lord Bingham CJ in *Street* [1997] 2 Cr App R (S) 309 at p. 311) and from academics (see, for example, David Thomas at [1997] *Criminal Law Review* 406). The Law Commission is currently working to that end. There can be no doubt that consolidation and restatement will have value in this area, where successive rapid amendments to earlier legislation have left the law in a state of some disarray. Consolidation, however desirable, cannot affect the principles which underlie sentencing, and where these are unclear or are in open conflict with each other, more fundamental rationalisation is required. Sentencing policy has become the playground for political gesturing, with constant switches of direction. The secure training order, which appeared on the statute book after publication of the 2nd edition of this book, is to be repealed by the CDB after being in force for only a few months. See further, Appendix 1. The sentencing of dangerous offenders is now an area of great complexity which, looked at in the round, can bear no rational explanation. The requirement in the Crime (Sentences) Act 1997 that a life sentence be imposed for the second 'serious offence', and that a minimum custodial sentence be imposed for repeat Class A drug trafficking, compounds an already complex sentencing choice between long determinate sentences, longer-than-normal sentences and discretionary life sentences.

Work on this edition was completed in mid February 1998 although I have been able to incorporate a few subsequent changes. I have tried to describe and explain the law as clearly as possible, but this has not always been easy since the obscurities are there and cannot be ignored. As always, I am grateful to the publishers for their efficiency, encouragement and, above all, their patience.

Preface to the First Edition

The sentencing of offenders is a subject which may be considered from many different points of view. There is the high philosophical approach, which seeks to explain and provide a moral justification for the infliction of punishment by society upon offenders. There is the criminological and sociological approach, which describes what the various forms of sentence entail as far as the person undergoing the sentence is concerned, and may also suggest what sentences are the most effective in deterring and/or reforming criminals. There is the approach which concentrates upon the decisions of the Court of Appeal, seeking to extract from those decisions an approved sentencing pattern for common types of crime. All these approaches are, of course, of great value, and the third especially is of considerable relevance to this book. However, my aim in writing is not encapsulated within any of the aforementioned approaches to sentencing. My aim is to describe, from a practical point of view, how offenders are sentenced in the Crown Court, magistrates' courts and juvenile courts; what procedures are gone through after conviction and before sentence is pronounced; what possible avenues of appeal are open to an offender who considers himself harshly treated; what powers of sentence are available to the courts and how they are likely, in practice, to exercise those powers. As Parliament has placed an ever more varied and complicated array of sentencing powers at the disposal of sentencers, so the need for a straightforward exposition of those powers has increased. It is my hope that this book will provide such an exposition, and will be of interest and value to students, to practitioners (especially the young ones who have not yet had time to learn by experience anything that these pages may be able to teach) and even, perhaps, to some sentencers.

Now is a particularly apt time to bring out a work on sentencing. Parliament has been especially active in the field in recent years, completely re-shaping the structure of sentences for young offenders; introducing a new form of sentence (part-suspended imprisonment) for offenders over 21, and making a host of other less important, but still significant, changes. In addition, the Court of Appeal has sought to influence sentencing at first instance more directly and forcefully than had hitherto been its practice. It has, for example, recommended a general reduction in the lengths of prison sentences for certain categories of crime, while for other offences (e.g. causing death by reckless driving and importing drugs) it has established sentencing brackets within which the penalty should normally fall. These developments are fully explained in the text. It was, in fact, written in the summer of 1984, and seeks to state the law as it then was, although I have been able to incorporate developments occurring up until late autumn.

My thanks are due, and gladly given, to a large number of people who have helped in the writing of what follows. Especially, I would like to thank those involved in various ways with sentencing who have answered my many questions on sentencing matters, and given much valuable background information. Particular mention must be made of the magistrates' court clerks, studying for their Bar Finals at the Inns of Court School of Law, who spared time from their revision to talk with me about sentencing practice in the courts where they work. My thanks as well to my publishers for their hard work and friendliness, and to all others involved in the production of the book. Finally, my thanks to my father for bearing patiently with the incessant clatter of typewriter keys, for making innumerable cups of tea, and for enabling me to concentrate all my energies upon writing.

Table of Cases

Table of Statutes

Table of Statutory Instruments

Table of Home Office Circulars

List of Abbreviations

BA	Bail Act
CA	Courts Act
CAA	Criminal Appeal Act
CDB	Crime and Disorder Bill
CICB	Criminal Injuries Compensation Board
CJA	Criminal Justice Act
CJPOA	Criminal Justice and Public Order Act
CLA	Criminal Law Act
CPIA	Criminal Procedure and Investigations Act
CPS	Crown Prosecution Service
C(S)A	Crime (Sentences) Act
CSP	*Current Sentencing Practice*
CYPA	Children and Young Persons Act
DPP	Director of Public Prosecutions
DSS	Department of Social Security
DTA	Drug Trafficking Act
DVLA	Driver and Vehicle Licensing Authority
FSA	Football Spectators Act
HMSO	Her Majesty's Stationery Office
IA	Immigration Act
MCA	Magistrates' Courts Act
MDA	Misuse of Drugs Act
MHA	Mental Health Act
MHRT	mental health review tribunal
NACRO	National Association for the Care and Resettlement of Offenders
OAPA	Offences against the Person Act
PACE	Police and Criminal Evidence Act
PCA	Proceeds of Crime Act
PCCA	Powers of Criminal Courts Act
POA	Prosecution of Offences Act
PSD	petty sessional division
RMO	responsible medical officer
ROA	Rehabilitation of Offenders Act
RTA	Road Traffic Act
RTOA	Road Traffic Offenders Act
SCA	Supreme Court Act
SOA	Sexual Offences Act

1 Introduction

Any attempt to describe the current body of sentencing law and sentencing principles must begin by acknowledging that the bulk and complexity of this topic have increased dramatically in recent years. This was made all the more challenging by the passing of the Criminal Justice Act 1991 (CJA 1991), which required all those involved in sentencing to re-think their assumptions about the subject. The aims of this chapter are as follows:

(a) To outline the current sentencing arrangements in England and Wales, describing those courts which, and those individuals who, are given the power to pass sentence upon persons convicted of criminal offences.

(b) To consider the range of aims which are traditionally associated with sentencing. A detailed discussion of sentencing philosophy lies outside the scope of this book, but without some explanation of that important debate modern developments in sentencing law and practice cannot fully be understood.

(c) To consider the existing legal framework for sentencing. This is an amalgam of statutory provision, appellate decisions and administrative and practical arrangements. The CJA 1991 represented a watershed in this context, and all the sentencing law and sentencing principles set out in this book must be seen against that background.

A reader wishing to gain an overview of the sentencing system should begin here. Someone already familiar with that system, or someone investigating a specific sentencing issue such as the powers available to the courts to pass a community service order, may prefer to start at the relevant section of the book. But, in the end, it is suggested, the detailed information can only be fully understood in the context of the material in this chapter.

Sentencing is closely connected with matters of criminal procedure. A general discussion of criminal procedure lies outside the scope of this book, although an outline of procedure as it directly affects sentencing is given in the following paragraphs. Readers seeking more detailed coverage are referred to *Emmins on Criminal Procedure*, by John Sprack.

1.1 AN OUTLINE OF PROCEDURE RELEVANT TO SENTENCING

Sentencing is about the way courts deal with a person *after* he has pleaded guilty or has been found guilty — in other words, it is about what happens from the moment when a person charged with an offence ceases to be merely 'the accused' and becomes 'the offender'.

1.1.1   Two methods of trial

Criminal trials in England and Wales take one of two forms — they are either summary trials or trials on indictment.

Summary trial takes place in a magistrates' court. The judges are magistrates (also known as 'justices of the peace'). Most magistrates are lay — i.e. unpaid — magistrates, but a minority are professional lawyers, paid a salary to work full-time as magistrates. The latter are known as 'stipendiaries'. A stipendiary may, and normally does, conduct a summary trial sitting alone, but a single lay magistrate has no jurisdiction to try a case. In fact a lay bench normally comprises three magistrates, although two is sufficient. The magistrates (whether lay or stipendiary) are assisted by a court clerk, who will be qualified as either a barrister or solicitor or will hold a Diploma in Magisterial Law. The clerk advises the magistrates on the law but must not otherwise interfere with their decisions.

A summary trial commences with the charge or *information* being put to the accused by the clerk. For this reason summary trial is also known as 'trial on information'. Where it is alleged that two or more persons acted together to commit an offence they may be jointly charged in one information, and will normally be tried together. This applies whether they were joint principal offenders or aiders and abettors or a combination thereof. An information must allege only one offence, but two or more informations may be tried together if *either* the accused (or all the accused where there is more than one) consent *or* the magistrates think that the informations are linked together so that the interests of justice are best served by a single trial. If the accused pleads guilty to the information, there is no need for evidence about the offence to be called, and the magistrates commence the procedures leading up to sentence being pronounced. If the accused pleads not guilty, the prosecution makes a short opening speech; the prosecution witnesses are called, each witness being first questioned 'in chief' by the prosecution legal representative and then cross-examined by the defence; the defence may, if they so wish, submit that there is no prima facie case against the accused, and if the magistrates agree they acquit forthwith; if no such submission is made or if one is made unsuccessfully, the defence may (but need not) call witnesses who may (but need not) include the accused; after the defence evidence (if any) the defence legal representative makes a closing speech and then the magistrates announce their verdict.

Trial on indictment takes place in the Crown Court. In legal theory the Crown Court is a single court, but in fact it sits in 91 different locations scattered throughout the country, the status of the locations depending on whether High Court judges sit there and whether there are facilities for civil as well as criminal work. The trial on indictment is nearly always preceded by *committal proceedings* which take place in a magistrates' court. The magistrates (who for these purposes are referred to as 'examining justices') receive the evidence the prosecution wish to put forward against the accused, and decide whether it discloses a prima facie case against that person in respect of any indictable offence, not necessarily the charge which was originally brought (see **1.1.2** for the meaning of 'indictable offence'). If there is no case to answer, the examining justices discharge the accused; if there is a case, they commit (i.e. send) the accused to the Crown Court to be tried. The committal may be in custody or on bail, at the examining justices' discretion.

Once the accused has been committed for trial an *indictment* is drawn up. This is done by a representative of the Crown Prosecution Service (CPS). An indictment contains one or more *counts*, each count charging the accused with a single indictable offence. The person drafting the indictment reads through the committal statements and includes counts for those offences which are disclosed by the evidence in the statements. The indictment is not restricted to counts for offences with which the accused was charged at the police station or in respect of which the examining justices found there was a case to answer. In general, an indictment should contain sufficient counts to represent fairly the criminal conduct alleged against the accused — it is not good practice, in a case where one piece of criminal conduct could be said to amount in law to several offences of roughly equivalent gravity, to include counts for all the offences. Ultimately, though, it is for the person drafting the indictment to decide whether an extra count would genuinely add something to the prosecution case or would merely overload the indictment.

A single count may allege that two or more persons committed an offence jointly, and there is no need to distinguish between principal offenders and aiders or abettors. Two or more counts against one accused may be put into one indictment provided the relevant offences are either founded on the same facts or comprise or form part of a series of offences of the same or a similar character. 'Founded on the same facts' covers cases where several offences are committed in a continuous piece of conduct (for example, if the accused opened a locked car door by use of a piece of wire, drove the car off without the owner's consent and, when spotted by a police car, drove at 60 mph on the wrong side of the road, one indictment could include counts for going equipped for theft, taking a motor vehicle without lawful authority and dangerous driving). In the example given the prosecution would seek convictions on all three counts, but two or more counts are also appropriate in cases where the prosecution are not sure which of several offences the accused is guilty of and merely seek a conviction on one count. Thus, if the prosecution case is that the accused pushed a glass into the victim's face causing a cut to the cheek which required 10 stitches, the evidence prima facie might justify a conviction either for the serious offence of wounding with intent to cause grievous bodily harm contrary to s. 18 of the Offences against the Person Act 1861 or for the less serious offence of unlawful wounding contrary to s. 20 of the 1861 Act. The indictment may include counts for both offences so that the jury can decide on which, if either, count to convict. Counts for assault occasioning actual bodily harm and common assault would not be justified because they would add nothing to the count for unlawful wounding, even though the prosecution evidence suggests that the accused is guilty of both offences (see the preceding paragraph on not overloading the indictment).

The second limb of the rule that counts may be included in one indictment if the offences are/form part of a series of offences of the same or a similar character has been generously interpreted by the courts. To be similar within the meaning of the rule, offences must be similar both legally and factually. Yet counts may be legally similar even though they allege contravention of different statutory provisions (see *Ludlow* v *Metropolitan Police Commissioner* [1971] AC 29 where the House of Lords approved joinder of counts for robbery and attempted theft on the basis that both offences involved the element of theft). As to factual similarity, *Ludlow* shows that even a tenuous link in the time, place, mode of commission etc. of the offences will satisfy the rule. Finally, it should be noted that even when the joinder of counts and/or defendants in a single indictment is legally justified the trial judge has a discretion to sever the indictment and order separate trials if a single trial would prejudice or embarrass the defence.

A trial on indictment begins with the clerk of court putting the counts in the indictment to the accused. If the plea is guilty to all counts, the court embarks upon the procedures leading up to the pronouncement of sentence. By pleading guilty the accused does not necessarily concede that the committal statements are entirely correct. A count merely sets out the bare essentials of the prosecution case, giving the name of the offence (e.g. 'Theft contrary to s.1(1) of the Theft Act 1968') and particulars of the offence (e.g. 'John Brown, on the 24th day of December 1997, stole a turkey belonging to Spencer and Marks Ltd'). The count says nothing about the *way* the offence was committed. Thus, if the committal statements indicate that John Brown stole the turkey by a sophisticated method suggesting that he is a 'professional' shoplifter, it is nevertheless open to the defence to argue that he stole on the spur of the moment, in a blatant and amateurish way.

If the accused pleads not guilty to all the counts in the indictment a jury is sworn in to try the case. A jury consists of 12 men and women, drawn largely at random from a wide (but not complete) cross-section of the adult population aged between 18 and 70. Generally jurors are summoned to attend at the Crown Court for a fortnight's jury service, and that may well be their only experience of the criminal courts. Their function is to bring in, at the end of the case, verdicts of guilty, not guilty or (sometimes) guilty of a lesser offence. They bring in a separate verdict in respect of each count in the indictment and each accused charged in a count. Of course, it is open to them to acquit on one count and convict on another, or they may acquit one accused and convict the other. Where the indictment charges an accused with offences of differing degrees of gravity arising out of one incident, the fact that the jury convict only on the less serious alternative has a considerable bearing on the appropriate sentence. The course of the trial is controlled by a professional Crown Court judge. The judge decides all questions of law and procedure which may arise (e.g. whether evidence is admissible and whether the indictment should be amended). The sequence of events is essentially the same as at a summary trial, save that the prosecution have a closing as well as an opening speech and the defence also sometimes have two speeches. After closing speeches and before the jury retire to consider their verdict, the judge sums up the case to the jury, telling them what the relevant law is and reminding them of the evidence they have heard. It will be apparent that a judge can have a considerable influence on the outcome of a case, but the fact remains that only the jury — not the judge — can find an accused guilty. It follows that if the jury convict an accused of only one offence out of several on the indictment the judge must sentence on the basis that the offence of which the accused has been convicted is the only offence the offender has committed, even if the judge thinks that the jury's verdict was perverse and the offender quite obviously committed all the offences alleged against him. As implied above, sentences in the Crown Court are determined by a Crown Court judge, sometimes assisted by lay magistrates. The jury's active role finishes the moment they have pronounced their verdict.

If the accused pleads guilty to some, but not all, of the counts on the indictment the prosecution have a choice. They can either agree not to proceed on the counts denied by the accused, arguing that the accused can properly and fairly be sentenced on the basis of the admitted offences, or they can insist that a jury be sworn in to try the not guilty pleas, in which case the guilty pleas still stand and the accused may be sentenced for those matters whatever the outcome of the jury trial. If the accused is considering pleading guilty to part of the indictment, defence counsel usually mentions the possibility to prosecuting counsel, who will indicate whether the proposed pleas are acceptable to the prosecution or not. If they are not, the accused might well decide to plead not guilty to the whole indictment. If they are, it is the general practice to ask the judge in private whether the proposed course is a suitable way of dealing with the case. Should the judge disapprove of the proposal the prosecution would almost certainly proceed on the whole indictment.

A final option sometimes open to the accused is to plead not guilty to the offence alleged in a count but guilty of some other (lesser) indictable offence which is expressly or impliedly included in the wording of the count (see Criminal Law Act 1967, s.6, as explained in

Wilson [1984] AC 242). It is clear, for example, that an accused may plead not guilty of murder but guilty of manslaughter; not guilty of robbery but guilty of theft; not guilty of rape but guilty of indecent assault, or not guilty of burglary by entering as a trespasser and stealing but guilty of theft. If the accused does tender such a plea the prosecution may reject it and insist that the accused be tried for the offence alleged in the count — the plea of guilty to a lesser offence is then impliedly withdrawn and a not guilty plea entered on behalf of the accused. Even if the prosecution are willing to accept a plea to a lesser offence the judge may refuse to allow it if it is considered that the evidence in the committal statements shows the accused to be guilty as charged. In all cases where the accused offered or could have offered a plea to a lesser offence the jury, on a not guilty plea, may find the accused not guilty as charged but guilty of the lesser offence (e.g. not guilty of murder, but guilty of manslaughter etc.).

Three simple points relevant to sentencing emerge from the above brief description of trial procedures. First, an offender is often sentenced on one occasion for several offences. This follows from the fact that the rules governing joinder of counts in one indictment and joint trial of several informations in the magistrates' courts frequently result in a single jury or a single bench of magistrates convicting an accused of a number of offences. Second, if the accused pleads not guilty, the sentencer (the Crown Court judge presiding over a trial on indictment or the bench of magistrates trying a case summarily) will hear evidence about the facts of the offence during the trial of the not guilty plea, whereas, if the accused pleads guilty, very limited information will be available at this stage about the offence. Third, the court has no control over the charges laid against the accused since it is the prosecution who are responsible for the laying of informations and the drafting of indictments. The judge's role in this context is essentially negative. The judge can prevent the prosecution dropping their case on the indictment as originally drafted in exchange for a plea of guilty to a lesser offence or a plea of guilty to some but not all the counts, but the judge cannot force the prosecution to put extra or more serious counts into the indictment even if as drafted it seems to under-represent the extent of the accused's criminal conduct.

1.2 AN OVERVIEW OF SENTENCING

1.2.1 What is a sentence?

At the end of a trial, the Crown Court judge or chairman of the bench of magistrates announces 'The sentence of the court is . . .', and then proceeds to specify how the convicted offender will be dealt with for his offence. The phrase 'the sentence of the court' is so familiar that we rarely pause to ask just what is meant by the word 'sentence'. A moment's reflection will show that defining the term is not as straightforward as it initally appears.

There is no statutory or case law definition of 'sentence' which is of general application. It is not, for example, a term defined in the Interpretation Act 1978. Certainly it must include the punishment, such as a fine or a custodial sentence, which the court imposes upon an offender for the offence. It should also include orders imposed upon the offender on conviction which cannot properly be described as punishments: a hospital order is a good example. Most lawyers would say that it should also include other orders which the court may make at the same time as imposing the punishment. These 'ancillary orders' are made against the offender to benefit individuals who have suffered loss or have been put to expense by reason of the offence. Examples are compensation orders and orders to pay costs. In this book the term 'sentence' is to be understood in the broad sense indicated here. Such a meaning is consistent with s. 50 of the Criminal Appeal Act 1968 (CAA 1968). Section 50 provides that, for the purposes of the CAA 1968 (which deals *inter alia* with the right to appeal to the Court of Appeal against sentence) 'sentence . . . includes any order made by a court when dealing with an offender including a hospital order . . . and a recommendation for deportation'. Thus s. 50 defines sentence to include punishments, orders in lieu of punishment and ancillary orders.

Wide though this definition is, there are a number of orders which a court may make against an offender which do not come within it. First, when a murderer is sentenced to life imprisonment, the judge may recommend that he serve a minimum term in prison before being considered for early release. It has been held that such a recommendation is not a sentence for the purposes of an appeal against sentence because it is not binding on the Parole Board, and so is not an order of the court (*Aitken* [1966] 1 WLR 1076). This stands in contrast with the power which a sentencer has to recommend the minimum period to be served by a discretionary life sentence prisoner, under C(S)A 1997, s. 28, which can be the subject of an appeal. Second, when a court orders that a legally aided offender pays a contribution to the costs incurred by the legal aid fund in providing him with representation, that is not part of the sentence because even an acquitted defendant may be ordered to make such a contribution (see *Raeburn* (1982) 74 Cr App R 21).

TABLE 1   MAXIMUM TERMS OF IMPRISONMENT

The primary purpose of this table is to indicate the maximum terms of imprisonment available for the most commonly encountered imprisonable offences. In addition the table shows whether the offences listed in it are triable only on indictment, triable either way, or triable only summarily. If there is an entry in column 3 but not in column 4 the offence is triable only on indictment; if there are entries in both columns 3 and 4 the offence is triable either way, and if there is an entry only in column 4 the offence is triable only summarily. Only a few summary offences appear in the table because the great majority of summary offences are non-imprisonable.

Offence	Statutory provision creating the offence [1]	Maximum prison term on indictment	Maximum prison term on summary conviction	Statutory provisions fixing maximum prison term [2]
HOMICIDE				
1. Manslaughter[3]	Common law	Life	—	OAPA 1861, s. 5
2. Infanticide	Infanticide Act 1938, s. 1	Life	—	Infanticide Act 1938, s. 1
3. Child destruction	Infant Life (Preservation) Act 1929, s. 1(1)	Life	—	Infant Life (Preservation) Act, s. 1(1)
4. Causing death by dangerous driving	Road Traffic Act 1988, s. 1	10 years	—	RTOA 1988, sch. 2
5. Causing death by careless driving while under the influence of drink or drugs	Road Traffic Act 1988, s. 3A	10 years	—	RTOA 1988, sch. 2
OFFENCES OF VIOLENCE				
6. Causing grievous bodily harm/ wounding with intent	OAPA 1861, s. 18	Life	—	OAPA 1861, s. 18
7. Administering poison with intent to endanger life	OAPA 1861, s. 23	10 years	—	OAPA 1861, s. 23
8. Administering poison with intent to injure	OAPA 1861, s. 24	5 years	—	OAPA 1861, s. 24
9. Unlawful wounding	OAPA 1861, s. 20	5 years	6 months	OAPA 1861, s. 20 and MCA 1980, s. 17
10. Assault occasioning actual bodily harm	OAPA 1861, s. 47	5 years	6 months	OAPA 1861, s. 47 and MCA 1980, s. 17
11. Assault with intent to resist arrest	OAPA 1861, s. 38	2 years	6 months	OAPA 1861, s. 38 and MCA 1980, s. 17

	Offence	Statutory provision creating the offence[1]	Maximum prison term on indictment	Maximum prison term on summary conviction	Statutory provisions fixing maximum prison term[2]
12.	Common assault and battery	CJA 1988, s. 39	—	6 months	CJA 1988, s. 39
13.	Assault on P.C. in execution of his duty	Police Act 1996, s. 89	—	6 months	Police Act 1996, s. 89
	SEXUAL OFFENCES				
14.	Rape	SOA 1956, s. 1	Life	—	SOA 1956, s. 37 and sch. 2
15.	Sexual intercourse with a girl under 13	SOA 1956, s. 5	Life	—	SOA 1956, s. 37 and sch. 2
16.	Sexual intercourse with a girl under 16	SOA 1956, s. 6	2 years	6 months	SOA 1956, s. 37 and sch. 2
17.	Incest	SOA 1956, ss. 10 and 11	7 years[4]	—	SOA 1956, s. 37 and sch. 2
18.	Indecent assault on a woman	SOA 1956, s. 14	10 years	6 months	SOA 1956, s. 37 and sch. 2 and MCA 1980, s. 17
19.	Buggery with a person under 16 or with an animal	SOA 1956, s. 12	Life	—	SOA 1956, s. 37 and sch. 2
20.	Buggery by a person aged 21 or over of a person aged under 18	SOA 1956, s. 12	5 years	—	SOA 1967, s. 3
21.	Buggery between persons aged 18 or over[5]	SOA 1956, s. 12	2 years	—	SOA 1967, s. 3
22.	Gross indecency between men[5]	SOA 1956, s. 13	2 years[6]	6 months	SOA 1956, s. 37 and sch. 2 and MCA 1980, s. 17
23.	Indecent assault on a man	SOA 1956, s. 15	10 years	6 months	SOA 1956, s. 37 and sch. 2
24.	Indecency with a child under 14	Indecency with Children Act 1960, s. 1	10 years	6 months	Indecency with Children Act 1960, s. 1; Crime (Sentences) Act 1997, s. 52
25.	Taking, distributing, publishing etc. indecent photographs of children	Protection of Children Act 1978, s. 1	3 years	6 months	Protection of Children Act 1978, s. 6
26.	Living on earnings of prostitution	SOA 1956, s. 30	7 years	6 months	SOA 1956, s. 37 and sch. 2
	OFFENCES OF DISHONESTY				
27.	Robbery	Theft Act 1968, s. 8(1)	Life	—	Theft Act 1968, s. 8(2)

No.	Offence	Statute	Maximum on indictment	Summary	Statute
28.	Assault with intent to rob	Theft Act 1968, s. 8(2)	Life	—	Theft Act 1968, s. 8(2)
29.	Blackmail	Theft Act 1968, s. 21(1)	14 years	—	Theft Act 1968, s. 21(3)
30.	Aggravated burglary	Theft Act 1968, s. 10(1)	Life	—	Theft Act 1968, s. 10(2)
31.	Burglary of a dwelling[7]	Theft Act 1968, s. 9(1)	14 years	6 months	Theft Act 1968, s. 9(3) and MCA 1980, s. 17
32.	Burglary of a building other than a dwelling	Theft Act 1968, s. 9(1)	10 years	6 months	Theft Act 1968, s. 9(3) and MCA 1980, s. 17
33.	Handling stolen goods	Theft Act 1968, s. 22(1)	14 years	6 months	Theft Act 1968, s. 22(2) and MCA 1980, s. 17
34.	Theft	Theft Act 1968, s. 1	7 years	6 months	Theft Act 1968, s. 7 and MCA 1980, s. 17
35.	Obtaining property by deception	Theft Act 1968, s. 15(1)	10 years	6 months	Theft Act 1968, s. 15(1) and MCA 1980, s. 17
36.	Obtaining services by deception	Theft Act 1978, s. 1	5 years	6 months	Theft Act 1978, s. 4
37.	Evasion of liability by deception	Theft Act 1978, s. 2	5 years	6 months	Theft Act 1978, s. 4
38.	Making off without payment	Theft Act 1978, s. 3	2 years	6 months	Theft Act 1978, s. 4
39.	Forgery and using a forged instrument	Forgery and Counterfeiting Act 1981, ss. 1 and 3	10 years	6 months	Forgery and Counterfeiting Act 1981, s. 6
40.	Possession of certain specified forged instruments[8]	Forgery and Counterfeiting Act 1981, s. 5(2)	2 years	6 months	Forgery and Counterfeiting Act 1981, s. 6
41.	Counterfeiting currency notes or protected coins and passing or tendering such notes or coin[9]	Forgery and Counterfeiting Act 1981, ss. 14(1) and 15(1)	10 years	6 months	Forgery and Counterfeiting Act 1981, s. 22
42.	Taking a motor vehicle without the owner's consent	Theft Act 1968, s. 12(1)	—	6 months	Theft Act 1968, s. 12(2)
43.	Aggravated vehicle taking[10]	Theft Act 1968, s. 12A	2 years (but 5 years if death results)	6 months	Theft Act 1968, s. 12A

Offence	*Statutory provision creating the offence*[1]	*Maximum prison term on indictment*	*Maximum prison term on summary conviction*	*Statutory provisions fixing maximum prison term*[2]
44. Interfering with a motor vehicle	Criminal Attempts Act 1981, s. 9(1)	—	3 months	Criminal Attempts Act 1981, s. 9(3)
45. Going equipped for burglary, theft or cheat	Theft Act 1968, s. 25(1)	3 years	6 months	Theft Act 1968, s. 25(2) and MCA 1980, s. 17
OFFENCES OF DAMAGE TO PROPERTY				
46. Destroying/damaging property where damage is more than £5,000	Criminal Damage Act 1971, s. 1(1)	10 years	6 months	Criminal Damage Act 1971, s. 4(2) and MCA 1980, s. 17
47. Destroying/damaging property where damage is not more than £5,000[11]	Criminal Damage Act 1971, s. 1(1)	—	3 months	Criminal Damage Act 1971, s. 4(2) and MCA 1980, s. 22 and sch. 2
48. Arson[12]	Criminal Damage Act 1971, s. 1(3)	Life	6 months	Criminal Damage Act 1971, s. 4(1) and MCA 1980, s. 17
49. Destroying/damaging property with intent etc. to endanger life	Criminal Damage Act 1971, s. 1(2)	Life	—	Criminal Damage Act 1971, s. 4(2)
OFFENCES AGAINST PUBLIC ORDER				
50. Riot	Public Order Act 1986, s. 1	10 years	—	Public Order Act 1986, s. 1(6)
51. Violent disorder	Public Order Act 1986, s. 2	5 years	6 months	Public Order Act 1986, s. 2(5)
52. Affray	Public Order Act 1986, s. 3	3 years	6 months	Public Order Act 1986, s. 3(7)
53. Fear or provocation of violence	Public Order Act 1986, s. 4	—	6 months	Public Order Act 1986, s. 4(4)
54. Intentionally causing harassment, alarm or distress	Public Order Act 1986, s. 4A	—	6 months	Public Order Act 1986, s. 4A
55. Harassment, putting person in fear of violence (stalking)	Protection from Harassment Act 1997, s. 4	5 years	6 months	Protection from Harassment Act 1997, s. 4

No.	Offence	Statute	Maximum on indictment	Maximum summary	Statute
56.	Harassment (stalking)	Protection from Harassment Act 1997, s. 2	—	6 months	Protection from Harassment Act 1997, s. 2
57.	Bomb hoax	Criminal Law Act 1977, s. 51(1)	7 years	6 months	Criminal Law Act 1977, s. 51(4)
58.	Contamination of goods	Public Order Act 1986, s. 38(1)	10 years	6 months	Public Order Act 1986, s. 38(4)
59.	Stirring up racial hatred	Public Order Act 1986, s. 18	2 years	6 months	Public Order Act 1986, s. 27(3)
	OFFENCES AGAINST ADMINISTRATION OF JUSTICE				
60.	Perverting the course of justice	Common law	Life	—	Common law
61.	Intimidation of witness, juror etc.	Criminal Justice and Public Order Act 1994, s. 51	5 years	6 months	Criminal Justice and Public Order Act 1994, s. 51
62.	Perjury	Perjury Act 1911, s. 1(1)	7 years	—	Perjury Act 1911, s. 1(1)
63.	Wasting police time	Criminal Law Act 1967, s. 5(2)	—	6 months	Criminal Law Act 1967, s. 5(2)
64.	Escape from legal custody	Common law	Life	—	Common law
65.	Assisting offenders[13]	Criminal Law Act 1967, s. 4(1)	3–10 years depending on the offence committed by the offender assisted	6 months	Criminal Law Act 1967, s. 4(3) and MCA 1980, s. 17
	DRUGS OFFENCES				
66.	Possessing a controlled drug in:	MDA 1971, s. 5(2)			MDA 1971, sch. 4
	Class A		7 years	6 months	
	Class B		5 years	3 months	
	Class C		2 years	3 months	
67.	Supplying/offering to supply a controlled drug and being in possession with intent to supply:	MDA 1971, ss. 4(3) and 5(3)			MDA 1971, sch. 4
	Class A		Life	6 months	
	Class B		14 years	6 months	
	Class C		5 years	3 months	

Offence	Statutory provision creating the offence[1]	Maximum prison term on indictment	Maximum prison term on summary conviction	Statutory provisions fixing maximum prison term[2]
DRIVING OFFENCES				
68. Dangerous driving	Road Traffic Act 1988, s. 2	2 years	6 months	RTOA 1988, sch. 2
69. Driving while disqualified	Road Traffic Act 1988, s. 103	—	6 months	RTOA 1988, sch. 2
70. Driving while unfit through drink or drugs	Road Traffic Act 1988, s. 4(1)	—	6 months	RTOA 1988, sch. 2
71. Being in charge of a motor vehicle when unfit through drink or drugs	Road Traffic Act 1988, s. 4(2)	—	3 months	RTOA 1988, sch. 2
72. Driving with excess alcohol in breath, blood or urine	Road Traffic Act 1988, s. 5(1)(a)	—	6 months	RTOA 1988, sch. 2
73. Being in charge of a motor vehicle with excess alcohol in breath, blood or urine	Road Traffic Act 1988, s. 5(1)(b)	—	3 months	RTOA 1988, sch. 2
74. Failing to provide specimen for analysis	Road Traffic Act 1988, s. 7	—	6 months[14]	RTOA 1988, sch. 2
OFFENCES CONCERNING WEAPONS				
75. Possession of firearm with intent to endanger life	Firearms Act 1968, s. 16	Life	—	Firearms Act 1968, sch. 6
76. Use of firearm to resist arrest	Firearms Act 1968, s. 17(1)	Life	—	Firearms Act 1968, sch. 6
77. Carrying firearm with intent to commit indictable offence	Firearms Act 1968, s. 18(1)	Life	—	Firearms Act 1968, sch. 6
78. Carrying loaded firearm in a public place	Firearms Act 1968, s. 19	7 years	6 months	Firearms Act 1968, sch. 6
79. Shortening a shotgun	Firearms Act 1968, s. 4(1)	7 years	6 months	Firearms Act 1968, sch. 6
80. Possessing a firearm without holding a firearm certificate	Firearms Act 1968, s. 1(1)	5 years[15]	6 months	Firearms Act 1968, sch. 6
81. Having an offensive weapon in a public place	Prevention of Crime Act 1953, s. 1	4 years	6 months	Prevention of Crime Act 1953, s. 1
82. Having article with blade or point in public place	CJA 1988, s. 139	—	6 months	CJA 1988, s. 139

MISCELLANEOUS

No.	Offence	Statute	Maximum on indictment	Maximum on summary conviction	Reference
83.	Bigamy	OAPA 1861, s. 57	7 years	6 months	OAPA 1861, s. 57 and MCA 1980, s. 17
84.	Communicating etc. information useful to an enemy	Official Secrets Act 1911, s. 1	14 years	—	Official Secrets Act 1911, s. 8(1)
85.	Disclosure of security information entrusted in confidence	Official Secrets Act 1989, s. 1	2 years	6 months	Official Secrets Act 1989, s. 10(1)
86.	Prison mutiny	Prison Security Act 1992, s. 1	10 years	—	Prison Security Act 1992, s. 1
87.	Obstructing a police officer in the execution of his duty	Police Act 1996, s. 89	—	1 month	Police Act 1996, s. 89
88.	Attempt to commit an indictable offence	Criminal Attempts Act 1981, s. 1	The maximum is the maximum which can be imposed for the offence attempted[16]	The maximum is the maximum which can be imposed upon summary conviction for the offence attempted	Criminal Attempts Act 1981, s. 4(1)
89.	Conspiracy to commit an offence	Criminal Law Act 1977, s. 1	The maximum is the maximum which may be imposed for the offence to which the conspiracy related	—	CLA 1977, s. 3
90.	Conspiracy to defraud	Common law	10 years	—	CJA 1987, s. 12
91.	Aiding and abetting an offence	Common law	The maximum is the maximum which may be imposed upon the principal offender	The maximum is the maximum which may be imposed upon the principal offender upon summary conviction	Accessories and Abettors Act 1861, s. 8

Where a statute creates an indictable offence and states that it is punishable with imprisonment but does not specify a maximum term, an offender may be sentenced to up to 2 years' imprisonment following conviction on indictment (PCCA 1973, s. 18(1)).

Notes

1. Where the offence is not created by statute but is an offence at common law the words 'Common law' are entered in column 2. Similarly if the maximum sentence is, by reason of common law, one of life imprisonment, the words 'Common law' are entered in column 5.

2. A reference to 'MCA 1980, s. 17' indicates that the offence is triable either way by reason of being listed in sch. 1 to MCA 1980. The maximum term imposable on summary conviction will therefore be 6 months' imprisonment, as provided in MCA 1980, s. 32.

3. The sentence for murder is not included in this table because the table lists maximum terms of imprisonment which may be imposed, and the sentence for murder (life imprisonment if the offender is over 21) is a mandatory one in respect of which the sentencer has no discretion.

4. If the incest was with a girl under 13, and the offence is so charged in the indictment, life imprisonment may be imposed.

5. Of course, no offence is committed if the homosexual acts are between consenting parties aged 18 or over and in private. (See SOA 1967, s. 1.)

6. If the offender is aged 21 or over and the other party is under 18 imprisonment for up to 5 years may be imposed.

7. If the burglary comprises the commission of, or an intention to commit, an offence which is triable only on indictment, then the burglary is also triable only on indictment. Further, if the burglary is in a dwelling, and any person in the dwelling was subjected to violence or the threat of violence, the offence is triable only on indictment (MCA 1980, sch. 1, para. 28).

8. The offence under the Forgery and Counterfeiting Act 1981, s. 5(3) of having equipment to make the forged instruments which it is an offence under s. 5(2) to possess is punishable with up to 10 years' imprisonment following conviction on indictment, and up to 6 months summarily.

9. The lesser offence under the Forgery and Counterfeiting Act 1981, s. 14(2) of making counterfeit notes or coins without lawful authority is punishable with up to 2 years' imprisonment following conviction on indictment, and up to 6 months summarily.

10. The maximum penalty on indictment is increased to 5 years where it is proved that the accident caused the death of the person concerned.

11. This provision is not applicable to cases of arson.

12. Aggravated arson, contrary to the Criminal Damage Act 1971, s. 1(2) and s. 1(3) is triable only on indictment.

13. This offence is triable either way where the offence to which the assisting relates is triable either way.

14. Where the offender was required to provide a specimen to ascertain the proportion of alcohol in his breath, blood or urine at a time when he was in charge of a motor vehicle (but not driving or attempting to drive it), the maximum term of imprisonment which may be imposed is 3 months.

15. Or, where the firearm was a shortened shotgun, 7 years.

16. SOA 1956, sch. 2 makes the maximum penalty for attempts to commit certain offences under the Act lower than the maximum for the completed offence.

TABLE 2   A SUMMARY OF SENTENCING POWERS

Nature of punishment	Offences for which imposable	Age groups for which imposable	Procedural requirements	Maximum and minimum terms	Sanctions for failure to comply with order	Statutory Authorities
1 IMPRISONMENT Detention in prison for a period specified by the court when passing sentence. Imprisonment may be for a determinate period, or for life. The actual period which is served by the offender is crucially affected by the rules as to early release.	All common law offences are imprisonable; statutory offences are imprisonable if the statute creating the offence so provides in the section dealing with punishment for the offence. 'Imprisonable offence', therefore, means an offence which is punishable with imprisonment in the case of an adult. The offence of murder has a penalty which is 'fixed by law' as life imprisonment.	21 is the minimum age for a sentence of imprisonment; there is no maximum age.	(a) The offender must be given the opportunity of legal representation before sentence (unless he has already served a sentence of imprisonment). (b) A pre-sentence report is required, unless the court is of the view that it is 'unnecessary' to obtain one. (c) A custodial sentence cannot be imposed unless either (i) the offence, or the combination of the offence and one or more offences associated with it, was so serious that only such a sentence can be justified, or (ii) the offence is a violent or sexual offence and only such a sentence would be adequate to protect the public from serious harm, or (iii) the offender is unwilling to comply with requirements in a community order which by law require his agreement. (d) The length of a custodial sentence (apart from one the length of which is fixed by law), or which falls within the presumptive sentence provisions of the C(S)A 1997, shall be either (i) for such term as is commensurate with the seriousness of the offence and other offences associated with it, or (ii) where the offence is a violent or sexual offence, for such longer term as in the opinion of the court is necessary to protect the public from serious harm. (e) Reasons must be given in open court for imposing the sentence.	Common law offences are punishable with imprisonment for life. If a statutory offence is punishable with imprisonment the statute creating the offence specifies the maximum term imposable. There is no minimum term. Magistrates' courts are limited to a maximum of six months for any offence, or the statutory maximum for the offence, whichever is the less.	Escape from prison is a common law offence punishable by imprisonment and fine. Breach of prison rules may result in loss of privileges or the addition of extra time to the sentence length.	(a) PCCA 1973, s. 21 (legal representation); (b) CJA 1991, s. 3(1), as amended by CJPOA 1994 (pre-sentence report); (c) CJA 1991, s. 1(2) and (3), as amended by C(S)A 1997 (imposition of custody); (d) CJA 1991, s. 2(2), as amended by C(S)A 1997 (custodial sentence length); (e) CJA 1991, s. 1(4) (giving reasons).

Nature of punishment	Offences for which imposable	Age groups for which imposable	Procedural requirements	Maximum and minimum terms	Sanctions for failure to comply with order	Statutory Authorities
2 SUSPENDED SENTENCE						
A sentence of imprisonment which will not be served unless during a period fixed by the court (the operational period) the offender commits a further imprisonable offence.	All imprisonable offences except those for which the sentence is fixed by law.	As for 1.	(a) A suspended sentence may not be passed unless a sentence of immediate imprisonment would otherwise have been appropriate, and where suspension of the sentence can be justified by the exceptional circumstances of the case. (b) A pre-sentence report is required, unless the court is of the view that it is 'unnecessary' to obtain one. (c) Procedural requirements (c), (d) and (e) in relation to immediate imprisonment also apply to suspended sentences. (d) Whenever a court passes a suspended sentence, it must consider whether also to impose a fine or an order for compensation.	The term suspended must not exceed two years. The operational period must be not less than one and not more than two years.	If the offender is convicted of an imprisonable offence committed during the operational period of a suspended sentence, the normal consequence is that the suspended sentence is brought into effect for its full term in addition to any penalty for the later offence.	PCCA 1973. ss. 22–24.
3 DETENTION IN A YOUNG OFFENDER INSTITUTION						
Detention in a young offender institution may be for a determinate period specified by the court when passing sentence, or it may be custody for life. The actual period which is served by the offender is crucially affected by the rules as to early release.	All imprisonable offences. In the case of custody for life, any offence which carries life imprisonment as the maximum penalty for an adult, or where the sentence is fixed by law.	Offenders aged between 15 and 20 inclusive but, in the case of custody for life, offenders aged 18, 19 or 20.	(a) Procedural requirements (a) to (e) in relation to imprisonment also apply here, but (a) is not subject to the restriction given there. (b) A sentence of detention in a young offender institution cannot be suspended.	(a) The maximum for an offender aged 15, 16 or 17 is 24 months. The maximum for an offender aged 18, 19 or 20 is the same as the maximum sentence of imprisonment available in the case of an adult. (b) The minimum sentence for an offender aged 15,	Escape from detention in a young offender institution is a common law offence punishable with imprisonment and fine. Breach of young offender institution rules may result in loss of privileges or the addition of extra time to sentence length.	(a) CJA 1982, s. 1A and s. 1B (maximum and minimum terms); (b) CJA 1982, s. 3 (legal representation); (c) CJA 1991, s. 3(1), as amended by CJPOA 1994 (pre-sentence report); (d) CJA 1991, s. 1(2) and (3), as amended by C(S)A 1997 (imposition of

Sentence	Age	Qualifying offences	Notes	Maximum/length	Statutory references
				16 or 17 is 2 months. The minimum for an offender aged 18, 19 or 20 is 21 days.	custody); (e) CJA 1991, s. 2(2), as amended by C(S)A 1997 (custodial sentence length); (f) CJA 1991, s. 1(4) (reasons); (g) CJA 1982, s. 8 (custody for life).

4 DETENTION UNDER CYPA 1933, s. 53(2)

Sentence	Age	Qualifying offences	Notes	Maximum/length	Statutory references
Detention in accordance with the Home Secretary's directions (e.g. in local authority secure accommodation, young offender institution or prison). The actual period served by the offender is crucially affected by the rules as to early release.	Offenders aged between 10 and 17.	Offences which are punishable with 14 years' imprisonment or more, excluding murder but including indecent assault and (where the offender is 14 or more) causing death by dangerous driving or causing death by careless driving while under the influence of drink or drugs. An offender convicted of murder who was under 18 when he committed the offence must be sentenced to be detained at Her Majesty's pleasure, under CYPA 1933, s. 53(1).	(a) Powers under s. 53(2) are limited to conviction on indictment. (b) Procedural requirements (a) to (e) in relation to imprisonment also apply here, but (a) is not subject to the restriction given there. (c) Detention under s. 53(2) may be ordered only if all the other methods of dealing with the offender are unsuitable.	The maximum term is the maximum term of imprisonment to which the offender could be sentenced were he aged 21.	(a) CYPA 1933, s. 53(2) (general powers); (b) CJA 1982, s. 3 (legal representation); (c) CJA 1991, s. 3(1), as amended by CJPOA 1994 (pre-sentence report); (d) CJA 1991, s. 1(2) and (3), as amended by C(S)A 1997 (imposition of custody) (e) CJA 1991, s. 2(2), as amended by C(S)A 1997 (custodial sentence length); (f) CJA 1991, s. 1(4) (reasons).

Nature of punishment	Offences for which imposable	Age groups for which imposable	Procedural requirements	Maximum and minimum terms	Sanctions for failure to comply with order	Statutory Authorities
5 FINE Payment to the state of a sum of money fixed by the court — normally payment must be made within a stated time or by instalments.	All offences except those for which the sentence is fixed by law.	All ages. The court must normally order that fines imposed on a person aged between 10 and 15 inclusive should be paid by that person's parent or guardian. The court has a discretion to do this where the offender is aged 16 or 17.	The court must have regard to the offender's ability to pay the fine, whether this has the effect of increasing or decreasing the amount to be paid.	Indictable offences are punishable with an unlimited fine; the maximum fine for a summary offence is fixed by reference to a standard scale of fines. Special rules govern the fining of juveniles.	Various enforcement procedures are available. The ultimate sanction for non-payment is custody in default.	(a) PCCA 1973, s. 32 (fines for indictable offences); (b) MCA 1980, s. 37 (standard scale); (c) CYPA 1933, s. 55 (payment by parent); (d) CJA 1991, s. 18 (requirement to have regard to means of offender).

6 PROBATION ORDER

An order placing the offender under the supervision of a probation officer for a period of time specified by the court. Various requirements may be written into the order (such as a requirement of residence or a requirement of treatment for a mental condition).	Any offence except those where the sentence is fixed by law.	The minimum age is 16. There is no maximum age.	(a) A probation order is a community order and the offence must be serious enough to warrant the use of a community order. (b) The order should (i) be the most suitable for the offender in all the circumstances and (ii) have restrictions upon liberty contained within it which are commensurate to the seriousness of the offence. (c) Probation must be desirable in the interests of (i) securing the rehabilitation of the offender, or (ii) protecting the public from serious harm or preventing the commission of further offences. (d) The offender must express a willingness to comply with any requirement of treatment for his mental condition or for his dependency on drugs or alcohol. (e) A pre-sentence report is desirable in all cases and is required before additional requirements are added to the order, unless the court is of the view that it is 'unnecessary' to obtain a report. (f) The court must explain the order to the offender in open court and in ordinary language.	The court fixes the period of probation. The minimum period is 6 months; the maximum is 3 years.	An offender who is in breach of a probation order (by failure to comply with any one of its requirements) may be fined up to £1,000, be made subject to a community service order or be made subject to an attendance centre order (provided he is aged between 16 and 20 inclusive); alternatively the probation order may be revoked and the offender re-sentenced. A person on probation who commits a further offence may be dealt with (in addition to the sentence for the new offence) by revocation of the order and re-sentencing.	(a) CJA 1991, ss. 6 and 7 (community orders); (b) PCCA 1973, s. 2 (general powers); (c) CJA 1991, sch. 2 (enforcement of community orders); (d) PCCA 1973, s. 3 and sch. 1A, as amended by C(S)A 1997 (requirements in probation orders).

Nature of punishment	Offences for which imposable	Age groups for which imposable	Procedural requirements	Maximum and minimum terms	Sanctions for failure to comply with order	Statutory Authorities
7 COMMUNITY SERVICE ORDER Performance of unpaid work in what would otherwise be the offender's spare time.	All imprisonable offences except those for which the sentence is fixed by law.	The minimum age is 16. There is no maximum age.	(a) Procedural requirements (a), (b) and (f) in relation to probation orders also apply here. (b) A pre-sentence report is required before the order is made, unless the court is of the view that it is 'unnecessary' to obtain one. (c) The necessary local arrangements need to be made for the work to be carried out and the offender must be suitable.	The minimum number of hours the court may order is 40; the maximum 240. Normally the order must be completed within 12 months.	An offender who is in breach of a community service order (by failure to carry out the work as specified) may be fined up to £1,000 or made subject to a further community service order; alternatively the community service order may be revoked and the offender re-sentenced. A person on community service who commits a further offence may be dealt with (in addition to the sentence for the new offence) by revocation of the order and re-sentencing.	(a) CJA 1991, ss. 6 and 7 (community orders); (b) PCCA 1973, s. 14 (general powers); (c) CJA 1991, sch. 2 (enforcement of community orders).

8 COMBINATION ORDER

| An order which places the offender under the supervision of a probation officer *and* requires the offender to perform unpaid work in what otherwise would be the offender's spare time. | All imprisonable offences except those for which the sentence is fixed by law. | The minimum age is 16. There is no maximum age. | (a) Procedural requirements (a)–(d) and (f) in relation to probation orders also apply here. (b) A pre-sentence report is required before the order is made, unless the court is of the view that it is 'unnecessary' to obtain one. (c) The necessary local arrangements need to be made for the work to be carried out under the community service part of the combination order, and the offender must be suitable. | The court fixes the period of probation, which must be between 12 months and 3 years. The minimum number of hours' community service the court may order is 40; the maximum 100. | An offender who is in breach of a combination order may be fined up to £1,000 or made subject to a community service order; alternatively the combination order may be revoked and the offender re-sentenced. A person under a combination order who commits a further offence may be dealt with (in addition to the sentence for the new offence) by revocation of the order and re-sentencing. | (a) CJA 1991, ss. 6 and 7 (community orders); (b) CJA 1991, s. 11 (general powers); (c) CJA 1991, sch. 2 (enforcement of community orders). |

Nature of punishment	*Offences for which imposable*	*Age groups for which imposable*	*Procedural requirements*	*Maximum and minimum terms*	*Sanctions for failure to comply with order*	*Statutory Authorities*
9 CURFEW ORDER An order which requires an offender to remain at a place specified in the order (such as the offender's home) for specified periods of time.	Any offence except those for which the sentence is fixed by law.	All ages.	(a) Procedural requirements (a), (b), and (f) in relation to probation orders are also applicable here. (b) A pre-sentence report is not required, but is desirable since the court must obtain information about the place to be specified in the order and the attitude of other persons likely to be affected. (c) Curfew orders may be enforced by electronic monitoring of the offender.	The court may require the offender to remain at the place (or places) specified in the order for specified periods of between 2 and 12 hours per day for a period of up to six months or, in the case of an offender aged 10 to 15, up to three months.	An offender who is in breach of a curfew order may be fined up to £1,000 or made subject to a community service order or, if the offender is under the age of 16, an attendance centre order; alternatively the curfew order may be revoked and the offender re-sentenced. A person under a curfew order who commits a further offence may be dealt with (in addition to the sentence for the new offence) by revocation of the order and re-sentencing.	(a) CJA 1991, ss. 6 and 7 (community orders); (b) CJA 1991, s. 12, as amended by C(S)A 1997 (general powers); (c) CJA 1991, s. 13 (electronic monitoring); (d) CJA 1991, sch. 2, as amended by C(S)A 1997 (enforcement of community orders).

10 ATTENDANCE CENTRE ORDER

An order which requires the offender to attend a centre (usually for sessions of two or three hours at weekends) under the supervision of the police or probation service, to take part in physical exercise and constructive activities.

All imprisonable offences except those for which the sentence is fixed by law.	Offenders aged between 10 and 20 inclusive.	(a) Procedural requirements (a) and (b) in relation to probation orders are also applicable here. (b) A pre-sentence report is not required. (c) The court must ensure that there is an attendance centre available to receive the offender, which is within reasonable travelling distance.	The number of hours of attendance must be specified by the court. The normal minimum number is 12, except where the offender is aged between 10 and 13 inclusive and a lesser minimum is appropriate. The normal maximum number of hours is also 12, except where that is inadequate, in which case the maximum is 24 hours where the offender is 10–15 inclusive, and 36 hours where the offender is aged 16–20 inclusive.	An offender who is in breach of an attendance centre order may be fined up to £1,000, or the order may be revoked and the offender re-sentenced.	(a) CJA 1991, ss. 6 and 7 (community orders); (b) CJA 1982, s. 17 (general powers); (c) CJA 1982, ss. 18 and 19 (enforcement of attendance centre orders).

Nature of punishment	*Offences for which imposable*	*Age groups for which imposable*	*Procedural requirements*	*Maximum and minimum terms*	*Sanctions for failure to comply with order*	*Statutory Authorities*
11 SUPERVISION ORDER An order which requires the offender to be supervised by a local authority social worker or a probation officer for a period of time which is specified by the court. Various requirements may be written into the order (such as a requirement of residence or a requirement that the offender participate in various schemes of intermediate treatment).	Any offence except those where the sentence is fixed by law.	Offenders aged between 10 and 17 inclusive.	(a) Procedural requirements (a) and (b) in relation to probation orders are also applicable here. (b) A pre-sentence report is required before additional requirements are added to the order, unless the court is of the view that it is 'unnecessary' to obtain a report. (c) A supervision order may be made by a youth court or the Crown Court but not by an adult magistrates' court.	(a) The duration of the order must be specified by the court. There is no minimum period. The maximum period is 3 years. (b) Require-ments of 'attendance' and of 'participation in specified activities' may last for a maximum of 90 days. A night restriction requirement cannot be imposed in respect of more than 30 separate days, or continue in operation for longer than three months.	An offender who is in breach of a supervision order may, if not yet 18, be fined up to £1,000 (whether or not the court also varies or discharges the order), or may be made the subject of an attendance centre order. If the offender has attained the age of 18, the court may impose any sentence (apart from custody) which it could have imposed if dealing with him for the original offence or, where the sentencing court specified that the supervision order was in lieu of custody, any sentence including detention in a young offender institution.	(a) CYPA 1969, s. 12 (general power); (b) CYPA 1969, ss. 12(2), 12A, 12AA, 12B, 12C and 12D (requirements in supervision orders); (c) CYPA 1969, s. 15 (breach of supervision orders).

12 DISCHARGE						
An absolute discharge discharges the offender with no conditions or qualifications. A conditional discharge discharges the offender subject to the condition that he does not commit a further offence during the period of the discharge.	All offences except those for which the sentence is fixed by law. The court must consider that it is inexpedient to inflict punishment.	Offenders of any age may be discharged.	(a) The court must consider that it is inexpedient to inflict punishment. No punishment can be combined with a discharge. (b) A discharge does not count as a 'conviction' for certain purposes.	The court fixes the period of a conditional discharge. The maximum period is three years; there is no minimum period.	An offender who commits an offence while subject to a conditional discharge may be sentenced for the original offence, in which case the discharge ceases to have effect.	(a) PCCA 1973, s. 1A (general powers); (b) PCCA 1973, s. 1B (breach of conditional discharge); (c) PCCA 1973, s. 1C (limited effect of conviction).

13 HOSPITAL ORDER AND GUARDIANSHIP ORDER

Nature of punishment	*Offences for which imposable*	*Age groups for which imposable*	*Procedural requirements*	*Maximum and minimum terms*	*Sanctions for failure to comply with order*	*Statutory Authorities*
An order authorising an offender's admission to and detention at a (mental) hospital specified in the order. His subsequent discharge from hospital is a matter for the doctor treating him. He also has a right to apply at specified intervals to a MHRT which may order his discharge. A guardianship order is similar to a hospital order but places the offender under the guardianship of the local authority or other named person.	All imprisonable offences except those for which the sentence is fixed by law.	Offenders of any age may be made the subject of a hospital order. Guardianship orders are available for offenders of at least 16 years of age.	(a) There must be oral or written evidence from two doctors (one a specialist in mental disorders) that the offender is suffering from mental illness, psychopathic disorder, mental impairment or severe mental impairment. (b) Arrangements must be made to ensure that the offender can be received at the hospital which is specified in the order.	The hospital order is for an indeterminate period, initially for six months, renewal for a further six months, and at yearly intervals thereafter. A guardianship order lasts for 12 months, but may be renewed.	An offender who is absent without leave from the hospital may be taken into custody and returned to the hospital, unless he has been absent for more than 28 days, in which case the order ceases to have effect and he is no longer liable to be detained.	MHA 1983, s. 37.

14 RESTRICTION ORDER

Where the Crown Court makes a hospital order, it may, in order to protect the public from the risk of serious harm, attach a restriction order to the hospital order. This makes discharge from the hospital subject to the decision of a MHRT.	As for 13.	(a) As for 13. (b) The restriction order must be justified by the need to protect the public from the risk of serious harm.	As for 13, but discharge subject to the decision of a MHRT.	As for 13.	MHA 1983, s. 41.

15 COMPENSATION ORDER

An order requiring the offender to pay the victim of his offence a sum of money to compensate him for personal injury, loss or damage resulting from the offence.	Any offence. Compensation may be imposed as an ancillary order or may stand alone.	Offenders of any age can be ordered to pay compensation. The court must normally order that compensation imposed on a person aged between 10 and 15 inclusive should be paid by that person's parent or guardian. The court has a discretion to do this where the offender is aged 16 or 17.	(a) A compensation order should be made only if the offender agrees he is liable to compensate the victim in the sum to be specified in the order *or* if there is material before the court clearly establishing liability to compensate in that sum. (b) The court must have regard to the offender's means before making a compensation order. (c) A compensation order should not be made where there are difficulties in assessing the size of the loss. (d) The court should give reasons for *not* awarding compensation. (e) Compensation takes priority over a fine. (f) The victim need not apply to the court for compensation.	Magistrates' courts are restricted to a maximum of £5,000 compensation for each offence. There is no limit in the Crown Court, subject only to the extent of the loss and the offender's ability to pay.	The court orders the offender to pay the compensation as a lump sum or by instalments. Various enforcement procedures are available. The ultimate sanction for non-payment is custody in default.

PCCA 1973, s. 35.

16 RESTITUTION ORDER

Nature of punishment	Offences for which imposable	Age groups for which imposable	Procedural requirements	Maximum and minimum terms	Sanctions for failure to comply with order	Statutory Authorities
An order requiring a person in possession of stolen goods to restore them to the owner (or anyone else entitled to possession of them). An order may also be made in respect of goods which represent the stolen goods (i.e. goods which could be the subject matter of 'tracing' in civil law). Also the offender convicted of stealing the goods may be ordered to pay to the person entitled to the goods the value of the goods, such payment being made out of any money taken from his possession when he was apprehended.	A restitution order may be made only when there has been a conviction 'with reference to the theft' of the stolen goods to which the order relates. Except in the case of orders to pay the value of the goods out of money taken from the offender's possession on apprehension, a restitution order may be made against non-offenders in possession of the goods. 'Stolen goods' include goods obtained by deception and by blackmail.	Offenders of any age may be ordered to make restitution.	(a) Restitution orders should not be made in cases of doubt where the money or property might belong to some third party (i.e. not to the offender or to the proposed recipient under the order). (b) In some cases the victim need not apply to the court for restitution.		Non-compliance with a restitution order amounts to a contempt of court and is punishable as such.	Theft Act 1968. s. 28.

17 FORFEITURE ORDER An order for the forfeiture of goods used in the course of an offence committed by the offender or intended for such use.	Any offence.	Offenders of any age.	(a) A forfeiture order must be based on proper evidence. (b) Other persons claiming true ownership of the property may apply to the court for return of the property, showing that they did not realise that the property would be put to unlawful use. (c) After passage of a period of time, property forfeited may be sold, and the proceeds paid to the victim of the offence.			PCCA 1973, s. 43; other specific powers of forfeiture exist under other statutes.
18 CONFISCATION ORDER: DRUG TRAFFICKING An order made by the Crown Court for the confiscation of profits derived by the offender from drug trafficking offences.	A drug trafficking offence, as defined in DTA 1994, s. 1.	Offenders of any age.	(a) The court must determine whether the defendant has benefited from drug trafficking. If so, the court must determine the amount, and then order the defendant to pay that sum, or such lower sum as can actually be realised. (b) The issue of confiscation should normally be resolved before sentence is imposed.	There is no maximum or minimum sum which may be recovered.	Various enforcement procedures are available. The ultimate sanction for non-payment is custody for default.	DTA 1994.
19 CONFISCATION ORDER: OTHER OFFENDING An order for the confiscation of profits derived by the offender.	Any indictable offence other than a drug trafficking offence, and a restricted range of summary offences.	Offenders of any age.	As for 18.	There is no maximum or minimum sum which may be recovered.	Various enforcement procedures are available. The ultimate sanction for non-payment is custody for default.	CJA 1988, Part VI, as amended by CJA 1993 and PCA 1995.

TABLE 3   OFFENDERS SENTENCED BY TYPE OF COURT, TYPE OF SENTENCE OR ORDER AND TYPE OF OFFENCE

England and Wales

Type of sentence or order	1995	1996						
		Number of offenders (thousands)				Percentage total offenders sentenced		
	Total	Total Indictable offences	Summary offences		Indictable offences	Summary offences		
			Offences (excluding motoring offences)	Motoring offences		Offences (excluding motoring offences)	Motoring offences	
Magistrates' court								
Absolute discharge	20.1	19.9	2.4	5.7	11.8	1	1	2
Conditional discharge	102.0	102.0	50.1	43.2	8.7	22	9	1
Fine	992.8	1,069.7	81.9	402.3	585.4	36	83	90
Community penalties								
Probation order	41.0	43.8	26.3	7.9	9.5	11	2	1
Supervision order	9.7	10.3	8.0	1.9	0.4	3	0	0
Community service order	37.8	36.8	19.7	8.1	9.0	9	2	1
Attendance centre order	7.4	7.4	5.3	1.9	0.1	2	0	0
Combination order	11.6	14.3	7.4	2.1	4.9	3	0	1
Curfew order	0.0	0.2	0.1	0.0	0.0	0	0	0
Young offender institution	10.6	11.2	7.4	1.9	1.9	3	0	0
Imprisonment								
Fully suspended	1.3	1.3	0.5	0.2	0.5	0	0	0
Unsuspended	28.2	30.0	14.6	4.4	11.0	6	1	2
Otherwise dealt with	17.6	17.3	5.6	6.6	5.0	2	1	1
Total	1,280.1	1,364.2	229.3	486.2	648.2	98	99	99
The Crown Court								
Absolute discharge	0.1	0.1	0.1	0.0	0.0	0	0	0
Conditional discharge	3.6	2.7	2.2	0.4	0.0	3	21	2
Fine	3.9	3.4	2.7	0.4	0.3	4	18	38
Community penalties								
Probation order	8.4	7.2	6.9	0.2	0.1	10	11	12
Supervision order	0.5	0.6	0.6	0.0	-	1	0	-
Community service order	10.5	9.0	8.6	0.4	0.0	12	19	6
Attendance centre order	0.1	0.1	0.1	0.0	-	0	0	-
Combination order	2.9	3.0	2.8	0.1	0.0	4	3	7
Curfew order	0.0	0.0	0.0	-	-	0	-	-
Young offender institution	8.2	9.5	9.3	0.1	0.0	13	7	3
Imprisonment								
Fully suspended	1.9	2.1	2.1	0.0	0.0	3	1	1
Unsuspended	32.2	33.4	33.5	0.3	0.2	47	16	24
CYPA 1933, s.53	0.4	0.6	0.6	-	-	1	-	-
Otherwise dealt with	1.6	1.5	1.4	0.1	0.0	2	3	6
Total	74.3	73.2	70.9	2.0	0.6	100	99	99

TABLE 3– *continued*

England and Wales

Type of sentence or order	1995	1996						
		Number of offenders (thousands)				Percentage total offenders sentenced		
	Total	Total	Indictable offences	Summary offences		Indictable offences	Summary offences	
				Offences (excluding motoring offences)	Motoring offences		Offences (excluding motoring offences)	Motoring offences
All courts								
Absolute discharge	20.2	20.0	2.5	5.7	11.8	1	1	2
Conditional discharge	105.6	104.7	52.3	43.6	8.7	17	9	1
Fine	996.7	1,073.0	84.6	402.7	585.7	28	82	90
Community penalties								
Probation order	49.4	50.9	33.1	8.2	9.6	11	2	1
Supervision order	10.1	10.9	8.5	2.0	0.4	3	0	0
Community service order	48.3	45.9	28.3	8.5	9.1	9	2	1
Attendance centre order	7.5	7.5	5.4	1.9	0.1	2	0	0
Combination order	14.6	17.3	10.2	2.1	4.9	3	0	1
Curfew order	0.0	0.2	0.1	0.0	0.0	0	0	0
Young offender institution	18.8	20.6	16.7	2.0	1.9	6	0	0
Imprisonment								
Fully suspended	3.2	3.4	2.6	0.2	0.5	1	0	0
Unsuspended	60.3	64.0	48.1	4.7	11.2	16	1	2
CYPA 1933, s. 53	0.4	0.6	0.6	–	–	0	–	–
Otherwise dealt with	19.1	18.8	7.0	6.7	5.1	2	1	1
Total	1,354.2	1,437.8	300.0	488.3	649.0	99	98	98

Source: *Criminal Statistics England and Wales 1996*, table 7.1.

TABLE 4   OFFENDERS SENTENCED FOR ALL OFFENCES BY TYPE OF
SENTENCE OR ORDER, 1991 to 1996

England and Wales   Thousands

Type of sentence or order	1991	1992	1993	1994	1995	1996
Absolute discharge	21.6	23.9	25.9	22.8	21.2	20.1
Conditional discharge	104.4	111.3	111.6	110.1	106.2	104.8
Fine	1,175.8	1,189.1	1,091.5	1,069.5	1,070.1	1,075.5
Probation order	48.4	44.5	43.8	50.9	49.4	50.9
Supervision order	6.4	6.0	7.3	9.3	10.1	10.9
Community service order	43.0	44.5	48.0	49.7	48.3	45.9
Attendance sentence order	8.3	7.2	6.8	7.3	7.5	7.5
Combination order	–	1.3	8.9	12.4	14.6	17.3
Curfew order	–	–	–	–	0.0	0.2
Care order	0.3	–	–	–	–	–
Young offender institution	17.0	15.1	15.2	16.9	18.8	20.6
Imprisonment						
Fully suspended	28.6	22.3	3.8	3.2	3.2	3.4
Partly suspended	1.1	0.6	–	–	–	–
Unsuspended	43.7	42.6	43.2	52.6	60.3	64.0
CYPA 1933, s. 53	0.1	0.1	0.3	0.4	0.4	0.6
Otherwise dealt with	19.9	20.2	18.7	18.9	19.3	18.8
All sentences or orders	1,518.6	1,528.7	1,425.0	1,424.0	1,429.4	1,440.5
Of which:						
Immediate custody	61.9	58.3	58.4	69.4	79.1	84.7
Community sentences	106.1	103.5	114.8	129.6	129.9	132.7

Source: *Criminal Statistics England and Wales 1996*, table 7A.

TABLE 5   CHANGE IN THE PROPORTIONATE USE OF VARIOUS SENTENCES
BETWEEN 1991 AND 1996, BY INDICTABLE OFFENCE GROUP AND TYPE OF
SENTENCE OR ORDER

England and Wales   Percentage points

Offence group	Type of sentence or order				
	Discharge	Fine	Community sentence	Fully suspended sentence	Immediate custody
Violence against the person	−5	−18	+17	−7	+14
inc. reclassified offences	–	−14	+15	−7	+7
Sexual offences	−4	−13	+6	−6	+16
Burglary	−3	−6	+2	−6	+13
Robbery	−2	−1	+3	−2	−3
Theft and handling of stolen					
goods	–	−9	+8	−5	+6
inc. reclassified offences	+1	−9	+7	−5	+6
Fraud and forgery	−3	−10	+15	−9	+8
Criminal damage	+5	−5	+6	−4	–
inc. reclassified offences	+8	−11	+5	−2	+1
Drug offences	+2	−12	+8	−4	+6
Other (ex. motoring)	+1	−9	+5	−4	+4
Indictable motoring offences	+1	−8	+7	−3	+3
inc. reclassified offences	−1	−18	+11	−9	+16
All indictable offences	−1	−7	+7	−5	+7
inc. reclassified offences	–	−8	+7	−5	+7

Source: *Criminal Statistics England and Wales 1996*, table 7b.

1.2.2 Age categories of offenders

A matter which may well have a crucial impact upon where the offence is to be tried and sentenced, and the powers available to the sentencing court, is the offender's age. Several age groups need to be distinguished. The terminology which is used in this book is as follows:

Adult offenders
aged 21 or over   adults
aged 18, 19 or 20   young adults

Juveniles
aged 14, 15, 16 or 17   young persons
aged 10, 11, 12 or 13   children

For the purposes of determining the method of trial and the appropriate sentencing court, the crucial dividing line is between adult offenders and juveniles. Adult offenders are dealt with in the Crown Court or in a magistrates' court, depending upon the seriousness of the offence charged. Juveniles are dealt with in the youth court. The CJA 1991 included 17-year-olds within the category of young persons (rather than adults) for a range of criminal justice purposes, so that 17-year-olds appear in youth courts. For the sentences available for various age categories of offenders see Table 2 on pp. 15 to 29.

What happens when the defendant's birthday occurs during the course of the proceedings? The determining factor in sentencing is normally the age of the offender on the date when he or she is convicted or found guilty. Thus if an offender is aged 15 when charged with an offence but is aged 16 when he is convicted or pleads guilty, the court's powers to deal with 16-year-olds but not 15-year-olds (such as a community service order) are available. So a birthday between charge and conviction will make a difference. On the other hand, a birthday between conviction and sentence will not make a difference. If an offender is aged under 21 when convicted but turns 21 before being sentenced, he or she should be treated as being under the age of 21 for sentencing purposes. This would mean that the appropriate custodial sentence would be one of detention in a young offender institution, rather than imprisonment (*Danga* [1992] QB 476). This decision has been followed in *Pesapane* (1992) 13 Cr App R (S) 438 and *Robinson* [1993] 1 WLR 168. When a court needs to determine the age of an offender before passing sentence it may consider any evidence which is available to it (Criminal Justice Act 1982 (CJA 1982) s. 1(6)). If the court imposes sentence on an assumption which subsequently turns out to be incorrect, the sentence is not rendered invalid by that mistake (*Brown* (1989) 11 Cr App R (S) 263). If there is a dispute about the offender's age, the best course is to adjourn until the matter can be resolved (*Steed* (1990) 12 Cr App R (S) 230). It is, of course, quite wrong, and would be regarded as an abuse of the process of the court, to adjourn a case simply so that an offender can attain a particular age in the meantime (*Arthur* v *Stringer* (1986) 8 Cr App R (S) 329).

1.2.3 Categories of offences

It is crucial to distinguish between sentencing for:

(a)   offences triable only on indictment,
(b)   offences triable either way, and
(c)   offences triable summarily.

Offences triable only on indictment must be dealt with in the Crown Court. Such offences include murder, manslaughter, rape and robbery.

Offences triable either way can, as their name implies, be dealt with either in the Crown Court or in a magistrates' court. Such offences include burglary, theft and assault occasioning actual bodily harm. The decision over where an offence triable either way will be dealt with is known as the *mode of trial* decision. Basically, an offence triable either way will be dealt with on indictment if *either* the accused relies upon his right to trial in Crown Court *or* the magistrates come to the view that the case is too serious for them (i.e. that if the accused is convicted of the offence charged a sentence will be required which is in excess of the magistrates' sentencing powers). When determining mode of trial, magistrates must make the decision on the basis of what has been alleged about the gravity of the offence(s) charged. If they think that their powers would be adequate to sentence the accused, then they should give the accused the option of summary trial. If they think that their powers would not be adequate, then they should embark upon committal proceedings with a view to trial on indictment.

A matter of terminology which often causes confusion is that in English law the term 'indictable offence' means an offence which is triable only on indictment *or* an offence which is triable either way (Interpretation Act 1978, sch. 1). So both murder and burglary are indictable offences. Similarly, a conviction in Crown Court is referred to as a 'conviction on indictment' whether or not the offence involved was an offence triable only on indictment or an offence triable either way.

Summary offences are (with certain exceptions dealt with below) dealt with exclusively in the magistrates' courts. These are the least serious offences and include many road traffic matters, regulatory offences and other assorted minor offences. Some offences which are triable only summarily cannot, however, be dismissed as trivial. Driving (or being in charge) of a vehicle while unfit through drink or drugs, driving with excess alcohol, taking a motor vehicle without consent and assaulting a police officer in the execution of his duty are all summary offences. Several of these offences were formerly triable either way and have been converted into summary offences in an attempt by Parliament to lighten the load of business in the Crown Court. There are two exceptions to the general rule that summary offences are tried and sentenced in the magistrates' court. First, if the magistrates are committing the offender for an offence triable either way, they may also commit for a summary offence at the same time, so as to avoid splitting the sentencing function between the magistrates' court and the Crown Court. This can only be done if the summary offence is punishable with imprisonment and arose out of circumstances which were connected with the offence triable either way (Criminal Justice Act 1988 (CJA 1988), s. 41). Secondly, certain summary offences (at present restricted to common assault, taking a motor vehicle without consent, driving while disqualified and criminal damage of £5,000 or less) may be included by the prosecution in the indictment along with the indictable offence to be dealt with in the Crown Court. The summary offence must be founded on the same facts or evidence as the indictable offence or be part of a series of offences of the same character as, or a similar character to, the indictable offence (CJA 1988, s. 40).

Summary offences are sometimes referred to as 'purely summary offences'. The word 'purely' adds nothing, but is sometimes included to reinforce a distinction being drawn between summary offences and offences triable either way. 'Summary conviction' means conviction in a magistrates' court, whether for a summary offence or for an offence triable either way.

The overall effect of the arrangements just described is that the great bulk of crime is dealt with in the magistrates' courts, serious crime is for the Crown Court, and crime of intermediate gravity is shared between the Crown Court and the magistrates' courts. A good picture of the distribution of sentencing responsibility is given by the 1996 *Criminal Statistics for England and Wales*. In 1996 magistrates' courts sentenced some 1,364,100 offenders; 229,400 of those had committed indictable offences, 648,400 had committed summary traffic offences and 486,300 had committed other summary offences. The Crown Court sentenced only 73,700 offenders, all but 2,700 of whom had committed indictable offences. Thus, approximately 6 per cent of offenders were sentenced in the Crown Court and 94 per cent were sentenced by magistrates. Even as regards indictable offences, 75 per cent of offenders were dealt with in the magistrates' courts and 25 per cent in the Crown Court. However, when one turns from sheer quantity of sentencing to the type of sentence passed, it is the work of the Crown Court which becomes the more significant. Sixty-one per cent of offenders sentenced in the Crown Court for indictable offences received an immediate custodial sentence, while in the magistrates' courts, the figure was 9 per cent. Moreover the average length of sentence of immediate custody imposed on adult males by the Crown Court for indictable offences was around 24 months, as compared with 2.7 months in the magistrates' courts. When dealing with summary offences, magistrates very rarely pass custodial sentences. In fact, most offenders sentenced by magistrates are fined — 36 per cent of those sentenced for indictable offences (as compared with 4 per cent in the Crown Court), 90 per cent of those sentenced for summary road traffic offences and 83 per cent of those sentenced for other summary offences (all statistics taken from Home Office, 1997b).

1.2.4 Courts sentencing adults

Adult offenders are sentenced either by the Crown Court or by a magistrates' court. An adult offender convicted on indictment will be sentenced by a Crown Court judge. The range of powers available to a Crown Court are set out in Table 2 on p. 15. An adult offender who is summarily convicted will normally be sentenced by the magistrates. The various limitations upon the sentencing powers of magistrates will be explained in the relevant parts of this book, but an overview can usefully be given here.

When magistrates convict an adult offender summarily of an offence triable either way they may pass a sentence of up to six months' imprisonment and/or a fine of up to £5,000. If the offender is aged under 21 neither the Crown Court nor a magistrates' court can pass a prison sentence, but they can sentence to an equivalent period of detention in a young offender institution. When they convict an adult summarily of two offences triable either way magistrates may sentence to an aggregate term of up to 12 months' imprisonment (or detention in a young offender institution) and/or a fine of up to £5,000 for each offence. Other methods of dealing with adult offenders are available to the magistrates in broadly the same circumstances as they are available to the Crown Court, except that magistrates cannot add a restriction order to a hospital order, or make a compensation order of more than £5,000 in respect of any one offence.

The decision over mode of trial has already been referred to. The level of gravity at which magistrates should refuse jurisdiction in respect of an offence triable either way is not susceptible to precise definition, but it is possible to gauge the kind of conduct which can properly be punished with a sentence of six months' imprisonment or less. Section 19 of MCA 1980 requires magistrates to have regard to the following matters in deciding whether an offence is more suitable for summary trial or trial on indictment:

(a)   the nature of the case,

(b)   whether the circumstances make the offence one of a serious character,

(c)   whether the punishment which a magistrates' court would have power to inflict for it would be adequate,

(d)   any other circumstances which appear to the court to make it more suitable for the offence to be tried in one way rather than the other, and

(e)   any representations made by the prosecution or the defence.

A practice note containing national mode of trial guidelines has been issued: *Practice Note (Mode of Trial: Guidelines)* [1990] 1 WLR 1439, which was revised and reissued in 1995. The Guidelines are designed to assist magistrates with their decision. They apply to all defendants aged 18 and over. General guidance given there on mode of trial is as follows:

(a)   the court should never make its decision on the grounds of convenience or expedition;

(b)   the court should assume for the purpose of deciding mode of trial that the prosecution version of the facts is correct;

(c)   the fact that offences are alleged to be sample counts is a relevant consideration, but the fact that the defendant if convicted will be asking for other offences to be taken into consideration is not;

(d)   where cases involve complex questions of fact or difficult questions of law, the court should consider committal for trial;

(e)   where two or more defendants are jointly charged with an offence each has an individual right to elect his mode of trial;

(f)   in general, except where otherwise stated in the Guidelines, offences triable either way should be tried summarily unless the court considers that the particular case has one or more of the features set out *and* that its sentencing powers are insufficient;

(g)   the court should also consider its powers to commit an offender for sentence, under MCA 1980, s. 38, if information emerges during the course of the hearing which leads them to conclude that the offence is so serious, or the offender such a risk to the public, that their powers to sentence him are inadequate.

The Guidelines then give specific advice on mode of trial for various individual offences. This advice is set out in relation to each of the offences considered in Chapter 12, where the sentencing pattern for a range of commonly encountered offences is explained.

If a person aged 18 or over is dealt with summarily, pleads guilty or is found guilty after summary trial, the magistrates will normally pass sentence. Sometimes, however, where the offender is convicted of an offence triable either way, the magistrates may commit to Crown Court for sentence. It will be remembered that the magistrates' decision on mode of trial was based on their view that their sentencing powers would be adequate in the event of conviction. Even so, further information may emerge during the course of the trial, or from the information received by the court after conviction, which inevitably affects the magistrates' provisional view and makes the offence(s) now seem more serious than at first sight. The magistrates may then commit for sentence to the Crown Court. This will normally be done under MCA 1980, s. 38, though there are other provisions which provide this power. The only justification for committal for sentence under s. 38 is that the offence(s) are more serious than at first appeared. Following a committal under s. 38, the Crown Court may deal with the offender as if he had just been convicted of the relevant offence(s) on indictment (PCCA 1973, s. 42(1)).

Section 38 applies where a person who is aged 18 or over has been convicted at summary trial of an offence which is triable either way. In order to commit to Crown Court for sentence the magistrates must be of the opinion that the offence is so serious that proper punishment for it would exceed their powers or, in the case where the offender has committed a violent offence or a sexual offence, a longer sentence than they can impose is required to protect the public from the offender. The usual reasons for committing for sentence under s. 38 are:

(a)   where the offender's previous convictions (which, of course, the magistrates will not have known about until they come to sentence him) place the offender in a less favourable light than if this had been his first offence, or they make the current offence seem more serious in the light of what has gone before, or

(b)   he asks for offences to be taken into consideration at that stage, the additional punishment for those taking the case above the magistrates' limit.

Magistrates should always think carefully before accepting a case which on the face of it seems likely to require a sentence close to their limit, not least because accepting it will lead the offender to expect to be sentenced in accordance with the lower court's powers. Having accepted jurisdiction, however, the magistrates can still change their minds about the case and commit for sentence. See *North Sefton Magistrates' Court, ex parte March* (1995) 16 Cr App R (S) 401, in which it was stated that the justices had an 'open-textured discretion' in the matter, a case which departed from the earlier more rigid approach in *Manchester Magistrates' Court, ex parte Kaymanesh* (1994) 15 Cr App R (S) 838.

Section 38A, which was inserted by the C(S)A 1997, deals with the case where there are several either-way offences charged against the defendant, to some of which he pleads guilty and some of which he intends to contest at trial. If the magistrates commit the defendant to Crown Court for trial, they can also commit for sentence the offences to which he pleads guilty, even though those offences standing alone would not have been serious enough to justify committal for sentence under s. 38.

1.2.5   Courts sentencing juveniles

Juveniles (i.e. persons who have not attained the age of 18) are normally sentenced by a youth court. Sometimes, however, they may be sentenced by an adult magistrates' court or by the Crown Court. As with adults, the general rule is that they are sentenced by the court in which they pleaded guilty or were found guilty but, again, this is subject to several exceptions.

When a juvenile charged with an offence is the only accused involved in the proceedings (or when any other accused are juveniles as well), he (or they) must be tried in a youth court unless either (i) the offence charged is murder, manslaughter or causing death by dangerous driving or (ii) the magistrates in the youth court consider that the prosecution allegations are such that, if convicted on indictment, the Crown Court could order the offender to be detained under CYPA 1933, s. 53(2). Section 53(2) empowers the Crown Court to order that juveniles convicted of certain grave crimes be detained for a period of time not exceeding the maximum prison term which could be imposed upon an adult for the offence (see **4.3.9**). Orders under s. 53(2) are appropriate only in very serious cases. Thus, provided no adult is involved in the offence, juveniles will be tried in a youth court unless the charge is a very serious one, in which event they must be tried on indictment.

Where the case of a juvenile is bound up with that of an adult, the position is more complicated. If they are jointly charged with an indictable offence and the adult is going to be tried on indictment, the magistrates have a discretion either to commit the juvenile for trial with the adult or to remit the case to a youth court for the juvenile to be tried there. If the adult and the juvenile are jointly charged with a summary offence or with an offence triable either way in respect of which the adult has elected summary trial, and if the adult pleads not guilty, then the juvenile must be tried with the adult in a magistrates' court. Where the adult pleads guilty and the juvenile pleads not guilty the magistrates' court may remit the juvenile to a youth court to be tried. If a juvenile and an adult are charged in a single set of proceedings with separate offences which are nevertheless linked together factually, and the adult is going to be tried summarily, then the magistrates have a discretion either to try the juvenile at the same time as the adult or to remit the juvenile to a youth court. The above is a summary of the effect of MCA 1980, s. 24 and CYPA 1933, s. 46.

Except where there is a committal for sentence under MCA 1980, s. 37 (see below), a juvenile who has a finding of guilt recorded against him in a youth court is also sentenced there. The sentencing powers of youth courts are almost as great as those of the Crown Court in respect of juveniles. The only major limitations are that a youth court cannot order detention under CYPA 1933, s. 53 and cannot pass a sentence of more than six months' detention in a young offender institution for one offence. The latter limitation is not particularly significant because 15 is the minimum age for detention in a young offender institution so many juveniles are too young for it, and even offenders aged 15, 16 or 17 cannot be sentenced by the Crown Court to more than 24 months' detention at a time. It should also be remembered that if a youth court is dealing with an offender aged 15, 16 or 17 for two or more indictable offences it may pass consecutive sentences of detention, provided that the aggregate term does not exceed 12 months. There will, however, sometimes be occasions when a youth court considers that more than six months' detention is called for but it is unable to pass such a sentence. In such cases MCA 1980, s. 37 enables the youth court to commit the offender to the Crown Court to be sentenced, and the Crown Court may then pass a sentence of up to 24 months' detention or deal with the offender in any way the youth court could have dealt with him (PCCA 1973, s. 42(2)). When the relevant provisions of the CDB become law and are brought into force, s. 37 will be repealed. The effect is that the youth court will still be able to impose a maximum sentence of six months' (or, in the case of two indictable offences, 12 months') custody on a 15, 16 or 17-year-old. The relevant custodial sentence will be a new sentence of a detention and training order. The Bill substitutes that sentence for the sentence of detention in a young offender institution for offenders under 18. The repeal of s. 37 will mean that sentences longer than six (or 12) months can be imposed on a 15, 16 or 17-year-old only after trial on indictment, where the Crown Court will be able to pass sentence of detention and supervision for up to 24 months or, in the case of a qualifying offence, impose a sentence of long-term detention under s. 53(2) of the CYPA 1933.

When a juvenile pleads guilty or is found guilty on indictment, all the sentencing powers available by law in respect of juveniles are at the Crown Court's disposal. However, CYPA 1933, s. 56 provides that, except in cases of homicide, if a juvenile is convicted otherwise than in a youth court he shall be remitted to that court unless the convicting court 'is satisfied that it would be undesirable to commit'. The rationale of s. 56 was that the magistrates sitting in a youth court had greater experience in sentencing juveniles than did Crown Court judges. Accordingly Crown Court judges used to be encouraged to remit to a youth court for sentence, unless it was thought that the juvenile should be given a sentence which a youth court had no power to impose or (at the other extreme) that the case could be dealt with leniently, such as by way of a discharge, and that prolonging the proceedings by remitting was pointless. In *Lewis* (1984) 6 Cr App R (S) 44, however, the Court of Appeal qualified its earlier approach. Lord Lane CJ regarded the idea that the youth court was the only court in which juveniles should be sentenced as out of place, and expressed the view that Crown Court judges would be justified in not remitting juveniles for sentence for, among others, the following reasons:

(a)   where the judge, having presided over the juvenile's trial, feels that he is better informed as to the facts and circumstances of the case than a youth court could be;
(b)   where an adult has been convicted as well as the juvenile, and remitting the juvenile might lead to disparity through co-offenders being sentenced in different courts;
(c)   where remitting the juvenile would lead to delay, duplication of proceedings and fruitless expense.

The last of these reasons could apply to virtually any case, so Lord Lane appears to have advocated that, notwithstanding CYPA 1933, s. 56, Crown Court judges should, as a general rule, themselves sentence juveniles convicted on indictment and should not remit them to a youth court for sentence.

Since s. 56 does not apply to cases of homicide, juveniles convicted of murder, manslaughter or causing death by dangerous driving will always be sentenced in the Crown Court.

Where a juvenile is convicted in an adult magistrates' court, that court's powers of dealing with the juvenile are very limited. The magistrates may impose a fine or a discharge, bind over the juvenile's parents, disqualify the juvenile from driving or endorse his licence, and make certain ancillary orders as to costs or compensation (CYPA 1969, s. 7(8)). Should these options not be appropriate, it will be necessary to remit to the youth court. An adult magistrates' court cannot remit a juvenile to the Crown Court.

1.2.6   Sentencers in the Crown Court

Sentence in the Crown Court is pronounced by a Crown Court judge. Normally the judge alone will conduct the trial and deal with sentencing, but there are some occasions on which the judge must, or may, sit with up to four lay justices. If the offender comes before the Crown Court as a result of being committed there for sentence, the Crown Court judge must sit with two lay magistrates (Supreme Court Act 1981 (SCA 1981), s. 74(1)) and may sit with up to four. If the appeal or committal for sentence is in respect of a juvenile, the justices must be members of a youth court panel and the court must include both a man and a woman. A magistrate who adjudicated in the same matter in the lower court cannot sit with the judge in the Crown Court. Lay justices will not normally be present at a trial on indictment, since the *Practice Direction (Crown Court: Allocation of Business)* [1995] 1 WLR 1083 indicates that justices should not sit with a High Court judge or in any case where the matter is listed for a plea of not guilty.

In those cases where justices may sit (proceedings listed for hearing by a circuit judge or a recorder and not listed for a plea of not guilty), the justices should play a full part in the decisions of the court, including the decision as to sentence (*Newby* (1984) 6 Cr App R (S) 148). In the event of disagreement, the majority view prevails (s. 73(3)). Thus, at least in theory, the justices can outvote the judge, but if an even-numbered court is evenly divided the judge has a casting vote. Also, the justices must accept directions from the judge on any questions of law relevant to a decision the court has to take (*Orpin* [1975] QB 283). The role the justices play as part of the court is the same whether their presence is optional or compulsory.

There are, if one excludes for the moment lay magistrates, five varieties of Crown Court judge:

(a) *High Court judges* Section 8(1)(a) of SCA 1981 provides that any High Court judge may sit in the Crown Court. On average, about 20 High Court judges will be sitting in the Crown Court at any one time. Normally a High Court judge asked to do Crown Court work will be one of the judges attached to the Queen's Bench Division, and will probably (but not necessarily) have gained knowledge of criminal practice during practice at the Bar.

High Court judges are asked to deal with the most serious criminal cases. The *Practice Direction* (*Crown Court: Allocation of Business*) [1995] 1 WLR 1083 provides a complex classification of Crown Court business for these purposes. A Class 1 offence must be tried by a Crown Court judge. These offences are treason, murder, genocide, an offence under s. 1 of the Official Secrets Act 1911 and incitement, conspiracy or attempt to commit any of those offences. Exceptionally, a case of murder (or incitement, conspiracy or attempt to commit murder) may be tried by a circuit judge approved by the Lord Chief Justice. A Class 2 offence may be tried by a High Court judge or an approved circuit judge. The most important of these offences are manslaughter, infanticide, child destruction, rape, sexual intercourse with a girl under 13, incest with a girl under 13 and an incitement, conspiracy or attempt to commit any of those offences. Offences which are neither necessarily reserved for High Court judges nor prima facie reserved for them (Class 3 and Class 4 offences) may none the less be put into a High Court judge's list if the facts alleged by the prosecution are particularly grave or a difficult issue of law is likely to arise.

(b) *Circuit judges* The office of circuit judge was created by the Courts Act 1971 (CA 1971), at the same time as the Crown Court itself. Together with recorders (see below) they handle the great bulk of Crown Court work. They also sit in the county courts, though the way a judge's time is split will vary from one to another. Like High Court judges (but unlike recorders), circuit judges are full-time judges appointed by the Queen on the Lord Chancellor's recommendation. Retirement is normally at the age of 72, although occasionally circuit judges are allowed to continue in office until they reach 75 (CA 1971, s. 17).

(c) *Recorders* Barristers or solicitors who have a 10-year Crown Court or county court qualification may be appointed to sit in the Crown Court as recorders. Again the appointment is by the Queen on the Lord Chancellor's recommendation, but the appointment is a part-time one for a certain period or for a specified number of days during the course of a year (CA 1971, s. 21(3)). When not sitting the recorder may, and usually does, revert to private practice. Retirement is at the age of 72 (CA 1971, s. 21(5)). Despite the fact that a solicitor is eligible for appointment as a recorder and is eligible to be appointed as a circuit judge after completing three years as a recorder, the great majority of circuit judges and recorders are drawn from the ranks of the Bar.

(d) *Deputy circuit judges and assistant recorders* Section 24 of CA 1971 empowers the Lord Chancellor to appoint retired Lord Justices of Appeal, retired High Court judges or retired circuit judges to act as deputy circuit judges. The Lord Chancellor may also appoint barristers or solicitors of at least 10 years' standing to act as assistant recorders. The purpose of such appointments is essentially to enable the Crown Court to cope with an unexpected rush of work or with an accumulated back-log of cases. For the period of appointment, a deputy circuit judge or an assistant recorder carries out the same functions as a circuit judge or recorder, as the case may be.

The effect of the above arrangements is that a small minority of very serious cases must be tried, or will normally be tried, by a High Court judge, while the great bulk of trials on indictment, sentencing following conviction on indictment and committals for sentence will be distributed between the other Crown Court judges as convenience dictates. Administrative staff at Crown Court locations may exercise an informal discretion so as to direct the more serious and/or complicated cases towards an experienced circuit judge rather than an inexperienced assistant recorder.

More generally from the sentencing point of view, however, it is clear that even in the Crown Court an offender may be dealt with by a relatively inexperienced sentencer. This raises the question: what training do Crown Court judges receive in sentencing? The Bridge Report in 1978 provided the impetus for the setting up of the Judicial Studies Board, the scope of which was revised and expanded in 1985, to provide training for the judiciary in the criminal field and in the civil and family jurisdictions. The Board has always given special prominence to training in matters related to sentencing. Induction seminars are now compulsory for all newly appointed assistant recorders, and refresher seminars are available for experienced circuit judges and recorders. A one-day conference, focussing primarily on sentencing, is run for all members of the full-time and part-time judiciary on each court circuit each year (see further on the JSB, Glidewell, 1992).

1.2.7 Sentencers in magistrates' courts

Sentence in the magistrates' courts is, of course, passed by magistrates. Most magistrates are lay men or women, often referred to as lay justices on account of their more formal title, 'justice of the peace'. 'Lay', in this context, simply means unpaid. Magistrates are entitled to an allowance for travelling and subsistence, and to compensation for loss of earnings (Justices of the Peace Act 1979, s. 12). Many lay justices are in full-time employment away from the court and so their availability to sit as justices is strictly limited. Normally magistrates are required to sit once a fortnight, but in some busy courts it may be once a week.

A small minority of magistrates, known as stipendiary magistrates, are appointed to act full-time. Unlike lay justices, stipendiaries are qualified lawyers who are paid a salary. Stipendiary magistrates are appointed by the Queen on the advice of the Lord Chancellor. They must be barristers or solicitors of at least seven years' standing. The Justices of the Peace Act 1979 permits the appointment of up to 60 metropolitan stipendiaries and up to 40 non-metropolitan ones. The metropolitan stipendiaries sit mainly in the central and inner London courts, where they dispose of a considerable proportion of the courts' business. Outside London, mainly in the large provincial cities, stipendiaries are becoming more popular.

For the purposes of summary trial and sentencing, a magistrates' court is duly constituted if it consists of a stipendiary magistrate or at least two lay justices (MCA 1980, s. 121(1)). A single lay justice cannot conduct a trial or pass sentence. Benches of three magistrates are preferable to benches of two because an uneven-numbered court is permitted to reach decisions by a majority, whereas if an even-numbered bench is split the case has to be remitted to a different bench.

Outside inner London, nearly all the business of the magistrates' courts is conducted by lay magistrates. They are appointed by the Lord Chancellor on the advice of local committees. Any person or organisation (e.g. a local political party) may submit to the secretary of the local advisory committee the name of a person who, in the view of the person or organisation, would make a good magistrate. The only significant category of persons to be excluded from appointment is undischarged bankrupts. Efforts are made to draw magistrates from as wide a range of ages, backgrounds, employments and ethnic groups as possible. The requirement that magistrates be available regularly for court duties which are unpaid does, however, result in a less than representative sample of people on the bench. Magisterial law, not least in the area of sentencing, is becoming more and more complex, and a minimum intellectual standard is required. A frequent criticism is that the upper classes and wealthier sections of society are overrepresented among the magistracy. At the age of 70 a magistrate in effect retires. Technically, their name is placed on the 'supplemental list', which means that, although retaining the status of justice of the peace, they cannot exercise jurisdiction. Stipendiary magistrates also retire at 70.

A magistrate is appointed to be a justice of the peace for the county in which he or she resides (in London there are six commission areas instead of counties). The counties are divided into petty sessional divisions (PSDs), with a magistrates' court in each one. Although a magistrate could in theory sit at any court in the county, magistrates are in practice assigned to the bench for the petty sessional division in which they live or work, and they would normally only sit in that division. Bench size varies considerably throughout the country. There is a trend towards larger courts, by amalgamation, for reasons of economy.

Each year the magistrates for a PSD elect, by secret ballot, a chairman and as many deputy chairmen as they consider to be necessary. Normally the chairman or one of the deputy chairmen presides at the sitting of every lay bench. The chairman announces the decision of the court. By statute, magistrates are often required to explain their decision on sentence to the offender in ordinary language, and that task also falls to the chairman.

At each sitting of a magistrates' court, the magistrates are assisted by a clerk. The duties of the clerk include putting the charge to the accused, noting down the evidence, explaining the procedure of the court to a party who is not legally represented and, most importantly, advising lay magistrates on matters of law. There is usually one justices' clerk for each PSD. The clerk must be a barrister or solicitor of at least five years' standing who has served for at least five years as assistant to a justices' clerk (Justices of the Peace Act 1979, s. 26). The justices' clerk will be aided by a deputy and by assistant clerks. The justices' clerk is required to carry out a range of administrative and managerial duties (these duties have increased since the commencement of cash-limiting in magistrates' courts in April 1992), and may be able to sit in court only infrequently. If the assistant clerks are to act as 'clerks in court' they must have some legal qualification, such as the specially designed diploma in magisterial law, but they are not required to have a law degree or to be professionally qualified. Despite the relatively low formal qualifications needed to be a clerk in court, lay magistrates rely heavily on their advice. In respect of sentencing, the *Practice Direction (Justices: Clerk to Court)* [1981] 1 WLR 1163 has summarised the duties of the clerk in court. The clerk must:

[Advise] the justices generally on the range of penalties which the law allows them to impose and on any guidance relevant to the choice of penalty provided by the law, the decisions of the superior courts or other authorities. If no request for advice has been made by the justices, the justices' clerk shall discharge his responsibility in court in the presence of the parties.

Thus the clerk will often be asked by the magistrates whether a particular form of sentence is open to the bench, or whether they have power to commit for sentence. Sometimes the advice is given in open court so that the parties can hear what is said. More frequently the clerk is asked by the justices to retire with them when they leave to consider their decision. Case-law stresses that the clerk's task is to *advise* the magistrates on matters of sentencing law and procedure, and not to *influence* their decision on the facts. In practice, however, this sharp distinction is a rather difficult one to achieve and, in some cases, the clerk may have a significant influence upon the bench's sentencing decision.

Some business relating to magistrates' courts (such as the appointment of clerks or the training of magistrates) needs to be organised on a county-wide basis. To administer such matters there are magistrates' courts committees, comprising representatives elected from the PSDs making up the county or district; plus circuit judges or recorders who may, with their consent, be co-opted on to a committee to act as the liaison judge. Appointment of magistrates, election of chairmen and deputy chairmen, composition of magistrates' courts committees and similar matters are all governed by the Justices of the Peace Act 1979 and rules made thereunder.

When lay magistrates are appointed they undertake to complete, within one year, a course of basic training. The training is organised by the magistrates' courts committee for the relevant county or district. Although it is the function of the Lord Chancellor's Department to oversee the training of magistrates, in practice the training officer is almost always one of the justices' clerks in the county, who enjoys considerable discretion over the matters to be covered. Training falls into two stages. The first stage, which must be completed before a new magistrate is allowed to take part in court work, consists of attending court sittings as an observer, listening to talks on the nature of a magistrate's duties and reading recommended literature. During the first stage a magistrate will be told about the sentencing options at the court's disposal and the kinds of situation in which each option is appropriately used. The second stage takes place after the magistrate has begun sitting in court. New magistrates from several PSDs may join together for lectures, discussions and practical exercises. A considerable proportion of the second stage is devoted to sentencing. A common teaching technique is the sentencing exercise, where magistrates are given details of imaginary sentencing cases, divided into groups and asked to report back their views on the appropriate sentences. Discussion then follows on differences which may have emerged. There are also required visits to custodial institutions and probation service facilities. In addition to the training on sentencing just described, there will be follow-up talks and exercises in subsequent years.

1.2.8 Sentencers in youth courts

Trial in a youth court is simply a special form of summary trial, so that the sentencers in youth courts are magistrates. Not all magistrates are entitled to sit in a youth court, however. Every three years the magistrates of a PSD meet together to elect on to the youth court panel those of their number whom they consider to be especially well suited for handling cases involving juveniles (CYPA 1933, sch. 2). Only members of the youth court panel may sit in the youth court.

A youth court must consist of two or three magistrates, preferably with both sexes represented. A stipendiary magistrate may not sit alone in a youth court. Upon election to the youth court panel a magistrate is given training in the work of that court because the training given upon appointment as a magistrate does not cover youth court work. When dealing with a juvenile offender, the magistrates do not 'convict' but 'record a finding of guilt' and, rather than 'sentencing', they 'make an order upon a finding of guilt' (CYPA 1933, s. 59).

1.3   AIMS OF SENTENCING

There has been much discussion in recent years concerning the proper aims of sentencing. Several different aims have been identified. Traditionally, sentencers have been largely free to pursue the sentencing approach which has seemed to them most appropriate, on a case by case basis, and there has been little attempt to regulate this. Indeed it has often been argued by sentencers themselves that the formulation of sentencing policy is a matter peculiarly within the remit of the judiciary. There has been a view that sentencing is 'an art rather than a science', that it has to be absorbed through the experience of doing it, rather than being addressed by way of a set of principles. This approach is still adhered to by some sentencers (the very words quoted were used by a member of the Court of Appeal in *Attorney-General's Reference (No. 4 of 1989)* (1989) 11 Cr App R (S) 517).

There are very few discussions at appellate level about the aims of sentencing. An exception is *Sargeant* (1974) 60 Cr App R 74, where Lawton LJ took advantage of a run-of-the-mill appeal against sentence to expound what he took to be the functions of, and the justifications for, sentencing. Giving the judgment of the Court of Appeal, Lord Justice Lawton referred to the 'classical principles of sentencing', which he said could be summed up in the four words 'retribution', 'deterrence', 'prevention' and 'rehabilitation'. The Court of Appeal, however, offered no explanation of how these aims were to be reconciled when they were in conflict with one another.

The sentencer who 'picks and chooses' among the various aims of sentencing has been called the 'eclectic sentencer' (Walker and Padfield, 1996). The problem, however, is that eclecticism leads inevitably to disparity. 'Sentencing disparity' arises when cases which are similar in relevant respects are dealt with differently, or where cases which are different in relevant respects are dealt with similarly. Disparity is a form of injustice, since it means that the sentence which a person receives for committing a particular offence will often turn on which particular judge or bench of magistrates is dealing with the case.

In a government White Paper, *Crime, Justice and Protecting the Public*, issued in 1990, the government demonstrated a willingness to address the question of sentencing aims in a more systematic fashion, with the avowed aim of achieving greater uniformity of approach amongst sentencers. The White Paper endorsed 'desert' (or retribution) as the guiding criterion in sentence selection. In making a number of clear statements on this matter, it is evident that the government intended that desert should be the dominant sentencing aim, ahead of deterrence, prevention and rehabilitation. Specifically, the White Paper was sceptical about relying upon deterrence as the basis for determining sentence. The principles in the White Paper formed the basis for the CJA 1991 but, in a number of respects, later developments have compromised the basic approach.

The imposition of punishment by the state will involve to one extent or another, depending on its precise nature, the imposition of hardship upon offenders. Another way of saying this is that sentences handed down by the court impose varying degrees of restriction of liberty upon offenders. Starting at the top of the range of punishments currently available to the courts in this country, imprisonment (or detention in a young offender institution for those under 21) obviously imposes the most severe restrictions upon liberty. Lesser, though still significant, restrictions are involved in the various community orders. Community service, for example, restricts liberty by requiring the offender to give up a proportion of leisure time to perform demanding unpaid work on a specified project of benefit to the community. A probation order (at its most basic) requires the offender to report to a probation officer at regular specified times, and keep the officer informed of any change of circumstances. This may seem a minimal restriction, but for an immature and disorganised individual it may impose a significant burden. Various conditions, more or less stringent, may be inserted into a probation order by the sentencer, such as requiring the offender to undergo treatment for a mental condition or for addiction to alcohol or drugs, or to attend a probation centre for education, practical advice or counselling (which may be designed to force the offender to face up to his offending behaviour). These requirements can be very demanding. Even financial penalties, designed to be a tax on an offender's spare income, are restrictions on liberty in the sense that the offender is deprived of cash which he or she would much have preferred to have spent on something else. For those on low incomes a fine can be a severe penalty, and sentencers are required to ensure that an offender's means are properly taken into account whenever a fine is imposed (see Chapter 6).

Once it is agreed that sentencing involves the deliberate infliction of hardship upon offenders, in the sense of restriction of liberty, the second step is to recognise that this practice stands in need of justification. How can the infliction of punishment by the courts, acting as instruments of the state, be justified? This is a question with which philosophers have grappled for many years. Broadly, two sets of ideas have emerged. They may be described as the reductivist approach and the desert approach.

1.3.1 The reductivist approach

The reductivist approach is that the imposition of hardship through punishment is justified whenever certain benefits are achieved by that punishment, and where those benefits outweigh the hardship and make its imposition, on balance, worthwhile. This is the principle of utility, expounded by Jeremy Bentham and others. In particular, the imposition of punishment is here designed to reduce the overall incidence of offending within society. The offender is thus being used as an instrument in an effort to achieve this beneficial result.

A number of distinct approaches shelter under the reductivist umbrella, and so a sentencer might impose a reductivist sentence by following one (or a mixture) of different lines of thought. The first line is that the punishment will act to deter the person sentenced (individual deterrence), so that the person will desist from offending through fear of repetition of the penalty in future. The second line is that the punishment will deter other like-minded people (general deterrence). They will decide not to commit an offence when they see what penalty has been inflicted on the offender on this occasion for doing so. The third line is that by imposing a sentence of a particular type, such as a lengthy prison term or a driving disqualification, the offender will be prevented from committing further offences in the future (incapacitation), at least for a limited period of time. The fourth line is that the sentence handed down by the court will bring about a change of attitude (reform, rehabilitation) on the part of the offender, so that he will desist from offending in future, not through fear of further punishment, but through a deeper realisation of the anti-social nature of offending.

All these arguments are offered by reductivists as justification for the practice of punishment generally and in individual cases. While it is helpful to draw distinctions between them, and there is a very substantial legal and philosophical literature on each, it will be apparent that a sentencer might, perfectly coherently, pursue more than one of these

[Handwritten margin notes: "deterrence, incapacitation, reform, rehabilitation ⎬ attempt to reduce level of offending in society."]

[Handwritten left margin: "= v. difficult.", "measuring crime levels (BCS)", "Do offenders take note of sentencing policy?"]

goals at the same time when passing a single sentence. What they have in common is the attempt, by the passing of the sentence, to reduce the general level of offending in society. The reductivist objective is, at least in theory, empirically testable. It might be possible to demonstrate that the passing of a particular sentence, or a policy of sentencing in a particular way, has 'worked', in that it has achieved a net benefit in terms of the number of offences which have thereby been prevented. In practice, however, such claims are very hard to prove or disprove. It is extremely difficult to measure the impact of a particular sentencing decision or group of decisions.

Sentencers sometimes claim that a particular form of offending has been 'stamped out' by severe deterrent sentences handed out to a few people who have offended in that way. Can such a claim be substantiated? Let us take house burglary as an example. Suppose that the official criminal statistics record a downturn for that offence in the months which follow a new practice of markedly more severe sentencing for burglary. It would be tempting to assume that the downturn was the result of the new sentencing policy. Such temptation should be resisted. For one thing, any such impact could not be measured by the official criminal statistics. These relate only to offences reported to the police and which are recorded by them. Unreported crime (a very much larger figure) is not recorded. So a decrease in reported house burglaries might conceal a real rise in the number of burglaries, or vice versa. The problem of the inadequacy of the statistics for recorded crime might in part be overcome by conducting regular victim surveys (such as the British Crime Survey) which would give a clearer picture of whether the decline in reported burglary was mirrored by a fall in the real level of such offending. Even if this could be shown to have happened, however, it would still be dubious to assume that the sentencing decision had brought about the change. The downturn may have been occasioned by some other factor, quite independent of sentencing, such as the growth of neighbourhood watch schemes, an advertising campaign for home security, a change in the economic climate of the country or simply a change in the fashions of offending. Further reflection reveals the lack of plausibility of claims that sentencing has a deterrent impact upon the real level of offending. The argument presupposes that burglars make choices about committing burglary based upon their knowledge of current sentencing practice. This may be true in some cases and, certainly, there is an important element of rational choice in the selection of targets for house burglary, particularly by so-called professional offenders. The general picture, however, is that most burglaries are committed by young men, often after drinking, without much forward planning and with little or no consideration of penalty levels. The criminological literature tells us that many young offenders tend to 'live for the moment' and rarely plan ahead or weigh the consequences of being caught against the excitement of breaking the law. In any event a burglar sufficiently well-informed to have read the sentencing reports will also know that the police clear-up rate for house burglary is very low. Penalty levels must become even less significant to offenders when they believe that they have little or no chance of being caught.

The argument about reductivist sentencing is not, however, solely about whether it can be shown to work. Let us take the burglary example again. Suppose a Crown Court judge imposes an exceptionally severe sentence upon a burglar in an attempt to deter. There is then the issue of the injustice of imposing a sentence which is more severe than this offender deserves (in comparison with sentences which have been imposed on others for doing the same) in an attempt to achieve a general effect. The moral point is a strong one. Some people may feel that even if the sentence's effectiveness could be convincingly demonstrated, and even if it could be shown that news of the severe sentence had travelled fast and had prevented, say, ten burglaries which would otherwise have taken place, the severe sentence should still be struck down on the ground that it is unjust to the sentenced offender. The fact that all reductivist strategies rely upon using the sentence imposed on the offender as a tool to achieve a wider social impact gives rise to a further criticism of reductivist approaches: they all contain a danger that the enthusiastic pursuit of the social goals may result in grave injustice to those few offenders who are caught, prosecuted and convicted. If severe sentences, contrary to expectation, do not appear to be having the desired effect of reducing crime, then this may result in even more severe sentences.

There has been much disillusionment with reductivist sentencing goals, particularly reform and rehabilitation, because the reductivist approach, which seemed in the 1960s and 1970s to be capable of achieving those goals, has manifestly failed to do so. As we have seen, reductivist goals are somewhat amenable to empirical testing, and this is particularly so in the case of reform. A famous survey of a large number of rehabilitative programmes was carried out in 1976. Its conclusions have been widely, though somewhat inaccurately, summarised with the dictum that 'nothing works' (Martinson, 1974; Brody, 1975). The evidence is carefully considered by Walker and Padfield (1996, ch. 7). In fact the survey found that rehabilitative programmes sometimes did 'work', by having a discernible impact upon the reconviction rates of those made subject to them, but often only for highly selected 'good risk' offenders (who might not have reoffended anyway), in rather specialised situations and over rather short follow-up periods. Many previously reported studies were dismissed by Martinson as being methodologically unsound. As a result, rehabilitation quickly went out of fashion as the central aim of sentencing, but it remains an important element in the appropriate use of community sentences and in the educational and training opportunities which ideally ought to be available as part of a custodial sentence. More recently there has been some reawakening of interest in the efficacy of rehabilitative programmes (see McGuire, 1995), but the reductivist goal which has attained most prominence in recent years is that of offender incapacitation. The CJA 1991, although having desert as its principal approach, also permits custody to be used, and longer-than-normal sentences to be imposed, on offenders convicted of violent or sexual crimes who appear to represent a serious risk to the public. It is incapacitation as a sentencing goal which leads to the promotion of electronic monitoring of offenders, and it was this objective which former Home Secretary Michael Howard had in mind when he insisted that 'Prison works'. The policy produced the so-called 'three strikes' laws in the United States (see Schichor, 1996) and has been influential in the introduction of some presumptive minimum sentences in the Crime (Sentences) Act 1997. Of course it is true that, for the period of incapacitation, reoffending by the offender is minimised, but claims in the United States that 'selective incapacitation' of high-risk offenders will have a significant impact on crime rates have promised much more than they have delivered. There are also substantial ethical questions about incapacitation which do not admit of easy answers. The main problem is that incapacitative sentencing requires a prediction to be made by the sentencer about the offender's future lawbreaking, on the basis of reports about him and what he has done in the past. Such predictions are, however, unreliable, with research evidence suggesting that risk assessments are, at best, as likely to be wrong as they are to be right (Floud and Young, 1991).

We can perhaps say of those who adhere to reductivist sentencing strategies that they do so often in the absence of convincing empirical evidence, and sometimes in the face of considerable ethical doubts. On the other hand, sentencers may need to feel that some good can result from the sentences handed down by the courts. Punishment can be seen as rather backward-looking and negative, whereas reductive strategies at least seem to offer ways of making the world a better or safer place in which to live. To abandon reductivist sentencing goals, then, may seem to make sentencing a more mechanical, or even pointless, exercise and reductivist views may be (and are) strongly held by many sentencers.

1.3.2   The desert approach

A second view can be set in contrast to the reductivist one. The desert approach to sentencing emphasises the moral requirement of maintaining a proper proportion between offence and punishment. It states that punishment involves censuring the offender for his wrongful behaviour. Thus the prime determinant of sentencing should be to ensure that the punishment imposed is that which is deserved for the offence, having regard to the seriousness of the harm caused or risked by the offender and the degree of the offender's culpability. It should be understood that, in contrast to the various reductivist approaches, desert principles do not require that sentencing practice should impinge upon overall crime levels. Although desert theorists would, of course, welcome any reduction in the incidence of crime generally, desert theory treats the sentencing of offenders as an issue distinct from tackling the roots of offending in the community. The view is that the 'crime problem' in society can and should be tackled by a combination of strategies including economic policy, social policy, housing policy, environmental design and education, but only to a rather limited extent through sentencing practice.

Desert theory has, at its heart, proportionality between the seriousness of the offence and the severity of the penalty imposed. This sounds a simple idea and, in some ways and in general terms, it is. But the working out of desert theory in the kind of rigorous and detailed way which is required in a complex sentencing system, such as that in England and Wales, brings with it considerable difficulty. 'Seriousness' is an elusive idea. What makes one offence more serious than another? A good starting point would be the kind of harm, and the amount of harm, occasioned to the victim. If the victim's life is taken that is clearly more serious than if the victim is injured but survives. That, in turn, is more serious than a case where the victim suffers only loss of property, or is merely inconvenienced or distressed by the offence. Various empirical studies of the public's perception of the relative seriousness of various crimes display a fair degree of consensus.

Intuitively most of us would agree that robbery is a more serious offence than theft. Indeed the legal definitions of the two crimes tell us that robbery is an aggravated form of theft: theft with the use of force or fear. But further reflection reveals that not all robberies are more serious than all thefts. A bag snatch involving minimal force and the loss of little of value would be regarded by most of us as less serious than the theft of £1 million from a bank. Many existing criminal offences describe criminal conduct in rather broad terms, and offences overlap with each other. This makes it difficult to draw up a hierarchy of offences for sentencing. One response might be to have more subdivision of existing offences. This subdivision need not be recognised in formal criminal law, but it could become accepted that a particular offence contained within it two or three seriousness bands, which should be kept distinct for sentencing purposes. As we will see, the offence of burglary is now formally divided for sentencing purposes into two: burglary of dwellings and burglary of other buildings, such as offices or shops. This distinction in relative seriousness was developed through courts' sentencing practice and only later reflected in legislation by the creation of different maximum sentences for the two forms of the offence (see **12.4.5**). There are other complications. One victim may suffer substantially more, or substantially less, harm from a crime than might have been expected. An elderly person, for example, might incur considerable hardship and distress from a house burglary from which a more resilient, and perhaps better insured, person would recover relatively quickly. How far should this differential impact affect our assessment of crime seriousness?

There is more to seriousness of crime than the harm incurred by the victim. The culpability of the offender is also of great importance. Criminal law *mens rea* terms such as intention, recklessness and negligence may play a further role here, but the offender's responsibility for the offence requires a fuller analysis at the sentencing stage. Sentencers distinguish a carefully planned crime from one committed on the spur of the moment, and between the ringleader in the offence and others who played a lesser role. Weight is given to other factors, such as provocation before the offence, and some regard can be given to the pressures which the offender may have been under at the time of the crime which, while not excusing it, may place what happened in a fuller and more revealing context. A further important point is that the two elements of crime seriousness, harm and culpability, do not operate independently. Each impinges on the other. To return to the earlier example, if the elderly victim of a burglary suffers very greatly, that may affect our view of the crime, but if it turns out that the offender targeted the house because he knew the householder was elderly, that may well affect it again. What is clear is that desert principles in sentencing force us to think in a systematic way about the relative seriousness of crime (both when comparing one category of offence with another, and one instance of an offence compared with a different instance).

Offence seriousness is on one side of the scale. On the other side is penalty severity. Again, intuitively, most of us would agree that five years' imprisonment is a more severe sentence than 100 hours of community service. But devising a scale of penalties in terms of severity is beset with difficulties just as acute as those of comparing the seriousness of offences. Penalties are very different. How can one compare imprisonment with a probation order or a fine? A useful starting point is to gauge all the various sentences in terms of their relative impact upon the average offender, or perhaps the extent to which they can be expected to impinge upon and restrict the average offender's liberty. This rough kind of scaling amongst sentences has always been part of the sentencing system in England and Wales, and it formed the basis of the description of the various sentencing powers available to the courts which was given earlier in this chapter. It is referred to in some of the texts on sentencing (particularly Thomas, 1979) as the sentencing 'tariff', reflecting, in a rather non-specific way, that more serious offences require more severe penalties. The traditional picture of sentencing is more complex than this, however. First, there is a degree of ambiguity about the meaning of the 'tariff'. Sometimes the term has been used to mean that an offender should progress up the sentencing ladder in the event of offence repetition. Thus a burglar who was sentenced to community service last time he was convicted of burglary must expect to receive something more severe if he reoffends. This approach, however, has much more to do with reductivist ideas of sentencing than with desert principles. Secondly, some of the available sentences were traditionally not regarded as punishments at all. The probation order is a clear example. The probation order was not regarded as occupying any particular place in the tariff. Indeed, until the CJA 1991 it was not strictly in law a 'punishment' or 'sentence' at all. It was an individualised measure addressed to the offender's needs, rather than to the seriousness of the offence. The strongly reductivist base of community sentences such as probation led probation officers to urge them upon sentencers in their social inquiry reports as being 'alternatives to custody', likely to produce a more beneficial (or at least less harmful) effect than imprisonment.

The failure of rehabilitation to deliver on the promise it seemed to offer in the 1970s was mentioned earlier in this chapter. At around the same time in the United States there emerged other concerns about reductivist goals in sentencing, which prompted a resurgence of interest in the principle of desert. The main concern was that, in the pursuit of reductivist goals, sentencers were imposing long and often indeterminate custodial terms. Much of the decision over sentence length was being left to members of parole boards who had been thought to be better placed than sentencers to judge the rehabilitative impact which the sentence might be making. The new desert movement protested at the injustice of incarcerating offenders for periods of time which bore no relationship to the seriousness of the offence which they had committed. This injustice was compounded by the paucity of evidence that these sentencing programmes actually worked. Accordingly in the United States from the mid-1970s onwards (marked in particular by the publication of the influential report *Doing Justice* (von Hirsch, 1976)) there has been a significant shift towards greater legislative involvement in sentencing goals and policies. Many states have introduced mandatory or presumptive sentencing guidelines which reduce sentencing discretion very considerably. The best known of these systems, that which operates in the state of Minnesota, is desert-based. Other systems, such as the Federal Sentencing Guidelines, have adopted a hybrid model, which tries to effect a compromise between the reductivist and desert approaches. The discretionary powers of parole boards in America have been reduced, and in some states they have been abolished altogether. In the wake of the American developments, and for similar reasons, many other countries have re-thought their sentencing principles. There have been important initiatives in Canada, Australia and several European countries, including Sweden and Eire (Clarkson and Morgan, 1995).

In England and Wales, as we have seen, comparable changes were signalled by the government in the White Paper, *Crime, Justice and Protecting the Public* (1990). This document proposed a comprehensive set of reforms of sentencing and early release arrangements. The aim was to create 'a coherent framework for the use of financial, community and custodial punishments'. The White Paper urged that proportionality should be the guiding criterion for deciding the severity of sentence (paras 1.6, 2.2 and 2.3) and was sceptical about relying on deterrence as the basis for determining sentence. The White Paper advocated the adoption of desert principles in respect of all these sentences. Within the new desert-based sentencing structure, the courts are to continue to decide upon the severity of penalty deserved for each particular type of offence, and will decide upon the weight to be attached to aggravating and mitigating circumstances in general, and in each particular case. The White Paper thus differed from the more radical American sentencing guideline models, where normally recommended sentence levels are set in advance by the legislature.

Most of the proposals in the White Paper found their way into the subsequent legislation, the CJA 1991. The best way of understanding that Act is to see it as laying down a basic framework for sentencing. It deals with custodial sentences, community sentences, fines, and discharges and other measures, and these should be seen as occupying more or less distinct levels in the sentencing scheme, with custodial sentences at the top and discharges at the bottom. Selection of the appropriate sentence is dependent, first and foremost, on the seriousness of the offence committed. A diagram representing the sentencing framework is set out at figure 1 on p. 52, and that framework is the subject of Chapter 2.

There have, of course, been a number of important legislative developments in sentencing since the 1991 Act, although the framework remains basically intact. These changes are dealt with where appropriate in this book, but it may be helpful to summarise the main ones here. The CJA 1993 represented something of a reversal of policy in sentencing after the 1991 Act. The 1993 Act abolished the system of 'unit fines' in magistrates' courts which had been introduced by the 1991 Act, and it also recast s. 29 of that Act, which deals with the relevance to offence seriousness of the offender's previous convictions or his failure to respond to previous sentences. This issue is discussed at **2.2.5**. The CJPOA 1994 introduced secure training orders, a new custodial sentence for juvenile offenders, but power to make those orders only became available in 1989, and the relevant provisions are to be repealed when the CDB becomes law. See further, *Appendix 1*. The 1994 Act made various other adjustments to the framework of the 1991 Act. In particular, by s. 48, it placed the circumstances in which a sentencing court should take account of the offender's guilty plea on a statutory footing, it substituted a new definition of 'sexual offence' in s. 31 of the 1991 Act, it relaxed somewhat the requirements in s. 3 of the 1991 Act that a pre-sentence report should be obtained before imposing a custodial or community sentence, it lowered the age at which an order for long-term detention under the CYPA 1933, s. 53(2), could be made, from 14 to 10, and it increased the maximum sentence of detention in a young offender institution which could be imposed on a 15, 16 or 17-year-old from 12 months to 24 months. The C(S)A 1997 made a range of further changes. These were, by s. 2, the introduction of an automatic life sentence for the second 'serious offence' and, by s. 3, a minimum sentence of seven years for the third Class A drug trafficking offence. Provision in s. 4 for a minimum sentence of three years for the third domestic burglary has not been brought into force. The 1997 Act abolished consent requirements for community orders, and made changes to fine enforcement. It also amended powers of Crown Court judges to indicate the period to be served by a discretionary life sentence prisoner before the prisoner could first be considered for early release. The CDB, which is currently before Parliament, contains provisions to introduce a new custodial sentence for young offenders, the detention and training order. This will replace detention in a young offender institution for offenders aged under 18, but that sentence will continue to be available for offenders aged 18, 19 or 20. The Bill proposes the introduction of two new community sentences, the drug treatment and testing order and the action plan order, together with a new non-custodial sentence, the reparation order. The Bill places a specific duty on the Court of Appeal to produce sentencing guidelines, and will establish a sentencing panel of experts to advise the court on the framing of those guidelines.

FIGURE 1
OUTLINE OF THE SENTENCING SCHEME

CUSTODIAL SENTENCES

Imprisonment (21 +)
Detention in a young offender institution (15–20)
Detention and training order (12–17)*
Detention under CYPA 1933, s. 53(2) (10–17)

CUSTODY THRESHOLD : 'so serious'
offence seriousness (s. 1(2)(a))
or
public protection following conviction for violent
or sexual offence (s. 1(2)(b))

COMMUNITY SENTENCES	FINES
Combination order (16 +)	
Community service (16 +)	
Drug treatment and testing (16 +)*	
Curfew order (10 +)	
Attendance centre order (10–20)	all age
Supervision order (10–17)	groups
Action plan order (10-17)*	

COMMUNITY SENTENCE THRESHOLD
'serious enough' (s. 6(1))

NON-CUSTODIAL SENTENCES

Reparation (10–17)*
Bind over (all age groups)
Discharge (all age groups)

SERIOUSNESS OF OFFENCE

*Sentences to be made available when the CDB is brought into force, at which time the sentence of detention in a young offender institution will become available only for offenders aged 18, 19 or 20.

2 Sentencing Law and Sentencing Principles

2.1 HOW SHOULD THE SENTENCER ARRIVE AT THE SENTENCE?

This entire book could be regarded as an explanation of how a sentencer arrives at the sentence. Yet by outlining, at this early stage, the major factors which should govern the sentencer's decision in a particular case, it will be possible to set in context the detailed discussion of sentencing procedure, powers and policy which follow in later chapters.

It is helpful to think of a sentencer asking himself or herself a sequence of four questions (see **2.1.1** to **2.1.4**):

2.1.1 Is the sentence for the offence fixed by law?

If statute prescribes a mandatory sentence for the offence of which the offender has just been convicted, the sentencer's task is simple. The sentence fixed by law is pronounced. Sentence is so fixed in very few cases.

(a) For high treason (Treason Act 1814, s. 1) and for piracy with violence (Piracy Act 1837, s. 2), the death penalty is retained. The death penalty cannot be carried out on a pregnant woman (Death Penalty (Expectant Mothers) Act 1931). Since prosecutions for treason and piracy are uncommon, to say the least, no further mention will be made of the death penalty. The CDB contains provisions for the repeal of these residual powers to impose the death penalty.

(b) For murder, the sentence must be one of life imprisonment (or custody for life, or detention during Her Majesty's pleasure, depending upon the age of the offender). The sentence for murder is considered at **4.5.2**, where the sentencer's retention of a degree of influence over a murderer's eventual release date is explained.

(c) The Crime (Sentences) Act 1997, s. 2, requires the Crown Court to impose a life sentence where an offender has been convicted of a second 'serious offence' as defined in the Act. Where an offender has been convicted for the third time of a Class A drug trafficking offence, s. 3 of the same Act requires the Crown Court to impose a custodial sentence of seven years or more. However, neither of these sentences is truly a 'mandatory' sentence, in that the court has a discretion under s. 2 to pass a different sentence if it finds that there are 'exceptional circumstances' in the case and, under s. 3, it need not impose the prescribed sentence if there are 'specific circumstances' which would render such a sentence unjust.

Statutes empowering the courts to deal with offenders by some means other than imprisonment often use a form of words to the effect that the sentence may be imposed for any offence not being an offence the sentence for which is fixed by law or which falls to be imposed under s. 2 or s. 3 of the Crime (Sentences) Act 1997. This formula makes explicit the fact that the sentencing power is not available to the court in the cases just described.

2.1.2   What powers are at the court's disposal?

Assuming that sentence is not fixed by law, the sentencer considers the sentencing options which are at the court's disposal. This exercise can raise numerous sub-questions, such as 'What is the maximum penalty for the offence permitted by law?', 'What is the offender's age?' and 'Have reports on the offender been prepared?' Magistrates must bear in mind the special restrictions on the sentencing powers of magistrates' courts to impose custody (see **4.1**) or to impose a fine (see **6.1**). A Crown Court judge dealing with an offender on a committal for sentence should ascertain the particular statutory provision under which the committal took place, for in some cases the Crown Court's powers are limited to those which the magistrates would have had if they had not committed for sentence.

As to the maximum penalties available, if the offence is statutory the relevant statute will specify the longest term of imprisonment which may be imposed or, by not referring to imprisonment, shows that the offence is non-imprisonable. Common law offences are punishable with imprisonment for life (i.e. the judge may pass a life sentence or may impose the appropriate fixed-term sentence or some lesser punishment). Offenders under 21 may not be sentenced to imprisonment. All offences (apart from murder) and offenders of any age may be dealt with by way of a fine. If the offence is summary, the statute creating it specifies the maximum amount of the fine: if it is indictable the potential fine is unlimited. All this is subject to the restrictions on the powers of magistrates to fine and the special rules relating to the fining of juveniles. For maximum penalties see Table 1 on pp. 7–14. The availability of other forms of sentence depends primarily upon the age of the offender, and upon whether the offence of which the offender has been convicted is imprisonable (i.e. punishable with imprisonment in the case of an adult).

The matters mentioned above are covered in detail in later chapters, and the courts' sentencing powers are conveniently summarised in Table 2 on pp. 15–29. The main point to appreciate here is that the maximum penalty available for an offence in the Crown Court is usually well in excess of anything the sentencer would wish to impose, except in a very small batch of cases where the offender's crime is just about the most serious of its type.

2.1.3   How serious is the offence?

Given that the sentencer is unlikely to want to pass the maximum sentence, the next question is: what level of sentence would properly reflect the seriousness of the offence? It is very difficult to define 'seriousness' in the abstract, and no attempt is made to do so in existing sentencing law. It is of great importance, however, for the sentencer to gauge the seriousness of one offence in relation to another, and to distinguish within each offence, for example one case of burglary from another case of burglary. Distinctions also need to be drawn between the respective roles played by co-defendants in a particular case. This is a demanding task for the sentencer, but it is central to the sentencing decision. It is perhaps not so difficult as it might sound. In assessing seriousness, the sentencer should have regard to the immediate circumstances of the offence, and the degree of the offender's culpability in relation to that offence. Sentencers are not entirely on their own in this task. They do not need to start from a blank sheet in every case. They will derive guidance on the assessment of offence seriousness, particularly where sentence is being imposed in the Crown Court, from the guideline judgments of the Court of Appeal and, where sentence is being imposed by magistrates, from the Magistrates' Association Guidelines (1997) and, perhaps, guidelines and norms produced by the particular bench. This guidance relates to sentencing for particular offences, and is set out where appropriate in Chapter 12, which deals with sentencing for a range of individual crimes.

The principle that a sentence should be in proportion to the seriousness of the offence committed, and that there is some recognised scale by which the appropriateness of a sentence can be judged, has long been an important consideration in sentencing, though it was given especial prominence by the CJA 1991. This scale has traditionally been known as the 'tariff'. This word should be used with caution. It has overtones of rigidity in sentencing ('slot-machine justice'), so that each of the Magistrates' Association Guidelines contain a warning that the Guidelines should be used with discretion and are not a 'tariff'. The term 'tariff' is also confusing because it is used on occasions to express a quite different proposition — that an offender who reoffends should, on each subsequent return to court, move 'up-tariff' and be sentenced more severely. This notion, in fact, tends to run contrary to the idea of proportionality in sentencing, and is at odds with the statutory framework of the CJA 1991. The tariff is not referred to in any statute, is only occasionally mentioned in sentencing case-law and has never been judicially defined. For these reasons, the term 'tariff sentence' and its companion term 'individualised sentence' are generally avoided in this book.

In determining the seriousness of the offence, the sentencer must always take into account any aggravating or mitigating factors which impinge upon the question of offence seriousness. Some of the factors apply across a range of offences. An example of a factor which tends to make an offence more serious is where the offender has committed the offence in 'breach of trust'. This has relevance in theft and deception offences, for example where a senior employee abuses his position of responsibility to embezzle funds or provide an outside team of offenders with a key to the stockroom. It also has relevance in sexual offences, for example where a schoolteacher or a social worker abuses that position of authority to commit a sexual offence on a child. An example of a general factor which tends to make an offence less serious is where there was provocation immediately before the offence. This factor may be relevant in a range of offences against the person or against public order. There are other factors which are relevant to seriousness in a more restricted range of offending. Thus, if the offence is one involving dishonesty, the court, as well as considering any breach of trust, will also be influenced by matters such as whether the offence was carefully planned or was committed on impulse, the value of the property involved and whether any, or how much, of it has been recovered. If the offence is one of violence, the court will be influenced by the severity of the injuries caused to the victim, the extent to which the victim has recovered, the offender's intention (or lack of it) to cause serious injury and the nature of the weapon (if any) which was used. By weighing up such factors as these, the sentencer will be able to reach a view on offence seriousness, and hence a provisional view on the appropriate sentence. According to the CJA 1991, offence seriousness is the key factor in determining whether the sentence will be a financial, community or custodial penalty. As we shall see, it is also a crucial factor in determining the size of the fine, the nature of the community sentence and the duration of any period of incarceration.

2.1.4 What mitigation is there?

The final matter for the sentencer's consideration is whether there are matters of mitigation personal to the offender which it is appropriate to take into account, even though these do not impinge upon the seriousness of the offence as such. Commonly encountered examples are where the sentencer gives credit for the offender's guilty plea, or the offender's clean (or nearly clean) criminal record. There are many other mitigating factors which may be considered, in the court's discretion. Information about the offender's personal circumstances might emerge from the facts of the offence, from the pre-sentence report or from the plea in mitigation advanced by the defence.

2.1.5 Consideration of the questions together

Of course a sentencer does not actually jump through the hoops of answering each of the above questions every time sentence is passed. The question at **2.1.1** is so basic that it answers itself. The question at **2.1.2** will, at least where an experienced Crown Court judge is concerned, require little more consideration, though it should not be thought that mistakes over the court's powers are never made. Sentencing law has become much more voluminous and complex in recent years, and there have been many changes, so that mistakes are perhaps not infrequent. The Court of Appeal has said on several occasions recently that it is the duty of counsel to correct the sentencer if it looks as if a mistake is about to be made. If nobody notices the error until after sentence is passed, but it emerges later, the court has 28 days in which to rectify it and re-sentence. A lay bench of magistrates will often need help from their clerk as to their available powers.

The questions posed at **2.1.3** and **2.1.4** are the difficult ones. Many sentencers in the past would not have separated them, but would have asked themselves something like: what is the range or bracket of sentences generally considered by the courts to be appropriate for persons of a background and character similar to those of this offender, who have committed offences roughly similar to that committed by him? From that range the sentencer would then select the sentence, influenced by his own personal attitude towards the aims of sentencing, and by the impression which defence mitigation makes on him on the day. The two-stage approach, of determining the penalty appropriate to the gravity of the offence, and then reducing it to allow for mitigation which is not related to the offence was, however, advocated by the Court of Appeal in *Fraser* (1982) 4 Cr App R (S) 254. Its great advantage is to emphasise that the sentence should not be out of proportion to the gravity of the crime for which the offender is being sentenced, however appalling the offender's character and record might be. Thus good character and other meritorious aspects of the offender's life which are placed before the court might serve to mitigate the sentence but his bad character should not aggravate it. The two-tier approach has, in effect, received statutory recognition in the CJA 1991.

2.2 THE STATUTORY FRAMEWORK OF SENTENCING

The outline of the process by which the sentencer should approach the sentencing decision given above is based upon the statutory framework for sentencing decisions laid down in the CJA 1991. It is now time to say something more about that framework.

2.2.1 The key concept of offence seriousness

Figure 1 on p. 52 is an attempt to represent in pictorial form the sentencing structure which has been in place since 1991. It tries to show the way in which the groups of criminal penalties are now related to each other. It will be seen that these groups are related more or less hierarchically, with custodial sentences at the apex and community sentences immediately below. At the lower levels are fines and discharges. The CJA 1991 requires that (with an exception relating to violent offences and sexual offences) a custodial sentence can be imposed only where the offence committed by the offender is 'so serious that only such a sentence can be justified' (CJA 1991, s. 1(2)(a)). This makes it clear that custodial sentences should be reserved for the most serious crimes, and that on every occasion when a sentencer is considering using custody he must ask himself whether 'only such a sentence can be justified': in other words that no lesser penalty, such as a community order, will do. The exception referred to above, where a sentencer may impose custody where the offender has committed a sexual offence or a violent offence, requires that 'only such a sentence would be adequate to protect the public from serious harm from him' (s. 1(2)(b)). The CJA 1991 also provides that a sentencer must justify the imposition of a community sentence (rather than something less severe) and the criterion here is that the offence committed by the offender is 'serious enough to justify such a sentence' (s. 6(1)). This makes it clear that community sentences should be reserved for that 'middle band' of offending which is serious enough to justify that approach but which is not so serious that the only possible sentence is a custodial one. The sentencing hierarchy is, then, primarily fixed by offence seriousness. It is offence seriousness which mainly determines the outcome at both the 'custody threshold' and the 'community sentence threshold'. The provisions relating to community sentences are described in more detail in Chapter 5. Fines and other non-custodial sentences are dealt with in Chapters 6 and 7, respectively.

When the sentencer is determining the seriousness of the offence, he is obliged by CJA 1991, s. 3(3)(a) to 'take into account all such information about the circumstances of the offence (including any aggravating or mitigating factors) as is available'. This must be done whenever the sentencer is considering the imposition of a custodial sentence (s. 3(3)) or a community sentence (s. 7(1)). It should be noted that the language of the CJA 1991 in this respect is mandatory, and imposes a *duty* upon the sentencer to give proper weight to factors relevant to offence seriousness. In addition, and by contrast, CJA 1991, s. 28(1) *permits* the sentencer also to have regard to any other matters in mitigation which are personal to the offender. Such matters will not relate to the seriousness of the offence, as such.

A sentencer might be expected to take into account a range of factors as being relevant to the seriousness of an offence. It is not possible (and it would be rather tedious to try) to give an exhaustive list. What follows is an indication of what the sentencing cases indicate to be the most important of these matters. Importance in this context can be measured both in terms of the range of offences to which they may be regarded as relevant, and to the extent of their likely impact upon sentence levels.

2.2.2 Factors which aggravate offence seriousness

(a) *Where the victim is especially vulnerable* It is widely accepted that where the offender has taken advantage of a relatively helpless person (i.e., someone very young, very old or handicapped) this aggravates the seriousness of the offence. An example is *Allen* (1988) 10 Cr App R (S) 466, where a custodial sentence of six years was upheld on offenders who robbed an 82-year-old woman in her own home. Another type of case is where confidence tricksters take advantage of elderly people to overcharge them for work done. An example is *Richards* (1989) 11 Cr App R (S) 286, where Hutchison J said that 'where victims selected are elderly or for some other reason vulnerable' offenders can expect custody 'despite youth or good character'. An issue of principle here is whether the offence is only to be regarded as aggravated where it can be shown that the offender actually knew that the victim was vulnerable, and had targeted them for that reason, or whether the offence is also aggravated when, say, an elderly householder suffers severe nervous shock when confronting a burglar in her home. It seems not unreasonable to take the view that any burglar may be assumed to know that victims may suffer distress, and must take the consequences of a greater than average degree of injury resulting from the offence. The Court of Appeal guideline case on house burglary, *Brewster* [1998] 1 Cr App R (S) 181, draws no sharp distinctions here, but it may perhaps be assumed that the offence is at its worst when a victim was targeted because of their vulnerability.

There is a category of people whose employment puts them in a position where they are more likely to be the victims of assault than the average person. Where persons such as police officers, taxi drivers, traffic wardens, late-night bus drivers and landlords of licensed premises are the victims of crime, this is often regarded by the courts as enhancing the seriousness of the offence. In *Tremlett* (1983) 5 Cr App R (S) 199 Kenneth Jones J said that 'What very substantially increases the seriousness of these offences is that they were directed towards a bus conductor doing his ordinary job on a bus shortly after midnight'. In *Robertson* (1990) 12 Cr App R (S) 278 the Court of Appeal observed that traffic wardens 'deserve the protection of the courts in carrying out their sometimes unpopular duties'. In *Rankin* (1993) 14 Cr App R (S) 636 the Court said that 'cab drivers are recognised as being vulnerable to attack and . . . sentences upon those who attack cab drivers have to reflect their vulnerability'.

(b) *Breach of trust*   This is a key aggravating factor. It is encountered in two main contexts.

First, it arises in sexual offences, where an offender has taken advantage of a person for whose care they were responsible. In *Usher* (1980) 2 Cr App R (S) 123 a schoolteacher, aged 30, was convicted of two counts of unlawful sexual intercourse and one of abduction of a pupil, aged 14, with whom he had formed an association. The Court of Appeal said that a custodial sentence was inevitable in this case and that 'it has to be made clear to persons occupying similar positions of trust, and to the parents of girls who are the recipients of that trust, that an abuse of it will receive stern treatment from the courts'. Many similar comments in later cases can be found. See, for example, *B* [1997] 2 Cr App R (S) 96, where the sexual offences were committed on a vulnerable child and 'were in gross breach of trust', and *Baker* (1989) 11 Cr App R (S) 513.

Secondly, it is relevant in offences of dishonesty, where a person has taken advantage of his office or employment to abuse trust which has been reposed in him. In *Dawson* (1987) 9 Cr App R (S) 248, when upholding a custodial sentence for theft of £64,000 by a stockbroker but reducing it from four years to three years for other reasons, Stephen Brown LJ said that breaches of trust 'undermine public confidence, because the matters of financial dealing with which this man was involved cannot be carried out unless confidence is reposed in those who carry out these transactions on behalf of members of the public'. For the guideline decision on theft in breach of trust see *Barrick* (1985) 7 Cr App R (S) 143 and **12.4.1**.

(c) *Premeditation and professionalism*   This aggravating factor suggests that, where the offence was committed after careful planning and/or by an offender experienced in perpetrating such offences, the offender's culpability is very high. The carefully planned offence stands at the other end of the scale of seriousness from offences which are committed on the spur of the moment and in response to immediate temptation (see **2.2.3**). A good contrast is between 'one-off' cases of pickpocketing, which are almost always dealt with by way of a fine or a conditional discharge, and carefully planned campaigns of pickpocketing (see *Tillett* (1987) 9 Cr App R (S) 411). A similar distinction is drawn in practice in shoplifting. See the cases discussed at **12.4.1**.

Planned offending may display 'a considered attack on social values, with greater commitment and perhaps continuity than a spontaneous crime' (Ashworth, 1995, p. 131). Such evidence may betoken the 'professional' offender, i.e. one who is committed to a criminal way of life, rather than one who drifts in and out of law-breaking. The fact that an offence is committed in the course of so-called organised crime is clearly an aggravating factor, but one problem of focussing on 'professionalism' as an aggravating factor in sentencing is that it is often difficult to distinguish it from simple persistence in offending. The conduct of the petty persistent offender lacks the elements of seriousness which characterise the professional, but it is unclear precisely when the sentencer may draw an inference from the pattern of an offender's criminal history that he displays the aggravating element of professionalism.

(d) *Gratuitous violence and injury* Where an offender has deliberately caused harm over and above that which is normally intrinsic in the commission of the particular offence, this is regarded as an aggravating feature of the case. In giving sentencing guidelines for rape in *Billam* (1986) 8 Cr App R (S) 48, for example, Lord Lane CJ indicated that in any case where violence was used over and above the force necessary to commit the rape, or where a weapon was used, or where the woman was subjected to sexual indignities apart from the fact of the rape, all those matters would aggravate the offence significantly. See further **12.3.1**. Such aggravating factors can also be identified in relation to the various types of assault, such as where the offender kicks and inflicts further injury on a victim who is already on the ground and is unable to defend himself. In *Ivey* (1981) 3 Cr App R (S) 185 Griffiths LJ said that 'The degree of injury likely to be caused by kicking a man in the head when he is down is of a wholly different degree to that which is likely to be suffered in the course of a fist fight.' Gratuitous violence and injury was at its worst in *Legge* (1988) 10 Cr App R (S) 208, where the offender forced the victim to remove his clothes before beating and kicking him, stabbing him in the leg and urinating on him. In that case a sentence of seven years' imprisonment was upheld. The matter is also relevant in house burglary, where ransacking, soiling and gratuitous damage in the house all make the offence more serious (*Brewster* [1998] 1 Cr App R(S) 181).

(e) *Group offending* Where an offence is committed by several people acting together, this is often regarded as a matter which aggravates the seriousness of the offence. This issue is most prominent in public order offences, where the offence label itself may well reflect the group nature of the offending. In *Rogers-Hinks* (1989) 11 Cr App R (S) 234, a sentence of eight years' imprisonment was upheld on an offender who took a leading part in inciting a disturbance by football supporters on a North Sea ferry. Fighting lasted for 45 minutes, damage to the value of £24,000 was caused, property worth a further £6,000 was stolen, and many passengers were put in fear. For other examples see **12.6.3**. The level of public fear generated by group offending is highly significant here. In addition, Ashworth suggests that 'group pressure to continue may make such offences less likely to be abandoned, and group dynamics may lead to greater harm or damage being caused (Ashworth, 1995, p. 130).

(f) *Offending whilst on bail*   In *Baverstock* [1993] 1 WLR 202 it was established that where the offence had been committed while the offender was on bail awaiting trial for another offence, that factor should be regarded as aggravating the later offence. Subsequently, a legislative provision to this effect was inserted by the CJA 1993 into the CJA 1991, s. 29(2), which now reads: 'In considering the seriousness of an offence committed while the offender was on bail, the court shall treat the fact that it was committed in those circumstances as an aggravating factor.' This provision is expressed in mandatory terms, but it has to be set against a further rule which states that consecutive sentences should be given for offences which are linked in this way. See further on this, **4.4.4**.

(g) *Offence prevalence*   It is possible to find comments in sentencing cases that the prevalence of an offence may justify an increased sentence, or that severe sentencing for a particular type of offence is appropriate in an area where it is presenting a special problem, on grounds of general deterrence. An example is *Bennett* (1995) 16 Cr App R (S) 438 ('joyriding' by juvenile offenders). In *Masagh* (1990) 12 Cr App R (S) 568, a case dealing with pickpocketing, Lloyd LJ doubted whether prevalence should be taken into account, and it is very hard to square the practice with the principles of the CJA 1991, which requires sentencers to address the seriousness of the case before them rather than the social problem represented by the totality of that kind of offending. In *Cunningham* [1993] 1 WLR 183, however, Lord Taylor of Gosforth CJ said that prevalence of a particular form of offending, and public concern about such offences, would be regarded as an aggravating factor when sentencing for an example of such an offence. In *Cunningham* Lord Taylor gave the example of violent sexual attacks being prevalent in a particular neighbourhood. Each such offence, he said, affects not only the immediate victim, but women generally in that area, putting them in fear and limiting their freedom of movement. Accordingly, in such circumstances, the sentence commensurate with the seriousness of the offence may need to be higher than had the offence taken place elsewhere. The point was restated in *Cox* [1993] 1 WLR 188. In fact, his lordship's comments may have less to do with prevalence as such, and more to do with addressing levels of community concern about a form of offending. Enhanced sentencing for so-called 'road rage' assaults are another example.

(h) *Racially motivated offending*   The Court of Appeal has made it clear on a number of recent occasions that where an offence is shown to have been racially motivated, that is an important aggravating factor. An example is *Attorney-General's Reference (Nos. 29, 30 and 31 of 1994)* (1994) 16 Cr App R (S) 698, where Lord Taylor CJ said that the racial element in these cases was a 'gravely aggravating feature'. The Magistrates' Association Guidelines (1997) make the same point. The presence of this motivation demonstrates a high degree of culpability in the offender in singling out the victim, and can also be seen as an additional harm to the victim, over and above the offence itself. The CDB proposes, in cl. 77, to require sentencing courts to treat racial motivation as an aggravating factor in sentencing, and to state in open court that the court has taken that matter into account. Also cll. 25 to 29 create new racially aggravated versions of existing assault, criminal damage, public order and harassment offences, attracting higher maximum penalties than the standard offences. Lord Taylor CJ in *Craney* [1996] 2 Cr App R (S) 336 doubted whether such special offences were really necessary, since the racial element in the offending could be dealt with appropriately and effectively by the sentencer in any event. Clause 77 will not be applicable when sentencing for the new racially aggravated offences, to avoid taking the same aggravating factor into account twice over.

2.2.3 Factors which mitigate offence seriousness

(a) *Offender has acted under provocation* While provocation is recognised in English law as a partial defence to murder (reducing that crime to manslaughter), in respect of all other offences it is relevant solely as a matter in mitigation. It is widely accepted that the offender's culpability for, say, an assault, may be significantly affected by his having received provocation before the act was committed. A sudden and impulsive violent reaction is regarded as less blameworthy than planned retaliation. The strength of the evidence of the provocation, of course, varies from case to case. In *Haley* (1983) 5 Cr App R (S) 9 the offender was a man of 45 and was of previous good character. He learned that, while he had been ill in hospital, his wife had formed an association with another man. The offender went to the man's house and, when he answered the door, he stabbed him four times. A sentence of three years' imprisonment was reduced to 18 months on a 'mild, inoffensive and unspectacular man suddenly . . . overwhelmed by circumstances and driven to do something which is wildly out of character' (per Lord Lane CJ). Another example is *Brookin* (1995) 16 Cr App R (S) 78 where the victim had attacked the offender's girlfriend and taunted him before the offender struck him. A custodial sentence was suspended in the light of the provocation. Where provocation is used as a mitigating factor, rather than as a partial defence to murder, it is more loosely interpreted by the courts and shades into cases where the offender has acted against a background of emotional stress.

(b) *Offender has acted under duress* Duress is a defence recognised in English law, but it is tightly circumscribed. In a case where an offender has been unable to found a defence of duress at his trial, it may nonetheless be possible to take those circumstances into account on sentence. In *Taonis* (1974) 59 Cr App R 160, for example, the offender was convicted of unlawful importation of cannabis. He had been forced into acting as a drug courier because of threats to beat and torture the woman he was living with and that he would be falsely accused of having stolen a considerable amount of money. The sentence was reduced from four years' imprisonment to two years, Scarman LJ commenting that 'The experience [the defendant] has gone through was described in the court below as truly terrifying'. Taonis could not on the facts avail himself of the defence of duress, since there was an interval between the time of the threats and the commission of the offence during which time he could have gone to the police, but the pressure he was under did significantly reduce his culpability.

(c) *Offender has acted in circumstances which, though not amounting to a defence in law, are relevant to culpability* The House of Lords in *Sang* [1980] AC 402 made it clear that circumstances of entrapment did not amount to a defence in English law, though on appropriate facts 'its mitigating value may be high'. In *Chapman* (1989) 11 Cr App R (S) 222 the offender pleaded guilty to conspiracy to supply amphetamine sulphate. Chapman had been in custody with respect to a different matter when he was placed in the same cell as a detective posing as a drug dealer. Later the detective met Chapman again and offered him £20,000 if Chapman could obtain amphetamine for him. Chapman undertook to do so, but subsequently withdrew from the agreement. Chapman's sentence of four years' imprisonment was reduced on appeal. Similarly, in *Mackey* (1993) 14 Cr App R (S) 53 sentence was reduced from seven years to five years on an offender who pleaded guilty to supplying heroin, since the offender had been encouraged to commit the offence by an informer.

The offender's mistake or ignorance of the law may sometimes provide powerful mitigation. A good example is *Universal Salvage* v *Boothby* (1983) 5 Cr App R (S) 428, where the offending company's fine for breaching road traffic regulations was reduced to take account of the fact that they had reasonably relied upon a letter from the appropriate government department informing them (incorrectly, as it turned out) that they were exempt from the regulations. Another example is *Surrey County Council* v *Battersby* [1965] 2 QB 194, discussed at **7.1.1**.

(d)   *Offender was intoxicated*   Surprisingly, there are few reported cases which deal with the relevance of an offender's intoxication at the time of the offence to his culpability and, hence, to the seriousness of the offence. The difficulty is that while the offender's intoxication may in some circumstances show that the offence was not a calculated one, and that the offender is therefore less blameworthy than he might otherwise have been, there is an element of culpability inherent in the fact of voluntary intoxication which tends to cancel this out or, in the eyes of some, make matters even worse.

One or two Court of Appeal decisions indicate that intoxication is *not* relevant. In *Kirkland* (1975) CSP C3-2D01 the offender, after having drunk 16 pints of beer, set fire to an unoccupied hostel and caused damage estimated at £440. Lawton LJ, in upholding a sentence of three years' imprisonment, said that 'The truth of the matter is that this offence came to be committed because the appellant had far too much to drink. The courts do not normally take drunkenness into account as a mitigating factor for criminal offences.' See also *Bradley* (1980) 2 Cr App R (S) 12. Despite these authorities, there are other examples where the offender's intoxication at the time of the offence has been interpreted by the courts to mean that there was less culpability on his part than there would have been if there had been a sober decision to commit the offence. An example is *Abrahams* (1980) 2 Cr App R (S) 10, where the theft of a plastic dinghy by the offender was described by the Court of Appeal as a 'drunken frolic rather than a premeditated crime of dishonesty'. So construed, the offence was not serious enough to require the activation of a suspended sentence imposed upon the offender in earlier proceedings. Another example is *Spence* (1982) 4 Cr App R (S) 175.

2.2.4   Personal mitigation

Offenders are rarely so bad that nothing can be said on their behalf. Usually the counsel or solicitor for the defence puts forward a plea in mitigation (see **3.6.1**), and even where the offender is unrepresented he is entitled to mitigate for himself. Once the sentencer has heard and considered the mitigation, sentence will often be reduced from the penalty which was originally in mind, to give credit for what the sentencer considers to be good mitigation. It must be remembered, however, that unlike matters which are relevant to offence seriousness, which must be taken into account by the sentencer under CJA 1991, s. 3(3)(a), allowance for matters of personal mitigation is not an entitlement; these matters may be taken into account at the sentencer's discretion, under CJA 1991, s. 28(1).

The cases indicate that sometimes an offence is so serious that mitigation can have no effect, or have only a marginal effect. This was stated in *Inwood* (1974) 60 Cr App R 70, where the offender, a man of previous good character, pleaded guilty to various counts of deception. Referring to the 'personal tragedy' of the offender, Scarman LJ said that:

We have listened, I hope with sympathy and understanding, to the mitigating factors urged upon us . . . But in the balance that the court has to make between the mitigating factors and society's interest in marking its disapproval for this type of conduct, we come to the irresistible though unpalatable conclusion, that we must not yield to the mitigating factors.

In respect of particular offences, matters in mitigation may be largely ignored for public policy reasons. An example is the general irrelevance of the offender's good character and clean record when sentencing drug couriers (see *Aramah* (1982) 4 Cr App R (S) 407). The reason is that, according to the Court of Appeal in that case, it is generally people of good character who are targeted for recruitment as couriers.

The cogency of certain forms of mitigation may vary from offence to offence. For example the tendering of a guilty plea is given special weight in sexual offences, since the victim is thereby spared the further ordeal of having to give evidence in court (*Billam* (1986) 8 Cr App R (S) 48). Assistance given by the offender to the police in catching the 'prime movers' justifies a substantial reduction when sentencing drug offenders who have played a role lower down the scale (*Aramah*). These special cases apart, normally the eventual sentence reflects such mitigating factors as the defence have been able to put before the sentencer.

Personal mitigation can affect the sentence in one of two ways. Sometimes it reduces the quantum of punishment, as when the offender is sent to prison for a shorter term, is given a smaller fine or ordered to perform fewer hours of community service than would have been the case had there not been mitigation. Sometimes mitigation will persuade the sentencer to impose a different form of sentence, such as a suspended sentence of imprisonment rather than an immediate term (though the circumstances in which this is appropriate must be exceptional) or a community sentence rather than a custodial one.

Section 28(1) of CJA 1991 provides that:

(1) Nothing in this Part shall prevent a court from mitigating an offender's sentence by taking into account any such matters as, in the opinion of the court, are relevant in mitigation of sentence.

On the face of it, this subsection gives sentencers complete freedom to have regard to any matter, or combination of matters, in mitigation when they think it appropriate to do so. It was confirmed in *Cox* [1993] 1 WLR 188 that in a case where the sentencer had decided that the seriousness of the offence was such that only a custodial sentence could be justified for it, it was still possible that the sentencer could avoid the imposition of custody by having regard to the offender's personal mitigation (see **4.2.4**). This decision underlines the importance of the two-stage form of reasoning outlined in **2.1.2**.

It is important to note that s. 28(1) does not allow for 'personal aggravation', allowing factors unrelated to offence seriousness to increase the sentence. It is wrong, for example, for a sentencer to increase sentence because (as in *Spinks* (1980) 2 Cr App R (S) 335) the offender has chosen to contest the case, or (as in *Evans* (1986) 8 Cr App R (S) 197) because of the manner in which he has conducted his defence (although of course the offender will not have the benefit of any discount which he would have received had he pleaded guilty). There is authority in *Loosemore* (1980) 2 Cr App R (S) 172 that a sentencer must deal with an offender on the basis of his offence and not on the basis of his 'feckless character and general behaviour'. A more plausible claim, perhaps, is that an offender's sentence may be aggravated by his record of previous offending. This issue is considered in **2.2.5**.

Some factors which may, at the court's discretion, be taken into account as mitigation are dealt with below.

(a)   *Offender is relatively young*   The effect of youth as a mitigating factor is somewhat unpredictable. On occasions it is arguable that the offender's relative youth might tend to reduce culpability (along with the matters mentioned at **2.2.3**). This might be reflected in the substantive sentencing rules, such as the lower maximum custodial sentences which are available for offenders under 18. It seems, though, that youth cannot *per se* affect culpability, and so it is more appropriately seen as a mitigating factor. This is reinforced by the fact that the offender's youth will be of less importance when the offence is a very serious one. In *Dodds* (1996), *The Times*, 28 January 1997, the Court of Appeal said that some earlier authorities exaggerated the importance of youth as a mitigating factor, and that if the offence was very serious, little or no reduction in sentence should be made for that reason. Youth is more significant as a mitigating factor when associated with other personal characteristics, such as a clean record and good character (see, for example, *Cox* [1993] 1 WLR 188). Where the offender is very young, the principle contained in CYPA 1933, s. 44(1), may still have some relevance: 'Every court in dealing with a child or young person who is brought before it, either as an offender or otherwise shall have regard to [his or her] welfare.' See *Secretary of State for the Home Department, ex parte Furber* [1998] 1 Cr App R (S) 208.

(b)   *Offender is relatively old*   In *Varden* [1981] Crim LR 272 the Court of Appeal upheld a reduction in sentence on a 71-year-old offender of low intelligence because his advanced years would probably make a term of imprisonment all the more unpleasant for him. In *Wilkinson* (1974) CSP C2-2B01 the offender pleaded guilty to various charges of indecent assault, indecency with a child and unlawful sexual intercourse with a girl aged under 13. All the offences were committed on the offender's grandnieces. Prison sentences of four years were reduced, 'as an act of mercy', to two and a half years, Roskill LJ stating that 'No court willingly sentences a man of 60 to spend a large part of the remainder of his life in prison.' See also *Nicholson* (1992) 14 Cr App R (S) 311, at (k) below. On occasions (such as where there is evidence of senility, or disordered thinking) it is arguable that the offender's relative age might tend to reduce culpability together with the matters mentioned at **2.2.3**. Ordinarily, though, age does not affect culpability, so that it is better regarded as personal mitigation.

(c)   *Offender has a good character, a clean record or relatively few previous convictions*   There are numerous decisions which can be taken to illustrate this point, and it offers one of the most frequently advanced matters in mitigation.

One of the most powerful matters which can be advanced in mitigation is the offender's good character and clean record. For such a person, the fact of conviction itself may be a sufficient penalty. Even where the offence is so serious that a custodial sentence is inevitable, there is an argument for reducing such a sentence for a first offender since 'for a man of good character undergoing his first prison sentence, conviction and a prison sentence are in themselves a substantial punishment' (per Lord Lane CJ in *Vinson* [1982] Crim LR 192). Lawyers try to mitigate on behalf of an offender who does have previous convictions by trying to show those convictions in a better light, such as by pointing out that they were committed some years ago (such as in *Cole* (1983) 5 Cr App R (S) 218, where the offender was aged 27 and the Court of Appeal said that a conviction as a juvenile 'can be disregarded for present purposes'), or were relatively trivial (in *Silver* (1982) 4 Cr App R (S) 48, a record of road traffic offences was said to be irrelevant when the current offence was manslaughter), or were of a quite different type to the current offence (in *Williams* (1983) 5 Cr App R (S) 244, an earlier conviction for rape not relevant to an offence of dishonesty). It seems that even a substantial list of convictions can be offset by evidence of a gap in the offending prior to the most recent offence, such a gap being indicative of an attempt by the offender to 'go straight'. In *Bleasdale* (1984) 6 Cr App R (S) 177 Hobhouse J commented that: 'What has to be said in favour of this appellant is that since serving the sentence [in 1978] he has kept out of trouble. This is an important feature in his favour.'

(d) *Offender has rendered substantial assistance to the police* Mitigation is appropriate, and may in some cases be very substantial, where an offender has disclosed information to the authorities which has led to the apprehension of others and the bringing against them of serious charges. The extent of the discount varies, depending on the degree of assistance given, the seriousness of the offender's offence and the seriousness of the other crimes cleared up. In *Lowe* (1977) 66 Cr App R 122 the offender pleaded guilty to four counts of robbery and other offences. He was sentenced to 10 years' imprisonment, with a suspended sentence of 18 months activated consecutively. The Court of Appeal held that he should have been given greater credit for his statements made to the police, in which he implicated no fewer than 45 other people in armed robbery, burglary, theft and handling offences. The sentence was reduced to a total of five years. In *King* (1985) 7 Cr App R (S) 22 a sentence of six years on a man who pleaded guilty to robbery and eight counts of burglary was reduced to four and a half years to give credit for the offender's assistance to the police, which had resulted in the conviction of 17 other offenders, and in *Saggar* [1997] 1 Cr App R (S) 167 sentence was reduced from seven years to four and a half years because of the help given by the offender, including testifying for the prosecution in related matters. On the other hand, in *Debbag* (1991) 12 Cr App R (S) 733 no discount was appropriate. The information had not been given to the police until after the offender, who vigorously contested the case, had been convicted and sentenced. The information, when produced, was already known to the police in any event.

(e) *Offender has performed some meritorious act unrelated to the offence, which shows him in a good light* This category of mitigation is a classic example of the court having regard to matters which are totally unrelated to the offence, and engaging in a kind of 'moral accounting'. Sentences have been reduced where the offender has failed in a valiant attempt to rescue three children from a burning house (*Reid* (1982) 4 Cr App R (S) 280), gone to the assistance of a wounded police officer (*Playfair* [1972] Crim LR 387), raised the alarm after prisoners escaped from a bus transporting them (*Dawn* (1993) 15 Cr App R (S) 720), and has previously shown great courage in apprehending armed men who had been carrying out a robbery (*Alexander* [1997] 2 Cr App R (S) 74).

(f) *Offender has shown remorse* The offender's remorse for the offence committed, particularly where it is more than a mere expression of sorrow but involves some more practical demonstration of contrition, may afford a degree of mitigation.

One difficulty with this head of mitigation is that statements of remorse are easy to make and their genuineness or otherwise is difficult for the court to assess. In some cases the offender's remorse will be associated with an early guilty plea, or with assistance to the authorities, in which case the combination becomes a more persuasive one. A frank admission to the police when questioned about the offence produced some mitigation in *Moores* (1980) 2 Cr App R (S) 317, but a stronger case is *Claydon* (1994) 15 Cr App R (S) 526, where the offender confessed to a scout leader and then gave himself up. The Court of Appeal indicated that sentence should be reduced by up to half in such a case.

It may be that by the time of sentence the offender has already made voluntary restitution to the victim. The strength of this mitigation will vary according to the relative difficulty for the offender in making such a payment, rather than the amount of compensation which the offender actually makes. It can also give rise to a danger that such mitigation will thereby be available only to offenders who have the money to pay. The Court of Appeal was aware of this dilemma in *Crosby* (1974) 60 Cr App R 234 and pointed out that to impose a custodial sentence on one co-defendant but to suspend sentence on the other since he had managed to find £3,600 to pay to the victim 'does not seem to us to be a firm foundation for the administration of justice'.

(g) *Offender has pleaded guilty* Undoubtedly the most important and most frequently relied upon matter in mitigation is the offender's guilty plea. It has importance in respect of all offences, both in the Crown Court and in magistrates' courts, but it has particular relevance in cases involving sexual offences, if it saves the victim the distress of having to give evidence (see *Billam* (1986) 8 Cr App R (S) 48, the guideline case on rape, at **12.3.1**). In some cases a guilty plea may be evidence of genuine remorse on the part of the offender (see (f) above). In the great majority of cases, however, the reason why the courts grant a substantial discount on sentence for a guilty plea is that, by cooperating in the smooth running of the criminal justice system, defendants who plead guilty help to shorten trials, reduce court backlogs and save the costs of legal aid. The authorities suggest that a guilty plea typically results in a sentence reduction in the Crown Court of between one quarter and one third in the length of a custodial sentence. Its effect in each particular case is a matter within the discretion of the sentencing court, and in an appropriate case the discount may be reduced or denied altogether. The Magistrates' Association Guidelines (1997) include sentence guides for offences dealt with summarily which are based on a first-time offender pleading not guilty. The Guidelines state that 'A timely guilty plea may attract a sentencing discount of up to one third but the precise amount of discount will depend on the facts of each case and a last-minute plea of guilty may attract only a minimal reduction'. The leading Court of Appeal decision is *Costen* (1989) 11 Cr App R (S) 182, where it was confirmed that the guilty plea discount might be lost in any of the following circumstances:

(i) If the protection of the public makes it necessary that a long sentence, possibly the maximum sentence, be passed, then the discount may be lost. An example is *McLaughlin* (1979) 1 Cr App R (S) 298, which involved a robbery committed at knifepoint. But there is a powerful counter-argument that the maximum sentence should not be imposed if there is significant mitigation in the case, such as a guilty plea. See, for example, *Greene* (1993) 14 Cr App R (S) 682.

(ii) Discount can be reduced or lost in cases of 'tactical plea', where the offender has delayed his plea until the final moment in a misguided attempt to secure some tactical advantage. In such a case, of course, much of the expense involved in arranging the trial has already been incurred. An example is *Hollington* (1985) 7 Cr App R (S) 364, where the offender had delayed his plea so as to enjoy the somewhat more congenial surroundings while on remand awaiting trial than he would have done if he had pleaded guilty from the start and been sent to prison.

(iii) If the offender has been caught red-handed and a plea of guilty is inevitable, the discount may be lost. This was the case in *Landy* (1995) 16 Cr App R (S) 908. The offender pleaded guilty to aggravated vehicle taking. After being pursued by the police at 90 mph he crashed the car into a fence and turned it upside down. Police officers pulled him out through the rear window.

There are other situations in which it seems that the discount can be reduced or lost. In *Byrne* [1997] 1 Cr App R (S) 165 it was held that an offender who had absconded and remained at large for 19 months was not entitled to expect a discount for his guilty plea when he was rearrested and brought back before the court. Also, some or all of the discount may be lost if the offender admits guilt but adduces a version of the facts at odds with the prosecution, requiring the court to conduct a *Newton* hearing (see **3.3.2**) to determine exactly what happened. Examples are *Stevens* (1986) 8 Cr App R (S) 297 and *Williams* (1991) 12 Cr App R (S) 415, in each of which the Court of Appeal accepted that some of the discount should be lost, not least because the victim was still required to give evidence.

The above principles are well established in the case law, but the CJPOA 1994, s. 48, makes specific provision as to reductions in sentences for guilty pleas:

(1)   In determining what sentence to pass on an offender who has pleaded guilty to an offence in proceedings before that or another court, a court shall take into account—

(a)   the stage in the proceedings for the offence at which the offender indicated his intention to plead guilty, and

(b)   the circumstances in which this indication was given.

(2)   If as a result of taking into account any matter referred to in subsection (1) above, the court imposes a punishment on the offender which is less severe than the punishment it would otherwise have imposed, it shall state in open court that it has done so.

(3)   In the case of an offence the sentence for which falls to be imposed under subsection (2) of section 3 of the Crime (Sentences) Act 1997, nothing in that subsection shall prevent the court, after taking into account any matter referred to in subsection (1) above, from imposing any sentence which is not less than 80 per cent of that specified in that subsection.

Section 3 of the C(S)A 1997 is considered at **4.3.3**. The reference to 'the stage of the proceedings' and the 'circumstances' in which the plea was tendered are sufficiently broad to be regarded as incorporating the case law described above, and so far there have been no Court of Appeal decisions to indicate any change in practice as a result of the section. It should be noted that this provision is not confined to custodial sentences. It seems to be relevant to any sentence. The Magistrates' Association Guidelines (1997) state that 'Discount may be given in respect of the fine or periods of community service' as well as custodial terms. It is clear that a guilty plea, particularly where associated with other mitigation, may form the basis for passing a community sentence rather than a custodial one (see, for example, *Cox* [1993] 1 WLR 188, described at **4.2.4**). On the other hand, reduction from an immediate prison sentence to a suspended sentence on the basis of a guilty plea is not permissible, since even an early guilty plea cannot amount to the 'exceptional circumstances' required before a prison sentence may be suspended (see **4.6.3**).

Section 48 places an obligation on judges and magistrates to state in open court that, in consequence of the guilty plea, the court has imposed a less severe sentence than it would otherwise have done. In *Fearon* [1996] 2 Cr App (S) 25 the Court of Appeal stressed that sentencers must always make it clear whether or not a reduction has been given.

(h)   *Adverse effects of sentence on offender have been especially severe*   In general the Court of Appeal has taken the view that the collateral effects upon the offender of conviction and sentence are not in themselves sufficient reason for mitigating the penalty normally appropriate for the offence. Thus in many cases of serious theft in breach of trust (see **12.4.1**) the offender may well lose his reputation, employment and the prospects of future employment in any position of responsibility. The general approach is to say that the offender should have considered those risks before embarking on the offending. Sometimes, however, where the collateral effects are particularly harsh and the original offence is not so serious as to preclude it, some mitigation will be available. In *Richards* (1980) 2 Cr App R (S) 119 the offender was a 57-year-old general medical practitioner, who was convicted of obtaining money from the health authority by submitting false expenses claims. The sum involved was £600. He was sentenced to 30 months' imprisonment. It was urged on the Court of Appeal that the sentence was too high, and that the sentencer had given insufficient weight to the fact that Richards faced professional disciplinary proceedings, would surely never work as a doctor again, would lose his pension rights and, given his age, would be unable to find comparable work. There were other tragic personal circumstances, such as that his wife had committed suicide. Sentence was reduced to 12 months. In contrast in *Lowery* (1993) 14 Cr App R (S) 485, where 'catastrophic consequences' ensued after the offender, a police officer, was convicted of false accounting, the Court of Appeal felt unable to suspend the prison sentence. In *Barbery* (1975) 62 Cr App R 248 sentence was reduced on a man who had been involved in an affray, during the course of which his own hand had been severed. In *Rees* (1982) 4 Cr App R (S) 71 it was accepted that the sentencer might take into account the fact that, as a result of his conviction, the offender would be discharged from military service, but a harder line was taken in *Ranu* [1996] 2 Cr App R (S) 334.

(i)   *Offender's serious illness*   The general view seems to be that the offender's illness is not a reason for mitigation, and should not form the basis for avoiding a custodial sentence which was otherwise merited. In *Moore* (1993) 15 Cr App R (S) 97 and in *Stark* (1992) 13 Cr App R (S) 548 the offenders had been diagnosed as HIV positive. In the former case the medical evidence as to the offender's condition was unclear, but in the second case it was accepted that he had recently developed AIDS and that his life expectancy was between one and two years. In both cases the Court of Appeal held that the correct sentences had been imposed and that the illness was a matter for the executive authorities and the Home Office, but not the courts. Nevertheless, in other cases, such as *Varden* [1981] Crim LR 272 the Court of Appeal has upheld a sentence reduction and, after reviewing the earlier authorities, the Court of Appeal in *Bernard* [1997] 1 Cr App R (S) 135 said that an offender's serious illness may exceptionally, as an act of mercy, allow the imposition of a lesser sentence than would otherwise be required.

(j)   *Severe adverse effect of sentence on offender's family*   There is authority that, in principle, the adverse effect upon the offender's family of the offender's conviction and sentence is not in itself a ground for mitigation. In *Ingham* (1974) CSP C4-2A01 Lord Widgery CJ said that '. . . imprisonment of the father inevitably causes hardship to the rest of the family . . . The crux of the matter is that part of the price to pay when committing a crime is that imprisonment does involve hardship on the wife and family, and it cannot be one of the factors which can affect what would otherwise be the right sentence.' On the other hand, such matters are regularly invoked in pleas in mitigation and, certainly where the effects upon the family would be unusually severe, they have been permitted to mitigate sentence.

The Court of Appeal has on occasions varied a custodial sentence so as to allow an offender's immediate release where there is evidence of acute hardship. In *Haleth* (1982) 4 Cr App R (S) 178, for example, the offender was convicted of affray and sentenced to 12 months' imprisonment. After sentence the offender's wife died from a kidney disease leaving their son, who was also very ill, uncared for. Sentence was varied to allow immediate release. In *Bellikli* [1998] 1 Cr App R (S) 135 a prison sentence was suspended by the Court of Appeal because the offender's child was very ill and would require major surgery in the near future. Another aspect of the same problem is where a custodial sentence on a woman will have the effect of leaving her children with nobody to look after them. Again, in principle, this factor is not relevant, but the Court of Appeal has adjusted sentence on some occasions to achieve a merciful outcome. *Vaughan* (1982) 4 Cr App R (S) 83 is one such case. More recently in *Whitehead* [1996] 1 Cr App R (S) 111 the Court of Appeal observed that there was always a reluctance to send the mother of small children to prison, although sometimes there was no choice. In this case, where both parents were given short prison terms, it was possible to vary the sentence on the mother so that she could be returned to her three young sons.

(k) *Lapse of time since the commission of the offence* Lapse of time since the commission of an offence has been taken into account in mitigation of sentence in several cases. It seems to be relevant for two reasons. The first is that where the offence is 'stale', the offender may, in a sense, be thought of as a different person from the one who committed it. An example is *Dashwood* (1994) 16 Cr App R (S) 733, where the offender was sentenced at the age of 29 for offences committed when he was 14. Second, the offender may have suffered considerable stress in having the matter hanging over him for so long. The argument for mitigation will be much less strong where the offence was a very serious one, and/or where the offender has taken active steps to avoid detection. It will be stronger where these factors are missing and/or there has been an unusually long delay in the prosecution and trial process. In *Tierney* [1982] Crim LR 53 there was a delay of some 18 months between the offender's arrest and his trial for burglary. Part of the delay was due to his being involved in a road accident and having to spend time in hospital. During the interval the offender had married and found a job. The Court of Appeal reduced the sentence of nine months' imprisonment to one of six months, suspended for two years, and said that the offender should be sentenced on the basis of his situation at the time of sentence and not at the time of the offence.

There are some offences, such as the commission of incest, which are by their nature unlikely to emerge until long after they have been committed. This, together with the serious nature of the offences themselves, means that any discount for the delay is likely to be minimal. In *Nicholson* (1992) 14 Cr App R (S) 311 the 64-year-old offender was being sentenced for a series of violent and sexual offences committed on his stepchildren 20 years before. A total sentence of nine years was reduced to seven years, to take account of the lapse of time and the age of the offender.

2.2.5 Relevance of previous convictions

The significance of the offender's previous convictions to the current sentence is a complex matter. Everyone accepts that the offender's record can often be of considerable importance in selecting the sentence, but there is little appellate discussion of the point, and it is not clear precisely what aspects of the offender's previous record should properly be regarded as relevant. The most settled point is that an offender who has a clean, or relatively clean, record is generally entitled to a degree of mitigation in that respect. Section 28(1) of CJA 1991, as we have seen, would allow mitigation in such a case. No precise formula as to the extent of such mitigation can be arrived at, but it seems obvious that the more serious the offence the less scope there will be for mitigation (see **2.2.4**). A more difficult issue is the extent to which a sentencer is entitled to pass a more severe sentence on an offender who does have a record. A number of pre-1991 Act Court of Appeal decisions, such as *Galloway* (1979) 1 Cr App R (S) 311 and *Bailey* (1988) 10 Cr App R (S) 231, displayed a general acceptance of the view that it is wrong to impose a sentence which is longer than would be indicated by the seriousness of the offence purely on the basis of previous record. A poor record should not, on that view, be regarded as an aggravating factor relevant to offence seriousness (see **2.2.2**).

One of the clearest statements of this principle can be found in *Queen* (1981) 3 Cr App R (S) 245. There the offender pleaded guilty to theft, forging a valuable security, uttering a forged document and attempting to obtain property by deception. The impressive list of charges belied a rather mundane activity. He had stolen a cheque which had arrived in a letter for another person who lived at the same address, signed the name of the payee on the back of the cheque and then attempted to cash it. The offender, who had a long list of offences of dishonesty going back 25 years, was given a prison sentence of 18 months. In the Court of Appeal Kenneth Jones J said that it was clear that the offender had been sentenced 'not merely for the offences which he committed, but for his record'. Such an approach was 'wrong in principle':

> Of course no prisoner is to be sentenced for the offences which he has committed in the past and for which he has already been punished. The proper way to look at the matter is to decide a sentence which is appropriate for the offence for which the prisoner is before the court. Then in deciding whether that sentence should be imposed or whether the court can extend properly some leniency to the prisoner, the court must have regard to those matters which tell in his favour, and equally to those matters which tell against him; in particular his record of previous convictions. Then matters have to be balanced up to decide whether the appropriate sentence to pass is one at the upper end of the bracket or somewhere lower down.

The sentence was varied so as to allow Queen, who at the time of the appeal had served a little over nine months of his sentence, immediate release from custody. This approach to previous convictions, often referred to as the 'theory of progressive loss of mitigation', holds that while a first offender may present a good case for mitigation in light of his record, the accumulation of previous convictions results in the progressive loss of that mitigation so that, by the time of the fourth or fifth conviction, all mitigation for a clean (or fairly clean) record is lost and the offender is sentenced in accordance with the seriousness of the offence. It also entails, however, that an offender's sentence should never be increased to a level disproportionate with the seriousness of the current offence simply because of his poor record. Despite the Court of Appeal authority listed above, this principle has never been fully accepted by sentencers who undoubtedly do still tend in practice to regard a list of previous convictions as an aggravating factor and, at least to some extent, to sentence offenders 'on their records'.

The relevant statutory provision is CJA 1991, s. 29(1), which states that:

> In considering the seriousness of any offence, the court may take into account any previous convictions of the offender or any failure of his to respond to previous sentences.

Section 29(2) is concerned with offending while on bail, and was considered in **2.2.2(f)**. Subsections (3) to (6) of s. 29 provide that for the purposes of the section the court may take into account previous convictions of the offender which have been dealt with by way of a probation order, or by the grant of a discharge. They also provide that the court may take into account any failure by the offender to respond to an earlier probation order or conditional discharge. These provisions are there to make it clear that such disposals do count as previous convictions, despite PCCA 1973, s. 1C, which states that they are convictions only for certain purposes. Section 1C is considered further at **7.1.4** and need not detain us here.

It can be seen that s. 29(1) provides the sentencer with a power to take into account the offender's previous convictions, where these impinge upon the seriousness of the offence to be sentenced. Unfortunately the subsection gives no indication of when the previous record is relevant for this purpose. Without delving into the history of this provision, it is helpful to realise that this is the second version of s. 29(1) and that the original version, in contrast, stated that an offence should *not* be regarded as more serious by reason of the offender's previous convictions or failures to respond to previous sentences, although there was a narrow exception in cases where the previous convictions revealed an aggravating feature of the new offence which otherwise might not have been apparent, such as a history of racially motivated offending. This original version was in line with desert theory in giving a very limited relevance to previous convictions, but it was subjected to sustained criticism when the 1991 Act was implemented. Despite the new version of s. 29(1) having been on the statute book since 1993 (when the CJA 1993 substituted the new wording) there has been no guidance from the Court of Appeal on its meaning. It is sometimes said that the new s. 29(1) gives sentencers complete flexibility to take account of previous convictions when sentencing, so that offenders can now be sentenced 'on their record'. This claim, however, ignores the fact that s. 29(1) is still tied to the concept of offence seriousness, and so the question still unanswered by Parliament and the Court of Appeal is: *When* can it properly be said that previous convictions of the offender, or previous failures of his to respond to past sentences, actually affect the *seriousness* of the new offence? The Magistrates' Association Guidelines (1997) advise magistrates to 'take care in using previous convictions or any failure to respond to previous sentences in assessing seriousness'. The Guidelines recommend that 'courts should identify any convictions relevant for this purpose and then consider to what extent they affect the seriousness of the present offence'. Wasik and von Hirsch (1994) have argued that the wording of the new s. 29(1) can still be squared with the principle of progressive loss of mitigation, but it is unclear whether the earlier Court of Appeal decisions, such as *Queen*, have any continuing relevance. It may also be noted that the *Practice Direction (Crime: Antecedents)* [1998] 1 Cr App R 213 states that 'In the Crown Court the police will provide brief details of the circumstances of the last three similar convictions, and/or of convictions likely to be of interest to the court, the latter being judged on a case by case basis.'

2.3 THE DUTY TO AVOID DISCRIMINATION

During the passage through Parliament of the Bill which became the CJA 1991, there was pressure for insertion into that Act of a specific legal duty on courts, and on other criminal justice agencies, to ensure that their decisions were in no way discriminatory as far as the race or gender of offenders was concerned, and to create an inspectorate to enforce such a provision. An amendment to the Bill to introduce a legal duty was, however, withdrawn in the face of a commitment by the government to consider how best such a principle should be enshrined in statute.

The rather disappointing result is the CJA 1991, s. 95. This places a duty on the Secretary of State 'each year to publish such information as he considers expedient' for the purpose of enabling criminal justice agencies to avoid discrimination 'on the ground of race or sex or any other improper ground'. The first publications issued in accordance with CJA 1991, s. 95 were produced in September 1992 and further publications have been produced on a regular basis since.

2.4 COSTS OF SENTENCING MEASURES

Section 95 of CJA 1991 also requires the Secretary of State to publish annually such information as he considers expedient for the purpose of 'enabling persons engaged in the administration of criminal justice to become aware of the financial implications of their decisions'. The first batch of information was released in October 1992.

2.4.1 Average costs of various sentences

According to the most recent government figures available, the costs of different sentencing disposals are:

custodial sentence	£2,190 per month
combination order	£270 per month
probation order	£190 per month
supervision order	£180 per month
community service order	£140 per month

It seems that these figures should be treated with a degree of caution, since experience has shown that actual expenditure resulting from a particular disposal varies considerably from case to case. The figures given for prison sentences do not include costing for the mandatory element of supervision where relevant.

3 Sentencing Procedure

Before selecting the appropriate sentence, the sentencer will require further information about the offence and about the offender. From the moment when the offender pleads guilty or is found guilty to the moment when the judge or bench of magistrates passes sentence, there is a period of time in which this information will be adduced. In simple, straightforward cases, particularly in magistrates' courts, the decision on sentence may be reached almost immediately. In more complex cases, the procedure between conviction and sentence may take several hours, involving the calling of witnesses and the close investigation of disputed facts. It may seem odd, at first sight, that an accused can be found guilty of an offence when important factual issues remain unresolved. It should be remembered, however, that where the accused has pleaded guilty, there will have been no trial and hence no examination of the circumstances of the offence in court. Even where there has been a full trial, it will have been confined to issues relevant to guilt. Other matters, not relevant to that issue, may still require examination before the proper sentence can be fixed. Consider offences of strict liability. Whether the accused committed the offences knowingly or not is irrelevant to liability, but it is of central importance when fixing the punishment. An example is *Lester* (1975) 63 Cr App R 144, where the offender pleaded guilty to strict liability offences under the Trade Descriptions Act 1968 and was sentenced on the assumption that he had *mens rea*. The Court of Appeal said that the assumption should not have been made without the offender having been given a chance to give evidence on the matter, and reduced the sentence from six months' imprisonment to a fine of £280. See also *Yorkshire Water Services* (1994) 16 Cr App R (S) 280.

The procedure between conviction and sentence is markedly different from that which pertains to the trial itself. The role of the judge or bench of magistrates changes from that of an umpire to one of a collector of information about the offence and the offender. Rules relating to the admissibility of evidence are somewhat relaxed, and the combative or adversarial style of the opposing lawyers is less marked. The judge takes a more central and active role in the gathering of information, which comes from a variety of sources, in reaching the sentencing decision. In fact there are relatively few legal rules governing the procedure between conviction and sentence: many of the practices discussed below have grown up through the day-to-day workings of the courts. Their operation is governed by a few statutory provisions, scattered appellate decisions and administrative guidance, especially a number of Home Office circulars.

The procedure between conviction and sentence may usefully be divided into three main stages, namely the determination of the facts of the offence and the hearing of evidence about the offender's character and antecedents; the reading by the court of reports prepared on the offender; and the presentation of defence mitigation. Before considering these three stages in detail, two preliminary matters must be mentioned: advance indications of sentence and adjournment before sentence.

3.1 ADVANCE INDICATIONS OF SENTENCE

In what circumstances may a Crown Court judge give an indication, in advance of the indictment being put to the accused, of the sentence the accused may expect to receive? This is a complex and difficult matter.

All lawyers (and many defendants) know that an accused who pleads guilty to a charge will, ordinarily, receive a lower sentence than he would receive if he were to contest the case and then be convicted. The reasons for this are threefold. First, to plead guilty saves a good deal of court time and public money. Second, in some cases, such as alleged sexual assault, witnesses will be spared the distress of reliving their experience in court. Third, at least in some cases, a decision to plead guilty will indicate the offender's regret for the offence (for discussion of the sentencing 'discount' for pleading guilty, see **2.2.4**). About two- thirds of accused in the Crown Court plead guilty and nine out of every ten accused in magistrates' courts do so. It is generally assumed that if the incentive to plead guilty were removed there would be many more contested trials, and some people claim that the administration of criminal justice would grind to a halt. Clearly it is one of the tasks of the defence lawyer to explain the sentencing discount fully and fairly to the accused (*Herbert* (1991) 94 Cr App R 233). The Code of Conduct of the Bar confirms that defence counsel should explain to the accused the advantages and disadvantages of pleading guilty. Strong advice to enter a guilty plea is permissible (*Peace* [1976] Crim LR 119). It should not, however, be so strong as to effectively deprive the accused of his free choice as to how he pleads (*Inns* (1975) 60 Cr App R 231). The danger, of course, is that an innocent accused may feel under great pressure to plead guilty believing that the plea will make the difference between a custodial sentence and a community sentence. Such pressure is all the greater if the accused, rightly or wrongly, gets the impression that the judge is involved as well.

The law in this area is governed by *Turner* [1970] 2 QB 321. That case states that the only circumstance in which the judge may give an advance indication of sentence is to say that the sentence will (or will not) take a particular form *regardless of how the accused pleads*. Usually defence counsel will go to see the judge in his private room and will ask him if he is prepared to give any indication of the type approved in *Turner*. In reply the judge may say that, regardless of plea, he is not considering a custodial penalty, or that the sentence will, in any event, be a fine, or will be one of the community orders. The judge may, on the other hand, decline counsel's request and he certainly should do so if he is not in possession of all the material facts (*Winterflood* (1978) 68 Cr App R 291). If an indication is given it is vital that it is not made conditional upon the plea. Where the judge indicates a community sentence in the event of a guilty plea but is silent as to the sentence which would follow conviction by a jury, this amounts to such an indication (*Ryan* (1977) 67 Cr App R 177). It will be seen that the judge may still take the plea into account, along with the range of other matters, in fixing custodial sentence *length* and in deciding what *level* of fine or *which* community sentence will be imposed. An indication from the judge that the sentence will be a community sentence, regardless of how the accused pleads may, then, be very helpful in a case where defence counsel suspects that his client really wants to plead guilty but is terrified that he will receive a custodial sentence. If the judge indicates that he is not considering a custodial sentence in any event, the accused may pluck up the courage to plead guilty.

A further point made in *Turner* is that anything the judge says privately to counsel must be passed on to the accused. It is inappropriate for matters of this sort to be communicated 'in confidence' between the judge and counsel (*Bird* (1977) 67 Cr App R 203). Indeed, the

Court of Appeal has said that no discussion of this sort should take place in the judge's private room without the presence of a shorthand writer or tape recordist to record exactly what is said (*Smith* [1990] Crim LR 354). Also, whenever defence counsel goes to see the judge privately, counsel for the prosecution should be present and the accused's solicitor may also be there. The accused is never present at these discussions but, again according to *Turner*, defence counsel may refer to any mitigating consideration, including something of which the accused is ignorant (such as the fact that the accused has a serious illness and may not have long to live). It seems that, apart from the limited circumstances specified in *Turner*, the rule is that any approach made by counsel to the judge for an indication of likely sentence is quite wrong (*Coward* (1979) 70 Cr App R 70). The judge should certainly never initiate a private meeting for this purpose (*Llewellyn* (1977) 67 Cr App R 148).

If a judge fails to comply with *Turner* and promises a community sentence in the event of a guilty plea, and either expressly says that the promise would not apply were the accused to be convicted by a jury, or simply gives no indication of what would happen in that event, then the accused is placed under intolerable pressure to plead guilty. A plea of guilty tendered in such circumstances would, on appeal, be treated as a nullity. The Court of Appeal would quash the conviction and order a re-trial at which, presumably, the accused would plead not guilty. Examples of such cases are *Ryan* (1977) 67 Cr App R 177 and *James* [1990] Crim LR 815.

An important implication of *Turner* is that any sentencing undertaking which is made by the judge must subsequently be honoured. The point is well illustrated by *Moss* (1984) 5 Cr App R (S) 209. Moss and two other young women were charged with shoplifting. Counsel asked to see the judge privately. The judge indicated that, regardless of what the pleas might be he was not considering a custodial sentence. In the event all three accused pleaded not guilty and were convicted by a jury. The judge adjourned for reports to be prepared. At the end of the period of adjournment the offenders appeared before a different judge to be sentenced. Although the reports recommended various community sentences, and although the sentencer was told of the first judge's inclination as to sentence, he still passed custodial sentences on all three young women. Since they each had several previous convictions for dishonesty, the sentences were in themselves not objectionable. The first judge had promised community sentences, however, and the Court of Appeal held that the promise was binding and substituted probation orders for the custodial sentences. See also *Keily* [1990] Crim LR 204.

The discussion of this topic has been entirely concerned with the Crown Court. No advance indications of sentence can be given in magistrates' courts. This is because magistrates, prior to the plea being tendered, are permitted to know nothing about the details of the prosecution case or the character and record of the offender, so obviously they are in no position to give undertakings about the sentence. A Crown Court judge, on the other hand, can familiarise himself with the case in advance by reading through the committal statements. The judge is also entitled before the plea is entered to see the accused's antecedents and list of previous convictions, which magistrates are not. Thus, the papers in the case may well give the judge an adequate basis for giving an indication as to sentence.

3.2 ADJOURNMENT BEFORE SENTENCE

The court does not necessarily sentence the offender on the day on which he or she pleads guilty or is found guilty. It has power to adjourn prior to passing sentence. This is, in fact, frequently done, for a range of reasons discussed below. Of course, adjournments are administratively inconvenient and can be disruptive and expensive. It is also quite likely, particularly in magistrates' courts, that the sentencer who ordered the adjournment will not be the same as the one who deals with the matter after adjournment, and this on occasions can cause difficulty. Such matters must, however, be outweighed by the need to take extra time in securing a just sentence.

The Crown Court's power to adjourn is one which it possesses by virtue of common law. It is distinct from its statutory power to defer sentence (see *Annesley* (1975) 62 Cr App R 113 and **3.10**). A magistrates' court's power to do so is governed by MCA 1980, s. 10(3). which permits a magistrates' court to adjourn 'for the purpose of enabling inquiries to be made or of determining the most suitable method of dealing with the case'. Adjournment for some other purpose, such as to put off making a difficult decision, or to allow the passage of time so that a young offender will become eligible for a prison sentence (as in *Arthur* v *Stringer* (1986) 8 Cr App R (S) 329), is unlawful. During the period of an adjournment before sentence, the offender will be remanded in custody or on bail. There is a prima facie right to bail by reason of the Bail Act 1976 (BA 1976), s. 4, but bail may be refused on any one of several grounds specified in that Act. In the present context all the grounds which may justify a refusal of bail before conviction apply here also, but an additional ground applies — that the adjournment is for the purpose of preparing a report and that it would be impracticable to do so if the offender were at liberty (BA 1976, sch. 1, Part 1, para. 7). Where an offender remanded for reports is granted bail the court may, in its discretion, include a condition that the offender makes himself available 'for the purpose of enabling inquiries or a report to be made to assist the court in dealing with him for an offence' (BA 1976, s. 3(6)(d)).

3.2.1 Adjournment for reports

Independent reports on offenders are often a vital factor in the sentencing decision. The most frequently encountered reports are pre-sentence reports and medical reports (see further on these **3.5.1** and **3.5.2**). Where the accused indicates an intention to plead guilty and it seems likely that the court will need reports before passing sentence, the reports are prepared before the hearing if possible. If, however, the accused is pleading not guilty it is unlikely that reports will be prepared. This is because an important element, in the pre-sentence report in particular, is consideration of the accused's attitude to the offence. If the accused is pleading not guilty then obviously this aspect cannot be investigated. Even if the accused is pleading guilty, the preparation of reports is not automatic. The circumstances in which the court is bound in law to obtain a pre-sentence report or a medical report are laid down by statute.

(a) *Pre-sentence reports* Broadly speaking, the Crown Court or a magistrates' court should normally obtain a pre-sentence report whenever the imposition of a custodial sentence is under consideration, or when the court is considering any of the following community sentences: a probation order which includes additional requirements, a community service order, a combination order, a supervision order which includes additional requirements, or a drug treatment and testing order. The role of pre-sentence reports is considered in detail in **3.5.1**. Apart from these specified cases where the court should not normally proceed to sentence without a pre-sentence report, there is a range of other circumstances where to pass the sentence without a report would not be good sentencing practice. In these circumstances, too, the court should adjourn for reports to be prepared.

When magistrates adjourn for reports it must be for not more than four weeks if the offender is remanded on bail, and not more than three weeks if he is remanded in custody (MCA 1990, s. 10(3)). The Crown Court can in theory adjourn for any period of time, but in practice adjournments are normally for two or three weeks. *National Standards* (Home Office, 1995b), issued pursuant to the CJA 1991, place emphasis upon the need to expedite the preparation of pre-sentence reports. As far as the Crown Court is concerned, the *National Standards* state that it should be possible for the probation service to provide an effective report-writing service for a broad range of cases at each Crown Court centre, including the preparation of some reports in writing on the day they are requested. In any event preparation of a pre-sentence report on an offender held on remand should be completed within seven days. As far as magistrates' courts and youth courts are concerned, the *National Standards* state that it is impracticable to provide 'dedicated PSR writing teams' for these courts, but that all reports should be prepared as speedily as possible, with priority being given to offenders who are being held in custody.

(b) *Medical reports* The circumstances in which a court can adjourn for a medical report are as follows. Written or oral evidence of two medical practitioners that the offender is suffering from mental disorder within the meaning of the Mental Health Act 1983 (MHA 1983) must be obtained before a court can make a hospital order under MHA 1983, s. 37(1), an interim hospital order under s. 38 or a hospital or limitation direction under s. 45A. One of the doctors making a report must be a psychiatrist approved by the Home Office (MHA 1983, s. 54). A report from at least one medical practitioner is required before a probation order with a requirement of treatment for a mental condition may be made (PCCA 1973, sch. 1A, para. 5). Whenever a Crown Court or a magistrates' court is considering imposing a custodial sentence upon an offender who is, or who appears to be, mentally disordered, the court should obtain and consider a medical report before passing a custodial sentence, and should consider the likely effect of a custodial sentence on that condition and on any treatment which may be available for it (CJA 1991, s. 4). Further, under MCA 1980, s. 30, a magistrates' court can adjourn for a medical report even before convicting the accused, if it is satisfied that the accused 'did the act or made the omission charged'. Under this provision the accused can be remanded for up to three weeks in custody or four weeks on bail. If the accused is granted bail, it must be made a condition of bail that he cooperates in the preparation of the report (MCA 1980, s. 30(2) and BA 1976, s. 3(6)(d)). Provisions in MHA 1983, ss. 35 and 36 allow the Crown Court or a magistrates' court to remand offenders to a hospital (rather than in custody or on bail) for reports to be prepared.

3.2.2 Adjournments where there are several offenders

There is a strong argument to be made that offenders who have jointly committed an offence, or offenders who have committed separate offences which arose out of the same circumstances or were otherwise factually linked, should be sentenced together by one judge on one occasion. To do so should ensure consistent treatment for them all, with any differences in the sentences received being justified by the different degrees to which they were involved in the criminal conduct, or by other material differences between them.

The procedural rules on joinder of defendants in one indictment make it likely that alleged confederates in crime will be charged in a single indictment and so initially will appear together to plead to that indictment. If they all plead guilty, or all plead not guilty, there is no problem about having them sentenced together. If, however, A pleads guilty and B pleads not guilty, then difficulties arise. Clearly B cannot be sentenced unless and until he is convicted by a jury. Jury trials are sometimes lengthy affairs. Nonetheless, the desirability of dealing with A and, if convicted, B together has led to a general rule that the sentence on A should be postponed until after the trial of B. This has the additional advantage of allowing the judge to hear the evidence called at B's trial, and proportion his sentences according to which, if either, of the accused played the leading role in the offence or offences. This general rule was established in *Payne* [1950] 1 All ER 102. In that case, however, Lord Goddard CJ stated that there was an exception to the general rule, where A was to 'turn Queen's evidence' and be called by the prosecution as a witness in the trial of B. In such a case, it was said, A should be sentenced straight away, so that there should be no suspicion of his evidence being coloured by the fact that, undoubtedly, he would hope for a lighter sentence as a reward for cooperating with the authorities and giving evidence against B.

While the general rule in *Payne* still represents the law, the scope of exception has been challenged in more recent cases. In *Weekes* (1980) 2 Cr App R (S) 377, in particular the Court of Appeal expressly stated that the prosecution's intention of calling A at the trial of B is not a sufficient reason for the Crown Court departing from the normal practice of sentencing A after B's trial is over. The statement in the case was, however, obiter. It is submitted that the decision as to when to sentence A should be left to the discretion of the trial judge, who is in the best position to balance the interests of B (that A, when he testifies, should have no motive for giving false evidence) against the wider interests of justice (that confederates in crime should be sentenced together so as to avoid unjustified differences in sentence). The existence of such a discretion is supported by the comments of Lord Denning MR in *Sheffield Crown Court, ex parte Brownlow* [1980] QB 520, where he suggested that the following matters (amongst others) might be relevant to whether or not to adjourn sentence upon A:

(a) A would have a very long wait before sentence could be passed, such as where B absconded; or

(b) A's offence was trivial in comparison with the charge against B; or

(c) there were more than usually strong reasons to think that A would perjure himself in giving evidence against B.

The situation discussed in this section also creates difficulty when the sentencer comes to determine the factual basis for passing sentence on the two offenders. Comments adverse to A's role in the offence may be made at B's trial which A may have little opportunity to refute. This issue is considered at **3.3.4**.

3.2.3 Adjournments where there are outstanding charges

It is desirable that an accused with several charges outstanding against him should be sentenced on one occasion for all matters in respect of which he is ultimately convicted. If he is sentenced piecemeal by different judges (or even by the same judge on different occasions) there is a danger that the aggregate sentence will be out of proportion to the overall gravity of the offending. There is also a danger that the first judge, dealing perhaps with the less serious offences, will pass a community sentence and thus create a dilemma for the second judge. The latter may feel that a custodial sentence is necessary for the offences with which he is dealing, but to pass such a sentence might prevent the earlier community sentence running its natural course. To avoid such difficulties, it is better that one sentencer should deal with everything on one occasion, even if this means adjournments and extra administrative work behind the scenes. Adjournment in these circumstances is entirely at the discretion of the court, and the accused may be remanded in custody or on bail (SCA 1981, s. 81(1)(c)).

Occasionally various charges against an accused may not have been consolidated into one indictment, perhaps because they are insufficiently linked to go into one indictment or simply because it is not realised at the time the first indictment is preferred that the accused is also to be indicted for trial on other charges. In *Bennett* (1980) 2 Cr App R (S) 96 Watkin J stressed that there was an obligation 'on solicitors, counsel and judges alike to do all within their power to ensure that as far as possible all outstanding charges against a defendant are dealt with in the same court, by the same judge upon a single occasion'. If it becomes known that there are charges against the accused other than the ones before the court, application should be made to the judge to have the accused's case adjourned to be dealt with later at that Crown Court or to be transferred to another Crown Court where the outstanding charges lie.

3.2.4 Sentence promises on adjournment for reports

Where the Crown Court or a magistrates' court adjourns for reports in circumstances which justifiably lead the offender to think that, if the report turns out to be favourable, a community sentence will be passed, then the court is bound by the implied promise which it has given. To resile from the promise would leave the offender with a legitimate sense of grievance.

This principle was first stated in *Gillam* (1980) 2 Cr App R (S) 267. The offender, who was nearing the end of a prison sentence, was before the court to be sentenced for two burglaries and one offence of reckless driving. It appeared likely that he would receive a further custodial sentence, but the judge adjourned so that Gillam's suitability for community service could be assessed. He also ordered that the offender should be released on bail once the custodial term he was serving came to an end. According to Watkins LJ, in the Court of Appeal, the main reason for the adjournment was 'to ascertain whether community service was available for such a person as the offender and whether he was a fit subject to perform that service'. In the event Gillam was assessed to be suitable for community service. Nonetheless the judge passed a sentence of six months' imprisonment. Watkins LJ indicated that the proper sentence in Gillam's case would have been immediate custody of about 15 months, but the appeal was allowed, since (at p. 269):

> . . . an important principle of sentencing is involved in this case . . . When a judge in these circumstances purposely postpones sentence so that an alternative to prison can be examined and that alternative is found to be a satisfactory one in all respects, the court ought to adopt the alternative. A feeling of injustice is otherwise aroused.

Gillam has been followed in several later cases. In *Ward* (1982) 4 Cr App R (S) 103, for example, the judge adjourned for three weeks so that Ward could stay at a probation hostel with a view to the making of a probation order with a condition of residence at that hostel. The report was favourable, and a custodial sentence, which was imposed by the judge despite that report, was quashed by the Court of Appeal. In *Wilkinson* (1988) 9 Cr App R (S) 468, on very similar facts, the offender came before a different judge after the adjournment. He took the view that the offence committed had been so serious that he was not prepared to incur public anger by taking such a lenient course. The Court of Appeal quashed the custodial sentence, saying that there was no alternative but to honour the first judge's promise, no matter what the public might think. Although these sentences were all imposed in the Crown Court, exactly the same principle applies to adjournments in magistrates' courts. An example is *Gutteridge* v *DPP* (1987) 9 Cr App R (S) 279.

The cases so far discussed all depend upon 'there having been something in the nature of a promise, express or implied, that if a particular proposal is recommended, it will be adopted' (per Croom-Johnson J in *Moss* (1983) 5 Cr App R (S) 209). So, if the judge ordering the adjournment makes it clear to the offender that no promise is being made, even if the report turns out to be favourable, then the offender can have no sense of grievance if the eventual outcome is a custodial sentence. Thus in *Horton* (1985) 7 Cr App R (S) 299 the offenders had been found guilty of snatching a handbag. The judge adjourned for three weeks for a social inquiry report and community service assessment to be compiled, but stated that he thought that custody would be the likely outcome. Community service was recommended, but the judge nevertheless imposed a custodial sentence. This sentence was upheld by the Court of Appeal. In *Horton*, the sentencer was bound by a statutory provision in force at that time to order a social inquiry report before proceeding to sentence, so this case clearly illustrates that it is certainly not in every case where an adjournment is made for reports that the judge is making a promise of a community sentence to the offender. The judge in *Horton* seems to have struck the correct balance: ordering the report, warning the offender not to expect too much, but leaving open the possibility of a community disposal should something exceptional in the report cause him to change his mind. This was the approach approved in *Chamberlain* (1994) 16 Cr App R (S) 473, where the Court of Appeal recommended that to avoid the sense of injustice referred to in *Gillam* the defendant must be told that he should not assume that he is likely to receive any form of treatment, or that a custodial sentence is ruled out, whatever the further report or inquiry may reveal.

3.3 THE FACTS OF THE OFFENCE

Having dealt with advance indications of the sentence and the procedure of adjournment, the remainder of this chapter is devoted to an examination of the proceedings between conviction and sentence. Although the description relates principally to proceedings in the Crown Court, the arrangements are little different in magistrates' courts; relevent differences are mentioned where appropriate.

3.3.1 Prosecution statement of facts

If the accused pleads guilty, the first stage in the procedure between conviction and sentence is the summary by the prosecutor of the facts of the offence. In the Crown Court this will be done by counsel for the prosecution, and in the magistrates' court by a representative of the Crown Prosecution Service (the CPS). This summary is designed to assist the court and to inform the offender and the public of the basis of the prosecution case. If the accused has pleaded not guilty this summary is dispensed with, since the facts of the offence will have emerged during the trial and will already be well known to the court.

An account will be given of the salient features of the offence. If it is an offence of theft, the value of the property taken should be pointed out and the amount of property recovered, if any, should also be mentioned. If it is an offence of violence, the injuries to the victim, whether the victim required hospital treatment and whether the victim made a full recovery should be stated. If it is an offence involving breach of trust, the position held by the offender should be indicated. If the offence involves drugs, their 'street value' and the offender's role in the offence should be explained. If it is a sexual offence, any previous relationship between the offender and the victim should be explained, and whether force was used over and above the force inherent in the offence itself should be made clear. The degree of planning which preceded any offence is relevant, as is any other aggravating factor such as the use of a weapon or the selection of a vulnerable victim. The circumstances of the offender's arrest, and his reaction, will be noted. If the offender cooperated with the police and promptly admitted guilt, this may tell in his favour on sentence. If the accused was interviewed at the police station, the record of the interview may be referred to or summarised.

The impact of the offence upon the victim is clearly an important consideration when the court is gauging the seriousness of the offence and in *Nunn* [1996] 2 Cr App R (S) 136, a case where the offender pleaded guilty to causing death by dangerous driving, the Court of Appeal said that it was an elementary principle of sentencing that the damaging and distressing effects of a crime upon the victim or, where the victim had been killed, the impact on the victim's family, should be made known to, and taken into account by, the sentencer. It is part of the duty of the prosecution to draw that impact to the sentencer's attention, but it will rarely be appropriate to call the victim as a witness (*Ashmeil* (1988) 10 Cr App R (S) 127). In *Hobstaff* (1993) 14 Cr App R (S) 605 the offender pleaded guilty to three counts of indecent assault, the offences having being committed on his neighbour's young daughters, who were aged between five and eight years. When opening the case, counsel for the prosecution said that the effects on the children had been 'horrific': one had suffered from nightmares and both had required treatment from a child psychologist. The sentencer made it clear when imposing sentence that he had borne that information in mind. The Court of Appeal said that while taking account of information about the victim's suffering was entirely appropriate, in this particular case it was improper, since there was no evidence before the court on the matter. Such evidence must be in proper form, whether as an expert's report or a witness statement or in some other appropriate form. The defence should, of course, see any such evidence in advance. It is not clear to what extent a sentencer may assume what the effects of a crime will have been on the victim without having heard evidence on the point (*O'S* (1993) 14 Cr App R (S) 632). Sometimes the victim may have forgiven the offender for the offence, and will want to urge leniency upon the court. This may be relevant as showing that the harm occasioned to the victim has been somewhat less than might have been expected (*Hutchinson* (1993) 15 Cr App R (S) 124).

The main point to notice is that, in principle, the prosecution is bound to take a *neutral* attitude during the stage between conviction and sentence. They are not concerned to influence the sentencer towards a heavy sentence; indeed to do so would be quite improper. On the other hand, if the offender in his statement to the police or in mitigation puts forward a version of the facts of the offence which does not accord with the evidence available to the prosecution, counsel should indicate that the defence version is not accepted by them. The Code of Conduct of the Bar states that whilst the prosecution have a duty to point out any aggravating features of the case, they are also duty bound to draw to the court's attention any matters, of which they are aware, which reflect to the offender's credit. This is particularly the case where the offender is unrepresented (see **3.11**). While the neutrality of the prosecutor is an essential feature of the English criminal justice system, and stands in contrast to the role of the prosecutor in other jurisdictions, the neutrality card can sometimes be overplayed. First, the prosecutor does have an important indirect influence upon sentencing outcome, through the initial selection of the charges to be brought and through any negotiations with the defence as to charges. Secondly, there is a recent trend in judicial decisions and statutory development towards the greater involvement of the prosecutor at the sentencing stage. The most obvious change was the introduction in the CJA 1988 of a prosecution power to draw the attention of the Attorney-General to an example of excessively lenient sentencing in the Crown Court, with a view to the Attorney-General referring the matter to the Court of Appeal. That development is considered further below (see **13.3**), but a number of other smaller, but collectively significant, changes have also taken place, and it is convenient to deal with those here.

(a)   In any case where the court is likely to make an order ancillary to the sentence, such as a compensation order under PCCA 1973, s. 35, a restitution order under the Theft Act 1968, s. 28 or a forfeiture order under PCCA 1973, s. 43, it seems that prosecution counsel must be ready to provide all the relevant information for the court. None of these orders can be made without an adequate factual basis being laid for them. In the case of a compensation order, for example, since the victim is not a party to the proceedings and may well not even be present in court, it will, in practice, fall to the prosecutor to provide the necessary facts. If personal injury, loss or damage has been occasioned to the victim, the onus is upon the prosecutor to adduce the amount, quantifying the loss so far as possible and producing evidence to substantiate the amount, such as receipts showing the cost of repairing property damaged by the offender (*Horsham Justices, ex parte Richards* (1985) 7 Cr App R (S) 158). The case of *Pemberton* (1982) 4 Cr App R (S) 328, dealing with forfeiture, contains a clear statement on the point. According to Kilner Brown J:

It is incumbent upon the prosecution to justify the application and it is incumbent upon the trial judge to put the prosecution to proof if they simply state baldly, without any supporting evidence, that they seek an order for forfeiture.

It is not, however, the duty of the prosecutor to investigate the offender's means (*Johnstone* (1982) 4 Cr App R (S) 141; *Phillips* (1988) 10 Cr App R (S) 419). If the victim's loss has not been quantified, or is in dispute, the court may adjourn so that further inquiries can be made.

Where the question of confiscation of the offender's assets arises, on his conviction of an offence of drug trafficking under the Drug Trafficking Act 1994 (DTA 1994) or his conviction of an offence of a relevant description under the CJA 1988, the statutes impose responsibility upon the prosecution to adduce full information about the offender's assets and to demonstrate the extent to which the offender has benefited from the offending before such an order can be made (for confiscation orders, see Chapter 9).

(b)   In a number of different circumstances the practice has been developing for sentencers to consult both defence and prosecution counsel, and invite submissions from them, before imposing a particular form of sentence. It seems that both counsel may, for example, be invited to address the judge on the appropriateness of imposing a life sentence upon the offender (*Virgo* (1988) 10 Cr App R (S) 427). The judge may also seek the views of both counsel before embarking on a *Newton* hearing into disputed facts (see further **3.3.2**).

(c)   Recent Court of Appeal decisions have made it clear that it is the duty of both prosecution and defence counsel to make themselves aware of any legal limitations on the court's sentencing powers so as to be in a position to assist the judge if necessary. In

Kennedy [1976] Crim LR 508 it was said that 'It is the duty of counsel to inform themselves what are the permissible sentences for the offences with which a defendant is charged, so as to be in a position to assist the judge if he makes a mistake.' This point was reinforced in *Komsta* (1990) 12 Cr App R (S) 63, and in *Richards* (1993) *The Times*, 1 April 1993, it was said to be 'particularly' the duty of counsel for the Crown to inform himself of the maximum sentence available for the offence being dealt with, and to correct the judge if he was about to make an error by exceeding it. Following these last-mentioned exhortations from the Court of Appeal, the Code of Conduct of the Bar indicates a more general duty upon prosecuting counsel to assist the sentencer in avoiding error. This goes beyond reminding the judge of maximum sentencing powers and extends to the increasingly complex range of statutory provisions on sentencing, and to Court of Appeal guideline judgments. The Code of Conduct suggests that such advice should be given either if asked for by the sentencer, or on counsel's initiative if it seems that a mistake of sentencing law is about to be made. In *Panayioutou* (1989) 11 Cr App R (S) 535 Hodgson J said that the time had come when judges were entitled to have guideline cases brought to their attention by counsel for the prosecution though, of course, the prosecutor could not ask for any particular penalty. This may cause difficulty for the prosecution in some cases, particularly if it involves drawing the sentencer's attention to an authority which suggests that the proposed sentence is too lenient.

3.3.2 Establishing the facts after a guilty plea

By pleading guilty the offender does not necessarily admit that the prosecution case against him is correct in its entirety. He admits, of course, that he committed the offences described in each of the counts of the indictment to which he enters a guilty plea, and if defence counsel says anything in mitigation which is inconsistent with the plea then the judge will either ignore it or will invite the defence to consider whether the plea should be changed. A change of plea may be accepted by the court at any time before sentence is passed (*S* v *Recorder of Manchester* [1971] AC 481), but whether the court should do so is a matter within its discretion. Generally a change is unlikely to be entertained, especially where the accused has been legally represented, and can be assumed to have received proper advice as to plea (*Drew* [1975] 1 WLR 914). The main issue here, however, is that many modern criminal offences are broadly drafted, and the particulars given in an indictment about an offence are likely to be so basic as to reveal little about whether the offence is a serious one, or a trivial one of its type. Thus, it sometimes happens that an offender quite properly pleads guilty and then, after the facts have been presented by prosecuting counsel, denies that his crime was as grave as has been alleged or might be assumed. Examples of such disputes, taken from decided cases, are: whether offenders had abandoned a conspiracy to rob before the police intervened to make commission of the robbery impossible anyway; whether an offence of unlawful wounding had been committed by the use of a knife or by fists alone; and whether a man who had caused grievous bodily harm to his wife had first been gravely provoked by taunts. It will be noted that in each of the examples given the accused, even on his own version of the events, was guilty as charged, but the sentence would be significantly affected by whether the judge accepted the prosecution statement of facts or the defence mitigation.

The leading case in this area is *Newton* (1982) 4 Cr App R (S) 388. The accused pleaded guilty to an offence of buggery, committed upon his wife. The prosecution summary of the facts stated that the offence had been committed without her consent. At the time of the case the offence was subject to a maximum sentence of life imprisonment, irrespective of consent, but clearly a case involving consent was far less serious than one where consent was absent. Defence counsel made it clear in mitigation that, according to his client, the wife had consented but the judge did not hear any evidence on the matter either from Newton or from the wife. He passed a sentence of eight years, which was clearly based upon an acceptance of the prosecution version of the facts. The Court of Appeal reduced the sentence to one year, which would result in Newton's immediate release from custody (he had by that time already served ten months in prison). Lord Lane CJ said (at p.15):

> On his own story Newton had to plead guilty to buggery, which left the vital issue of consent unresolved . . . There are three ways in which a judge in these circumstances can approach his difficult task of sentencing. It is in certain circumstances possible to obtain the answer from a jury . . . The second method which could be adopted by the judge in these circumstances is himself to hear the evidence on one side and another, and come to his own conclusion, acting so to speak as his own jury on the issue which is the root of the problem. The third possibility is for him to hear no evidence but to listen to the submissions of counsel and then come to a conclusion. But if he does that . . . then where there is a substantial conflict between the two sides . . . the version of the defendant must so far as possible be accepted.

On the facts of *Newton* the first option was unavailable, since this was a guilty plea rather than a conviction after a trial, but the judge had failed to adopt either of the other two courses, which had been open to him. He had simply sentenced the offender on the basis that the acts were non-consensual, without hearing any evidence on the point at all.

The basic propositions in *Newton* have been elaborated in other decisions of the Court of Appeal, and the procedure advocated by Lord Lane has become known as a '*Newton* hearing'. The following main points have emerged:

(a)　In *Newton* cases the burden of proof rests upon the prosecution to establish its version of the facts beyond reasonable doubt. The clearest authority on the point is *Ahmed* (1984) 6 Cr App R (S) 391, where Parker LJ referred to 'the broad principle, which is so clearly recognised in *Newton*, that the accused should be given the benefit of the doubt', and then added:

> The accused is given the benefit of the doubt (if there is one) by the necessity for the Crown Court to direct itself (or any jury) that the accused's account must be accepted *unless that court is sure that it is untrue.* (emphasis added)

In *Kerrigan* (1993) 14 Cr App R (S) 179 it was accepted to be 'clear beyond any argument' that the criminal standard was the appropriate one. In that case it was also said that it was better for the judge to direct himself openly as to the relevant burden and standard of proof, although failure to do so was not necessarily fatal. It is the duty of the defence to notify the Crown in advance that a plea of guilty will be tendered but that the prosecution version of the facts will be disputed at the sentencing stage. This will enable the prosecution to take steps to ensure that the necessary witnesses are present in court (*Mohun* (1993) 14 Cr App R (S) 5).

(b)　In *Newton* Lord Lane CJ said that the principles were applicable where there was a 'a substantial conflict between the two sides'. It follows that where the factual difference is insignificant and would make no real difference to the sentencing outcome, there is no need for a *Newton* hearing to resolve it. An example is *Bent* (1986) 8 Cr App R (S) 19, where the offender received a sentence of six months' youth custody for assaulting a store detective who was trying to arrest him. The prosecution stated that B had struck the detective with a stick, whilst Bent claimed that he had only threatened the victim with it. The sentencer took the view that the gravamen of the charge was the resisting of arrest and that it mattered little whether the stick had actually struck the detective or not. In a case such as this, for the avoidance of doubt, it is probably better for the sentencer to make it clear that he is sentencing on the basis of the defence version of the facts, as was recommended by Lincoln J in *Hall* (1984) 6 Cr App R (S) 321 at p. 324.

(c)   A series of cases following *Newton* have made it clear that there are some situations in which the defence version of the facts is so implausible that the judge may reject it out of hand rather than being obliged to conduct a *Newton* hearing into the matter. In *Hawkins* (1985) 7 Cr App R (S) 351, the offender's account of his involvement as the get-away driver in a joint offence of burglary, committed by himself and two others, was that he was unaware until the very end of the incident that the reason the others had asked him to drive them to specified premises and then collect them an hour later was so that they could break in and be assisted to escape with the proceeds. The judge declined to hear evidence on the matter and sentenced Hawkins on the prosecution version of the facts, which was that Hawkins had been a knowing participant throughout. The Court of Appeal upheld the decision, agreeing that H had made an 'incredible assertion'. (See also the situation dealt with at the end of **3.6.1**.) The judge's decision to reject the defence version out of hand must not, however, be taken lightly. In *Costley* (1989) 11 Cr App R (S) 357 C pleaded guilty to inflicting grievous bodily harm. The prosecution claimed that C had struck the victim about the head and body with a piece of wood. The defence version was that fists only had been used, and that there had been very considerable provocation. The Court of Appeal said that the defence version of the facts should not have been rejected out of hand, that there was a difference of importance between the sides, and that this should have been resolved by a *Newton* hearing.

(d)   In a case where a *Newton* hearing is appropriate, the judge is under a duty to hold one. The judge may hear submissions from counsel as to the appropriateness of that course, but the decision is then one for the judge. Thus a hearing may go ahead even if the defence is against that course (*Williams* v *Another* (1983) 5 Cr App R (S) 134). The parties are given the opportunity to call witnesses, if they wish to do so, and to cross-examine the witnesses of the other side. The offender is a competent witness for the defence at the sentencing stage (Criminal Evidence Act 1898, s. 1(1) and *Wheeler* [1917] 2 KB 283), but cannot be called by the prosecution. The defence may, of course, sit back and wait to see if the prosecution can discharge its burden of proof. The whole *Newton* hearing procedure has more in common with trial procedure than the normal arrangements between conviction and sentence. The hearing itself should follow adversarial lines (*McGrath* (1983) 5 Cr App R (S) 460, at p. 463). The judge should preside over the matter and direct himself as if he were directing a jury (*Gandy* (1989) 11 Cr App R (S) 564). He should not assume an inquisitorial role and, if asking questions of the offender, should normally wait until both counsel have completed their questioning (*Myers* [1996] 1 Cr App R (S) 187). It is unclear how many of the substantive rules of criminal evidence would also apply to *Newton* hearings, but *Gandy* indicates that, where identification is in issue, the judge should direct himself in accordance with the guidelines in *Turnbull* [1977] QB 224, which would have been applicable at trial.

(e)   It will be clear from the last paragraph that a *Newton* hearing may be ordered by the sentencer even where the prosecution and defence are agreed upon the facts on which the plea was based. In *Beswick* [1996] 1 Cr App R (S) 343 the judge was not prepared to accept the factual basis which had been agreed by the two sides. On appeal the Court of Appeal said that sentence should always be passed on a factual basis which is true. The prosecution must not lend itself to any agreement with the defence which was based on an unreal set of facts. If that had occurred, the judge could properly order a *Newton* hearing, and it was the duty of the prosecution to assist the judge by presenting the prosecution evidence and challenging the defence version.

(f)   One result of contesting the facts by way of a *Newton* hearing is that the offender may lose some of the discount which he would otherwise have received for pleading guilty (see **2.2.4 (g)**). The offender ought to be told about this, but the judge should be careful not to give the impression of having already decided against the offender's version of the facts (*Satchell* [1996] Crim LR 351).

It is one of the most fundamental principles of sentencing that an offender who has pleaded guilty to an offence must only be sentenced for *that* offence. Where the prosecution accepts a plea of guilty to a lesser offence, or accepts a plea of guilty to one of several counts which were originally preferred against the accused, the judge must be careful to sentence only for the matters admitted or specifically proved against the offender. In *Lawrence* (1981) 3 Cr App R (S) 49 the offender pleaded guilty to possession of cannabis and a count for possession with intent to supply was not proceeded with. The Court of Appeal varied a short prison sentence to a fine because it was felt that the sentencer had failed to 'banish from his mind' the possibility that L was growing the cannabis in order to sell it.

A difficult problem is posed by the bringing of sample counts against an accused. After a period of some uncertainty, it is now clearly established by the Court of Appeal in *Canavan* [1998] 1 Cr App R 79 that the sentencer is bound to impose sentence purely on the basis of the sample counts proved against the offender or admitted by him, unless the defence concede that the counts are merely part of a wider pattern, or ask for the other offences to be taken into consideration. For further discussion of sample counts see **3.9**.

3.3.3   Establishing the facts after a verdict of guilty

Post-conviction disputes about the circumstances of the offence are not limited to cases where the offender pleads guilty, for a jury's verdict of guilty after a not guilty plea is not necessarily a total vindication of the prosecution's case. Consider, for example, the position if an accused denies a charge of assault occasioning actual bodily harm. The victim gives evidence for the prosecution that he was attacked with a knife, and the accused admits striking the victim but says that he was acting in reasonable self-defence and did not use a weapon. A verdict of guilty will merely show that, in the jury's view, the admitted assault was not a justified act of self-defence. It will not resolve the issue, highly relevant to sentence, of whether a weapon was used.

In such cases it is for the judge to form his own view of the evidence adduced before the jury, and decide what the facts of the offence were. In general, it seems, he should not ask the jury the reasons for their verdict or ask them what facts they find proved. In earlier times it was common practice for the judge to ask a jury to elaborate on the factual basis for its decision, to deliver a 'special' rather than a 'general' verdict. A case often cited as authority that this practice is now improper is *Larkin* [1943] KB 174, although examples of trial judges doing it may be found in later cases, such as *Lamb* [1967] 2 QB 981 (at p. 984), *Frankum* [1984] Crim LR 434, *Baldwin* (1989) 11 Cr App R (S) 139 and *McGlade* (1990) 12 Cr App R (S) 105. With the exception of *McGlade*, these are all cases of manslaughter, a crime which may be legally established in a number of different ways. It may be that manslaughter cases represent an exception to what the Court of Appeal in *Stosiek* (1982) 4 Cr App R (S) 205 (at p. 208), called 'the usual and proper practice' of 'refrain[ing] from inviting juries to explain their verdicts'. The reason for doubting this practice in England is the rather strange ground that investigation by the judge into the precise reason for the jury's verdict may reveal that different members of the jury have based their conviction on materially different versions of the facts. If it emerges that this has happened, the accused's conviction must be quashed (see *Brown* (1984) 79 Cr App R 115). In *McGlade* the relevant issue was the same as in *Newton*: whether an act of buggery had been consensual or not. The judge invited the jury to add a rider to their verdict to indicate their finding on this matter, and the Court of Appeal did not indicate any disapproval of what the judge had done. Seeking guidance from the jury was said to be 'not necessarily wrong' in *Cranston* (1993) 14 Cr App R (S) 103. There remains the possibility that the jury may, unsolicited, volunteer their reasoning to the judge (as in *Jama* (1968) 52 Cr App R 498) or make their opinion clear in some other way, such as by adding a rider to the verdict.

One way of avoiding the practice of the judge questioning the jury to determine the facts is for the prosecution to anticipate the problem, and insert an additional count in the indictment, which is designed to resolve the ambiguity on the main count. While this is often possible in theory, in practice it is difficult to achieve. Thus, it has been suggested that if in *Newton* (see **3.3.2**) the prosecution had included an additional count of assault occasioning actual bodily harm, the jury's verdict on that count might have resolved the issue of whether the sexual offence was consensual or not. Even so, on the prosecution version of the facts, the wife had received other injuries consistent with an attempt to escape from her husband, so it seems that a verdict of guilty on the assault charge would not necessarily have settled the 'vital issue of consent'. In *Efionayi* (1995) 16 Cr App R (S) 380, however, such a course should have been possible. There the defendants were charged with neglect of a child 'on a day between the 1st and 14th day of September'. The prosecution resisted a defence request to include a further count of neglect relating to a particular day or days. The jury convicted and sentence was passed on the basis that neglect occurred throughout the period, but the Court of Appeal said that the indictment could and should have been amended so as to secure the jury's finding on that point.

The view of the facts which the judge adopts must be consistent with the jury's verdict. If the jury refuse to find the accused guilty as charged but convict him of a lesser offence, the sentence must be appropriate to that lesser offence, notwithstanding that the judge is convinced that there should have been a conviction for the more serious offence (*Hazelwood* (1984) 6 Cr App R (S) 52). In *Baldwin* (1989) 11 Cr App R (S) 139 the Court of Appeal reduced sentence on the offender, who was indicted for murder but convicted of manslaughter after stabbing the victim in the chest with a lock-knife, from ten years to seven years, to be faithful to the jury's 'perplexing' view that Baldwin had no intent to inflict grievous bodily harm.

Where several interpretations of the jury's verdict are possible, the judge is not bound to accept that version of events which is most favourable to the offender. In *Triumph* (1984) 6 Cr App R (S) 120 the jury found the offender not guilty of attempted murder but guilty of causing grievous bodily harm with intent. The defence claimed that injuries to the victim's legs had been caused when the gun had gone off accidentally, and that a stab which the victim had also received had been inflicted by another offender without Triumph's knowledge. The judge rejected the defence version in favour of a finding that the offender had shot the victim deliberately, even though he had not intended to kill him. This decision was upheld by the Court of Appeal. This case must, however, be read in the context of other decisions, particularly *Stosiek* (1982) 4 Cr App R (S) 205, which make it clear that the sentencer must be 'extremely astute' to give the benefit of any doubt about the facts of the offence to the offender. In *Stosiek* the offender was convicted of an assault upon a plain-clothes police officer. A prison sentence of 12 months was imposed, on the basis that Stosiek realised that his victim was a police officer. In fact, as the Court of Appeal explained, there was a 'reasonable possibility' that he had not realised that, and had overreacted to what he took to be a member of the public picking a quarrel with him. The custodial sentence was quashed and a fine was substituted.

3.3.4   Establishing the facts after a verdict of guilty, where a co-accused pleads guilty

The development of the procedures outlined above has generated difficulty in the case where A has pleaded guilty but is not sentenced and B, who has pleaded not guilty, is convicted at his trial. The problem is that when sentencing B the judge is, of course, under a duty to determine the proper factual basis for sentencing both offenders.

In *Smith* (1988) 10 Cr App R (S) 271 the offender pleaded guilty to involvement in the supply of stolen credit cards to the three co-accused. One of the co-accused pleaded guilty, while the other two were found guilty by a jury after their defence, that they were acting under duress from Smith, was rejected. At sentence, the judge stated that he had taken the view that Smith was the ringleader in the enterprise, based in part upon the evidence which the two co-accused had given in their own defence. The judge offered Smith the opportunity to testify in his own defence at the sentencing stage, but this was turned down. A sentence of 21 months' imprisonment was imposed upon Smith, while the three co-accused were all given community service orders. The Court of Appeal upheld the sentences, saying that the sentencer was entitled to take account of all the evidence he had heard at the trial of B in fixing the appropriate sentence on A. It was important that A be given the chance to give evidence about the extent of his involvement, and this had been done. Lord Lane CJ said that it was important that the sentencing judge should bear in mind the obvious risk that self-serving statements made by the offenders might be untrue. A *Newton* hearing might offer a way of resolving any significant factual dispute, but in the case the offender had turned down the opportunity to present his version of events on oath. The judge had, therefore, 'handled this difficult situation impeccably'. In *Winter* [1997] 1 Cr App R (S) 331 six offenders were charged with conspiracy to cause grievous bodily harm with intent. One offender pleaded guilty while the others were convicted after a trial and received eight-year or six-year sentences. The offender who had pleaded guilty appealed against his six-year term on the basis that he had been given no credit for his plea and that the factual basis for that plea, which was that he had used no violence against the victim, had been ignored. The Court of Appeal, reducing the sentence from six years' imprisonment to five, said that the offender should at least have been given the opportunity to give evidence if he had wished. This had not been done.

3.4   ANTECEDENTS EVIDENCE AND CRIMINAL RECORD

After the prosecution summary of the facts or, in the case of a not guilty plea, immediately after the verdict of guilty, evidence will normally be given by the prosecution about the 'character and antecedents' of the offender. Antecedents evidence covers general information about the offender's background and circumstances, and is prepared in a standard form. On a separate sheet, attached to the antecedents evidence, is a list of the offender's previous convictions, if there are any.

In the Crown Court, the traditional procedure was for a police officer to give evidence of antecedents and criminal record, but the prosecutor will now normally summarise the accused's antecedents and record in his opening of the facts, provided that no dispute is anticipated. If some material in the antecedents is in dispute, a police officer is usually called to give evidence, and is then cross-examined by the defence. In the magistrates' courts a list of previous convictions is prepared, and this is handed by the prosecution to the bench. No antecedents report will be prepared in minor traffic cases, such as where the defendant is pleading guilty by post, or in other cases regarded as trivial. There may also be no report where a summary offence is prosecuted by an agency other than the CPS (Prosecution of Offences Act 1985 (POA 1985), s. 6(1)).

3.4.1 Antecedents

The antecedents material is now on a set of standard forms which are prepared in advance by the police, and are subject to guidance provided by the *Practice Direction (Crime: Antecedents)* [1998] 1 Cr App R 213. The Practice Direction lays down minimum standards applicable for the provision of this information in the Crown Court and magistrates' courts and these were agreed between the Lord Chancellor's Department, the CPS and the Association of Chief Police Officers. Where local practice has been to provide fuller information, that practice should continue. The antecedents must contain personal and other details relating to the defendant, most of which will be completed by the police on the basis of information supplied by the defendant, such as to the custody officer on arrest, or upon committal by the magistrates to Crown Court. This information would normally include the defendant's date of birth rather than just his age, especially where the defendant is a juvenile and his age will crucially affect the sentencing options available (*Rossi* [1955] 1 WLR 109), his address, home circumstances and employment details, together with date of arrest. The antecedents must also contain information about the defendant's previous convictions and previous findings of guilt, if any, derived from the Police National Computer (see further **3.4.2**). Where appropriate, in the Crown Court these should contain brief details of the facts of the last three similar convictions. Spent convictions should be specially marked as such, but spent convictions are not erased from the record itself (see **3.4.4**). Details of any previous formal cautions will appear on a separate sheet (**3.4.3**). Seven copies of the antecedents documents are prepared in the Crown Court. Two copies are sent directly to the CPS, and the remainder are sent to the court which will be dealing with the case. The court then sends one copy of the antecedents to the defence and one to the probation service. Case law indicates that the defendant should see a copy of the antecedents as soon as possible, especially where the document contains material which is likely to be disputed (*Wilkins* (1977) 66 Cr App R 49). The remaining copies are for the court's use, including one for the note-taker. The antecedents documents must be served within 21 days of committal in every case. Any points of dispute arising from the information in the antecedents should be raised with the police, by the defence, at least seven days before the hearing, so that wherever possible the matter can be cleared up before the hearing itself. Seven days before the listed hearing date the police will check the conviction information against their computer-held data and will supply information to the court on any additional convictions, together with any other outstanding matters. The antecedents should also contain information on the date of last discharge from prison or other custodial institution, any court orders to which the defendant is currently subject, any outstanding offences, and liability for driving disqualification. Outstanding fines, however, are not shown. Where relevant, information should be given on the time which has been spent by the defendant on remand in custody on the impending matter.

Some portion of the antecedents material is quite often read out in court. As explained above, the material will have been supplied or verified by the defendant and in most cases proves to be entirely uncontroversial. In the past, problems have arisen where the police have included material in the antecedents which has gone well beyond that indicated in the Practice Direction. An illustrative case is *Wilkins* (1977) 66 Cr App R 49, where Wilkins was found guilty of living on the earnings of prostitution. He had been running 'escort agencies' which were, in fact, a cover for prostitution. The evidence at the trial indicated that some women had, with Wilkins's approval, worked as prostitutes. The antecedents statement, however, indicated much more widespread offending and suggested that some women had become prostitutes as a *result* of working for the offender. The antecedent evidence clearly influenced the judge, who passed a prison sentence of three and a half years. The Court of Appeal reduced it to two years, commenting that much of the antecedents evidence was hearsay and highly prejudicial. Another example is *Sargeant* (1974) 60 Cr App R 74, where the defendant disputed a suggestion in the antecedents that he had been dismissed from his last employment for drunkenness. Lawton LJ said that if it was thought that the information really would help the sentencer, information in support of the allegation should have been provided for the court. A third example is *Bibby* [1972] Crim LR 513, where the Court of Appeal said that it was unfair for the antecedents material to contain a general statement that the defendant 'mixed with criminals'. The basic principle to be derived from these cases is that, should the defence challenge information in the antecedents, the prosecution are required to prove the matter according to the normal criminal standard. If they are unable to do so, the sentencer should make it clear that he has disregarded the disputed material (*Campbell* (1911) 6 Cr App R 131). It follows that if there is no proper proof of an allegation prejudicial to the defendant, it should not be made in the first place.

3.4.2 Previous convictions

Evidence of the offender's previous convictions, if there are any, is always made available to the court when it turns to consider sentence. There is no doubt that information about previous convictions, and the offender's response to previous sentences, is highly influential in sentence decision-making. If an offender has no previous convictions, or is lightly convicted, or has a conviction-free gap prior to the commission of the latest offence, these are matters which the court may (and usually will) weigh in the offender's favour in the court's discretion under s. 28(1). If the offender does have a poor record, however, its precise relevance is more difficult to state. Certainly the offender is not entitled to the mitigation which he could have claimed on the basis of a clean record. It is not clear, however, in what circumstances, or to what extent, the court may view the offender's poor record as making the new offence more serious, and therefore deserving of a heavier punishment. Section 29(1) of the CJA 1991 simply states that 'the court may take into account any previous convictions of the offender or any failure of his to respond to previous sentences' when considering the seriousness of the latest offence. This provision, and the background to it, was considered at **2.2.5**.

Attached to the antecedents form will be the list of the offender's previous convictions. This list also contains previous 'findings of guilt'. A finding of guilt is the equivalent of a conviction, but made against a juvenile who has pleaded guilty or has been found guilty in a youth court or in a magistrates' court (CYPA 1933, s. 59). If the offender has now attained the age of 21, any findings of guilt which were recorded against him when he was under the age of 14 are excluded from the criminal record (CYPA 1933, s. 16(2)). For each conviction, the previous convictions form gives the court at which the offender was convicted, the date of the conviction, the offences of which the offender was convicted, the sentence passed (generally including the amount of any fine, the duration of any custodial or community sentence and the number of hours of any community service ordered) and any alteration made as the result of an appeal. The date of release from the last custodial sentence, if any, is also given.

Previous convictions are taken to be those in existence before the commission of the offence for which the offender is now to be sentenced. Any convictions between the commission of the offence and the hearing relating to that offence should, technically, not appear in the list of previous convictions, but should still appear in the antecedents. There must, of course, never be mention on the form of any arrests, charges or prosecutions which have not ended in conviction (*Burton* (1941) 28 Cr App R 89). Offences taken into consideration are not convictions, and those incurred by the offender on previous occasions should be listed separately (see **3.8**). Formal cautions (**3.4.3**) are not convictions, but any which have been incurred by the offender during the last three years will appear on a separate list. The payment of a fixed penalty without prosecution under the Road Traffic Offenders Act 1988 does not count as a conviction and so should not appear in the convictions list. No order should appear in the list of previous convictions which was not made consequent upon conviction (Rehabilitation of Offenders Act 1974, s. 7(5)). The best example of such an order would be where a person is bound over to keep the peace or to be of good behaviour, without having been convicted of any offence (see **7.2.1**). Even so, it seems that such orders are sometimes included in criminal records (Law Commission, 1987, pp. 66–8). Another example is a prosecution which has ended in a finding of unfitness to plead, or a finding of not guilty by reason of insanity, but, again, it seems that these findings are often included in the list. It may be thought that a conviction followed by an absolute or conditional discharge should not be included in the list of previous convictions because of the effect of PCCA 1973, s. 1C, which states that, for a range of purposes, an offender who is so sentenced is deemed not have been convicted of the offence (see **7.1.4**) but ROA 1974, s. 1(4), defines 'conviction' so as to include conviction followed by discharge. See also CJA 1991, s. 29(3) to (6), mentioned at **2.2.5**.

The list of the previous convictions will also include, where this is known to the police or CPS, information about any breaches of a suspended sentence, probation order, conditional discharge or breach of licence conditions following an offender's early release from custody, provided that these have been the subject of court proceedings. Where breach proceedings are brought against an offender following his failure to comply with the requirements of a probation order, for example, no further offence has been committed and so the matter might not be known about by the police or CPS. The supervising probation officer will bring the matter back to court and will, in effect, act as prosecutor. If it is apparent from the evidence of previous convictions that the offender committed his present offence during the operational period of a conditional order (a suspended sentence, a community order or a conditional discharge), then he should be asked whether he admits the breach of the sentence. Assuming that he does so, the court can then deal with him for that matter as well as for the current offence, in accordance with the statutory provisions dealing with breach and revocation of the particular conditional order. If the offender refuses to admit the breach, or indeed if he challenges any of the evidence about previous convictions, the prosecution must prove beyond reasonable doubt that the evidence challenged is correct. Otherwise it should be ignored by the judge when sentence is passed, and the judge should make it clear that this is being done (*Butterwasser* [1947] 2 All ER 417). An offender who admits a previous conviction but wishes to be allowed to explain it more fully should be permitted by the court to do so (*Metcalfe* (1913) 9 Cr App R 7). This may perhaps be more conveniently done in the plea in mitigation, rather than by challenging the antecedents.

In most cases, the information about previous convictions is clear and is not disputed by prosecution or defence. Sometimes, however, there can be difficulties. The prosecution may wish to show that the offender has other convictions, such as very recent ones, which do not appear on the record. The records are sometimes inaccurate or incomplete in other ways, and for other reasons. In *Powell* (1980) (unreported), an offender was given a prison sentence of nine months because of a mix-up over criminal records. His record had been confused with another person with a similar name, and Powell was released after serving one month. In *Brumwell* (1980) *The Guardian*, 17 November 1980 the offender was given a sentence of six months' imprisonment. He was released when it came to light that an error on his record had credited him with eight previous convictions while, in fact, he had only two.

An alleged previous conviction which is disputed by the offender may be proved by:

(a)   producing a certificate of conviction signed by the clerk of the court in which the conviction took place, and

(b)   adducing evidence to show that the person named in the certificate is the person whose conviction it is sought to establish (PACE 1984, s. 73).

It will thus be for the prosecution to prove that the offender before the court is the person named in the certificate of conviction that has been produced. This might be done through the evidence of a police officer, or prison officer, who was present in court on the occasion of the conviction, and who can therefore testify that the offender now in the dock is the same person he previously saw convicted. Alternatively the evidence may take the form of further certificates which between them establish that the fingerprints of the person to whom the certificate of conviction relates and the fingerprints of the offender are identical (Criminal Justice Act 1948, s. 39). For previous convictions on indictment, the certificate of conviction will give the substance of the indictment upon which the conviction took place. For summary convictions, it will consist of a copy of the document recording the conviction (PACE 1984, s. 73(2)). In addition, there is a special provision to cater for proof of previous convictions of a person convicted of a summary offence where that person does not attend court. A notice must be served on the person, not less than seven days before the hearing, stating the alleged previous convictions which it is proposed to bring to the attention of the court. The court may, if the offender does not dispute the convictions, then take account of them in the offender's absence. Endorsements on a driving licence may be produced as prima facie evidence of the matters endorsed (Road Traffic Offenders Act 1988 (RTOA 1988), ss. 3(1) and 44(1)). An order of disqualification from driving may be proved, under the Magistrates' Courts' Rules 1981, r. 68, by the production of an extract from the court register certified by the clerk of the court.

3.4.3 Previous formal cautions

As an alternative to initiating a prosecution the police may decide to issue a formal caution. A formal caution should be distinguished from an informal warning given to the person by a police officer as part of the officer's 'on the street' discretion. The practice of administering a formal caution is subject to guidelines set out in a series of Home Office circulars, the most recent being Home Office Circular 18/1994. Clause 61 of the CDB provides for a new system of reprimands and warnings to replace the current system of formal cautions. For the present, however, a formal caution involves four elements. First, the person cautioned must fully admit guilt. Second, there must be enough evidence against the person at that time to provide a realistic prospect of conviction if a prosecution were brought. Third, the person must consent to being cautioned rather than being prosecuted; the effect of the person's consent to accepting a caution must be explained to him, and he must be told that cautions may be cited in court in the event of future offending. Fourth, certain procedural requirements must be complied with:

(a) the caution must normally be administered at a police station, by an officer of at least the rank of inspector;

(b) in the case of a juvenile, the juvenile's parent or guardian should normally be present;

(c) a standard form should be completed by the police officer, and signed by the person cautioned, as a record of what has taken place.

It should be noted that the cautioning power rests with the police and not the prosecuting authorities, although, of course, the CPS have an important discretion to discontinue proceedings against a person, even where the police have passed the papers to them with a view to prosecution.

The rapid growth in the use of formal cautioning, rather than prosecution, especially for juvenile offenders, has been an important feature of modern criminal justice policy. There are thought to be strong policy reasons for delaying a juvenile's entry into the criminal justice system for as long as possible, in the hope that he will grow out of his offending behaviour and never enter the system at all. The percentage of males aged 10–13 inclusive cautioned for indictable offences in 1996 (as a percentage of those found guilty or cautioned) was 86 per cent. The equivalent figure for those aged 14–17 inclusive was 55 per cent, for those aged 18–20 inclusive it was 33 per cent and for those aged 21 and over it was 18 per cent. The cautioning rate for adults varies considerably across the country. In Dorset in 1996, for example, the figure was 11 per cent, whereas in the Metropolitan Police area it was 39 per cent.

Before a formal caution is administered the position of the victim should be considered, by obtaining his views about the offence, and considering the extent of any loss or damage. One factor to be borne in mind is that if a suspect is formally cautioned rather than prosecuted there is no opportunity for a court to make a compensation order.

Formal cautions are not convictions, and so should not appear in the list of previous convictions. All police forces, however, record juvenile and adult cautions administered locally. Previous cautions which were issued for offences committed by the offender (whether a juvenile or an adult) within the three years preceding the current offence may be cited in court (Home Office Circular 59/1990). That Circular also makes it clear that cautions and convictions, although presented to the court at the same time, should not appear on the same sheet, so as to preserve a distinction between them. The lack of full national records of formal cautions means that those administering them, and the courts, may not know that the offender has been cautioned before, especially where the caution was given in another police force area. Clause 62 of the CDB provides that reprimands or warnings, which will replace formal cautions in due course, 'may be cited in criminal proceedings in the same circumstances as a conviction of the person may be cited'.

3.4.4 Spent convictions

The Rehabilitation of Offenders Act 1974 (ROA 1974) was passed with the aim of helping ex-offenders to 'live down' the stigmatising effect of previous convictions. The main effect of the Act is that, once a certain time (the 'rehabilitation period') has elapsed from the date of the offender's conviction, the conviction becomes 'spent' and the offender, in respect of that conviction, is a 'rehabilitated person' (ROA 1974, s. 1(1)). As a rehabilitated person he is, for most purposes, treated as if he had never committed or been convicted of the offence (s. 4(1)). Thus, if he is questioned on a job application about his criminal record he need not mention spent convictions, and if a newspaper were to reveal in an article that he had a spent conviction he could maintain an action for libel against the newspaper. 'Conviction' is, for the purposes of the ROA 1974, widely defined to include 'any finding in criminal proceedings other than one linked with a finding of insanity' (s. 1(4)). It includes 'findings of guilt' made against juveniles.

On its face, the ROA 1974 does not apply to a wide range of judicial proceedings, including criminal proceedings (s. 7(2)). This is misleading. In the case of criminal proceedings, *Practice Direction (Crime: Spent Convictions)* [1975] 1 WLR 1065 endorsed the spirit of the Act in stating that neither counsel nor judge should refer to a spent conviction where 'such reference can reasonably be avoided'. Mention of a spent conviction requires the judge's authority and that authority should be given only where the interests of justice so require. At the sentencing stage, the list of previous convictions given to the court should mark those which are spent. They are usually stamped over with the word 'SPENT' (though what is written underneath remains readable). When passing sentence the judge should say nothing about spent convictions unless it is vital to do so to explain the penalty decided upon. *Practice Direction (Crime: Spent Convictions)* has no direct application to magistrates' courts but, following advice issued by the Secretary of State (in Home Office Circular 98/1975) comparable practice is followed in the lower courts.

Whether a previous conviction is capable of becoming spent and, if so, the length of the rehabilitation period, are governed by the sentence imposed for the offence. Thus, if the offender serves a sentence of more than 30 months' imprisonment or detention in a young offender institution (including a life sentence) the conviction can never become spent. If he serves a sentence of more than six months but not more than 30 months, the conviction becomes spent after 10 years. At the other end of the scale, if he is given an absolute discharge the rehabilitation period is only six months. A full list of rehabilitation periods is given at **13.6.1**, together with some of the other provisions in the Act, such as the reduced rehabilitation periods for some sentences which apply to offenders who were under 18 years of age when convicted.

It is important to realise that for a conviction to become spent the rehabilitation period must be conviction-free. If an offender is convicted of an offence (other than a purely summary offence) during the rehabilitation period for an earlier conviction, then (unless the later conviction can never become spent) the two convictions both become spent on the later of the two relevant rehabilitation dates (s. 6(4)). This usually means that the earlier conviction does not become spent until the date on which the later conviction becomes spent. It follows that regular offenders tend to have no spent convictions, since the rehabilitation periods for early convictions are extended by the later convictions. The ROA 1974 has its main practical effect then where a person collects a conviction early in life and this is followed by a long conviction-free period.

A further complexity of the ROA 1974 lies in the wide range of exceptions to its out-of-court application. These were first set out in the Rehabilitation of Offenders Act 1974 (Exceptions) Order 1975 and have been added to since. See **13.6.2**.

3.5 REPORTS

Once evidence has been given concerning the offender's antecedents and previous convictions the sentencer will turn to consider any reports which have been prepared on the offender. In general terms, the purpose of reports is to provide additional factual information for the sentencer about the circumstances of the offence and the character of the offender. Sometimes sentence may properly be passed without the benefit of reports, but there are now many occasions upon which the court is placed under an obligation to obtain and consider them, and other cases in which it is good sentencing practice to do so.

The relevant reports may have been obtained prior to conviction or hearing, in which case, in the Crown Court, they will probably have been read by the judge in advance. If they have not been obtained, it may be appropriate for the sentencer to adjourn for them to be prepared (see **3.2.1**). A pre-sentence report (see below) on an accused who intends to plead not guilty will not generally be prepared in advance. This is because to do so would be a wasted effort if the accused is acquitted, and because important matters which should appear in the report, such as the extent of the accused's culpability and the accused's attitude to the offence, cannot be investigated. In these cases, adjournment after conviction is the general rule.

In the discussion which follows the main emphasis is placed upon the pre-sentence report because this is the document most commonly encountered in practice and in many cases will be the only report which the court will have. Depending on the issues raised by the case, however, the pre-sentence report may be supplemented by other reports.

3.5.1 Pre-sentence reports

Section 3(5) of CJA 1991 provides that a pre-sentence report is a report in writing which:

(a) with a view to assisting the court in determining the most suitable method of dealing with an offender, is made or submitted by a probation officer or by a social worker of a local authority social services department; and

(b) contains information as to such matters, presented in such manner, as may be prescribed by the Secretary of State.

Reports on those over 21 are compiled by probation officers. Local authority social workers prepare reports on children aged under 13. For intermediate ages, responsibility is shared, with the arrangements varying from area to area (CYPA 1969, ss. 9 and 34(3)). Whenever a court requests a report, it is the duty of the probation service or local authority to provide one. A copy of the pre-sentence report must be given to the offender or to his lawyer so that any controversial matters in it can be challenged and a further copy should be given to the prosecutor (C(S)A 1997, s. 50). Ordinarily the court should not read out a pre-sentence report in full (*Smith* (1968) 51 Cr App R 376). If matters in the report are in dispute the writer should be called. Otherwise, and particularly if it is uncontroversial, the report may be presented by a court liaison officer. Any matters relating to the report should be dealt with before counsel for the defence enters the plea in mitigation, so that counsel can question the report writer if necessary and refer to the content of the report in the mitigation (*Kirkham* [1968] Crim LR 210). In practice, lawyers often base their pleas in mitigation on material in the report. This is natural enough, but has sometimes occasioned criticial comment.

The CJA 1991 gives little information about the form and content of pre-sentence reports. The Home Office National Standard (Home Office, 1995) fills in much of the detail. A pre-sentence report must be 'in writing'. This excludes the possibility of presentation of an oral 'stand-down' inquiry in any of the cases where a pre-sentence report is referred to by statute (see below). Stand-down inquiries (i.e. brief verbal reports following an interview at court during an adjournment) were permitted before the 1991 Act came into force but were comparatively unusual. Perhaps an oral report could still be given, in appropriate circumstances, where a pre-sentence report is not otherwise required.

Important provisions in Part I of CJA 1991 require a sentencing court to obtain and consider a pre-sentence report in the following circumstances. As far as custodial sentences are concerned, it should be borne in mind when looking at (a) and (b) below that, subject to the normal requirement that the court 'shall obtain and consider a pre-sentence report' (CJA 1991, s. 3(1)), the court may dispense with such a report if, in the circumstances of the case, the court is of the opinion that it is unnecessary to obtain one (s. 3(2)). The discretion to dispense with a report is subsequently narrowed in respect of an offender who is under the age of 18. Unless the offence is one which is triable only on indictment, the court cannot decide that a pre-sentence report on a juvenile is unnecessary unless a report was prepared earlier and the court has seen it (s. 3(2A)). Section 3(4) provides that no sentence shall be invalidated by failure of the court to comply with s. 3(1), but on appeal against a custodial sentence passed without the court having obtained and considered a pre-sentence report, the appellate court must obtain and consider one unless, in accordance with s. 3(4A), that court thinks that the court below was justified in not calling for a report or, even if it was not justified, in the circumstances of the case at the time the matter is before the appellate court, it is unnecessary to obtain one. Again, however, the appellate court cannot take this line with a juvenile not convicted of an offence triable only on indictment. In such a case the appellate court must order a report, or have sight of a recent one prepared on the juvenile (s. 3(2A)).

(a) *When making a decision whether a custodial sentence is justified.* In assisting the sentencer to make this decision the report should address, and the sentencer should have regard to, those matters which the sentencer is bound to consider under CJA 1991, s. 1(2)(a) (whether the offence was 'so serious' that only a custodial sentence can be justified for it) or, under s. 1(2)(b) (where the offence was a violent offence or a sexual offence, whether only a custodial sentence would be adequate to protect the public from serious harm from the offender). The court must take into account 'all such information about the circumstances of the offence (including any aggravating or mitigating factors) as is available to it (s. 3(3)(a)). The pre-sentence report is a prime source for this information. Where the court is dealing with an offender convicted of a violent offence or a sexual offence, it may 'take into account any information about the offender which is before it' (s. 3(3)(b)). More generally, CJA 1991, s. 28(1) provides that nothing 'shall prevent a court mitigating an offender's sentence by taking into account any such matters as, in the opinion of the court, are relevant in mitigation of sentence', and s. 29 permits the court to have regard to the offender's previous convictions and response to previous sentences. Material in the pre-sentence report may be relevant to all of these matters.

(b) *When making a decision on the appropriate length of a custodial sentence.* The court must take into account 'all such information about the circumstances of the offence (including any aggravating or mitigating factors) as is available to it (CJA 1991, s. 3(3)(a)). Where the court is dealing with an offender convicted of a violent offence or a sexual offence, it may 'take into account any information about the offender which is before it' (s. 3(3)(b)). Again, CJA 1991, s. 28(1) provides that nothing 'shall prevent a court mitigating an offender's sentence by taking into account any such matters as, in the opinion of the court, are relevant in mitigation of sentence', and s. 29 permits the court to have regard to the offender's previous convictions and response to previous sentences. Material in the pre-sentence report may be relevant to all of these matters.

(c) *When making a decision to impose one of the more onerous community orders.* In this context CJA 1991, by s. 7(3), identifies:

(i)   a probation order which includes additional requirements authorised by PCCA 1973, sch. 1A;
(ii)   a community service order;
(iii)   a combination order;
(iv)   a supervision order which includes requirements imposed under CYPA 1969, s. 12, 12A, 12AA, 12B or 12C; or
(v)   when the relevant provisions of the CDB 1998 become law and are brought into force, a drug treatment and testing order.

The CJA 1991 states that a court should not impose a community sentence unless it is of the opinion that the offence 'was serious enough to warrant such a sentence' (s. 6(1)) and that the restrictions imposed upon the offender by the community sentence 'are commensurate with the seriousness of the offence' (s. 6(2)(b)). When imposing a community sentence the court is also bound, by s. 6(2)(a), to select that sentence which is the 'most suitable for the offender'. Section 28(1), referred to above in relation to custodial sentences, also applies to community sentences, so that the court may consider any matter in mitigation which is drawn to its attention, and s. 29 permits the court to have regard to the offender's previous convictions and response to previous sentences.

As far as the orders listed here are concerned, it should be borne in mind that, subject to the normal requirement that the court 'shall obtain and consider a pre-sentence report' (CJA 1991, s. 7(3)), the court may dispense with such a report if, in the circumstances of the case, the court is of the opinion that it is unnecessary to obtain one (s. 7(3A)). The discretion to dispense with a report is subsequently narrowed in respect of an offender who is under the age of 18. Unless the offence is one which is triable only on indictment, the court cannot decide that a pre-sentence report on a juvenile is unnecessary unless a report was prepared earlier and the court has seen it (s. 7(3B)). Section 7(4) provides that no sentence shall be invalidated by failure of the court to comply with s. 7(3), but on appeal against a custodial sentence passed without the court having obtained and considered a pre-sentence report, the appellate court must obtain and consider one unless, in accordance with s. 7(5), that court thinks that the court below was justified in not calling for a report or, even if it was not justified, in the circumstances of the case at the time the matter is before the appellate court, it is unnecessary to obtain one. Again, however, the appellate court cannot take this line with a juvenile not convicted of an offence triable only on indictment. In such a case the appellate court must order a report, or have sight of a recent one prepared on the juvenile.

Even for those community sentences where a pre-sentence report is not normally required it will often be good sentencing practice to obtain one, in order to consider further information both about the offence and the offender.

In what circumstances could a sentencer properly take the view that a pre-sentence report is unnecessary? Some help may be derived from case law pre-dating the Act, but relating to similar wording in earlier statutory provisions. In *Massheder* (1983) 5 Cr App R (S) 442 a 15-year-old pleaded guilty to arson involving £5,000 worth of damage. No report was available on the offender because of industrial action amongst social services staff. The judge passed a sentence of 18 months' detention under CYPA 1933, s. 53(2). On appeal, the Court of Appeal had the benefit of a report which recommended a supervision order. It was held that the judge had been wrong to pass sentence as he did. According to MacPherson J:

> The whole purpose of obtaining a report is to give help and balance to the consideration of all available courses open to the court. In this case, in spite of the difficulty faced by the court, the matter should have been adjourned to see whether a report was produced.

If anything, the circumstances in which a sentencer could properly find that a report was 'unnecessary' will be narrower after the CJA 1991 than before. A sentencer might be tempted to dispense with a report in a case where, on the facts of the offence, he regards a custodial sentence as inevitable. Yet CJA 1991, s. 3(1) makes information in the report relevant to sentence length as well as to choice of sentence. It would, therefore, be a rare case indeed where the sentencer could predict that nothing in a pre-sentence report could affect his decision on sentence length either.

The Home Office National Standard requires that reports should be prepared as quickly as possible, should take no more than seven days where the defendant has been remanded in custody and should, in any event, normally be completed within four weeks. The National Standard also hints at the necessity for improving disclosure of information to the probation service by the CPS and the need to allow report writers swifter access to defendants held on remand.

The National Standard, at least in theory, removed the report writer's prerogative to make a recommendation on sentence. This was common practice in social inquiry reports before the 1991 Act, and research studies showed a high correlation between recommendations made and sentences passed. The making of sentence recommendations has always been controversial, and in some Court of Appeal decisions probation officers were criticised for making 'unrealistic' proposals (e.g. *James* [1982] Crim LR 59). It remains to be seen how much difference the formal removal of the power to make a recommendation will actually make, since the National Standard still encourages the report writer to discuss the availability of community sentences and indicate which community option, in the writer's experience, would be the most suitable for the offender. This discussion should, however, be 'realistic and appropriate in relation to seriousness'.

The national standard states that reports should be 'crisp, clear, easy to understand and relevant' and, at another point, 'concise, free of jargon and exclude unnecessary detail'. Where possible, the Home Office National Standard urges, a pre-sentence report should be no more than two pages long. The first task of the report writer is to summarise the offence 'factually and objectively' and then to 'analyse the offender's behaviour and attitude to the offence'. This information must be provided 'impartially', to present a 'balanced picture'. The offender 'should be interviewed on one or more occasions' to provide information for the report. Typically the report should address the offender's explanation for the offence, acceptance of responsibility and feelings of guilt and remorse, attitudes, motivations, character, criminal history, relationships (e.g. contacts with family, friends and associates), personal problems such as alcohol or drug misuse, financial, housing, or employment difficulties, and medical or psychiatric problems. The report should contain only information which is relevant to the sentencing decision and should provide 'a clear indication of the source of main facts and whether they have been verified.'

3.5.2 Medical reports

There is a range of circumstances in which a court will have before it a medical report prepared upon the offender. Medical reports are generally prepared in advance on any offender charged with murder or manslaughter, a serious violent or sexual offence or arson. Apart from these cases, a request for a medical report may be initiated by the defence, or sometimes by the sentencer. A court must obtain medical reports before it can make a hospital order or a guardianship order under MHA 1983, s. 37 or before it can insert into a probation order or a supervision order a requirement of medical treatment (see Chapter 11).

A court must order a medical report to be prepared on any offender who is, or appears to be, mentally disordered, before a custodial sentence (apart from a mandatory life sentence for murder or a sentence under C(S)A 1997, s. 2) is passed on him (s. 4(1)). Failure to comply with this requirement does not render the sentence invalid but, if there is an appeal, the appellate court must obtain a medical report (s. 4(4)). The court need not obtain a report if it thinks this is 'unnecessary' (s. 4(2)). This exception is somewhat wider than the equivalent exception relating to pre-sentence reports (s. 3(2)), which is confined to cases where the offence is triable only on indictment. In any event, before passing a custodial sentence on such an offender, the court must consider any information before it (whether in a medical report, a pre-sentence report or otherwise) which relates to the offender's mental condition and the likely effect of a custodial sentence on that condition and the availability of treatment for it (s. 4(3). A medical report may be submitted orally or in writing by a registered medical practitioner who is duly approved for the purposes of MHA 1983, s. 12, as having special experience in the diagnosis and treatment of mental disorder (s. 4(5)). Section 4 does not affect the decision of the Court of Appeal in *Hook* (1980) 2 Cr App R (S) 353, which was to the effect that a sentencer cannot recommend that an offender serve a custodial sentence at the psychiatric prison, Grendon Underwood.

The court may adjourn for the preparation of a medical or psychiatric report on the offender. Adjournment for reports is considered in **3.2.1**. When the report has been prepared, a copy should be given to the clerk of the court and to the defence lawyer. The offender will not see the report, but if he is not legally represented he should be told the gist of what is in it (MHA 1983, s. 54(3)). Although the report should not be read out in court, there may be discussion in court of its contents. The defence may require the report writer to be called to give evidence, and evidence can be called to rebut what is in the report. A study of the use of psychiatric reports in the Crown Court (Mackay, 1986) found that the vast majority of requests for reports came from the defence, in the context of providing material for mitigation. Reports seemed to be given considerable weight by sentencers, and clear recommendations for psychiatric disposal were overridden by the sentencer in only a very few cases; custody being imposed because of the seriousness of the offence.

3.5.3 Other reports

Information may on occasion be derived from other reports. Custodial establishments may submit a report to the Court of Appeal which relates to the offender's behaviour while in custody. Sometimes information about an offender's reaction to his first few weeks of custody is a factor which weighs with the appellate court in reducing sentence (see further **13.2**).

Before passing a community service order or a combination order, the court must have an assessment of the offender's suitability for that disposal. So, in addition to the pre-sentence report which is required in any event, there will be a short report from a probation officer indicating whether the offender seems to have the necessary skills and motivation to perform work under the order and whether there is suitable work available in the local area. For details see the discussion of the various community orders in Chapter 5.

A youth court will frequently remand a juvenile in care for two or three weeks so that a report can be prepared. The school the juvenile attends (or fails to attend) may also submit a report.

3.6 DEFENCE MITIGATION AND OTHER REPRESENTATIONS

After the judge has read and considered the reports, the defence has the opportunity to present the 'plea in mitigation' on behalf of the offender. The prosecution, on the other hand, has no opportunity to present a 'plea in aggravation'. It was explained earlier that sentencing procedure is quite different from trial procedure, and the lack of an adversarial approach here is a further illustration of that point.

3.6.1 The plea in mitigation

There is no set pattern for mitigation. According to Comyn J in *Gross* v *O'Toole* (1982) 4 Cr App R (S) 283, mitigation is 'purported to be the province of the most junior of counsel' but 'is in fact amongst the most difficult tasks any barrister can ever face'. The purpose of the plea in mitigation is to make known to the sentencer any aspects of the case which tend to reduce its gravity, whether this relates to the precise facts of the offence (any significant differences between prosecution and defence versions of the facts should already have been resolved: **3.3**), the offender's attitude to the offence, his individual circumstances, any feelings of remorse, willingness to make reparation or other mitigating factors. On the other hand, it is important that the lawyer advancing mitigation should be 'realistic' about his client's case, and be frank about the aggravating features of the case as well. In a case where the judge may have in mind a sentence which counsel may not have considered, the judge should give the lawyer notice of that fact before mitigation is begun, so that he may address that specific point. Examples are where the judge is considering imposing a life sentence on the offender (*Morgan* (1987) 9 Cr App R (S) 201) or a longer-than-normal custodial sentence under CJA 1991, s. 2(2)(b) (*O'Brien* (1995) 16 Cr App R (S) 556). Another is disqualification from driving for life, rather than for a fixed term of years (*Scott* (1989) 11 Cr App R (S) 249). A fourth is where the judge is considering imposing a separate custodial sentence for failure to surrender to bail (*Woods* (1989) 11 Cr App R (S) 551).

The plea in mitigation generally takes the form of a single address, but it is open to the defence to call witnesses to speak to the offender's generally good character (e.g. an employer who says that he is willing to continue employing the offender), or to comment upon the circumstances of the offence. This evidence may be called at the beginning, in the middle, or at the end of the speech (per Comyn J in *Gross* v *O'Toole*). The offender will not normally be called at this stage unless there is a dispute about the facts of the offence, or if it is a road traffic case and the offender is subject to mandatory disqualification unless he shows special reasons for not being disqualified from driving (see **10.1**). If the lawyer decides to call his client at this stage, it is not appropriate for the judge to discourage it (*Cross* [1975] Crim LR 591). It is perfectly proper for counsel to cite guideline sentencing decisions of the Court of Appeal when giving the speech in mitigation (*Ozair Ahmed* (1993) 15 Cr App R (S) 286). There is in fact great variation in the style, length and content of pleas in mitigation. What ought to be said will obviously vary considerably from case to case, and the lawyer's common sense and experience will be the guide as to what is better left unsaid. Even where there appears to be little which can be said in favour of the offender, it is the lawyer's duty to present whatever mitigation can be found, and the sentencer's duty to listen to those representations, without excessive interruption (*Jones* [1980] Crim LR 58). The plea in mitigation will normally be heard in open court, but there is power to clear the court of members of the public to hear sensitive matters of mitigation in camera. This is a 'wholly exceptional' course to take (*Ealing Justices, ex parte Weafer* (1981) 3 Cr App R (S) 296). Where a matter is to be put forward in mitigation which the offender does not wish to have made public, the information may be written down and handed to the sentencer, with a copy being given to the prosecution (*Ealing Justices* (above); *Beckett* (1967) 51 Cr App R 180). If the defendant contested the case but was convicted, it is wrong for counsel to repeat the defendant's claim to be innocent in the speech in mitigation (*Wu Chun-piu* v *The Queen* [1996] 1 WLR 1113). During the speech in mitigation, counsel must not make statements which are 'merely scandalous or intended or calculated to vilify, insult or annoy' any person (Code of Conduct of the Bar, para. 610(e)). Section 58 of the Criminal Procedure and Investigations Act 1996 states that the judge may make an order to prevent the reporting by the press of any false or irrelevant assertions made during a speech in mitigation. Of particular concern here are suggestions made in the speech that the victim of the offence was a person of less than upright character, or was at least partly responsible for what happened.

As we have seen, offence seriousness is the key criterion under the CJA 1991 when determining both the form of sentence (custodial, community or financial penalty) and the appropriate degree of restriction of liberty, if a custodial or community sentence is selected. This approach is often reflected in pleas in mitigation. The lawyer will tend initially to address matters of offence seriousness, pointing out in particular those matters which make the offence less serious than other examples of the particular offence committed. Perhaps the offence was committed on the spur of the moment, rather than planned, or, if several offenders were involved, the offender's role was a peripheral one or, if the offender has committed an assault, this followed a degree of provocation from the victim. After the circumstances of the offence and the offender's degree of involvement have been discussed, the lawyer may then turn to more general matters in mitigation. Of particular importance will be credit for a guilty plea, for a clean record and for full co-operation with the police. In a case where the seriousness of the offence indicates that a community sentence is the likely outcome, the offender's attitude to the offence and his willingness to comply with any community penalty would be important matters. Recent or impending changes in the offender's circumstances may be brought to the court's attention. In all these matters the lawyer may refer the sentencer to relevant passages in the pre-sentence report. All these matters are discussed further in Chapter 2.

Sometimes difficulties arise where an assertion is made in the plea in mitigation which is hard for the sentencer to accept, since it conflicts with other information which has been received. In *Gross* v *O'Toole*, the offender was convicted of offering his services as a driver at Heathrow Airport contrary to a by-law. In mitigation it was contended that he had offered his services innocently, and free of charge. Before passing sentence the magistrates commented that they disbelieved the mitigation, no doubt because the offender had many previous convictions for the same sort of offence. One of the points argued on appeal against sentence was that the bench should have given the defence warning that they were minded to reject the mitigation. The Divisional Court said that the prime responsibility was on the defence advocate to 'make good the submission', whether by a speech or by calling evidence. The bench was not obliged to warn the lawyer of its provisional view, but it might be 'good practice' to do so.

As was explained in **3.3**, where conflicting versions of the facts of the offence are advanced by prosecution and defence, and acceptance of one version rather than the other would result in a material difference to the sentence, the sentencer is required to make a choice between them, and a *Newton* hearing should be held for this purpose. Suppose, however, that the prosecution is not in a position to refute mitigation urged by the defence, such as where it relates to matters not directly connected with the commission of the offence. In *Ogunti* (1987) 9 Cr App R (S) 325, for example, the defence claimed that the offender had committed the offence (possession of drugs with intent to supply) because a stranger who had given him the drugs had threatened him with violence if he did not comply. Even though the mitigation was consistent with Ogunti's statements to the police, the Court of Appeal held that the sentencer was certainly not bound to accept the defence assertion. In such a case the burden is on the defence to prove their version of events, on the balance of probabilities (*Guppy* [1994] Crim LR 614). This may be contrasted with a 'true' *Newton* case, where the prosecution is positively involved in offering a different version of facts from the defence and the burden of proof rests upon them to establish their version beyond reasonable doubt.

3.6.2 Other representations to the sentencer

(a) *The Jury* The jury has no direct role to play in sentencing. Their task is to return a verdict of guilty or not guilty or, where appropriate, guilty of a lesser offence. The traditional view is that the jury should be discouraged, in cases where they convict, from trying to influence the judge's decision on sentence. In *Sahota* [1980] Crim LR 678, for example, the Court of Appeal criticised a Crown Court judge who simply wrote 'yes' on a note he had been sent by the jury, which asked if they could add a rider to their verdict recommending leniency. The accused had been charged with causing grievous bodily harm to his wife. The evidence had shown that he had been provoked by her, and the jury were clearly reluctant to convict unless they could be assured that the offender would not be dealt with too harshly. None the less, the Court of Appeal said that the jury should have been told that sentencing was not their concern. The effect of this rule is that a jury may be tempted to acquit perversely; if this happens, there is no method of appeal. Alternatively the jury may, perversely, convict of a lesser offence. A different line was taken by the Court of Appeal on this matter in *Attorney-General's Reference (No. 8 of 1992)* (1993) 14 Cr App R (S) 130. The jury convicted the offender, who was aged 17 at the time of the offence, of manslaughter on an indictment for murder, but asked that the judge be made aware that they had 'great sympathy' for the offender. A probation order was imposed. It was accepted by the Attorney-General for the purposes of the sentencing reference to the Court of Appeal, and by the appellate court itself, that 'the judge was right to give effect to the recommendation of mercy, or at least of sympathy, expressed by the jury'. Lord Taylor CJ said that the sentencer had been 'absolutely correct' in his view that he 'had to have regard to the jury's recommendation'. None the less the Court of Appeal felt that the sentence was unduly lenient in all the circumstances, and increased it to one of two years' detention in a young offender institution. See also **3.3.3**.

(b) *The victim*   The Court of Appeal stated clearly in *Nunn* [1996] 2 Cr App R (S) 136 that the opinion of the victim or members of the victim's family about the appropriate level of punishment for the offender could not provide a sound basis for sentencing. Otherwise, cases with identical features would be dealt with in widely differing ways. It has been held in Scotland that it is wrong for a sentencer to seek the views of the victim of an offence as to the appropriate sentence for the offender (*HM Advocate* v *McKenzie* 1990 SLT 28). The reason given by the court in that case was that it would be 'invidious to expose the complainer to a risk of public pressure by passing any comment on matters that lie outside her expertise'. Although some North American jurisdictions do allow victims to have their say on sentence, there are obvious dangers in that approach. The victim is hardly likely to bring the necessary degree of detachment required to reach a proper sentencing decision, and the criminal offence is a wrong against society as a whole as well against an individual victim. Sometimes, however, the views of the victim of the offence will become known to the court. For example, the victim may have forgiven the offender and now be urging leniency. If so, there may be some scope to take account of the victim's representations in mitigation of sentence under CJA 1991, s. 28(1), but the court may properly pass a sentence which disregards those views if the seriousness of the offence dictates otherwise (*Hutchinson* (1993) 15 Cr App R (S) 124). In the unusual circumstances that the sentence passed by the judge has had the effect of increasing the anguish occasioned to the victim or his family, the sentence can be reduced on appeal (see *Nunn*, where the offender and the victim had been friends and the custodial sentence had made the victim's death harder to bear, and *Attorney-General's Reference (No. 8 of 1994)* (1995) 16 Cr App R (S) 327). Conversely, the victim's interest in the offender receiving a severe sentence may be apparent from evidence given at trial or, perhaps, from an application to the court for compensation from the offender. Again, the court's prime concern is to fix a sentence appropriate to the seriousness of the offence and the culpability of the offender. For compensation orders see **8.1**.

(c) *The offender*   When the plea in mitigation is concluded, it is the habit of some sentencers to ask the offender whether he (rather than his lawyer) has anything to say to the court.

3.7   PRONOUNCING SENTENCE

A Crown Court judge sitting alone will normally pronounce sentence immediately after defence mitigation is concluded. If the judge is sitting with lay magistrates (e.g. on a committal for sentence) and the decision is a difficult one, they sometimes retire to consider the sentence. Similarly, a lay bench of magistrates may wish to retire to consider the sentence. They may ask their clerk to retire with them to advise them on their sentencing powers (see **1.2.7**). In a magistrates' court the decision on sentence may be taken by a majority but it is pronounced by the chairman of the bench, without any mention of the fact that it is not unanimous.

In a number of situations courts are now required to justify their sentencing decision by reference to specific statutory sentencing criteria. Examples are:

(a)   Whenever a magistrates' court or the Crown Court imposes a custodial sentence (including a suspended sentence, but excluding a case where custody results from the offender's failure to express his willingness to comply with a condition in a community order which requires an expression of such willingness) it is the court's duty to state in open court its view that custody is justified under either or both of the criteria in CJA 1991, s. 1(2), to explain why it is of that opinion and to explain to the offender in open court and in ordinary language why it is passing a custodial sentence (CJA 1991, s. 1(4)). For magistrates' courts, this must be specified in the warrant of commitment and entered in the register (s. 1(5)). See further **4.2.3**.

(b)   Whenever a magistrates' court or the Crown Court imposes a custodial sentence which is for a term longer than is commensurate with the seriousness of the offence(s) (including a discretionary life sentence, a sentence of custody for life or a sentence of detention under CYPA 1933, s. 53(2)), the court must state that in its view the criterion in CJA 1991, s. 2(2)(b) applies, explain why it is of that opinion and explain to the offender in open court and in ordinary language why the sentence is for such a term. See further **4.2.6**.

(c)   A court which is dealing with an offender who is in breach of a suspended sentence and which chooses not to activate the sentence in full must give reasons for taking a more lenient approach (PCCA 1973, s. 23(1)). See further **4.2.6**.

(d)   A court which has power to make a compensation order on the offender must, if it does not do so, explain why compensation has not been ordered (PCCA 1973, s. 35(1)).

(e)   Section 48 of the CJPOA 1994 requires sentencers to state in open court that the sentence imposed has been reduced in consequence of the offender's guilty plea. See **2.2.4(g)**.

(f)   When sentencing a juvenile aged under 16 the court should normally bind over the parent or guardian of that offender and, if it does not do so, explain why not (CJA 1991, s. 58(1)). See **7.2.5**.

(g)   The CDB proposes that where the court has power to make a reparation order, under powers in cl. 54(11) of the Bill, the court must explain why it did not make such an order. See **7.4.1**.

(h)   Where a court, for 'special reasons', exercises its discretion not to disqualify the offender from driving or not to order endorsement, it must state its grounds for doing so in open court and if it is a magistrates' court it must enter these reasons in the register. The same requirements apply if, because of 'mitigating circumstances', a court does not disqualify, or disqualifies for a period shorter than six months. See further **10.1**.

Apart from these specific cases, Crown Court judges are in any event generally encouraged to give reasons for deciding upon a particular sentence. They should certainly give reasons when the sentence on the face of it may seem unduly severe (*Newman* (1979) 1 Cr App R (S) 252) or unduly lenient, given the circumstances of the case. In *Attorney-General's Reference (No. 23 of 1992)* (1993) 14 Cr App R (S) 759 the Court of Appeal, dealing by way of an Attorney-General's Reference with a Crown Court sentence alleged to be unduly lenient, criticised the sentencer for not specifying reasons or explaining the process by which a 'derisory' sentence had been arrived at. In the past some sentencers have tended to follow the letter, rather than the spirit, of the requirement to give reasons, and such reasons have been perfunctorily expressed. As the Court of Appeal pointed out in

Attorney-General's Reference (No. 23 of 1992), not only does the requirement of giving reasons make it easier, in the event of an appeal, for the appellate court to understand the thought processes of the sentencer, it also tends towards greater clarity in the initial sentencing decision. It is to be hoped that the increasing number of statutory requirements to give reasons will prompt sentencers to give fuller explanations for sentence in all cases. In addition to the requirement to give reasons, there are also numerous provisions in sentencing legislation where courts are required to explain the import of the sentencing decision to the offender in ordinary, non-technical language. There are also a few cases in which an expression of willingness to comply with the order of the court must be expressed by the offender before a particular sentence may lawfully be passed. Again, these require that the court explain the implications to the offender in ordinary language.

Occasionally the sentencer's comments when passing sentence reveal that an irrelevant or inappropriate consideration has been taken into account. This may then form the basis for an appeal. There are occasionally cases which are seized upon by the press, where a judge expresses himself inappropriately, such as by stating that a female hitch-hiker who was raped was guilty of 'contributory negligence', thereby justifying a lower sentence for the offender (see now the guideline case of *Billam* (1986) 8 Cr App R (S) 48, discussed at **12.3.1**, which makes it clear that sentence should not be reduced in such cases). In earlier times it was quite common for judges to deliver sentencing 'homilies' upon the offender, in which the judge might express a view about the offender's general moral character and suggest ways in which he ought to adjust his life-style to avoid further conflict with the criminal law. Some odd statements are still made from time to time by judges, but sentencing homilies have been criticised by the Court of Appeal and are now much rarer than they were.

3.8 TAKING OTHER OFFENCES INTO CONSIDERATION

One of the most fundamental sentencing principles, which emerges from the material in this chapter, is that the offender must only be sentenced for those offences for which he has been found guilty or to which he has pleaded guilty. There is a limited exception to this principle, which applies where other offences are taken into consideration.

Other offences taken into consideration when sentence is passed (or 't.i.c.'s as they are generally known) are offences of which the offender is never convicted, but which are admitted by him in court and, at his request, are borne in mind by the judge when sentence is passed for the offences in respect of which there is a conviction (hereinafter referred to as the 'conviction offences'). The sequence of events leading up to offences being taken into consideration will vary from case to case, and the procedure is a matter of convention and court practice rather than statutory regulation (*Walsh* (1973) CSP L3.3A01). The practice is one of long standing (see, for example, *Syres* (1908) 1 Cr App R 172) and it has been referred to in several statutory provisions, such as CJA 1991, s. 31(2). Typically, it will involve a suspect, who has been arrested on suspicion of one or more crimes, admitting at the police station that he committed the crimes alleged and making it obvious that he intends to plead guilty. The police may then ask him about other similar offences which they believe he might have committed, but which, in the absence of an admission from him, they would find difficult to prove. Since he is resigned to having to plead guilty to the offences for which he was arrested, the suspect often decides to make a clean breast of everything on the understanding that some or all of the offences he is now being asked about will not be the subject of separate charges but will merely be taken into consideration. A list is then drawn up of the offences to be taken into consideration, and the suspect signs the list. The offences for which he was arrested and with which he was charged are then prosecuted in the normal way. Copies of the list are given to the prosecutor and to the defence. In *Wheeldon* (1988) *The Times*, 13 May 1988, one of the grounds for allowing an appeal against sentence was that the defence had not been provided with the list.

At court, the accused duly pleads guilty. Then, at some stage during the prosecution's statement of the facts, the prosecutor will mention to the sentencer that the offender wants to have other matters considered. The sentencer will then be handed the list of the offences signed by the offender and the sentencer, or the court clerk, will ask the offender in open court whether he admits them, and whether he wants them taken into consideration (*Anderson* v *DPP* [1978] AC 964). If the offender answers 'yes' to both questions the sentencer may, and probably will, comply with the request. Agreement must come from the offender, rather than his lawyer (*Davis* [1943] KB 274). The offender should admit the offences in open court (*Griffiths* (1932) 23 Cr App R 153). It is not necessary to put the particulars of the offences to the offender one by one. Usually the offender is asked whether he signed the list, whether he agrees that he committed the offences and whether he wants them taken into consideration. It is essential that the offender fully understands what is being done. In *Walsh* (1973) CSP L3.3A01 it emerged later that some of the 259 't.i.c.'s which W had admitted had in fact been committed at a time when Walsh was in prison. Any offences which the offender denies must be deleted. In *Burfoot* (1990) 12 Cr App R (S) 252 an appeal against sentence was allowed where B had been sentenced on the basis of a list of no less than 600 't.i.c.'s which B had signed at the police station but subsequently denied at court.

The prosecution should be in a position to provide the sentencer with brief details of any offence taken into consideration. The sentence which is eventually passed will be somewhat more severe than it would have been in the absence of the 't.i.c.'s (*Batchelor* (1952) 36 Cr App R 64). The addition to the sentence will, however, be considerably less than the penalty would have been if they had been prosecuted separately. If, in a magistrates' court, the new information about the 't.i.c.'s now makes the case one which should attract a punishment greater than the magistrates are empowered to impose, and provided the offence is triable either way and the offender is aged 18 or over, the case may be committed to the Crown Court for sentence (MCA 1980, s. 38: see also **1.2.9**).

It will be seen that the system of taking offences into consideration has advantages for offenders. It allows the offender to 'clear the slate' and to receive a lesser sentence than might otherwise have been the case. It also has advantages for the police, because they 'clear up' offences which might otherwise have remained unsolved. The following additional points about taking offences into consideration should be noted:

(a) When the sentencer is deciding whether an offence is, or offences are, so serious that only a custodial sentence can be justified, the court may consider the conviction offences or a combination of the conviction offences and the offences taken into consideration (CJA 1991, s. 1(2)(a): see also **4.2.3**). If the sentencer decides that a custodial sentence is justified on this ground, then all the conviction offences and all the 't.i.c.'s should be weighed when determining the appropriate sentence length (CJA 1991, s. 2(2)(a): see also **4.4**). If, on the other hand, the sentencer decides that the offence is, or the offences are, not so serious as to require custody, a community sentence may be imposed, but only where serious enough to justify that course, rather than a financial penalty or a discharge. When deciding whether the offence is, or offences are, so serious that a community sentence is required, the court may similarly have regard to the 't.i.c.'s as well as the conviction offences (CJA 1991, s. 6(1): see also **5.1**). If the sentencer decides that a community sentence is justified on this ground, then all the conviction offences and all the 't.i.c.'s should be weighed when determining the appropriate degree of restriction upon the offender's liberty (CJA 1991, s. 6(2)(b): see also **5.1**).

(b) The sentence the court may pass is restricted to the maximum permissible for the offence(s) of which the offender has been convicted (*Hobson* (1944) 29 Cr App R 30 and, for custodial sentences, CJA 1991, s. 2(2)(a)). In practice it is almost always possible to add something to the sentence for the conviction offences to reflect the existence of the 't.i.c.'s, without approaching the maximum sentence.

(c) Which offences to charge and which to refrain from charging in anticipation of their eventually being taken into consideration is a matter within the discretion of the police and prosecution authorities. It is common for there to be up to ten 't.i.c.'s, but on occasions the 't.i.c.'s may vastly outnumber the conviction offences. In *Oyediran* [1997] 2 Cr App R (S) 277 the offender had claimed social security benefit for three years without revealing that he was also in receipt of a student grant. He pleaded guilty to five counts of false accounting and asked for 68 additional offences to be taken into consideration. Each time Oyediran had signed the benefit form he had committed a further offence. Another common situation in which there will often be a large number of 't.i.c.'s is credit card and chequebook fraud, where each dishonest use of the card or chequebook is a further offence. The sentencer should state, when passing sentence, how many offences have been taken into consideration.

(d) Since the taking of an offence into consideration does not, as a matter of law, amount to a conviction, the offender would not be able to resist a subsequent prosecution for the offence by reliance upon a plea of *autrefois convict* (that he has already been convicted of that charge, and so cannot be charged again) (*Nicholson* [1947] 2 All ER 535). In practice, however, prosecutions should never be brought for offences which have been taken into consideration. In a case where, by error, one was brought, the Court of Appeal recommended that there be 'no additional penalty' for it (*North* (1971) CSP L3.1B01).

(e) Although the 't.i.c.' system is designed primarily for offenders pleading guilty, there is nothing to stop the prosecution requesting a short adjournment after the accused has been found guilty, following a not guilty plea, to ask him whether, given the outcome of the trial, he would now like other offences considered.

(f) The court is not obliged to comply with a request to take offences into consideration. Magistrates should not take offences into consideration which are triable only on indictment (*Simons* [1953] 1 WLR 1014). More generally, it is bad practice to take offences into consideration which are more serious than the conviction offences; nor should the 't.i.c.'s be of a different type from the conviction offences. The court should never take offences into consideration which carry endorsement or disqualification unless the conviction offences are also so punishable (*Collins* [1947] KB 560) because the sentencing powers of the court are limited to those it possesses in respect of the conviction offences.

(g) A compensation order may be passed by the court in respect of an offence taken into consideration (PCCA 1973, s. 35(1)). In a magistrates' court, the total sum which may be ordered by way of compensation where the offender has 't.i.c.'s must not exceed the maximum which could be ordered for the offences, apart from the 't.i.c.'s (MCA 1980, s. 40(1)). (The maximum compensation which may be ordered for any offence by magistrates is £5,000.) A restitution order may be passed in respect of an offence taken into consideration (Theft Act 1968, s. 28(1)). A forfeiture order may be imposed, *inter alia*, where the offender asks to have an offence taken into consideration which involves unlawful possession of property which has since been lawfully seized from him or was in his possession or under his control when he was apprehended (PCCA 1973, s. 43(1)(b)).

3.9   SAMPLE COUNTS

Where the prosecution alleges that the offender has committed a large number of very similar offences over a substantial period of time, they may wish to proceed on the basis of 'sample counts'. A few of the alleged offences will be charged and then the sentencer will be invited to pass sentence on the basis of the whole scale of the offending. This may be seen as an alternative to presenting a list of 't.i.c.'s. Provided that the defence accepts the wider allegations and the offender pleads guilty to the sample counts, the sentencer may pass sentence on that basis. If, however, the defence says that the charges brought represent the total of the offending, the sentencer is not entitled to hear evidence from either side as to which version is correct. To do so would involve sentencing the offender for offences with which he has not been charged, which is quite improper.

The leading authority is *Canavan* [1998] 1 Cr App R 79, where the Court of Appeal dealt with a number of appeals giving rise to the same issue. Lord Bingham of Cornhill CJ said that it was 'inconsistent with principle that a defendant should be sentenced for offences neither admitted nor proved by verdict'. His lordship could find nothing in the CJA 1991 which would support any contrary interpretation of the law (indeed ss. 2(2)(a) and 31(2) of the CJA 1991 both indicate that the court should not take into account offences other than those of which the offender has been convicted or which he has had taken into consideration), and nor could his lordship see any relevant difference between the approach to be taken after a trial or when sentencing after a guilty plea. Thus, in respect of one appellant, a sentence of two years' imprisonment imposed on the basis that there had been repeated intimidation of a witness could not be sustained where the offender had been convicted of a single count of intimidation. Noting the common practice of prosecutors to proceed by way of specimen counts, his lordship continued: 'prosecuting authorities will wish, in the light of this decision . . . to include more counts in some indictments. We do not think this need be unduly burdensome or render the trial unmanageable.' The Court of Appeal approved earlier decisions to the same effect in *Hutchison* [1972] 1 WLR 398 and *Clark* [1996] 2 Cr App R (S) 351, and disapproved other cases, especially *Bradshaw* [1997] 2 Cr App R (S) 128, which suggested that the judge might pass sentence on the basis that the offending was in reality far more extensive than that revealed by the sample counts. In *Huchison* [1972] 1 WLR 398 the offender pleaded guilty to one count of incest with his daughter. The daughter's statement to the police indicated that sexual intercourse had taken place regularly over a period of years, but the defence claimed that it was limited to the one occasion alleged in the indictment. The judge passed a sentence of four years' imprisonment on the basis that the offence had been repeated, but the Court of Appeal halved the sentence. The judge was bound to sentence only on the offence admitted; the only other course open to him might have been to adjourn so that counts for the other occasions could be added to the indictment.

3.10   DEFERMENT OF SENTENCE

Both magistrates' courts and the Crown Court have powers to adjourn before passing sentence (see **3.2**). A comparable, though distinct, power to defer sentence is provided for both courts by PCCA 1973, s. 1. Section 1(1) provides that a court may defer passing sentence on an offender for the purpose of enabling it to have regard, in dealing with him, to his conduct after conviction (including, where appropriate, the making by him of reparation for his offence) or to any change in his circumstances.

The exercise of this power is subject to the offender giving his consent (s. 1(3)). The deferment must not exceed six months (s. 1(2)) and, subject to one exception mentioned in a moment, sentence may be deferred only once. The date to which sentence is deferred should be announced at the time of the deferment, but if the offender is not dealt with on that date the court does not thereby lose its power to sentence (*Ingle* [1974] 3 All ER 811). Should the offender be convicted of a further offence during the period of the deferment, the court which deferred sentence may issue a summons or warrant for arrest immediately (i.e. the court need not wait until the deferred sentence date) so as to bring him before it to be dealt with for the deferred sentence offence. Alternatively, the court dealing with the new offence may also deal with the deferred sentence offence, except that a magistrates' court cannot deal with an offence in respect of which the Crown Court deferred sentence (s. 1(4A)). If the Crown Court deals with an offence in respect of which a magistrates' court deferred sentence, the Crown Court is limited to the sentencing powers of the magistrates. At the end of a period of deferment, a magistrates' court may commit the offender to the Crown Court to be sentenced in preference to dealing with him themselves (s. 1(8)) and if it wishes, the Crown Court may then itself defer sentence (s. 1(8A)); this is the one exception to the rule that sentence may be deferred only once. When deferring sentence the court may not remand the offender (s. 1(6A)), it simply allows him to go free on the understanding that he will return on the day to which sentence has been deferred. If he fails to do so, a summons or warrant can be issued to secure his attendance. Whenever an offender is dealt with in respect of an offence for which sentence was deferred, the court may deal with him in any way the court which deferred sentence could have dealt with him (s. 1(8)). The court should always make it clear that it is deferring sentence under these powers rather than simply adjourning (*Fairhead* [1975] 2 All ER 737).

In the case of *George* [1984] 1 WLR 1083 Lord Lane CJ gave important guidance on how the courts should use the power to defer sentence. The case provides a useful summary of points made in several earlier decisions and these are outlined below:

(a)   A court deferring sentence should make it clear to the offender what its purposes in doing so are and what conduct is expected of the offender during the period of the deferment. A careful note of these matters must be made for the assistance of the court which eventually passes sentence. Ideally, a copy of the note should be given to the offender. Common reasons for deferring sentence are to establish whether the offender will make genuine efforts to find work or will stay in work, will save money so as to be in a position to make reparation to the victim of the offence, will give up drinking to excess or will contact and take advice from a probation officer. The reasons given for deferring sentence must always come within the terms of PCCA 1973, s. 1(1); deferment should not be used as a device for substantially restricting the offender's control over his own life during the period of deferment (e.g. by requiring that the offender reside at a mental hospital as a voluntary patient: *Skelton* [1983] Crim LR 686).

(b)   When the offender appears to be sentenced at the end of the period of deferment, the court passing sentence will know what the reasons for deferring were (if necessary, the sentencer may refer to the note which was made at the time sentence was deferred). If the material before the sentencing court (e.g. a pre-sentence report and the defence mitigation) shows that the offender has substantially complied with the requirements or expectations of the deferring court, then an immediate custodial sentence should not be imposed. If he has not, then the court is not so restricted, but it must state precisely how the offender failed. If this explanation is not given, any custodial sentence which is imposed may be quashed on appeal (even though otherwise justified by the seriousness of the offence), because of the unfairness to the offender (*Glossop* (1981) 3 Cr App R (S) 347).

(c)   Whenever possible the judge or the magistrates who deferred sentence should make themselves available to pass sentence (*Gurney* [1974] Crim LR 472). Counsel who represented the offender at the deferment should also strive to attend at sentencing (*Ryan* [1976] Crim LR 508). It is precisely because this will not always (or often) be possible, that the elaborate requirements in (a) and (b) have been devised by the Court of Appeal. Every effort should be made to sentence the offender on the deferred date but, in exceptional circumstances, an adjournment (rather than a deferment) even to a date more than six months from the date of deferment is permissible (*Anderson* (1984) 78 Cr App R 251). The sentence eventually passed should be reduced to take account of the delay.

(d)   Deferring sentence is not meant to be 'an easy way out for a court which is unable to make up its mind about the correct sentence' (Lord Lane CJ in *George*). In particular, the court should consider carefully whether the objectives of deferment could not be more efficiently achieved by passing an immediate sentence, such as a probation order with certain specific requirements included within it (see **5.2.3**). Deferment should be preserved for those cases where the court needs to know how the offender will behave in the near future, but its expectations of him (e.g. that he will try hard to find employment) are too imprecise to be put into a probation order. It should also be remembered that since the decision in *George*, statutory restrictions imposed by the CJA 1991 upon the proper use of a probation order mean that probation can now be appropriate only in a case where the passing of community sentence is justified by the seriousness of the offence(s) committed.

3.11   LEGAL REPRESENTATION

An unrepresented offender may, of course, put forward his own plea in mitigation. Such a person is likely to be at a disadvantage, however, because of ignorance as to the relevance of mitigating factors which may weigh with the court. Legal representation is of especial importance where the offender is at risk of a custodial sentence. There is special legislative provision, therefore, that, subject to an exception mentioned below, when a magistrates' court or the Crown Court is dealing with an offender who is not legally represented in court, the court must give that person an opportunity to apply for legal aid before doing any of the following:

(a)   passing a sentence of imprisonment if the offender has never before received such a sentence (PCCA 1973, s. 21);

(b)   passing a sentence of detention in a young offender institution under CJA 1982, s. 4 (CJA 1982, s. 3);

(c)   passing a sentence of custody for life under CJA 1982, s. 8(2) (CJA 1982, s. 3);

(d)   making an order for detention under CYPA 1933, s. 53(2) (CJA 1982, s. 3);

(e)   making a detention and training order (CDB, sch. 8, para. 36).

Paragraph (a) above also applies to the passing of a suspended sentence, but a suspended sentence imposed on the offender in the past which never took effect is ignored when deciding whether the offender has previously received a prison sentence (PCCA 1973, s. 21(3)). Note that in paras (b) to (e) the requirement of legal representation before sentence is passed is not restricted to the first occasion upon which the sentence is passed on the offender.

These provisions use identical words in framing the exception to the restriction, namely that the court must not pass the relevant sentence on an unrepresented offender unless either:

(a)   he applied for legal aid and the application was refused on the ground that it did not appear his means were such that he required assistance; or

(b)   having been informed of his right to apply for legal aid and had the opportunity to do so, he refused or failed to apply.

For these purposes a person is to be treated as legally represented if he has the assistance of counsel or a solicitor to represent him at some time after he is found guilty and before he is sentenced. The offender's legal aid may relate to the whole proceedings or just in relation to sentence.

If a magistrates' court imposes a custodial sentence without complying with these provisions and the offender appeals to the Crown Court against sentence, it was held in *Birmingham Justices, ex parte Wyatt* [1976] 1 WLR 260 that the Crown Court must pass a sentence which the lower court could lawfully have passed, which must necessarily be a non-custodial sentence. On the other hand, where the Crown Court proceeded without complying with the provisions, it was held that the Court of Appeal might uphold the custodial sentence if it thought that it was the correct one in all the circumstances (*McGinlay* (1975) 62 Cr App R 156; *Hollywood* (1990) 12 Cr App R (S) 325).

3.12   COMMENCEMENT AND VARIATION OF SENTENCE

A sentence imposed by the Crown Court takes effect from the beginning of the day on which it is imposed, unless the court directs otherwise (SCA 1981, s. 47(1)). The court cannot order a sentence to take effect earlier than the day on which it was pronounced (*Gilbert* [1975] 1 WLR 1012). There is, however, a discretion to order the sentence to begin at a specified later date, usually at the expiration of another period of custody to which the offender is already subject. An unusual example of the use of this power arose in *Fairbrother and Hughes, The Times,* 29 June 1991 (news item) where the judge passed custodial sentences (of two months and six weeks) on company directors who had pleaded guilty to revenue offences. In an attempt to avoid the collapse of the business, the sentencer ordered the custodial sentence on one offender to commence at such time as the other offender was released.

The Crown Court may vary or rescind a sentence imposed or other order made within 28 days of its being passed (SCA 1981, s. 47(2)). The variation must be made by the Crown Court judge who originally passed the sentence (s. 47(4)). If he was then sitting with lay justices they need not be present for the variation. If the offender was jointly indicted with other accused, the period is 56 days from the passing of the sentence or 28 days from the conclusion of the joint trial, whichever expires the sooner (s. 47(3)). The offender should be present in court when sentence is varied (*Cleere* (1983) 5 Cr App R (S) 465) unless there is some good reason for his absence, such as in *McLean* (1988) 10 Cr App R (S) 18, where the good reason was that McLean had absconded. Any variation should be made in open court, so that nobody can be left in doubt as to what sentence has been passed; it should not be done behind the scenes, or by sending a message (*Dowling* (1988) 88 Cr App R 88). It is clear that the power to vary sentence may be used to correct an error in the original sentence. Thus, in *Iqbal* (1985) 7 Cr App R (S) 35, an unlawful sentence of 30 months' youth custody imposed upon a juvenile was replaced by an equivalent term under CYPA 1933, s. 53(2). It may also be used to replace one form of sentence with a quite different one. In *Sodhi* (1978) 66 Cr App R 260 a prison sentence of six months was replaced by a hospital order plus restriction order.

The extent to which a sentence may be varied substantially to the offender's detriment is less clear. In *Grice* (1978) 66 Cr App R 167 the Court of Appeal's view was that a susbstantial increase to the original sentence was not permissible. The judge had passed a suspended sentence upon receiving an undertaking from the offender that he would not go near his adopted daughter, with whom he had committed unlawful sexual intercourse. Grice did in fact contact his daughter and, since the contact took place within the 28-day period, the judge varied the sentence to one of immediate imprisonment. The Court of Appeal restored the sentence to what it had originally been. However, other cases suggest that *Grice* takes a too restrictive view of the power to vary. In *Hart* (1983) 5 Cr App R (S) 25, for example, Hart was given a suspended prison sentence, partly on the basis of evidence that he was leaving the country to start a new life abroad. Shortly afterwards a newspaper reported Hart as saying that this story had been a lie, told to the judge to trick him into passing a lenient sentence. The judge brought Hart back to court and replaced the suspended sentence with immediate custody. The variation had to be quashed because it was done outside the 28-day period, but the Court of Appeal said that, had it been done in time, this was 'one of the plain cases for which s. 47(2) is designed'.

Magistrates' courts may also vary or rescind a sentence under MCA 1980, s. 142. Again the variation must be made within 28 days of the sentence being passed. The court varying sentence must either be identical to the original court or, where the original court consisted of three or more justices, a majority of those must be present for the variation. In *Jane* v *Broome* (1987) *The Times*, 2 November 1987 the Divisional Court held that magistrates were entitled to exercise their powers under s. 142 in a case where they had originally found special reasons for not disqualifying J from driving, but had later come to the view that their findings of fact could not amount in law to special reasons. They reconvened the court and disqualified J for 12 months.

Once the statutory period for variation has expired, a court may not vary its sentence even if, through inadvertence, it has failed to include in the sentence an order which it really should have made (*Menocal* [1980] AC 598). In *Stillwell* (1992) 13 Cr App R (S) 253 the sentencer rescinded the original sentence within the time limit but did not impose a new one until the period had expired. It was held that no valid sentence was in place and the offender was released on appeal. The court may, however, correct the terms of an order which is lawful in substance though defective in form (*Saville* [1981] 1 QB 12), since it has an inherent jurisdiction to remedy minor mistakes.

3.13 REWARDS

The Crown Court has power to order the payment of a sum of money to any person who has been 'active in or towards the apprehension of any person charged with an arrestable offence' (Criminal Law Act 1826, s. 28). The amount of any such reward should be sufficient to compensate that person for any 'expenses, exertion and loss of time' involved in that apprehension. Such an award might well be made at the time of sentencing an offender. For an example see *Alexander* [1997] 2 Cr App R (S) 74.

4 Custodial Sentences

The imposition of custodial sentences, whether by a magistrates' court or the Crown Court, is governed by the general statutory sentencing framework laid down in the CJA 1991 and a range of specific statutory provisions and case-law dealing with particular forms of custodial sentencing. For a discussion of the general sentencing framework see Chapter 2. This chapter describes in detail the law which governs the imposition of custodial sentences.

For adult offenders (aged 21 and over) the appropriate custodial sentence is imprisonment. A sentence of imprisonment cannot be passed on anyone aged under 21 (CJA 1982, s. 1(1)). There is no upper age limit for imprisonment. Those aged under 21 cannot be sentenced to imprisonment for any reason, even, for example, the non-payment of a fine, but if a person under 21 is remanded in custody or committed for trial or sentence in custody and there is no remand centre available, he may be committed to prison for the period before the case is disposed of (s. 1(2)). Some offenders under the age of 21 do actually serve their custodial sentence in a prison, but if the offender is under 18 this must only be for a temporary purpose (CJA 1982, s. 1C). The Divisional Court held in *Accrington Youth Court, ex parte Flood* [1998] 1 WLR 156 that it was unlawful to require a 16-year-old girl to serve the whole of her eight-month sentence in an adult prison. The serving by a person under 21 of some or all of a sentence in prison does not alter the fact that the sentence being served is not one of imprisonment. The custodial sentences which are available for offenders 'aged under 21 are detention in a young offender institution, detention under CYPA 1933, s. 53, custody for life under CJA 1982, s. 8(2) and, when the relevant provisions of the CDB become law and are brought into force, a detention and training order. In determining a person's age, and the sentence available, the relevant date is the date of conviction. A person aged 20 when convicted but aged 21 when sentenced cannot be given a prison sentence (*Danga* [1992] QB 476). Where there is doubt about the age of an offender before the court, CJA 1982, s. 1(6) provides that:

> For the purposes of any provision of this Act which requires the determination of the age of a person by the court or the Secretary of State his age shall be deemed to be that which it appears to the court or the Secretary of State (as the case may be) to be after considering any available evidence.

When a court imposes a sentence on an assumption of the offender's age made under s. 1(6), the sentence is not rendered unlawful if it is discovered subsequently that the assumption was incorrect (*Brown* (1989) 11 Cr App R (S) 263). In *Harris* (1990) 12 Cr App R (S) 318 the offender appeared to the judge to be 21, and he imposed a suspended sentence of imprisonment, a penalty only available to adults, on that basis. In this case, however, the wording of the antecedents form which was before the judge indicated that the offender was only 20 and, in those circumstances, s. 1(6) could not rescue the sentence and it was quashed. If there is a dispute about the offender's age, the best course is for the court to adjourn until the matter can be resolved (*Steed* (1990) 12 Cr App R (S) 230).

4.1 FORMAL REQUIREMENTS BEFORE CUSTODY MAY BE IMPOSED

Whenever the court is considering the imposition of a custodial sentence, it must abide by the following statutory requirements.

4.1.1 Offence must be imprisonable

The most obvious limitation on the availability of a custodial sentence is that the offence must be an imprisonable offence in the case of an adult. All common law offences are punishable with imprisonment. A statutory offence is so punishable if the statute creating it specifies imprisonment as one of the methods of dealing with offenders who commit the offence. Thus, if the statute mentions only a fine, or perhaps a fine plus disqualification from driving, as the penalties for the offence, it is non-imprisonable. Virtually all indictable offences are imprisonable; offences under the Forgery and Counterfeiting Act 1981, ss. 18 and 19, which proscribe the putting into circulation of imitation currency notes and coins without permission, are two exceptions. The more serious summary offences are also imprisonable. Drink/driving offences carry up to six months' imprisonment (Road Traffic Offenders Act 1988, sch. 2) assaulting a police officer in the execution of his duty carries six months (Police Act 1964, s. 51(1)) and interfering with a motor vehicle carries three months (Criminal Attempts Act 1981, s. 9). Most summary road traffic offences (such as careless driving, speeding, using a vehicle without insurance and failing to stop after an accident) are non-imprisonable. There is a also a great mass of minor offences, such as dropping litter, which are non-imprisonable.

If an offence is not imprisonable in the case of an adult, a custodial sentence cannot be imposed upon an offender aged under 21.

4.1.2 Legal representation

Section 21 of PCCA 1973 provides that a court shall not pass a sentence of imprisonment on an offender who is not legally represented, and who has not previously been so sentenced, unless he has applied for legal aid but his means have made him ineligible for it, or he has been informed of his right to apply for legal aid and has failed to make any application. Lord Bridge of Harwich explained the importance of this matter for the unrepresented defendant in *McC (A Minor)* [1985] AC 528:

> No one should be liable to a first sentence of imprisonment . . . unless he has had the opportunity of having his case in mitigation presented to the court in the best possible light. For an inarticulate defendant, such presentation may be crucial to his liberty.

It should be noted that s. 21 applies to the imposition of a suspended prison sentence as well as to immediate custody. Section 21(3), however, states that where a person has in the past received a suspended prison sentence, which was not activated, such sentence must be disregarded when deciding whether the offender is now facing the prospect of his first prison sentence.

A sentence passed contrary to the provisions of s. 21 is prima facie invalid (*Birmingham Justices, ex parte Wyatt* [1976] 1 WLR 260), but in *Hollywood* (1990) 12 Cr App R (S) 325 the Court of Appeal felt itself able to uphold a custodial sentence passed in circumstances where s. 21 had been overlooked by the sentencer, on the basis that 'no other sentence would have been appropriate'. That case was followed in *Wilson* (1995) 16 Cr App R (S) 997 where the difficulty was that the defendant sacked one firm of lawyers after another.

Comparable restrictions (in the CJA 1982, s. 3) apply whenever the court is considering imposing a custodial sentence on an offender aged under 21. There is a difference, however, in that for young offenders s. 3 is *not* limited to the imposition of the *first* custodial sentence, as is s. 21 for imprisonment. Compliance with s. 3 is thus a prerequisite for passing any custodial sentence on an offender aged under 21. Custodial sentences on offenders under 21 cannot be suspended, so there is no equivalent provision to s. 21(3) in their case.

4.1.3 Compliance with statutory criteria

Before passing a custodial sentence, the court must be satisfied that it is justified in doing so in accordance with the criteria in CJA 1991, s. 1(2). Put shortly, these criteria are that the custodial sentence is justified either on the basis of the seriousness of the offence committed or, where a violent or sexual offence has been committed, on the ground of public protection. See further **4.2**.

4.1.4 Pre-sentence report

In order to determine whether the statutory criteria in s. 1(2) are satisfied, the court must obtain and consider a pre-sentence report, unless the court considers that to obtain such a report is 'unnecessary' (CJA 1991, s. 3(1)). Material in the report is also relevant when deciding upon custodial sentence length. Although no sentence is invalidated by a failure to comply with s. 3(1), in the event of an appeal against a custodial sentence imposed without one, the appellate court should normally obtain and consider one (s. 3(4)). Pre-sentence reports are considered in detail at **3.5.1**.

4.1.5 Other relevant material

In addition to considering the pre-sentence report, the court must 'take into account all such information about the circumstances of the offence (including any aggravating or mitigating factors) as is available to it' (CJA 1991, s. 3(3)(a)), and may take into account any matter of mitigation personal to the offender (CJA 1991, s. 28). These matters are discussed further below.

4.1.6 Stating reasons

It is surely a basic requirement of justice that proper reasons be given for sentencing decisions. Apart from the general desirability of sentencers giving reasons (a matter the importance of which has been stressed by the Court of Appeal on numerous occasions, such as in *Attorney-General's Reference (No. 23 of 1992)* (1993) 14 Cr App R (S) 759), the number of occasions on which courts are required by statute to give their reasons for sentence has been increasing in recent years. Any court passing a custodial sentence is now required by CJA 1991, s. 1(4)(a) to state in open court that such a sentence is justified under either s. 1(2)(a) (offence seriousness) or s. 1(2)(b) (public protection), or both. It must explain why it has come to that view. The court must also, by s. 1(4)(b), explain to the offender in open court and in ordinary language why it is imposing a custodial sentence. There is a further requirement in a magistrates' court that the reason must be recorded in the warrant of commitment and in the court register.

In *Baverstock* [1993] 1 WLR 202 the Court of Appeal said that in general a two-stage process of explanation by the sentencer is not necessary to comply with s. 1(4). In most cases the judge should be able at one and the same time to explain in ordinary language the reasons for his conclusion and tell the offender why he is passing a custodial sentence. Lord Taylor CJ said that, when complying with the second of these requirements, the judge would be addressing the offender directly and if, in complying with s. 1(4)(a) he had not used ordinary language, it would be necessary for him to do so in order to comply with subsection 1(4)(b). The Court of Appeal stressed that the precise words used by the judge were not critical, and that the statutory provisions 'are not to be treated as a verbal tightrope for judges to walk'. Provided that the judge's approach is in accord with the statutory provisions, the Court of Appeal will not be sympathetic to appeals based upon 'fine linguistic analysis' of the sentencing remarks.

4.2 JUSTIFYING THE IMPOSITION OF CUSTODY

Section 1 of the CJA 1991 creates a set of criteria to assist the courts in determining when the imposition of a custodial sentence is appropriate. The key provision is CJA 1991, s. 1(2), which restricts the powers of the Crown Court and magistrates' courts to impose a custodial sentence to cases where the court is of the opinion either:

(a)   that the offence, or the combination of the offence and one or more offences associated with it, was so serious that only such a sentence can be justified for the offence; or

(b)   where the offence is a violent or sexual offence, that only such a sentence would be adequate to protect the public from serious harm from him.

These provisions have general application in the Crown Court and in magistrates' courts, and they apply to all 'custodial sentences'. This expression is defined in CJA 1991, s. 31. For a person of or over 21, 'custodial sentence' means 'a sentence of imprisonment', which includes discretionary life imprisonment and a suspended sentence of imprisonment (but it does not include a committal or attachment for contempt of court). For a person under 21 it means a sentence of detention in a young offender institution, detention under CYPA 1933, s. 53(2), a sentence of custody for life under CJA 1982, s. 8(2) and, when the relevant provisions of the CDB become law and are brought into force, a detention and training order.

These custodial sentences are dealt with, in turn, in the following paragraphs. First, however, it should be noted that there are two exceptions to the application of CJA 1991, s. 1(2).

4.2.1   Murder cases and cases under s. 2 or s. 3 of the Crime (Sentences) Act 1997

Section 1(2) of the CJA 1991 naturally does not apply where the sentence for the offence is fixed by law (CJA 1991, s. 1(1)). This, in practice, means the offence of murder, where the penalty is fixed at imprisonment for life for an adult by the Murder (Abolition of Death Penalty) Act 1965, s. 1(1) (see further **4.5.2**). Custody for life (CJA 1982, s. 8(1)) and detention during Her Majesty's pleasure (CYPA 1933, s. 53(1)) are the equivalent sentences in the case of offenders aged under 21 who are convicted of murder. Nor does s. 1(2) apply where the Crown Court is, subject to exceptional circumstances, obliged by s. 2 of the C(S)A 1997 to impose a life sentence on an offender for his 'second serious offence' (see **4.3.5**) or is, subject to specific circumstances which would make the sentence unjust, required to impose a custodial sentence of at least seven years on an offender for his third Class A drug trafficking offence under s. 3 of the C(S)A 1997 (see **4.3.3**).

4.2.2 Offender failing to express willingness to comply with requirement in community sentence

In a limited range of cases, before a community sentence may be imposed on an offender, he must express his willingness to comply with a requirement which the court intends to insert into that order. If the offender is not willing to do so, s. 1(3) of the CJA 1991 states that nothing in s. 1(2) shall prevent the court from passing a custodial sentence instead. The relevant cases in which an expression of willingness to comply are so required are:

    (a)   where the court proposes to insert into a probation order a requirement that the offender undergo treatment for a mental condition (PCCA 1973, sch. 1A, para. 5);

    (b)   where the court proposes to insert into a probation order a requirement that the offender undergo treatment for drug or alcohol dependency (PCCA 1973, sch. 1A, para. 6);

    (c)   where the court proposes to insert into a supervision order, a requirement that an offender aged 14 or over undergo treatment for a mental condition (CYPA 1969, s. 12B); and

    (d)   (when the relevant provision of the CDB becomes law and is brought into force) where the court proposes to make a drug treatment and testing order (see **5.6**).

More general requirements in the earlier law that the offender must consent to the imposition of a range of community orders, including probation orders and community service orders, were abolished by the C(S)A 1997, s. 38. Earlier case law indicated that an offender should be given a fair opportunity to choose whether to consent to the community sentence (see, for example, *Marquis* [1974] 1 WLR 1087). This surely still holds good under the new provisions, as does the observation of the Court of Appeal in *Barnett* (1986) 8 Cr App R (S) 200 that the offender's agreement is not vitiated by his knowledge that, if he does not agree, a custodial sentence might be imposed instead. In these circumstances, a grudging consent is an adequate legal consent.

4.2.3 Justifying a custodial sentence under s. 1(2)(a)

We turn now to consider the criteria for imposing a custodial sentence in CJA 1991, s. 1(2), on the assumption that neither of the exceptions discussed in the last two paragraphs apply to the case. The first alternative ground is:

    (a)   that the offence, or the combination of the offence and one or more offences associated with it, was so serious that only such a sentence can be justified for the offence.

This paragraph is best seen as a custody threshold provision (see Chapter 2). It provides the key justification in the CJA 1991 for a sentencer to select a custodial sentence rather than a community sentence. The Act also requires the sentencer to have regard to aggravating and mitigating factors of the case which impinge upon the seriousness of the offence, and permits the sentencer to take account of any other mitigating (but not aggravating) factor. It is clear from the decision in *Cox* [1993] 1 WLR 188 that factors which are *not* associated with offence seriousness may operate to save the offender from custody, by pulling the offender back from the custody threshold, but can never provide the impetus for custody if the offence is not in itself sufficiently serious to justify it. See **4.2.4**.

4.2.4   Seriousness and the single offence

Under CJA 1991, s. 1(2)(a), the offender must have been convicted of at least one offence, and this of course covers both conviction after a trial and a guilty plea (*Cole* [1965] 2 QB 388). Taking first the case of an offender being dealt with for a single offence, in *Cox* [1993] 1 WLR 188 Lord Taylor of Gosforth CJ adopted the following words of Lawton LJ in the pre 1991 Act case of *Bradbourn* (1985) 7 Cr App R (S) 180, as providing an indication of the meaning of the phrase 'so serious that only such a sentence can be justified for the offence':

> The kind of offence which . . . would make all right thinking members of the public, knowing all the facts, feel that justice had not been done by the passing of any sentence other than a custodial one.

In *Bradbourn*, Lawton LJ formulated even this degree of guidance with reluctance, commenting that 'courts can recognise an elephant when they see one, but may not find it necessary to define it'. Criticism of the vagueness of the test is, however, well-founded. It is too general to be of much practical help to the courts. As Ashworth and von Hirsch (1997) have pointed out, if it is meant simply to be an appeal to public opinion, the test should be rejected, because the statute requires the sentencer to gauge the 'seriousness' of the offence, and not just to follow a popular clamour for certain offenders to be imprisoned. If, on the other hand, it is meant to be a 'reasonable person' test, it appears to be circular and to add nothing useful, since we have to assume that all sentencers are trying their best to be 'reasonable' when deciding questions about the custody threshold.

In contrast to the rather unhelpful general test for the custody threshold which has so far been developed, there is a substantial and important body of case law, developed by the Court of Appeal in guideline judgments both before and after the CJA 1991, which determines in what circumstances the commission of particular offences could properly be regarded as so serious that only a custodial sentence can be justified. This case law is considered in the context of sentencing for particular offences in Chapter 12. The decisions tend to discuss the seriousness of a particular offence category in the context of a range of aggravating and mitigating factors which might apply, generating a series of 'starting points' for different levels of seriousness within a particular offence. Thus, in *Billam* (1986) 8 Cr App R (S) 48, the Court of Appeal stressed that the offence of rape calls for a custodial sentence other than in wholly exceptional circumstances, and then proceeded to describe three broad categories of the offence with appropriate starting points. A number of aggravating and mitigating factors were then spelt out. In *Aramah* (1987) 9 Cr App R (S) 360, a case amended and refined in several later decisions, the Court of Appeal indicated appropriate starting points for sentences for importation, supply and possession of Class A, B and C drugs. In *Barrick* (1985) 7 Cr App R (S) 142, another case recently updated, Lord Lane CJ said that offenders who steal or obtain property by deception in the course of their employment should, notwithstanding their previous good character, be given a custodial sentence unless the sum involved is small. The court then proceeded to indicate three starting points, determined by reference to the amount of money involved. In *Brewster* [1998] 1 Cr App R (S) 181 the Court of Appeal explained why an offence of house burglary is normally so serious that only custody can be justified, and then proceeded to spell out the major aggravating and mitigating factors which tend to arise in such cases.

Whenever a court decides, under s. 1(2)(a), whether to impose a custodial sentence, s. 3(3)(a) requires that the court 'shall take into account all such information about the circumstances of the offence or (as the case may be) of the offence and the offence or offences associated with it (including any aggravating or mitigating factors) as is available to it'. A range of aggravating and mitigating factors relevant to offence seriousness have developed through the case law, and these factors were discussed at **2.2.2** and **2.2.3** above. Additionally, s. 28(1) provides that 'Nothing in this Part shall prevent a court from mitigating an offender's sentence by taking into account any such matters as, in the opinion of the court, are relevant in mitigation of sentence'. The more commonly encountered matters of personal mitigation were considered at **2.2.4** above.

It is clear that although an offence may be regarded as so serious that only a custodial sentence can be justified, mitigating factors which are personal to the offender may mean that the offender can still be dealt with in a less severe way, and custody can be avoided. Such mitigation may pull the offender back from the custody threshold. An example is *Cox* [1993] 1 WLR 188. There the offender pleaded guilty to theft and reckless driving. He had been riding a motor cycle without lights and carrying a pillion passenger. In attempting to avoid a pursuing police car, he mounted the pavement, which he drove along for 50 metres, executed a dangerous manoeuvre in front of a car, ignored a 'Give way' sign, and then lost control of the cycle and fell off. He had with him various items of stolen property, which he had taken from a garage earlier in the evening. The Court of Appeal agreed with the sentencer that the offences were so serious that only a custodial sentence could be justified, but also found that the sentencer had given insufficient attention to personal matters of mitigation, such as the offender's age (he was 18 at the time of the offence), the fact that there was only one previous court appearance on his record and the suggestion of probation in the pre-sentence report. A probation order for 12 months was substituted.

4.2.5 Seriousness and multiple offences

The preceding discussion of s. 1(2)(a) has been based on the assumption that the offender has been found guilty of, or has pleaded guilty to, one offence. Section 1(2)(a) also refers to the judgment of seriousness being made on the basis of 'the combination of the offence and one or more offences associated with it'. When considering the gravity of a combination of offences, CJA 1991, s. 31(2) provides that one offence is to be regarded as 'associated with' another offence if the offender is convicted of the offences in the same proceedings, or is sentenced for the offences at the same time, or when convicted and sentenced he asks to have one or more other offences taken into consideration. Clearly the implication is that a custodial sentence may be justified when the court is looking at more than one offence when it would not be so justified in respect of any one of the offences standing alone.

The limitations inherent in the phrase 'associated with' are important ones. In *Baverstock* [1993] 1 WLR 202 the offender was being dealt with for two offences. The second had been committed while the offender was on bail in respect of the first. Since the offender was being sentenced for the two offences on the same occasion, they were clearly 'associated' offences for the purposes of s. 31(2). It was established in *Godfrey* (1993) 14 Cr App R (S) 804 that where a sentencer is sentencing for a new offence and, at the same time, revokes a community sentence and resentences the offence for which it was imposed, the new offence and the earlier offence are associated offences. This is also true where the sentencer sentences for a new offence and resentences for breach of a conditional discharge. On the other hand, in *Crawford* (1993) 98 Cr App R 297 the offender was committed to the Crown Court for sentence for an offence of theft from a supermarket. The commission of that theft had placed him in breach of a suspended sentence of imprisonment imposed for an earlier offence of theft. The Court of Appeal held that these two offences were not 'associated'. The sentencer, when deciding whether a custodial sentence was appropriate for the second theft, should have left the first theft out of account. The sentencer should have sentenced for the new offence standing alone, and then turned to consider what effect the new sentence should have on the suspended sentence. This case was followed and applied in *Cawley* (1994) 15 Cr App R (S) 25. Finally, in *Canavan* [1998] 1 Cr App R 79 it was clearly established that where the offender has been convicted on an indictment charging him with offences alleged to be representative of other similar offences (sample counts), the offender cannot be sentenced for offences of which he has not been convicted or which he has not asked to have taken into consideration. As Lord Bingham of Cornhill CJ put it, 'unindicted, unadmitted offences' cannot be 'associated' offences. See further, on the issue of sample counts, **3.9**.

Once the court has decided that a custodial sentence is justified, the next question is how long that custody may properly be. That matter is discussed at **4.4** below.

4.2.6   Justifying a custodial sentence under s. 1(2)(b)

A custodial sentence may be justified under CJA 1991, s. 1(2)(b), if the court is of the opinion:

> (b)   where the offence is a violent or sexual offence, that only such a sentence would be adequate to protect the public from serious harm from [the offender].

This provision permits the Crown Court or a magistrates' court to impose a custodial sentence on an offender convicted of a violent or sexual offence, on the basis of a prediction of the offender's future predilection to commit violent or sexual offences. It is thus a 'predictive' rather than a 'desert' based test, and may be regarded as an exception to the general framework of the provision of the CJA 1991. (For a discussion of the general principles underlying the Act see Chapter 2.) The CJA 1991 provides a definition of 'serious harm', as well as definitions of 'violent offence' and 'sexual offence' (see below).

The great majority of custody decisions are made under the 'seriousness' criterion in s. 1(2)(a) rather than under s. 1(2)(b). In particular, there are very few cases where it will be appropriate for a magistrates' court to impose custody on the basis of s. 1(2)(b). This is because the relative shortness of custodial sentences available to magistrates could rarely achieve the envisaged public protection. Presumably the legislature anticipated that there would be some such cases, for it would not otherwise have given this power to the lower courts. The inclusion of s. 1(2)(b) in the statutory scheme presupposes that there are some violent or sexual cases where the offence or offences committed by the offender are not in themselves sufficiently serious to justify custody under s. 1(2)(a). If that were not so, s. 1(2)(b) would be superfluous. A case where s. 1(2)(b) might be used is where the offender has committed an offence not in itself requiring custody (such as a minor indecent assault), but information about the offender, including details of his previous convictions, leads the court to believe that custody is required in order to protect the public from the risk of future offending.

4.2.7 Meaning of 'violent offence' and 'sexual offence'

Section 1(2)(b) of CJA 1991 must be interpreted in the light of s. 31(1), which provides that a 'violent offence' means an offence:

> which leads, or is intended or likely to lead, to a person's death or to physical injury to a person, and includes an offence which is required to be charged as arson (whether or not it would otherwise fall within this definition).

This provision covers cases which range from those where death or physical injury is actually caused by the offender, even where that outcome was not intended or even likely to occur, to cases where no harm at all is occasioned but where such harm was a likely consequence of the offender's conduct. There is no requirement that the physical injury caused or risked need be 'serious', but an offence which results, or is likely to result, only in psychological harm is not a violent offence for these purposes.

In respect of many criminal offences the application of these criteria will be perfectly clear. Other offences, however, will sometimes qualify as 'violent' offences, but sometimes not. The Court of Appeal in *Robinson* [1993] 1 WLR 168 confirmed that whether a particular offence falls within the definition of a 'violent offence', thereby permitting the sentencer to consider the imposition of custody under s. 1(2)(b), depends not upon the offence category as such but rather upon the individual facts of each case. This has given rise to a number of rather strange decisions. In *Cochrane* (1994) 15 Cr App R (S) 708 the Court of Appeal held that on the facts before it, the particular robbery at knifepoint committed by the offender was a 'violent offence', since it had been likely to lead to injury, even though no injury had been inflicted or, apparently, intended. In *Bibby* (1995) 16 Cr App R (S) 127, however, the Court of Appeal doubted whether an offender who had threatened staff in building society branches with a knife, and had demanded cash, had committed a 'violent offence', since the evidence was that Bibby had neither used the knife nor had any intention of doing so. In *Khan* (1995) 16 Cr App R (S) 180 the carrying of an unloaded firearm in the course of a robbery was held not to constitute a violent offence. Using an imitation firearm to threaten the victim in the course of a raid on a sub-post office was held not to constitute a violent offence in *Palin* (1995) 16 Cr App R (S) 88.

Apart from robbery, another offence giving rise to problems in this context is that of threatening to kill, In *Richart* (1995) 16 Cr App R (S) 977 the offender made numerous telephone threats to the victim, threatening to kill her, and also sent her a bullet with her name on it through the post. The Court of Appeal found that in this case no 'violent offence' had been committed, since there was no physical injury or evidence that the threats were intended or likely to lead to physical injury. The Court invited Parliament to amend the definition, so as to include cases which, on the face of it, would lead to a reasonable apprehension of violence.

Section 31(1) states that 'an offence which is required to be charged as arson' (i.e., the offence of criminal damage when committed by fire) always qualifies as a 'violent offence'.

It was held in *Guirke* [1997] 1 Cr App R (S) 170 that all offences of *attempted* arson are also included. This seems doubtful, however. Since attempted arson is not mentioned in s. 31(1), it appears that such an offence may qualify as a violent offence only where it leads, or is intended or likely to lead, to death or physical injury.

It is clear from the decision in *Robinson* [1993] 1 WLR 168 that the categories of 'violent offence' and 'sexual offence' overlap, and are not mutually exclusive. That case involved a rape committed by a 16-year-old offender on an elderly woman after he had tricked his way into her home. The offender received a sentence of eight years' detention under CYPA 1933, s. 53(2). The judge had proceeded on the basis that this was both a 'violent' and a 'sexual' offence, and his view was upheld by the Court of Appeal.

Section 31(1), as amended by the CJPOA 1994, provides that 'sexual offence' means:

   (a)   an offence under the SOA 1956, other than an offence under ss. 30, 31, or 33 to 36 of that Act;

   (b)   an offence under s. 128 of the MHA 1959;

   (c)   an offence under the Indecency with Children Act 1960;

   (d)   an offence, under s. 9 of the Theft Act 1968, of burglary with intent to commit rape;

   (e)   an offence under s. 54 of the CLA 1977;

   (f)   an offence under the Protection of Children Act 1978;

   (g)   an offence, under s. 1 of the CLA 1977, of conspiracy to commit any of the offences in paras (a) to (f) above;

   (h)   an offence under s. 1 of the Criminal Attempts Act 1981 of attempting to commit any of those offences;

   (i)   an offence of inciting another to commit any of those offences.

It will be seen that Parliament has adopted a quite different approach in defining 'sexual offence' from that used to define 'violent offence'. Whether an offence counts as a 'sexual offence' or not turns entirely on the category of offence with which the offender is convicted. The list of offences originally set out in s. 31 of the CJA 1991 turned out to be defective in a number of ways, and a revised list was substituted by the CJPOA 1994. Subsequently, the Court of Appeal in *Wrench* [1996] 1 Cr App R (S) 145 noted that the offence of child abduction under the Child Abduction Act 1984 was not a 'sexual offence' within the meaning of s. 31, and described this as a 'grave omission'. As later pointed out in *Newsome* [1997] 2 Cr App R (S) 69, that offence might, depending on the precise facts, nonetheless amount to a 'violent offence'. The list of offences includes within category (a) most serious sexual offences, including rape, incest, sexual intercourse with under-age females, and indecent assault. It excludes offences such as living on the earnings of prostitution (SOA 1956, s. 30), offences related to the keeping of brothels (ss. 31 and 33 to 36 of the 1956 Act) but, controversially, includes other sexual offences not regarded as particularly serious, such as gross indecency between men, which is an offence under s. 13 of the 1956 Act. The offence referred to in (b) is unlawful sexual intercourse with a mental patient by a member of staff; the offence in (c) is the commission of an act of gross indecency with or towards a child; the offence in (e) is a form of incest; and offences under (f) are taking, permitting to be taken, or distributing indecent photographs of a child.

Reliance upon s. 1(2)(b) requires an assessment by the court that, in the light of the offender's conviction for a violent or sexual offence, only a custodial sentence would be adequate to 'protect the public from serious harm from him'. It is clear from this wording that the sentencer must consider that the public require protection from this particular offender, rather than just from offenders of his type. 'Serious harm' is defined for these purposes by s. 31(3) to mean 'death or serious personal injury, whether physical or psychological, occasioned by further such offences' committed by the offender. The reference to 'further *such* offences' makes it clear that it is the commission of further violent or sexual offences by the offender from which the public need to be protected. While the statute makes it clear that there must be a risk of serious harm, there is no indication of how substantial that risk must be perceived to be to justify sentencing under s. 1(2)(b). It will be seen that while the causing of psychological harm cannot amount to a violent offence, the prospects of causing such harm in the future may be included when considering the risk to the public posed by the offender. Section 3(3)(b) allows the court to take into account any information about the offender when making this assessment. The court will normally have obtained and considered a pre-sentence on the offender by this stage. If the offender is, or appears to be, mentally disordered, a medical report must be obtained (CJA 1991, s. 4(1)). In making its assessment of the offender's dangerousness the court may take the offender's previous convictions into account. These issues are considered further in **4.4.3**.

In *Baverstock* [1993] 1 WLR 202 the Court of Appeal said that a sentencer should not pass a sentence in reliance upon s. 1(2)(b) without giving an express indication to counsel that this was being considered.

4.3 VARIETIES OF CUSTODIAL SENTENCES

4.3.1 Determinate sentences of imprisonment

A determinate sentence of imprisonment is the normal custodial sentence for adult offenders. Between 1986 and 1996 the proportionate use made by the courts of immediate imprisonment when sentencing for indictable offences has increased significantly, especially in the case of violent or sexual offences and burglary. The change in the use of immediate custody between 1986 and 1996 for the main categories of offending is as follows:

		1986	1996
(1)	violence against the person	11 per cent	23 per cent
(2)	sexual offences	27 per cent	52 per cent
(3)	burglary	16 per cent	26 per cent
(4)	robbery	38 per cent	34 per cent
(5)	theft and handling	6 per cent	11 per cent
(6)	fraud and forgery	13 per cent	19 per cent
(7)	criminal damage	8 per cent	8 per cent
(8)	drug offences	19 per cent	17 per cent
(9)	motoring offences	10 per cent	11 per cent
	All offending	10 per cent	16 per cent

These figures do not include suspended sentences of imprisonment.

The maximum term of imprisonment which may be imposed for a statutory offence is almost always laid down by the statute which creates that offence. For summary offences and for offences triable either way which are tried summarily, general limits on the power of magistrates' courts to impose imprisonment are specified by MCA 1980, ss. 31 and 32. The minimum prison sentence which may be imposed by a magistrates' court in any case is five days (MCA 1980, s. 132). The maximum in respect of any one offence is six months, unless the statute which creates the offence prescribes a lower maximum or the offence is non-imprisonable. The maximum aggregate term which magistrates can impose is also six months, unless two of the terms imposed are for offences triable either way, in which case the maximum aggregate term is 12 months (MCA 1980, s. 133). Thus the maximum term of imprisonment which a magistrates' court can impose for an offence triable either way is less, indeed often much less, than the Crown Court can impose following conviction on indictment.

A table of maximum prison terms available for a range of commonly encountered offences is set out at Table 1 on pp. 7–14. Table 1 does not reveal a rational pattern; the Advisory Council on the Penal System (Advisory Council on the Penal System, 1978) conducted a review of maximum penalties in 1978 and commented that:

> The system of maximum penalties is not the product of a rational and consistent scheme, but rather the result of piecemeal legislation over more than a century, in response to many different pressures such as, for example, transient Parliamentary concern with a specific crime.

It will be seen from Table 1 on pp. 7–14 that the available maxima are generally very high. For many offences nothing like the maximum sentence is approached in day-to-day Crown Court sentencing practice. There are exceptions, so that very long determinate sentences or life sentences are not uncommon for very grave crimes such as manslaughter or armed robbery. Generally speaking, however, the average length of prison terms actually imposed for offences is well below half the maximum term which may lawfully be imposed. For males aged 21 and over who were sentenced for indictable offences in the Crown Court and received a sentence of immediate imprisonment in 1996, the average sentence length for burglary was 20.3 months (maximum either 10 or 14 years depending on the nature of the premises burgled), for theft/handling stolen goods it was 11.9 months (maximum for theft seven years, and for handling 14 years) and for robbery it was 52.5 months (maximum life). Related to the point that maximum sentences are, in general, very high, is the point that the maximum term available for a given offence is only a very approximate guide to its gravity relative to other offences. The maximum sentence for perjury, for example, is seven years, which is significantly less than the maximum of 14 years for handling stolen goods. The Court of Appeal has said on several occasions that a custodial sentence is almost inevitable for an offence of perjury (see, for example *Hall* (1982) 4 Cr App R (S) 153) whereas that is certainly not the case for handling. The reduction in the maximum penalty for theft from 10 years to seven years by CJA 1991 made the maximum sentence of 10 years for obtaining property by deception (given the substantial overlap between the two offences, especially since *Gomez* [1993] AC 442) look rather anomalous. The maximum sentence for non-consensual buggery of a man over 16 was, prior to the CJPOA 1994, 10 years. That Act extended the legal definition of rape so as to include so-called 'male rape', thereby in effect increasing the maximum sentence for the former offence to life imprisonment.

The maximum penalty available for dealing with a particular offence is no real guide at all to the normal sentencing bracket for that offence. The Court of Appeal has stated that imposition of the maximum sentence is appropriate only when sentencing for 'the worst example of that offence which is likely to be encountered in practice' (*Byrne* (1975) 62 Cr App R 159). Even so, when the sentencer is considering whether a particular offence is one of the worst examples of its kind, regard should be had to the range of cases actually encountered in practice, rather than to unlikely or hypothetical examples (*Ambler and*

Hargreaves (1971) CSP A1-4C01). A second proposition which follows from the general principle mentioned above is that, if there is substantial mitigation present in a case, imposition of the maximum prison sentence must be incorrect (*Thompson* (1980) 2 Cr App R (S) 244). Sometimes sentencers have chafed against this principle, usually because they were confronted in a particular case with an available maximum sentence which was anomalously low. This was the case in *Carroll* (1995) 16 Cr App R (S) 488, where the judge, after imposing the maximum sentence of two years' detention in a young offender institution on an offender who had pleaded guilty to aggravated vehicle-taking, commented that the maximum sentence provided was too low. The Court of Appeal, in reducing the sentence to 18 months, said that sentencers must abide loyally by the maximum sentences provided, that the maximum sentence should be reserved for the most serious examples of that offence and that an appropriate discount (such as for a guilty plea) should be made from the sentence which was commensurate with the seriousness of the offence. The case is one of several which makes it clear that the maximum sentence should not be imposed where the offender has pleaded guilty. In *Greene* (1993) 14 Cr App R (S) 682 the maximum sentence of five years' imprisonment for violent disorder was reduced to three years for this reason, and in *Barnes* (1983) 5 Cr App R (S) 368 a maximum sentence for attempted rape was reduced on the grounds of the guilty plea and saving the victim from the further ordeal of giving testimony.

It is an important principle that an offender who falls to be sentenced after the maximum penalty for the offence has been increased, but in respect of an offence committed before that increase, must be sentenced on the basis that the former maximum applies, unless there is a clear legislative intent that the new maximum should apply retrospectively (*Penwith Justices, ex parte Hay* (1979) 1 Cr App R (S) 265). In *Street* [1997] 2 Cr App R (S) 309 the 73-year-old offender pleaded guilty to several counts of indecent assault on a girl committed many years earlier. The Court of Appeal reduced the custodial sentences imposed because the sentencer had overlooked the fact that the offences had been committed before the maximum penalty for indecent assault was increased from two years to 10 years by the CJA 1988. In *S* (1991) 13 Cr App R (S) 306 the offender was convicted of indecent assault. It was unclear on what day the assault had taken place and the period within which it was alleged by the prosecution that the offence had taken place covered the period before and after the increase in the maximum penalty came into force. The Court of Appeal held that the offender must be sentenced on the basis of the former maximum penalty. If the reverse problem occurs and the maximum penalty has been reduced, the court should seek guidance from the relevant statute or commencement order. See *Shaw* [1996] 2 Cr App R (S) 278.

There are a number of special rules relating to maximum penalties:

(a) *Statutory offence: no maximum specified* If a person is convicted on indictment of a statutory offence and is liable to be sentenced to imprisonment, but the sentence is not limited to a specified term by that statute, the maximum prison sentence is deemed to be two years (PCCA 1973, s. 18). This provision does not, however, apply to common law offences, such as kidnapping, perverting the course of justice and incitement, where the penalty is at the discretion of the court.

(b) *Statutory conspiracies* Under the Criminal Law Act 1977 (CLA 1977), s. 3, a person guilty of conspiracy to commit murder, conspiracy to commit any offence for which the maximum penalty is life imprisonment or conspiracy to commit any indictable offence punishable with imprisonment where no maximum term is specified is subject to a maximum penalty of life imprisonment. The maximum penalty for other statutory conspiracies is the same as the maximum period provided for the relevant offence. These provisions do not apply to common law conspiracies (preserved by CLA 1977, s. 5), which are subject to a penalty at the discretion of the court. By the CJA 1987, s. 12, however, the maximum penalty for conspiracy to defraud is 10 years.

(c) *Attempts*   Section 4 of the Criminal Attempts Act 1981 provides that the maximum penalty for attempted murder is life imprisonment; other indictable offences are subject to the same maximum as applies on conviction on indictment for the offence attempted. If the offence is triable either way, the maximum penalty on summary conviction is the same as the maximum penalty available for that offence tried summarily. Certain exceptions are provided for in s. 4(5). By reference to the Sexual Offences Act 1956, s. 37 and sch. 2, a maximum sentence of two years is provided for attempted incest by a man with a female over the age of 13 and for attempted incest by a woman; in each case the maximum penalty for the full offence is seven years. A maximum sentence of seven years is specified for attempted sexual intercourse with a girl aged under 13, where the maximum penalty for the full offence is life imprisonment.

4.3.2   Detention in a young offender institution

Detention in a young offender institution is by far the most commonly imposed custodial sentence for offenders aged under 21. It replaced several sentences which were formerly available for young offenders, such as youth custody, detention centre orders and borstal training. All these earlier sentences have now been abolished by statute.

The percentage of offenders aged 14 but under 17 who were sentenced to immediate custody for indictable offences declined significantly from 13 per cent in 1986 to around 9 per cent in the early 1990s, but has since then risen steadily to a figure of 12 per cent in 1996. The same trend is even more marked for offenders aged 17 or over, but under 21, where there was a decline from a custody rate of 20 per cent in 1986 to around 14 per cent in the early 1990s, but this has increased to over 22 per cent in 1996.

The sentence of detention in a young offender institution is available for offenders aged between 15 and 20 inclusive, whenever the offender has been convicted of an offence which is punishable with imprisonment in the case of an adult (CJA 1982, s. 1A). The other custodial sentences which are available for offenders within this age group (detention under CYPA 1933, s. 53 and custody for life under CJA 1982, s. 9) are used in only a small minority of cases, where exceptionally serious offences have been committed. A scheme of minimum and maximum terms for the sentence of detention in a young offender institution is provided by CJA 1982, ss. 1A and 1B. The position may be summarised as follows.

The sentence is available for male or female offenders aged between 15 and 20 inclusive. The normal *maximum* term for an offender aged 15, 16 or 17 is 24 months. For offenders aged 18, 19 or 20 the *maximum* sentence of detention in a young offender institution is of the same duration as the maximum sentence of imprisonment which would be available in the case of an adult being sentenced for the same offence. The normal *minimum* term is two months where the offender is aged 15, 16 or 17, or 21 days where the offender is aged 18, 19 or 20. This differential in minima looks odd at first, but is designed to achieve the effect that an offender aged 15, 16 or 17 should only receive the sentence in circumstances where the offence is sufficiently serious to require detention for at least two months. Where a magistrates' court passes a sentence of detention in a young offender institution, that court is, of course, restricted to the maximum term it could impose if the offender were aged 21 or over (i.e. for one offence, a magistrates' court can never impose more than six months' detention in a young offender institution, while the aggregate term for two or more offences must not exceed 12 months.

Perhaps the most important aspect of these provisions is that an offender aged 15, 16 or 17 may not be given more than 24 months' detention in a young offender institution, even though the maximum term of imprisonment for the offence is longer. The limitation to 24 months was increased from 12 months by the CJA 1991. If the court passes a sentence which is in contravention of this provision, CJA 1982, s. 1B(5) operates so that the sentence takes effect as one for 24 months. This happened in *Smithyman* (1993) 14 Cr App R (S) 263, where the sentencer purported to pass a sentence of three and a half years' detention on a 16-year-old offender who was convicted of false imprisonment and a very serious indecent assault on a female. The effect of the statute being automatic, there was nothing that the Court of Appeal could do to rescue the original sentence, notwithstanding that the sentencer could have passed a sentence under CYPA 1933, s. 53(2) for the longer period. In *Marriott* (1995) 16 Cr App R (S) 428 the sentencer passed a sentence of 'seven years' detention' for robbery. The Court of Appeal said that it was clear from the context that the sentencer meant to impose a term under s. 53(2) rather than a sentence of detention in a young offender institution. It followed that s. 1B(5) did not operate. In *AM* [1998] 1 WLR 363 the Court of Appeal reminded sentencers of the need to make it clear which of the two sentences was being passed.

As we have seen, it is a general sentencing principle that imposition of the maximum sentence is appropriate only when sentencing for the worst example of that offence which is likely to be encountered in practice, and that the presence of mitigating factors (including the offender's guilty plea) renders the imposition of the maximum penalty contrary to principle. It should be borne in mind that, following the commission of one of a number of grave crimes, and subject to certain other limitations, a custodial sentence in excess of 24 months may be imposed by the Crown Court upon a young offender by virtue of CYPA 1933, s. 53(2). This exceptional power is considered at **4.3.5**. The Court of Appeal has dealt with a number of cases where the maximum sentence of 24 months has been imposed on a young offender aged under 18, and the following points have emerged. The first issue is where the nature of the offence is such that the offender could have received a sentence of detention in excess of 24 months under the CYPA 1933, s. 53(2), but where the sentencer, taking the mitigation including the guilty plea into account, has decided that a term of 24 months is appropriate. In that case the proper sentence is one of 24 months' detention in a young offender institution. In *AM* [1998] 1 WLR 363 the Court of Appeal confirmed that where the court had imposed such a sentence it ought not to be inferred that the sentencer had failed to give credit for the guilty plea. Clearly, however, in a case where the judge is imposing a sentence of 24 months on an offender aged under 18, it is desirable for him to explain how that figure has been arrived at. This was done in *Kearsley* (1992) 13 Cr App R (S) 295, where the young offender and two accomplices entered a shop wearing stocking masks and carrying a knife. The maximum sentence of detention in a young offender institution was upheld, the Court of Appeal commenting that 'if there had not been a plea of guilty, a sentence of detention under s. 53(2) would have been fully justified'. A second issue arises where detention under s. 53(2) is not available for the offence which has been committed (for the details see **4.3.5** but, broadly, such sentence cannot be imposed unless the offence is punishable with at least 14 years' imprisonment in the case of an adult) or where the offence is not quite serious enough to justify a sentence in excess of the 24-month limit. Here, it seems, the sentencer should give credit for mitigation including a guilty plea, and the passing of the maximum sentence will be regarded as wrong in principle. This seems to have been the reasoning in the case of *Storey* (1986) 8 Cr App R (S) 301, where a

16-year-old offender pleaded guilty to unlawful wounding. Detention under the CYPA 1933, s. 53(2) was not available since the maximum penalty for the offence is five years' imprisonment in the case of an adult. The judge imposed the maximum term of detention in a young offender institution which could be imposed on Storey, but the Court of Appeal said that it should be reduced from the maximum to reflect the guilty plea.

If an offender aged 18 is sentenced to detention in a young offender institution for a period longer than 24 months, he has no basis for complaint that, had he been 17, the maximum sentence would have been 24 months. Similarly, there would be no unacceptable disparity in sentence where an 18-year-old and a 17-year-old who were equally implicated in an offence received sentences which fell either side of the 24 month maximum applicable to the younger offender (*Tyre* (1984) 6 Cr App R (S) 247).

4.3.3 Custodial sentence for a third Class A drug trafficking offence

When passing a determinate sentence of imprisonment, or a term of detention in a young offender institution, the sentencer will take account of the maximum sentence available for the offence and any restrictions on sentencing powers which result from the age of the offender, and then pass a custodial sentence which is commensurate with the seriousness of the offence while making allowance for matters of personal mitigation. There are few occasions on which sentencers must also have regard to statutory requirements as to the *minimum* length of custodial sentence which can be passed. One exception, the minimum term of detention in a young offender institution which may be imposed on an offender under 18, was referred to in **4.3.2**. A further restriction of this kind is now created by s. 3 of the Crime (Sentences) Act 1997.

The section states that where a person has been convicted of a Class A drug trafficking offence and, at the time of that offence he was aged 18 or over, and he had previously been convicted of two other Class A drug trafficking offences, and one of those had been committed after he was convicted of the other, the Crown Court *must* impose a custodial sentence of at least seven years. The relevant custodial sentence will be imprisonment in the case of an adult, or detention in a young offender institution in the case of an offender under 21. This provision is, however, not mandatory, since the court may impose a lesser sentence if it finds that there are 'specific circumstances' relating to the offending or to the offender which would make a seven-year term 'unjust in all the circumstances'. Section 3 came into force in October 1997 and there is, as yet, no case law to define the scope of the exception. Its wording is to be slightly amended by the CDB, sch. 7, para. 48. 'Drug trafficking offence' is defined in the DTA 1994 (see **9.1.1**).

If the offender pleads guilty, there is a question about how credit for his plea can be given where the minimum sentence is prescribed by statute. This problem has been dealt with by Parliament in the C(S)A 1997, by amending s. 48 of the CJPOA 1994 (see **2.2.4** at (g)) so as to permit a discount of up to 20 per cent of the sentence of seven years or more which would otherwise have been imposed by the sentencer under s. 3. Power to pass sentence under s. 3 is dependent on proof that the offender has been convicted twice before for similar lawbreaking. It may be worth noting that if either of the earlier offences was dealt with by way of discharge or (if the conviction was imposed before the CJA 1991 came into force) a probation order, that conviction would not count for these purposes. See further **7.1.4**.

4.3.4 Mandatory life sentences for murder

Life imprisonment is the mandatory sentence for murder when committed by an offender aged 21 or over (Murder (Abolition of Death Penalty) Act 1965, s. 1(1)). An offender under the age of 21 who is convicted of murder must be sentenced to custody for life under the CJA 1982, s. 8(1), unless the offender was under the age of 18 at the time the offence was committed, in which case the sentence is detention during Her Majesty's pleasure, under the CYPA 1933, s. 53(1). These three sentences are all mandatory sentences, so that the judge has no discretion whatever over choice of sentence when sentencing for murder. Murder is the only crime which is subject to a mandatory sentence in this way. The mandatory sentence does not even apply to closely related crimes, such as attempted murder or conspiracy to murder. The sentence of custody for life will normally be served in a young offender institution until the offender attains the age of 21, when he should be transferred to prison (CJA 1982, s. 12). A sentence under s. 53(1) is served 'in such place and under such conditions as the Secretary of State may direct or arrange', which is likely to be a specialised secure unit for young offenders.

The existence of the fixed penalty for murder is clearly anomalous in our sentencing system, and it has been the subject of considerable criticism from the judiciary and from commentators in recent years. The sentence can be attacked on the basis that it fails to allow judicial discretion in the sentencing of a crime where offender culpability can vary significantly, and where that ought to be reflected in the sentence passed by the court. The arrangements for early release of mandatory life sentence prisoners have also been heavily criticised, mainly because they give a politician, the Home Secretary, a decisive influence over judicial matters. The report of the House of Lords select committee, *Murder and Life Imprisonment* (House of Lords Papers, Session 1988–89, 78), recommended that the mandatory penalty should be abolished, and the House of Lords in its legislative capacity voted to abolish it during the passage through Parliament of the Bill which became the CJA 1991. Most recently in the Divisional Court, Lord Bingham of Cornhill CJ, when considering an application by the Moors murderer Myra Hindley for judicial review of the Home Secretary's decision that she should never be released from prison, commented that:

There [is] room for serious debate whether the task of determining how long convicted murderers should serve in prison as punishment for their crimes should be undertaken by the judiciary, as in the case of discretionary life prisoners or, as now, by the executive. That [is] in large measure a political and constitutional debate, not a question for decision by the court. The applicant clearly felt that she was held hostage to public opinion, condemned to pass the rest of her life in prison, although no longer judged a danger to anyone, because of her notoriety and the public obloquy which would fall on any Home Secretary who ordered her release. (*Secretary of State for the Home Department, ex parte Hindley, The Times*, 19 December 1997).

The House of Commons has resisted these objections throughout, however, and at the moment there seems to be little prospect of change.

Although these three sentences are mandatory, they very rarely require the offender to serve the rest of his or her life in custody. At some point during the sentence the offender will probably be released back into the community, although remaining under supervision and recall. For this reason, the sentences are perhaps better referred to as 'indeterminate' rather than 'life' sentences, but because the latter term is in general usage it will also be used in this book. When a sentencer passes a sentence of life imprisonment for murder the period of time to be served in custody is determined by the Home Secretary as advised by the Parole Board (see C(S)A 1997, s. 29), but the sentencing judge has some influence over that issue. The court is empowered under s. 1(2) of the Murder (Abolition of Death Penalty)

Act 1965, to 'declare the period which it recommends to the Secretary of State as the minimum period which in its view should elapse' before licence. This recommendation is not strictly binding on the executive authorities, who will actually determine the date of release and, since it is not a sentence in itself, there is no right of appeal against this recommendation (*Leaney* [1996] 1 Cr App R (S) 30). It was said in *Flemming* [1973] 2 All ER 401 that if the sentencer would be content to see the offender at liberty in under 12 years he should make no recommendation. Apart from the power to make a recommendation in each case the sentencing judge is required to indicate in writing the 'tariff' period which in his view is necessary to meet the requirements of retribution and deterrence in the case. This report goes to the Lord Chief Justice, who also records his views, and then to the Home Secretary. These indications do not, however, bind the Home Secretary, who may set a lower or higher tariff than is indicated by the judges. Such a change should be made only exceptionally, and may be challenged in the courts by the prisoner to whom it relates (*Secretary of State for the Home Department, ex parte Doody* [1994] 1 AC 531; *Secretary of State for the Home Department, ex parte Stafford* (1997) *The Times*, 28 November 1997). The Court of Appeal held in *Secretary of State for the Home Department, ex parte Hindley* (1997) *The Times*, 19 December 1997, that the Home Secretary is entitled to fix a 'whole life tariff', which would mean that the offender would never be released from prison, but the decision could not be made in such a way as to prevent its being reopened, either by the same Home Secretary at a later date, or by a successor in that office. The Home Secretary does not have power to increase a tariff period which has already been determined and told to the life sentence prisoner (*Secretary of State for the Home Department, ex parte Pierson* [1997] 3 WLR 492).

If the murder was committed by an offender aged under 21, the appropriate mandatory sentence is custody for life under the CJA 1982, s. 8(1), and s. 1(2) of the 1965 Act does not apply, but there is a broadly equivalent power provided by the C(S)A 1997, s. 28. This section provides that the sentencer may specify at the time of sentence what part of the sentence should expire before the offender becomes eligible for consideration for early release. The sentencer should do this by working out what determinate sentence he would have imposed if he had not been required to pass the sentence of custody for life, and he should then specify a period of time somewhere between a half and two thirds of that notional determinate sentence. When fixing that period the sentencer should give credit for any relevant mitigating factors in the case, including a guilty plea and the young age of the offender, and reduce the period by any time which was spent by the offender on remand in custody. The Parole Board would begin to consider the case for the possibility of early release upon the expiry of that period of time.

If the murder was committed by an offender who was under 18 at the time of the offence, the appropriate mandatory sentence is detention during Her Majesty's pleasure under s. 53(1) of the CYPA 1933. Twenty-six young offenders were so sentenced during 1996. As with the sentence of custody for life when imposed as the mandatory sentence for murder, the judge has the power provided by the C(S)A 1997, s. 28 to specify at the time of sentence what part of the sentence should expire before the offender becomes eligible for consideration for early release. The House of Lords in *Secretary of State for the Home Department, ex parte Venables* [1997] 2 WLR 67 stressed that when passing such a sentence on a very young offender the welfare of that child or young person is also of great importance, and there should be flexibility in the early release arrangements so that the executive authorities could review the case in the light of progress during the period of detention. See further on s. 28 **4.5.2.**

4.3.5 Automatic life sentence for the second serious offence

Under the Crime (Sentences) Act 1997, s. 2, the Crown Court is required to impose a life sentence on an offender who is convicted of a 'serious offence' which has been committed after October 1997 (when s. 2 came into force) if, at the time when that offence was committed, the offender was aged 18 or over and had already been convicted of another 'serious offence'. Where the offender is aged 21 or over the relevant life sentence is life imprisonment, and where the offender is aged from 18 to 20 inclusive the relevant life sentence is custody for life under the CJA 1982, s. 8(2). These life sentences are not mandatory life sentences in the same sense as mandatory life sentences imposed for the crime of murder (see **4.3.4**). The sentencing court may pronounce a different sentence if it finds that there are 'exceptional circumstances' relating to either of the offences, or to the offender, which justify its not imposing a life sentence. If the court does not impose a life sentence, it must state what the 'exceptional circumstances' are which it has relied upon. Nothing in the C(S)A 1997 explains what might constitute exceptional circumstances and there are, as yet, no decisions of the Court of Appeal to provide any guidance on the matter.

It will be seen from the wording of s. 2 that the first serious offence may have been committed before that section was brought into force. The age of the offender when he committed that first offence is irrelevant, and there is no requirement that the two offences be of the same kind, nor any restriction on the period of time which must have elapsed between them. It is possible, of course, that such matters may be relevant when a judge is deciding whether there are 'exceptional circumstances' applicable to the case.

'Serious offence' has a particular meaning here. The offences which qualify as 'serious offences' for the purposes of s. 2 are listed in s. 2(5). They are:

    (a)   attempted murder, conspiracy to murder or incitement to murder;
    (b)   soliciting murder;
    (c)   manslaughter;
    (d)   wounding or causing grievous bodily harm with intent;
    (e)   rape or attempted rape;
    (f)   sexual intercourse with a girl under 13;
    (g)   an offence under s. 16, 17 or 18 of the Firearms Act 1968; and
    (h)   robbery where, at some time during the commission of the offence the offender had in his possession a firearm or imitation firearm within the meaning of the 1968 Act.

All these offences already carry life imprisonment as their maximum penalty. It is clear, therefore, that Parliament is not providing additional powers for the Crown Court in s. 2 but, rather, is seeking to ensure that ('exceptional circumstances' apart) the courts will impose such a sentence where a 'serious offence' has been committed for the second time. A discretionary life sentence cannot be passed unless the offence which has been committed is a violent or a sexual offence, and in nearly every case where an offence qualifies as a serious offence it will also qualify as a 'violent offence' or a 'sexual offence' as defined in CJA 1991, s. 31(2) (see **4.2.7**). One possible exception is an offence of robbery using an imitation firearm, which qualifies as a 'serious offence', but was held not to amount to a 'violent offence' on the particular facts of *Palin* (1995) 16 Cr App R (S) 888.

Whether the life sentence imposed under s. 2 is a sentence of life imprisonment or a sentence of custody for life under CJA 1982, s. 8(2), the sentencer may exercise the power under C(S)A 1997, s. 28, to specify what part of the sentence must expire before the offender is to be considered for early release. See further on s. 28, **4.5.2**.

4.3.6   Discretionary life imprisonment

A discretionary life sentence may be passed in respect of any offence for which life imprisonment is provided as the maximum penalty (see Table 1 on pp. 7–14 for examples of such offences). The relevant discretionary life sentence for an offender aged 21 or over is life imprisonment. For an offender aged from 18 to 20 inclusive the relevant sentence is custody for life under CJA 1982, s. 8(2) and, if the offender is under 18, the relevant sentence is detention for life under the CYPA 1933, s. 53(2). The statutory criteria in CJA 1991 for determining whether the imposition of a custodial sentence is justified, and, if so, for fixing its length, apply to discretionary life sentences as they do to determinate sentences. Since the life sentence is an indeterminate sentence, it is very difficult to see how its imposition, rather than that of a determinate sentence of imprisonment, could be justified in terms of s. 2(2)(a) as being 'commensurate with the seriousness of the offence'. A discretionary life sentence may now be justified only under s. 2(2)(b), as being 'necessary to protect the public from serious harm from the offender'. It therefore follows that an indeterminate sentence can be passed only where the offender has committed a violent offence or a sexual offence (as defined in CJA 1991, s. 31). This has now been confirmed by the Court of Appeal in *Robinson* [1977] 2 Cr App R (S) 35, where the offender pleaded guilty to possessing an imitation firearm with intent to commit a burglary. A discretionery life sentence was quashed on the basis that the offence was neither a sexual offence nor, on the facts, a violent offence. See also *Meek* (1995) 16 Cr App R (S) 1003. Statutory criteria apart, there are several offences punishable with life imprisonment which never in practice result in such a sentence. This is especially true of common law offences, which carry life as the maximum penalty unless statute provides to the contrary. The offences most likely to lead to a sentence of discretionary life imprisonment are manslaughter, rape and arson.

It might be thought that the principle that the maximum penalty should be reserved for the gravest instances of an offence reasonably likely to occur would lead to the conclusion that the most serious offences of rape, robbery, arson or manslaughter would be punished with life imprisonment while those which are less serious would merit a fixed-term sentence. That is not, however, the approach of the courts. Crimes which, though grave, are not necessarily the gravest of their type sometimes result in a life sentence for the offender. Conversely, unless the conditions outlined below are satisfied, even the gravest examples are normally dealt with by determinate sentences, albeit very long ones. Thus in *Wilson* (1964) 48 Cr App R 329, better known as the 'Great Train Robbery', in which the Glasgow to London mail train was held up and £2,600,000 in used notes was stolen, only a fraction of which was ever recovered, life sentences were not passed. Concurrent terms of 30 years (for the robbery) and 25 years (for the associated conspiracy) were imposed by the judge. If life imprisonment was not seen as appropriate in such a case, when could it be appropriate? The Court of Appeal has developed several important sentencing principles over the years which relate to the imposition of the discretionary life sentence. These principles are well known and appear in the main to be well settled.

The starting point is that 'life sentences for offences other than homicide should not be imposed unless there are exceptional circumstances in the case' (per Lawton LJ in *Pither* (1979) 1 Cr App R (S) 209). What constitutes such exceptional circumstances? From the leading cases of *Hodgson* (1968) 52 Cr App R 113, *De Havilland* (1983) 5 Cr App R (S) 109 and *O'Dwyer* (1986) 86 Cr App R 313, it can be seen that life imprisonment has been deemed to be appropriate only where the following conditions have been satisfied:

(a)   the offence or offences are in themselves serious enough to require a very long sentence;

(b)   it appears from the nature of the offences, or from the offender's criminal history, that he is a person of mental instability who, if at liberty, would probably reoffend and present a grave danger to the public;

(c)   the offender will remain unstable and a potential danger for a long and/or uncertain period of time.

The continuing relevance of these criteria was confirmed in *J* (1992) 14 Cr App R (S) 500 and *Attorney-General's Reference (No. 34 of 1992)* (1994) 15 Cr App R (S) 167. Although in *Hodgson* (1968) 52 Cr App R 113 it was said that a life sentence was proper only where the offence was itself grave enough to justify a very long sentence, and in *Attorney-General's Reference (No. 32 of 1996)* [1997] 1 Cr App R (S) 263 it was stated that there could be 'no question' of a life sentence unless a very serious offence had been committed, in *Ashdown* [1974] 1 WLR 270 a life sentence was upheld even though the Court of Appeal observed that the fixed-term sentence proportionate to the gravity of the offence would have been five years. In that case the accused was convicted of armed robbery when he stole £2 from a man whom he threatened with an air pistol. Similarly in *Blogg* (1981) 3 Cr App R (S) 114 the offender had set fire to a box in an empty office block. The Court of Appeal upheld a life sentence for 'the almost trifling offence of arson which was committed', by having regard to the offender's perceived dangerousness, in the light of his history of arson offences committed over 30 years. It might be thought that life sentences imposed following conviction for such offences would now be inconsistent with the 'seriousness' criterion for the imposition of custody in the CJA 1991, ss. 1(2)(a) and 2(2)(a). The sentences could, however, be justified in accordance with the 'public protection' criterion in ss. 1(2)(b) and 2(2)(b). It will be recalled that the public protection criterion can be relied on only where the offender has committed a violent offence or a sexual offence.

The second condition for the imposition of a life sentence is that the offender be perceived as a real danger to the public. Life sentences have been imposed in the past following psychiatric evidence of the offender's 'immaturity and sexual maladjustment' in a case of repeated rape (*Thornett* (1979) 1 Cr App R (S) 1), psychopathic disorder not susceptible to treatment (*De Havilland* (1983) 5 Cr App R (S) 109), personality disorder (*Finney* (1979) 1 Cr App R (S) 301), latent schizophrenia and a long history of eccentric and inconsequent behaviour (*Scott* (1981) 3 Cr App R (S) 334) and paedophilia not susceptible to treatment (*Hatch* [1997] 1 Cr App R (S) 22). On the other side of the line are cases such as *Blackburn* (1979) 1 Cr App R (S) 205, where a life sentence for conspiracy to rob was varied to one of eight years' imprisonment; the offender was described in medical reports as having 'a severe personality problem', as 'impulsive' and 'capable of dishonesty', but the evidence did not point to mental instability. In *Wilkinson* (1983) 5 Cr App R (S) 105, the Court of Appeal held that, in the absence of evidence of mental instability, the accused, who had carried out numerous burglaries, sometimes threatening occupants with violence, had to be sentenced like any other 'bad burglar or robber', a term of 11 years being substituted for the life sentence. The fact that an offender is of 'borderline subnormal intelligence' has been held not of itself to be enough to fulfil the mental instability criterion (*Laycock* (1981) 3 Cr App R (S) 104), nor is the fact that the offender is a chronic alcoholic (*Stewart* (1989) 11 Cr App R (S) 132). In *Roche* (1995) 16 Cr App R (S) 849, a case involving attempted murder and indecent assault on a woman, the medical evidence did not disclose any abnormal mental state, and so the Court of Appeal held that a life sentence could not be justified. Medical evidence should normally be considered by the court when an assessment of dangerousness is being made (*Pither* (1979) 1 Cr App R (S) 209) although it is not necessary to show that the offender is suffering from a specific mental disorder within the meaning of the MHA 1983. In an appropriate case the sentencer may impose a life sentence without hearing any medical evidence at all (*Stevenson* (1993) 14 Cr App R (S) 22).

Whether the third condition, that there must be a potential danger, exists may be ascertained by the court from the facts of the offence, details of the offender's previous convictions and the medical evidence. The danger in question will usually be a danger to the public generally, but a specific threat to a particular person may be sufficient. Thus in *Allen* (1987) 9 Cr App R (S) 169 the offender had been found in possession of a loaded sawn-off shotgun shortly after attempting to trace a woman whom he had kidnapped and treated with violence on a previous occasion; the real and immediate danger to her justified a life sentence. In *Attorney-General's Reference (No. 32 of 1996)* [1997] 1 Cr App R (S) 261 the offender was convicted of causing grievous bodily harm with intent, an offence committed the day after he had been released on home leave from a life sentence for murder. Imposing a further life sentence for the assault the Court of Appeal stressed that the offender would pose a serious danger for an indefinite period of time. The offender's dangerousness will justify a life sentence where the medical evidence is that the offender's condition will not improve through treatment or the passage of time (*Virgo* (1988) 10 Cr App R (S) 427). Conversely, where there is evidence that the offender's mental state will improve during a specified period, and a sentence proportionate to the seriousness of the offence would thereby provide sufficient protection for the public, that sentence, rather than a life sentence, should be passed (*Hercules* (1980) 2 Cr App R (S) 156).

Even in cases where the above three conditions are met it is quite likely that the court will have available an alternative which may be seen as more suitable than life imprisonment. The alternative is a hospital order made under the provisions of the MHA 1983, s. 37 (see **11.3**). The effect of a hospital order, in the case of a dangerous offender, would be his compulsory detention in a mental hospital. It is likely that special restrictions would, by s. 41 of the Act, be placed upon his discharge from hospital. The following conditions must, however, be satisfied if a court is to make a hospital order:

(a)   the offender must be diagnosed as suffering from one or more of the forms of mental disorder specified in the MHA 1983;

(b)   there must be a suitable hospital prepared to offer him admission; and

(c)   the court must consider that treatment rather than punishment is appropriate in view of the extent to which the offender was responsible for his actions.

A mentally unstable offender will not necessarily be suffering from mental disorder within the meaning of the MHA 1983; even if he is, there may not be room for him in hospital. In such circumstances the court may be thrown back upon what is regarded as the 'least wrong' sentence in the circumstances, life imprisonment.

If the judge is considering imposing a discretionary life sentence, he should as a matter of good practice alert counsel to that fact, so that the matter may be addressed in argument by them. This is clearly of particular importance for defence counsel (*McDougall* (1983) 5 Cr App R (S) 78), but in *Virgo* (1988) 10 Cr App R (S) 427 the judge heard submissions from both counsel. While warning counsel in this way is good practice, it should not be regarded as an absolute requirement, since there may be cases where the passing of a life sentence is an obvious possibility to all concerned in the case (*Allen* (1987) 9 Cr App R (S) 169).

A life sentence and a fixed-term sentence may run concurrently. In *Nugent* (1984) 67 Cr App R 93 the imposition of two determinate prison sentences to run consecutively but concurrently with a life sentence was approved by the Court of Appeal. A fixed-term sentence may not run consecutively to a life sentence (*Foy* [1962] 1 WLR 609) and an implication of this is that life sentences cannot run consecutively to each other. Neither may a life sentence run consecutively to a fixed term (*Jones* v *DPP* [1962] AC 635).

4.3.7 Custody for life

As was explained in **4.3.4**, an offender under the age of 21 who is convicted of murder *must* be sentenced to custody for life (CJA 1982, s. 8(1)), unless he was under the age of 18 at the time of commission of the offence, in which case the proper sentence is detention during Her Majesty's pleasure. An offender aged 18, 19 or 20 who is convicted of an offence which is punishable in the case of an adult with a maximum sentence of life imprisonment *may* be sentenced to custody for life (CJA 1982, s. 8(2)). In many respects this sentence is parallel to the discretionary life sentence for adult offenders. The sentence of custody for life is distinguished from the imposition of a determinate sentence of detention in a young offender institution by the requirement that custody for life should be imposed only in exceptional circumstances, and only where the offender displays a degree of mental instability the duration of which is unclear and which makes the offender a danger to the public. The Court of Appeal has stressed that custody for life must not be seen as a more merciful disposal than a fixed-term sentence (*Lynas* (1992) 13 Cr App R (S) 363). These requirements are very similar to the traditional requirements for the imposition of a life sentence upon an adult.

One case where the Court of Appeal quashed a sentence of custody for life is *Hall* (1986) 8 Cr App R (S) 458, since there was 'no real evidence' that the offender, who pleaded guilty to arson, was 'suffering from any mental illness or abnormality, although he was immature and a young criminal who had committed many offences'. A second case is *Powell* (1989) 11 Cr App R (S) 113, where the offender pleaded guilty to wounding with intent, taking a conveyance and violent disorder but again there was 'an insufficient degree of mental instability, or dangerousness, to call for the exceptional course which the judge felt obliged to take'; the sentence was varied to eight years. On the other hand, in *Busby* (1992) 13 Cr App R (S) 291 the offender pleaded guilty to buggery, committed on a girl aged three. The 18-year-old offender was described in reports as 'flat and detached' and as showing no remorse. He had committed two earlier assaults on young children and, in the light of that, it was held that the sentence of custody for life was appropriate to protect the public from him.

4.3.8 Detention for life under CYPA 1933, s. 53(2)

An offender aged under 18 who is convicted of an offence which is punishable in the case of an adult with a maximum sentence of life imprisonment may be sentenced to detention for life under the CYPA 1933, s. 53(2) (*Abbott* [1964] 1 QB 489). In many respects the sentence is parallel to the discretionary life sentence for adult offenders and the sentence of custody for life under CJA 1982, s. 8(2) for those aged 18, 19 or 20. In *Bryson* (1973) 58 Cr App R 464 a sentence of detention for life was upheld on a 14-year-old who pleaded guilty to arson causing damage worth £20,000 and considerable risk to life. In *Carr* [1996] 1 Cr App R (S) 191 the defendant was a 15-year-old girl who pleaded guilty to causing grievous bodily harm with intent, having stabbed another schoolgirl in the back with a knife. Two other offences, in which she had tried to strangle other schoolgirls, were taken into consideration. Reports revealed other instances of disturbed and aggressive behaviour and indicated that the defendant was 'exceptionally dangerous'. An indeterminate sentence under s. 53(2) was upheld. See also *Lomas* (1995) 16 Cr App R (S) 955 and *Secretary of State for the Home Department, ex parte Furber* [1998] 1 Cr App R (S) 208 both manslaughter cases.

Only one young offender was sentenced to detention for life under CYPA 1933, s. 53(2) during 1996.

Section 53(2) of the CYPA 1933 gives the Crown Court a discretionary power to sentence juveniles convicted of certain grave offences to detention for a term not exceeding the maximum prison term carried by the offence in question. A striking contrast may be made with the sentence of detention in a young offender institution where the maximum sentence of detention which may be imposed on an offender aged 15, 16 or 17 is 24 months. In contrast sentences imposed under s. 53 may sometimes be for life and are rarely for less than three years, although a number of shorter sentences are imposed under s. 53(2) on offenders aged under 15, for whom the sentence of detention in a young offender institution is not available.

4.3.9   Detention for a fixed term under CYPA 1933, s. 53(2)

While the proportion of offenders given sentences under s. 53(2) is still relatively small (609 such sentences were passed in 1996 compared to 20,600 sentences of detention in a young offender institution), s. 53(2) is very important because it gives the Crown Court power to deprive a young offender of his or her liberty for a substantial period of time. Of the 609 cases, 275 followed conviction for robbery, 97 were for offences of violence, 51 for sexual offences, 101 for burglary and 33 for arson. The use of this sentence has been increasing sharply in recent years. Only 102 such orders were made in 1991.

The availability of the sentence under s. 53(2) depends upon a complex interlocking of s. 53(2) with various other provisions. The first point to note is that the power is reserved to the Crown Court after the young offender has been convicted on indictment. A youth court cannot pass such a sentence in any circumstances, nor may the Crown Court do so if the offender is remitted there for sentence after a finding of guilt in a youth court (*McKenna* (1985) 7 Cr App R (S) 348). In a case where the offence merits a greater penalty than is permitted by the scheme of maximum penalties for detention in a young offender institution provided for in the CJA 1982, ss. 1A and 1B (see **4.3.2**), or where the offender is aged under 15 and so is ineligible for a sentence of detention in a young offender institution in any event, the proper course is for the magistrates in the youth court to commit to Crown Court for trial. An error was made in *Learmonth* (1988) 10 Cr App R (S) 229, where the 16-year-old offender pleaded guilty before the youth court to assault with intent to rob. He was committed by that court to the Crown Court for sentence, where three years' detention under s. 53(2) was ordered. This sentence had to be quashed on appeal, since Learmonth had not been convicted of the offence on indictment. The Court of Appeal has stressed the importance of this point on several occasions, such as in *Billam* (1986) 8 Cr App R (S) 48, in respect of offences of rape committed by juveniles, and again more generally in *AM* [1998] 1 WLR 363.

The second point is that the offender must be aged from 10 to 17 inclusive. Since no offender aged under 15 can receive a sentence of detention in a young offender institution, it will be apparent that, until the detention and training order provisions in the CJB become law and are brought into force (see **4.3.10**), the sentence of detention under s. 53(2) remains as the only available custodial sentence for offenders aged under 15.

The third point is that the young offender must have been convicted of one of a range of offences specified in s. 53(2). This list of 'relevant offences' has been subject to recent statutory changes, and now comprises:

(a) any offence punishable in the case of an adult with imprisonment for 14 years or more, but not murder;

(b) an offence of indecent assault, whether committed on a man or on a woman;

(c) if the defendant is aged between 14 and 17 inclusive, an offence of causing death by dangerous driving (RTOA 1988, s. 1) or causing death by careless driving while under the influence of drink or drugs (RTOA 1988, s. 3A).

Relevant offences include, therefore, manslaughter, arson, wounding with intent, robbery, burglary committed in a dwelling and handling stolen goods, but not theft, obtaining by deception, burglary committed other than in a dwelling (see *Brown* (1995) 16 Cr App R (S) 932), aggravated vehicle taking, even where death results, unlawful wounding, or assault occasioning actual bodily harm. Offences in (a) and (b) above are specially listed since, although they may attract a sentence under s. 53(2) in an appropriate case, they carry a maximum sentence of less than 14 years' imprisonment in the case of an adult.

The fourth and final point is that s. 53(2) expressly provides that the sentence should not be imposed unless no other method of dealing with the offender (such as detention in a young offender institution) is appropriate. This requirement is considered further below.

The maximum term of detention which may be ordered under s. 53(2) is the maximum prison term which could be ordered for the relevant offence if committed by an adult. If the offence carries imprisonment for life, then detention for life may be ordered (*Abbott* [1964] 1 QB 489 and **4.3.8**). There is no minimum term fixed by statute, but it is obvious from the restricted circumstances in which the sentence is available that detention under s. 53(2) is only meant to be used in those rare cases in which a person aged 15, 16 or 17 deserves to lose his liberty for a substantial period of time or where an offence committed by a juvenile under 15 is so serious that only custody can be justified for it. The effect of the sentence is that the detainee is liable to be kept 'in such a place and under such conditions' as the Secretary of State considers appropriate. Depending on the age of the detainee, that place might be local authority secure accommodation, a young offender institution or a prison. If the offender is suffering from a mental disorder, he might be sent to a suitable hospital.

The Court of Appeal has stated clearly on several occasions that the power to order detention under s. 53(2) is to be used sparingly, as a last resort, reflecting the language of s. 53(2) that it should be used only where 'none of the other methods in which the case may legally be dealt with is suitable'. Traditionally, long-term detention has been used for offences involving grave violence or where there is danger to the public. Thus in *Storey* [1973] 1 WLR 1045 the Court of Appeal upheld 20 years' detention for the 16-year-old ringleader of a group of youngsters who had, for no reason, set upon a man in the street. Storey had dragged the man into an alley, hit him and kicked him in the head. The group left him lying there, but on two occasions later in the evening returned to him and Storey kicked him again repeatedly and hit him with a brick. The victim's injuries were very severe. The Court of Appeal decided that Storey must be detained until such time as he had matured, and could be trusted not to behave in such an appalling way again. Examples of cases in which sentences under s. 53(2) have been imposed under the 1991 Act criteria for violent or sexual offences (see **4.2.6**) are *Taylor* (1995) 16 Cr App R (S) 570, where seven years' detention was reduced to six years for robbery committed with great violence by a

17-year-old on a 70-year-old man, and *K* (1995) 16 Cr App R (S) 966, where a six-year term of detention was appropriate for an offender aged 16 who raped his six-year-old sister. The medical report in the latter case 'gave a disturbing picture of sexual fantasising' and indicated that the offender would remain a risk to the public for at least the next decade.

The circumstances in which s. 53(2) detention is appropriate for non-violent but serious offences of dishonesty has not been entirely clear. In *Oakes* (1983) 5 Cr App R (S) 389 the Court of Appeal said that Parliament did not intend s. 53(2) to be used for simple offences of dishonesty, however despicable they might be. In that case the Court of Appeal substituted a sentence of 12 months for 30 months' detention under s. 53(2) in a case where a 16-year-old had been convicted of burgling the homes of several old people by tricking his way in and then stealing any items of value while his accomplice kept the victim occupied. In *Simmons* (1995) 16 Cr App R (S) 801, however, five years' detention was upheld in the case of a 16-year-old who pleaded guilty to seven counts of house burglary and asked for a large number of offences to be taken into consideration, including 67 burglaries and attempted burglaries. It was held by the Court of Appeal that the sentence was appropriate to reflect both the gravity of the offending and its persistence. In *Bennett* (1995) 16 Cr App R (S) 438, five years' detention was upheld on a boy aged 15 for damaging property, being reckless whether life was endangered, and for aggravated vehicle taking. He took a van from a garage and drove it at high speed, starting a police chase during which the van was driven at police vehicles, causing damage to the value of £3,500. The offender had committed over 100 previous offences, and the sentence was upheld on punitive and deterrent grounds, having regard to the prevalence of that kind of offending in the area in question.

The last case also raises the question of sentencing an offender who stands convicted of more than one offence, but where only one of those offences is punishable under s. 53(2). In *Bennett* a sentence under s. 53(2) could not have been passed for the aggravated vehicle taking offence on its own. This issue was clarified by the Court of Appeal in *Walsh* [1997] 2 Cr App R (S) 210, where there were five offenders, all girls aged 14 or 15. They pleaded guilty to false imprisonment and unlawful wounding, committed while carrying out a sustained and violent attack on another girl aged 14. Sentences of detention under s. 53(2) were imposed for terms varying between three and a half years and three years and 11 months. It was argued on appeal that the sentences were wrong, since the real gravity of the offending lay in the unlawful wounding of the victim, but that was an offence for which s. 53(2) was not available. The Court of Appeal, however, said that the two offences were 'associated offences' (see **4.2.4**) and, since s. 53(2) was available in respect of the false imprisonment, it was also available when the two offences were being dealt with together. The approach taken in *Walsh* was endorsed in *AM* [1998] 1 WLR 363.

Further important guidance on the use of the power under s. 53(2) was provided by the Court of Appeal in *Fairhurst* [1986] 1 WLR 1374, in which Lord Lane CJ stated that, given the restriction on the maximum term of detention in a young offender institution which could lawfully be imposed on an offender under 15, 16 or 17 (which was at the time of that case 12 months, but which has since been increased by the CJPOA 1994 to 24 months), '. . . it is not good sentencing practice to pass a sentence of detention under s. 53(2) simply because a [24] months' sentence seems to be on the low side for the particular offence committed'. Subsequently this was interpreted by the Court of Appeal in *Wainfur* [1997] 1 Cr App R (S) 43 to mean that for offenders within this age group, the court should be satisfied before imposing a sentence under s. 53(2) that a sentence 'substantially greater' than 24 months is appropriate. In the important case of *AM* [1998] 1 WLR 363, however, the Court of Appeal signalled a different approach. Lord Bingham of Cornhill CJ stated that the earlier law had the effect of creating a 'sentencing no-man's land' between the maximum sentence of detention in a young offender institution and the shortest term which might appropriately be imposed under s. 53(2). Accordingly, his lordship said that while a Crown Court sentencer should not exceed the 24-month limit without careful thought, if it was concluded that a longer term, even if not much longer, was needed, then the court should impose whatever it considered the appropriate period of detention under s. 53(2) to be. For further consideration of cases where the sentencer has to choose between imposition of the 24-month maximum term of detention in a young offender institution and a sentence under s. 53(2) see **4.3.2**.

The imposition of a sentence under s. 53(2) is subject to the statutory criteria for determining the imposition of custodial sentences, and for determining their length, which are laid down in CJA 1991. The cases discussed above illustrate that there are some occasions on which recourse to s. 53(2) is justified by the seriousness of the offence and others where the protection of the public is the triggering factor. All the decided cases on s. 53(2) must, however, be read with the statutory limitations in mind. Clearly, unless the term is being imposed for the protection of the public, the duration of detention under s. 53(2) should be in proportion to the seriousness of the offence. Indeed, for a very young person, it seems that if possible the sentence should be shorter than that which would be appropriate for an adult (this approach was advocated in *Storey* (1984) 6 Cr App R (S) 104).

The decision in *Fairhurst* [1986] 1 WLR 1374 was also clear authority that a sentence of detention under s. 53(2) should not be imposed consecutively to, or concurrently with, a sentence of detention in a young offender institution, and that case was applied in several subsequent cases, including *Basid* [1996] 1 Cr App R (S) 421. In *AM* [1998] 1 WLR 363, however, the Court of Appeal decided to relax this rule. The original reason for it, as explained in *Fairhurst*, was that there were a number of important differences between the two sentences, particularly with regard to the establishments within which the sentences were to be served, and arrangements for early release, which made it impracticable for them to be mixed together. In *AM*, however, Lord Bingham CJ noted that various statutory changes, especially those made to early release arrangements by the CJA 1991, meant that there is now little difference in these respects between the two sentences. Accordingly, when, a sentencer is dealing with an offender convicted of two offences, one of which would attract a determinate sentence within s. 53(2) but the other merited a sentence of detention in a young offender institution, the sentencing court could properly, and without causing administrative problems to the authorities, order one sentence to run consecutively to the other. As far as concurrent sentences are concerned, his lordship said that it is still generally undesirable to have the two sentences running together. If an offender is being sentenced for an offence which attracts a sentence under s. 53(2) as well as for associated offences which do not, it would normally be preferable to impose no separate penalty for the lesser offences and to pass a sentence of detention under s. 53(2) which takes them into account. Finally, it was pointed out that if the offender is aged 15 it is undesirable for the sentences to be mixed either concurrently or consecutively, since the offender might be detained under s. 53(2) in secure local authority accommodation, and administrative problems would be caused by also imposing a sentence of detention in a young offender institution.

4.3.10 Detention and training order

When the relevant provisions of the Crime and Disorder Bill become law and are brought into force a new custodial sentence for offenders aged from 10 to 17 inclusive, the detention and training order, will be introduced. The main, and very significant, effect of the order will be to replace the sentence of detention in a young offender institution as far as offenders under 18 are concerned. That sentence will thereafter be restricted to offenders aged 18, 19 or 20. The detention and training order will also supersede the secure training order. This form of sentence was created by the CJPOA 1994, but the relevant provisions (ss. 1 to 4 of that Act) were brought into force for only a short period of time and the CDB will repeal them. The detention and training order will (subject to certain specific conditions referred to below) be available for young offenders aged 10 to 14 inclusive, an age group in which the sentence of detention in a young offender institution has not been available and where the only applicable custodial sentence has been that of long-term detention under the CYPA 1933, s. 53(2), a sentence available only to the Crown Court after conviction on indictment. Implementation of the detention and training order is not expected before summer 1999.

The detention and training order will be available to youth courts and to the Crown Court, and it can be imposed on any offender under the age of 18 who has been convicted of an offence punishable with imprisonment in the case of an adult where the normal criteria for imposing a custodial sentence under the CJA 1991, s. 1(2)(a) or (b) apply, or where the offender has failed to express his willingness to comply with a requirement in a community order which requires such an expression of willingness (CJA 1991, s. 1(3)). The detention and training order is a 'custodial sentence' for the purposes of the 1991 Act, so that it will be subject to provisions in that Act which normally require the court to obtain a pre-sentence report before the order can be imposed (s. 3) and to obtain a medical report in any case where the offender is or appears to be mentally disordered (s. 4). Clause 69(1) states that, subject to CYPA 1933, s. 53 (detention during Her Majesty's pleasure and sentences of long-term detention of juveniles convicted of certain serious offences), and to CJA 1982, s. 8 (custody for life), where the offender qualifies for a custodial sentence, the 'sentence that the court is to pass' is the detention and training order, rather than a sentence of detention in a young offender institution. Clause 69(2) further provides that the court shall not make a detention and training order on an offender under the age of 15 unless it is of the opinion that he is a 'persistent offender', and the court shall not make such an order on an offender under the age of 12 unless it is of the opinion that 'only a custodial sentence would be adequate to protect the public from further offending by him'. In either of these cases the sentencer must state in open court that it is of the necessary opinion. This requirement is in addition to the normal obligation on the sentencer under CJA 1991, s. 1(4) to give reasons for imposing a custodial sentence (see **4.1.6**). Rather strangely, the Bill offers no guidance on the meaning of 'persistent offender', and its interpretation seems to have been left entirely to the courts. The Bill envisages that the courts will not be empowered to impose a detention and training order on an offender aged under 12 until the Secretary of State makes a further order to that effect.

The term of detention and training which may be imposed can be four, six, eight, 10, 12, 18 or 24 months (cl. 69(5)). Specifying particular sentence lengths in this way is a novel sentencing development, and it appears to be linked to ease of calculation, since all such orders will fall naturally into two equal parts, the 'period of detention' and the 'period of training'. Clause 69(5) is made subject to cl. 69(6), which states that the order must not exceed the maximum term of imprisonment which may be imposed upon an adult for the offence. The legislative intention here must surely be to limit the maximum term of a detention and training order to the period specified in cl. 69(5) or the maximum penalty for the offence, whichever is the shorter (as does the current equivalent wording in CJA 1982, s. 1B(2)). That is not, however, what cl. 69(5) says and, on the face of it, it seems to allow terms of detention and training for periods of up to life depending on the maximum penalty carried by the offence committed. To avoid confusion the Bill really ought also to state that the stated periods in cl. 69(5) are subject to the normal rule about the maximum length of custodial sentences.

When these provisions are brought into force, CJA 1982, s. 1B, which specifies a maximum term of 24 months' detention in a young offender institution for offenders aged 15, 16 or 17, will be repealed. It will be replaced by very similarly worded provisions. Clause 69(5), as we have seen, envisages that the longest term of detention and training which will be imposed is 24 months and cl. 70, while permitting a court to pass concurrent and consecutive terms of detention and training, states that no such order shall render the offender subject to an aggregate term which exceeds 24 months. If, by error, a sentencer does exceed that limit, the excess term shall be remitted (cl. 70(4)). This replicates the effect of CJA 1982, s. 1B(2) and (5), discussed at **4.3.2** except, of course, that it will apply to all offenders sentenced to a detention and training order rather than being restricted, as at present, to offenders aged 15, 16 or 17.

The 'period of detention' is to be served in a young offender institution, a secure training centre, local authority accommodation or any other accommodation approved by the Secretary of State (cl. 71). The 'period of supervision' will normally start at the halfway point in the sentence and normally end when the full term of the order expires (cl. 72(1)). During that time the offender will be supervised by a probation officer, a social worker or a member of a youth offending team (cl. 72(2)).

Breach of the supervision requirement of a detention and supervision order may be dealt with by imposing a fine not exceeding £1,000, or by ordering the offender to be returned to custody for the remainder of the full term of the order, or for three months, whichever is the shorter period (cl. 73(3)). If a person subject to a detention and training order commits during the supervision period of the order a further offence which is punishable with imprisonment in the case of an adult, the court dealing with him for the new offence may, whether or not it imposes any other sentence, order the offender to be detained for a period which begins with the date of the court's order and is equal in length to the period of the full order which remained unexpired at the time when the new offence was committed. This new period of detention must either be served before, or concurrently with, any sentence which is imposed for the new offence. These arrangements for returning an offender to custody in light of the commission of a further offence during the currency of a custodial sentence are very similar to those under CJA 1991, s. 40, which applies where the original sentence was one of imprisonment, detention in a young offender institution or a term of detention under the CYPA 1933, s. 53(2). For discussion of the operation of s. 40 see **4.5.1**.

4.4 FIXING THE LENGTH OF CUSTODIAL SENTENCES

4.4.1 Statutory criteria

Once the court has reached a decision that the particular case before it has to be dealt with by a custodial sentence in accordance with the criteria indicated in CJA 1991, s. 1, the next decision for the court is to fix the length of the custodial sentence. Prior to the 1991 Act there was no statutory guidance on this matter. It is worth mentioning the Court of Appeal decision in *Bibi* [1980] 1 WLR 1193 at this point, however. That case articulated the important general principle that, where loss of liberty is inevitable, the custodial sentence should be kept as short as possible. As Lord Lane CJ said:

It is no secret that our prisons are at the moment dangerously overcrowded. So much so that sentencing courts must be particularly careful to examine each case to ensure, if an immediate custodial sentence is necessary, that the sentence is as short as possible, consistent only with the duty to protect the interests of the public and to punish and deter the criminal. Many offenders can be dealt with equally justly and effectively by a sentence of six or nine months' imprisonment as by one of 18 months' or three years.

The principle enunciated in that case was reinforced by the CJA 1991.

The CJA 1991 provides statutory criteria for determining sentence length, which are set out in s. 2 of the Act. They apply to all custodial sentences, including discretionary life sentences and suspended sentences, whether imposed by the Crown Court or by magistrates' courts and whether passed on adults or on young offenders. Any sentence imposed must, of course, be within the statutory maximum provided for the offence and, if sentence is being imposed in a magistrates' court, must accord with the restrictions on the powers of that court to pass custodial sentences of a particular length. The different statutory maxima which apply to young offenders (see **4.3.2**) must also be borne in mind. Section 2(1) of the CJA 1991 excludes from the ambit of the section cases where the sentence for the offence is fixed by law (i.e. murder) and cases where sentence falls to be imposed under s. 2 or s. 3 of the C(S)A 1997 (see **4.3.3** to **4.3.5**). Section 2 further provides as follows:

(2) ... the custodial sentence shall be—

(a) for such term (not exceeding the permitted maximum) as in the opinion of the court is commensurate with the seriousness of the offence, or the combination of the offence and one or more offences associated with it; or

(b) where the offence is a violent or sexual offence, for such longer term (not exceeding that maximum) as in the opinion of the court is necessary to protect the public from serious harm from the offender.

(3) Where the court passes a custodial sentence for a term longer than is commensurate with the seriousness of the offence, or the combination of the offence and one or more offences associated with it, the court shall—

(a) state in open court that it is of the opinion that subsection (2)(b) above applies and why it is of that opinion; and

(b) explain to the offender in open court and in ordinary language why the sentence is for such a term.

(4) A custodial sentence for an indeterminate period shall be regarded for the purposes of subsections (2) and (3) above as a custodial sentence for a term longer than any actual term.

Section 3(1) of the CJA 1991 requires that, for the purposes of forming an opinion under s. 2(2)(a) or (b) as to the appropriate length of a custodial sentence, the court 'shall obtain and consider a pre-sentence report' unless, in the circumstances of the case, the court is of the opinion that it is unnecessary to obtain one (s. 3(2)). For pre-sentence reports generally, see **3.5.1**. Section 3(3)(a) states that the court must have regard to any information about the circumstances of the offence (including any aggravating or mitigating factors) which have a bearing on the seriousness of that offence. The court may also have regard to any relevant mitigating (but not aggravating) factor which does not impinge upon offence seriousness but which relates to the offender (s. 28(1)). Where the criteria under consideration by the court are those in s. 2(2)(b), the court 'may take into account any information about the offender which is before it' (s. 3(3)(b)). For discussion of these general provisions see Chapter 2.

4.4.2 Custodial sentence length under CJA 1991, s. 2(2)(a)

Turning first to s. 2(2)(a), it will be seen that the criterion for sentence length embodies the key principle of the CJA 1991 that sentence length should be commensurate with the seriousness of the offence. In the great majority of cases where custodial sentences are imposed, sentence length will be determined in accordance with s. 2(2)(a) rather than s. 2(2)(b). Section 2(2)(a) may be relied upon even where the offence is a violent or sexual offence, since s. 2 merely gives an option to the sentencer of justifying custodial sentence length under s. 2(2)(b) in these cases, but does not require the sentencer to do so. Given the emphasis in s. 2(2)(a) upon the requirement that the sentence be 'commensurate with the seriousness of the offence', and the wording of s. 2(4), it is difficult to see how the imposition of a discretionary life sentence could be justified under s. 2(2)(a).

In *Cunningham* [1993] 1 WLR 183, Lord Taylor CJ said that the purpose of a custodial sentence had primarily to be to punish and deter, and the phrase 'commensurate with the seriousness of the offence' in s. 2(2)(a) meant 'commensurate with the punishment and deterrence which the seriousness of the offence' required. The reference here to deterrence is potentially misleading, and it is important to understand the implications of Lord Taylor's remark. It permits reference by the sentencer to deterrence (whether individual or general deterrence) as an objective in sentencing only insofar as a deterrent effect may be achieved by imposing the commensurate custodial sentence. It does *not* permit the sentencer to exceed the commensurate sentence in an attempt to achieve a greater deterrent impact. Indeed Lord Taylor stated specifically in *Cunningham* that the wording of s. 2(2)(a) prohibits adding extra length to the commensurate sentence so as to make a special example of the defendant (so-called 'exemplary sentencing'). Prevalence of the offence is, however, a legitimate factor in determining the length of a custodial sentence (see **2.2.2(g)**).

Section 2(2)(a) states that the court may have regard to 'the combination of the offence and one or more offences associated with it' when determining the length of a custodial sentence. Section 31(2) makes provision as to when one offence may properly be regarded as for these purposes as 'associated with' another, and was considered at **4.2.5**. Where the offender is being sentenced for several offences (and perhaps asks for several others to be taken into consideration), the danger of sentencing on the basis of the totality of the offending is that it could lead to a total sentence which is disproportionate to the nature of the offending behaviour. CJA 1991, s. 28(2)(b), in an attempt to avoid this, declares that nothing shall prevent a court 'in a case of an offender who is convicted of one or more other offences, from mitigating his sentence by applying any rule of law as to the totality of sentences'. This rather obliquely worded provision gives statutory recognition to the 'totality principle', which has been developed over the years by the Court of Appeal. For discussion of this principle see **4.4.4**.

The offender's previous convictions and response to previous sentences is relevant when the court is considering sentence length. For a discussion of this see **2.2.5**.

4.4.3 Custodial sentence length under CJA 1991, s. 2(2)(b)

Section 2(2)(b) deals with the extent to which the court is permitted to depart from the general principle of commensurability set out in s. 2(2)(a). The court may impose a longer sentence, but not one which exceeds the statutory maximum for the offence, in the case of a custodial sentence passed for a violent offence or a sexual offence, where the court is of the opinion that a custodial sentence of that length is necessary to protect the public from serious harm from the offender. Definitions of 'violent offence', 'sexual offence' and 'serious harm' are provided in s. 31 of the CJA 1991 and were considered at **4.2.6**. The longer sentence which is imposed in reliance upon s. 2(2)(b) may be a determinate sentence which is longer than could be justified in reliance upon s. 2(2)(a) or, when sentencing for an offence which carries life imprisonment as its maximum penalty when committed by an adult, it may be a discretionary life sentence. Only where a violent offence or a sexual offence has been committed, where the public protection criterion is made out, and where the further criteria for the imposition of a discretionary life sentence have been made out (see **4.3.6**) may such a sentence be passed.

It should be clear that s. 2(2)(b) provides the court with a *power* to impose a custodial sentence which is longer than that which would be commensurate with the seriousness of the offence. It does not require the court to do so, and it may well be that in the ordinary run of sentencing for violent offences or sexual offences a sentence commensurate with the seriousness of the offence imposed under s. 2(2)(a) will be a perfectly appropriate response. Given the statutory language of 'public protection', the circumstances in which it would be appropriate for a magistrates' court (which is, of course, normally limited to a maximum custodial sentence of six months) to rely upon s. 2(2)(b) will arise very rarely, if ever. The Crown Court may impose a sentence under s. 2(2)(b) on an offender convicted in the magistrates' court and committed to Crown Court for sentence. An example is *Etchells* [1996] 1 Cr App R (S) 163.

Where reliance is placed upon s. 2(2)(b), s. 2(3) requires that the sentencer must state in open court that the court is of the opinion that s. 2(2)(b) applies and why it is of that opinion. The sentencer must explain to the offender in open court and in ordinary language why the sentence is for such a term. These requirements may be compared to those which apply in respect of a decision to impose a custodial sentence (see **4.1.6**). In that context, in *Baverstock* [1993] 1 WLR 202, Lord Taylor CJ said that a two-stage process of explanation was not strictly necessary and that the precise words used by the judge when doing so were not critical. The Court of Appeal would not be sympathetic to appeals based upon a fine linguistic analysis of the judge's sentencing remarks. A magistrates' court is additionally required to specify in the warrant of commitment, and to enter in the register, its reason for passing a custodial sentence (s. 1(5)), but it is not required to specify its reasons for determining the length of the custodial sentence.

The general rule in sentencing (violent and sexual offences included) remains that the sentence should be proportionate to the seriousness of the offence but, exceptionally, the court may impose a longer-than-normal sentence where special risk to the public is made out and where the imposition of a proportionate sentence would not provide adequate protection for the public (*Christie* (1995) 16 Cr App R (S) 469). In *Crow* (1995) 16 Cr App R (S) 409 the Court of Appeal said that if the offence was an isolated example, or there is no good reason to fear a substantial risk of further offending, s. 2(2)(b) would not be applicable. This point is also clear from *Bestwick* (1995) 16 Cr App R (S) 268, where two offenders had been involved in a series of arson offences. One was given a proportionate sentence of 30 months' in a young offender institution, but the other received five years' imprisonment, passed as a longer-than-normal sentence. An appeal on the basis of disparity between the two sentences was dismissed, the Court of Appeal noting that the offender who received the longer sentence had a seriously disturbed personality and an obsession with lighting fires and represented a real risk to the public. The other offender had a normal personality and hence fell to be sentenced in accordance with the seriousness of his offending.

Although the imposition of a longer-than-normal sentence should not, then, be regarded as the normal course for the sentencer to take when dealing with a violent or sexual offence, it has been held that, where a defendant is clearly eligible for a longer-than-normal sentence, the court's decision not to impose one (or its failure to appreciate that it might have done so) may be regarded as the imposition of an unduly lenient sentence. In *Attorney-General's Reference (No. 9 of 1994)* (1995) 16 Cr App R (S) 366 the Court of Appeal upheld a prosecution appeal and said that a longer-than-normal sentence of 10 years, rather than a commensurate sentence of six years, should have been passed. The offender had committed a series of sexual offences against young boys, and he represented a real and continuing danger.

Before imposing a sentence under s. 2(2)(b) the court must be sure that it is basing its decision on accurate information about the offender, if necessary by holding a *Newton* inquiry into any important factual issue (*Oudkerk* (1995) 16 Cr App R (S) 172). The evidential basis for passing a longer-than-normal sentence under s. 2(2)(b) will normally be found in a psychiatric report prepared on the offender, or in his previous convictions, or both. Normally both these elements will figure in the court's consideration, but it seems that an offender who has no previous convictions may still receive a longer-than-normal sentence provided that the medical evidence is clear (*Crow* (1995) 16 Cr App R (S) 409). On the other hand, in a case where the previous convictions speak eloquently of the offender's dangerousness, a longer-than-normal sentence may be passed without obtaining a medical report (*Hashi* (1995) 16 Cr App R (S) 121). Where the previous convictions are being relied on, the court must of course ensure that the information which it has about the circumstances of those earlier offences is accurate, and it may be necessary to investigate the previous offences to see whether the offender really does represent a serious risk or whether he can properly be sentenced on a proportionate basis (*Samuels* (1995) 16 Cr App R (S) 856). It seems from the cases that information about the current offence standing alone, without inferences drawn from previous offences and without the benefit of a psychiatric report, is unlikely to be enough to justify such a sentence.

A number of important principles have emerged from the Court of Appeal decisions on the appropriate use of longer-than-normal sentences under s. 2(2)(b). It should be recalled that the subsection states that a longer-than-normal sentence shall be for such longer term (not exceeding the maximum available for the offence) '. . . as in the opinion of the court is necessary to protect the public from serious harm from the offender'. The first point, then, is that the court must be clear that it is *this offender* who poses the risk — the threat must come from him. So, the court cannot use a longer-than-normal sentence simply to mark its disapproval of a particularly unpleasant offence, or to register concern at the type of offending involved. The court must base its view on the information which it has concerning the offence and the offender. Thus, in *Walsh* (1995) 16 Cr App R (S) 204, a longer-than-normal sentence was held to be inappropriate in a case where the offender had committed sexual offences on a 13-year-old boy, but where the offence was 'out of character' for the offender and repetition was unlikely. Secondly, it must be shown to be necessary to protect *the public* from serious harm from the offender. While in the ordinary case the risk will be to members of the public generally, it has been accepted in some cases a longer-than-normal sentence can properly be passed for the protection of a small group of individuals or a particular person. In *Hashi* (1995) 16 Cr App R (S) 121 the threat was to the offender's ex-wife and any male friends that the offender might see her with. In *Nicholas* (1994) 16 Cr App R (S) 381 the offender had in the past persistently assaulted his wife but had never assaulted anyone else. Although the principle was accepted in *Nicholas* that a longer-than-normal sentence could be imposed in such a case, on the facts it was not justified since the wife now had a court order restraining the offender from molesting her and the offender had apparently now accepted that their marriage was over. Another aspect of this issue arose in *L* (1994) 15 Cr App R (S) 501, where the offender admitted sexually abusing his stepdaughters, aged 10 and 12, over a period of 20 months. The Court of Appeal quashed a longer-than-normal sentence of seven years and substituted a proportionate term of three years on the basis that the offending had been confined within the family, that the offender had no other convictions and would have no future contact with the victims. In the circumstances the court did not think that the offender represented a risk 'to the public'. Thirdly, it has to be shown that in the particular case before the court the public needs to be protected from *serious harm* from the offender. As we have seen, the 1991 Act states that this phrase should be 'construed as a reference to protecting members of the public from death or serious personal injury, whether physical or psychological, occasioned by further such offences committed by the offender' (s. 31(3)). What matters here is not so much the likelihood of further offences occurring, nor necessarily the seriousness of the current or previous offences committed by the offender (though both of these will of course weigh with the court), but rather the anticipated seriousness of future offending. Also, that the sentencer must anticipate the commission of 'further *such* offences', i.e., further violent or sexual offences, being committed by the offender. In *Creasey* (1994) 15 Cr App R (S) 671 the offender pleaded guilty to indecent assault on a 13-year-old boy, attempting to masturbate him by rubbing his hand on the boy's trousers. Creasey had previous convictions for similar offences, but the Court of Appeal quashed a longer-than-normal sentence of five years and substituted a proportionate sentence of 21 months. The offending was 'unpleasant and distressing' but, in the view of the court, did not require the protection of the public from serious harm. The case may be contrasted with *Bowler* (1994) 15 Cr App R (S) 78, where the defendant pleaded guilty to indecent assault, having put his hand up a young girl's skirt and fondled her. He had eight previous convictions for very similar offences, committed on women and girls. In this case a longer-than-normal sentence of six years was upheld by the Court of Appeal, on the basis that the court must bear in mind the possibility of future victims more vulnerable to such conduct than the average, who might suffer psychological harm. The distinction between these two cases is difficult to see. *Bowler* was distinguished in *Fishwick* [1996] 1 Cr App R (S) 359, where the offender had a history of relatively minor physical assaults of a non-sexual nature, and where the Court of Appeal felt that there was no basis to conclude that future victims were likely to suffer serious psychological injury. A longer-than-normal sentence of three years was, accordingly, reduced to a proportionate sentence of 18 months.

The question of the appropriate additional length to be added to a custodial term under s. 2(2)(b), to take account of the risk to the public, has been considered in several Court of Appeal decisions, but a clear pattern has not yet emerged. In *Mansell* (1994) 15 Cr App R (S) 771 the Court of Appeal said that in each case the sentencer had to try to balance the need to protect the public on the one hand, with the need to look at the totality of the offending on the other. It was, the Court of Appeal said, impossible to provide more precise guidance. In *Crow* (1995) 16 Cr App R (S) 409 it was said that, when fixing the length of a longer-than-normal sentence, account should be taken of the age of the offender (in that the risk which the offender represented to the public might be expected to decline over time), some allowance should normally be made for a guilty plea (even in the worst case) and a sentence imposed under s. 2(2)(b) should still bear a 'reasonable relationship' to the offence for which it was imposed, but in *Bowler* (1994) 15 Cr App R (S) 78 the Court of Appeal said that when a sentence is being passed to protect the public, matters of mitigation, such as a guilty plea, the impulsive nature of the offence and the offender's limited intelligence, would carry less weight than in the case of a proportionate sentence. The decisions in *Campbell* [1997] 1 Cr App R (S) 119 and *Gabbidon* [1997] 2 Cr App R (S) 19 make it clear that, in cases where a very long proportionate sentence imposed under s. 2(2)(a) would in any event be justifiable on the facts of the offence (proportionate custodial terms of 15 years would have been appropriate for rape in the former case and for robbery in the latter case), the court may still pass a longer-than-normal sentence under s. 2(2)(b) where the criteria for such a sentence are made out, even though commensurate sentences of such length would already contain a significant element of public protection. Care should be taken, however, to ensure that the balance referred to in *Mansell* is preserved: the need to protect the public should not produce a sentence which is out of all proportion to the offending behaviour. A total sentence of 20 years was reduced to 17 years in *Campbell*, and 27 years reduced to 20 years in *Gabbidon*. At the other end of the scale, in *Carpenter* [1997] 1 Cr App R (S) 4, where the proportionate sentence for the offence of indecent assault would, in the view of the Court of Appeal, have been no more than two years on a guilty plea, but where a longer-than-normal sentence was appropriate in light of the offender's record and the risk which he posed, the addition of a further 12 months was the maximum that could be justified having regard to the offence.

4.4.4 Concurrent and consecutive custodial sentences and the totality principle

When an offender is convicted on more than one count, the court should pass separate sentences on each count. If custodial sentences are passed in respect of two or more offences the court may order that the sentences must be served either at the same time as, or successively to, each other. In the former case the sentences are said to be *concurrent*; in the latter case they are said to be *consecutive*. Where sentences are concurrent, the aggregate term will be the longest of the individual terms passed. Where sentences are consecutive, the aggregate term will be the total of the individual terms. These principles apply to sentences of imprisonment, to terms of detention in a young offender institution (see CJA 1982, s. 1A(5)) and, when the relevant provisions of the CDB become law and are brought into force, a detention and training order. It is open to the sentencer to make some terms run concurrently with each other but consecutively to other terms. In some cases this may lead to a complex sentencing pattern (see, for example, *Prime* (1983) 5 Cr App R (S) 127, below). If a sentencer fails to state when passing sentence whether a term is to be served concurrently or consecutively to another term, the sentences are presumed to be concurrent. Similarly, if an offender is already serving a custodial sentence when he appears to be sentenced for a further offence, the court may make any further custodial sentence it imposes for the new offence concurrent or consecutive to the term being served, though this is subject to CJA 1991, s. 40 (see **4.5.1**).

A determinate custodial sentence may not run consecutively to a life sentence (*Foy* [1962] 1 WLR 609) nor vice versa (*Jones* v *DPP* [1962] AC 635). Where sentence is passed on an offender under CJA 1991, s. 2(2)(b), a custodial sentence imposed at the same time for other matters must be ordered to run concurrently with and not consecutively to it (*Walters* [1997] 2 Cr App R (S) 87). Terms of imprisonment may be made to run consecutively to each other even though the result is that the aggregate term exceeds the maximum which could have been imposed for any one of the offences concerned. Thus in *Blake* [1962] 2 QB 377 the offender was convicted of five offences under the Official Secrets Act 1911, and an aggregate sentence of 42 years was upheld, even though the maximum sentence available for a single offence was 14 years. Similarly, in *Prime* an aggregate sentence of 38 years was passed (on one indictment) for seven offences contrary to the Official Secrets Act 1911 and (on a second indictment) three offences of indecent assault. The offender was sentenced to 14 years on each of two counts on the first indictment, to run consecutively, and to seven years on each of the remaining five counts, to run concurrently with each other but consecutively to the other terms. The total sentence on the first indictment was, therefore, 35 years. On the second indictment the total sentence was three years, made to run consecutively to the 35 years, making a grand total of 38 years.

It will be recalled that the maximum sentence of detention in a young offender institution which can be imposed upon an offender aged 15, 16 or 17 is 24 months (see **4.3.2**). This restriction cannot be circumvented by imposing shorter consecutive sentences whose total exceeds 24 months. Section 1B(4) of CJA 1982 states that a court shall not pass a sentence of detention in a young offender institution upon an offender to whom the 24-month maximum applies where its effect is to impose a total term in excess of that period. In the event of such a sentence being passed, so much of the term as exceeds 24 months is treated as remitted. When the sentence of detention in a young offender institution is replaced by the sentence of detention and training for offenders in this age bracket (see **4.3.10**) the same principle will continue to apply to the new sentence.

It is wrong in principle to pass consecutive custodial terms for two or more offences if to do so would, in effect, punish the offender twice for what was really one crime. Thus in *Coker* [1984] Crim LR 184 the offender attacked a young woman as she was walking across a field. He struck her repeatedly about the face, tore off most of her clothing, and indecently assaulted her. He was sentenced to two years' imprisonment for the indecent assault and three years consecutive for assault occasioning actual bodily harm. The Court of Appeal held that, as the facts of the two offences were inextricably linked, the terms should have been concurrent. Even where, unlike *Coker*, the offender has committed two quite distinct offences, sentences imposed should still be concurrent where the offences arise out of the same set of facts: the 'same occasion' or the 'same transaction', as it is sometimes put. Thus in *Jones* (1980) 2 Cr App R (S) 152 the Court of Appeal held that consecutive terms of 12 months and six months respectively for driving while disqualified and driving with excess alcohol could not be justified, since the two offences were committed on the same occasion. The decisions in this area are not consistent, however. In *Wheatley* (1983) 5 Cr App R (S) 417, a sentence of 12 months for driving while disqualified was ordered to run consecutively to a sentence of six months for driving with excess alcohol. The reasoning behind the sentence was that, if the sentences were concurrent, Wheatley, who was a persistent offender, might think that he could drive with excess alcohol and incur no additional penalty for the breach of disqualification. This case was followed and applied in *Jordan* [1996] 1 Cr App R (S) 181.

It is well established that sentencers must have regard to the total length of the sentence passed, particularly where consecutive sentences have been imposed, to ensure that the sentence properly reflects the overall seriousness of the behaviour. This effect will not be achieved merely by adding the sentences of a multiple offender together, for this will soon result in a total sentence out of all proportion to the kind of offending which has taken place. This principle, which has its clearest application in relation to custodial sentences, has achieved oblique recognition in CJA 1991, s. 28(2)(b), which states that nothing shall prevent a court 'in the case of an offender who is convicted of one or more other offences, from mitigating his sentence by applying any rule of law as to the totality of sentences'. The Court of Appeal's development of the totality principle has been most associated with custodial sentencing, but the statutory provision clearly also applies to fines and to community orders.

If offences are committed on different occasions, or are not part of the 'same transaction', there is no objection to imposing consecutive sentences, but this approach should not be regarded as inevitable. In *Hill* (1983) 5 Cr App R (S) 214 a sentence of six months' imprisonment for burglary from a factory on 30 July 1982 was said to have been rightly imposed consecutively to a sentence of 12 months for burglary from a garage on 7 August 1982. Bearing in mind the totality principle, it may be more convenient for the sentencer, particularly when sentencing for a series of similar offences, to pass a proportionate sentence for the most serious offence, coupled with shorter, concurrent terms for the less serious matters. In that way the various terms reflect the relative seriousness of the offences for which they are imposed, but the overall punishment remains in proportion to the overall gravity of the offender's criminal conduct. There are some situations in which the Court of Appeal has stressed the need to impose consecutive custodial terms. This approach should be taken, *inter alia*, where the offender has used violence against a police officer to resist arrest for another offence (e.g. *Fitter* (1983) 5 Cr App R (S) 168) or has used violence against a householder to make good his escape from the scene of a burglary (e.g. *Bunch* (1971) CSP A5-2C01). Sentences should also normally be consecutive where the offender carries a firearm while committing another offence (*French* (1982) 4 Cr App R (S) 57). In *Attorney-General's Reference (No. 1 of 1990)* (1990) 12 Cr App R (S) 245 the Court of Appeal said that consecutive sentences for indecent assault and perverting the course of justice should have been imposed in a case where the offender had written to the victim of the indecent assault from prison, while on remand, in an attempt to dissuade him from giving evidence. A custodial sentence imposed for escaping from custody should run consecutively to the sentence which was being served at the time of the escape (*Clarke* (1994) 15 Cr App R (S) 825). There is authority in *Young* (1973) CSP A5-2FO1 and in *Hunnybun* (1979) CSP A5-2FO2 that consecutive sentences should normally be passed where the offender commits one offence on bail which was granted in respect of the other offence. It is not clear how this squares with the principle that the second offence must be regarded as more serious by virtue of it having been committed by an offender on bail (see **2.2.2(f)**).

4.4.5 Taking account of time served on remand

A sentencer passing a custodial sentence on an offender may not infrequently be dealing with a person who has already spent weeks or months on remand in custody awaiting trial and/or sentence. Section 67 of the Criminal Justice Act 1967 (CJA 1967) provides that, if an offender spends time in custody awaiting trial and/or sentence, the term of any sentence of imprisonment ultimately passed on him shall be treated as reduced by the period in custody. If an offender is remanded in custody by magistrates prior to summary trial or committal proceedings, and/or is committed for trial or sentence in custody, and/or is remanded in custody after conviction and before sentence, the period for which he is thus detained is deducted from the sentence which he eventually has to serve. Occasionally this can mean, in a case where the sentence is short, that the term has already been served by the date on which it is imposed, so that the offender is entitled to release immediately after sentence.

Although CJA 1967, s. 67 is expressed in terms of the effect of time spent on remand upon a sentence of imprisonment, it is clear that it also counts towards a sentence of detention in a young offender institution, a determinate sentence imposed under CYPA 1933, s. 53(2) and, when the relevant provisions of the CDB become law and are brought into force, a detention and training order. It should also be noted that a suspended sentence is a sentence of imprisonment, so a sentencer passing a suspended sentence should take account of any time spent by the offender in custody on remand when fixing the length of the term which is to be suspended (*Practice Direction (Crime: Suspended Sentence)* [1970] 1 WLR 259). In one sense this has no direct impact on the offender, but if the suspended sentence were subsequently to be activated, the reduction would have practical effect.

Of course CJA 1967, s. 67 does not apply if the offender would have been in custody anyway for the relevant period, such as where he was serving a custodial term for an earlier offence. Nor does it apply to time spent in custody in a foreign country awaiting extradition to this country in respect of the offence being dealt with. Section 47 of CJA 1991 makes it clear that the sentencer has a discretion to take such period, or part of such period, into account when fixing sentence length. In *Scalise* (1985) 7 Cr App R (S) 395 this was said by Lawton LJ to be the 'normal' approach. In *Stone* (1988) 10 Cr App R (S) 322 the Court of Appeal upheld the judge's decision to take only part of the period into account, in view of the offender's challenge to the extradition proceedings. CJA 1967, s. 67 does not extend to a case where the offender is held in custody in respect of an offence which is subsequently taken into consideration, though in *Towers* (1987) 9 Cr App R (S) 333 it was said to be appropriate to make some allowance in those circumstances.

The operation of these provisions has given rise to problems of interpretation recently, in respect both of consecutive and concurrent sentences. In *Secretary of State for the Home Department, ex parte Naughton* [1997] 1 Cr App R (S) 151 the Divisional Court dealt with a case where the applicant had been sentenced to 18 months' imprisonment for each of two offences, and the sentences had been ordered to run consecutively. The offender had spent 81 days on remand in custody in respect of the first offence, and a further 239 days on remand in custody for both offences. The issue was the extent of the 'relevant period' which had to be deducted. The Divisional Court, having regard to CJA 1967, s. 104(2), held that the relevant period for the purposes of s. 67(1) was not two times 239 days, as the offender had contended, but 81 *plus* 239 days. Section 104(2) provides that for the purpose of the 1967 Act references 'to the term of imprisonment or other detention to which a person has been sentenced or which, or part of which, he has served, consecutive terms and terms which are wholly or partly concurrent shall be treated as a single term'. At the time of the decision in *Ex parte Naughton*, the position in respect of an offender sentenced to concurrent terms of imprisonment for two offences, who had spent time on remand in custody for the first offence but no time on remand in custody for the second offence, was that the remand time did not affect the sentence for the second offence and thus had no impact on the concurrent sentence at all. This could clearly operate very unfairly in some cases, and the relevant authorities were doubted in *Ex parte Naughton*. Subsequently, in *Governor of Brockhill Prison, ex parte Evans* [1997] 1 Cr App R (S) 282, the Divisional Court changed the rule and held that where concurrent sentences are imposed on a defendant in respect of offences for which he has spent separate periods on remand in custody, the term which he is required to serve would be reduced by the remand time relating to the first offence *plus* the remand time relating to the second offence, provided that these remand periods do not overlap. An overlapping period would count once, not twice.

The C(S)A 1997 contains provisions which, if brought into force, will repeal CJA 1967, s. 67 and replace it with new arrangements for the crediting of periods of remand in custody under s. 9 of the 1997 Act.

4.5 SENTENCING AND EARLY RELEASE

While the sentencer is responsible for fixing the length of the custodial sentence and for announcing that term in open court, the actual period to be served by the offender is affected by the operation of early release arrangements and, in some cases, by subsequent decisions made by the Parole Board. Traditionally, there was a strongly held view that sentencing decisions and early release decisions were entirely separate matters, the former for the judiciary and the latter for the executive authorities, and that the sentencer should put considerations about remission and parole (as they were then termed) out of his mind when sentencing for the offence (*Maguire* (1956) 40 Cr App R 92; *Oules* (1986) 8 Cr App R (S) 124). This was true whether the adjustment which the sentencer was minded to make would involve shortening or lengthening the sentence. Thus in *Kenway* (1985) 7 Cr App R (S) 457, Taylor J said that 'it is well established that to take account of parole when passing sentence is improper'. The main reason for this was that since the operation of remission and parole was highly discretionary, there was no certainty whether an offender being sentenced would subsequently benefit from them.

Important changes were brought about by the CJA 1991 which apply to offenders sentenced after 1 October 1992 and so have taken some years to filter through the entire custodial population. The CJA 1991 brought about a radical overhaul of the arrangements for early release, implementing many of the recommendations of the Carlisle Committee Report (1988). As a result, subject to their good behaviour when in custody, most offenders who receive custodial sentences now know at the time of their sentence what their actual release date will be. There is much greater correlation for short-term prisoners between the sentence imposed and the time served. On the other hand, some discretion over the release date for long-term prisoners remains in the hands of the executive authorities. The sanctions for breach of licence and for the reinstatement of the unexpired part of a sentence upon commission of a further offence under CJA 1991, s. 40, may well operate more severely than was the case before the Act.

A new relationship between sentencing and early release decisions, encouraged in the Carlisle Committee Report, can now be seen, but has taken some years to come about. After the 1991 Act Lord Taylor of Gosforth CJ issued an important *Practice Statement (Crime: Sentencing)* [1992] 1 WLR 948, in which he explained that it would henceforth be necessary for sentencers to have regard to the period in custody which would actually be served by the offender in consequence of the early release provisions of the Act, as compared to the period in custody which the offender would have served subject to remission and parole. See further on this, **4.5.3**. The Act itself also extended the situations in which a sentencer may exercise a direct influence over early release arrangements. Crown Court sentencers are, by the Murder (Abolition of Death Penalty) Act 1965, s. 1(2), able to make a recommendation as to the minimum period to be served under a mandatory sentence of life imprisonment for murder. Under CJA 1991, s. 34 (a provision subsequently repealed and replaced by the C(S)A 1997, s. 28) a sentencer in the Crown Court may (and normally will) specify what period of a discretionary life sentence must expire before the case is first referred to the Parole Board. Section 28 is described further at **4.5.2**. Also, by s. 44 of the 1991 Act, when sentencing for a 'sexual offence', a sentencer may require that the offender, after release on licence, must serve out the full term of his sentence under supervision rather than, as would otherwise be the case, receiving unconditional release after serving three quarters of the full term. Section 44 is described further at **4.5.4**.

The Carlisle Committee Report envisaged that sentencers would routinely explain to offenders (and to the public) how much of the custodial sentence would actually be served in custody and how much in the community. This step has now, belatedly perhaps, been taken, with the issuing of a further Practice Direction, this time by Lord Bingham of Cornhill CJ. The *Practice Direction (Custodial Sentences: Explanations)* [1998] 1 WLR 278 has, apparently, been issued mainly in response to Home Office research indicating widespread misconceptions about sentencing, which were said to be undermining public confidence in the sentencing system:

> It was desirable that when sentence was passed the practical effect of the sentence should be understood by the defendant, any victim and any member of the public who was present in court or read a full report of the proceedings.
>
> In future, whenever a custodial sentence is imposed on an offender, the court should explain the practical effect of the sentence in addition to complying with existing statutory requirements. That would be no more than an explanation; the sentence would be that pronounced by the court.
>
> Sentencers should give the explanation in terms of their own choosing, taking care to ensure that the explanation is clear and accurate. No form of words is prescribed. Annexed are short statements which might, adapted as necessary, be of value as models.

In the following paragraphs the current system for early release from custodial sentences is outlined, and attention is drawn to the implications of these matters for sentencing.

4.5.1 Determinate sentences and the Criminal Justice Act 1991, s. 40

The CJA 1991 abolished the long-established distinction between remission and parole and put in its place the single concept of early release. The abolition of remission requires that disciplinary offences in prison, formerly sanctioned by loss of remission, are now dealt with by the award of additional days in custody (CJA 1991, s. 42).

Adult determinate sentence prisoners fall into one of three categories:

(a) offenders serving a sentence of less than 12 months;
(b) offenders serving terms of 12 months or more but less than four years (short-term prisoners);
(c) offenders serving terms of four years or more (long-term prisoners).

For an offender serving a sentence of less than 12 months, release is automatic after half the sentence has been served, unless release is delayed because additional days have been added. There is no supervision on licence. For short-term prisoners, release is automatic after serving half the sentence, again, unless release is delayed because additional days have been added, but there is supervision under licence by a probation officer for these offenders, which will last until the three-quarter point of the sentence. Failure by a short-term prisoner to comply with the conditions of a licence is made a summary offence punishable by a fine (CJA 1991, s. 38(1)) but it may also be dealt with by termination of the licence and recall to prison. A long-term prisoner must be released after serving two thirds of the sentence, and there may be discretionary release at a point somewhere between one half and two thirds of the sentence, to be determined in accordance with a recommendation made in each case by the Parole Board. Supervision on licence will last from the point of release until the three-quarter point of the sentence. In the event of breach of licence conditions by a long-term prisoner, the Home Secretary may revoke the licence and recall the prisoner to custody where it appears to be expedient to do so. This may be done with or without the recommendation of the Parole Board. A breach of licence by a long-term prisoner may not be dealt with by way of a fine. For all practical purposes these arrangements also apply to young offenders given a custodial sentence of detention in a young offender institution or a determinate sentence under CYPA 1933, s. 53(2).

The Parole Board retains its pivotal role in the system of early release, but its workload is much reduced in comparison with the arrangements which applied before the implementation of the CJA 1991. It retains a discretion over the actual date of release in many fewer cases than before that Act. The Parole Board now needs to make such a decision in respect only of long-term offenders (serving sentences of four years or more). Local Review Committees, which exercised discretion over release in the case of shorter sentence prisoners prior to the CJA 1991, have been abolished. The Home Secretary sits at the apex of the parole machinery, and the Parole Board makes its recommendations on early release to him. The Home Secretary is not able to release an offender without such a recommendation but, in the case of any offender serving a custodial sentence of seven years or more, is not bound to follow the Board's positive advice. This power in the Home Secretary (known as the 'veto') is controversial. The Carlisle Committee recommended that this particular power should be abolished and that Parole Board decisions should be final, but this suggestion was not adopted by the government. In the case of an offender serving at least four years but less than seven years a recommendation for release from the Parole Board is binding on the Home Secretary (see CJA 1991, s. 50).

For any prisoner, whether short-term or long-term, who commits a further offence punishable with imprisonment during the period from the date of release from custody until the expiry of the full term of the sentence, the sentencing court dealing with the new offence 'may, whether or not it passes any other sentence on him, order him to be returned to prison' (CJA 1991, s. 40(2)). Section 40 has been the subject of recent judicial interpretation, and is set out here in full. It provides that:

(1)   This section applies to a short-term or long-term prisoner who is released under this Part if—

(a)   before the date on which he would (but for his release) have served his sentence in full, he commits an offence punishable with imprisonment; and

(b)   whether before or after that date, he is convicted of that offence ('the new offence').

(2)   Subject to subsection (3) below, the court by or before which a person to whom this section applies is convicted of the new offence may, whether or not it passes any other sentence on him, order him to be returned to prison for the whole or any part of the period which—

(a)   begins with the date of the order; and

(b)   is equal in length to the period between the date on which the new offence was committed and the date mentioned in subsection (1) above.

(3)   A magistrates' court—

(a)   shall not have power to order a person to whom this section applies to be returned to prison for a period of more than six months; but

(b)   subject to section 25 of the Criminal Justice and Public Order Act 1994, may commit him in custody or on bail to the Crown Court for sentence and the Crown Court to which he has been so committed may make such an order with regard to him as is mentioned in subsection (2) above.

(4)   The period for which a person to whom this section applies is ordered under subsection (2) to be returned to prison—

(a)   shall be taken to be a sentence of imprisonment for the purposes of this Part;

(b)   shall, as the court may direct, either be served before and be followed by, or be served concurrently with, the sentence imposed for the new offence; and

(c)   in either case, shall be disregarded in determining the appropriate length of that sentence.

Section 40 only applies where the original sentence was a determinate sentence of imprisonment, a term of detention in a young offender institution, or a term of detention under CYPA 1933, s. 53(2). When the relevant provisions become law and are brought into force, a provision equivalent to s. 40 will be applicable to offenders who commit a further offence during the period of supervision of a detention and training order (see **4.3.10**). Section 40 is not applicable where the original sentence was an indeterminate one. It should be noted that s. 40 applies whether or not the conviction for the new offence takes place after the expiry of the full term of the original sentence; what matters is whether the new offence was committed before that date. The exercise of the power to return the offender to prison is discretionary, and the court may order the offender to be returned for the full period indicated in the section, a lesser period, or not at all.

It was held in *Harrow Justices, ex parte Jordan* [1997] 1 Cr App R (S) 410 that, where an offender who is liable to be returned to custody under s. 40 is convicted in a magistrates' court, the magistrates should deal with both the sentence for the new offence and the order for return to custody, or should commit the offender to the Crown Court in respect of both matters. Lord Bingham of Cornhill CJ, in the Divisional Court, stated that committal to the Crown Court would be appropriate where the new offence is one of any gravity and where a significant part of the licence period is unexpired. This might sometimes entail that the magistrates would be committing a purely summary offence for the Crown Court to deal with. In *Worthing and District Justices, ex parte Varley* [1998] 1 Cr App R (S) 175 the issue arose whether a magistrates' court could both make an order returning an offender to custody under s. 40 and impose the custodial sentence for the new offence to run consecutively to it where the aggregate exceeded the maximum aggregate term of imprisonment which that court could impose (normally six months: Magistrates' Courts Act 1980, s. 133). The Divisional Court held that it could do so, since an order that the offender be returned to custody under s. 40 is not, in any ordinary sense, a sentence of imprisonment, but is an order to reactivate custody from which the offender had been prematurely released. Section 40(4)(a), which states that a period of return ordered under s. 40 'shall be taken to be a sentence of imprisonment' is not relevant. Its purpose is to deem the reactivated term to be a term of imprisonment for purposes of the early release provisions of the 1991 Act. If a custodial sentence is imposed for the new offence, the section makes it clear that the sentence may run concurrently with, or consecutively to, the reinstated period, but that the reinstated period cannot run consecutively to the sentence for the new offence (s. 40(4) and *Clerkenwell Crown Court, ex parte Feely* [1996] 2 Cr App R (S) 309). If the sentence imposed for the new offence is a sentence passed for a violent or sexual offence under CJA 1991, s. 2(2)(b), any reinstated period required to be served under s. 40 should run concurrently with the sentence for the new offence. This is because a sentence under

s. 2(2)(b) is imposed for reasons of public protection, and it makes no sense to order such a sentence to start from a future date (*Johnson* [1997] Crim LR 609). In *Foran* [1996] 1 Cr App R (S) 149 the Court of Appeal considered the application of s. 40 in the case of an offender aged 15, 16 or 17, for whom the total term of detention in a young offender institution must not exceed 24 months (CJA 1982, s. 1B(2) and see **4.3.2**). The Court held that when exercising the power under s. 40 in such a case the full duration of the reinstated period and the sentence for the new offence must not, taken together, exceed 24 months.

4.5.2 Life sentences and the Crime (Sentences) Act 1997, s. 28

It is necessary to distinguish between the early release arrangements for offenders aged 18 and over serving a mandatory life sentence for murder, and those serving other forms of life sentence. The mandatory sentence of life imprisonment (for those of 21 and over) and the mandatory sentence of custody for life for murder (for those aged 18, 19 or 20) were discussed at **4.3.4**, and will not be further considered here.

When imposing any other form of life sentence the sentencer is given power under the C(S)A 1997, s. 28, to specify the period which must elapse before the offender serving the life sentence can be considered for early release. The life sentences in respect of which the power under s. 28 may be exercised are, then, an automatic life sentence imposed under C(S)A 1997, s. 2 for the second 'serious offence' (see **4.3.5**), a discretionary sentence of life imprisonment (see **4.3.6**), a discretionary sentence of custody for life under the CJA 1982, s. 8(2) (see **4.3.7**), a sentence of detention for life under the CYPA 1933, s. 53(2) (see **4.3.8**) and (although that sentence is applicable only in murder cases) a sentence of detention during Her Majesty's pleasure under CYPA 1933, s. 53(1). The part of the sentence specified in the order shall, by C(S)A 1997, s. 28(3), be:

... such part as the court considers appropriate, taking into account—

(a) the seriousness of the offence, or the combination of the offence and other offences associated with it, and

(b) the effect of any direction which it would have given under section 9 above [not yet in force] if it had sentenced him to a term of imprisonment [and

(c) the provisions of this section as compared with those of sections 33(2) and 35(1) of the 1991 Act].

The effect of specifying part of the sentence under s. 28 is that the life prisoner will not become eligible to be considered for early release until the expiry of that period. If the sentencer does not order that s. 28 shall apply in respect of the life prisoner, 'the Secretary of State shall direct that this section shall apply to him as soon as he has served a part of his sentence specified in the direction' (s. 28(4)). For a person serving more than one discretionary life sentence the court may make an order under s. 28 in respect of each of those sentences, with that person becoming eligible for consideration for early release 'after he has served the relevant part of each of those sentences' (s. 34(1)). If the court does not make an order in respect of each of the sentences, s. 28(4) will apply.

The power in s. 28 to specify a part of the sentence to be served by a discretionary life sentence offender before he can be considered for early release replaces the equivalent power in CJA 1991, s. 34, which was repealed by the 1997 Act. It is important to note that s. 28 is applicable in respect of offenders sentenced on or after 1 October 1997, irrespective of the date on which the offence was committed (1997 Act, s. 34(2)).

Given the close similarities between s. 28 of the 1997 Act and s. 34 of the 1991 Act, it may be helpful to refer to some of the Court of Appeal guidance on the operation of s. 34. In *Practice Direction (Crime: Life Sentences)* [1993] 1 WLR 223, Lord Taylor of Gosforth CJ said that the sentencer should normally specify the relevant period, the only exception being the rare case where the sentencer thinks that the offender should never be released, and that if the judge decided not to specify a period he should state this in open court when passing sentence. A decision not to specify might be the subject of an appeal (*Hollies* (1995) 16 Cr App R (S) 463). When specifying the relevant period the judge should have regard to the specific terms of the section, and should indicate the reasons for the decision. It was also established with respect to s. 34 that before specifying the relevant period the sentencer should permit counsel for the defence to address the court on the appropriate length of the relevant part. It was held that an order under s. 34 may be the subject of an appeal (*D* (1995) 16 Cr App R (S) 564).

Section 28(3)(a) mirrors an equivalent provision in s. 34(2)(a). In *Lundberg* (1995) 16 Cr App R (S) 948 the Court of Appeal emphasised that, when having regard to the seriousness of the offence, or the combination of the offence and other offences associated with it, the section permitted the sentencer to look at the totality of the associated offences, rather than just the offence for which the life sentence was being passed, and to consider whether, if a life sentence had not been given, the sentences for the associated offences would have been consecutive to the main sentence. See also *Haan* [1996] 1 Cr App R (S) 267.

Section 28(3)(b) makes reference to s. 9 of the 1997 Act. Section 9 is not in force. If it is brought into force, s. 9 will replace CJA 1967, s. 67 (effect of time spent in custody on remand: see **4.4.5**). When fixing the period to be served by a discretionary life sentence prisoner under s. 34 of the 1991 Act the sentencer was required to take into account any period spent by the offender in custody on remand which would be deducted from a determinate sentence under the CJA 1967, s. 67. By para. 5(1) of sch. 5 to the Crime (Sentences) Act 1997, it is provided that:

> In relation to any time before the commencement of section 9 of this Act, section 28 of this Act shall have effect as if, in paragraph (b) of subsection (3), for the words 'of any direction it would have given section 9 above' there were substituted the words 'which section 67 of the Criminal Justice Act 1967 would have had'.

Therefore, whether or not s. 9 is brought into force, s. 28(3)(b) requires the sentencer to take account of any period spent by the offender in custody on remand. The position is, therefore, effectively the same as it was in relation to s. 34 of the 1991 Act.

Section 28(3)(c) mirrors an equivalent provision in s. 34(2)(b). It will be noted that para. (c) as set out above appears in square brackets. This is because sch. 5, para. 5(2), provides that:

> In relation to any time before the commencement of Chapter I of Part II of this Act, section 28(3) of this Act shall have effect as if after paragraph (b) the words 'and (c) the provisions of this section as compared with those of s. 33(2) and 35(1) of the 1991 Act' were inserted.

Since it now seems clear that Chapter I of Part II of the 1997 Act (which would have restructured the arrangements for early release of prisoners) will not be brought into force, s. 28(3) is set out, above, as if it contained those additional words. Their effect is to require a sentencer exercising power under s. 28 to take into account the fact that under ss. 33(2) and 35(1) of the 1991 Act a prisoner who has received a determinate long-term sentence is entitled to be released after serving two thirds of his term and may be released after serving only a half of his term. The position is, therefore, effectively the same as it was in relation to s. 34 of the 1991 Act. Court of Appeal guidance indicated that the period specified under s. 34 of the 1991 Act should be set at between one half and two thirds of the determinate sentence. It seems that when identifying the notional determinate sentence the judge should make appropriate allowance for any mitigating factors in the case, such as the offender's guilty plea (*Meek* (1995) 16 Cr App R (S) 1003). In *Attorney-General's Reference (No. 6 of 1993)* (1994) 15 Cr App R (S) 375 the Court of Appeal held that, in respect of a 20-year-old offender convicted of rape and robbery, who had previous convictions for rape, sexual assault and burglary, having regard to the seriousness of the latest offences and apart from the element of risk, the proper determinate sentence in the case would have been 12 years. This was, however, 'a case in which the only sentence which could possibly be contemplated, in terms of protecting the public, is a life sentence' (Lord Taylor of Gosforth CJ, at p. 380). The relevant period to be fixed under s. 34, therefore, had to fall somewhere between a half and two thirds of 12 years, and the court accordingly specified eight years as the relevant period. In *O'Connor* (1994) 15 Cr App R (S) 473, where the offender was given a life sentence after being convicted of manslaughter on the ground of diminished responsibility, the Court of Appeal reduced the period specified by the trial judge from 12 years to seven years, observing that the judge may well have taken the first step of fixing the determinate sentence, but had perhaps then failed to take the second step of deciding upon such proportion of that determinate sentence as fell between a half and two thirds of the determinate sentence. Other decisions on s. 34 include *Richards* [1996] 1 Cr App R (S) 167, *Brandy* [1997] 1 Cr App R (S) 38, *Razzaque* [1997] 1 Cr App R (S) 154 and *Parker* [1997] 1 Cr App R (S) 259.

Unlike s. 34 of the 1991 Act, the power conferred by s. 28 of the 1997 Act is not, on the face of it, confined to cases where the discretionary life sentence is imposed for a violent or sexual offence within the meaning of s. 31 of the 1991 Act. It is now clear that a discretionary life sentence can only be imposed for a violent or sexual offence (see **4.3.6**) so this change of wording has no effect as far as discretionary life sentences are concerned. However, in the case of an automatic life sentence imposed for the 'second serious offence', under the C(S)A 1997, s. 2, there is no requirement that the second such offence which, subject to exceptional circumstances, will trigger the automatic life sentence, need be a violent or sexual offence within the meaning of s. 31 (see **4.3.5**).

4.5.3 Practice Statement on early release arrangements

It was readily apparent that when the CJA 1991 was implemented early release arrangements would, without appropriate adjustment to sentencing levels, have resulted in many offenders serving longer, sometimes substantially longer, terms in custody than those given similar sentences before 1 October 1992. The offenders who would have been most affected by these changes were those given sentences in the range between 12 months and up to four years, whose early release cannot now occur until half the term has been served. Formerly, a substantial number of those offenders were granted discretionary parole after they had completed one third of their sentence. In *Practice Statement (Crime: Sentencing)* [1992] 1 WLR 948, issued to coincide with the coming into force of the CJA 1991, Lord Taylor of Gosforth CJ stated that:

It has been an axiomatic principle of sentencing policy until now that the court should decide the appropriate sentence in each case without reference to questions of remission or parole. I have consulted the Lords Justices presiding in the Court of Appeal (Criminal Division) and we have decided that a new approach is essential. Accordingly, from 1 October 1992, it will be necessary, when passing a custodial sentence in the Crown Court, to have regard to the actual period likely to be served and, as far as practicable, to the risk of offenders serving longer under the new system than would have been normal under the old. Existing guideline judgments should be applied with these considerations in mind.

In *Cunningham* [1993] 1 WLR 183 Lord Taylor of Gosforth CJ emphasised that the 1992 *Practice Statement* did not require 'an arithmetically precise calculation to be made'. Its object was to alert sentencers to the changed regime of early release and to require them to have regard to the possible effects of passing sentences after October 1992 of the same length as those they would have passed before. The Court of Appeal, he said, would be concerned in an appropriate case with whether the custodial term imposed by a sentencer was correct under the criteria contained in the CJA 1991, but would be unmoved 'by nice arithmetical comparisons between periods under the old and new regimes'.

Apart from this general advice on custodial sentence length, earlier decisions which permitted a sentencer to adjust sentence length to avoid an unusual and adverse effect upon an offender's release date would still appear to be valid (see *Waite* (1992) 13 Cr App R (S) 26 and *Cozens* [1996] 2 Cr App R (S) 321). In the latter case the Court of Appeal dealt with a case where a sentence of six months for breach of bail had been ordered to run consecutively to a sentence of 42 months for importation of cannabis. The effect was to make the offender a long-term prisoner, and to require him to serve up to an additional 11 months in custody. In order to avoid that effect the Court of Appeal reduced the sentence for the bail offence to three months. On the other hand, it seems that nothing in the 1992 *Practice Statement* should be taken to detract from the general principle that a sentencer should not increase sentence length merely to bring an offender within a different early release category (see *Kenway* (1985) 7 Cr App R (S) 457). Such a course would appear to be contrary to the general requirement of proportionality in CJA 1991, s. 2(2)(a).

As was explained in **4.5** above, the Court of Appeal has now issued a *Practice Direction (Custodial Sentences: Explanations)* [1988] 1 WLR 278, which requires a sentencer who imposes a custodial sentence to explain its practical effect in terms of the actual period to be served in custody.

4.5.4   Sexual offences: extension of licence period

Where an offender is sentenced to imprisonment, detention in a young offender institution or a determinate sentence under CYPA 1933, s. 53(2), the sentence is for 12 months or more and the whole or part of the custodial sentence is imposed for a 'sexual offence' (as defined in CJA 1991, s. 31: see **4.2.7**), the sentencer may, at the time of passing sentence, also make an order under CJA 1991, s. 44. Its effect is that the offender, after release from custody, will remain on licence for the whole term of the sentence, rather than such licence expiring (as would otherwise be the case) at the three-quarter point of the sentence.

In making such an order, the court must have regard to the need to protect the public from serious harm and the desirability of preventing the commission by the offender of further offences and of securing his rehabilitation. The restriction to sentences of 12 months or more means that this power is effectively confined to Crown Court sentencers. The Court of Appeal has indicated the appropriate use of the power under s. 44 in a number of cases. In particular, in *Attorney-General's Reference (No. 7 of 1996)* [1997] 1 Cr App R (S) 399 it increased a sentence of seven years' imprisonment together with an order under s. 44 for burglary with intent to rape, which had been imposed as a commensurate sentence under CJA 1991, s. 2(2)(a), to a sentence of 12 years, passed as a longer-than-normal sentence under s. 2(2)(b) of that Act. The offender had a long record of serious offending, including two convictions for rape. The Court also upheld the trial judge's order under s. 44 and applied it to the whole of the increased sentence, Lord Bingham of Cornhill CJ commending its use in appropriate cases to sentencers. His lordship stated that this was a section which gave the authorities additional control over an offender, since it affected both the period which an offender will serve if he is recalled to prison after release on licence and the period for which a prisoner will be supervised after release on licence. He added that in some parts of the country it was too little used. Other cases in which orders under s. 44 have been upheld are *Kennan* [1996] 1 Cr App R (S) 1 and *Samuels* (1995) 16 Cr App R (S) 856.

4.5.5 Sexual or violent offences: extended sentences

When the relevant provisions of the Crime and Disorder Bill become law and are brought into force, the power under s. 44 of the CJA 1991 described in **4.5.4** will be repealed and replaced by new powers to impose 'extended' custodial sentences on offenders convicted either of sexual or violent offences. The terms 'violent' and 'sexual' offences have the same meanings as in the CJA 1991, s. 31 (see **4.2.6**). The purpose of the proposed new provision is to allow the court to pass an 'extended sentence' in a case in which it thinks that the offender would otherwise be subject to a licence period which is inadequate for the purposes of (a) preventing the commission by him of further offences and (b) securing his rehabilitation. That extended sentence will be the sum of the custodial term which the court would otherwise have passed ('the custodial term') and a further period ('the extension period') during which the offender will be subject to a licence and which is itself of a length necessary to achieve the purposes (a) and (b) indicated above. The effect of clause 55 is to add a licence period to the end of the custodial sentence which the court would have imposed anyway, either as a proportionate sentence under CJA 1991, s. 2(2)(a) or as a longer-than-normal sentence for a violent or sexual offence under s. 2(2)(b). If the offence is a violent offence, the court shall not pass an extended sentence which is less than four years, and the extension period (i.e., the additional licence period) must not exceed five years. If the offence is a sexual offence there is no specified minimum for the length of the custodial term, but the extension period must not exceed 10 years (cl. 55(3) and (4)). In no case can the extended sentence exceed the maximum sentence for the offence committed (cl. 55(5)).

Where the court passes an extended sentence under cl. 55, cl. 56 explains what the effect of that will be on the offender's early release prospects. Clause 56 proposes to substitute a new s. 44 in the CJA 1991 (see **4.5.4**). According to cl. 56, the question whether the offender is a short-term or a long-term prisoner is to be determined by the overall length of the extended term imposed by the court. If the offender would otherwise have been released unconditionally (i.e., the extended term is for less than 12 months), the effect of an order will be that his release will be on licence until the end of the extension period. If the offender would otherwise have been released on licence (i.e., the extended term is for 12 months or more), the effect of an order under this clause is that the licence period, rather than ending at the three-quarter point of the sentence, will last until the end of the extension period. If the offender commits a new offence while on licence and the court, in addition to dealing with him for the new offence, decides to return the offender to custody under CJA 1991, s. 40 (see **4.5.1**), it appears from the new s. 44 that the extension period must be included when determining the duration of the period to be reinstated (cl. 47(2)). This means that an order under s. 40 can be made if the new offence is committed at any time within the entire licence period, including the 'extension period'.

4.6   THE SUSPENDED SENTENCE

A suspended sentence of imprisonment is one which will not be brought into effect unless the offender is convicted of an imprisonable offence committed during a period of time fixed by the court when it suspends the sentence. It is very important to notice that only a determinate sentence of imprisonment may be suspended: it is not possible to suspend any other custodial sentence, such as a sentence of detention in a young offender institution. The absence of such a power in respect of young offenders was regretted by Lord Lane CJ in *Dobbs* (1983) 5 Cr App R (S) 378, but there is now no prospect of the power of suspension being extended to other custodial sentences. Since suspended sentences are treated as sentences of imprisonment (PCCA 1973, s. 22(6)), and since all the statutory restrictions upon the imposition of immediate imprisonment also apply to them, it is appropriate to describe them in the part of this book dealing with custodial sentences. It will be apparent, however, that these sentences are merely *potentially* custodial. The court's hope when it suspends a sentence of imprisonment is that the question of activating it will never arise, because the offender will be deterred from further offending by the knowledge that he is subject to the suspended sentence. As we shall see, conviction for a further imprisonable offence during the operational period of a suspended sentence normally means that the suspended sentence is activated and served in full.

Suspended sentences were introduced by the CJA 1967. The present legislation on suspended sentences is contained in PCCA 1973, ss. 22–5, though these provisions were amended by the CJA 1991, most importantly by requiring that courts should impose a suspended sentence only in a case where there are 'exceptional circumstances'. This change has resulted in a sharp decline in the use of the suspended sentence.

Suspended sentences used to be popular with sentencers; they were imposed on over 21,000 offenders convicted of indictable offences in 1991, and by the Crown Court in 16 per cent of indictable offences. In 1996 the equivalent figures were 2,600 and 3 per cent. The main difficulty is that the suspended sentence, rooted as it is in a theory of achieving compliance through deterrence, sits uneasily within the desert framework of the CJA 1991. Another problem is the absurdity of allowing for suspension of prison sentences where sentences of detention in a young offender institution cannot be suspended, particularly since the CJA 1991 made the criteria for justifying custody the same for both classes of offenders.

4.6.1   The term which is to be suspended

The maximum term of imprisonment which may be suspended is *two years* or the maximum immediate term which the court could impose, whichever is the less (PCCA 1973, s. 22(1)). Thus a magistrates' court is normally limited to the imposition of a suspended sentence of no more than six months in length, since that is the normal maximum term of imprisonment which such a court can impose. There is no minimum fixed for the length of a prison sentence which may be suspended, but since the minimum sentence of immediate imprisonment which can be imposed by a magistrates' court is five days (MCA 1980, s. 132), this must also represent the shortest suspended sentence which can lawfully be passed by that court.

Where a court is dealing with an offender for several offences and it passes consecutive sentences of imprisonment for two of those offences, it may suspend the sentences only if the total term is less than two years. This is because PCCA 1973, s. 57(2) states that consecutive terms of imprisonment, and terms which are wholly or partly concurrent, shall be treated as single terms unless the context otherwise requires. In *Arkle* (1972) 56 Cr App R 722 the offender had been sentenced to three terms of nine months, all to run consecutively, and the court had purported to suspend the aggregate term of 27 months. It was held that the suspension was a nullity, with the consequence that commission of a further offence by the offender did not put him at risk of having the sentence activated. It seems that if a sentencer purports to suspend a sentence which he has no power to suspend, the sentence takes effect as a sentence of immediate imprisonment (*Arkle*). Oddly enough, it appears that a term of imprisonment imposed under the Vagrancy Act 1824, s. 10 may not be suspended, since the condition of being an incorrigible rogue is a status and not an offence (*Theophile* (1975) CSP A11-2B01).

The length of the term which is to be suspended must be that length which would have been appropriate had an immediate sentence of imprisonment been imposed instead. Thus a sentencer should not lengthen (nor, presumably, shorten) the term merely because it is to take effect as a suspended rather than an immediate sentence of imprisonment. This point was underlined in *Mah-Wing* (1983) 5 Cr App R (S) 347. Since sentence length has to be justified in terms of the criteria laid down in CJA 1991, s. 2 (primarily the seriousness of the offence), it follows that the length of the suspended term must also reflect the seriousness of the offence.

When fixing the length of the term, the sentencer should take into account any period of time already spent in custody by the offender in respect of that offence (*Practice Direction (Crime: Suspended Sentence)* [1970] 1 WLR 259). In a case where the offender has already been held in custody on remand for a period equivalent to the appropriate term of imprisonment for the offence, the sentence should be such as to secure his immediate release (*McCabe* (1988) 10 Cr App R (S) 134). Indeed, it is wrong in these circumstances to impose a suspended sentence at all (*Peppard* (1990) 12 Cr App R (S) 88).

4.6.2 The operational period

The operational period of the suspended sentence is that period during which commission of a further imprisonable offence will put the offender at risk of having the suspended sentence activated. That period must be not less than one and not more than two years (s. 22(1)). The precise length of the operational period is fixed by the court when it passes the suspended sentence. The period runs from the date of the sentence. In practice, operational periods tend to be three months, six months, 12 months, 18 months or two years. There appears to have been no appellate discussion of what principles might underlie the selection of operational period length. It is not clear, therefore, whether this period should reflect primarily the seriousness of the offence (as should the length of the term), or whether other matters, such as the sentencer's perception of the likelihood of the offender remaining conviction-free during a lengthy operational period, may properly be taken into account.

4.6.3   Justifying the imposition of a suspended sentence

PCCA 1973, s. 22(2), provides as follows:

(2)   A court shall not deal with an offender by means of a suspended sentence unless it is of the opinion —
(a)   that the case is one in which a sentence of imprisonment would have been appropriate even without the power to suspend the sentence; and
(b)   that the exercise of that power can be justified by the exceptional circumstances of the case.
(2A)   A court which passes a suspended sentence on any person for an offence shall consider whether the circumstances of the case are such as to warrant in addition the imposition of a fine or the making of a compensation order.

Section 22(2)(a) contains an important principle of sentencing in relation to the use of suspended sentences. A suspended sentence must not be imposed by a court unless the imposition of an immediate prison sentence would have been available to the sentencing court, and would have been appropriate for use in the particular case, in the absence of the power to suspend. A suspended sentence cannot be ordered unless all the statutory provisions as to the imposition of a sentence of immediate imprisonment, including those contained in CJA 1991, ss. 1–3, have been complied with. The court must be clear that it would have passed a sentence of immediate imprisonment in the absence of the power to suspend, and that such sentence would have been for a term of two years or less. It is important to remember that the power to impose a suspended sentence in a magistrates' court is limited just as the magistrates' powers to impose a sentence of immediate imprisonment are limited.

The question of whether a particular case would properly have been dealt with by an immediate custodial sentence in the absence of the power to suspend is, of course, a matter of judgment. The key question which must be asked is whether the offence, or the combination of the offence and one or more offences associated with it, was so serious that only a prison sentence could be justified. As Lord Parker CJ explained in *O'Keefe* [1969] 2 QB 29 (at p. 32):

it seems to this court that before one gets to a suspended sentence at all, the court must go through the process of eliminating other possible courses such as absolute discharge, conditional discharge, probation order, fines, and then say to itself: this is a case for imprisonment, and the final question, it being a case for imprisonment, should be: is immediate imprisonment required, or can a suspended sentence be given?

This principle still holds good after the CJA 1991.

The Court of Appeal has on numerous occasions quashed a suspended sentence because it did not accept that immediate imprisonment would have been correct on the facts of the particular case and considered that the imposition of a suspended sentence was therefore wrong. In *Watts* (1984) 6 Cr App R (S) 61, for example, a sentence of three months' imprisonment, suspended for two years, was reduced on appeal to a conditional discharge for 12 months; the offender had allowed her premises to be used for smoking cannabis in circumstances which, according to the Court of Appeal, were 'not by any means the gravest for this sort of offence', she had no previous convictions involving cannabis and none at all for 15 years. In *Jeffrey* (1985) 7 Cr App R (S) 11 a suspended sentence was said to be 'wholly inappropriate' in respect of a man with a clean record who stole an electric fire from his landlady. In *Bedborough* (1984) 6 Cr App R (S) 98 the Court of Appeal quashed a sentence of 18 months' imprisonment, suspended for two years, where the offender pleaded guilty to buggery committed in a public lavatory with a consenting adult; since immediate imprisonment has been held to be generally wrong in such cases (see *Tosland* (1981) 3 Cr App R (S) 365), suspended imprisonment was also wrong. A striking case is *Smith* (1990) 12 Cr App R (S) 85, in which the sentencer imposed a suspended sentence so as to ensure that the offender, who had obtained employment as a supply teacher by using the name and qualification of a friend without her knowledge, would be prevented from obtaining further employment as a teacher. The Court of Appeal said that a fine was the proper sentence for the deception. A suspended sentence ought never to have been passed, the sentencer having disregarded the statutory restrictions. It was also said to be improper to pass a suspended sentence in an attempt to deny the offender future employment.

It is contrary to principle to impose a suspended sentence in a case where a fine is the proper sentence, solely because the offender lacks the means to pay. In *Whitehead* (1979) 1 Cr App R (S) 187 a conditional discharge was substituted for a sentence of six weeks' imprisonment, suspended for one year, for shoplifting. The suspended sentence was 'quite wrong in principle'; the offender was a woman with a clean record who was dependent upon social security benefits and there were other mitigating factors of substance. Conversely, a suspended sentence should not be imposed for an offence for which a fine would normally be the correct penalty, solely on the ground that the offender is well-off and the fine would have little impact upon him (*Hanbury* (1979) 1 Cr App R (S) 243). While this decision still holds good today, the issue is now less likely to arise since CJA 1991, s. 18(5), permits courts to vary the level of a fine upwards to increase its impact on a well-to-do offender (see **6.1.5**).

PCCA 1973, s. 22(2)(b) requires the sentencer to impose a suspended sentence only in a case where that can be 'justified by the exceptional circumstances of the case'. This phrase was inserted into s. 22 by the CJA 1991, and was designed to ensure that the suspended sentence 'should be used far more sparingly than it had been in the past' (*Lowery* [1993] Crim LR 225). The statute provides no hint of what might be regarded as 'exceptional circumstances'. In *Okinikan* [1993] 1 WLR 173, the first occasion on which the Court of Appeal was able to consider the matter, Lord Taylor CJ declined to lay down a definition of the phrase, stating that what amounted to exceptional circumstances would depend on the facts of each case. He did say, however, that 'taken on their own or in combination, good character, youth and an early plea' were *not* exceptional circumstances justifying a suspended sentence, since they were common features of many cases and hence could not be characterised as 'exceptional'. These comments were cited with approval in *Weston* [1996] 1 Cr App R (S) 297. In *Armstrong* [1997] 1 Cr App R (S) 255 Simon Brown LJ commented that where the offence itself was of a particularly serious nature, circumstances to justify suspending the inevitable prison sentence would have to be not merely 'exceptional', but 'unique'.

There has been a steady trickle of appeals to the Court of Appeal on the question of 'exceptional circumstances', but the Court has continued to deal with the matter on a case-by-case basis with little attempt to formulate more general principles. Indeed in *Thomas* (CA unreported, 6 February 1995) Lord Taylor of Gosforth CJ expressly declined an opportunity to elaborate further:

It might be thought helpful if we were to give guidance as to the circumstances in which it would be appropriate to suspend a sentence. However, the provisions of s. 5 [of the CJA

1991] make it clear that it has to be considered on a case-by-case basis. What amounts to exceptional circumstances has to be considered in relation to all the facts of the case. The circumstances which could produce a justification for suspension may not be any one particular matter but a combination of matters. It must be left open to individual judges in individual cases to decide when the circumstances contemplated by the section have arisen.

The result is that the cases are very hard to reconcile with one another.

One case in which no 'exceptional circumstances' could be found is *Sanderson* (1993) 14 Cr App R (S) 361, where the offender pleaded guilty to an offence of unlawful wounding, and the sentence of six months' imprisonment was upheld, the Court of Appeal stating that the offender's good character, family circumstances and a measure of provocation before the offence were all relevant to sentence length, but not to suspension of the sentence. A second example is *Frow* (1995) 16 Cr App R (S) 609, where the court declined to suspend a prison term of nine months for dangerous driving, despite the fact that the offender had incurred serious leg injuries in the accident which he had caused. A third is *Murti* [1996] 2 Cr App R (S) 152, where suspension of a sentence of eight months' imprisonment was inappropriate in the case of a Post Office counter assistant who had permitted other women to cash DSS benefit vouchers which she knew had been stolen, despite the fact that the offender was the mother of two small children, had suffered from post-natal depression at the time of the offence, and had cooperated fully with the prosecuting authorities.

In contrast, a case in which 'exceptional circumstances' were found so as to justify suspending the sentence is *Cameron* (1993) 14 Cr App R (S) 801, where the offender pleaded guilty to assault occasioning actual bodily harm on his five-year-old son. The Court of Appeal suspended the prison sentence of 12 months in the light of a decision made by social workers to try to rehabilitate the family under supervision. In *French* (1994) 15 Cr App R (S) 194 exceptional circumstances were found in the offender's financial and emotional difficulties before the offence, which was a conspiracy relating to an insurance fraud, and the fact that the offender was now undergoing treatment for depression. In *Oliver* [1997] 1 Cr App R (S) 125 the relevant exceptional circumstances were that the offender, who pleaded guilty to possession of amphetamine with intent to supply, had been the victim of a multiple shooting awaiting trial. His life was still in danger from one of the bullets, which could not be surgically removed. In *Bellikli* [1998] 1 Cr App R (S) 135 the offender was convicted of facilitating illegal entry, but the sentence of two years' imprisonment was suspended by the Court of Appeal on the basis that the offender's child was very ill and would probably require major surgery in the near future. In *Brookin* (1995) 16 Cr App R (S) 78, where the offender pleaded guilty to unlawful wounding, there was found to be sufficient provocation both before and at the time of the offence to justify suspension of a sentence of six months' imprisonment. Finally, in *Snelling* [1996] 2 Cr App R (S) 56, where the offender agreed to help a physically handicapped friend to move to another area by burning down her house, and as a result was trapped in the burning house and suffered burns to her back and legs, the case fell 'four square' within the power to suspend. According to Leggatt LJ in the Court of Appeal, in this case suspension 'not only could but should have been exercised' by the sentencer.

4.6.4 Concurrent and consecutive suspended sentences

If an offender is already serving a prison sentence, it is wrong to pass a suspended sentence upon him, whether this is intended to run concurrently with, or consecutively to, it (*Baker*

(1971) 55 Cr App R 182). Where two suspended sentences are passed on the same occasion, the court must make it clear whether they are to run concurrently or consecutively (*Wilkinson* [1970] 1 WLR 1319). If they are to run consecutively, they constitute a single suspended sentence (*Gall* (1970) 54 Cr App R 292). If an offender is already under a suspended sentence, and the sentencer passes a further suspended sentence on him, the sentencer should give no indication whether, if activated, the sentences are to run concurrently or consecutively, since that is for the sentencer ordering the activation on a later occasion to decide (*Blakeway* [1969] 1 WLR 1233).

More generally, it is bad sentencing practice to allow suspended sentences to accumulate in respect of an offender. In a case where more than one suspended sentence is activated in respect of an offender at the same time, the overall term is subject to the totality principle (*Smith* (1971) CSP A11-6C01).

4.6.5 Combining a suspended sentence with other sentences or orders

An immediate prison sentence and a suspended sentence should not be imposed on the same occasion (*Sapiano* (1968) 52 Cr App R 674) nor should a suspended sentence be passed in respect of a person already serving a prison sentence (*Baker* (1971) 55 Cr App R 182).

A suspended sentence and a probation order may not be imposed by the court on an offender, whether or not the offences are charged in the same indictment (PCCA 1973, s. 22(3)), though a similar effect may be achieved by passing a suspended sentence supervision order (see **4.6.6**). It would seem, therefore, that a suspended sentence may not lawfully be imposed at the same time as a combination order, since insofar as combination orders impose supervision requirements they shall be regarded 'as if they were probation orders' (CJA 1991, s. 11(3)(a)). A suspended sentence may lawfully be combined with a community service order or with a curfew order when passing sentence for a single offence or when sentencing for two separate offences on the same occasion, but it is very doubtful whether such mixes would constitute good sentencing practice (see *Campbell* (1993) 14 Cr App R (S) 401).

A fine may be combined with a suspended sentence; indeed this is a combination specifically encouraged by PCCA 1973, s. 22(2A). It is important to remember, however, that it is wrong to combine them where a fine standing alone would have been the proper sentence. To do so would conflict with the principle in PCCA 1973, s. 22(2)(b), discussed in **4.6.3**. Another way of stating this is to say that 'a fine may be added to a suspended sentence, but a suspended sentence may not be added to a fine'. The correct reasoning was explained in *Genese* [1976] 1 WLR 958 at p. 964:

> if the court decides that there is no other appropriate method of dealing with the offender than imprisonment and imposes a prison sentence, the court can then, in the appropriate case, go on to consider that the sentence should be suspended. . . . If the court does go on to consider that the sentence should be suspended . . . the court can also consider whether an additional penalty by way of a fine is justified.

In the ordinary case the fine will be added as a kind of 'sting in the tail' of the suspended sentence, so that the offender has an immediate penalty to pay for the offence as well as the deterrent threat of the suspended sentence hanging over him. If a fine is added to a suspended sentence the court must, of course, have proper regard to the means of the offender (*King* [1970] 1 WLR 1016).

A suspended sentence cannot be combined with a discharge when sentencing for a single offence (*Savage* (1983) 5 Cr App R (S) 216). This is because a discharge is imposed only 'where it is inexpedient to inflict punishment', but a discharge could be given for one offence when a suspended sentence was passed in respect of another offence sentenced on the same occasion.

A compensation order may be imposed in addition to any other sentence (PCCA 1973, s. 35(1)), so such an order may be mixed with a suspended sentence, whether in respect of a single offence or for different offences sentenced on the same occasion. The combination of suspended sentence and compensation order is expressly encouraged by PCCA 1973, s. 22(2A). It should be borne in mind, however, that it would be contrary to principle to pass a suspended, rather than an immediate, custodial sentence, merely because of the offender's ability to pay compensation. Regard should also be had to the fact that if the offender reoffends within the operational period of the suspended sentence, the activation of that sentence may well bring to an end any prospect of compensation being paid (*McGee* [1978] Crim LR 370).

Apart from compensation, other ancillary orders may be combined with a suspended sentence, such as a forfeiture order, a restitution order, or an order to pay costs. If the offence is so punishable, a suspended sentence may be combined with an order for disqualification from driving

4.6.6 Suspended sentence supervision orders

Section 26 of PCCA 1973 provides that where a court passes a suspended sentence of more than six months for a single offence it may order that, for a period not exceeding the operational period of the suspended sentence, the offender shall be placed under the supervision of a probation officer. The probation officer will be one assigned to work in the petty sessions area in which the offender lives (s. 26(3)). The offender is under a duty to keep in touch with the officer in accordance with the latter's instructions and notify him of any change of address (s. 26(4)). If he fails to do so, a summons or warrant for arrest may be issued to bring him before the magistrates' court for the relevant petty sessions area, and the magistrates may fine him up to £1,000 (s. 27). Should the offender be convicted of an imprisonable offence committed during the operational period of the suspended sentence, the normal rules about activation of the suspended sentence still apply (see **4.6.7**). If the sentence is brought into effect the supervision order automatically terminates (s. 28(6)). Where the offender is fined by the magistrates for failing to keep in touch with the probation officer, the supervision order is unaffected and there is, of course, no question of activating the suspended term.

There is provision in PCCA 1973, s. 26(9) for the early discharge of a suspended sentence supervision order on application of the offender or the probation officer concerned. Application would normally be made to the magistrates' court, but to the relevant Crown Court if that Court reserved to itself the power of discharge when it passed the sentence.

In some ways the suspended sentence supervision order provides a means of combining a suspended sentence and a probation order, a mix which is otherwise prohibited. In contrast to a probation order, however, where several different kinds of requirements may be included within it, a suspended sentence supervision order may include only the basic requirement of keeping in touch with the probation officer. The Home Office National Standards state that supervision of an offender under a suspended sentence supervision order should be conducted in accordance with the standard on probation order supervision (see **5.2.2**). The provision that a supervision order may be attached to a suspended sentence only where the latter is for a term of more than six months for one offence has the effect that magistrates have no power to pass a suspended sentence supervision order. In *Seafield* (1988) *The Times*, 21 May 1988, the Court of Appeal suggested that the power was not available where a term of exactly six months had been suspended, and noted that this mistake had required correction by the Court of Appeal on several occasions. It was held in *Baker* (1988) 10 Cr App R (S) 409 that a suspended sentence supervision order may not be passed where sentences which are each shorter than six months are imposed consecutively to make an aggregate sentence of more than six months.

Relatively few suspended sentence supervision orders are made each year and there is no appellate guidance to speak of. In *Terry* (1992) *The Times*, 156 JP 795, the Court of Appeal observed that a suspended sentence supervision order should not be used as an alternative to a probation order, nor should it be seen as a 'probation order with teeth'. Clearly this is correct since, as we have seen, the sentencer must have regarded the offence as so serious that a custodial sentence was the only appropriate means of dealing with it, and hence rejected all community orders (including the probation order), before the option of the suspended sentence came into view.

4.6.7 Breach of suspended sentences

An offender who is convicted of an imprisonable offence during the operational period of a suspended sentence is thereby in breach of the suspended sentence, and is at risk of being ordered to serve the suspended term in prison. In 1996, 14 per cent of suspended sentences imposed by the courts were breached.

It is important to note that conviction for a non-imprisonable offence will not constitute breach. Thus in *Melbourne* (1980) 2 Cr App R (S) 116 activation of a suspended sentence was overturned by the Court of Appeal where the defendant was convicted before magistrates during the operational period of a suspended sentence of two offences which were punishable only by a fine on summary conviction. It was said to be irrelevant that the offences could have attracted a prison sentence on conviction on indictment. It is also clear that conviction for an offence committed *before* the offence for which the offender was given the suspended sentence will not suffice to justify activation of the suspended sentence (*Daurge* (1972) CSP A13-2A01). On the other hand, conviction for an imprisonable offence committed during the operational period does amount to a breach even if the conviction is not until after the expiry of the operational period. In such circumstances, however, it is likely that the court would exercise its discretion not to activate the suspended sentence. In what follows, the offence for which the suspended sentence was passed is referred to as the 'original offence' and the offence which puts the offender in breach of the suspended sentence is referred to as the 'subsequent offence'.

The options which are available to a court dealing with an offender for breach of a suspended sentence are listed in PCCA 1973, s. 23(1):

(a) to order that the suspended sentence shall take effect with the original term unaltered; or

(b) to order that the sentence shall take effect with a lesser term substituted for the original term; or

(c) to vary the original suspended sentence by making the operational period run until a date not more than two years from the date of the variation; or

(d) to make no order with respect to the suspended sentence.

The court *must*, however, activate the suspended sentence with its term unaltered (that is, choose (a) above) unless it is of the opinion that, in all the circumstances, including the facts of the subsequent offence, it would be unjust to do so (s. 23(1)). Where it is of the opinion that it would be unjust to activate the sentence with its term unaltered, the court must state its reasons. This applies both to the Crown Court and to magistrates' courts. In 1996, breaches of suspended sentence were dealt with by immediate imprisonment in 75 per cent of cases.

Before looking at these options in detail, two points should be made about the powers of the court dealing with the subsequent offence. First, if that court were to impose a discharge for the subsequent offence, there is then no power to deal with the suspended sentence at all, since (by PCCA 1973, s. 1C), there is deemed to have been no 'conviction' in respect of the subsequent offence (*Moore* [1995] QB 353 and see **7.1.4**). Secondly, if the court defers sentence for the subsequent offence there is no power to deal with the suspended sentence in that situation either, since it remains open to the court to deal with the subsequent offence by way of a discharge at the end of the period of deferment (*Salmon* (1973) 57 Cr App R 953).

There are four steps in a court's consideration of the options available to it under s. 23 when dealing with an offender who is in breach of a suspended sentence. The first step is that the sentencer must consider the appropriate penalty for the subsequent offence (*Ithell* [1969] 1 WLR 272). If the appropriate penalty is a custodial sentence, then the second step is to determine the appropriate length of that sentence. The third step is to consider whether the suspended sentence should be activated. Bearing in mind that s. 23(1) requires the sentencer to bring the suspended sentence into effect with its term unaltered unless it would be unjust to do so, this will probably be the appropriate course to take. According to Russell J in *Craine* (1981) 3 Cr App R (S) 198, 'it cannot be made too plain that when suspended sentences of imprisonment are imposed they mean what they say. Only in exceptional circumstances, if further offences involving imprisonment are committed, will those suspended sentences not be activated' and numerous other observations in support of the statutory language may be found. The fourth and final step is to consider whether the suspended term should run consecutively to, or concurrently with, the term for the subsequent offence. In *Ithell* Edmund Davies LJ said (at pp. 273-4) that 'unless there are some quite exceptional circumstances, the suspended sentence should be ordered to run consecutively to the sentence given for the current offence'. The sentencer must make sure, however, that the overall effect of the sentence is not too severe and does not breach the totality principle (see **4.4.4**). To avoid that effect, the sentencer may either reduce the term which he originally had in mind for the subsequent offence, or may substitute a lesser term for that originally suspended (that is, choose option (b) rather than (a) (*Bocskei* (1970) 54 Cr App R 519).

The rule in s. 23(1) that upon breach of a suspended sentence the term suspended should be activated in full has, on the whole, been strictly endorsed by the Court of Appeal. The Court has not been easily convinced on appeal that activation in full was unjust and, in particular, has held on several occasions that the subsequent offence being different in type from the original offence does not by itself render activation of the full term unjust. In *Clitheroe* (1987) 9 Cr App R (S) 159 the offender was subject to a sentence of six months' imprisonment, suspended for two years, imposed for handling stolen goods. The subsequent offence, committed 14 months after the suspended sentence was passed, was for wounding with intent. The police were called to a domestic incident involving the offender and a woman who was the mother of his son and the offender stabbed a police officer with a wallpaper stripping knife. The sentencer imposed a sentence of four years for the subsequent offence and activated the suspended sentence in full and consecutively. The Court of Appeal upheld the sentence. Lord Lane CJ observed that 'the mere fact that the subsequent offence was wholly unrelated to the earlier is no ground for not activating the suspended sentence in full and consecutively'. An offender is more likely to succeed where he argues against activation on the basis that the subsequent offence was a relatively trivial one, so that if he is required to serve the whole suspended term plus a short term for the subsequent offence the overall penalty will be out of proportion to the gravity of the conduct. Such an argument will be all the stronger if it can be shown that the subsequent offence was both relatively trivial and dissimilar to the original offence (*Moylan* [1970] 1 QB 143). In such a case, it seems, the sentencer might consider either not activating the suspended sentence at all or activating it but with a much reduced term. An example is *Abrahams* (1980) 2 Cr App R (S) 10, where the offender was in breach of a suspended sentence of 18 months which had been imposed for burglary. The subsequent offence involved theft of a plastic dinghy whilst on holiday and in 'a drunken frolic'. Here the Court of Appeal quashed the order for activation of the suspended sentence. Another good argument for non-activation is that the subsequent offence was committed right at the end of the operational period of the suspended sentence. In *Carr* (1979) 1 Cr App R (S) 53 the offender had completed 22 months of the two-year period of suspension before being convicted of a subsequent offence, for which he received two years' immediate imprisonment. The activation of the 12-month suspended sentence in full and consecutively was disapproved by the Court of Appeal, which ordered that it should run concurrently with the new sentence.

The sentencer may decide that the subsequent offence is not so serious that only custody can be justified for it. If the sentencer selects a community order as the appropriate means of dealing with the subsequent offence, the general rule seems to be that activation of the suspended sentence is not appropriate. One reason for this is that it is generally illogical and undesirable to mix together custodial and community sentences. Thus in *McElhorne* (1983) 5 Cr App R (S) 53 the offender was subject to a sentence of two months' imprisonment, suspended for two years, for possession of 5.66 g of cannabis and 5 mg of diamorphine. One year later, in breach of the suspended sentence, he pleaded guilty to possession of 127 mg of cannabis resin. He was sentenced to 50 hours' community service for the subsequent offence and the suspended sentence was activated. The Court of Appeal said that activation was inappropriate. Skinner J indicated that it was a general rule that the suspended sentence should not be activated in such a case. In *Brooks* (1990) 12 Cr App R (S) 756 the offender pleaded guilty to possession of a small quantity of cannabis resin. He was then in breach of a sentence of nine months' imprisonment, suspended for two years, for possession of cannabis with intent to supply. The sentencer passed a sentence of imprisonment of one month for the subsequent offence and activated the suspended sentence in full. The Court of Appeal said that the proper way to have dealt with the subsequent offence was by way of a fine and that, in those circumstances, activation of the suspended sentence was inappropriate. Auld J commented that:

the fact that a subsequent offence does not warrant a custodial sentence is a strong argument for not activating the suspended sentence . . . this is not a matter of principle but a matter of strong argument for counsel when mitigating in such a case . . . Whilst the argument is particularly strong when a later offence is of a different character from the earlier one as well as being comparatively trivial . . . it is not confined to such a case.

In *Brooks* the main reason for not activating the suspending sentence was not the incompatibility of the sentence for the subsequent offence with the activated term of imprisonment, but an acceptance that where the subsequent offence can properly be dealt with by way of a fine, activation of the suspended sentence is generally inappropriate. *Brooks* has been followed in later cases, such as *Burnard* (1994) 15 Cr App R (S) 218, but in other cases the Court of Appeal has upheld implementation of the suspended sentence in full. See, for example, *Calladine* (1994) 15 Cr App R (S) 345 and *Stacey* (1994) 15 Cr App R (S) 585.

A court activating a suspended sentence is not empowered to suspend part of it (*Senior* (1984) 6 Cr App R (S) 15).

4.6.8 When a court may deal with breach of suspended sentence

If an offender appears before the Crown Court to be sentenced for an offence, whether following conviction on indictment or following a committal for sentence from the magistrates, and he is in breach of a suspended sentence, the Crown Court may deal with the breach whether the suspended sentence was originally imposed in the Crown Court or in a magistrates' court (PCCA 1973, s. 24(1)). On the other hand, a magistrates' court can deal with breach of a suspended sentence only if that sentence was imposed by itself or another magistrates' court.

If a magistrates' court deals summarily with an offender for an offence which puts him in breach of a suspended sentence imposed by the Crown Court, the magistrates may choose one of two options. The first and more usual course is to commit the offender to Crown Court to be dealt with for the breach (s. 24(2)). If this option is chosen the magistrates will also commit the offender (under MCA 1980 s. 38 or CJA 1967, s. 56) to be sentenced by the Crown Court for the subsequent offence. In this way the Crown Court will deal with both matters at the same time. The second option is to give written notice to the Crown Court that the conviction has occurred (s. 24(2)). If this option is chosen, the magistrates will sentence for the subsequent offence, thereby hinting strongly their view that the suspended sentence should not be activated. Once the Crown Court receives notice, it may issue a summons or warrant for arrest to secure the offender's appearance before it (s. 25). Difficulties may then arise if the Crown Court is of the view that the suspended sentence should be activated, particularly if the magistrates have imposed a sentence for the subsequent offence which is generally incompatible with activation. First, if the magistrates have dealt with the subsequent offence by granting a discharge in respect of it, there is no power to deal with the suspended sentence at all, since by PCCA 1973, s. 1C, there is deemed to have been no 'conviction' in respect of the subsequent offence (*Moore* [1995] QB 353 and see further **7.1.4**). Second, it is undesirable for the magistrates to impose a community order for the subsequent offence (as happened in *Stewart* (1984) 6 Cr App R (S) 166), or to pass a second suspended sentence (as happened in *Hamilton* (1984) 6 Cr App R (S) 451), since that renders the task of the Crown Court dealing with the original suspended sentence much more difficult. In such cases it is better for the magistrates to select the first option, and commit the offender to the Crown Court so it may deal with the whole matter.

5   Community Sentences

Community sentences lie within a central band of available sentencing options, appropriate in cases where the offender has committed an offence of an intermediate degree of seriousness. Community sentences are imposed where the sentencer takes the view that the nature of the offence is not such as to require custody, but that it does require something more than the mild penalty of a bind over or a discharge. A community sentence is a sentence which includes one or more community orders (though these may, in turn, be mixed with other measures, particularly fines and compensation). The various community orders are a diverse group, since they have been introduced by legislation at different times during the century, against a changing penological background. It is possible to see in all of the community orders the twin ideas of rehabilitation of the offender and punishment in the community. In the past the former of these ideas was predominant, particularly in measures such as the probation order, which was regarded as lying outside the 'tariff', an individualised measure geared towards rehabilitation of the offender away from crime. Until 1991 the probation order was not even legally a 'sentence' and could not be combined with any other order of the court which contained a punitive element within it (such as a fine). The emphasis was shifted significantly by the CJA 1991, and the probation order has been brought within the tariff, but the conflicting underlying objectives still remain.

5.1   COMMUNITY SENTENCES IN GENERAL

It must be appreciated that not all sentences that are by nature non-custodial, are 'community sentences'. The latter phrase is now a term of art, defined in CJA 1991, s. 6(4) so as to encompass the probation order, the community service order, the combination order, the curfew order, the attendance centre order, the supervision order and, when the relevant provisions of the CDB are brought into force, the drug treatment and testing order and the action plan order. Other sentencing options, particularly fines and discharges, are not technically community sentences; they are considered in Chapters 6 and 7. While community orders display a large degree of diversity, the CJA 1991 now ensures that they share a common legal framework. This framework relates both to the circumstances in which they may be selected by the sentencer in a particular case and, for the most part, to the consequences for an offender who finds himself in breach of a community order. This common framework is described next, and then the legal provisions and principles of sentencing applicable to the individual community orders are dealt with in the remainder of this chapter.

The CJA 1991 requires that the imposition of any community order must be justified by the court in accordance with certain statutory criteria. Section 6(1) provides that:

(1) A court shall not pass on an offender a community sentence, that is to say, a sentence which consists of or includes one or more community orders, unless it is of the opinion that the offence, or the combination of the offence and one or more offences associated with it, was serious enough to warrant such a sentence.

The requirement in s. 6(1) that the court must consider 'the offence, or the combination of the offence and one or more offences associated with it' mirrors the provision in CJA 1991, s. 1(2)(a), which relates to the court's requirement to justify the imposition of custody (see **4.2.3**). A definition of the phrase 'associated with' is provided by CJA 1991, s. 31(2), and was considered at **4.2.3**. An offence which is taken into consideration at the time of sentence may count as an offence to be weighed in accordance with s. 31(2). Unlike the justification for imposing a custodial sentence, however, the seriousness of the offence, or offences, is here the sole criterion for imposing a community sentence. There is no equivalent provision to s. 1(2)(b) (which permits the imposition of a custodial sentence on the basis of public protection following the offender's conviction for a violent offence or a sexual offence).

It will be noted that while s. 6(1) states that a community sentence may be imposed only where the offence is 'serious enough' to warrant such a sentence, the imposition of a custodial sentence requires that the offence be 'so serious that only' a custodial sentence can be justified. This is a significant difference in wording. It means that at the lower threshold of the community sentence band there is some degree of overlap between community sentences and fines. A particular offence may be 'serious enough' to qualify for a community sentence but, in all the circumstances of the case, the court may still properly impose a fine. A further complication is provided by C(S)A 1997, s. 37, relating to 'persistent petty offenders', whereby a community service order or a curfew order can be imposed instead of a fine on an offender who already has outstanding fines (see **6.6**).

Section 6(2) provides that:

(2) Subject to subsection (3) below, where a court passes a community sentence—
    (a) the particular order or orders comprising or forming part of the sentence shall be such as in the opinion of the court is, or taken together are, the most suitable for the offender; and
    (b) the restrictions on liberty imposed by the order or orders shall be such as in the opinion of the court are commensurate with the seriousness of the offence, or the combination of the offence and one or more offences associated with it.

It will be noted that, in parallel with the criteria relating to custodial sentence length, the court may look at the whole pattern of offending in determining whether to impose a community order and, if so, which community order or orders to impose (see **4.4.2**). Where several offences are involved, a danger of this approach is that it could lead to a total sentence which is disproportionate to the overall seriousness of the offending behaviour. Section 28(2)(b) of the CJA 1991, in an attempt to avoid this, makes reference to the totality principle (see **4.4.4**) by stating that the sentencer may mitigate the sentence by 'applying any rule of law as to the totality of sentences' and this applies to community sentences as well as custodial ones. There is a good deal of potential difficulty with s. 6(2). The twin objectives of 'suitability' and 'seriousness' are likely on some occasions to conflict, and the statute gives no indication of which objective should prevail where that is the case.

In forming its opinion that a community sentence is justified under CJA 1991, s. 6(1), and in determining the appropriate restrictions on liberty imposed by the community order or orders comprising the community sentence, s. 7(1) requires the court to 'take into account all such information about the circumstances of the offence (including any aggravating or mitigating factors) as is available to it'; by s. 7(2)), in forming an opinion about the suitability of the community order or orders for the offender, the court 'may take into account any information about the offender which is before it'. Further, by CJA 1991, s. 28(1) nothing shall prevent a court from 'mitigating an offender's sentence by taking into account any such matters as, in the opinion of the court, are relevant in mitigation of sentence' and, by s. 28(2)(a) and without prejudice to the generality of s. 28(1), the court may mitigate any penalty included in an offender's sentence by taking into account any other penalty included in that sentence. For discussion of mitigation and aggravation see **2.2**; for the rules relating to combining individual community orders with other sentences or orders see the detailed discussion of the particular community orders below.

By CJA 1991, s. 7(3), the obtaining of a pre-sentence report is normally required whenever the court is considering imposing:

(a)   a probation order which includes additional requirements authorised by PCCA 1973, sch. 1A;

(b)   a community service order;

(c)   a combination order;

(d)   a supervision order which includes requirements imposed under CYPA 1969, s. 12, 12A, 12AA, 12B or 12C; or

(e)   a drug treatment and testing order.

It follows that a pre-sentence report is not normally required whenever the court is considering imposing:

(f)   a probation order which does not include additional requirements;

(g)   a supervision order which does not include the specified requirements indicated at (d) above;

(h)   a curfew order;

(i)   an attendance centre order; or

(j)   an action plan order.

In many of the cases falling within (f) to (j), however, it would no doubt constitute good sentencing practice to obtain a pre-sentence report before passing such a sentence. This is echoed in the Home Office National Standard (1995), which states that such a report is of value 'in advising the court about suitability for community sentences for which a pre-sentence report is not required by law, and in seeking to ensure that supervision, if ordered, is able to start promptly and effectively'.

Section 7(3) is made subject to s. 7(3A), which states that the court may dispense with a pre-sentence report in any case where the offender is aged 18 or over and the court considers such a report to be 'unnecessary'. For those under the age of 18, s. 7(3B) says that, in a case where the offence is punishable only on indictment the court may dispense with a pre-sentence report, but if the offence is not so punishable the court should not dispense with a report unless there exists an earlier pre-sentence report on the offender and the sentencer has seen that and taken it into account. Subsection (3B) was inserted into s. 7 in response to complaints from some sentencers that, in a case where a custodial sentence for the offender is inevitable given the seriousness of the offence, it can be a waste of time to order a report.

Even in those cases where the obtaining of a pre-sentence report is normally required, CJA 1991, s. 7(4) states that no community sentence shall be invalidated by the failure of the court to comply with s. 7(3), but, in the event of an appeal being brought against a community sentence passed without the court having obtained and considered such a report, the appellate court must then obtain and consider one unless it believes that the sentencer was justified in not calling for one or that, although proceeding without a report was not justified at the time, in light of the current circumstances it is unnecessary to obtain one.

Former provisions requiring that an offender must consent to the imposition of certain community sentences before they could be imposed were abolished by the C(S)A 1997, s. 38. For further details see the text relating to specific community orders.

The number of community sentences rose by 2 per cent to 133,000 in 1996. Following rises of 13 per cent in 1994 and 11 per cent in 1993, the number of community sentences has changed little between 1994 and 1996. Just over a third of community sentences were for summary offences.

5.2 PROBATION ORDERS

5.2.1 The probation service and the probation order

The origins of the probation service go back to the latter part of the nineteenth century when voluntary church societies appointed 'police court missionaries' to assist in the reformation of drunkards and others who appeared in the inner city courts. The practice then grew up of magistrates releasing petty offenders without sentencing them, on the understanding that they would accept help from the missionary. The practice was put on a statutory footing by the Probation of Offenders Act 1907, which enabled courts to make probation orders in a form rather similar to that of the basic order which is still used today. Also, magistrates' courts were allowed to appoint probation officers who, instead of being supported by voluntary societies, would be paid by the local authority.

Probation officers today are officers of the court. In addition to supervising offenders sentenced to probation, they have a wide (and increasing) range of other duties. They supervise offenders under early release from custody, they organise the work performed by offenders under community service and combination orders, they run probation centres and probation hostels and prepare pre-sentence reports for the courts. They are not employed by central or local government, but by the area probation committee.

Neighbouring magistrates' courts join together to form units of a convenient size, known as probation areas. Each probation area has a probation board comprising magistrates, one or more Crown Court judges appointed by the Lord Chancellor and co-opted members. The area probation board is responsible for appointing a sufficient number of probation officers for its area, for paying those officers out of monies provided and for ensuring that their general conditions of work are satisfactory. In addition to the probation boards, each magistrates' court has a probation liaison committee, consisting of magistrates from the division, who review the work of the probation officers in their area and discuss with them matters of common concern. Probation boards are funded by local authorities who, in turn, are reimbursed by central government subject to strict cash limiting.

The role of central government in the organisation and funding of the probation service has increased greatly since 1907, and it now exercises a considerable measure of control. During the 1960s the social work or welfare ideology was clearly dominant in probation practice, and there has always been an important element of offering practical help to the offender, by assistance in finding employment, for example. More recently the service has been required to implement clearer management objectives and to accept national standards to govern the ways in which the community orders are administered, and in the preparation of pre-sentence reports for the courts. Independent external review is provided by HM Inspectorate of Probation.

Between 1986 and 1996 the proportionate use of probation orders for indictable offences has been increasing steadily. This holds true for nearly all the main categories of offending, though in some of these there was a greater use in the proportionate use of probation during the early 1990s which appears now to have tailed off. The percentage change in the use of probation orders between 1986 and 1996 for the main categories of offending is as follows:

		1986	1996
(1)	violence against the person	5 per cent	10 per cent
(2)	sexual offences	15 per cent	17 per cent
(3)	burglary	11 per cent	14 per cent
(4)	robbery	2 per cent	3 per cent
(5)	theft and handling	10 per cent	14 per cent
(6)	fraud and forgery	13 per cent	15 per cent
(7)	criminal damage	10 per cent	14 per cent
(8)	drug offences	6 per cent	8 per cent
(9)	motoring offences	5 per cent	4 per cent
All offending		9 per cent	11 per cent

This in fact translates into a modest decline in the numbers of offenders receiving probation orders (33,100 in 1996 as compared with 34,800 in 1986) but this reflects a marked decline in the overall number of offenders being sentenced by the courts.

5.2.2 Power to make a probation order

A probation order may be made by the Crown Court, by an adult magistrates' court or by a youth court. Its effect is that the offender is required to be under the supervision of a probation officer for a period specified in the order, of not less than six months nor more than three years. During that period the offender must keep in touch with the probation officer, follow such instructions as he is given by that officer and notify him of any change of address (PCCA 1973, s. 2(6)). This is the 'basic' probation order. The government requires that probation orders should be seen to be more demanding than has sometimes been the case in the past, when the measure was dismissed by some as a 'soft option'; the order should require the offender to face up to his offending, and should be more rigorously and consistently enforced. The Consultation Paper *Strengthening Punishment in the Community* (Home Office, 1995a) commented that 'both courts and the public have found some difficulty in squaring their concept of the probation order with the notion of a punishment involving a significant restriction of liberty'. The Home Office National Standard (1995b) states:

Effective probation order supervision requires high standards both from probation services and from individual probation staff and should generally entail establishing a professional relationship, in which to advise, assist and befriend the offender with the aim of:

(i)   securing the offender's co-operation and compliance with the probation order and enforcing its terms;

(ii)   challenging the offender to accept responsibility for his or her crime and its consequences;

(iii) helping the offender to resolve personal difficulties linked with offending and acquire new skills; and

(iv)   motivating and assisting the offender to become a responsible and law-abiding member of the community.

The National Standards for probation orders require that there be frequent meetings between the probation officer and the offender (between six and 12 meetings in the first three months, and at least one meeting a month thereafter). The National Standards envisage that the offender and the probation officer will, at the first meeting, together draw up in writing a 'supervision plan' based upon the requirements of the order and any assessment and outline proposals made in the pre-sentence report. This plan should identify the offender's motivation and pattern of offending, his or her relevant problems, the risk of reoffending or serious harm to the public and the requirements of the order. It should then set out an individual programme designed to tackle these issues, identifying the appropriateness of individual or group work for the offender, referral to a specialist probation team or facility (such as a probation centre or drug or alcohol group) and referral to, or involvement with, other resources and opportunities in the community (such as employment, training, education, health, social services, housing and community groups). A time-scale for achieving these objectives should be set and records must be kept of all meetings.

In practice, most probation orders are for a period of between 12 months and two years. The criteria for fixing the length of a probation order are unclear, but presumably its duration would be affected both by the court's perception of the seriousness of the offence and the needs of the offender. A short probation order might be appropriate where the offender has immediate problems (such as financial difficulty) which require resolution. The White Paper, *Crime, Justice and Protecting the Public* (Home Office, 1990), pointed out that 'a comparatively short order may make more severe demands on some offenders than more severe orders would on others'. Where appropriate, a probation order may be discharged early (see **5.2.10**). In addition to this 'basic' probation order, the court may choose to insert various specific requirements into the order. These are considered at **5.2.3**.

The conditions which must be established before a probation order may be made by the court are as follows.

(a)   Since a probation order is a 'community order' within the meaning of CJA 1991, s. 6(4), the imposition of a probation order in any case requires justification by the court in terms of the seriousness of the offence, or the offence and one or more offences associated with it. This general requirement for all community orders is dealt with at **5.1**.

(b)   The offender must be aged 16 or over. The age requirement was lowered from 17 to 16 by the CJA 1991. As a result of this change offenders aged 16 or 17 are now eligible for both probation orders *and* supervision orders (as to the latter see **5.8**). There is as yet no statutory or appellate guidance on the appropriate choice between these measures for such offenders. The 1990 White Paper said that 'courts should be able to select either of these disposals according to the maturity of the offender and the arrangements available locally', but the Home Office National Standards suggest that in practice the supervision order should normally be preferred for offenders aged 16 and 17. There is no upper age limit for the probation order.

(c)   The probation order is available for offenders convicted of any offence, subject only to the crime of murder and to the two presumptive sentences under the C(S)A 1997. The offence does not need to be imprisonable. On the other hand, the requirement that the offence, or the offence and one or more offences associated with it, must be sufficiently serious, together with the limited resources of the probation service, mean that the imposition of a probation order by the court for a trivial offence is inappropriate.

(d)   If the court has it in mind to include within the probation order any of the requirements specified in PCCA 1973, sch. 1A, it should normally first obtain a pre-sentence report (CJA 1991, s. 7 and **5.1**). Even if no such additional requirements are proposed, it would seem that before a basic probation order is passed, it will often be good sentencing practice to obtain a pre-sentence report.

(e)   The court must be of the opinion that supervision of the offender by a probation officer is desirable in the interests of securing the rehabilitation of the offender, protecting the public from harm from him or preventing the commission by him of further offences (PCCA 1973, s. 2(1)).

(f)   The court must explain to the offender in ordinary language the effect of the order (including the effect of any additional requirements to be included in the order), the consequences for the offender of breach of the order and that the court has power to review the order later, on the application either of the offender or the supervising probation officer (PCCA 1973, s. 2(3)).

(g)   The court must give copies of the order to the probation officer in attendance at the court, who must then pass on copies to the offender, the probation officer who will supervise the offender and the person in charge of any hostel or other institution in which the order obliges the offender to live. It is unlikely that a failure to comply precisely with these requirements would invalidate the probation order (see, by analogy, *Walsh* v *Barlow* [1985] 1 WLR 90, considered at **5.3.1**).

Once the probation order is made by the court, the Home Office National Standard indicates that supervision should commence promptly: normally within five working days. If practicable, the first appointment should be made before the offender leaves court.

On making a probation order the court may, if it thinks it expedient for the purpose of reformation of the offender, allow any person who agrees to do so to give financial security for the good behaviour of the offender (PCCA 1973, s. 12(1)). This option seems to be very rarely used by the courts.

5.2.3   Requirements in probation orders

The court may require that, during the whole or part of the probation order, the offender must comply with such additional requirements in the order as the court considers desirable in the interests of securing the offender's rehabilitation, protecting the public from harm from him or preventing the commission by him of further offences (PCCA 1973, s. 3(1)). This is a generally expressed provision, so that it would seem that any reasonable condition might be inserted by the sentencing court. One example would be the inclusion by the court of a requirement that the offender shall not, during the period of the probation order, possess, use or carry a firearm: Firearms Act 1968, s. 52. The generality of s. 3(1) is subject, however, to s. 3(2), which states that the payment of compensation to the victim must not be included as a requirement of a probation order (though there is no objection to making a compensation order and a probation order at the same time and, indeed, this is commonly done). In *Rogers* v *Cullen* [1982] 1 WLR 729 Lord Bridge indicated that no requirement should be included in a probation order which would 'introduce a custodial or other element', and that any discretion conferred on the probation officer to regulate the probationer's activities should be 'confined within well defined limits'. In a *Practice Note* (1952) 35 Cr App R 207 Lord Goddard CJ deprecated 'vague' conditions being written into probation orders. There is no power to include in a probation order a condition that the offender leave the country never to return (*McCartan* [1958] 1 WLR 923).

Schedule 1A to the 1973 Act provides statutory authority for a number of specific requirements which may be inserted into the basic probation order. It should always be remembered that to the extent that the insertion of such requirements makes the probation order more onerous for the offender, it may only be justified in accordance with the terms of CJA 1991, s. 6(2): that the particular order or orders comprising the community sentence must be such as in the opinion of the court is, or are, the most *suitable* for the offender, *and* the restrictions on liberty imposed by the order or orders are commensurate with the seriousness of the offence, or the combination of the offence and one or more offences associated with it. In particular, complex and onerous conditions should not be included within a probation order unless they are justified by the relative degree of seriousness inherent in the offence for which the probation order is imposed.

In practice around 70 per cent of probation orders are made without the insertion of specified requirements.

5.2.4   Requirements as to residence

A probation order may require the offender to live at a certain private address, or in an approved probation hostel, or in some other named institution (PCCA 1973, sch. 1A, para. 1). A probation hostel provides supervised accommodation for offenders on probation, as well as for those on licence following early release from custody and defendants who are on bail. Some are operated by the probation service and some by the voluntary sector. The Home Office National Standards set requirements for the management, rules and regime, induction and record-keeping of such hostels. According to the National Standard, the purpose of approved hostels is to provide an enhanced level of supervision to enable bailees and offenders to remain under supervision in the community. Hostel residents are normally expected to go to work or to attend projects, training courses or treatment facilities in the community.

A residence requirement may last for the whole or part of the duration of an order; but the period for which it will last must be stated in the order. Often the residence period is several months shorter than the full term of the order, to allow a reasonable period of supervision after residence in the hostel has ceased. Before inserting a residence condition into a probation order, the court must consider the home surroundings of the offender, the pre-sentence report being the obvious source for such information. A requirement of residence at a hostel might be appropriate where the offender's home environment is particularly bad, or where he represents more of a risk to the public than the average probationer, so that requiring him to live in approved accommodation supervised by the probation service is some additional safeguard for the public. It is clear that approved hostels should thus be reserved for those who require this enhanced degree of supervision, and that they are not meant simply as convenient accommodation for homeless offenders. They should provide a structured and supportive environment within which their residents can be supervised effectively. They are not secure, however, and so cannot provide the same degree of protection for the public as do most prison service establishments.

5.2.5 Requirements as to activities, etc.

A probation order may require an offender to report to a person specified in the order, at a place specified in the order (such as a centre run by the probation service or an associated agency such as NACRO), to participate in specified activities. This provision makes it possible to require the offender to participate in a variety of schemes and activities offered by the probation service. Alternatively, or in addition, the condition may require that the offender refrain from participating in specified activities (such as attending football matches, where the offending arose from violence at such events).

A requirement of participation in activities may not involve the probationer for more than a total of 60 days. Before making such a requirement, the court must be satisfied that it is feasible to secure the offender's compliance (PCCA 1973, sch. 1A, para. 2(2)) and that he can attend at times which do not interfere with work or school commitments, if applicable. The place specified in the order must be one approved by the relevant probation board as providing facilities suitable for persons subject to probation orders (para. 2(5)) though, of course, persons who are not probationers may be attending at the same time. In any case where an activity will involve a person other than the probationer and the probation officer, the consent of that person to the arrangement should be obtained. A requirement that the offender refrain from a particular activity may be imposed in respect of a certain day or days within the currency of the order, or extend for a portion of the order, or the whole of it (para. 2(1)(b)).

Where an offender has been convicted of a sexual offence (as defined in CJA 1991, s. 31(1): see **4.2.7**), the normal limit (60 days) for attendance for participation in specified activities under para. 2 does not apply. The duration may, in the case of such an offender, be for 'such greater number of days as may be specified in the direction' and thus may extend for the full duration of the probation order.

5.2.6 Requirement of attendance at probation centre

The probationer may be required, during the probation order, to attend at a probation centre specified in the order (PCCA 1973, sch. 1A, para. 3). A 'probation centre' is described in para. 3(7) as:

premises—
(a) at which non-residential facilities are provided for use in connection with the rehabilitation of offenders; and
(b) which are for the time being approved by the Secretary of State as providing facilities for persons subject to probation orders.

Prior to the coming into force of the CJA 1991, probation centres were called 'day centres'. In 1988, 2,700 of the probation orders made contained a requirement of attendance at a day centre. The diversity of organisation and objectives to be found in day centres was criticised by a Home Office research study (Mair, 1988). Such centres formerly had to be approved by the local probation committee. The change to approval by the Secretary of State was an attempt to impose greater central control and standardisation of facilities.

Before making a requirement of attendance at a probation centre, the court must consult a probation officer, ensure that arrangments can be made for the offender's attendance and that the manager of the centre agrees to the inclusion of the requirement (para. 3(2)). A requirement imposed under para. 3(1) may involve attendance at the centre for a maximum of 60 days during the course of the order, during which the probationer must comply with the instructions of staff at the centre (para. 3(3)). Attendance arrangements must, so far as possible, avoid times when the offender would otherwise be at work or school.

Where an offender has been convicted of a sexual offence (as defined in CJA 1991, s. 31(1): see **4.2.7**), the normal limit (60 days) for attendance at a probation centre under para. 3 does not apply. The duration may, in the case of such an offender, be for 'such greater number of days as may be specified in the direction' and thus may extend for the full duration of the probation order. It is clear that the purpose of this is to encourage the courts to deal with offenders convicted of the less serious sexual offences by closer supervision in the community, rather than by custody.

5.2.7   Requirement as to treatment for mental condition etc.

The imposition of a requirement of this kind is provided for in PCCA 1973, sch. 1A, para. 5. Probation orders containing such a requirement are often termed 'psychiatric probation orders'. They are considered, together with other sentencing provisions for mentally disordered offenders, at **11.1**.

5.2.8   Requirements as to treatment for drug or alcohol dependency

Under PCCA 1973, sch. 1A, para. 6, a probation order may include a requirement of treatment for drug or alcohol dependency where the court is satisfied (para. 6(1)):

(a)   that the offender is dependent on drugs or alcohol;
(b)   that his dependency caused or contributed to the offence in respect of which the order is proposed to be made; and
(c)   that his dependency is such as requires and may be susceptible to treatment.

Probation is often seen as the appropriate sentence where an offender convicted of an offence of intermediate seriousness has exhibited a willingness to receive treatment for alcohol or drug abuse. Moxon found that 'treatment for addiction' was the single factor which most affected the Crown Court sentencer's selection of probation rather than some other non-custodial sentence (Moxon, 1988, p. 44). Before such a requirement can be imposed the court must ensure that arrangements can be made for the treatment to be carried out, and the offender must express his willingness to comply with the requirement (para. 6(4) as substituted by the C(S)A 1997, s. 38).

In these provisions 'dependency' is widely construed, and includes cases where the offender has 'a propensity towards the misuse of drugs or alcohol' (para. 6(9)). Treatment for the dependency must be carried out at a place specified in the order (para. 6(3)). It may continue for the whole period of the probation order or for such specific part of it as is required by the court (para. 6(2)). Clearly the treatment is the main purpose of the order, and the probation officer's normal supervision duties are relevant only insofar as is necessary for the purpose of revocation or amendment of the order (para. 6(5)). It would seem from the words 'caused or contributed to the offence' in para. 6(1) that the court is not confined in the use of these powers to cases where the offender has been convicted of an offence which was committed when the offender was affected by alcohol or drugs or which is otherwise directly related to alcohol or drugs. The powers could, for example, be used where an offender has committed theft or assault in order to obtain money to purchase a supply of alcohol or drugs, or has committed burglary or robbery in a chemist's shop in order to obtain drugs. Of course, in any of these cases, the court might properly regard the offence as being so serious that only a custodial sentence could be justified.

5.2.9 Combining probation orders with other sentences or orders

It is not permissible to combine a probation order with a sentence of immediate custody, whether in respect of the same offence or for different offences sentenced on the same occasion (*Mullervy* (1986) 8 Cr App R (S) 41 and *Duporte* (1989) 11 Cr App R (S) 116). It is also impermissible to combine a probation order with a suspended sentence (PCCA 1973, s. 22(3)); the suspended sentence supervision order (see **4.6.6**) provides a means of mixing a suspended sentence with an element of supervision. A probation order may be combined with a fine when sentencing for a single offence, or when sentencing for different offences sentenced on the same occasion. A probation order may not be combined with a community service order when sentencing for a single offence (CJA 1991, s. 6(3)), except where imposed in a specified mix to form a combination order (see **5.4**). There would seem to be no legal restriction on passing a probation order in respect of one offence and a community service order in respect of a second offence sentenced on the same occasion (see *Harkess* (1990) 12 Cr App R (S) 366), but objection may be made that to do so would have the effect of circumventing specific statutory provisions on combination orders and hence would be bad sentencing practice. Since a probation order forms part of a combination order, it would seem to be illogical to combine those two orders together. A probation order may, however, be combined with a curfew order whether in respect of the same offence or different offences sentenced on the same occasion. A probation order may not be be combined with a conditional discharge or an absolute discharge when sentencing for a single offence, since a discharge is appropriate only when 'it is inexpedient to inflict punishment' (PCCA 1973, s. 1A(1)) but a probation order and a discharge may be used for sentencing different offences on the same occasion.

A probation order may be combined with a compensation order or an order for costs (PCCA 1973, s. 12(4)), or an order for disqualification from driving (RTOA 1988, s. 46(1)). It may also be combined with an order for deportation (Immigration Act 1971, s. 6(3)), or an exclusion order in respect of licensed premises (Licensed Premises (Exclusion of Certain Persons) Act 1980, s. 1(2)). A probation order may be combined with an order for forfeiture of property under PCCA 1973, s. 43 or a restitution order under the Theft Act 1968, s. 28.

When combining sentencing measures, regard should always be had to CJA 1991, s. 28(2)(a) which states that 'nothing shall prevent a court from mitigating any penalty included in an offender's sentence by taking into account any other penalty included in that sentence'. It may also be useful to refer to the White Paper (Home Office, 1990), in which it was stated that 'For most offenders only one of these orders will be necessary, or justified by the seriousness of their offences. For more serious offenders, however, more than one community penalty could be imposed.'

5.2.10 Early termination of probation order

According to the Home Office National Standards, early termination of a probation order should be considered whenever the offender has made good progress in achieving the objectives set out for the order, and where there is not considered to be a significant risk of reoffending and/or of serious harm to the public. An application for early termination should not normally be sought before half-way through the term of the order, but such action should be considered by the time two-thirds of the term has elapsed, unless there are clear reasons for not doing so. There appear to be two possible procedures here.

The first is where application is made to the magistrates' court by the offender with the support of the supervising probation officer, under CJA 1991, sch. 2, para. 7. During the application the officer will present a report outlining the offender's good progress under the order. It is desirable, though not apparently essential, that the probationer be present at this time. The magistrates' court, if it made the order, and having taken into account the extent to which the probationer has complied with the order, may now decide to revoke it (para. 7(2)). If the Crown Court made the order, it seems that the applicant must be released on bail until he can appear before the Crown Court. Stone (1994) indicates that some Crown Court judges are willing to hear applications for early termination of a probation order in chambers on a direct application by the supervising officer.

The second procedure is under PCCA 1973, s. 11, where application is made to the magistrates' court for the probation order to be discharged and for a conditional discharge to be substituted. Application under this section is appropriate where it is felt that the probation order can serve no further useful purpose but where it is too early in the term of the order to seek revocation. Application cannot be made while any appeal against the probation order is pending (s. 11(1A)). Under s. 11 the offender is not required to attend court provided that the supervising officer can assure the court that the probationer consents to the application being made and understands what the effect of the order will be. Substitution can be made by the magistrates' court even where the Crown Court made the probation order, unless when it made the order the Crown Court expressly reserved to itself the power of discharging it. A person in respect of whom an order under s. 11 has been made is to be treated, for so long as the conditional discharge continues, in all respects (and especially for the purposes of commission of a further offence) as if the original order had been a conditional discharge and not a probation order. The reason for this is that the powers of the court when dealing with a breach of a conditional discharge are different from those when dealing with revocation of a probation order after commission of a further offence. The conditional discharge expires at the time when the probation order would otherwise have expired (s. 11(1)). Presumably the discharge counts as a 'conviction' only for limited purposes (PCCA 1973, s. 1C; see **7.1.3**).

5.3 COMMUNITY SERVICE ORDERS

5.3.1 Power to make a community service order

A community service order is a 'community order' and the court cannot impose a community service order unless the conditions which apply to the passing of a community order are first satisfied. In particular, by CJA 1991, s. 6(1), the court must be satisfied that the offence committed is serious enough to warrant a community order (see **5.1**).

Community service orders were introduced into English law in 1972. The relevant powers of the courts to pass community service orders are now to be found in PCCA 1973, s. 14. A community service order is an order that requires the offender to perform unpaid work in the community. Its main purposes, according to the Home Office National Standards are to 're-integrate the offender into the community through (i) positive and demanding work, keeping to disciplined requirements, and (ii) reparation to the community by undertaking socially useful work which, if possible, makes good damage done by offending'. It should be noted that the court does not have power to order that the offender shall perform community service for any particular victim injured by his offence. Reparation here is meant in the sense of reparation to society generally for the offence committed. The National Standards do, however, envisage that appropriate work may include the amelioration of damage which has been criminally caused, e.g. by the removal of grafitti from walls.

Between 1986 and 1996 the proportionate use made by the courts of community service orders for sentencing for indictable offences has remained steady across most of the main categories of offending. Increased use of community service in burglary cases during the early 1990s has since tailed off. The percentage change in the use of community service orders for indictable offences between 1986 and 1996, for the main categories of offending is as follows:

		1986	1996
(1)	violence against the person	7 per cent	14 per cent
(2)	sexual offences	2 per cent	3 per cent
(3)	burglary	13 per cent	11 per cent
(4)	robbery	5 per cent	3 per cent
(5)	theft and handling	7 per cent	9 per cent
(6)	fraud and forgery	8 per cent	16 per cent
(7)	criminal damage	7 per cent	7 per cent
(8)	drug offences	2 per cent	7 per cent
(9)	motoring offences	12 per cent	9 per cent
All offending		8 per cent	9 per cent

This represents a modest fall in its use over that period from 30,500 offenders to 28,300. The community service order is used in fewer cases than the probation order (33,100 in 1996), but in more cases than the other community orders put together.

A community service order may be made by the Crown Court, by an adult magistrates' court or by a youth court. The offender must be aged 16 or over. There is no upper age limit, but in practice this measure tends to be used mainly for offenders in their late teens or twenties. The offender must have committed an offence which is punishable with imprisonment in the case of an adult. The total number of hours community service to be performed must be specified in the order, and must be between 40 and 240 hours. The number of hours ordered by the court should reflect primarily the seriousness of the offence committed. Normally, according to the Home Office National Standard, the first work session should be under way within ten days of the making of the order. A minimum work rate of five hours per week should be achieved throughout the order, but normally no more than 21 hours should be worked in any one week. Work must be completed within the period of 12 months from the date of the order but, unless revoked, the order remains in force until all the hours are in fact completed. The 12-month period may be extended by application to the court (CJA 1991, sch. 2, para. 15). If the offender is in employment the community service must be arranged for evenings or weekends or such other times as do not clash with the offender's working hours. If the offender is unemployed, the order should not conflict with his or her entitlement to welfare benefits, and should not prevent the offender from being available to seek or take up employment. The court should not normally impose a community service order without first obtaining a pre-sentence report (CJA 1991, s. 7 and **5.1**).

Before making the order the court must be satisfied that the offender is a suitable person to perform community service (for example, that he is physically fit enough to do so) and that there is work available locally. Formerly there was a legal requirement that the offender must consent before the order was made, but that requirement was abolished by the C(S)A 1997, s. 38, the government arguing that the requirement was 'anomalous . . . and a derogation from the authority of the court' (Consultation Document, *Strengthening Punishment in the Community* (1995)). There were two reasons for the consent requirement. One was that to pass a community service order when an offender is not motivated to comply with it merely stores up trouble for the future. The second was that without the requirement of consent it was thought that the community service provisions could infringe art. 4(2) of the European Convention on Human Rights, which states that 'No one shall be required to perform forced or compulsory labour'. Although art. 4(3) goes on to exempt work 'required to be done in the ordinary course of detention . . . or during conditional release from such detention', it does not exempt work done under sentence in the community. According to its Consultation Document (1995) the government does not believe that removal of the requirement of consent will be regarded as a breach of the article since 'a community sentence does not involve detention and is, therefore, less restrictive' than work required of a sentenced prisoner.

The community service order must specify the petty sessions area in which the offender lives. The court must explain to the offender in open court and in ordinary language the purpose and effect of the community service order, the consequences of failure to comply with it and the fact that the court has power to review the order subsequently on the application of either the offender or the probation officer (PCCA s. 14(4) and (5)). The court must then give copies of the order to the probation officer and the offender. Non-compliance with these provisions does not, apparently, invalidate the order. In *Walsh* v *Barlow* [1985] 1 WLR 90 it was argued by the offender, unsuccessfully, that a community service order imposed upon him was ineffective, since no copy of it had been delivered to him. The Court of Appeal held that such delivery was not a prerequisite of the coming into force of the order.

5.3.2 Community service arrangements

Community service orders are administered by the probation service. That service is reponsible for all the administrative arrangements, including liaison with a wide range of local groups to which offenders on community service orders are attached from time to time. For this purpose many probation service areas have a designated community service unit or a number of officers organised into the community service team. The community service work itself may be directed by supervisors employed by the probation service, or by a local voluntary or public body. Some tasks involve offenders working alongside volunteers. The Home Office National Standards require that the probation service should arrange a variety of community service work placements, which should be 'demanding in the sense of being physically, emotionally or intellectually taxing, of benefit to the community and, if possible, personally fulfilling for offenders and designed to secure public support for the supervision of offenders in the community'. The sort of work available varies considerably but examples include helping in outdoor conservation or reclamation projects, refurbishing community facilities, building adventure playgrounds, making toys which are then sold to raise money for charity, decorating flats and houses for the elderly or handicapped, and helping disabled people. Work done under community service schemes should not be of a type which a business might be interested in carrying out on a paid basis; community service must not be permitted to undercut ordinary commercial enterprise. Community service is imposed 'as punishment' not 'for punishment', so it is not the intention that the work 'should deliberately be made unpleasant in the expectation that this will deter' (Home Office, 1990). The probation service is also made responsible by the National Standards for ensuring that the risk to the public of placing offenders on community service is minimised. Community service may be undertaken in individual placements, which should be designed to emphasise to the offender his or her own personal responsibility, or group placements which allow offenders to take part in a team project.

The probation service is responsible for enforcing the order and securing the offender's compliance with its terms. An offender's failure to comply with the terms of the order must be investigated by the probation officer. If there is no adequate explanation for the failure to comply, the incident must be recorded. According to the National Standards, action should normally be taken to enforce the order after no more than three instances of failure to comply (see further the Community Service and Combination Order Rules 1992). The offender is not actually under probation supervision during the period of the order, but there will be times where personal contact between the probation service and the offender is appropriate in order to deal with problems arising during the time of the order and to help the offender maintain a commitment to completion of the order. By PCCA 1973, s. 15(1), the offender is required to keep in touch with the relevant probation officer and notify him of any change of address. A failure to do so would be a failure to comply with the order. If an offender requires a more formal element of supervision in addition to the community service requirement, this may be achieved by the court passing a combination order.

5.3.3 Concurrent and consecutive sentences of community service

Section 14(3) of PCCA 1973 allows for the possibility of the court passing community service orders in respect of two or more offences, and specifying that those orders shall either run concurrently with, or consecutively to, each other. It seems clear that the principles underlying the choice between concurrent and consecutive sentencing are the same as those which inform the choice between concurrent and consecutive custodial sentencing (see **4.4.4**). Section 14(3) also requires that the total number of hours of community service to be completed by the offender must not exceed the maximum which could be imposed for a single offence, which is 240. This provision has direct application where the court is imposing two community service orders on the same occasion. In *Siha* (1992) 13 Cr App R (S) 588 the Court of Appeal said that while s. 14(3) did not actually apply to the case where an offender is already serving a sentence of community service and subsequently has a further community service order imposed upon him, sentencers imposing a second community service order on an offender in such circumstances should remember that Parliament had prescribed 240 hours as the maximum to be imposed on a single occasion. In *Anderson* (1989) 11 Cr App R (S) 147 it was made clear that it was the total number of hours imposed on the offender (rather than the number of hours which remained to be served) which must not exceed 240.

5.3.4 Combining community service orders with other sentences or orders

A community service order should not be imposed on the same occasion as an immediate custodial sentence, whether the sentences relate to different counts or to separate indictments

(*Starie* (1979) 69 Cr App R 239) and a community service order should not be combined with a suspended sentence of imprisonment (*Ray* (1984) 6 Cr App R (S) 26). A community service order may be combined with a fine. A community service order and a probation order may not be combined for a single offence except in the form of a combination order (CJA 1991, s. 6(3)). There would seem to be no objection in law to imposing a community service order in respect of one offence and a probation order in respect of another, when sentencing on the same occasion. This was permissible before the implementation of the CJA 1991 (*Harkess* (1990) 12 Cr App R (S) 366) and nothing in that Act prevents it, but it is arguable that such a mix is undesirable since it would allow the court to circumvent the specific provisions relating to combination orders. It is possible to combine a community service order with a curfew order. It is clear from PCCA 1973, s. 14(8) that a community service order may be combined with an order for costs, a disqualification of any kind imposed on the offender, a compensation order or a forfeiture order made under PCCA 1973, s. 43. A community service order cannot be combined with an absolute or conditional discharge when sentencing for a single offence, since a discharge can be imposed only where 'it is inexpedient to inflict punishment' (PCCA 1973, s. 1A(1)), but these two measures may, of course, be used for sentencing different offences on the same occasion.

When combining sentencing measures regard should always be had to CJA 1991, s. 28(2)(a), which states that 'nothing shall prevent a court from mitigating any penalty included in an offender's sentence by taking into account any other penalty included in that sentence'. Regard may also be had in this context to the White Paper (Home Office, 1990), where it was stated that 'For most offenders, only one of these orders will be necessary, or justified by the seriousness of their offences. For more serious offenders, however, more than one community penalty could be imposed.'

5.3.5 Community service orders: sentencing principles

The Court of Appeal has endorsed the use of community service for some younger offenders who have committed offences which lie close to the custody threshold, such as non-residential burglary. In *Brown* (1981) 3 Cr App R (S) 294 community service was said to be 'tailor-made' for a 19-year-old offender with no previous convictions who, in breach of trust, and together with a co-defendant, had committed burglary of his employer's premises, with loss of goods to the value of £2,850. In *Lawrence* (1982) 4 Cr App R (S) 69 the offender, together with three others, had taken a car without authority and driven to another town. There they had broken the window of a shop and stolen television sets, video recorders and tape recorders. The Court of Appeal took account of a period of five years without convictions which preceded the current offences, and the fact that the offender was 'a man who really has all the marks of someone who, at this stage in his life, is capable of settling down and remaining a good and useful member of the community'. The offender was 'ideally suited' to a community service order of 190 hours, though this was varied to 150 hours to take account of time which he had already spent in custody. There are few recent decisions on the use of community service orders in burglary cases. In *Tetteh* (1994) 15 Cr App R (S) 46 the offender was seen coming out of the cellar at a YMCA club, where the spirits store was found to have been broken open. Nothing had been stolen. Despite the defendant's poor record the Court of Appeal thought that this case did not cross the custody threshold and that a community sentence would have been appropriate. A similar case is *Carlton* (1994) 15 Cr App R (S) 335. Where the property involved is a house, rather than a factory, office or shop, the offence will normally be regarded by the courts as being above the custody threshold (for the relevant guideline case see **12.4.5**). Community service will then only be appropriate where the offender has a clean record, has played a peripheral role, or where there is other substantial mitigation. One example is *Mole* [1991] Crim LR 220, where the offender, a youth of 17 with no previous convictions, acted as lookout while two others ransacked a house and stole valuables. A sentence of three months' detention in a young offender institution was quashed and a community service order for 100 hours was substituted. See also *Suker* (1990) 12 Cr App R (S) 290, where the 19-year-old offender, affected by drink and looking for money to pay his taxi fare home, attempted to climb through the bathroom window of a house in the early hours of the morning and was detained by the householder.

Occasionally community service has been upheld for less serious offences of violence. An example is *McDiarmid* (1980) 2 Cr App R (S) 130, where an offender, aged 18 and of previous good character, threw a beer glass at a man in the course of a disturbance in a public house. A custodial sentence was varied to 75 hours' community service by the Court of Appeal. A community service order is not a suitable sentence for offences involving serious violence, however. In *Attorney-General's Reference (No. 49 of 1996)* [1997] 2 Cr App R (S) 144, the offender pleaded guilty to causing grievous bodily harm with intent after attacking a man in the street with a bottle and then punching and kicking him on the ground. The Court of Appeal said that the sentence was unduly lenient and varied it to nine months' imprisonment. Another example is *Attorney-General's Reference (No. 30 of 1993)* (1995) 16 Cr App R (S) 318, where the offender, a man with a bad record for violence, had struck a man in the face with a pool cue and had then tried to kick him when he fell to the ground. After having been convicted of wounding with intent the sentence was 240 hours of community service together with a compensation order. The Court of Appeal said that the sentence would 'undermine public confidence in the administration of justice' and increased it to 18 months' imprisonment. A community service order of 150 hours imposed for robbery in a contested case was held to be unduly lenient in *Attorney-General's Reference (No. 39 of 1996)* [1997] 1 Cr App R (S) 355. The offender and a co-defendant had encountered a youth riding a mountain bike. They kicked and punched the victim several times and took the bike, abandoning it at the side of the road shortly afterwards. The Court of Appeal increased the sentence to 12 months' imprisonment. A community service order was also said to be wrong in *Attorney-General's Reference (No. 6 of 1994)* (1995) 16 Cr App R (S) 343, where robbery of an 18-year-old victim was committed at night by threatening to use a knife. A sentence of 18 months' imprisonment was substituted.

Community service may be appropriate in a wide range of property crimes. It is this group which seems to form the main catchment area for community service sentencing, whether or not offenders have previous convictions. In *Graham* (1988) 10 Cr App R (S) 352 the offender continued to draw unemployment benefit for 12 months after gaining employment. The total sum involved was over £1,500, and 120 hours' community service was said to be appropriate. In a case where offenders sprayed paint on carriages at a London Underground depot (*Ferreira* (1988) 10 Cr App R (S) 343) the Court of Appeal replaced custodial sentences with community service orders of 120 hours, Farquharson J commenting that community service was 'designed' for such a case. A sentence of 60 hours' community service was said to be correct in *Hamilton* (1988) 10 Cr App R (S) 383, where the offender stole goods and property worth £180 and the same sentence was approved in *Zaman* (1992) 12 Cr App R (S) 657, where a 19-year-old stole a radio from a car. In *Small* (1993) 14 Cr App R (S) 405 the 19 year-old offender pleaded guilty to three counts of theft, committed while he was employed as operations manager by a firm supplying pizzas. He failed to pay into the bank three sums of money totalling just over £1,000. The sentencer passed a sentence of three months' detention in a young offender institution but the Court of Appeal, bearing in mind the offender's youth and inexperience, his good record and the fact that, in the view of the court, too much responsibility had been placed on him at work without adequate supervision, varied the sentence to a community service order.

Community service is appropriate for some road traffic offences. In *Eynon* (1988) 10 Cr App R (S) 437 the offender, a man of good record, pleaded guilty to dangerous driving after his car, pursued by a police car, mounted a pavement and nearly knocked down pedestrians. A sentence of 180 hours' community service, together with disqualification from driving and orders for compensation and costs, was upheld. The case may be contrasted with *Attorney-General's Reference (No. 36 of 1994)* (1995) 16 Cr App R (S) 723 where a community service order of 240 hours together with disqualification from driving for three years was imposed on a goods driver, a man with a clean record, for causing death by careless driving having consumed alcohol above the prescribed limit. The defendant's vehicle had mounted a verge at the side of a dual carriageway after dark and had struck and killed a young man walking on the verge. Sentence was varied to two years' imprisonment.

It is clear from the place which community service has been assigned in the framework of the CJA 1991 that it should be regarded by sentencers as one of the more demanding forms of community sanction. This is in line with earlier sentencing practice, where Moxon found that community service assumed a higher place in the tariff than any other non-custodial sentence (Moxon, 1988), although that research was carried out before the introduction of combination orders. In a borderline case, where it was felt that custody could just be avoided, community service was the first alternative which sprang to mind. It is also clear that the number of hours required of the offender should reflect the seriousness of the offence (or offences) committed. There were very few appellate observations on appropriate community service sentence length before the CJA 1991. A rare example is the old case of *Lawrence* (see above), where the Court of Appeal said that 190 hours was appropriate for a burglary that might otherwise have attracted 9–12 months' imprisonment. Now that seriousness is the central issue in sentencing, more detailed guidance from the Court of Appeal would be helpful, but has not been forthcoming.

As has been explained above, there is relatively little direct involvement by the probation service with an offender carrying out a community service order. Community service, then, would seem to be an appropriate sentence only where there is a low requirement of social work intervention (see Figure 2 below). It is unclear to what extent factors personal to the offender might properly affect the number of hours ordered. Some sentencers take the view, apparently, that it is right to increase the number of hours on an unemployed offender. Although there may be 'a certain logic' in the view that a penalty based upon deprivation of leisure time should take into account the amount of spare time available (Moxon, 1983), the practice does seem discriminatory, and if so, should be seen as being wrong in principle.

5.4 COMBINATION ORDERS

By CJA 1991, s. 11, magistrates' courts and the Crown Court have power to pass a combination order on an offender who is of or over the age of 16 in any case where the offence is punishable with imprisonment. This sentence is a mix between a probation order and a community service order. A combination order is a 'community order', and the court cannot impose a combination order unless the conditions which apply to the passing of a community order are satisfied. In particular, by CJA 1991, s. 6(1), the court must be satisfied that the offence is serious enough to warrant the passing of a community order (see **5.1**).

FIGURE 2

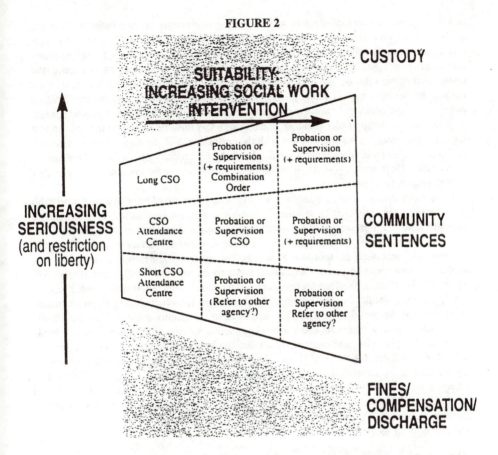

Figure 2 is reproduced from the Home Office National Standards for the Supervision of Offenders in the Community

The combination order was introduced by the 1991 Act, although powers to mix probation and community service had been available in Scotland for some years. The White Paper (Home Office, 1990) suggested that the order 'would enable the courts to introduce an element of reparation but, at the same time, to provide the probation service with an opportunity to work with offenders, to reduce the likelihood of future offending'.

The courts have made good use of this sentencing option, with combination orders as sentences for indictable offences increasing sharply from 900 cases in 1992 (the first year in which the measure was available to the courts) to over 6,000 cases in 1993 and 10,200 in 1996. This total is still small, however, compared with probation orders and community service orders standing alone.

5.4.1 Power to make a combination order

The sentence contains elements of probation and community service. The legislation provides that the probation element shall be dealt with in law as if it were a probation order and the community service element as if it were a community service order (CJA 1991, s. 11(3)). The probation element within the order may last for a period of between one year and three years (as compared to between six months and three years for an ordinary probation order) and the community service element of the order must require the completion of between 40 and 100 hours (as compared to between 40 and 240 hours for a community service order standing alone). The court may also insert into the combination order any of the additional requirements provided for in PCCA 1973, sch. 1A, which might be added to a probation order standing alone, though this must be subject to the proviso that these requirements are not inconsistent with the performance of the community service part of the order. For these requirements see **5.2.3** and the Community Service and Combination Order Rules 1992, which give details of work arrangements for the community service part of the combination order.

Unlike a probation order, a combination order may be imposed only in a case where the offender has been convicted of an offence punishable with imprisonment. The court should normally consider a pre-sentence report before passing a combination order (CJA 1991, s. 7 and **5.1**). Formerly, the offender's consent was required before a combination order could be imposed, since such consent was needed before either a community service order or a probation order could be made. The consent requirement for those sentences was abolished by the C(S)A 1997, s. 38. That section does not mention combination orders, but it can be safely assumed that the consent requirement for combination orders has by implication also been removed. Section 6(3) of CJA 1991 states that 'a community sentence shall not consist of or include both a probation order and a community service order'. The effect of this is to ensure that probation and community service can be mixed together only in the form of a combination order. Neither s. 6(3) nor s. 11 would seem to prevent a court from sentencing an offender to community service for one offence and probation for another when two offences are dealt with on the same occasion. This was possible prior to the implementation of the CJA 1991 (*Harkess* (1990) 12 Cr App R (S) 366), but may now be regarded as undesirable sentencing practice since it would be against the spirit of s. 11, which permits the mix only in restricted circumstances.

5.4.2 Combining combination orders with other sentences or orders

In principle, since a combination order is itself a complex order which may involve a range of requirements, it is submitted that it will generally be undesirable to combine it with other sentences or orders. There seems little doubt that it should not be mixed with custody, whether immediate or suspended. It would seem to be illogical to mix it with a probation order or a community service order. It can be assumed that it could be mixed with a fine, with a compensation order, with a disqualification or with an order for forfeiture, since either a community service order or a probation order standing alone may be so mixed. A combination order could be mixed with a curfew order. A combination order may not be combined with a conditional discharge or an absolute discharge when sentencing for the same offence, since a discharge is appropriate only where 'it is inexpedient to inflict punishment' (PCCA 1973, s. 1A(1)), but a combination order and a discharge may be used for sentencing different offences on the same occasion.

When combining sentencing measures regard should always be had to CJA 1991, s. 28(2)(a) which states that 'nothing shall prevent a court from mitigating any penalty included in an offender's sentence by taking into account any other penalty included in that sentence'. Regard may also be had in this context to the White Paper (Home Office, 1990), where it was stated that 'For most offenders, only one of these orders will be necessary, or justified by the seriousness of their offences. For more serious offenders, however, more than one community penalty could be imposed.'

5.4.3 Combination order: sentencing principles

The aim of this sentence is to provide a demanding community sentence to cater for some offenders who otherwise would receive immediate custody. The White Paper (Home Office, 1990) specifically mentioned 'persistent property offenders . . . sentenced for burglary, theft, handling, fraud and forgery [who] have three or more previous convictions'. According to CJA 1991, s. 11(2), a combination order should be imposed where it is desirable in the interests of 'securing the rehabilitation of the offender' or 'protecting the public from harm from him or preventing the commission by him of further offences'. These are the same statutory objectives as for a probation order (PCCA 1973, s. 2(1)). Further useful comment and advice may be found in the Home Office National Standards, which contain a section on combination orders. The National Standards suggest that a combination order is most likely to be regarded as suitable for an offender who:

(a) has committed an offence which is amongst the most serious for which a community sentence may be imposed;

(b) has clearly identified areas of need that have contributed to the offending and which can be dealt with by probation supervision; and

(c) has a realistic prospect of completing such an order, including both the probation and community service elements.

They also suggest that amongst those offenders who might not be regarded as suitable for a combination order would be those whose lifestyle is particularly chaotic (as a result of drug or alcohol addiction, for example) and who might have particular difficulty in keeping to a programme of community service work. Conversely, also excluded might be offenders with well ordered lifestyles who have little need of, or little prospect of responding to, probation supervision. Combination orders which contain additional requirements within the probation element are likely to be particularly onerous, and are likely to prove to be difficult to complete, especially for younger offenders. An early study on the use made by courts of combination orders (HM Inspectorate of Probation, 1993) looked at 160 cases and found that well over half had been imposed on offenders aged 21 or over. Thirty-three per cent of cases so dealt with were for burglary, 16 per cent for theft or handling, 16 per cent for motoring offences and 12 per cent for violence.

The National Standards also stress the importance of good management arrangements in the administration of combination orders, to ensure that the two parts of the order, including enforcement, are properly coordinated.

There is also little guidance from the Court of Appeal on the appropriate use of the combination order. Such a sentence was held to have been an unduly lenient sentence for robbery by mugging in *Attorney-General's Reference (No. 74 of 1995)* [1996] 2 Cr App R (S) 436. The offender and a co-defendant, wearing overalls and balaclavas, attacked the 17-year-old victim and stole his pay packet. The Court of Appeal increased the sentence to 12 months' detention in a young offender institution. Another case of robbery where the Court of Appeal varied a combination order to a custodial sentence is *Attorney-General's Reference (No. 2 of 1994)* (1995) 16 Cr App R (S) 117.

5.4.4   Early termination of combination order

The Home Office National Standards suggest that early termination may be considered only after completion of the community service element of the order, and then in accordance with the criteria for early termination of probation orders (see **5.2.10**).

5.5   CURFEW ORDERS

By CJA 1991, s. 12, magistrates' courts and the Crown Court have power to impose a curfew order on an offender of any age who is convicted of any offence except murder or an offence attracting a prescriptive minimum sentence under the C(S)A 1997. A curfew order is a 'community order' and the court is not able to impose a curfew order unless the conditions relating to the passing of a community order are satisfied. In particular, by CJA 1991, s. 6(1), the court will have to be satisfied that the offence committed is serious enough to warrant the passing of a community order (see **5.1**). A curfew order should not be confused with the power to attach a curfew condition to the grant of bail; a curfew order is a final disposal, not a measure pending trial or sentence.

The history of curfew orders has been closely associated with the use of electronic monitoring. Although the powers to impose curfew orders date from the CJA 1991, they were not brought into force until January 1995, by the CJPOA 1994. That Act allowed for the introduction of pilot trials on the use of curfew orders enforced by electronic monitoring, on an area-by-area basis. Trials commenced in July 1995 and were extended in November 1995. Until March 1998 the orders are available only in the trial areas, which are: (a) Greater Manchester, North Cheshire, Salford and Rochdale; (b) Berkshire, parts of the Thames Valley and outer London; (c) Norfolk, Suffolk and north Essex. The *Criminal Statistics* indicate a total of around 200 offenders who were so sentenced during the course of 1996, with an equal split between summary and indictable offences.

5.5.1   Power to impose a curfew order

A curfew order may be imposed by the Crown Court, by an adult magistrates' court or by a youth court on an offender who is convicted of any offence, subject only to the crime of murder and to the two presumptive sentences under the C(S)A 1997. A previous restriction on the use of curfew orders to offenders aged 16 or over was removed by the C(S)A 1997, s. 43, and the order is now also available for offenders aged from 10 to 15 inclusive. The curfew order may specify different places of curfew or different periods of curfew on different days, but the curfew order cannot last for longer than six months from the date of the making of the order or, in the case of an offender under the age of 16, three months from the date of the order (s. 12(2A)). It must not involve curfew periods of less than two hours' duration, or more than twelve hours' duration, in any one day during that period (CJA 1991, s. 12(2)). The curfew arrangements must not, so far as possible, interfere with the times when the offender attends work or school, or conflict with the requirements of any other community order to which he may be subject (s. 12(3)). The order must name a person who is to be responsible for monitoring the offender's whereabouts during the periods of curfew (s. 12(4)).

The court must explain to the offender in ordinary language the effect of the order and the consequences of failure to comply with its requirements (s. 12(5)). A former requirement that the offender must consent before a curfew order could be imposed was removed by the

C(S)A 1997, s. 38. The court must have information about the place or places to be specified in the order, including information about the attitudes of persons likely to be affected by the enforced presence there of the offender under curfew (s. 12(6)) and in the case of an offender aged under 16 the court is required to obtain additional information about the young offender's family circumstances and the likely effect of such an order on those circumstances (s. 12(6A)). The obtaining of a pre-sentence report is not normally required before a curfew order is passed (see **5.1**) but since the court must have the information referred to in s. 12(6) and (6A) the obtaining of such a report is likely to be regarded as good sentencing practice.

The government explained in the White Paper (Home Office, 1990) that it was not the purpose of curfew orders to keep people at home for most of the day. The aim is:

> to enable them to go to work, to attend training courses or probation centres, to carry out community service or to receive treatment for drug abuse. Curfews could be helpful in reducing some forms of crime, thefts of and from cars, pub brawls and other types of disorder. A curfew order could be used to keep people away from particular places, such as shopping centres or pubs, or to keep them at home in the evenings or at weekends.

A subsequent White Paper (Home Office, 1996a) noted that 'the curfew order is a significant restriction on liberty with the courts empowered to sentence for up to 2,000 hours over a period of six months'.

It may be noted in this context that courts currently have other powers to prevent offenders from frequenting specified places, under the Licensed Premises (Exclusion of Certain Persons) Act 1980 (see **10.4**), the Public Order Act 1986 (exclusion orders relating to certain designated football matches) and the Football Spectators Act 1989 (see **10.5**). More specifically in relation to juveniles a 'night restriction order' (a form of curfew) may be included as a condition of a supervision order (CYPA 1969, s. 12A(3)(b): see **5.8.4**), though these conditions are little used in practice. As mentioned above, the C(S)A 1997 has extended the availability of curfew orders to juveniles under 16. Although not a sentencing power, it may be noted that the CDB proposes to give powers to local authorities to set up local child curfew schemes, under which children under 10 can be banned from public places in the evenings and at night unless they are under the control of a responsible person aged 18 or over.

5.5.2 Combining a curfew order with other sentences or orders

It seems clear from the observations in the White Paper cited in the last paragraph that the government envisages the curfew order as operating in tandem with other community orders, such as probation or community service, although it can stand on its own. If a curfew order is being considered as part of a package of measures, the court should always remember that the overall effect should be to pass a total sentence which is proportionate to the seriousness of the offence committed. When combining sentencing measures, CJA 1991, s. 28(2)(a) states that 'nothing shall prevent a court from mitigating any penalty included in an offender's sentence by taking into account any other penalty included in that sentence'. A curfew order can be combined with a fine, a compensation order, an order for disqualification from driving or an order for forfeiture. In practice it seems to have been assumed, perhaps because of the difficulties of ensuring compliance with a curfew, that such orders will routinely carry a requirement of electronic monitoring (see **5.5.3**).

It can safely be assumed that a curfew order could not be combined with an immediate custodial sentence and that the restrictions upon the use of suspended imprisonment means that a combination with it is unlikely. A curfew order could not be combined with an absolute or conditional discharge since a discharge cannot be combined with a punitive measure for the same offence (PCCA 1973, s. 1A), though there would be nothing to prevent a curfew order being imposed in respect of one offence and a discharge in respect of another offence sentenced on the same occasion.

The general provisions as to mitigation (CJA 1991, s. 28(2)(a)) and the White Paper's comments on combining community sentences (see **5.4.2**) should be borne in mind in addition to the matters mentioned above.

5.5.3 Electronic monitoring

A curfew order imposed under CJA 1991, s. 12 may include requirements for securing the electronic monitoring of the offender's whereabouts during the curfew periods specified in the order in accordance with the terms of CJA 1991, s. 13. Electronic monitoring is not a sentence in its own right, but solely a means of enforcing a curfew order which is imposed under s. 12. The difficulties of ensuring compliance with a curfew order without including a condition of electronic monitoring were referred to above. Section 12(4A) of the CJA 1991, which was inserted by the CJPOA 1994, states that 'A court shall not make a curfew order unless the court has been notified by the Secretary of State that arrangements for monitoring the offender's whereabouts are available in the area'. This subsection suggests that a curfew order cannot be made by a court unless electronic monitoring is available to it. On the other hand, s. 12(5) refers to electronic monitoring as an 'additional requirement', suggesting that a court might make a curfew order without recourse to electronic monitoring where it is otherwise satisfied that the order will be complied with.

The issue of electronic monitoring of offenders has attracted a good deal of attention. Various schemes of this sort have been operational in the United States for some years, where there has been long experience of 'house arrest' as a form of sentence. In this country the Home Office ran three experimental schemes of electronic monitoring during 1990, though it was then used as a means of reinforcing bail conditions rather than as part of the sentencing exercise (see Mair and McNee, 1990). The pilots were not very successful, being characterised by a low take-up rate from the three courts and a high rate of equipment failure and defendant violation. Further trials, to test the electronic monitoring of curfew orders, have been running since 1995 in the three pilot areas referred to above, in order to test further the technical arrangements and costs of general introduction of the measure. The government has said in its White Paper, *Protecting the Public* (Home Office, 1996a) that:

> It is still too early to make a final evaluation of the trials so far, but they have already proved the potential value of electronic monitoring as a highly flexible, restrictive community sentence with a part to play in punishing offenders and reducing crime . . . The technology has so far proved successful in monitoring offenders whom the courts want off the streets, and has ensured that the courts' sentences cannot be evaded without serious consequences. The slightest breach of a curfew order or attempt to tamper with the equipment is detected, and investigated by the contractors immediately. No violations are ignored, with warnings given for the most minor infringement. Offenders who continue not to comply are returned to court.

This statement misleads in suggesting that electronic monitoring is in itself a sentence — as we have seen, it is not. The government is considering the scope for wider application of electronic monitoring generally, and the CDB contains provisions for electronic monitoring of prisoners on release under licence.

5.6 DRUG TREATMENT AND TESTING ORDERS

Part IV of the Crime and Disorder Bill contains provisions which, when they become law and are brought into force, will create a new community order — the drug treatment and testing order.

When the relevant provisions are implemented the drug treatment and testing order will be a 'community order', and the court will not be able to impose such an order unless the conditions relating to the passing of a community order are satisfied. In particular, by CJA 1991, s. 6(1) as amended by the CDB, sch. 7 the court will have to be satisfied that the offence committed is serious enough to warrant the passing of a community order (see **5.1**). The court should not normally impose a drug treatment and testing order without first obtaining a pre-sentence report (CJA 1991, s. 7 as amended by CDB, sch. 7).

5.6.1 Power to impose a drug treatment and testing order

A drug treatment and testing order may be imposed by the Crown Court, by an adult magistrates' court (or, presumably, by a youth court) on an offender aged 16 or over who is convicted of any offence, subject only to the crime of murder and to the two presumptive sentences under the C(S)A 1997 (CDB, cl. 57(1)). The court may, by cl. 57(5) make such an order where it is satisfied:

    (a)   that [the offender] is dependent on or has a propensity to misuse drugs; and

    (b)   that his dependency or propensity is such as requires and may be susceptible to treatment.

For the purposes of cl. 57(5) the court may require the offender to provide samples, in order to establish whether the offender has any drug in his body. This requirement cannot be made unless the offender expresses his willingness to comply with it (cl. 57(6)). Before making a drug treatment and testing order the court must explain to the offender in ordinary language the effect of the order and the consequences of failure to comply with its requirements (cl. 60(1)), and the order itself cannot be made unless the offender expresses his willingness to comply with it. Copies of the order must be provided for the offender, the person who will provide the treatment under the order and the probation officer (cl. 60(2)). It is unlikely, however, that non-compliance with this last requirement would be fatal to the order: see *Walsh v Barlow* [1985] 1 WLR 90, considered at **5.3.1**. The order will have effect for a period specified in the order of not less than six months nor more than three years (cl. 57(2)).

The order has two elements to it. The first is the 'treatment requirement', which is that the offender should, during the whole time of the order undergo treatment with a view to tackling the offender's dependency on, or propensity to misuse, drugs. Such treatment may be as a resident at a place specified in the order, such as a hospital or clinic, or as an out-patient. The second element is the 'testing requirement', which is the provision of further regular samples by the offender during the course of the order. During the order the offender will be under the supervision of a probation officer. The offender is required to keep in regular contact with the probation officer and to provide the officer with the results of the tests carried out on the samples which the offender has supplied, but supervision is carried out by the officer only to the extent necessary to enable reports on the offender's progress to be made to the court, and to deal with any questions of amendment or revocation of the order which may arise (cl. 58(8)).

Clause 59 of the Bill requires that periodic reviews of the offender's progress under the order be made by the court at intervals of not less than one month. These reviews, at least initially, will involve the offender's attendance at a 'review hearing' in court, at which the offender's test results, the supervising officer's report on his progress, and the views of the person providing the treatment will be considered by the court (cl. 59(1)). If, at a review hearing, it appears that the offender's progress is satisfactory, subsequent reviews may be carried out by the court without a full review hearing (in the case of the Crown Court, by a judge, and in the case of a magistrates' court, by a justice of the peace) but, if progress subsequently becomes unsatisfactory, a further review hearing in court must be convened (cl. 59(8)). At the review hearing the court may revoke the order and resentence the offender, giving credit for any period of the order which has been successfully completed (cl. 59(4)) or, with the agreement of the offender, amend any requirement or provision of the order, but not so as to make the length of the order less than six months or more than three years. Any amendment to the treatment or testing requirements of the order require the offender's willingness to comply (cl. 59(3)).

The court cannot make a drug treatment and testing order unless arrangements have been made in that court area for the treatment to be specified in the order to be carried out (cl. 58(3)).

This order may be compared with a requirement as to treatment for drug or alcohol dependency which may be inserted as a requirement of probation order (see **5.2.8**). Clearly the two orders are very similar. The differences seem to be (a) that the probation requirement extends to alcohol misuse, whereas the drug treatment order is presumably confined to misuse of drugs; (b) that the drug treatment order has the 'testing requirement' which the probation order does not; and (c) that the provisions for the probation requirement state that the offender's dependency should have 'caused or contributed to the offence', while no such causal link is specified for the drug treatment order.

5.7 BREACH, REVOCATION AND AMENDMENT OF CERTAIN COMMUNITY ORDERS

The arrangements for enforcement (breach, revocation and amendment) of several of the community orders are to be found in CJA 1991, s. 14 and sch. 2. The community orders so dealt with are the probation order, the community service order, the combination order, the curfew order and (when the relevant provisions of the CDB become law and are brought into force) the drug treatment and testing order. The government's stated intention in the White Paper which preceded the 1991 Act (Home Office, 1990) was to bring greater consistency to the area of enforcement and so very similar provisions are applicable in respect of these five community orders. The provisions for enforcement of the three other community orders — attendance centre orders, supervision orders and (when the relevant provisions of the CDB become law and are brought into force) the action plan order — are somewhat different, and are dealt with as part of the description of each of those orders, at **5.8.4**, **5.9.10** and **5.10.3** respectively. The provisions dealing with breach of conditional discharge and breach of reparation orders are different again, since neither of these orders is a community order. For breach of conditional discharge see **7.1.5** and for breach of reparation orders see **7.4.3**.

An important distinction should be drawn at the outset between breach, revocation and amendment of community orders. 'Breach' refers to the situation where enforcement action is taken against an offender in consequence of a failure to comply with one of more of the requirements of the relevant community order, such as a failure to notify the probation officer of a change of address or a failure to carry out properly the work specified under a community service order. 'Revocation' refers to the situation where application is made to the court to bring the relevant community order to an end. This may be for one of a number of reasons, such as early termination where progress under the order has been good. It also covers the case, however, where the offender has committed a further offence during the currency of the order. As part of the court's response when dealing with the new offence, it may decide to revoke the original community order. An example would be where a custodial sentence is passed for the new offence, a sentence incompatible with the continuance of the community order. Commission of a further offence is thus relevant to revocation, rather than to breach. In contrast to breach and to revocation, either the offender or the relevant officer may make application to the court for amendment of a community order. This covers cases where some change of circumstance has occurred since the order was imposed, and an adjustment to the terms of the order is thus requested.

In the White Paper (Home Office, 1990) the government indicated the 'careful balance' which has to be achieved in the use by the courts of breach and revocation powers:

> If the procedures are too lax, confidence in the effectiveness of these community penalties will be undermined. On the other hand, if these procedures are too strict, for example if they allow minor disciplinary infractions to be punished with custody, there is a danger that offenders who are otherwise not at risk of custody will find themselves in prison. There should be three stages in enforcing the requirements of an order: warnings and possible administrative sanctions by the supervisor; a decision, if necessary, to take the offender back to court; and the court's decision.

The Home Office National Standards suggest that, in general, action should be taken to return an offender to court for breach of the relevant community order where there have been no more than *three* unacceptable failures to comply with the requirements of the order. For details see the text relating to each of the specific community orders.

Before turning to consider the enforcement arrangements for community sentences in more detail, it may be worth indicating what percentage of offenders given various community sentences are subsequently returned to court, and how frequently the court then imposes a custodial sentence. According to the *Criminal Statistics* (Home Office, 1997b), during 1996, 12 per cent of offenders given probation orders were subsequently returned to court and, of those, 31 per cent received a custodial sentence instead. Of offenders given community service orders, 28 per cent were returned to court, of whom 19 per cent received custody, and 36 per cent of those given combination orders were returned to court, with 38 per cent of those returned receiving custody. No figures are provided for other community orders. The *Statistics* compare the rate of recall to court and the percentage use of custody across the last 10 years, and the figures are somewhat surprising. For community service orders the 'failure rate' has increased from 18 per cent to 28 cent, but the rate of use of custody in response has declined from 36 per cent to 19 per cent. These trends suggest that community service orders are being more rigorously enforced, with offenders being returned to court where once they might only have warned. The courts, however, tend increasingly to fine the offender and continue with the order, rather than impose custody. Care should be taken with these figures, since the relevant table in the *Criminal Statistics* (Table 7.25) refers to the rate of 'breach' of community orders, but it appears that the figures also include cases where the order has been 'revoked' for commission of a further offence, a distinction which was explained above.

5.7.1   Breach of certain community orders

Where there is evidence of breach of the terms of a probation order, a community service order, a combination order, a curfew order, or a drug treatment and testing order, a justice of the peace may issue a summons or warrant for the offender's appearance. The offender must appear before a magistrates' court acting for the petty sessions area concerned or, in the case of a drug treatment and testing order, the court which made the order. The Crown Court has no jurisdiction to deal with breach of a community order unless the matter has first come before the magistrates. Any breach must be admitted by the offender or be formally proved. The prosecution must be in a position to put before the court the facts of the original offence as well as the circumstances of the alleged breach (*Clarke* [1997] 2 Cr App R (S) 163). If it is proved to the magistrates' court before which the offender appears that he has failed without reasonable excuse to comply with the requirements of the probation order, community service order, combination order, curfew order, or drug treatment and testing order the court may then adopt any one of four courses of action set out in CJA 1991, sch. 2, para. 3(1).

(a)   It may impose a fine on the offender not exceeding £1,000 (para. 3(1)(a)). The original community order would continue.

(b)   It may make a community service order of not more than 60 hours on the offender. The original community order would continue. If the offender is being dealt with for breach of an existing community service order, this option is still available, but the total number of hours under both orders must not exceed 240 hours (paras. 3(1)(b) and 6(3)). It can perhaps be assumed that this total of 240 refers to the total number of hours ordered, rather than the total number which remain to be served, by analogy with *Anderson* (1989) 11 Cr App R (S) 147 (see **5.3.3**).

(c)   Where the offender is in breach of a probation order or a curfew order where the offender is under the age of 16, and it is a case where the offender is eligible for an attendance centre order (see **5.8**), the court may make an attendance centre order (para. 3(1)(c)). The original community order would continue.

(d)   Where the original order was made by a magistrates' court (for cases where the original court was the Crown Court, see below), the court may revoke the order and deal with the offender, for the offence in respect of which the community order was passed, in any manner in which it could deal with him if he had just been convicted by the magistrates' court of that offence (para. 3(1)(d)).

Options (a) to (c) are without prejudice to the continuation of the original order. They are simply penalties for the offender's failure to comply with the order's requirements, and do not amount to sentencing the offender for the original offence. In principle there seems no reason why a court might not exercise options (a) to (c) more than once in respect of subsequent breaches of the same community order. If, however, the offender can be said to have 'wilfully and persistently failed to comply' with the order, the court may choose to follow option (d). Note also that the court has no power, when dealing with breach of a community order, to extend the operational period of that order.

Under option (d), the court may revoke the community order in the light of the breach, and pass sentence again for the original offence. When dealing with an offender under para. 3(1)(d) the court, according to para. 3(2):

(a) shall take into account the extent to which the offender has complied with the requirements of the relevant order; and

(b) may assume, in the case of an offender who has wilfully and persistently failed to comply with those requirements, may impose a custodial sentence notwithstanding anything in section 1(2) of this Act.

There is perhaps an assumption that, once the court turns to para. 3(1)(d), the offender will then be facing a custodial sentence. This is likely, but not inevitable, particularly where, having regard to para. 3(2)(a), the offender has in fact completed a substantial part of the community order. Paragraph 3(2)(b) is printed above as amended by the C(S)A 1997. The CJA 1991 gives statutory recognition to the principle developed in earlier cases on breach of community service orders that the court should have regard to the offender's progress under the order when considering how to deal with the breach. In *Paisley* (1979) 1 Cr App R (S) 196 six months' custody, consequent upon breach and revocation, was varied to allow an offender's immediate release, where he had completed 61 of his 100 hours of community service, although he had on three occasions failed to comply with the order's requirements. Even if good progress under the order cannot dissuade the court from revoking the order and imposing custody, it should properly serve to reduce the length of the term imposed. While the desirability of giving credit is most compelling when the offender has completed a high proportion of the order, in *Whittingham* (1986) 8 Cr App R (S) 116 the Court of Appeal said that some credit should have been given where only a third of the hours had been completed successfully. Apparently, hours of community service completed after breach proceedings have been initiated may still be of some value in mitigation (*Tebbutt* (1988) 10 Cr App R (S) 88).

If a custodial sentence is imposed consequent upon breach of a community order, the court must, of course, have regard to the normal limitations upon the imposition of custodial sentences (such as the restriction on the maximum custodial sentence which can be imposed by a magistrates' court). It seems that the breach court should normally also observe the statutory restrictions in the CJA 1991, ss. 1(2) and 2(2) on the imposition and length of custodial sentences. This means that custody should only be given consequent upon breach where the original offence was so serious that only custody could be justified for it. It was explained by the Court of Appeal in *Oliver* [1993] 1 WLR 177 that the mere fact that the offender has received a community sentence does not mean that the offence itself was below the custody threshold. The court which imposed the community sentence may have taken into account matters of personal mitigation which, at the time, saved the offender from custody, but these may seem less persuasive now in light of his failure to comply with the community order. If, however, the court is relying on para. 3(2)(b), that the offender has 'wilfully and persistently failed to comply' with the requirements of the community order, it is clear from the wording of that sub-paragraph that the court is not required to justify custody in accordance with s. 1(2) of the 1991 Act.

Whenever a custodial sentence is imposed following breach of a community order, allowance should be given for any period of time which was spent by the offender in custody on remand before the community sentence was passed, although the extent of the allowance is a matter for judicial discretion. This point has been made on a number of occasions by the Court of Appeal. On the latest occasion, in *Henderson* [1997] 2 Cr App R (S) 266, Stuart White J in the Court of Appeal added that the breach court should always indicate the extent to which the time served on remand has been taken into account.

In the preceding discussion of court proceedings for breach of a community order, the assumption has been that the magistrates' court will be dealing with the breach itself. All breaches of community orders must come before a magistrates' court initially, but that court has discretion to send the offender to be dealt with in the Crown Court whenever the community order was originally passed by the Crown Court (sch. 2, para. 3(3)). The Crown Court's powers on breach are identical to those stated above in relation to magistrates' courts except that, in a case where the Crown Court chooses to revoke the order and exercise the power equivalent to that in para. 3(1)(d) (which for the Crown Court can be found in para. 4(1)(d)), the Crown Court is empowered to deal with the offender in any manner in which it could deal with him if he had just been convicted by the Crown Court of that offence. The upshot of this is that there is little point in magistrates sending an offender to the Crown Court to be dealt with for breach of a community sentence originally imposed by the higher court unless the magistrates expect the Crown Court to revoke the order and sentence for the original offence. The Crown Court, in dealing with an offender under para. 4(1)(d) must have regard to matters equivalent to those in para. 3(2) (see above).

A person sentenced by magistrates under para. 3(1)(d) may appeal to the Crown Court against the sentence (para. 3(5)).

5.7.2   Revocation of certain community orders

A probation order, a community service order, a combination order, curfew order, or a drug treatment and testing order may be revoked for any one of a number of reasons relating to the offender's change of circumstances since the order was imposed. A probation order may be revoked, for example, in the light of the offender's good progress. A community service order may be revoked because the offender can no longer carry out the work required under the order (e.g. since he has injured his back: *Fielding* [1993] Crim LR 229). A community order may also be revoked as a consequence of breach (see **5.7.1**). Commission of a further offence also forms the factual basis for revocation of the order, and the following discussion concentrates on this aspect of revocation. The use of revocation in contexts other than commission of a further offence must, however, be borne in mind when looking at the following provisions.

A magistrates' court acting for the petty sessions area concerned may revoke a probation order, a community service order, a combination order or a curfew order, or deal with the offender in some other way for the offence, where, on the application of the offender or the responsible officer, it appears to be in the interests of justice to do so. In the case of a drug treatment and testing order, however, this function can only be performed by the court which actually made the order. Unless the offender is making the application, the court must summon the offender to appear or, if he does not appear, issue a warrant for his arrest. By CJA 1991, sch. 2, para. 7(2), a magistrates' court, if the original community order was made in a magistrates' court, may either, under para. 7(2)(a)(i), simply revoke the order or, under para. 7(2)(a)(ii), revoke it and deal with the offender for the offence in respect of which the order was made in any manner in which it could have dealt with him if he had just been convicted by that court. In the latter case the magistrates must take into account the extent to which the offender has complied with the terms of the original order (e.g. the number of hours of community service which the offender has completed successfully). This principle is parallel to the rule discussed at **5.7.1** in relation to breach of community orders. If the original order was made in the Crown Court, a magistrates' court may commit the offender to Crown Court under para. 7(2)(b).

The issue of revocation of a probation order, a community service order, a combination order, a curfew order, or a drug treatment and testing order may come before the Crown Court in one of three different ways, which are listed in CJA 1991, sch. 2, para 8. First, an offender in respect of whom a relevant community order is in force may be convicted before the Crown Court of a further offence. Second, the offender may have been convicted of a further offence by a magistrates' court and committed for sentence to the Crown Court. Third, the magistrates may have committed the offender to Crown Court under para. 7(2)(b) because the original order was made by the Crown Court, and a magistrates' court may not revoke a Crown Court order. In any of these situations the Crown Court may either (a) simply revoke the community order or (b) revoke the community order and resentence for the original offence. If it resentences, the Crown Court must take into account the extent to which the offender has complied with the requirements of the order (para. 8(4)).

It is somewhat unclear on the face of these provisions whether the Crown Court, when revoking and resentencing an offender in respect of a community order which was originally imposed by a magistrates' court, is restricted to the powers of the lower court. After a series of conflicting decisions on this point the Court of Appeal ruled in *Ogden* [1996] 2 Cr App R (S) 386 that it is so restricted. Where a custodial sentence is passed consequent upon revocation of a community order, allowance should be made for any period spent by the offender on remand in custody before the community order was passed, though the extent of such allowance is a matter for judicial discretion (*McDonald* (1988) 10 Cr App R (S) 458 and the decision in *Henderson* [1997] 2 Cr App R (S) 266, see **5.7.1**). The case law indicates that where a community order is revoked in consequence of the commission of a further offence, it is almost always desirable for the court to deal fully and finally with the original offence for which the community order was passed (see *Rowsell* (1988) 10 Cr App R (S) 411). If custodial sentences are imposed both for the new offence and in consequence of resentencing for the original offence, such custodial terms may run consecutively, but subject to the usual totality principle (*Cook* (1985) 7 Cr App R (S) 249 and, for an explanation of this principle, see **4.4.4**).

A couple of further complications have arisen in the cases. One is where the offender commits a further offence during the operational period of a community order but has completed all the requirements of that order before being convicted of the new offence. Here the answer is straightforward: the court has no power to revoke the order or to deal with the offender for the original offence (*Cousin* (1994) 15 Cr App R (S) 516). The second is where the offender is convicted of an offence during the operational period of a community order but it turns out that the offence was in fact committed before the community order was imposed. The Court of Appeal has wavered on this one, but the prevailing view is that, although the court dealing with the new offence may revoke the community order, it is wrong to resentence for the original offence, since the offender did not break the terms of the community order by committing a further offence while he was subject to it (*Saphier* [1997] 1 Cr App R (S) 235, but see *Day* [1997] 2 Cr App R (S) 328).

5.7.3 Amendment of certain community orders

There is a range of circumstances in which application may be made to amend one or other of the requirements contained within a probation order, a community service order, a combination order, a curfew order or a drug treatment and testing order. Such application should be made to the local magistrates' court, by the offender or by the relevant officer. Unless the offender is making the application he should be summoned and, if he does not appear, the magistrates' court may issue a warrant for his arrest (CJA 1991, sch. 2, para. 17(1)), subject to the exception in para. 17(2) (cancellation, or reduction in a requirement, of an order and amendment relating to a change of petty sessions area or place specified in the order). The offender's expression of a willingness to comply with any amendments to the order is normally required. Paragraph 12 allows for amendment of a probation order, community service order, combination order or curfew order to take account of a change in the offender's area of residence. Paragraph 13 deals with the possibility of making amendments to the conditions or duration of a probation order or a curfew order. Paragraph 14 relates to probation orders which contain a condition of mental treatment or a condition of treatment for alcohol or drug dependency and provides for variation or cancellation of that requirement. Paragraph 14A allows for amendments to be made to requirements in a drug treatment and testing order. Paragraph 15 allows for the extension of the period of a community sentence order beyond 12 months, for reasons such as the ill-health or changed work commitments of the offender.

5.7.4   Reciprocal enforcement of certain community orders

Schedule 3 to CJA 1991 deals with certain detailed matters relating to the carrying out of community orders made by the courts in England and Wales by offenders who will be resident after sentence in either Scotland or Northern Ireland and the transfer to England and Wales of corresponding orders made in Scotland or Northern Ireland.

5.8   ATTENDANCE CENTRE ORDERS

An attendance centre order may be imposed on an offender between the ages of 10 and 20 inclusive. It may be made by the Crown Court, an adult magistrates' court or a youth court. It requires the offender to attend at a specified attendance centre for a specified number of hours. An attendance centre order is a 'community order' and the court cannot impose an attendance centre order unless the conditions relating to the passing of a community order are satisfied. In particular, by CJA 1991, s. 6, the court must be satisfied that the offence committed is serious enough to warrant a community order (see **5.1**).

Between 1986 and 1996 the proportionate use made by the courts of attendance centre orders when sentencing for indictable offences has remained steady at 2 per cent, though given the decline in the total number of offenders being sentenced, the number receiving attendance centre orders has declined from 9,400 to 5,400 over that period.

5.8.1   Power to impose an attendance centre order

Power to pass an attendance centre order derives from CJA 1982, s. 17. Such an order may be made by the Crown Court, an adult magistrates' court or a youth court, in any case where an offender aged between 10 and 20 inclusive is being sentenced for an offence punishable with imprisonment in the case of an adult. A former restriction on the use of attendance centre orders, limiting them to cases where the offender had no previous custodial experience, was removed by the CJA 1988.

The number of hours for which the offender must attend the centre is fixed by the court when it makes the order. The minimum number of hours is 12, except in a case where the offender is aged under 14 and the court is of the opinion that 12 hours would be excessive (s. 17(4)). The maximum number is 24, where the offender is aged under 16, or 36 hours where the offender is 16 but under 21 (s. 17(5)). Where an offender is dealt with for several offences on one occasion by means of two or more attendance centre orders, it is the aggregate number of hours which must be not less than 12 nor more than 24 or 36. If, on the other hand, an offender is already subject to an attendance centre order made on a previous occasion and the court dealing with him for a further offence also wishes to make such an order, the number of hours which he is to attend under the second order may be fixed without taking into account the hours he still has to attend under the first order (i.e. the combined total may exceed 24 or 36) (s. 17(6)). This rule stands in contrast to that which applies in relation to community service orders (see **5.3.3**).

Both the centre which the offender must attend and the time of his first attendance are specified by the court when it makes the order (s. 17(1) and (9)). Thereafter he has to attend in accordance with the direction of the person in charge of the centre (s. 17(10)). Interference with school or working hours must, as far as practicable, be avoided, and the offender may not be ordered to attend for more than three hours on any one occasion or more than one occasion on any one day (s. 17(11)). Periods of two or three hours on each occasion are normal, with periods of two hours being favoured for offenders aged under 18. A copy of the order should be provided for the offender and another for the officer in charge of the centre (s. 17(12)). The conduct of attendance centre staff and offenders is subject to the Magistrates' Courts (Attendance Centre) Rules 1958, as amended by the Magistrates' Courts (Attendance Centre) Rules 1992.

The court must have been notified that an attendance centre is available in the relevant area to receive a person of the age and sex of the offender, and it must be satisfied that the attendance centre which is named in the order is reasonably accessible to the offender (s. 17(1) and (7)). The Home Office has recommended that an order should not be made if the offender would have to travel more than 15 miles to reach the centre or if the journey would take him more than an hour and a half (if the offender is under 14, the recommended maxima are 10 miles and an hour's journey).

5.8.2 Attendance at the centre

An attendance centre is defined in CJA 1982, s. 16(2) as 'a place at which young offenders under 21 years of age may be required to attend and be given, under supervision, appropriate occupation or instruction'. Most centres are run by police officers, prison officers or teachers in their off-duty hours, at premises such as schools, youth clubs and church halls. They are usually open on alternate Saturday mornings or afternoons, and the effect of a typical attendance centre order is that the offender has to go to the centre named by the court for a number of three-hour sessions on separate Saturdays. Thus, the offender is punished by having his normal Saturday activities interfered with. One obvious use of the attendance centre order is to keep a young person convicted of disorder connected with football matches away from such matches. This possibility was specifically referred to in Home Office Circular 69/1990, where using an attendance centre order in conjunction with a football exclusion order (see **10.5**) was advocated as an appropriate means of dealing with such cases. The object of an attendance centre order is not, however, entirely punitive. According to the Home Office, attendance at an attendance centre should benefit the offender by 'bringing him under the influence of representatives of the authority of the state' and 'teaching him something of the constructive use of leisure'. Firm discipline, periods of strenuous physical exercise and instructions in handicrafts, citizenship, first aid, motor-cycle maintenance or such like are typical of the attendance centre regime. Each scheme of activities must be approved by the Secretary of State.

The imposition of an attendance centre order does not require the consent of the offender. The obtaining of a pre-sentence report before the passing of such a sentence is not required but, no doubt, there is a range of such cases where the obtaining of a report would constitute good sentencing practice.

In the past most attendance centres have catered for male juveniles. The government has in recent years encouraged the opening of more attendance centres for juvenile males and for girls. In 1992 there were 66 'junior attendance centres', which take males under the age of 17, 18 'junior mixed attendance centres', which take males and females under the age of 17, and 26 'senior attendance centres', which take males aged between 17 and 20 (Home Office Circular 30/1992).

As well as being used as a community sentence for an offence, attendance centre orders can be used as a means of enforcement in respect of a range of other sentencing measures. The importance of this role for attendance centre orders has increased significantly in recent years. An attendance centre order may now be used:

(a)   for those who default in payment of a fine, a compensation order etc., who are aged under 25 (CJA 1982, s. 17(1)) — formerly this option was restricted to offenders aged under 21, but the age limit was raised to under 25 by the C(S)A 1997 and is the only circumstance in which offenders over 20 may be sent to an attendance centre;

(b)   for breach of a probation order, where the offender is aged under 21 (CJA 1991, sch. 2, para. 3);

(c)   for breach of a curfew order, where the offender is aged under 16 (CJA 1991, sch. 2, para. 3);

(d)   for breach of a supervision order (CYPA 1969, ss. 15(3) and 16A);

(e)   when the relevant provisions become law and are brought into force, for breach of an action plan order (CDB, sch. 4, para. 3(2)); and

(f)   when the relevant provisions become law and are brought into force, for breach of a reparation order (CDB sch. 4, para. 3(2)).

In the case of money order defaulters, payment of the whole sum discharges the attendance centre order, and payment of a proportion of the sum reduces the number of hours to be served by the same proportion, rounded down to the nearest complete hour (CJA 1982, s. 17(3)).

5.8.3   Combining attendance centre orders with other sentences or orders

It is inappropriate to combine an attendance centre order with any form of custodial sentence. Since an attendance centre order is one of the methods open to the court when dealing with an offender aged under 21 who is in breach of one of a range of community sentences, it would seem that such orders when imposed on a person under that age should not be made at the same time as an attendance centre order. There seems to be no objection to imposing a fine, a compensation order, an order for disqualification from driving or an order for forfeiture at the same time as an attendance centre order. Adding a football exclusion order to an attendance centre order will be an attractive option in appropriate cases (see Home Office Circular No 69/1990). An attendance centre order cannot be combined with an absolute or conditional discharge when sentencing for a single offence, since discharges are imposed only where 'it is inexpedient to impose punishment' (PCCA 1973, s. 1A(1)), but these two measures may certainly be used when sentencing for different offences dealt with on the same occasion.

When combining sentencing measures regard should always be had to CJA 1991, s. 28(2)(a) which states that 'nothing shall prevent a court from mitigating any penalty included in an offender's sentence by taking into account any other penalty included in that sentence'. Regard may also be had in this context to the White Paper (Home Office, 1990), where it was stated that 'For most offenders, only one of these [community] orders will be necessary, or justified by the seriousness of their offences. For more serious offenders, however, more than one community penalty could be imposed.'

5.8.4 Discharge and variation of attendance centre order

An attendance centre order can be discharged early, either on application by the officer in charge of the attendance centre, or on the application of the offender, to a magistrates' court acting for the petty sessions area in which the centre is situated or to the court which actually made the order (CJA 1982, s. 18(3)). The Crown Court may reserve to itself the power to discharge the order (s. 18(4)). The power of discharge includes the option of dealing with the offender, for the original offence, in any manner in which he could have been dealt with by the court which made the attendance centre order (s. 18(4A)). This might allow the court, for instance, to impose an alternative penalty where there has been a change in the offender's circumstances (e.g. he has obtained employment which includes Saturday working) which mean that he is no longer able to carry out the order. Further, the relevant magistrates' court may, on application by the officer in charge or the offender, vary the starting day or hour of the order (s. 18(5)), or may substitute a different attendance centre (s. 18(6)). This will be appropriate if the offender changes his address or if the attendance centre named in the order closes.

5.8.5 Breach of attendance centre order

If the offender has failed to attend, or has committed a breach of the rules for the regulation and management of attendance centres (see Attendance Centre Rules 1994) which cannot adequately be dealt with under those rules, proceedings for breach of the attendance centre order may be initiated. A justice of the peace acting for the petty sessions area in which the attendance centre named in the order is situated, or, if the order was made by a magistrates' court, the petty sessions area for which that court was acting, may issue a summons requiring the offender to appear, or may issue a warrant for his arrest, requiring him to be brought before the court (CJA 1982, s. 19(1)).

If the order was made by a magistrates' court, the magistrates' court before which the offender is brought has power to impose a fine not exceeding £1,000 and continue with the order, or to revoke the order and deal with the offender for the original offence in any manner in which he could have been dealt with for that offence by the court which made the order (s. 19(3)(a)). If the order was made by the Crown Court, the magistrates' court may commit him in custody or release him on bail until he can appear before the Crown Court (s. 19(3)(b)). The magistrates' court should provide a certificate signed by a justice of the peace giving details of the case (s. 19(4)), though this is not conclusive of the breach, which must be specifically proved before the Crown Court. The Crown Court has powers to revoke the order and to deal with the offender for the original offence. In reaching its decision on the appropriate action to deal with the breach, the court must always take into account the extent to which the offender has complied with the requirements of the attendance centre order (s. 19(5A)(a)), such as the number of hours successfully completed prior to the breach. Further, if the court finds that the offender has 'wilfully and persistently failed to comply' with the requirements of the order, the purpose of s. 19(5A)(b) is to allow the court to deal with the offender by way of a custodial sentence. This subsection should have been amended by the C(S)A 1997 but appears to have been overlooked.

The offender may appeal against the sentence imposed for the original offence, after revocation of the attendance centre order, if the sentence was imposed by the magistrates' court, by virtue of s. 19(6) or, if imposed by the Crown Court, by virtue of CAA 1968, s. 9.

5.9   SUPERVISION ORDERS

Supervision orders are broadly equivalent to probation orders but cater for younger offenders. A supervision order may be passed by the Crown Court or a youth court (but not an adult magistrates' court) on an offender aged between 10 and 17 inclusive. For offenders aged 16 or 17, both orders are available. The Home Office National Standards and Home Office Circular 30/1992 taken together suggest that, while both a supervision order and a probation order are intended to assist an offender to become more responsible and to keep out of trouble, the clearest feature distinguishing them is that the supervision order is also intended to help a young person to develop into an adult, whereas a probation order is more appropriate for someone who is already emotionally, intellectually, socially and physically an adult. The National Standards suggest that 'since many 16 and 17 year olds are still very much in the stage of transition into adulthood, the supervision order may often in practice be the more suitable form of supervision'. Other relevant matters are the degree of offenders' independence from parents, whether they lead an independent life or have their own family reponsibilities, how they might be influenced by other offenders whom they may meet at group sessions and whether assistance is currently being received, or is needed, from social services.

The percentage use of supervision orders in the case of male offenders aged 14 and under 17 who are convicted of indictable offences increased from 11 per cent to 19 per cent between 1986 and 1996, and increased from 17 per cent to 25 per cent for male offenders aged 10 and under 14 who are convicted of indictable offences. These changes have to be seen in the context of a shrinking sentenced population for these age groups. In the former group the sentenced population has shrunk from 63,400 in 1986 to 36,500 in 1996 and the latter group has shrunk from 6,100 in 1986 to 2,600 in 1996. This is the result of demographic changes and the greatly increased use of formal cautioning for juveniles.

Supervision orders are designed to provide a demanding but constructive sentencing option for young people. Section 44 of CYPA 1933 sets out the principle that all courts must have regard to the welfare of the child or young person who appears before them. The CJA 1991 brings 17-year-old offenders within the scope of this provision, but the National Standards make it clear that the younger the offender the more important the welfare requirement is.

A supervision order is a 'community order' and the court will not be able to impose a supervision order unless the conditions relating to the passing of a community order are satisfied. In particular, by CJA 1991, s. 6, the court will have to be satisfied that the offence committed is serious enough to warrant a community order (see **5.1**). A pre-sentence report is normally required before imposing a supervision order which includes requirements imposed under CYPA 1969, s. 12, 12A, 12AA, 12B or 12C (CJA 1991, s. 7(3)), and in any other case where a supervision order is made it may be considered good sentencing practice to obtain a report. A supervision order does not require the offender's consent, but the court may not insert a requirement of treatment for a mental condition under s. 12B on an offender who has attained the age of 14 unless the offender expresses his willingness to comply with it.

5.9.1 Power to impose basic supervision order

The powers to make supervision orders are to be found in CYPA 1969. By s. 7(7)(b) of that Act, a court dealing with a child (aged 10 to 13 inclusive) or a young person (aged 14 to 17 inclusive) for any offence other than murder may make a supervision order in respect of him. This is subject to s. 7(8), which prohibits an adult magistrates' court from dealing with a juvenile by any means other than a fine, a conditional or absolute discharge, a recognisance taken from the juvenile's parents or orders which may be combined with any of the first three. Thus, an adult magistrates' court may not make a supervision order. The Crown Court may make one, but it should consider whether or not CYPA 1933, s. 56 makes it desirable to remit the offender to a youth court rather than passing sentence itself. The mandatory sentence in murder cases where the offender was under 18 at the time of the offence is detention during Her Majesty's pleasure. For this, and for long-term detention of juveniles convicted of other serious crimes, see **4.3.5**. The youth court is the court in which the great majority of supervision orders are made.

A supervision order will last for three years from the date on which it was made, or for such shorter period as may be specified in the order (CYPA 1969, s. 17(a)). In practice supervision orders tend to be for one year or two years. There is no minimum period. The order places the juvenile under the supervision of either a local authority social worker or a probation officer (s. 11). A local authority must not be designated as a supervisor unless the person to be supervised resides in that area (s. 13(1)). If the juvenile is under 14 years of age the supervisor must be a local authority, unless the probation service has already had dealings with the family of the juvenile in the past (s. 13(2)). Where a probation officer is the supervisor, he will be one of those working in the petty sessions area where the juvenile lives. In every case the supervisor's duty is to 'advise, assist and befriend the supervised person' (s. 14). A local authority carries out this task through the social workers in its employment. The Home Office National Standards envisage that supervision should start within five working days of the making of the order, should involve frequent appointments (where practicable and appropriate, there should be 12 in the first three months), accurate and timely record-keeping of appointments and prompt and effective action to enforce the order, including breach action where behaviour is unacceptable. The National Standards state that wherever possible the supervisor should work together with the offender and the offender's parent or guardian and should involve them at all stages of the order.

The order described above may be characterised as a 'basic supervision order' into which a number of basic requirements, set out at **5.9.9**, are normally inserted. A range of further special requirements may be included within the order at the court's discretion.

5.9.2 Requirement as to residence

A supervision order may require the juvenile to reside with an individual who is named in the order (CYPA 1969, s. 12(1)). The person so named must agree to the requirement being made. Any residence requirement imposed under s. 12(1) is subject to the supervised person being obliged from time to time to reside elsewhere by virtue of a requirement imposed under one of the other subsections of s. 12.

5.9.3   Requirement as to intermediate treatment

Requirements as to intermediate treatment are usually made under s. 12(2). The effect of a requirement made under s. 12(2) is that, for a certain number of days, the person supervised is liable to be directed by the supervisor to:

(a)   live at a place specified by the supervisor; and/or
(b)   attend (but not live at) a place specified; and/or
(c)   take part in specified activities.

The number of days in respect of which the supervisor may give directions is specified by the court when the order is made, up to a maximum of 90 days, which need not necessarily be consecutive (s. 12(3)). The name 'intermediate treatment' is attached to these requirements because, by virtue of them, the supervisor may ensure that for a short time the person supervised is taken away from his home environment, or at least is kept usefully occupied while still at home, so an order which includes such a requirement has some of the characteristics of a care order, being 'intermediate' in its effect between a basic supervision order and a care order. In fact the making of a care order is now exclusively within the domain of the civil courts, since the Children Act 1989 removed the power of criminal courts to pass a care order as part of a sentence. Typically, intermediate treatment requirements involve individual counselling or group discussion; there is an educational and skills-based approach. Particular projects may be used by supervisors to put the persons supervised into situations where they face new challenges and have the opportunity to develop their abilities and to be involved in worthwhile activities. Juveniles might be directed to take part in a course to learn a new skill (such as horse riding or canoeing) or might be sent on an adventure-type holiday, such as walking the Pennine Way or, more mundanely, might be required to attend a youth club on a certain number of evenings a week (for a much fuller description and analysis see Bottoms et al., 1990). It will be seen that intermediate treatment is not envisaged as punitive in itself. The aim is to give juvenile offenders the opportunity to develop more constructive use of their leisure time which does not involve the committing of criminal offences. The implementation of intermediate treatment ordered under s. 12(2) is very much within the discretion of the supervisor, and is hence sometimes referred to as 'discretionary intermediate treatment'.

Intermediate treatment requirements may, alternatively but not additionally, be included within a supervision order by virtue of s. 12A(3)(a). In such a case, the court itself may require the offender to do anything which the supervisor might have required the supervised person to do under s. 12(2); for example, it may nominate where the juvenile is to live or which activities he is to take part in. Intermediate treatment requirements imposed under s. 12A(3)(a) are sometimes referred to as 'stipulated intermediate treatment'. The maximum number of days is again 90, and the court must consult with the proposed supervisor to ensure that it will be feasible to ensure compliance with the proposed scheme. Stipulated intermediate treatment was introduced by the CJA 1982, in response to complaints from magistrates that some supervisors would either fail to give directions under s. 12(2) or not give the sort of directions the magistrates thought should have been given. In practice, however, intermediate treatment requirements are more frequently included by virtue of

s. 12(2), perhaps because deciding whether the offender should spend time learning to ride a horse or learning how to manage a canoe hardly seems appropriate to the judicial function. The Crime and Disorder Bill contains provisions which will allow the court to insert a requirement, under a new s. 12A(3)(aa), that the young offender shall make specified reparation to the victim of the offence (the offender's consent to this is required) or to the community at large. Before making an order under s. 12A(3) the court must be satisfied that securing compliance with the order is feasible and, if the person is aged under 16, the court must obtain and consider information about his family circumstances and the effect of the order on those circumstances.

Whenever the court imposes a requirement under s. 12A(3)(a) and it is of the view that it would have imposed a *custodial sentence* on the offender if it had not imposed the supervision order, it should state in open court that it is making the supervision order 'instead of a custodial sentence' (s. 12D(1)). In doing so the court should be satisfied that the offence of which the offender has been convicted, or the combination of that offence and one or more offences associated with it, was so serious that only a supervision order containing such a requirement or a custodial sentence can be justified for that offence, or that the offence was a sexual offence or a violent offence and only a supervision order containing such a requirement or a custodial sentence would be adequate to protect the public from serious harm from the offender. The court must also explain why it is so satisfied. The terms of s. 12D(1) are those which are used in Part I of the CJA 1991 (e.g. the meaning of 'violent offence' and 'sexual offence') and should be similarly construed (s. 12D(1A)). The making of such a statement under s. 12D is a prerequisite of the court imposing a custodial sentence on the supervised person under s. 15(4A) (i.e. in consequence of any breach of the supervision order: see **5.9.11**).

5.9.4 Requirements imposing night restriction

The courts are empowered under CYPA 1969, s. 12A(3)(b) to require the supervisee, on not more than 30 separate occasions within the first three months of the supervision order, to be indoors by a certain hour in the evening and not thereafter to go out until the next morning (s. 12A(10) and (11)). The supervisee must not, however, be required to remain at a place for longer than 10 hours on any one night (s. 12A(9)). The place, or one of the places, specified in the order must be the home of the person supervised (s. 12A(8)). The supervised person may only leave the place during the relevant period if accompanied by his parent, guardian, supervisor or some other person specified in the order (s. 12A(12)).

These 'night restriction' or 'curfew' orders have been little used, largely because the social services and probation authorities have been reluctant to recommend them to courts in pre-sentence reports and to administer them. There is a reluctance on the part of these services to adopt a 'surveillance' role, which is seen as devoid of social work content. Before making an order under s. 12A(3) the court must be satisfied that securing compliance with the order is feasible but the fact is that, in many cases, night restriction requirements are in practice unenforceable and, in contrast to curfew orders (see **5.5**), there is no provision of electronic monitoring of juveniles under night restriction requirements. Before making such an order on a person under 16 the court must consider the likely effect of it upon the supervised person's home circumstances.

5.9.5 Requirement as to refraining from activities

By CYPA 1969, s. 12A(3)(c), the court may insert a requirement that the offender refrain from participating in certain specified activities on specified days or for a specified period.

5.9.6   Requirement as to residence in local authority accommodation

By CYPA 1969, s. 12AA(1) (which was inserted by the Children Act 1989), where certain conditions are satisfied (see below), a supervision order may contain a requirement that a juvenile live for a specified period in local authority accommodation. The order must specify the local authority in whose area the offender lives and the authority must be consulted first (s. 12AA(2) and (3)). The maximum period of residence is six months (s. 12AA(5)). A residence requirement may also specify that the juvenile may *not* live with a particular person (s. 12AA(4)).

The conditions which must be met before a requirement of residence in local authority accommodation can be imposed are:

(a)   that a supervision order has previously been made in respect of the offender;

(b)   that the previous order imposed a requirement under s. 12A(3) (stipulated intermediate treatment, night restriction order or order to restrain the offender from participating in specified activities) or a residence requirement;

(c)   that the offender is found guilty of an offence which was committed while that supervision order was in force, the offence is punishable by imprisonment if committed by an adult and, in the opinion of the court, is serious; and

(d)   that the court is satisfied that the behaviour which constituted the offence was due, to a significant extent, to the circumstances in which he was living.

Condition (d) does not have to be satisfied if the offender is already subject to a residence requirement.

A requirement of residence in local authority accommodation should not be made unless the juvenile is legally represented or, if not so represented, unless he has had the opportunity to apply for legal aid (s. 12AA(9)). A supervision order imposing a requirement of residence in local authority accommodation may also include any requirement imposed under s. 12, 12A, 12B or 12C of the Act (s. 12AA(11)).

5.9.7   Requirement as to treatment for a mental condition etc.

Under CYPA 1969, s. 12B, a requirement of treatment for a mental condition may be inserted into a supervision order. The supervised person, if aged 14 or over, must consent to the insertion of such a requirement. This requirement is fully discussed at **11.2**.

5.9.8   Requirement as to education

Where the supervised person is of compulsory school age, a requirement may be inserted into the basic supervision order imposed under CYPA 1969, s. 6(7) requiring that person to comply, for as long as he is of that age and the order remains in force, 'with such arrangements for his education as may from time to time be made by his parent, being arrangements for the time being approved by the local education authority' (s. 12C(1)). The court must secure the agreement of the education authority (s. 12C(2)). The consent of the offender is not required.

5.9.9   Other requirements

By CYPA 1969, s. 18(2)(b), the offender may be required to comply with such provisions (prescribed in r. 29(3) of the Magistrates' Courts (Children and Young Persons) Rules 1992) as the court considers appropriate for facilitating the performance by the supervisor of his functions under s. 14 of the Act, to notify the supervisor of any change of residence or employment, and/or to keep in touch with the supervisor in accordance with his instructions and, if the supervisor so requires, to receive visits from the supervisor at home.

5.9.10 Discharge or variation of supervision order

Provision as to the discharge or variation of supervision orders is contained in CYPA 1969, s. 15.

During the currency of a supervision order in respect of a person who has not yet reached the age of 18, a youth court (or, in the case of a person who has reached that age, an adult magistrates' court) may, on the application of the supervisor or the supervised person, make an order for early termination by discharging the supervision order (s. 15(1)). The Home Office National Standards suggest that early termination of a supervision order should be considered where the offender has made good progress in achieving the objectives set out in the order and where there is not considered to be a significant risk of reoffending and/or of serious harm to the public. An application for early termination should normally be considered by the time two-thirds of the term of the order has elapsed unless there are clear reasons for not doing so.

The relevant court may also vary the supervision order by cancelling any requirement included in it under CYPA 1969, s. 12, 12A, 12AA, 12B, 12C or 18(2)(b) or by inserting any provision into the order which could have been included in the original order. The relevant court is not empowered, however, to insert a requirement under s. 12A(3)(b) (night restriction order: see **5.9.4**) in respect of any day which falls outside the period of three months beginning with the date on which the order was made. There are also limitations on the court's powers to vary a requirement under s. 12B, relating to medical treatment (see **11.2**).

5.9.11 Breach of supervision order

The powers of the court to deal with breach of supervision orders may be found in CYPA 1969, s. 15.

The Home Office National Standards state that any apparent failure to comply with requirements in a supervision order should be followed up promptly by the supervising officer, normally within two working days. If the offender's explanation (or lack of one) is not considered acceptable, the incident must formally be recorded as an instance of failure to comply. Immediate action in respect of a breach may be appropriate in some cases of failure to comply, such as a failure to notify a change of adddress when it is clear that the failure was an attempt to avoid carrying out the order. In other cases the supervising officer should normally take such action after no more than *three* instances of failure to comply. When action is taken the supervising officer has an important role in the process of proving the breach before the court and advising the court on further action. The National Standards state that the officer should be clear as to what action he or she would like the court to take. This advice should be contained, as required, in an oral or written report to the court, which should also include an account of the offender's response to supervision thus far, and the extent to which the offender has successfully completed the order. If thought necessary, the officer may complete a further pre-sentence report prior to the breach hearing.

If breach action is brought against a supervised person who has not yet attained the age of 18 the appropriate court to deal with the breach is the youth court. By s. 15(3)(a), where it is proved to the satisfaction of the youth court, on the application of the supervisor, that a supervised person who has not attained the age of 18 has failed to comply with any of the requirements of the order included pursuant to CYPA 1969, s. 12, 12A, 12AA, 12C or 18(2)(b) then, whether or not it also varies or discharges the supervision order (see **5.9.10**), the court may order payment of a fine not exceeding £1,000, or £250 for a child under 14, or may make an attendance centre order.

If breach action is brought against a supervised person who has attained the age of 18, the appropriate court to deal with the breach is the adult magistrates' court. By s. 15(3)(b), if the person supervised has attained the age of 18 and an adult magistrates' court discharges the supervision order consequent upon its breach, it may impose any punishment upon him (apart from a sentence of detention in a young offender institution) which it could have imposed if it had then the power to try him for the offence for which he was given the supervision order and had convicted him. If the punishment which is imposed is a fine, the fine shall not exceed £5,000.

By s. 15(4), if the breach is in respect of a failure to comply with a requirement imposed under s. 12A(3)(a) ('stipulated intermediate treatment'), and the court which made the supervision order made a statement under s. 12D(1) (that the supervision order was in lieu of a custodial sentence: see **5.9.3**) and the court discharges the order following breach by the offender, it may impose any punishment upon him (including a sentence of detention in a young offender institution) which it could have imposed if it had then the power to try him for the offence for which he was given the supervision order and had convicted him. If the punishment which is imposed is a fine, the fine shall not exceed £5,000.

If the case falls within s. 15(3)(b) or (4) and the offence in question is one which the court has no power to try (i.e. the offence is triable only on indictment) or has no power to try without the appropriate consents (i.e. the offence is triable either way), s. 15(5) provides that the punishment imposed shall not exceed that which a court having power to try such an offence could have imposed, and must not in any event exceed:

(a)   where the case falls within s. 15(4), a custodial term of six months and/or a fine not exceeding £5,000;

(b)   where the case falls within s. 15(3)(b), a fine not exceeding £5,000.

The relevant court must always take account of the extent to which the person supervised has complied with the requirements of the supervision order (s. 15(8)). This provision is comparable with provisions on breach of certain other community orders under CJA 1991, sch. 2, para. 3(2)) (see **5.7.1**).

5.10   ACTION PLAN ORDERS

The Crime and Disorder Bill contains provisions in Part IV which, when they become law and are brought into force, will create a new community order applicable to offenders under the age of 18 — the action plan order. A pilot scheme is to be introduced to run for 18 months from Autumn 1998. In the White Paper, *No More Excuses* (Home Office, 1997a), the government describes the action plan order as 'a short intensive programme of community intervention combining punishment, rehabilitation and reparation to change offending behaviour and prevent further crime. The order will be available for 10 – 17-year-olds and will impose requirements designed to address the specific causes of offending. Each order will last for three months.'

When the relevant provisions are implemented the action plan order will be a 'community order', and the court will not be able to impose such an order unless the conditions relating to the passing of a community order are satisfied (cl. 65(11)). In particular, by CJA 1991, s. 6(1), as amended by CDB, sch. 7, the court will have to be satisfied that the offence committed is serious enough to warrant the passing of a community order (see **5.1**). The court may pass an action plan order without first obtaining a pre-sentence report, but by cl. 66(1) the court is required, before making such an order, to obtain and consider a written report by a probation officer, a social worker or a member of a youth offending team. The report must indicate the requirements which that person proposes to include in the action plan order, the benefits to the offender which those requirements are designed to achieve, the attitude of a parent or guardian of the young offender to the proposed requirements and, where the offender is under the age of 16, information about the young offender's family circumstances and the likely effect of the order on those circumstances.

5.10.1 Power to impose an action plan order

An action plan order may be imposed by the Crown Court or a youth court on any offender aged under 18 who is convicted of any offence, subject only to the law on sentencing for the crime of murder and the presumptive minimum sentences under the C(S)A 1997. The court may make an action plan order if it is of the opinion that this is desirable in the interests of securing the young offender's rehabilitation, or of preventing the commission by him of further offences (cl. 65(2)). The order will (a) require the young offender for a period of three months, commencing with the date of the order, to comply with the specified action plan (which is a series of requirements with respect to his actions and whereabouts during that time); (b) place him under supervision; and (c) require him to comply with directions given by the supervisor (who will be a probation officer, a social worker or a member of a youth offending team) as to the implementation of the action plan. Require-ments to be made of the young offender, any or all of which may be included by the court in a particular action plan (cl. 65(5)), are:

(a) to participate in specified activities at specified times;
(b) to present himself to a specified person at a specified place and time;
(c) to attend at an attendance centre for a specified number of hours;
(d) to stay away from a place or places specified in the requirements;
(e) to comply with any specified arrangements for his education;
(f) to make reparation to a specified person or to the community at large; and
(g) to attend any hearing fixed by the court under cl. 66(3) below.

Requirement (c) above cannot be included unless the offence committed by the young offender is punishable with imprisonment in the case of an adult (cl. 65(7)), and requirement (f) cannot be included unless a person has been identified as a victim of the offence or a person otherwise affected by it and that person consents to the reparation being made (cl. 65(8)). The requirements included in the action plan order must, so far as possible, not interfere with the times when the offender attends school or conflict with his religious beliefs or with the requirements of any other community order to which he may be subject (on this see **5.10.2**). The White Paper (Home Office, 1997a) indicates that the requirements in the action plan order will be tailored to the individual young offender, reflecting consultation with the offender, his family and perhaps the victim, and 'it may include elements such as motor projects, anger management courses, alcohol or drug treatment programmes or help with problems at home or at school or in finding accommodation, training or employment'.

The court must explain to the offender in ordinary language the effect of the order and the requirements to be inserted into it and the consequences of failure to comply with the order (cl. 66(2)). For the powers of the court on breach of the order see **5.10.3**. Immediately after making an action plan order the court may fix a further hearing for a date not more than 21 days after the date of the order (cl. 66(3)) at which time the supervising officer will submit a progress report, indicating the extent to which the order has been implemented and its effectiveness. In the light of that report the court may cancel any of the existing requirements or insert new ones. The young offender may be required to attend that hearing.

5.10.2   Combining an action plan order with other sentences or orders

Clause 65(4) of the CDB states that an action plan order shall not be made if the offender is already the subject of such an order or if the court proposes to pass a custodial sentence, a probation order, a community service order, a combination order, a supervision order, or an attendance centre order. Reparation orders are not included in this list but, since an element of reparation may be included within an action plan order, mixing the two orders together would seem to be undesirable. There is nothing to prevent an action plan order being combined with a fine, a compensation order, a forfeiture order or a restitution order but, more generally, the compendious nature of the action plan order makes it unlikely that courts would wish to combine it with other sentences or orders.

5.10.3   Discharge or variation of an action plan order

Arrangements for discharge or variation of an action plan order are set out in sch. 5 to the CDB. Paragraph 2 of sch. 5 provides that while an action plan order is in force the young offender or the supervisor may make application to the youth court for an order to discharge that order, or to vary it by cancelling any provision within it or by inserting any fresh provision. Ordinarily the young offender should be present in court at the time the application is made (para. 4(1)), but his attendance is not necessary where, for instance, the court is discharging the action plan order or cancelling a requirement in it (para. 4(9)). If an application for discharge is made, and is dismissed by the court, no further application for discharge can be made without the consent of the court.

5.10.4   Breach of an action plan order

Arrangements for dealing with failure to comply with the terms of an action plan order are set out in sch. 5 to the CDB. When dealing with the young offender for breach of an action plan order the relevant court must take into account the extent to which he has complied with the order (para. 3(7)). The young offender should be present in court (para. 4(1)).

Paragraph 3 of sch. 5 provides that where it is proved that the young offender has failed to comply with any of the requirements of the order the youth court (a) whether or not it also discharges the order, may fine the offender an amount not exceeding £1,000, or make an attendance centre order, or a curfew order on him, or (b) if the original order was made by a youth court, may discharge the order and deal with the young offender in any manner in which he could have been dealt with for the offence, or (c) if the original order was made by the Crown Court, the youth court may commit the young offender in custody or on bail until he can appear before the Crown Court (para. 3(2)). The Crown Court must then revoke the action plan order and deal with the young offender in any manner in which he could have been dealt with by that court for the offence (para. 3(4) and (5)).

6 *Fines and Forfeiture*

A fine is an order that the offender shall pay a sum of money to the state, and it is the most commonly imposed penalty in the courts. In 1996 the fine was the selected sentence in 36 per cent of indictable offences in magistrates' courts and 4 per cent of such offences in the Crown Court. It was used in 83 per cent of summary (non-motoring) cases in magistrates' courts and for summary motoring cases heard there it was used in 90 per cent of cases. Although these figures appear to be very high, the importance of the fine in sentencing should not be overstated. These figures are skewed because of the almost exclusive use of the fine as the sentence for minor offences, regulatory offences and road traffic offences. Crimes of violence, sexual offences and serious crimes against property are unlikely to be dealt with by way of a fine, since their seriousness renders the fine an unsuitable punishment. Figures for the relative use of different sentencing options, for a range of different offences, are given in Chapter 12. The proportionate use of the fine has declined over the last ten years. The percentage of male offenders aged over 21 who were sentenced for indictable offences and received a fine has decreased from 41 per cent of the total in 1986 to 33 per cent in 1996. For male offenders aged 18 but under 21 the percentage fined has fallen from 41 per cent in 1986 to 29 per cent in 1996. The decline in the rate of use of the fine for female offenders, in both these groups, has been even more marked. This change seems to be taking place at the same time as a substantial increase in the proportionate use by the courts of the conditional discharge and, to a lesser extent, the probation order and community service order.

In terms of the sentencing structure provided by the CJA 1991, the fine occupies a somewhat ambivalent position. It is clear that if the offence committed is so serious that only a custodial sentence would be an adequate penalty then a fine cannot be used. In general, too, the fine can be regarded as occupying a lower tier in the sentencing framework than the community orders, but that will not always be the case. CJA 1991, s. 6(1) merely requires that a community sentence shall not be imposed unless the offence is serious enough for that approach to be justified, but does not require that the offence be too serious for it to be dealt with by way of a fine. There is thus a degree of overlap between the fine and the community sentences, so that the court will sometimes have to make a choice between them. It is submitted that in making a choice between a community order and a fine the main criterion for the court to consider will be whether a simple financial penalty ('hitting the offender in the pocket') is a proper and adequate response to the case, or whether the nature of the offence and the character of the offender requires more intensive intervention by the state in the life of the offender, by requiring his supervision, community service or whatever. For special provision in relation to persistent petty offenders see **6.6**.

When a fine is imposed, payment is normally made, whether by cash or a cheque, to the clerk of the appropriate magistrates' court, who at periodical intervals accounts for the revenue which has been received to the Secretary of State (Justices of the Peace Act 1979, s. 61). The fine is one of the very few sentencing options that actually generates income for the state.

All offences, apart from murder, and the two presumptive sentences under the C(S)A 1997 are punishable by fine. The great majority of summary offences, as they were originally drafted, provided for punishment by way of a fine not exceeding a certain stated sum. Changing these sums across a myriad of summary offences, to take account of changes in the value of money, was a complex matter. As a result of the CJA 1982, all statutes creating summary offences which provide for a financial penalty have been amended, so as to permit a fine to be imposed which does not exceed the amount shown at a certain level on a 'standard scale' of fines (i.e. the statutes no longer refer to a sum of money). The standard scale is set out at **6.2.1**. The advantage of this development is that changes over time to the value of money may be taken into account by adjustment to the standard scale, rather than by having to amend all the individual provisions so affected. If a statute mentions only imprisonment as a means of dealing with offenders for a summary offence, a fine not exceeding level 3 may none the less be imposed as an alternative (MCA 1980, s. 34(3)). In the cases of indictable offences, PCCA 1973, s. 30(1) empowers the Crown Court, following conviction on indictment, to fine the offender in lieu of, or in addition to, dealing with him in any other way. This power does not apply, however, where:

(a)   the sentence is fixed by law, i.e. after conviction for the offence of murder; or

(b)   the sentence is an automatic life sentence imposed under the C(S)A 1997, s. 2 or is the prescribed minimum custodial sentence imposed under the C(S)A 1997, s. 3; or

(c)   where the use of some other power precludes the use of the fine (e.g., a discharge, or a hospital order).

6.1   FINES IN THE CROWN COURT

6.1.1   Maximum fines in the Crown Court

Where an offender has been convicted on indictment, there is no statutory limit to the amount of the fine which may be imposed by the Crown Court (CLA 1977, s. 32(1)). In *Ronson* [1991] Crim LR 794 the Court of Appeal upheld a fine of £5 million (in addition to a prison sentence). No statutory limit applies if the offender has been committed to the Crown Court for sentence under MCA 1980, s. 38, following summary conviction in a magistrates' court of an offence triable either way.

There are, however, some circumstances in which the maximum fine which the Crown Court can impose is restricted to the maximum fine which is available in the magistrates' courts. These circumstances are:

(a)   where the offender is convicted on indictment of a summary offence dealt with on indictment by virtue of CJA 1988, s. 40 (see further **1.2.3**);

(b)   where an offender is committed for sentence for a minor offence under CJA 1967, s. 56 (various minor offences: see Appendix 2);

(c)   where the Crown Court resentences an offender for an offence for which he was previously conditionally discharged by a magistrates' court or was previously sentenced by a magistrates' court to a community sentence (see further **5.6.2** and **7.1.5**); and

(d)   where a fine is imposed on the disposal of an appeal against conviction or against a sentence passed in a magistrates' court.

6.1.2 Crown Court's duty to fix term in default

A term of imprisonment or detention to be served in default must be fixed in every case where the Crown Court imposes a fine (PCCA 1973, s. 31(2)), unless the offender is under 18 years of age. If the offender is aged between 18 and 20 inclusive, the term in default takes the form of a term of detention under CJA 1982, s. 9. If such an offender eventually has to serve the term, he may be detained in a prison, young offender institution or remand centre at the discretion of the authorities (CJA 1982, s. 12(10)). No term of detention in default can be ordered in respect of a juvenile (*Basid* [1996] 1 Cr App R (S) 421).

Despite the apparently mandatory nature of the duty to fix a term in default, it has been held that a failure to fix such a term does not invalidate the fine itself (*Hamilton* (1980) 2 Cr App R (S) 1). The term which is fixed by the court should relate to the whole sum of the fine, rather than to any instalment (*Power* (1986) 8 Cr App R (S) 8). Where fines are imposed in respect of more than one offence, the terms to be served in default may be ordered to run concurrently or consecutively (*Savundra Nayagan* [1968] 1 WLR 1761). Also, the court may order that the term(s) to be served in default can run concurrently with, or consecutively to, any term of imprisonment (or detention in a young offender institution) to which the offender is sentenced at that time by the court, or which he is currently serving (PCCA 1973, s. 31(4)). A term of imprisonment in default may be imposed consecutively to a maximum prison sentence imposed for the same offence (*Carver* [1955] 1 WLR 181). Consecutive custodial terms are, however, subject to the totality principle (*Savundra Nayagan* and *Benmore* (1983) 5 Cr App R (S) 468), and the total term (i.e. the term of imprisonment for the offence plus the term in default) should not be disproportionate to the overall gravity of the offending. This principle is discussed at **4.4.4**.

Where the Crown Court imposes a fine on committal for sentence from a magistrates' court, in circumstances where the powers of the Crown Court are limited to those of the magistrates' court (see **6.1.1**), the Crown Court must nevertheless specify the term to be served in default (PCCA 1973, s. 31(6)).

The maximum terms of imprisonment or detention which may be ordered by the Crown Court are set out in PCCA 1973, s. 31(3A).

Size of fine	Maximum term in default
Not exceeding £200	7 days
Over £200, not exceeding £500	14 days
Over £500, not exceeding £1,000	28 days
Over £1,000, not exceeding £2,500	45 days
Over £2,500, not exceeding £5,000	3 months
Over £5,000, not exceeding £10,000	6 months
Over £10,000, not exceeding £20,000	12 months
Over £20,000, not exceeding £50,000	18 months
Over £50,000, not exceeding £100,000	2 years
Over £100,000, not exceeding £250,000	3 years
Over £250,000, not exceeding £1 million	5 years
Over £1 million	10 years

These are maximum periods and, of course, the Crown Court has discretion to fix shorter terms. An appropriate period from within the band should be selected (*French* (1995) 16 Cr

App R (S) 841). If the offender serves the entire default term the fine is expunged. If any amount of the fine is paid, the default period will be reduced proportionately by the amount paid (s. 31(3B)). The only exception to this is that part payment cannot have the effect of reducing the period to be served to less than seven days (s. 31(3C)). Where, exceptionally, a magistrates' court is empowered to fix a term in default of payment of a fine, the same periods apply, except that a default term in excess of 12 months cannot be exceeded by the magistrates (MCA 1980, sch. 4).

6.1.3 Crown Court fines: allowing time to pay

When imposing a fine (or forfeiting a recognisance, or making an order for the payment of compensation or costs), the sum becomes due for payment immediately and some offenders pay before leaving the court, by cash or cheque. Whether a cheque is accepted as payment is, of course, at the clerk's discretion. The Crown Court (and magistrates' courts) are, however, usually under a duty to give the offender 'time to pay'. This might be done by fixing a date by which the whole sum must be paid or, more likely, by making arrangements for the payment of the sum by instalments. Even where it is not strictly under such a duty, the court always has a discretion to allow time to pay (PCCA 1973, s. 31(1)). If time to pay is granted, and it almost invariably is, enforcement is the responsibility of the magistrates' court (see **6.5**). The only occasions on which the Crown Court (or a magistrates' court) may refuse to allow an offender time to pay are when, by PCCA 1973, s. 31(3):

(a)   the offence is punishable with imprisonment and the offender appears to have sufficient means to pay the sum forthwith, i.e., in practice, on the same day (PCCA 1973, s. 34A(2));
(b)   it appears to the court that the offender is unlikely to remain long enough at a place of abode in the United Kingdom to enable payment of the sum to be enforced by other methods; or
(c)   the offender is already serving a custodial sentence or a term of detention under CJA 1982, s. 9, or is given a custodial sentence by the court at the same time as it imposes the fine.

The court may order that the offender be searched (by a police officer of the same sex as the offender), so that money found on him can be used to pay the fine (PCCA 1973, s. 34A). Such money cannot be used if the court is satisfied that the money does not belong to the offender. When a court grants time to pay, it either fixes a period within which the entire sum must be paid or it orders that the sum be paid by fixed instalments.

Where a court allows payment of a fine by instalments, the general rule is that the fine should be capable of being paid off by the offender within 12 months (*Knight* (1980) 2 Cr App R (S) 82 and *Nunn* (1983) 5 Cr App R (S) 203). This is certainly not a rigid rule, however, and in *Olliver* (1989) 11 Cr App R (S) 10 Lord Lane CJ said:

. . . there is nothing wrong in principle with the period of payment being longer, indeed much longer than one year, providing it is not an undue burden and so too severe a punishment having regard to the nature of the offence and the nature of the offender. Certainly it seems to us that a two-year period will seldom be too long, and in an appropriate case three years will be unassailable, again of course depending on the nature of the offender and the nature of the offence.

Where payment is fixed by instalments, the offender is in default as soon as he fails to meet any one of the instalment payments.

On the rare occasions when a Crown Court refuses time to pay and the offender does not produce the money at once, the offender will be detained, first at court, and then by committal to prison until he pays or has served the term which was fixed in default. Serving the term in default expunges the fine. Any part-payment of the fine results in a proportionate reduction of the default term to be served.

6.1.4 Crown Court fines: fine should reflect the seriousness of the offence

The first principle of sentencing in relation to the use of the fine in the Crown Court is that the selection of the fine rather than some other punishment, and the determination of the appropriate level of the fine, if selected, should reflect, primarily, the seriousness of the offence (CJA 1991, s. 18(2)).

Clearly, a fine is an inappropriate penalty where the seriousness of the offence requires an immediate custodial sentence. An example is *Attorney-General's Reference (No. 41 of 1994)* (1995) 16 Cr App R (S) 792, where fines totalling £350 had been imposed on the offender, who had pleaded guilty to wounding with intent to cause grievous bodily harm. He had struck the victim on the head with a bottle, causing a wound which required stitches, and subsequently threatened him with a knife. The Court of Appeal held that the sentence was 'absurd', unduly lenient, and substituted a custodial term of 30 months. On the other hand, there are cases where the facts do not disclose a degree of seriousness sufficient to justify a fine. A discharge may well be the proper sentence in that case. In *Jamieson* (1975) 60 Cr App R 318 the offender, who had a clean record and substantial personal mitigation, was convicted of theft of a half bottle of whisky from a supermarket and fined £300 with £100 costs. The Court of Appeal varied the sentence to a conditional discharge and an order to pay costs not exceeding £50.

As far as the level of the fine is concerned, this should also reflect primarily the seriousness of the offence (CJA 1991, s. 18(2)). In parallel to the principle which applies in relation to custodial sentences, it is clear that the imposition by the court of the maximum fine should be reserved for the most serious instances of the offence which are reasonably likely to occur. An illustration of this point is *Universal Salvage v Boothby* (1983) 5 Cr App R (S) 428 which, although a magistrates' court decision, is certainly applicable to the Crown Court as well. In that case the company was fined for breach of regulations requiring it to have in its lorry proper equipment to record the journeys made by the lorry. It was accepted that, in reliance on a letter from the relevant government department, the company had reasonably believed that the lorry was a 'specialised breakdown vehicle', and as such was not required to carry the recording equipment. The offence being one of strict liability the company was none the less guilty. The magistrates imposed the maximum available fine, which was £200. The Divisional Court, on an appeal by way of case stated, held that the circumstances surrounding the offence, particularly the reasonable reliance upon the letter, provided considerable mitigation. In a case where such mitigation was present it was an error of law for the magistrates to have imposed the maximum sentence.

In all cases involving fines it is the 'first duty' of the sentencer to 'measure that fine against the gravity of the offence' (per Kenneth Jones LJ in *Messana* (1981) 3 Cr App R (S) 88), having regard to all relevant matters in aggravation and mitigation. As with custodial sentences, there is no precise tariff, only a degree of consensus over how large or how small particular fines should be. In *Cleminson* (1985) 7 Cr App R (S) 128 the offender pleaded guilty to handling stolen goods, some jewellery which had been stolen in a burglary. The jewellery was recovered. She was fined £1,000. According to Boreham J, 'judged by the gravity of the crime itself, this was a penalty which, in our judgment, was excessive . . . the appropriate fine is £150'. At the other end of the scale, in *F. and M. Dobson Ltd* (1995) 16 Cr App R (S) 957, a fine of £25,000 had been imposed on a confectionery manufacturer for failing to detect the blade of a Stanley knife in one of its products. The Court of Appeal said that the relevant considerations were the level of culpability involved plus the need to reflect an element of deterence. The fine was reduced to £7,000. In *Fairbairn* (1980) 2 Cr App R (S) 315, where the offender was convicted of seven counts of theft from his employers of goods estimated to be worth between £600 and £700, and received a prison sentence of nine months together with fines totalling £7,500, the Court of Appeal, while not disapproving the custodial sentence, pointed out that 'the amount of the fine was over 10 times the value of the goods stolen, and . . . is out of scale in relation to the gravity of the offence of which he was convicted'. This last case should certainly not be taken to say that the amount of the fine should equate to the value of the property taken, but there will be many cases in which a rough equivalence will be appropriate. In any event, these cases must now be read subject to CJA 1991, s. 18(5), which requires the Crown Court to adjust the level of a fine to take account of the offender's means. In the case of a well-off offender convicted, say, of a minor theft, the level of the fine is likely to be significantly more than the value of the property stolen. In *Roberts* (1980) 2 Cr App R (S) 121, where the judge apparently calculated the fine on the basis of the compensation which would have been received if the victim had made application to the Criminal Injuries Compensation Board, the Court of Appeal disapproved that approach.

6.1.5   Crown Court fines: amount of the fine should be adjusted to take account of means

The court is required by CJA 1991, s. 18(1) and (3) to inquire into the financial circumstances of the offender, and take those into account when fixing the level of the fine. Of course, a fine is meant to be a punishment, and it is perfectly proper that the offender should have to endure a degree of 'hardship', as Lord Lane CJ put it in *Olliver* (1989) 11 Cr App R (S) 10, since 'one of the objects of the fine is to remind the offender that what he has done is wrong'. Such hardship might properly involve the offender giving up other expenditure and leisure activities or postponing the purchase of some item in order to pay. But a fine which is so large that the offender will not be able to pay it and, at the same time, provide for the necessities of life, is counter-productive. The offender may, indeed, be tempted into more crime in order to pay the fine. The main point, however, is that if a court imposes a fine at an unrealistically high level it is not in reality imposing a fine at all — it is really imposing a custodial sentence, since the offender will end up going to prison in default of payment. To take this course is wrong in principle because the seriousness of the offence did not require custody in the first place. Clearly, the principle of adjusting the fine to meet an offender's ability to pay will, on occasions, conflict with the principle expressed at **6.1.4**, and great care is needed in its exercise.

A number of important sentencing principles should be noted here. Where the offender lacks the means to pay the fine proportionate to the seriousness of the offence, it is clearly contrary to principle to impose a custodial sentence instead. According to Roskill LJ in *Reeves* (1972) 57 Cr App R 366, where the offender had pleaded guilty to obtaining £600 by deception and had received a prison sentence of nine months, the comments made by the sentencer 'must plainly have indicated to the appellant . . . that he was being sent to prison not because the offence itself merited a sentence of immediate imprisonment but because he had not the financial wherewithal to pay a substantial fine. That . . . is, of course, completely wrong.' The same principle applies to the imposition of a suspended prison sentence in these circumstances, since such a sentence should be passed only where a prison sentence would have been appropriate in the absence of a power to suspend (see **4.6.3**). Whenever the use of custody is inappropriate for this reason, there are three alternatives which the court might consider. The first is to ask whether the offender's lack of means might in some cases justify the selection of a community sentence instead. This might be appropriate so long as the offending is 'serious enough to warrant such a sentence' (CJA 1991, s. 6(1)). If so, the court should then select that community order which is the 'most suitable for the offender' (CJA 1991, s. 6(2)(a)) and which involves a level of restriction upon the offender's liberty which is commensurate with the seriousness of the case (CJA 1991, s. 6(2)(b)). See further the provisions on persistent petty offenders (see **6.6**). A second possibility is to move to a conditional discharge instead. A third is to adjust the level of the fine downwards, to a sum which the offender can reasonably afford to pay. A good example of consideration of these options was provided by the Court of Appeal in *Ball* (1981) 3 Cr App R (S) 283. The 18-year-old offender had been convicted of shoplifting. The Court of Appeal disapproved, as too severe a punishment, the suspended prison sentence which had been passed by the sentencer. The pre-sentence report which had been prepared did not recommend a probation order because, its author said, the offender was 'a basically honest young woman' and was not, apparently, in need of supervision. In this case a conditional discharge was not appropriate either, since the offender was, as a result of her conviction for shoplifting, now in breach of a conditional discharge imposed for her only other previous offence, handling stolen goods. The Court of Appeal therefore selected 'the least wrong course which is open to us', imposing a £25 fine, with six months in which to pay. There is no precise formula to determine the sum to which the fine should be reduced in such circumstances.

Where the offender is well-off and the fine appropriate to the offence would create little inconvenience for him, it is contrary to principle to impose a custodial sentence for that reason (*Gillies* [1965] Crim LR 64). It is, however, right to raise the level of the fine in such a case, so as to increase its penal 'bite'. Section 18(5) of CJA 1991 makes it clear that the level of the fine should be adjusted to reflect the offender's means whether this has the 'effect of increasing or reducing the amount of the fine'. The Magistrates' Association Guidelines (1997) state that 'the principle behind determining the amount of a fine should be that of equality of hardship rather than equality of monetary penalty. Punishment does not lie in the amount of a fine but in the degree of hardship and inconvenience caused by the need to pay it'. Section 18(5) does not, of course, affect the principle that an offender who is well-off should not be dealt with by financial penalty where the offence itself merits custody and a person who is less well-off would have gone to prison (*Markwick* (1953) 37 Cr App R 125). The principle that a rich offender must not be seen to 'buy his way out of prison' is a fundamental one, and it applies equally where the offender has friends or family who are able to meet a substantial fine (*Curtis* (1984) 6 Cr App R (S) 250).

The principle that the level of the fine should be adjusted according to the offender's means entails that the court should not assume that somebody else will pay the fine. In *Charambous* (1984) 6 Cr App R (S) 389, where a fine was imposed on a married woman who had limited income of her own, the Court of Appeal stressed that the fine must reflect the offender's means and was not a fine on the family.

Section 18(1) of CJA 1991 requires the court to inquire into the offender's financial circumstances before fixing the level of the fine. Section 20 of the CJA 1991 provides that a court may, for that purpose, make a 'financial circumstances order' requiring him to provide for the court a statement of his financial circumstances. Failure to comply without reasonable excuse is an offence, as is furnishing a statement known to be false in a material particular.

6.1.6   Crown Court fines: the totality principle

In *Chelmsford Crown Court, ex parte Birchall* (1989) 11 Cr App R (S) 510 the offender, an independent haulage contractor, pleaded guilty before a magistrates' court to ten offences of using a goods vehicle whose gross weight exceeded the weight shown on the plating certificate, the degree of overweight varying on these occasions between 15 per cent and 25 per cent. He was fined a total of £7,600. The fines were calculated by a formula which took a basic fine of £400 as a starting point, then added a further £20 for each 1 per cent by which the overweight exceeded the permitted maximum. The offender's appeal against this sentence to the Crown Court was dismissed. He applied for judicial review of the Crown Court's decision (see **13.1.3**) The Divisional Court said that it found the sentence 'truly astonishing'. The appropriate sentence for the total wrongdoing was said to be a fine of £1,300, allotted between the different offences by imposing a fine £400 on one and £100 on each of the others, the fine to be paid at the rate of £55 per month. The court emphasised that the application of a 'rigid formula' was incorrect when imposing a fine, even for a single offence, and it was wrong to apply it to each of ten offences and then add the sentences up. The court had to consider all the circumstances and apply the principles of sentencing which, it said, were 'well known'. The main importance of this decision is its clear endorsement of the 'totality principle' in relation to fines: that the sentencer must review the total sentence, and ensure that it remains proportionate to the totality of the offending, as well as being within the offender's capacity to pay.

Ex parte Birchall continues to apply to both the Crown Court and to magistrates' courts, but since that decision the totality principle has now received statutory recognition. The CJA 1991, s. 28(2)(b) reinforces the common law by stating that nothing shall prevent a court 'in a case of an offender who is convicted of one or more other offences, from mitigating his sentence by applying any rule of law as to the totality of sentences'.

6.2.   FINES IN MAGISTRATES' COURTS

6.2.1   Maximum fines in magistrates' courts

Where an offender has been summarily convicted of an offence triable either way which is listed in MCA 1980, sch. 1, the magistrates may fine him an amount not exceeding the 'prescribed sum' (MCA 1980, s. 32(1)). By s. 32(9), 'the prescribed sum' means £5,000. If the offender has been summarily convicted of an offence triable either way and the statute creating the offence prescribes a maximum penalty upon summary conviction which is greater than £5,000, the magistrates may fine him an amount not exceeding that higher maximum (s. 32(2)), and subject to the exception of certain drug offences listed in s. 32(5). There are also some 'continuing offences', where a fine prescribed in the relevant statute may be levied for each day on which the offence continues after the conviction (s. 32(4)). Where the maximum penalty indicated in the statute creating the offence is expressed to be 'the statutory maximum', that maximum shall be the prescribed sum, i.e. £5,000 (CJA 1982,

s. 74). In the case of an offender under 18 years of age, a special maximum fine applies (see **6.3**). Where magistrates are dealing with an offender for two or more offences (whether triable either way or triable summarily), there is no objection to them imposing fines which in the aggregate exceed what they could have imposed for any one offence, subject to their statutory duty to have regard to the offender's means.

The maximum fine which may be imposed for a summary offence is normally set out in the statute which creates the offence. If the statute refers only to punishment by means of imprisonment, a fine not exceeding level 3 may, nevertheless, be imposed as an alternative (MCA 1980, s. 34(3)). The 'standard scale' of maximum fines for summary offences is contained in CJA 1982, s. 37(2), and is as follows:

Level on the scale	Amount of fine
1	£200
2	£500
3	£1,000
4	£2,500
5	£5,000

A fine which is punishable at level 1 on the standard scale is generally known as a 'level 1' offence, and so on. Examples of *level 1* offences are: dog being on a designated road without being on a lead; holding on to a vehicle in order to be towed or carried; and pedestrian failing to give his name and address to a constable directing traffic after failing to stop. Examples of *level 2* offences are: not wearing a seat belt; riding a motor cycle without a helmet; and removing a fixed penalty notice attached to a vehicle. Examples of *level 3* offences are: speeding; failing to provide a specimen of breath for a breath test; misuse of a disabled person's badge; and cycling when unfit through drink. Examples of *level 4* offences are: careless driving; dangerous cycling; driving after making a false declaration as to physical fitness to drive. Examples of *level 5* offences are: driving with excess alcohol; driving while disqualified; and fitting of defective or unsuitable vehicle parts.

6.2.2 Magistrates' courts: normal requirement not to fix term in default

When a magistrates' court imposes a fine it should not normally fix a term of imprisonment (or detention under CJA 1982, s. 9) in default. This is in sharp contrast to the Crown Court duty to fix such a period (see **6.1.2**). If, however, the case is of a kind where the court is not obliged to allow the offender any time to pay (and by MCA 1980, s. 82(1) and (2), these are the same as the occasions set out in PCCA 1973, s. 31(3) in respect of the Crown Court: see **6.1.3**), it should fix such a term.

6.2.3 Magistrates' courts: sentencing principles

The sentencing principles applicable in relation to the use of the fine in magistrates' courts are the same as those which apply in the Crown Court, and which were described in **6.1.4** to **6.1.6**. The Magistrates' Association Guidelines (1997) state that:

Fines are appropriate for cases which are neither serious enough to attract a community penalty nor so serious that only custody is appropriate. The level of fine for any offence must be commensurate with the seriousness of the offence and must take the offender's means into account. Before fixing the amount of the fine, the court must enquire into the offender's financial circumstances and we recommend the regular use of means forms.

Guideline fines are indicated in the Guidelines and are reprinted where appropriate in Chapter 12 below. They are set at three levels:

Low income — about £100 net per week from all sources.
Medium income — about £250 net per week from all sources.
High income — about £600 net per week from all sources.

The guideline fines assume that the case has been contested. Appropriate discount of up to one third should be given for a 'timely guilty plea'.

A system of 'unit fines', applicable to magistrates' courts but not the Crown Court, was introduced by the CJA 1991. The scheme was controversially abolished by the CJA 1993. For further information see the 2nd edition of this book, Appendix 1.

6.3   FINING JUVENILES

There are special provisions relating to the appropriate level of fines for juveniles, and in some circumstances the parents or guardian of a juvenile may be ordered to pay a fine imposed in respect of an offence committed by that juvenile.

Where a person under 18 years of age pleads guilty or is found guilty by a magistrates' court of an offence in respect of which the court would normally be empowered to impose a fine exceeding £1,000, the amount of the fine imposed must not exceed £1,000 (MCA 1980, s. 36(1)). If the offender is under the age of 14 and the court could otherwise have imposed a fine exceeding £250, the amount of the fine imposed shall not exceed £250 (MCA 1980, s. 36(2)). There is no limit upon the fine which may be imposed by a Crown Court upon a juvenile convicted on indictment.

The parent or guardian of a person under 18 may be ordered to pay a fine (or a compensation order or costs) imposed upon the juvenile, by virtue of CYPA 1933, s. 55(1). If such an order is made it is, of course, the means of the parent rather than the means of the juvenile, which are taken into account in determining the level of the fine (CJA 1991, s. 57(3)). If the juvenile is aged under 16, however, it is the *duty* of the court to order that the fine, compensation or costs is paid by the parent or guardian rather than by the juvenile himself. The court *may* make such an order (or, in the case of a juvenile under 16, *must* make such an order), unless the court is satisfied either:

(a)   that the parent or guardian cannot be found; or
(b)   that it would be 'unreasonable to make an order for payment, having regard to the circumstances of the case'.

Section 55(1A) of CYPA 1933 provides that, where a juvenile would otherwise be required to pay a fine for failure to comply with a requirement in a supervision order or for breach of the requirements of a community service order, the court shall order the fine to be paid by the parent or guardian, subject to the same qualifications as appear in s. 55(1). In the case of a juvenile who is aged 16 or 17, however, the effect of s. 55(1B) is to convert the court's duty to require payment by the parent or guardian into a *power* to do so. The government explained in a White Paper (Home Office, 1990) the reasons behind these provisions. Many 16 and 17-year-old offenders are in a position to pay the fine or compensation themselves, and it is appropriate that they should. If not, the parent should pay, especially where the order is for compensation and the victim would otherwise lose out. In respect of younger offenders, who are clearly unable themselves to pay, the court should not simply make the order and assume that a parent will pay. It is right that the parent should by order be required to pay, since this will have the effect of bringing home to them 'the reality of the consequences of their children's behaviour, and the implications for their own actions'. The *Criminal Statistics* show that, in 1996, 9 per cent of parents were ordered by the court to a pay a fine imposed on their child for an offence, and 21 per cent of parents were so ordered in respect of a compensation order. These are overall figures, and for younger juveniles the percentage of parents ordered to pay is much higher. For juveniles aged at least 10 but under 14, the equivalent figures were 36 per cent and 51 per cent.

The court should not make an order under s. 55 against a parent without first considering their means (*Lenihan* v *West Yorkshire Metropolitan Police* (1981) 3 Cr App R (S) 42) or without giving the parent an opportunity of being heard (s. 55(2)). It may in the circumstances be 'unreasonable' for the court to make an order under s. 55 in a case where the parent has done all that he or she reasonably could to prevent the offending. In *Sheffield Crown Court, ex parte Clarkson* (1986) 8 Cr App R (S) 454 it was held that any assessment made by the court about the financial position of the parents, or of the extent to which they had been neglectful of their offspring, must be made on the basis of properly admissible evidence. The Court of Appeal said that it was wrong simply to draw inferences about these matters from the pre-sentence report which had been prepared on the young offender. In *TA* v *DPP* [1997] 1 Cr App R (S) 1 a mother was required by the court to pay £100 compensation for criminal damage committed by her daughter, when she kicked the door panel of a police car which had arrived to arrest her boyfriend. The Court of Appeal heard that the incident occurred at a local authority home. The daughter was living there temporarily, as the mother was unable to control her behaviour. Since the mother had, in practice, no control over what her child was doing at the relevant time, the order under s. 55 was incorrect and was quashed.

In the last-mentioned case the daughter was not in care, but in any case where a local authority has 'parental responsibility' for a juvenile within the meaning of the Children Act 1989, s. 3 and the juvenile is in their care or is provided with accommodation by them, that local authority will come within the scope of CYPA 1933, s. 55. Where the local authority is required to pay a fine (or a compensation order or costs), the usual requirement that the court must have regard to the offender's means does not apply but the court still has a discretion not to make an order where, having regard to the circumstances of the case, it would be unreasonable to do so (s. 55(5)). Accordingly, the Divisional Court in *D* v *DPP* (1995) 16 Cr App R (S) 1040 said that orders under s. 55 should not have been made where the relevant authority had, on the facts, done all it reasonably and properly could to keep the young offender from criminal ways and to protect the public. In *Bedfordshire County Council* v *DPP* [1996] 1 Cr App R (S) 322 the Divisional Court stated that before ordering the authority to pay it was normally necessary to establish some causal link between any fault proved against the council and the commission of the particular offences. The court also stressed that, where a youth court was considering making an order that a local authority should pay a fine or compensation, the relevant authority must be given notice and informed of its right to make representations to the court.

An appeal against an order made by a magistrates' court under s. 55 lies to the Crown Court (s. 55(3)), and an appeal against an order made by the Crown Court lies to the Court of Appeal (s. 55(4)).

6.4   COMBINING FINES WITH OTHER SENTENCES OR ORDERS

Apart from the restrictions referred to in PCCA 1973, s. 30(1) there is no general restriction on combining fines with imprisonment or other custodial sentences, whether in respect of the same offence or different offences sentenced on the same occasion, but in practice this will often not be a desirable combination, since incarceration may well deprive the offender of the means to pay the fine. In any event a fine and a custodial sentence will be an inappropriate combination where the offender lacks the means to pay the fine, and hence will serve the term fixed in default of payment (*Maunde* (1980) 2 Cr App R (S) 289), or where the offender will be saddled with a significant financial burden on his release from prison.

In several cases in the 1980s the Court of Appeal approved the addition of a fine to an immediate custodial sentence as a means of removing a 'substantial financial benefit' made by the offender from his offending (*Forsythe* (1980) 2 Cr App R (S) 15). In *Garner* (1985) 7 Cr App R (S) 285 Hodgson J described the fine in these cases as 'a rough and ready method of confiscating the profits of crime'. A more sophisticated approach to the removal of the proceeds of offending, which was not available to the courts at the time of these decisions, is to make a confiscation order: see Chapter 9.

A court which imposes a suspended sentence of imprisonment may also impose a fine for the same offence, but the offence must be one which would have been properly dealt with by way of immediate custody in the absence of a power to suspend the sentence (see **4.6.3**). A fine imposed in such circumstances is usually added by the court as a 'sting in the tail' of the suspension, and to provide an immediate penalty to counter any suggestion that the offender has received a complete 'let-off'. In every case in which a suspended sentence is imposed the court is required to consider 'whether the circumstances of the case are such as to warrant in addition the imposition of a fine or the making of a compensation order' (PCCA 1973, s. 22(2A)). There are, however, dangers inherent in this combination (see **4.6.3**). Where the fine is being so used (as a subsidiary part of punishment), it is difficult to know how the court should gauge the proper level of the fine. One thing is clear, however. The court, as always, must have proper regard to the offender's means (*King* [1970] 1 WLR 1016).

It seems clear that a fine may, in principle, be combined with any of the community orders individually, or with any mix of community orders. Statutory restrictions which existed before the CJA 1991 on combining a fine with a probation order, or with a community service order, were removed by that Act. A fine may not be combined with an absolute or conditional discharge, however, since a discharge may only be imposed where it is 'inexpedient to inflict punishment' (and see *McClelland* [1951] 1 All ER 557), but a fine and a discharge may be imposed on the same occasion for different offences.

A fine and a compensation order may be combined. The PCCA 1973, s. 35(4A) provides that, where the offender has insufficient means to pay both the appropriate fine and appropriate compensation, the court shall give preference to compensation. In a particular case this will mean that the level of the fine is reduced to enable the full compensation order to stand, or that no fine is ordered and the compensation order stands alone (see further **8.1.8**). Fines may be combined with other financial orders, such as an order to pay the costs of the prosecution, though the court must consider the total effect of the orders it is making and should ensure that the whole sum the offender has to pay is not beyond his means. There is some authority to the effect that a small fine should not be combined with a large order for costs (*Whalley* (1972) 56 Cr App R 304). A fine may also be combined with a restitution order under the Theft Act 1968, s. 28(1), a forfeiture order under PCCA 1973, s. 43, or an order for disqualification from driving where the vehicle was used for the purposes of crime under PCCA 1973, s. 44.

A fine cannot be combined with a hospital order (MHA 1983, s. 37(8)).

6.5 ENFORCEMENT OF FINES

Enforcement of all fines rests with magistrates' courts, whether the fine was originally imposed in a magistrates' court or in the Crown Court. When ordering a fine, the Crown Court must fix a term to be served in default but a magistrates' court should not normally do so (see **6.1.2** and **6.2.2**). The procedure for enforcement of fines is contained in MCA 1980, ss. 75 to 91. As a result of the wide definition of 'fine' in MCA 1980, s. 150, the same procedures also apply to enforcement of compensation orders.

The magistrates' court responsible for enforcement is that court which imposed the fine or, if the fine was imposed by the Crown Court, the court specified in the fine order or, if none was specified, the court which committed the offender for trial or sentence to the Crown Court. Where the offender is now residing in a different petty sessions area, a transfer of fine order may be made (MCA 1980, s. 89).

When a fine is imposed it becomes due for payment immediately. The court may, however, allow time for payment or order payment by instalments (s. 75(1)). Subsequently, further time may be given (s. 75(2)). If the court orders payment by instalments, default in any one instalment is taken to be a default of all instalments then unpaid (s. 75(3)). Where a magistrates' court allows time (or further time) for payment, it may fix a day on which the offender must appear in person (unless he is serving a custodial sentence) to enable a means enquiry to be conducted (MCA 1980, s. 86). The offender must be present at such an inquiry, and his attendance can be secured by summons or by issuing a warrant for his arrest. Offenders cannot be imprisoned for default without such further inquiry into their means and full consideration of other methods of enforcement.

6.5.1 Immediate enforcement of fines

The magistrates' court may use the following methods to enforce *immediate* payment of the sum:

(a) The court may order the offender to be searched for money to meet the fine, with any balance being returned to the offender (s. 80(1)). Such money, which includes money found on the offender at the time of his arrest or at the time of his reception into prison or detention (s. 80(2)), must not be used for payment of the fine if the court is satisfied that the money does not belong to the offender, or if it is satisfied that 'the loss of the money would be more injurious to his family than would be his detention' (s. 80(3)).

(b) Where the offence is punishable with imprisonment, the court may order the offender to be *detained* at a police station until 8 a.m. of the following day (s. 136).

(c) The court, on the occasion of the conviction or on a subsequent occasion, may make a *money payment supervision order* (MCA 1980, s. 88), which should specify the terms of the payment. Such an order places the defendant under the care of a person, usually a probation officer, whose duty is to 'advise and befriend the offender with a view to inducing him to pay and thereby avoid imprisonment' (Magistrates' Courts Rules 1981, r. 56). There is no requirement that the offender consent to the making of the order. A money payment supervision order may be imposed on a juvenile as well as an adult, and in the case of an offender aged under 21 it must be used before committing to detention, unless it is undesirable or impracticable to do so (s. 88(4)). If the court commits an offender under 21 to detention without having first issued a money payment supervision order, it shall state in the warrant of commitment the reasons for so doing (s. 88(5)). The court shall not commit to prison in default a person in respect of whom a money payment supervision order has been made before taking reasonable steps to obtain a report from the supervisor (s. 88(6)).

(d)   The magistrates may issue a *warrant of distress*, authorising the seizure and sale of goods belonging to the offender, using the proceeds to meet the sum outstanding (s. 76). Where it appears that the offender has assets available to satisfy the sum outstanding, a distress warrant should be used rather than committal to prison (*Birmingham Justices, ex parte Bennett* [1983] 1 WLR 114). The court may also postpone the issue of a warrant if it thinks it expedient to do so, until such time and on such conditions as the court thinks just (s. 77).

(e)   In the case of an offender who is in employment and with his consent the court may make an *attachment of earnings order* directing that the employer make deductions from the offender's wages after deduction of tax, and remit them to the court. If the magistrates have this option in mind they should first consult with the clerk, who must obtain relevant details about the offender and his employment (the procedure is governed by the Attachment of Earnings Act 1971, as amended by the CPIA 1996, s. 53. If the offender changes his employment, he is required to notify the court so that the new employer can make the appropriate deductions (1971 Act, s. 15). An attachment of earnings order may be imposed on a person aged under 18 as well as on a person aged 18 or over.

(f)   The court may order the offender's *immediate imprisonment* (or, in the case of an offender aged 18 or over but under 21, detention under the CJA 1982, s. 9) for the term specified as being the time to be served in default or, if no such time was specified, a term specified by the court having regard to the table in the MCA 1980, sch. 4. This table corresponds to the first seven entries listed in the PCCA 1973, s. 31(3A), which is set out at **6.1.2**. It should be noted that the periods specified in the table are the maximum periods which may be ordered, and shorter periods may be ordered at the discretion of the court. The minimum period of imprisonment which can be imposed in any case is five days (s. 132). By MCA 980, s. 82(1), immediate committal to custody cannot be ordered unless:

(i)   in the case of an offence punishable with imprisonment, the offender appears to the court to have sufficient means to pay the sum forthwith, or

(ii)   whether the offence is punishable with imprisonment or not, it appears to the court that the offender is unlikely to remain long enough at a place of abode in the United Kingdom to enable payment of the sum to be enforced by other methods, or

(iii)   the offender is being sent to prison or detention on the same or another charge, or if the offender is already serving a prison sentence or sentence of detention.

The court should announce its reason(s) for making an immediate committal and the reason(s) should be entered in the court register and on the committal warrant. Failure to specify reasons may result in the committal being challenged successfully by way of judicial review (*Oldham Justices, ex parte Cawley* [1996] 1 All ER 464). If, even at this stage, the defendant tenders payment of the fine to court staff or other officials, payment should be received from him, and he is entitled to be released.

The default period can be ordered to be served concurrently with or consecutively to another sentence already being served. If ordered to run consecutively it is not unlawful for the addition of the default period to the custodial term already imposed to exceed the statutory maximum for magistrates' courts (*Green* [1977] 1 All ER 353), but consecutive terms are subject to the totality principle (see **4.4.4**). If more than one fine is being enforced, the periods of imprisonment or detention in default may run consecutively to each other, except that the total period to be served must not exceed the maximum stated in the table in sch. 4 to the 1980 Act as being appropriate for the aggregate sum and, again, this is subject to the totality principle (*Southampton Justices, ex parte Davies* [1981] 1 All ER 722).

Where the offender serves the whole of the term in default this has the effect of expunging the fine. Payment of the sum in default means that the person must be released (s. 79(1)). Part payment of the sum by the offender will result in a proportionate reduction in the term to be served in default (s. 79(2) and (3)).

6.5.2 Enforcement pursuant to means inquiry

If the offender fails to pay the whole or any part of the sum within the time allowed by the court, the magistrates' court may issue a summons or warrant requiring the offender to appear or issue a warrant to arrest him and bring him before the court to conduct a means inquiry to investigate the defendant's ability to pay (s. 83). The court may require that the defendant produce evidence of his income and outgoings. If the court orders the defendant to produce a statement of means and the defendant fails to do so, such failure is an offence punishable by a fine not exceeding £1,000 (s. 84(2)). If the offender knowingly or recklessly furnishes a statement which is false in a material particular, or knowingly fails to disclose any material fact, this is an offence punishable with imprisonment not exceeding four months, a fine not exceeding £1,000, or both (s. 84(3)).

In the light of information received by the court at the means inquiry, the magistrates may grant further time to the offender for payment of the fine, or arrange payment by instalments, or reduce the amount of each instalment (s. 75). The court may remit the whole or any part of the fine having regard to any change in his circumstances since the offender's conviction (s. 85(1)). The court may also remit or reduce the fine where the fine was imposed in the absence of adequate information about his means either because he was convicted in his absence or failed to comply with an order to furnish information concerning his means. In no circumstances can the court increase the fine in consequence of holding a means inquiry. If the Crown Court imposed the fine, the magistrates may only remit the fine in whole or in part if they first obtain the consent of the Crown Court. It should be noted that the power to remit is restricted to fines, and there is no equivalent power in respect of compensation orders (s. 85(2)).

Pursuant to a means inquiry, the magistrates' court may enforce payment by the following methods:

(a) to (f) above.

(g) In respect of offenders aged 18 or over, the court may make an order for the *deduction from the offender's income support payments* in accordance with the Criminal Justice Act 1991, s. 24. The court makes application to the appropriate district office of the Department of Social Security for this to be done. Detailed arrangements are set out in the Fines (Deduction from Income Support) Regulations 1992 (SI 1992/2182).

(h) In respect of offenders aged 10 or over but under 21, the court may make an attendance centre order (CJA 1982, s. 17 and see **5.8.2**). By the C(S)A 1997, s. 36, amending

s. 17 of the 1982 Act, an attendance centre order may also be made in default of payment in respect of a person aged 21 or over but under 25.

(i)   In respect of offenders aged 16 or over the court may, by the C(S)A 1997, s. 35, which came into force on 1 January 1998, make a community service order. The minimum number of hours community service which may be ordered under s. 35 is 20 (s. 35(5)). By s. 35(6), in the case of a sum in default not exceeding £200 the number of hours of community service shall not exceed 40, for a sum exceeding £200 but not exceeding £500 the number of hours shall not exceed 60, and for a sum exceeding £500 the number of days shall not exceed 100. A magistrates' court shall not make an order under this section unless notified by the Secretary of State that arrangements for implementing such orders are available in the relevant area (s. 35(11)). On payment of the whole sum in default the order ceases to have effect and on a payment of part of the sum the number of hours shall be reduced proportionately (s. 35(13)).

(j)   In respect of an offender aged 16 or over the court may, by the C(S)A 1997, s. 35, which came into force on 1 January 1998, make a curfew order. By s. 35(9), in the case of a sum in default not exceeding £200 the number of days to which the curfew order may relate shall not exceed 20, for a sum exceeding £200 but not exceeding £500 the number of days shall not exceed 30, for a sum exceeding £500 but not exceeding £1,000 the number of days shall not exceed 60, for a sum exceeding £1,500 but not exceeding £2,500 the number of days shall not exceed 90, and for a sum exceeding £2,500 the number of days shall not exceed 180. A magistrates' court shall not make an order under this section unless notified by the Secretary of State that arrangements for implementing such orders are available in the relevant area (s. 35(11)). On payment of the whole sum in default the order ceases to have effect and on a payment of part of the sum the number of hours or days shall be reduced proportionately (s. 35(13)).

(k)   By the C(S)A 1997, s. 40, which came into force on 1 January 1998, the court may order the person in default to be disqualified from holding or obtaining a driving licence for such period, not exceeding 12 months, as the court thinks fit. A magistrates' court shall not make an order under this section unless notified by the Secretary of State that the power to make such orders is exercisable by the court (s. 40(3)). On payment of the whole sum in default the disqualification ceases to have effect and on a payment of part of the sum the period of disqualification shall be reduced proportionately (s. 40(4)).

(l)   The court may order the offender's *immediate imprisonment* (or, in the case of an offender aged 18 or over but under 21, detention under the CJA 1982, s. 9) for the term originally specified as being the time to be served in default or, if no such time was specified, a term specified by the court having regard to the table in the MCA 1980, sch. 4. This table corresponds to the first seven entries listed in the PCCA 1973, s. 31(3A), which is set out at **6.1.2.** An immediate committal to custody can only be ordered where since the conviction the court has inquired into the offender's means in his presence on at least one occasion and where:

(i)   in the case of an offence punishable with imprisonment the offender appears to the court to have sufficient means to pay the sum outstanding forthwith, or

(ii)   the court is satisfied that the default is due to the offender's wilful refusal or culpable neglect and the court has considered or tried all other methods of enforcing payment of the sum and it appears to the court that they are inappropriate or unsuccessful (1980 Act, s. 82(4)).

Further restrictions on the use of immediate committal to prison are set out in section 82(5) to (5F). The court must have 'considered or tried' all other methods of enforcement:

these words must be complied with and allow no room for the exercise of discretion (*Norwich Magistrates' Court, ex parte Lilly* (1987) 151 JP 689). The warrant of commital should state the grounds on which the court was satisfied that it was undesirable or impracticable to use the other methods of enforcement (*Oldham Justices, ex parte Cawley* [1996] 1 All ER 464). For offenders aged over 18 but under 21 the CJA 1982, s. 1(5A) further requires the justices to specify in the warrant their reasons for concluding that detention is the only appropriate method of dealing with the defaulter. 'Wilful refusal', which means a deliberate defiance of the court order, or 'culpable neglect', which means a reckless disregard of the court order, must be established by proof beyond reasonable doubt (*South Tyneside Justices, ex parte Martin* (1995) *The Independent* 20 September 1995).

6.6 PERSISTENT PETTY OFFENDERS

The Crime (Sentences) Act 1997, by s. 37, introduces new powers for magistrates' courts and the Crown Court applicable in a case where, ordinarily, the court would have imposed a fine on the offender as the penalty commensurate with the seriousness of the offence, but where the evidence is that the offender already has outstanding fines against his name. In these circumstances it may seem pointless to impose a further financial burden on the offender, so s. 37 permits the court to impose a community service order, or a curfew order, instead. 'Community service order' and 'curfew order' have the same meaning here as they have when the measures are used as straightforward community orders, except that while a curfew order used as a community sentence may be imposed on an offender under 16, here it applies only to those aged 16 and over. Community service orders are, of course, only available to those aged 16 and over in any event. As was explained in **5.5**, curfew orders are ordinarily enforced by electronic monitoring, which is currently available only in some parts of the country. Accordingly, a court cannot impose a curfew order under s. 37 unless arrangements for implementing those orders are in place in the relevant area.

The term 'persistent petty offenders' is not used in the section itself, but appears in the section heading and must be intended to give some indication of the audience at which these measures are meant to be targeted. Operation of the provision, by s. 37(2), requires:

    (a)   that one or more fines imposed on the offender in respect of one or more previous offences have not been paid; and
    (b)   if a fine were imposed in an amount which was commensurate with the seriousness of the offence, the offender would not have sufficient means to pay it.

Paragraph (a) is a rather token attempt to capture the element of 'persistence', requiring that the offender has now committed at least three offences, and the meaning of 'petty' is also contentious. It clearly means that these offences are ordinarily punishable by way of fine, but is says nothing about the level of the fine. If s. 37 is really to be confined to 'petty' cases, why was it made available to the Crown Court? Objection might be made to the section that it breaches the important principle in the 1991 Act, that a community sentence should be imposed only where the offence is 'serious enough' to justify it. This is presumably why s. 37(3) states that the community order may be imposed on a petty persistent offender 'notwithstanding anything in section 6 of the 1991 Act'. As explained above, however, there has always been a degree of overlap between fines and community sentences and, provided that the community order does not create onerous obligations out of all proportion to the nature of the offending, it is not objectionable to use that alternative where extracting the fine from the offender has proved very difficult. As we have seen, these same community sentences may now be used as methods of fine enforcement (**6.5.2**). Section 37 could be viewed as a more honest approach to the problem, avoiding the complexity and delay of fine enforcement procedures, which may have led to the same result in any event.

6.7 FORFEITURE ORDERS UNDER THE POWERS OF CRIMINAL COURTS ACT 1973

The main power of the courts to order the forfeiture of property which has been connected with the commission of an offence is created by PCCA 1973, s. 43(1). In addition, there is a range of other powers of forfeiture which arise only upon conviction for certain offences; these are considered at **6.8**. The power under s. 43(1) may be exercised by the Crown Court, a magistrates' court or a youth court in respect of any offence. Unlike a compensation order or a restitution order, which are orders ancillary to sentence, a forfeiture order is part of sentence. It is best regarded as a species of fine, which takes the form of removal of an item of the offender's property (which was connected with the offence) rather than a sum of money. The order operates to deprive the offender of his rights in the property, and the property is required to be taken into police possession, if it is not already there. In many cases it will be quite clear that the property in question has been used for the criminal purpose. The sawn-off shotgun and the house-breaking implements can clearly be forfeited as 'tools of the trade'. The powers extend somewhat further than this, however.

Forfeiture orders are used in a relatively small percentage of cases (apart from their use in drug-related offences, where separate powers exist: see **6.8.1**). Forfeiture orders were made in 8 per cent of robbery cases, 8 per cent of cases involving violence against the person and 3 per cent of burglary cases sentenced in the Crown Court in 1996.

6.7.1 Power to make forfeiture order

Power to make a forfeiture order arises where a person has been convicted of any offence. It may be made in respect of any property which has been lawfully seized from the offender or was in the offender's possession or under his control, either at the time when he was apprehended for the offence or when a summons in respect of it was issued (PCCA 1973, s. 43(1)(a)). The property must have been used for the purpose of committing, or facilitating the commission of, any offence, or must have been intended by the offender to be so used (s. 43(1)(b)). The power does not extend to real property, such as the offender's home (*Khan* (1982) 4 Cr App R (S) 298).

In a typical case, the property will have been used for the purposes of the offence which has led to the offender's conviction, but s. 43 clearly contemplates the offender being deprived of property which he used for a quite different offence. The power does not extend, however, to property which was associated with an offence committed by some person other than the offender (*Neville* (1987) 9 Cr App R (S) 222). On the other hand, in *Coleville-Scott* (1992) 12 Cr App R (S) 238 it was held that the power did extend to £125,000 which was found on the offender when he was arrested, and which had been paid to him as a reward for his involvement in the offences with which he had been convicted. 'Facilitating the commission of an offence' includes taking steps after the offence has been committed to dispose of the proceeds or to avoid detection (s. 43(2)). When considering whether to make a forfeiture order, the court must always have regard to the value of the property and the likely financial and other effects on the offender of making the order (s. 43(1A)).

6.7.2 Forfeiture orders and motor vehicles

Forfeiture orders have been used in a number of cases to confiscate an offender's car. Under s. 43(1B) and (1C), in any case where the offender has been convicted of an offence involving 'driving, attempting to drive, or being in charge of a vehicle' (which may include any offence under the RTOA 1988 which is punishable with imprisonment, manslaughter and an offence of wanton and furious driving (under the Offences against the Person Act 1861, s. 35), or failing to provide a specimen for analysis (RTOA 1988, s. 7) or failing to stop and give information or report an accident (RTOA 1988, s. 170), the vehicle involved is to be regarded as having been used for the purpose of committing the offence. Subsections (1B) and (1C), however, in no way limit the courts' power to order forfeiture of the offender's car under the general provision in s. 43(1). The main issue there is whether the use of the car was merely peripheral to the offence, in which case there is no power to order forfeiture, or whether it can fairly be said that it was used for the purpose of the offence. In *Lucas* [1976] Crim LR 79 the offender offered a woman a lift in his car and drove her to a place near some wasteland. They left the car and had sexual intercourse, apparently with the woman's consent. He then indecently assaulted her in a manner to which she did not consent. He was convicted of indecent assault and deprived of his car. The Court of Appeal quashed the order on the basis that the use of the car was part of the background to the offence, but it had not been used to commit or facilitate the offence. A comparable case is *McDonald* (1990) 12 Cr App R (S) 408, where the offender indecently assaulted a young girl on the street and tried to drag her to his car. An order for forfeiture of the car was quashed, since there was insufficient connection between the vehicle and the offence. By contrast, in *Buddo* (1982) 4 Cr App R (S) 268 the offender had driven himself and his accomplice to a chemist's shop, with the intention of breaking in and stealing drugs. The vehicle used was a motor caravan which belonged to the offender. The Court of Appeal found that the 'use of the motor caravan was an integral part of the offence of burglary' (though the order was quashed for other reasons: see **6.7.4**).

6.7.3 Forfeiture orders: procedural matters

In deciding whether to make an order under s. 43, the court may proceed on its own initiative, or the prosecution may apply for the order to be made (*Pemberton* (1982) 4 Cr App R (S) 328). Evidence must be laid before the judge on the issue of forfeiture, and 'full and proper investigation' must be made (*Pemberton*). Where any item of substantial value is to be made the subject of an order, the sentencer must have proper information about its value. The use of forfeiture orders should be confined to 'simple, uncomplicated cases'; in *Troth* (1980) 71 Cr App R 1 it was held that an order should not have been made in respect of property which was subject to joint ownership. In that case the offender was convicted of theft of coal, using a tipper lorry which was co-owned by himself and his partner and used in the course of their joint business as coal merchants; there was no suggestion that the partner was involved in the theft.

The effect of an order under s. 43 is to deprive the offender of his rights in the property (s. 43(3)). It does not affect the rights of any other person, who may apply to the court for recovery of that property. The normal avenue of redress would be the Police (Property) Act 1897, but no such application may be made more than six months from the date of the making of the forfeiture order. The claimant must satisfy the court either that he had not consented to the offender having possession of the property or, where the order was made under s. 43(1)(a), that he did not know, and had no reason to suspect, that the property was likely to be used for criminal purposes.

Section 43A allows the court, where the offender has been convicted of an offence which has resulted in a person suffering 'personal injury, loss or damage' or where such an offence is taken into consideration by the court, to order that any proceeds which accrue from the disposal of the forfeited property shall (up to a certain specified sum) be paid to that person (s. 43A(1)). The court should exercise this power only in a case where it would have made a compensation order (of that specified sum) in that person's favour, but was unable to do so because of the offender's lack of means (s. 43A(2)). This special provision apart, it must be remembered that a forfeiture order is a penalty in its own right, and cannot be used as security for the payment of a fine or compensation (*Kingston Justices, ex parte Hartung* (1981) 72 Cr App R 26).

An offender in respect of whom a forfeiture order has been made may appeal against the order in the same way as against any other order or sentence of the court.

6.7.4   Forfeiture orders: sentencing principles

When considering whether to make a forfeiture order, the court must always have regard to the value of the property, and to the likely financial and other effects on the offender of making the order (s. 43(1A)). In *Highbury Corner Justices, ex parte Di Matteo* (1990) 12 Cr App R (S) 594, the Court of Appeal found that no proper inquiry as to the likely financial or other effects of making the order had been undertaken by the sentencer, and hence the order was quashed. It must always be remembered that the forfeiture order forms part of the sentence for the offence, and other component elements of the punishment must be adjusted accordingly if forfeiture, especially of a substantial item, is also ordered.

This important principle has been applied by the Court of Appeal in several cases. In *Buddo* (1982) 4 Cr App R (S) 268, in addition to a total prison sentence of two years, the offender was deprived of his rights in a motor caravan in which he and an accomplice had driven to the scene of a burglary. The Court of Appeal said that although such an order could properly be made on the facts, to do so in this case was 'overdoing the punishment' and the order was accordingly quashed. A similar case is *Joyce* (1989) 11 Cr App R (S) 253. Where the order would have a disproportionately severe impact upon an offender, it should not be made. In *Tavernor* [1976] RTR 242 an order depriving an offender of his rights in a car, imposed in addition to a suspended sentence and a fine, was quashed in view of the offender's physical disability and the fact that his car was specially adapted for his use.

In a case where several offenders are equally implicated in an offence and receive comparable sentences, it is wrong to impose a forfeiture order on only one of them (*Ottey* (1984) 6 Cr App R (S) 163). This may be contrasted with the principle applicable to ancillary orders, such as compensation orders where only one offender has the means to pay compensation (see *Beddow* (1987) 9 Cr App R (S) 235, at **8.1.5**). The main purpose of a forfeiture order is to punish the offender, rather than to compensate the victim.

6.7.5   Combining forfeiture orders with other sentences or orders

It seems that a forfeiture order may be combined with any other punishment, provided that the sentencing principle described in the last paragraph is observed by the court. A forfeiture order cannot be combined with an absolute discharge (*Hunt* [1978] Crim LR 697) or a conditional discharge (*Savage* (1983) 5 Cr App R (S) 216) since a discharge may only be used where it is 'inexpedient to inflict punishment'. A forfeiture order may be combined with a compensation order, and provision is made under PCCA 1973, s. 43A to allow the sale of property connected with the offence to finance the compensation (see **6.7.3**).

6.8 FORFEITURE ORDERS UNDER OTHER STATUTES

Several statutes empower the criminal courts to make forfeiture orders with respect to their subject matter.

6.8.1 Misuse of drugs

By the Misuse of Drugs Act 1971 (MDA 1971), s. 27(1), the court by or before which a person is convicted of an offence under the MDA 1971 (or a drug trafficking offence, as defined in the DTA 1994, s. 1(3)) may order anything shown to the satisfaction of the court to relate to the offence to be forfeited, and either destroyed or dealt with in such manner as the court may order. 'Anything', in this context, is restricted to tangible items of personal property, including money, of which physical possession can be taken by persons authorised to do so (*Cuthbertson* [1981] AC 470). The power does not extend to seizure of real property such as a house (*Pearce* [1996] 2 Cr App R (S) 316). It does not extend to intangibles, such as money in bank accounts, nor to personal property which is situated abroad. The item to be forfeited must be shown to relate to the offence with which the offender has been convicted, and it is not enough to show that it relates to some other offence, whether planned or already committed (*Ribeyre* (1982) 4 Cr App R (S) 165; *Boothe* (1987) 9 Cr App R (S) 8). It does not apply to offenders convicted of a conspiracy to contravene the provisions of the MDA 1971, since conspiracy is not an offence under the Act (*Cuthbertson*). The court must adopt a judicial rather than a whimsical approach when determining how the items seized are to be disposed of (*Beard*).

The court has a duty to hear evidence before making an order under s. 27(1) (*Churcher* (1986) 8 Cr App R (S) 94). Provided the other requirements of s. 27(1) are made out, property may be forfeited even though it belongs to a person other than the offender (*Menocal* [1980] AC 598). In that case, however, any such person claiming ownership may apply to the court to be heard (s. 27(2)).

Orders under s. 27(1) are limited in their scope. If the court wishes to make an order designed to remove the profits of drug offending, a more appropriate option is to make a confiscation order under the DTA 1994 (see **9.1**). That power, however, is not available in magistrates' courts. There is no power under s. 27(1) to order compensation to be paid from any proceeds of property seized.

In 1996, 50 per cent of offenders sentenced for indictable drug-related offences in magistrates' courts had forfeiture orders made against them, and 65 per cent of offenders so sentenced in the Crown Court had forfeiture orders made against them. The number of forfeiture orders has increased dramatically between 1986 and 1996 (from 1,292 to 12,187 in magistrates' courts and from 237 to 6,426 in the Crown Court).

6.8.2 Firearms and other weapons

Section 52 of the Firearms Act 1968 applies where a person:

(a)   is convicted of an offence under that Act; or

(b)   is convicted of any other offence for which he is given a custodial sentence; or

(c)   has been ordered to enter into a recognisance to keep the peace or be of good behaviour, on condition that he shall not possess, use or carry a firearm; or

(d)   is subject to a probation order which contains a requirement that he shall not possess, use or carry a firearm.

In any such case, the court by or before which the person is convicted, or by which the order is made, may make such order as to the forfeiture or disposal of any firearm or ammunition found in his possession as it thinks fit, and may cancel any firearms certificate or shot-gun certificate held by him.

The wording of s. 52 is broad, and it does not require that the offender was in possession of the firearm at the time of the offence nor, indeed, that the firearm was in any way related to the offence.

By the Prevention of Crime Act 1953, s. 1(2), when any person is convicted of an offence under s. 1(1) (possession of offensive weapon in a public place without lawful authority or reasonable excuse), the court may make an order for the forfeiture or disposal of any weapon in respect of which the offence was committed. A person convicted under the Crossbows Act 1987 may be liable to the forfeiture and disposal, as the court thinks fit, of any crossbow or part of a crossbow in respect of which the offence was committed (Crossbows Act 1987, s. 6(3)) as may a person convicted of an offence under CJA 1988, s. 139, of having an article with a blade or a sharp point in a public place or on school premises.

6.8.3   Written material

A range of forfeiture provisions exist in relation to offences involving written material:

(a)   A court may, on a conviction for seditious libel, make an order for the disposal of all copies of the libel seized (Criminal Libel Act 1918, s. 2).

(b)   Under the Incitement to Disaffection Act 1934, s. 3, the court may order any documents connected with an offence under that Act to be destroyed, or otherwise disposed of.

(c)   Where articles are seized under the Obscene Publications Act 1959, s. 1(4), and a person is convicted of having those publications for gain, the court must order forfeiture of those goods.

(d)   Where indecent photographs of children are seized, under the Protection of Children Act 1978, the Indecency with Children Act 1978, s. 5 or the CJA 1988, s. 160, the photographs must be seized and destroyed. 'Photographs' now includes computer-generated images.

(e)   Under the Public Order Act 1986, where a person is convicted of specified offences relating to the incitement of racial hatred, the court must order written material or recordings relating to the offence to be seized.

Note that in several of these examples the court, subject to certain conditions specified in the statutes, is under a duty, rather than merely given a power, to seize the material.

6.8.4 Other statutes

There are a number of other powers of forfeiture, including the following. A person convicted of certain offences under the Forgery and Counterfeiting Act 1981 is liable to have any property which is shown to the satisfaction of the court to relate to the offence to be forfeited and either destroyed or dealt with in such other manner as the court may order (Forgery and Counterfeiting Act 1981, ss. 7(3) and 24). A person convicted on indictment of an offence of assisting illegal entry into the UK, if he is at that time the captain or the owner (or director or manager of a company which is the owner) of a ship, aircraft or vehicle used or intended to be used in connection with that offence, may be subject to forfeiture of that ship, aircraft or vehicle, in the discretion of the court (Immigration Act 1971, s. 25 and Customs and Excise Management Act 1979, ss. 49 and 68).

CJPOA

7 Discharge, Bind Over, Reparation and Parenting Orders

In Chapters 4, 5 and 6 of this book the sentences which appear in the three key levels of the sentencing framework created by the CJA 1991 were described. We turn now to consider the non-custodial penalties of discharge and bind over, which have their place towards the foot of the sentencing structure, and the reparation order and parenting order, which will be introduced when the CDB becomes law. These measures are appropriate in cases where the offence is not sufficiently serious to justify the imposition of a community sentence. Courts are then often faced with a choice between a fine and a non-custodial order.

7.1 ABSOLUTE AND CONDITIONAL DISCHARGE

The court's power to pass absolute or conditional discharges may be found in PCCA 1973, s. 1A. The power to discharge is available whatever the age of the offender and whatever the offence committed, subject only to the crime of murder and to the two presumptive sentences under the C(S)A 1997. It is a power enjoyed by the Crown Court, an adult magistrates' court and a youth court. Powers of discharge are not community orders. There is no requirement that the court obtain a pre-sentence report. The only effective limitation on the use of the discharge is the requirement in s. 1A(1) that the court, having had regard to the circumstances, including the nature of the offence and the character of the offender, must conclude that it is 'inexpedient to inflict punishment' before a discharge can be ordered. A discharge is not, then, technically a punishment at all (although a conditional discharge might perhaps be characterised as a 'mild' penalty). There is no reported judicial consideration of the phrase 'inexpedient to inflict punishment'. One effect of it, however, is to restrict the other sentences or orders with which a discharge may be combined (see **7.1.3**).

7.1.1 Use of the absolute discharge

Where a court grants an absolute discharge, the offender leaves court with no effective penalty at all. The absolute discharge must, of course, be distinguished from an acquittal, since in the latter case no conviction has been recorded. An absolute discharge is a sentence imposed upon conviction, and will be recorded in the offender's list of previous convictions. Two qualifications to that statement should, however, be noted. First, an absolute discharge may be granted by a criminal court in a case where a person has been charged with an offence and has not been convicted, but has either been found unfit to plead or not guilty by reason of insanity. This matter is dealt with in **11.3.7**. Second, by PCCA 1973, s. 1C, wherever a conviction is followed by a discharge (whether absolute or conditional) that conviction counts as a conviction for a limited range of purposes only (see **7.1.4**).

Absolute discharges are infrequently awarded by the courts. Taking the figures for all courts for 1996, the absolute discharge was used in 1 per cent of indictable offences, 1 per cent of non-motoring summary offences and 2 per cent of summary motoring offences. It may be tempting to think of the absolute discharge simply as being the sentence appropriate in trivial cases. This is true to some extent, but there are perhaps three different types of case in which an absolute discharge has been seen as appropriate:

(a) In cases where the offence is trivial, and/or the offender is virtually blameless for what has occurred and/or the public interest does not require that the offender should suffer any penalty beyond the recording of guilt. In *Surrey County Council* v *Battersby* [1965] 2 QB 194 the Divisional Court recommended that magistrates should absolutely discharge a woman convicted of the offence of failing to register a fostering arrangement because, before entering into the arrangement in question, she had sought, and received, official advice that no such registration was required in her case. An absolute discharge was held to be appropriate in a case of possession of a small amount of a controlled drug, where the offender originally had acquired the drug lawfully and subsequently forgotten its whereabouts (*King* [1977] Crim LR 627). Where a defendant company had committed an offence of strict liability without any degree of culpability, and where it was doubtful if the public interest had been served in prosecuting, an absolute discharge was appropriate (*Smedleys Ltd* v *Breed* [1974] AC 839).

(b) Where the court wishes to register its disapproval of police methods used in the particular case, and the discharge is addressed as much to the police as to the offender. In *Willcock* v *Muckle* [1951] 2 KB 844 an absolute discharge was 'emphatically approved' where the police had exercised special powers to demand identity documents from the offender in inappropriate circumstances. It was also upheld in *Browning* v *Watson* [1953] 1 WLR 1172, where the offenders had been trapped by the police into committing the offence. Criticism may also be directed by the court at the prosecuting authorities, such as where charges for very trivial, stale or technical offences have been brought. It may be noted in this context that the Code for the Crown Prosecution Service, issued pursuant to POA 1985, s. 10, indicates that, where the circumstances of an offence are not particularly serious and a court would be likely to impose a purely nominal penalty, Crown Prosecutors should consider carefully whether the public interest would be better served by dropping the prosecution.

(c) The absolute discharge is also employed as an administrative measure by some courts when dealing with an offender convicted of a number of offences on a single occasion. In road traffic cases particularly, the court may pass the 'real' sentence for the most serious of the offences, and deal with a number of other lesser offences by way of absolute discharge. Other courts use the device of 'no separate penalty' to achieve the same effect, though this seems to have no statutory or judicial authority (*Burnham Justices, ex parte Ansorge* [1959] 1 WLR 1041). Yet another method is to adjourn the proceedings 'sine die'.

7.1.2 Use of the conditional discharge

When a discharge is conditional, the sole condition is that the offender should commit no further offence during the period of the conditional discharge. No other condition or requirement may be inserted. The period of the conditional discharge is fixed by the court, up to a maximum of three years. In practice conditional discharges are usually for periods of six months or 12 months. If an offender is convicted of an offence during that period, he will be in breach of the conditional discharge and will be liable to be sentenced for the offence in respect of which he received the discharge as well as being sentenced for the new offence. Before making an order for conditional discharge, the sentencing court must explain the consequences of breach to the offender in open court and in ordinary language (PCCA 1973, s. 1A(3)). In *Wehner* [1977] 1 WLR 1143 it was said to be sound practice for the court to explain this to the offender personally, but delegation of that task to the offender's lawyer was not prohibited, provided that the court was satisfied that the explanation had been made and understood before the order was made. The Court of Appeal adopted this approach when substituting a conditional discharge on an offender who had appealed against sentence (*Whitehead* (1979) 1 Cr App R (S) 187).

The conditional discharge is widely used by the courts. Taking the figures for all courts for 1996, the conditional discharge was used in 17 per cent of indictable offences, 9 per cent of summary non-motoring offences and 1 per cent of summary motoring offences.

The conditional discharge is the most important sentencing option, apart from the fine, lying beneath the community sentence threshold. There is very little appellate authority on the choice between the fine and the conditional discharge, or indeed on the conditional discharge at all. It would seem that where the offence is not serious enough to warrant the use of a community sentence, a fine will continue to be the first choice for sentencers. Indeed, in magistrates' courts, the fine is often regarded as the presumptive penalty. Despite the requirement in s. 1A(1) that it should be used only where 'it is inexpedient to inflict punishment', the conditional discharge may also usefully be regarded as a penalty, albeit a mild one, in the form of a warning. In *Whitehead* (1979) 1 Cr App R (S) 187 the offender was convicted of shoplifting a tin of ham, a tin of steak and a pair of tights. She had an 'unblemished character' and was living in difficult domestic and financial circumstances. She was bringing up on her own two children, one of whom was mentally handicapped, and she was reliant upon social security payments. The Court of Appeal said that the appropriate sentence in such a case was a conditional discharge for 12 months, not least because of the offender's straitened circumstances. In *McGowan* [1975] Crim LR 113 the Court of Appeal approved the use of the conditional discharge where a fine would otherwise have been the proper sentence, but the offender lacked the means to pay. The threat inherent in the conditional discharge, that the offender will be sentenced for the original offence if he fails to keep out out of trouble during the period of the discharge, is clearly an important aspect of the sentence. In *Watts* (1984) 6 Cr App R (S) 61 the Crown Court judge had imposed a suspended prison sentence of three months on the offender, who had allowed her premises to be used for the purposes of smoking cannabis. It was accepted that she did not smoke cannabis herself, but had allowed a friend of hers to do so when he visited her. She had some previous convictions, but none during the last 15 years, during which time she had led 'an honest and perfectly respectable life'. The Court of Appeal said that the suspended sentence was contrary to principle since the offence was not serious enough to justify custody, but that 'some sanction to prevent her from permitting any repetition of the offence in her house' was required. A conditional discharge for 12 months would supply that requirement, and was the proper sentence for the judge to have imposed.

On making an order for conditional discharge, the court may, if it thinks it expedient for the purpose of the offender's reformation, allow any person who consents to do so to give security for the offender's good behaviour (PCCA 1973, s. 12(1)). It is thought that this power is rarely exercised.

7.1.3 Combining a discharge with other sentences or orders

It has been held that a discharge, whether absolute or conditional, cannot be combined with a punitive measure for the same offence (*Savage* (1983) 5 Cr App R (S) 216), except where such a mix is expressly permitted by statute. Thus a discharge cannot be combined with any custodial sentence, any community sentence or a fine. The incompatibility of the fine and the discharge was made clear in *McClelland* [1951] 1 All ER 557 and was confirmed in *Sanck* (1990) 12 Cr App R (S) 155. For the same reason, apparently, a discharge cannot be combined with an order to disqualify a person from acting as a company director (*Young* (1990) 12 Cr App R (S) 262) although it can be questioned whether a disqualification like this is properly thought of as a punishment. These restrictions on combining a discharge with other sentences are not so restrictive as they might at first appear, however, since where an offender is being dealt with for more than one offence, the court is free to discharge for one offence and exercise its normal sentencing powers with respect to other offences (*Bainbridge* (1979) 1 Cr App R (S) 36). A discharge can in any event be combined with a compensation order, an order for costs (PCCA 1973, s. 12(4)) or a restitution order (PCCA 1973, s. 1C(4)). It may also be combined with a recommendation for deportation (*Akan* [1973] 1 QB 491), or with orders for endorsement or disqualification from driving under the Road Traffic Act (RTOA 1988, s. 46) but not, oddly enough, with disqualification from driving under the PCCA 1973, s. 44 (**10.1.9**) or under the C(S)A 1997, s. 39 (**10.1.10**).

7.1.4 Limited effect of conviction where discharge is granted

Where an offender pleads guilty or is convicted of an offence and is dealt with by way of discharge, he is deemed not to have been convicted of the offence unless and until he is subsequently sentenced for it, i.e. where the discharge is a conditional one and he is later in breach of it (PCCA 1973, s. 1C and *Moore* [1995] QB 353). This provision used to extend to probation orders as well as to discharges. The former orders were excluded from its ambit by the CJA 1991, but a probation order imposed on an offender before 1 October 1992 (when the CJA was brought into force) would still count only for limited purposes. The rule in s. 1C has the effect, for example, that a person granted a discharge for a particular offence would not be debarred from holding an office from which persons convicted of that offence are normally barred.

Another (perhaps unintended) effect is that, if a person commits an imprisonable offence during the operational period of a suspended sentence, and receives an absolute or conditional discharge for that new offence, the offender cannot be dealt with for breach of the suspended sentence since power to activate a suspended sentence arises only where there has been a 'conviction' for the subsequent offence (*Tarry* [1970] 2 QB 561). In practice a court which imposed a discharge for the new offence might well be minded not to activate the suspended sentence in any event, but the authorities indicate that the relative triviality of the new offence is not, in itself, sufficient reason for not activating the suspended sentence. In respect of other sentences which become available only where the offender is shown to have relevant previous convictions, an earlier discharge will not count for this purpose. For an example see **4.3.3**.

It should be noted that, quite apart from s. 1C, the operation of the Rehabilitation of Offenders Act 1974 may mean that an offender can deny that he has been convicted of an offence once his conviction becomes 'spent' (see **13.6.1**).

Section 1C does not prevent a person who is granted a discharge from appealing against conviction or against sentence (MCA 1980, s. 108(1) and CAA 1968, s. 50(1A)).

7.1.5 Breach of conditional discharge

A conditional discharge can be breached only by the conviction of the offender of a further offence committed during the period of the discharge (PCCA, s. 1B(1)). In every case the breach must be clearly admitted by the offender or be proved (*Devine* (1956) 40 Cr App R 45). This will normally present no problem, since the date of the offender's conviction for the further offence will be a matter of record. Breach must always be dealt with by sentencing for the original offence. The percentage of offenders originally dealt with by way of conditional discharge who are subsequently dealt with for the original offence in consequence of breach has remained remarkably consistent over the last ten years. It has stayed at around 10 per cent throughout that period. It has been said that the sentence for the original offence should normally be more than a nominal one (*Stuart* [1964] 1 WLR 1381). No detailed breakdown of disposals following breach of conditional discharge is available, but it may perhaps be assumed that the most frequently used penalty in these circumstances is a fine. The criminal statistics do, however, record the proportionate rate of use of custody following breach of conditional discharge. Over the last ten years the annual figure has declined from 23 per cent to 14 per cent. The proportion in 1991 was 18 per cent. This figure does not include offenders who have received custody for the new offence, rather than for the original offence. Sentencing for the original offence always terminates the conditional discharge, but any order for compensation or for costs which was made at the time of the conditional discharge remains valid (*Evans* [1963] 1 QB 979).

If a magistrates' court is sentencing for the new offence, it should sentence for the original offence either if it imposed the discharge or if a different magistrates' court imposed the discharge and the agreement of that court is obtained. If the discharge was imposed by the Crown Court the magistrates may commit the offender to the Crown Court. If the Crown Court is sentencing for the new offence it may sentence for the original offence whether the discharge was imposed by the Crown Court or by a magistrates' court.

When dealing with the breach, the court may sentence the offender for the original offence in any manner in which it could have dealt with the offender if he had just been convicted before the court of that offence (s. 1B(6)) except that the Crown Court dealing with a person conditionally discharged by a magistrates' court is limited to the lower court's powers (s. 1B(7)).

If a juvenile offender has been conditionally discharged by a magistrates' court for an offence which is triable only on indictment in the case of an adult, any court dealing with him for the original offence consequent upon breach of the conditional discharge after he has attained the age of 18 may use only the powers to sentence for the original offence which would have been available for an offence triable either way which was tried summarily (s. 1B(9)). For the purposes of these provisions, the age of an offender is deemed to be that which it appears to the court to be after considering any available evidence (s. 1B(10)).

7.2 BINDING OVER TO KEEP THE PEACE

There is a range of powers available to English sentencers which are conveniently grouped together under the heading of 'bind over'. All these powers take the form of a suspended financial penalty, on the basis of an undertaking by the person bound over to comply with certain (sometimes rather vague) requirements of the court.

The powers which a magistrates' court possesses to bind over a person to keep the peace (or to be of good behaviour) derive from two different sources. The first is where an action in the form of a complaint is brought before the court, pursuant to MCA 1980, s. 115. If the court finds the complaint to have substance, it may bind over the person in respect of whom the complaint was brought (and, incidentally, if the court finds cause, the complainant as well: *Wilkins* [1907] 2 KB 380). The procedure is more closely analogous to civil rather than criminal procedure and cannot in any circumstances result in a conviction and sentence. This form of bind over is, accordingly, not considered further here. The second form of bind over to keep the peace stems from an ancient common law power, the existence of which has been recognised in several statutes, notably the Justices of the Peace Act 1361. These powers arise only in criminal proceedings. They are very wide and, in addition to being used as part of a sentence, may be exercised by the justices at any time before the conclusion of the proceedings. The Justices of the Peace Act 1968, s. 1(7) makes it clear that 'any court of record having a criminal jurisdiction has, as ancillary to that jurisdiction, the power to bind over to be of good behaviour'. The Crown Court is a court of record (Courts Act 1971, s. 4(1)), and hence possesses power to bind over, and it has been established that this power also extends to the Court of Appeal (*Sharp* [1957] 1 QB 552).

7.2.1 Scope of power to bind over

Common law powers to bind over may be used at the time of withdrawal of the case by the prosecution, on a decision by the prosecution to offer no evidence, on an adjournment or, even, upon the acquittal of the defendant (*Inner London Crown Court, ex parte Benjamin* (1986) 85 Cr App R 267) as well as, after conviction, on sentence. A survey of the courts' use of powers to bind over in October 1983 (Law Commission, 1987) found that in three-quarters of the cases where the power was exercised it was used other than on sentence. Use of the powers was patchy, however. Nearly 40 per cent of the courts in the survey did not use their powers to bind over at all during the month of the survey. Subsequently, the Law Commission recommended that these powers should be abolished because they are anomalous (Law Commission, 1994). The proposal has not been acted upon.

The powers may be exercised whenever the court considers that a person's conduct has been such that there might be a breach of the peace in the future, whether committed by that person or by others or (at least in a magistrates' court) where that person's behaviour was *contra bones mores* (*Hughes* v *Holley* [1987] Crim LR 253). The traditional explanation for the breadth of these powers has been the court exercising 'preventive justice' (*Veator* v *Glennon* [1981] 1 WLR 567). A common law bind over may be used against a witness before the court (*Sheldon* v *Bromfield Justices* [1964] 2 QB 573). It may not, however, be used against a person who came to court as a witness but was not called (*Swindon Crown Court, ex parte Pawittar Singh* (1983) 5 Cr App R (S) 422).

The effect of the order is that the person bound over is required to enter into an undertaking (or, as it is normally called, a recognisance) that he will keep the peace and/or be of good behaviour for a specified period, upon pain of forfeiting a certain sum of money if he fails to do so. The period for which a bind over to keep the peace (or to be of good behaviour) may run is entirely within the court's discretion. A bind over may name a person or persons for whose special protection the bind over is made (*Wilson* v *Skeock* (1949) 65 TLR 418); otherwise, the cases indicate that courts should not insert specific conditions into bind overs. In *Randall* (1986) 8 Cr App R (S) 433, a condition that the person bound over did not teach, or try to teach, anyone under the age of 18 was held to be invalid. In *Goodlad* v *Chief Constable of South Yorkshire* [1979] Crim LR 51 a condition forbidding the possession, carrying or use of a firearm was held to be invalid, but this cannot be squared with the Firearms Act 1968, s. 52, which specifically envisages that such an order may be made (see **6.8.2**). In any event, such conditions must be reasonable, and it has been held that there is no power to bind over a person on condition that they leave the jurisdiction and do not return (*Ayu* [1958] 1 WLR 1264), though see **7.3**. The sum of money to be forfeited upon breach of the bind over is also within the court's discretion. There appears to be no limit, save that the sum should be reasonable in all the circumstances. It is clear, for instance, that a person may be bound over in a sum which is greater than the maximum fine available for the offence of which he stands convicted (*Sandbach Justices, ex parte Williams* [1935] 2 KB 192).

Powers to bind over to keep the peace may also be imposed after conviction, on sentence. The powers exercisable at that stage appear to be indistinguishable from those which may be exercisable at earlier stages of the proceedings. Remarkably, it is unclear whether a convicted offender may be dealt with by way of a bind over to keep the peace (or to be of good behaviour) standing alone on sentence, or whether the passing of some other sentence upon him is required in addition. The wording of the Justices of the Peace Act 1968, s. 1(7) (see **7.2**) indicates that the bind over is 'ancillary' to the court's criminal jurisdiction, and this may mean that a court should determine the penalty for the offence before the ancillary power of binding over to keep the peace is considered. The Law Commission found evidence, however, that bind overs are sometimes imposed on sentence without any additional penalty.

When the court proposes to bind over a person convicted of an offence in anything other than a trivial sum, the court should have regard to his means and other personal circumstances, and should allow him to make representations in respect of those matters (*Central Criminal Court, ex parte Boulding* [1984] QB 813). The court should fix the period of the recognisance and the sum of money to be forfeited upon breach at the time when it imposes the bind over.

Under the Magistrates' Courts (Appeals from Binding Over) Act 1956, there is a right of appeal to the Crown Court against a bind over to keep the peace (or to be of good behaviour) made by a magistrates' court. Where the bind over is imposed by the Crown Court on sentence, a right of appeal lies to the Court of Appeal by virtue of CAA 1968, s. 50(1).

7.2.2 Use of bind over to keep the peace

Little is known about the actual operation of the power to bind over to keep the peace, and it is very difficult to disentangle the use of the power as a sentencing option from use at earlier stages of the criminal process. Speaking generally, the Law Commission identified three areas of law-breaking where the courts tended to favour the use of bind overs:

(a)   the less serious matters of violence and public disorder;

(b)   relatively minor matters involving annoyance and distress, including certain forms of sexual behaviour in public; and

(c)   neighbour and domestic disputes.

The Criminal Statistics for 1996 indicate that magistrates' courts use their powers to bind over on sentence almost entirely in respect of summary, rather than indictable, offences. The summary offences are broken down no further in the statistics, but the bulk of the indictable offences dealt with by way of bind over on sentence were offences of violence against the person. The Law Commission's survey suggested that in 1983 the average recogisance was about £100, and the average duration of a bind over was about 12 months. The survey's figures do not distinguish between bind overs imposed on sentence and those imposed at an earlier stage, and no more recent figures are available.

Since the rationale for the use of powers to bind over to keep the peace and/or be of good behaviour is 'preventive justice', it follows that such powers should not be used where there is no reasonable apprehension by the court of such conduct in the future. It may be argued that binding over should not be used where a person is convicted of matters unconnected with violence or public disturbance, actual or potential. In *Middlesex Crown Court, ex parte Khan* (1996) *The Times*, 24 January 1997 the Divisional Court said that before binding over an acquitted defendant the court should be satisfied beyond reasonable doubt that the defendant posed a threat to other persons and was a man of violence.

7.2.3 Refusal or failure to enter into recognisance

Whenever the court requires a person to be bound over to keep the peace (or to be of good behaviour), that person must consent to being so dealt with. The sanction for refusal to enter into a recognisance proposed by the court is imprisonment. There appears to be no limit to the duration of the term of custody which may be imposed where the court acts under its common law powers, but the normal limitations upon magistrates' courts powers to impose custody would surely apply where the bind over was imposed by magistrates upon a convicted offender.

It was made clear in *Conlan v Oxford* (1983) 5 Cr App R (S) 237 that the court may bind over an offender who consents even though the court would have no power to send that person to prison for refusal to consent (i.e. where the offender is aged under 21). Provided that there is consent, it seems that an offender of any age may be bound over. Problems have arisen where the court has sought to bind over an offender whom it had no power to imprison, but who refused to consent. It seems that a person aged from 18 to 20 who refuses to consent to be bound over by a magistrates' court may be detained under the CJA 1982, s. 9 instead (see **6.5**). There is no power to order detention of a person under the age of 18 in these circumstances, but an attendance centre order could be made (CJA 1982, s. 17(1)). The Crown Court may deal with a refusal to be bound over as a contempt of court.

7.2.4 Failure to comply with bind over

If a person who has been bound over is adjudged to have failed to comply with the conditions of the order, the court may deal with him by forfeiting the whole or part of the recognisance in its discretion, together with costs. It may allow time for payment, or direct payment by instalments of the sum forfeited (PCCA 1973, s. 31(1)). It is important to realise that the court is *not* empowered to impose custody for failure to comply with the conditions of a bind over (*Finch* (1962) 47 Cr App R 58; *Gilbert* (1974) CSP D10-3A01). This is in contrast to the court's powers to impose custody where a person refuses to be bound over. A court, when forfeiting a recognisance, must fix a term of imprisonment or detention not exceeeding 12 months, to be served in the event of default of payment (PCCA 1973, s. 31(2), (3) and (3A)). It seems that a recognisance can be declared to be forfeit only by way of an order on complaint (MCA 1980, s. 120), irrespective of the power which the court was exercising when the bind over was first imposed. Also, by s. 120, only that magistrates' court which imposed the bind over may forfeit the recognisance.

Proceedings for breach of bind over are civil in character and require only the civil standard of proof (*Marlow Justices, ex parte O'Sullivan* [1984] QB 381). The person concerned should, nevertheless, be told the nature of the breach alleged and be given an opportunity to present evidence, call witnesses or adduce an explanation (*McGregor* [1945] 2 All ER 180). There appears to be no right of appeal against an adjudication of forfeiture (*Durham Justices, ex parte Laurent* [1945] KB 33), although there is the possibility of making an application for judicial review.

7.2.5　Binding over parent or guardian of offender aged under 16

Section 58 of CJA 1991 places an obligation upon magistrates' courts and the Crown Court to bind over the parent or guardian of an offender who is under the age of 16, whenever the court is satisfied that to do so would be desirable in the interests of preventing the commission by the young offender of further offences. If the court is not satisfied of that, on the facts of the particular case, it should state in open court that it is not so satisfied, and give reasons for its view. Section 58 replaces infrequently used powers in CYPA 1969, s. 7(7)(c), to bind over the parent or guardian of a young offender. In the White Paper which preceded the 1991 Act (Home Office, 1990) the government said that such powers 'could play an important part in ensuring that parents do all they can to stop their children reoffending'. It is envisaged that the bind over will normally be imposed on parents at the same time as a sentence (such as a supervision order) is imposed on the juvenile.

By s. 58, the court is empowered to order the parent or guardian to enter into a recognisance, in a sum not exceeding £1,000, to take proper care of the offender and exercise proper control over him. The maximum duration of the recognisance is until the offender reaches the age of 18, or for a period of three years, whichever is the shorter period (s. 58(2) and (3)). Entry into the recognisance requires the consent of the parent or guardian, but if consent is refused and the court considers the refusal to be unreasonable, the parent or guardian may be punished by a fine not exceeding level 3 on the standard scale (s. 58(4)). In fixing the level of the recognisance, the court should take into account, among other things, the means of the parent or guardian, whether such consideration has the effect of increasing or reducing the level of the recognisance fixed upon (s. 58(5)).

As far as forfeiture of the recognisance is concerned, s. 58(3) states that MCA 1980, s. 120 shall apply in relation to a recognisance under s. 58 as it does to a recognisance to keep the peace (see **7.2.4**). The court may, therefore, order forfeiture of the whole or part of the recognisance in its discretion, together with costs. A right of appeal to the Crown Court against an order made under s. 58 which is made by a magistrates' court is created by s. 58(6); where the order is made by the Crown Court, there is a right to appeal to the Court of Appeal (s. 58(7)).

7.3　BINDING OVER TO COME UP FOR JUDGMENT

A common law power enjoyed by the Crown Court (but not a magistrates' court or a youth court) is to bind over a person to come up for judgment to be sentenced on a certain later day, or on a day to be specified to him later, on recognisance on certain specified conditions. If the offender breaks one or more of the conditions, he will be brought back before the court for sentencing for the original offence but, if he does not break any of the conditions within the specified period, he will either not be sentenced for the original offence at all, or will receive a nominal penalty for it.

A bind over to come up for judgment is made in lieu of sentence and it is therefore wrong to impose it in addition to the sentence (*Ayu* [1958] 1 WLR 1264). An offender should consent to the bind over, although such consent is not vitiated by a reasonable expectation of a custodial sentence in the alternative (*Williams* [1982] 1 WLR 1398). It is a 'sentence' made on conviction on indictment (*Abrahams* (1952) 36 Cr App R 147), and therefore an appeal against it lies to the Court of Appeal (CAA 1968, s. 50(1)).

This power is anomalous and would appear to have very limited use. It has a long history, pre-dating all the modern non-custodial disposals. Figures made available to the Law Commission by the Home Office relating to 1980 suggest that it is never used, or very rarely used, in the majority of Crown Courts (Law Commission, 1987), though in one urban area the Crown Court used it no less than 113 times during that year. According to the *Criminal Statistics* the Crown Court bound over defendants in 278 cases in 1996, but it is not clear how many of these were bind overs to come up for judgment as opposed to bind overs to keep the peace. The power bears some similarity to the courts' powers to defer sentence (see **3.10**), but deferment is a statutory power and really ought to be used in preference. In many cases the effect of binding over to come up for judgment may be achieved by imposing a probation order, where the offence is serious enough to justify that course, or a conditional discharge. The sentence may also be compared to the bind over to keep the peace or be of good behaviour, the main difference lying in the Crown Court's power to impose a range of conditions within a bind over to come up for judgment. It is in the possibility of such conditions that the residual usefulness of this power may be found. From time to time it has been used in respect of offenders who are prepared to leave the country, where the sentencer also wishes that course to be followed but cannot make a recommendation for deportation because the offender is a British subject.

In *Hodges* (1967) 51 Cr App R 361 the offender had been sentenced to five years' imprisonment for offences of dishonesty. He had a history of similar offending. The Court of Appeal heard that the offender showed genuine signs of reformation and that his cousin, a farmer in Southern Ireland, wanted the offender to go to live with him. The Court of Appeal wished to allow the offender to take up this offer, but wanted to ensure that he would go to Ireland and stay there. They quashed the prison sentence, and bound the offender to come up for judgment on condition that he left immediately for Dublin and did not re-enter the UK for ten years. In contrast, in *Williams* [1982] 1 WLR 1398 the offender was a youth of 18 who was born in England to Jamaican parents. He was convicted of theft and had a number of previous convictions and findings of guilt. He was bound over to come up for judgment in his own recognisance, on condition that he accompanied his mother to Jamaica and did not return to the UK for five years. On appeal, Lord Lane CJ disapproved the sentence, since Williams was reluctant to go to Jamaica and had agreed to this course of action at trial only when the sentencer had told him that the alternative was custody. The Court of Appeal said that the bind over should normally be used in such a case only where the offender would be going to a country of which he was a citizen or an habitual resident. The bind over was replaced by a conditional discharge.

If the offender is in breach of a bind over to come up for judgment, he is liable to forfeit the recognisance as well as being sentenced for the original offence. Where a person is brought back before the court on the ground that a recognisance entered into by him has been broken, the breach must be proved beyond reasonable doubt (*McGarry* (1945) 30 Cr App R 187). The person bound over is entitled to be heard on the matter (*David* [1939] 1 All ER 782).

7.4 REPARATION ORDERS

The Crime and Disorder Bill contains provisions in Part IV which, when they become law and are brought into force, will create a new order applicable to offenders under the age of 18 — the reparation order. A pilot scheme will be introduced to run for 18 months from Autumn 1998. In the White Paper, *No More Excuses* (Home Office, 1997a) the government describes the reparation order as:

> . . . a new penalty . . . which courts will have to consider imposing on young offenders in all cases where they do not impose a compensation order. The order will require reparation to be made in kind, up to a maximum of 24 hours' work within a period of three months. The reparation might involve writing a letter of apology, apologising to the victim in person, cleaning graffiti or repairing criminal damage. Of course not all victims want reparation. The government's proposals will ensure that the victim's views will be sought before an order is made. Where a victim does not want direct reparation, the reparation may be made to the community at large.

Reparation to the victim is the central feature of this order, although it will be recalled that a reparation requirement may be included as one element within an action plan order (also introduced by the CDB: see **5.10**). The government envisages that the reparation order will be appropriate where a compensation order cannot be made, most likely because the young offender has no means to pay. It is important to note that, when the legislation is implemented, the reparation order (unlike the action plan order) will *not* be a 'community order'. The reparation order may, therefore, be used in respect of an offence which is not serious enough to justify the passing of a community sentence although there seems no reason why, in an appropriate case, it might not be used as an alternative to one of the less onerous forms of community sentence. See further **7.4.2**. Clause 63(6) states that the number of hours of work required of the young offender and, presumably, the nature of that work, must be such as in the opinion of the court are commensurate with the seriousness of the offence or offences committed. The court may pass a reparation order without first obtaining a pre-sentence report but, by cl. 64(1), before making a reparation order the court must obtain and consider a report from a probation officer, a social worker or a member of a youth offending team indicating the type of work that is suitable for the young offender and the attitude of the victim or victims to the requirements to be included in the order.

7.4.1 Power to impose a reparation order

A reparation order may be imposed by the Crown Court or a youth court on any offender aged under 18 who is convicted of any offence, subject only to the crime of murder and the operation of the two presumptive sentences under the C(S)A 1997. The order will require the young offender to make reparation specified in the order either to a named victim or victims of the offence (subject to their agreement), or to the community at large (cl. 63(2)). The order shall not require the offender to work for more than 24 hours in total (cl. 63(5)). The reparation must be carried out under the supervision of a probation officer, a social worker, or a member of a youth offending team (cl. 63(8)). Presumably where the reparation is to be made to the community at large the relevant community service team will make arrangements for suitable work to be found.

The requirements in the reparation order must not, so far as possible, interfere with the times when the young offender works or attends school, or conflict with his religious beliefs or with the requirements of any other order to which he may be subject (cl. 63(7), and on this see **7.4.2**).

The court must explain to the offender in ordinary language the effect of the order and the requirements to be inserted into it and the consequences of failure to comply with the order (cl. 64(2)). For the powers of the court on breach of the order see **7.4.3**. If the court does not make a reparation order in a case where it had power to do so, cl. 63(11) requires the court to give reasons why it did not do so. This requirement is similar to that which operates in relation to compensation orders.

7.4.2 Combining a reparation order with other sentences or orders

Clause 63(4) states that a reparation order shall not be made if the court proposes to pass a custodial sentence, a community service order, a combination order, a supervision order which includes requirements under ss. 12 to 12C of the CYPA 1969, an action plan order or a compensation order. The clause is not entirely clear, but the restriction seems to apply not just to mixing the orders when sentencing for a single offence, but also to imposing the orders at the same time for separate offences. In addition to the measures listed in cl. 63(4) it is clear that a reparation order could not be combined with an absolute or conditional discharge since a discharge cannot be combined with a punitive measure for the same offence (PCCA 1973, s. 1A), though there would be nothing to prevent a reparation order being imposed in respect of one offence and a discharge in respect of another offence sentenced on the same occasion. The list envisages that a reparation order might in an appropriate case be imposed on an offender at the same time as a probation order, a supervision order which does not contain the particular requirements referred to, an attendance centre order, a fine, a forfeiture order or a restitution order.

Clause 63(4) forbids passing a reparation order and a compensation order on the young offender at the same time. If both orders were in respect of the same victim such a course might well be objectionable on the ground of double compensation, but it seems unfortunate that a reparation order to the community at large cannot be made at the same time as a compensation order to the actual victim (whether this is to be paid by the offender or, if he lacks the means, by his parent under CYPA 1933, s. 55 — see **6.3**). There seems also to be a problem of sentencing principle here. The court has for some years been required to give reasons why it does not make a compensation order in a particular case and, as we have seen it is now required to give reasons for not making a reparation order. Presumably it is sufficient reason for making one of these orders that the court has made the other. Yet these measures are not directly comparable in the way envisaged by the legislation. A reparation order is certainly a punishment (as confirmed by the existence of proportionality requirements in cl. 63(6)), but a compensation order is an ancillary order, not a punishment at all.

7.4.3 Discharge or variation of a reparation order

Arrangements for discharge or variation of a reparation order are set out in sch. 5 to the CDB. Paragraph 2 of sch. 5 provides that while a reparation order is in force the young offender or the supervisor may make application to the youth court for an order to discharge that order, or to vary it by cancelling any provision within it or by inserting any fresh provision. Ordinarily the young offender should be present in court at the time the application is made (para. 4(1)), but his attendance is not necessary where, for instance, the court is discharging the reparation order or cancelling a requirement in it (para. 4(9)). If an application for discharge is made, and is dismissed by the court, no further application for discharge can be made without the consent of the court.

7.4.4   Breach of a reparation order

Arrangements for dealing with failure to comply with the terms of a reparation order are set out in sch. 5 to the CDB. When dealing with the young offender for breach of a reparation order the relevant court must take into account the extent to which he has complied with the order (para. 3(7)). The young offender should be present in court (para. 4(1)).

Paragraph 3 of sch. 5 provides that where it is proved that the young offender has failed to comply with any of the requirements of the order the youth court (a) whether or not it also discharges the order, may fine the offender an amount not exceeding £1,000, or make an attendance centre order, or a curfew order on him, or (b) if the original order was made by a youth court, may discharge the order and deal with the young offender in any manner in which he could have been dealt with for the offence, or (c) if the original order was made by the Crown Court, the youth court may commit the young offender in custody or on bail until he can appear before the Crown Court (para. 3(2)). The Crown Court must then revoke the reparation order and deal with the young offender in any manner in which he could have been dealt with by that court for the offence (para. 3(4) and (5)).

7.5.   PARENTING ORDERS

The Crime and Disorder Bill contains provisions in Part I which, when they become law and are brought into force, will create a power in the youth court and the Crown Court to make a parenting order. A pilot scheme will be introduced to run for 18 months from Autumn 1998. The order will require a parent or guardian of a person under 18 who, *inter alia*, has been convicted of an offence, to attend counselling or guidance sessions and to comply with certain specified requirements. The parent can be required to attend the counselling or guidance sessions, in accordance with instructions given by the responsible officer (who will be a probation officer, social worker or member of the youth attending team specified in the order), not more than once a week and for no longer than three months overall. The specified requirements, however, may remain in force for up to 12 months. These can take whatever form the court considers to be desirable in the interests of preventing the child from re-offending, and might commonly include requirements that the parent ensure that the child is accompanied to school each day and is indoors by a certain hour in the evening.

By cl. 10, if a child under the age of 16 has been convicted of an offence and the court is satisfied that a parenting order would help to prevent a recurrence of the child's offending behaviour, the court is under a duty to make such an order against the parent or guardian, unless the court thinks that to make an order would not help prevent the commission of further offences by the juvenile, in which case there is an obligation to explain why the order has not been made. This is clearly an important area of discretion for the court, and a pre-sentence report or other report will have to be made available so that the court can make an informed decision. There will certainly be cases where the court will take the view that the home circumstances of the young offender are such that a parenting order is either unnecessary or will be counter-productive. Before making a parenting order on the parent of a juvenile under 16 convicted of an offence, the court must take into account information about the family circumstances and shall explain the effect and consequences of the order, including the consequences which may flow from breach of the order, to the parent or guardian in ordinary language.

The order may subsequently be discharged or varied by the court, on the application of the parent or the responsible officer. The order can be cancelled, such as in the case of good progress, or varied by cancelling a requirement or adding a fresh requirement. Breach of the parenting order, which is constituted by failure by the parent without reasonable excuse to comply with any requirement in the order, is punishable by a fine not exceeding level 3 on the standard scale. Commission of a further offence by the juvenile would not constitute a breach of the order (cl. 10(7)). Clause 11 provides that the parent or guardian may appeal against the making of a parenting order in the same way as they could appeal against a conviction or sentence.

8 Compensation and Restitution

While the great bulk of this book is concerned with the legal framework of punishments which may be imposed upon an offender in consequence of his offence, this chapter is concerned with what many perceive to be an equally important task to be undertaken at the sentencing stage: providing for appropriate compensation for the victim of crime.

Since most criminal offences are also civil wrongs, victims, at least in theory, will often be able to sue their offender in a civil court for damages. In reality, however, this is rarely done. A civil remedy is, of course, not available where the perpetrator of the crime has not been identified. Even where he has been caught, however, relatively few people who have been the victims of crime are prepared to take on the considerable further burden of pursuing that person for redress through the civil courts. In a case where the perpetrator has been prosecuted and convicted and the facts of the matter are before the criminal court, it would seem to be an unnecessary duplication to require in addition that the victim sue the offender for compensation. It makes good sense, at least in cases which are factually clear and straightforward, for the criminal court to make an award of compensation to the victim at the same time as it imposes appropriate punishment on the offender. The power to make compensation orders is contained in PCCA 1973, s. 35 to 38. Section 35 provides that, instead of or in addition to dealing with the offender in any other way, the Crown Court, an adult magistrates' court or a youth court may require the offender to pay compensation to the victim for any 'personal injury, loss or damage resulting from the offence'. It should be clear from the explanation given here that the punishment and compensation functions of the criminal court are in principle quite separate, being designed to achieve different objectives. In practice, however, they are not always so clearly distinguished.

The compensation order is one of the ways in which the victim of an offence may be compensated for the crime which has been committed against them. The other main avenue is for the victim to make an application for compensation under the State funded Criminal Injuries Compensation Scheme. That scheme, which has been in existence since 1964 but was re-established on a statutory basis by the Criminal Injuries Compensation Act 1995, is confined to cases where the victim has suffered physical injury as a result of a 'crime of violence'. There are restrictions on applicants, such as that the applicant must have cooperated fully with the investigating authorities and must not have contributed to the crime himself. There are further restrictions in respect of domestic violence cases, especially where the victim is a child, which are designed to ensure that the payment of compensation does not fall into the hands of the perpetrator. Clearly this scheme offers compensation to a narrower range of claimants than compensation orders, being confined to victims of violent crime. In another way, though, it is more extensive than compensation orders, since under the state scheme the victim may receive compensation even though the perpetrator has never been caught. The principal drawback of compensation orders is that they are restricted to cases where offenders have been caught, prosecuted and convicted, and where it is established that they have the means to pay the victim. If the perpetrator of the offence has received a formal caution rather than being prosecuted and convicted, no opportunity to make a compensation order arises. On the other hand, compensation may be ordered in respect of offences which are taken into consideration. In those cases where a criminal court is able to make a compensation order, to take that approach may be seen as particularly appropriate, and properly reflective of personal responsibility, since it is the offender himself who is being required to pay compensation to the victim, rather than the State being relied upon to do that job.

In a case where a victim for whose benefit a compensation order has been made does not feel that the order reflects the true extent of his loss, there is nothing to prevent the victim also making application to the Criminal Injuries Compensation Authority or claiming damages against the offender in a civil court. Clearly, however, the rules cannot permit the victim to recover twice, so the award of damages will be reduced by the amount actually paid under the compensation order, and a plaintiff victim may enforce judgment for an amount by way of a compensation order only where the civil court gives leave (PCCA 1973, s. 38). Similarly, any award which a victim receives from the State scheme, or any payment which a victim receives via any relevant insurance policy, will be reduced by the amount of the compensation order.

The percentage of offenders sentenced during 1996 who were also required to pay compensation to their victim is recorded in the criminal statistics and is shown in the Table below:

Offence category	*Magistrates' court*	*Crown Court*
violence against the person	53 per cent	18 per cent
sexual offences	24 per cent	1 per cent
burglary	29 per cent	4 per cent
theft and handling	17 per cent	9 per cent
fraud and forgery	35 per cent	13 per cent
criminal damage	56 per cent	17 per cent

8.1 COMPENSATION ORDERS

8.1.1 Power to make a compensation order

The central aim of making a compensation order was explained by Scarman LJ in *Inwood* (1975) 60 Cr App R 70, when he said that it was to provide victims of crime with 'a convenient and rapid means of avoiding the expense of resorting to civil litigation, when the criminal clearly has means which would enable the compensation to be paid'. Since the compensation order is ancillary to sentence, it should not be regarded as part of the punishment for the offence (even though the offender who is required to pay may not always appreciate the difference between compensation and a fine), and hence its imposition does not require any adjustment in the sentence per se. In particular, compensation orders should not provide an escape route by which wealthy offenders may buy their way out of the normal consequences of their crime (see *Barney* (1989) 11 Cr App R (S) 448, discussed at **8.1.4**).

Also, compensation orders are not an appropriate device for depriving an offender of the fruits of his crime. In a case where the court has this aim in mind, a confiscation order (see Chapter 9) or a fine are the appropriate options to pursue.

There is no limit to the amount of compensation which the Crown Court may order, though it is an important principle of sentencing that the sentencer must always have regard to the offender's ability to pay compensation (PCCA 1973, s. 35(4): see further **8.1.5**). In a magistrates' court, MCA 1980, s. 40(1) provides that the maximum sum which may be ordered by way of compensation for any offence is £5,000. Section 40(1) also places a limit on the total sum which may be ordered by way of compensation in a magistrates' court where the offender asks for offences to be taken into consideration. The total amount ordered must not exceed the maximum which could be ordered for the offences in respect of which the offender has been formally charged and convicted. It seems that the court should make clear which amounts of compensation relate to which offences. Thus the fixing of a 'global figure' for compensation is normally inappropriate (*Oddy* [1974] 1 WLR 1212). The only exception seems to be where the offences were all committed against the same victim (*Wharton* [1976] Crim LR 520). Where there are competing claimants for available funds, the total compensation available should normally be apportioned on a pro rata basis (*Miller* (1976) 63 Cr App R 56). This approach seems preferable to that adopted in *Amey* (1982) 4 Cr App R (S) 410, where the court selected some claimants for compensation and excluded others. Where there are co-defendants, it is preferable to make separate orders against each of them (*Grundy* [1974] 1 WLR 139).

Compensation may be ordered for 'any personal injury, loss or damage' resulting from the offence. This phrase has been liberally construed by the courts. Although, as was mentioned above, many criminal offences are also civil wrongs and the main aim of making a compensation order is to save the victim the inconvenience of pursuing a civil claim, it has been held that it is not a prerequisite of making a compensation order that the offender would be liable in civil law for the loss (*Chappell* (1984) 80 Cr App R 31). 'Personal injury, loss or damage' has been taken to include distress and anxiety (*Bond* [1983] 1 WLR 40, where an order for £25 was upheld in respect of a householder who had been terrified when the offender threw a stone through her window). 'Loss' has been held to include a sum by way of interest (*Schofield* [1978] 2 All ER 705), but it seems that calculation of interest will be appropriate only where the sum involved is substantial and the relevant period is a lengthy one. A compensation order may be made whenever it can fairly be said that a particular loss results from the offence (*Rowlston v Kenny* (1982) 4 Cr App R (S) 85). A common sense test should be applied in deciding such cases, without having regard to technical issues of causation (*Thomson Holidays* [1974] QB 592). Thus in *Taylor* (1993) 14 Cr App R (S) 276 it was held to be appropriate to require the offender to pay £50 compensation to a man who had been kicked in the course of an affray, in which the offender and four others had accosted another group of men and a fight developed. It could not be established that Taylor had kicked the victim, but it was said to be 'artificial and unjust to look narrowly at the physical acts of each defendant' (see also *Denness* [1996] 1 Cr App R (S) 159). A case which fell on the other side of the line was *Derby* (1990) 12 Cr App R (S) 502 where the offender had threatened the victim with a knife and his co-defendant had seriously injured the victim by attacking him with a piece of wood. It was held that a compensation order for £4,000, made against the offender, was improper, since the offender had clearly not been responsible for inflicting the injuries.

In cases where no injury, loss or damage can be established (such as where a stolen article has been recovered, returned undamaged, and is of no less value to the owner than before it was taken), no compensation order can be made (*Hier* (1976) 62 Cr App R 233). Conversely, where there has been damage or loss to the victim, a compensation order is not precluded by the fact that the offender has made no profit from the offence.

A compensation order in respect of bereavement may only be made for the benefit of a person who could claim damages for bereavement under the Fatal Accidents Act 1976, s. 1A (i.e. the spouse of the deceased or, in the case of a deceased minor, his parents, or mother if the minor is illegitimate), and the amount of that compensation shall not exceed the sum specified in the Fatal Accidents Act 1976, s. 1A(3) (currently £7,500) (s. 35(3C) and (3D)). A compensation order in respect of funeral expenses may be made for the benefit of anyone who incurred the expenses (s. 35(3B)).

The victim does not have to apply to the court before a compensation order can be made; in fact victims relatively rarely do so. The court is required by the PCCA 1973, s. 35(1) to consider awarding compensation in every case, and if it does not do so, reasons why no order has been made should be given. The *Victim's Charter* states that the police will give the victim a form to fill in and return so that compensation can be considered.

8.1.2 Procedural requirements

Section 35(1A) of PCCA 1973 states that compensation shall be of such amount as the court considers appropriate, 'having regard to any evidence and to any representations that are made by or on behalf of the accused or the prosecutor'. Thus the amount of the victim's loss should either be agreed by the defendant, or be established by the evidence. In *Horsham Justices, ex parte Richards* (1985) 7 Cr App R (S) 158, Neill LJ said:

in my judgment the court has no jurisdiction to make a compensation order without receiving any evidence where there are real issues raised as to whether the claimants have suffered any, and if so what, loss.

In practice, however, courts do sometimes proceed on fairly flimsy evidence in their anxiety to provide compensation for victims wherever possible. Where the case raises complex factual issues, the court should not embark on a complex inquiry into the scale of loss, since compensation orders are designed to be used only in clear, straightforward cases: see further **8.1.7**.

In the case of an offence under the Theft Act 1968 where the property in question is recovered, any damage to the property occurring while it was out of the owner's possession is normally treated as having resulted from the offence, however and by whomsoever it was caused (s. 35(2), applied in *Quigley* v *Stokes* [1977] 1 WLR 434). In *Ahmad* (1992) 13 Cr App R (S) 212, however, an 18-year-old offender pleaded guilty to taking a conveyance, reckless driving and driving while disqualified. A compensation order for £99, for repairing damage done to the vehicle was upheld, but insofar as the order related to the loss of property which had been in the vehicle (valued at £300) it was quashed, as the offender had not been found guilty of theft. A compensation order may only be made in respect of injury, loss or damage which was due to an accident arising out of the presence of a motor vehicle on a road (other than loss suffered by a person's dependants in consequence of his death), if either it is damage which falls within s. 35(2) or it is in respect of injury, loss or damage for which the offender is uninsured in relation to the use of the vehicle and compensation is not payable under any arrangements to which the Secretary of State is a party, i.e. the Motor Insurers' Bureau Agreements (s. 35(3)). Under that scheme the first £175 of loss is not covered, and so in an appropriate case a compensation order in that amount can be made (see *Austin* [1996] 2 Cr App R (S) 191). In the exceptional cases where a compensation order can be made in respect of such an accident, the compensation may include a sum representing the whole or part of any loss of or reduction in preferential rates of insurance attributable to the accident, i.e. the victim's no claims bonus (s. 35(3)). A vehicle which is exempted from insurance (e.g. a vehicle which belongs to the Crown) is not uninsured for these purposes (s. 35(3A)).

The victim of the offence will not receive any compensation until there is no further possibility of an appeal by which the order could be varied or set aside (PCCA 1973, s. 36(1)). By s. 37, at any time before the offender has paid into court the whole amount due under the order, the magistrates' court having power to enforce the order may, on application of the offender, discharge the order or reduce it on the ground that:

(a) the injury, loss or damage in respect of which the order was made has been held in civil proceedings to be less than it was taken to be for the purposes of the order;

(b) property the loss of which was the subject of the order has now been recovered;

(c) the means of the offender are insufficient to satisfy both the compensation order and a confiscation order made against him in the same proceedings under CJA 1988 (see Chapter 9 for confiscation orders); or

(d) the offender's means have suffered a substantial reduction which was unexpected at the time of making the order.

Before the magistrates may act under (c) or (d) to discharge or reduce a Crown Court order, they must have the consent of that court.

Section 35(1) contains a further important procedural requirement, which is that in every case where a court has power to make a compensation order but does not do so, it must give reasons why no such order has been made. Such reasons might include the incompatibility of the sentence imposed for the offence (see **8.1.8**), the offender's lack of means (**8.1.5**), or the complexity of the case (**8.1.7**).

8.1.3 Enforcement of compensation orders

Enforcement of compensation orders is the function of magistrates' courts. The maximum terms of imprisonment which a magistrates' court may impose in default of payment of compensation orders are specified in MCA 1980, sch. 4. These are the same periods which apply in the case of fines (set out at **6.1.2**) and, as with fines, magistrates have no power to specify a term in default in excess of 12 months. Magistrates have discretion to fix a lower term. The Crown Court is not empowered to make an order fixing the term to be served in default of payment of a compensation order (in contrast to its duty to do so in respect of fines: *Komsta* (1990) 12 Cr App R (S) 63 and see **6.1.2**). The maximum terms indicated in sch. 4 will thus normally also apply in default of payment of compensation orders imposed by the Crown Court. Exceptionally, however, if the Crown Court makes a compensation order for an amount in excess of £20,000 and considers that a maximum default term of 12 months is inadequate, it may fix a longer period, not exceeding the term specified for the equivalent amount in PCCA 1973, s. 31(3A). As with fines, part payment of the compensation order will result in proportionate reduction in the term to be served in default.

Where a child or young person is convicted of an offence and the court makes an order for compensation, it may, under CYPA 1969, s. 55 order the parent or guardian of the child or young person to pay the compensation order. See **6.3** for further information on this provision, which also operates in respect of fines imposed on a child or young person.

8.1.4 Compensation orders are not to be regarded as punishment

As has been explained above, the making of a compensation order should not in principle affect the punishment imposed for the offence. In particular, it would be quite wrong that the payment of compensation should 'permit the offender to buy his way out of a custodial sentence'. This principle has been stated on many occasions, and is well illustrated in *Barney* (1991) 11 Cr App R (S) 448. In that case the sentencer said to the offender 'Were you in a position to pay compensation, I would reduce the sentence for that . . .'. In the Court of Appeal, Ognall J stated that the impression given by that remark was incorrect and that:

> It must never be thought that the convicted criminal can buy his way out of imprisonment or any part of it. The significance of an offer to pay compensation is that it may be treated as some token of remorse on the defendant's behalf as well as redressing the private loss of the victim. To that extent and no further it sounds in the sentencing exercise. But it must be clearly recognised that compensation orders are otherwise wholly independent of that exercise.

This important principle is not, however, always rigidly followed by the courts, and there have been cases where, for example, a sentence of imprisonment has been suspended on the basis that if the offender goes to prison he will thereby be deprived of the means of paying compensation to the victim of the offence. This point was conceded in *Huish* (1985) 7 Cr App R (S) 272 by Croom-Johnson LJ, but its importance was re-emphasised by Lord Taylor CJ in *Attorney-General's Reference (No. 5 of 1993)* (1993) 15 Cr App R (S) 201.

The general principle that compensation should not displace punishment is, in any event, subject to PCCA 1973, s. 35(4A), which applies in a case where the court decides that the appropriate penalty for the offence is a fine but wishes to make a compensation order in addition. If the offender would have insufficient means to meet his obligations under both orders, s. 35(4A) requires the court to give priority to the imposition of a compensation order. This, in a strict sense, permits the offender to 'buy his way out of the penalties for crime', but it may be regarded as a legitimate exception allowing, as it does, for the offender's limited resources to be channelled towards the victim rather than the state. Section 35(4A) has no application to sentences other than fines.

8.1.5 Compensation orders and the means of the offender

The next important principle is that a compensation order should be made only where the sentencer is satisfied that the offender has the means to pay. This principle may be found in PCCA 1973, s. 35(4) but is sometimes overlooked by the courts, to judge from the number of occasions upon which the Court of Appeal has had to quash or reduce compensation orders on that ground. Part of the trouble stems from a failure to follow the general principle expressed at **8.1.4**. The defence in mitigation often stresses the offender's willingness to pay compensation, in the hope that this will lead the court to pass a community sentence rather than a custodial one. Later, it transpires that the offer to pay compensation was unrealistic, and the Court of Appeal, on an appeal by the offender, is then asked to quash the order. An example of such a case is *Roberts* (1987) 9 Cr App R (S) 275. If it is clear that the offender has misled his legal advisers about the availability of funds to pay the compensation, the Court of Appeal has declined to quash the orders imposed (e.g. *Dando* [1996] 1 Cr App R (S) 155).

It is the responsibility of the offender to inform the court of his resources, and not for the sentencer to initiate inquiries into the matter (*Bolden* (1987) 9 Cr App R (S) 83). Nor is it the duty of the prosecutor to establish the offender's means (*Johnstone* (1982) 4 Cr App R (S) 141), but where the offender's lawyer advances mitigation on the basis that the offender will pay substantial compensation, the defence is under an obligation to ensure that the necessary means do in fact exist (*Coughlin* (1984) 6 Cr App R (S) 102). It may be thought that to place defence counsel under a duty to check that the offer of compensation is genuine is inconsistent with the commonly accepted view that counsel, subject to not deliberately misleading the court, acts on the client's instructions whether they seem credible to counsel or not.

It is generally wrong to make a compensation order which will require the sale of the offender's home (*Harrison* (1980) 2 Cr App R (S) 313). On the other hand, it is not unreasonable to expect the offender to sell items of personal property to pay the compensation (*Workman* (1979) 1 Cr App R (S) 335); in such a case the court should ascertain a realistic value for the asset (*Chambers* (1981) 3 Cr App R (S) 318). An order should not be made on the basis of sale of an asset unless it is quite clear that the offender will be able to dispose of that asset (*Hackett* (1988) 10 Cr App R (S) 388, where the relevant asset was the family home, which was in joint ownership). Nor should one be made on the basis of an uncertain promise of work or on the prospect of seasonal work which may not materialise (*Coughlin* (1984) 6 Cr App R (S) 102).

It follows from the above principles that co-defendants may be required to pay different sums by way of compensation if their capacity to pay is different. A good example is *Beddow* (1987) 9 Cr App R (S) 235, where the offender was one of two defendants who pleaded guilty to being carried in a vehicle taken without consent by a third defendant, who had fallen asleep at the wheel, causing the van to crash. The offender was conditionally discharged and ordered to pay £300 in compensation. The other two defendants received a suspended sentence and a conditional discharge respectively, but neither was required to pay compensation. The Court of Appeal approved the sentences on the basis that the offender was the only one of the defendants who was in work and could afford to pay. See also *Stapleton and Lawrie* [1977] Crim LR 366. A compensation order should not be imposed on the assumption that persons other than the offender will pay, or will contribute to, the order (*Hunt* [1983] Crim LR 270).

8.1.6   Compensation order should be complied with within a reasonable time

The court may allow the offender time to pay the sum due under the compensation order, or direct payment of the sum by instalments of such amounts and on such dates as the court may specify (PCCA 1973, s. 34 and MCA 1980, s. 75(1)), but a compensation order should not be made which involves payments by instalment over an unreasonable length of time. In *Bradburn* (1973) 57 Cr App R 948, Lord Widgery CJ said that, in general, compensation orders 'should be sharp in their effect rather than protracted' and that an order which would take four years to complete was 'unreasonably long'. A batch of decisions including *Bradburn* and *Makin* (1982) 4 Cr App R (S) 180 have indicated that payment should not normally extend over a period longer than 12 months, but in *Olliver* (1989) 11 Cr App R

(S) 10 the Court of Appeal said that a fine (or compensation order) might properly be repaid over a period of up to as long as three years. Lord Lane CJ in that case said that: 'Certainly it seems to us that a two-year period will seldom be too long, and in an appropriate case three years will be unassailable.' The Magistrates' Association Guidelines (1997) state that an order for compensation should 'normally be payable within 12 months'. The court should also consider whether a protracted order is in the interests of the victim.

8.1.7 Compensation orders to be made only in clear cases

Compensation orders should be made only in clear, straightforward cases. The criminal court should not embark on complex issues of quantum of damages which are suitable only for a civil court. The importance of this point is clear when it is remembered that the vast majority of compensation orders are ordered by lay magistrates, who are inexperienced in such matters.

In *Donovan* (1981) 3 Cr App R (S) 192 the offender pleaded guilty to taking a conveyance, having hired a car for two days and failed to return it. The car had suffered no damage. He was fined £250 with £100 costs and £1,388 compensation, on the basis of the hire company's loss of use of the car. On appeal, Eveleigh LJ said that 'A compensation order is designed for the simple, straightforward case where the amount of the compensation can be readily and easily ascertained'. Since the amount of damages in a civil case of loss of use 'is notoriously open to argument', the compensation order was quashed and the hire company was left to pursue its civil remedy if it wished to do so. See also *Hyde v Emery* (1984) 6 Cr App R (S) 206, where the offender pleaded guilty to three charges of obtaining unemployment benefit by false representation. There was a dispute over whether the sum claimed in compensation by the DHSS should be reduced by the amount of supplementary benefit which he could legitimately have claimed. Watkins LJ said in the Divisional Court that the magistrates should have declined to deal with the matter. Another example is *White* [1996] 2 Cr App R (S) 58, where the offender made an insurance claim in respect of a burglary at his home but the claim was found, in part, to have been fraudulent. The insurance company applied for a compensation order for the amount which they had paid under the claim but were awarded a lesser sum equivalent to the value of property which the police had found hidden at the offender's house. Owen J said that the order should not have been made, it having been established in 'countless cases' that compensation orders should not be made when there were complex issues as to liability.

8.1.8 Combining compensation orders with other sentences or orders

Compensation orders may be imposed 'instead of or in addition to dealing with the offender in any other way' (PCCA 1973, s. 35(1)). For the avoidance of doubt, it is expressly provided that a compensation order may be combined with an absolute or conditional discharge (s. 12(4)).

While a compensation order may be combined with a sentence of immediate custody where the offender is clearly able to pay the compensation or has excellent prospects of employment on his release from custody (*Townsend* (1980) 2 Cr App R (S) 328), it is often inappropriate to impose a compensation order as well as a custodial sentence. It may well be undesirable for a compensation order to be hanging over the offender's head after release, and the order may be 'counterproductive, and force him back into crime to find the money' (*Inwood* (1974) 60 Cr App R 70). While it is not wrong to combine a compensation order with a suspended sentence and, indeed, that combination is positively encouraged by PCCA 1973, s. 22(2A), regard should be had to the fact that if the offender is in breach of the suspended sentence its activation may bring to an end any prospect of the payment of compensation (*McGee* [1978] Crim LR 370). It would appear to be contrary to principle to suspend a custodial sentence merely because of the offender's ability to pay compensation (see **8.1.4**).

Where it would be appropriate both to impose a fine and to make a compensation order, but the offender has insufficient means to pay both, the court must give preference to compensation, though it may impose a fine as well (s. 35(4A)). This entails that the fine should be reduced or, if necessary, dispensed with altogether so as to enable the compensation to be paid. A compensation order may, thus, stand alone on sentence. It looks strange, perhaps, that a criminal court may dispose of a case purely by way of compensation. Although interesting in theory, there are relatively few cases so dealt with in the courts. In 1996 around 100 offenders were dealt with by way of compensation as the 'sole or main penalty' in the Crown Court, out of a total of over 5,700 offenders who were given compensation orders ancillary to their main sentence. In magistrates' courts in 1996, the equivalent figures were 6,500 cases out of 89,100. For both courts these figures exclude summary motoring offences. Where the court proposes to make a compensation order and a confiscation order under the CJA 1988 (see Chapter 9 for confiscation orders), and the offender has insufficient means to pay both, the court must, by virtue of s. 72(7) of the CJA 1988, order that the compensation order shall be paid from sums recovered under the confiscation order.

8.1.9 Compensation: guidelines

Suggested starting points for the award of compensation are provided in Tables which are published in Home Office Circular 53/1993.

Revised guidelines are reproduced in the Magistrates' Association Guidelines (1997):

Type of Injury		*Suggested Award*
Graze	Depending on size	Up to £50
Bruise	Depending on size	Up to £75
Black eye		£100
Cut (no permanent scarring)	Depending on size and whether stitched	£75–500
Sprain	Depending on loss of mobility	£100–1,000
Loss of a non-front tooth	Depending on cosmetic effect and age of victim	£250–500
Other minor injury	Causing reasonable absence from work (2–3 weeks)	£550–850
Loss of front tooth	—	£1,000
Facial scar	However small (resulting in permanent disfigurement)	£750 +

Type of Injury		Suggested Award
Jaw	Fractured (wired)	£2,750
Nasal	Undisplaced fracture of the nasal bone	£750
Nasal	Displaced fracture of bone requiring manipulation	£1,000
Nasal	Not causing fracture but displaced septum requiring sub-mucous resection	£1,750
Wrist	Simple fracture with complete recovery in a few weeks	£1,750–2,500
Wrist	Displaced fracture (limb in plaster for some six weeks: full recovery 6–12 months)	£2,500+
Finger	Fractured little finger; assuming full recovery after a few weeks	£750
Leg or arm	Simple fracture of tibia, fibula, ulna or radius with full recovery in three months*	£2,500
Laparotomy	Stomach scar 6–8 inches long (resulting from exploratory operation)	£3,500

*The reference in the Circular to full recovery in 'three weeks' is an error.

Circular 85/1988 emphasises that these suggestions are only guidelines and that there may be factors which could cause any of the awards to be substantially increased (such as the effect of an assault upon an elderly or disabled person). It is for the criminal courts to decide what use should be made of the information, but a sentencer certainly cannot be criticised for having had recourse to it (*Broughton* (1986) 8 Cr App R (S) 379).

8.2 RESTITUTION ORDERS

8.2.1 Power to make restitution order

The Crown Court, an adult magistrates' court or a youth court may make a restitution order. The relevant law is contained in Theft Act 1968, s. 28. A restitution order is an order which is imposed by the court as ancillary to the sentence for the offence, and may be made in combination with any other sentence passed, including a deferment of sentence (s. 28(1)). Its basic object is simple compensation: to return stolen property from the offender to the victim from whom it was taken. The legal provisions are, however, rather complex since they must allow for the possibility that the offender has disposed of the goods in the meantime. Restitution orders have declined in importance since the introduction of compensation orders (see **8.1**), which in general are a much more flexible remedy, but restitution orders are still a potentially useful means of providing redress for the victim of property crime.

Power to make a restitution order arises where goods have been 'stolen'. This term is construed widely, to include not just theft and offences where theft is a constituent element, such as robbery and burglary, but also offences where the goods were obtained by blackmail or deception (s. 24(4)). A restitution order can be made where goods have been stolen and the offender has been convicted of an offence 'with reference to the theft', or where such an offence has been taken into consideration when sentencing the offender for a different offence. An offence 'with reference to' the theft of stolen goods includes handling them, and would probably extend to conspiring to steal them or to assisting the thief to avoid arrest under CLA 1967, s. 4(1). Provided that it is sufficiently established that the goods were stolen, a restitution order may be made even though nobody has been convicted of the theft itself.

When the court is entitled to make a restitution order, it can order the offender (or anyone else who is in possession of the goods or has control over them) to restore them to any person who is entitled to them (s. 28(1)(a)). It may well be that the police will have taken possession of the stolen goods on arresting the offender, so the enforcement of the order will create no practical problems. Where the offender no longer has the stolen goods, but is in possesssion of goods which directly or indirectly represent them, he may be ordered to transfer to any person entitled to them the goods representing those which have been stolen (s. 28(1)(b)). Thus, if an offender steals a television set, sells it and buys a video recorder with the proceeds, the victim of the theft may apply to the court for an order that the video recorder be transferred to him. This form of order may be made only where the proposed beneficiary makes an application. Lastly, the court may order that, out of any money taken from the offender at the time of his apprehension, a sum not exceeding the value of the stolen goods should be paid to any person who would have been entitled to them if they had still been in the offender's possession (s. 28(1)(c)).

An order may be made of the court's own motion under s. 28(1)(a) without an application being made. If an order is made under s. 28(1)(a), it will be inappropriate to order restitution under s. 28(1)(b) or (c) in addition, since the person will thereby recover more than the value of the goods (*Parsons* (1976) CSP J3.2F01). For an order under s. 28(1)(a), the person in 'possession or control' need not be the offender, and might be an innocent purchaser. Where a person has, in good faith, bought the relevant goods from the person convicted, or has, in good faith, lent money to the convicted person on the security of the goods, the court may order payment of compensation to that person out of money taken from the offender under s. 28(1)(c) (s. 28(3)). Under s. 28(1)(b), an application must be made by the person claiming, and may not relate to goods held by a third party. Where the offender is no longer in possession of the goods, orders may be made under both s. 28(1)(b) and (c), with reference to the same goods, providing that the person does not thereby recover more than the value of the goods (s. 28(2)). An order may be made under s. 28(1)(c) with or without an application being made by the victim. The phrase 'taken out of his possession on his apprehension' in s. 28(1)(c) has been generously construed to extend to money seized from the offender after he has been arrested. In *Ferguson* [1970] 1 WLR 1246, the sum of £2,000, which was taken from the offender's safe deposit box 11 days after his arrest, was held to have been in his possession at the time of his apprehension. On the other hand, money seized prior to the offender's apprehension may not be the subject of an order (*Hinde* (1977) 64 Cr App R 213, a case decided in relation to forfeiture orders but applicable by analogy here). There is no need to show that the money is the proceeds of the relevant offence; all that is necessary is that it be shown that it is money belonging to the offender (*Lewis* [1975] Crim LR 353). It was also established in *Lewis*, where the offenders split the proceeds of a robbery between them, that a restitution order under s. 28(1)(c) may be made against one offender for a greater sum than he actually received as a result of the offence, provided that this is not for a greater amount than the total loss. This is in contrast to *Grundy* [1974] 1 WLR 139, a case which establishes that joint and several liability should not apply in the closely related context of compensation orders.

8.2.2 Procedure

The factual basis for making a restitution order may be established from evidence given at the offender's trial, from witness statements before the court in a case where he pleads guilty or from admissions made by the offender or by anyone else who would be adversely affected by the making of the order. Orders should, however, be made only in cases where the evidence is clear and has been given before sentence is imposed (s. 28(4) and *Church* (1970) 55 Cr App R 65). In particular, a restitution order should not be made where the question of title to the goods is unclear. According to Woolf J in *Calcutt* (1985) 7 Cr App R (S) 385 at p. 390:

> . . . the criminal courts are not the appropriate forum in which to satisfactorily ventilate complex issues as to the ownership of such money or goods. In cases of doubt it is better to leave the victim to pursue his civil remedies or, alternatively, to apply to the magistrates' court under the Police (Property) Act 1897.

This point has been made in several cases, and is well established. Under the Police (Property) Act 1897, the police or any person claiming property at the end of criminal proceedings may invoke that Act and a magistrates' court can then make an order for the delivery of the property to the person who appears to the court to be the owner. If the owner cannot be ascertained the court may make such order in relation to the property as it thinks fit (s. 1(1)). This includes its sale or destruction in a case where no owner has been ascertained.

If a magistrates' court commits the offender for sentence to the Crown Court, the power to make a restitution order passes to the Crown Court, and should not be exercised by the magistrates (CJA 1967, s. 56(5)). An offender may appeal against the making of a restitution order, as against any other sentence (MCA 1980, s. 108 and CAA 1968, s. 50(1)). Such an order is, however, subject to a unique proviso. Where the order is passed on conviction on indictment, it is made subject to an automatic suspension for 28 days from the date of conviction (unless the trial judge specifically directs to the contrary on the ground that 'the title to the property is not in dispute': CAA 1968, s. 30(1)) or, further, until the determination of any appeal. If the restitution order is made by a magistrates' court, it is subject to an automatic suspension for 21 days from the date of conviction (unless the court directs to the contrary as above: CJA 1972, s. 6(5)) or, further, until the determination of any appeal.

8.2.3 Combining restitution orders with other sentences or orders

Since a restitution order is an ancillary order it would seem that it may be combined with any other sentence. A restitution order and a compensation order might be made at the same time, such as where the goods which are the subject of the restitution order are returned but have been damaged.

9 Confiscation

Confiscation orders may be made under the Drug Trafficking Act 1994 (DTA 1994), which consolidates earlier provisions, under the CJA 1988, and under the prevention of terrorism legislation. The legislation is designed principally to allow the courts to confiscate the profits of lucrative offending such as drug trafficking.

The drug trafficking legislation was passed to remedy defects in the law disclosed by the decision in *Cuthbertson* [1981] AC 470. That case revealed a startling inability of the criminal courts to use their existing powers of fine and forfeiture (see Chapter 6) to deprive an offender of the profits of his crime and, as a result, the House of Lords had, with 'considerable regret', to quash an order for forfeiture made under the Misuse of Drugs Act 1971 (MDA 1971), s. 27 (see **6.7.1**) under which the sentencer had sought to confiscate assets of the offenders to the value of £750,000, which included cash, cars, paintings and deposits of money and securities in bank accounts abroad. It was held that s. 27 could not extend to such assets. In consequence of that decision, a committee was set up under the chairmanship of Sir Derek Hodgson, which produced its final report in June 1984. Following recommendations in that report (Hodgson Committee, 1984), Parliament introduced important new powers for the courts to order confiscation of assets, initially in drug trafficking cases, and subsequently in respect of other kinds of lucrative offending.

The powers in the DTA 1994 are complex in form and draconian in effect. Many feel that the seriousness of this kind of offending, and the desirability of confiscation of profits derived from it, are such that massive powers are appropriate. They are thought to be necessary to ensure that drug traffickers cannot hide away their profits in such a way that they are beyond the powers of the criminal courts to seize. It may be, however, that notwithstanding the laudable goals of the Act, its draconian provisions 'invite judges to ignore precepts central to our system of criminal justice' (Sallon and Bedingfield, 1993) and that this does damage to the sentencing system as a whole. The provisions are anomalous in requiring the prosecuting authorities to take the initiative in investigation and enforcement, a role at odds with the prosecution's traditional and much vaunted neutrality at the sentencing stage and the applicable standard of proof is the civil one of balance of probability, rather than proof beyond reasonable doubt.

Part VI of the CJA 1988 provides the courts with power to order the confiscation of the proceeds of an offender's wrongdoing. The powers are available to the Crown Court for any indictable offence and, in a limited range of circumstances, to magistrates' courts. The order, which may be seen as a replacement for criminal bankruptcy orders, which were available to the courts from 1973 to 1988, is designed to remove the profit from lucrative offending. The power does not apply where the defendant has benefited from drug trafficking, since the more particular scheme under the DTA 1994 applies. The CJA 1993 and the Proceeds of Crime Act 1995 (PCA 1995) have amended and further strengthened the relevant provisions of the CJA 1988.

In 1996, 1,557 confiscation orders were made under the DTA 1994, from a total number of 7,373 eligible cases, producing a total of nearly £10.5 million. The percentage of drug trafficking cases in which orders have been made has remained steady over recent years at about 25 per cent, and most of the orders have been for relatively small sums. In 1996, 1,334 of the orders were for less than £3,000 but there were two cases in which an order for more than £1 million was made. There is less evidence about sums actually recovered as a result of these orders. There appear to be no published statistics on the courts' use of confiscation powers under the CJA 1988.

There is much in common in the ways in which the confiscation order provisions in the DTA 1994 and the CJA 1988 are drafted, but there are also some significant differences. Since they are mutually exclusive orders, it is necessary to deal with the two types of confiscation orders separately in this chapter, although this approach does involve a degree of repetition.

9.1 CONFISCATION ORDERS: DRUG TRAFFICKING

9.1.1 Outline of powers

According to Lord Lane CJ in *Dickens* (1990) 12 Cr App R (S) 191 at p.194, the Crown Court's powers to order confiscation of the assets of those convicted of drug trafficking offences are 'intentionally draconian'. The provisions are certainly also complex. The Crown Court must follow a set procedure, and the mandatory nature of these requirements was stressed in *Stuart* (1989) 11 Cr App R (S) 89. Normally the prosecutor will be asking the court to proceed in this way, but the court may do so without the prosecutor's invitation.

(a) Under the DTA 1994, s. 2, where a defendant has been convicted before the Crown Court of a 'drug trafficking offence', or where he has been committed by the magistrates for sentence under MCA 1980, s. 38 in relation to such an offence, the Crown Court may determine whether or not the defendant has benefited from drug trafficking. The court *must* proceed to do this if the prosecutor so requests, or the court may itself decide to do so (s. 2(1)(a) and (b)). By s. 2(3), the test of whether the defendant has so benefited is whether the defendant has 'at any time . . . received payment or other reward in connection with drug trafficking carried on by him or another person'. In making this determination the court may make certain 'required assumptions' set out in s. 4(3). These assumptions *must* be made unless they are shown to be incorrect in the defendant's case, or if serious injustice would be caused by so doing.

(b) The prosecutor is required by s. 11 of the DTA 1994, in every case in which the prosecutor has asked the court to proceed under the Act, or in any other case in which the court asks the prosecutor to do so, to tender a 'prosecutor's statement' of any matters which are relevant to the determination of whether the defendant has benefited from drug trafficking. Any admission by the defendant of an allegation in the prosecutor's statement may be treated by the court as 'conclusive'. If the defendant does not admit any allegation, the court may require him to provide any information which he wishes to rely on, within a specified period. If he fails to do so, the court can treat such failure as an acceptance of the relevant allegation.

(c) If, having heard the evidence and considered the statements, the court determines that the defendant has benefited from drug trafficking, it must then determine 'the amount to be recovered' in accordance with the terms of s. 5 of the DTA 1994, as elaborated in ss. 6 to 8. The court must determine the value of the defendant's proceeds of drug trafficking, and that sum is prima facie the amount to be recovered under the order. When the court has determined the value of the defendant's proceeds it should make a confiscation order in that sum, unless the court is satisfied that 'the amount that may be realised' from the defendant is a lesser sum. In determining the amount that may be realised the court must comply with the provisions of s. 6 of the DTA 1994, which defines the amount that may be realised as the total value of all realisable property held by the defendant at the time of the confiscation order, together with the total value of all 'gifts' made by him which are caught by the Act, less the total value of any obligations which have priority at that time.

(d)   A confiscation order in the appropriate sum can then be made. Determination of the sum to be paid should normally be done *before* sentencing the defendant for the drug trafficking offence. The confiscation order should be taken into account before fixing any fine or other sentence involving forfeiture or deprivation of property, but otherwise the court should leave the confiscation order out of account when determining the sentence (s. 2(5)).

'Drug trafficking offences' are defined in s. 1(3) of the DTA 1994 to mean offences under MDA 1971, ss. 4(2) and (3), 5(3) and 20 (production, supply and possession for supply of controlled drugs), the Customs and Excise Management Act 1979, ss. 50(2) and (3), 68(2) and 170 (improper importation, exportation, fraudulent evasion of prohibition on importation or exportation of controlled drug), the Criminal Justice (International Cooperation) Act 1990, ss. 12, 14 and 19, and ss. 49 to 51 of the DTA 1994 (concealing or transferring proceeds of drug trafficking etc. — 'laundering') together with conspiracy, attempt, incitement and participation in relation to those offences.

The object of the legislation is to ensure that the convicted drug trafficker is parted from the proceeds of his offending. The court should proceed in any case where the defendant might have so benefited, whether or not the benefit relates directly to the drug trafficking offence with which he has just been convicted. Where the prosecutor asks the court to proceed, the provisions of the DTA 1994 are mandatory and all must be fully complied with. The only exception is where the prosecutor does not ask the court to proceed, in which case the court still has a discretion whether to do so, the judge making a preliminary assessment of whether or not it is a 'benefit' case. The evidence from the trial, or the facts which emerge from the trial papers if there has been a guilty plea, should be enough to allow the judge to form this preliminary assessment. Sometimes the judge will hear evidence from prosecution witnesses (such as Customs and Excise officials) on the matter. The court's powers to fine, to make a compensation order or an order for costs or to make a forfeiture order under PCCA 1973, s. 43 or MDA 1971, s. 27 are unaffected by these powers of confiscation, but s. 2(5) makes it clear that the issue of confiscation has priority, and must be resolved first. This means that where the bulk of the defendant's assets are required to meet the confiscation order, there may well be insufficient funds to meet any other financial order. Further, s. 2(6) provides that no statutory provision restricting the court from combining sentences or orders shall prevent the Crown Court from dealing with the offender 'in any way the court considers appropriate in respect of a drug trafficking offence'. This means that the imposition of a confiscation order does not entail that the penalty for the offence, such as a custodial sentence, should thereby be reduced. The confiscation order is ancillary to sentence. The DTA 1994, by s. 3, provides for the possibility of a 'postponed determination', whereby the Crown Court may decide that it needs further information before determining whether the defendant has benefited from drug trafficking, or to what extent. It may then postpone making that determination for up to six months (s. 3(3)). In such a case the court may pass sentence immediately but must not impose a fine or make a forfeiture order (s. 3(7) and (9)).

These powers are available where the offender has been dealt with on indictment or on committal for sentence under MCA 1980, s. 38. Section 2(7) provides that they shall not be available where the offender is committed to the Crown Court for sentence under MCA 1980, s. 37(1), or otherwise where the court's powers are limited to dealing with the defendant in any way in which a magistrates' court might have dealt with him, such as on an appeal by the defendant to the Crown Court against conviction or sentence.

9.1.2 Determining whether the defendant has benefited from drug trafficking

By s. 4 of the DTA 1994, any 'payments or other rewards' received by a person at any time in connection with drug trafficking carried on by him or another person are his proceeds of drug trafficking, and the value of his proceeds of drug trafficking is the aggregate of the values of his payments or other rewards. Where there is more than one defendant before the court, a separate assessment of the proceeds of each defendant must be made but, in the absence of evidence to the contrary, the sentencer may assume that the proceeds were equally shared. A confiscation order cannot be imposed on two defendants jointly and severally (*Porter* (1990) 12 Cr App R (S) 377). In assessing the value of the defendant's interest in property which is jointly owned (such as a house), the sentencer should determine the extent of the defendant's own interest (*Buckman* [1997] 1 Cr App S 325). The meaning of 'payment or other reward' has been considered in a number of cases. In *Osei* (1988) 10 Cr App R (S) 289 the Court of Appeal rejected an argument that the phrase was limited to payment by way of reward, and held that it simply meant any payment or, as it was put in *Smith* (1989) 11 Cr App R (S) 55, 'any payment in money or kind'. A defendant's expenses must not be deducted from his proceeds when making an assessment of the value of the 'payments or other rewards': the court should take account of gross profits rather than actual or net gains. These cases were all decided on the legislation as it stood before consolidation into the DTA 1994, but the Court of Appeal in *Banks* [1997] 2 Cr App R (S) 110 confirmed that they have continuing effect.

In order to ease the problems of proof in such cases for the prosecution, s. 4(2) provides that certain 'required assumptions', set out in s. 4(3), must be made by the court regarding the defendant, except where these can be shown to be incorrect in the defendant's case or there would be a serious risk of injustice if such an assumption were to be made (s. 4(4)). The court should, for the purpose of determining whether the defendant has benefited from drug trafficking and, if he has, of assessing the value of his proceeds of drug trafficking, assume (s. 4(3)):

   (a) that any property appearing to the court —
      (i) to have been held by the defendant at any time since his conviction; or
      (ii) to have been transferred to him at any time since the beginning of the period of six years ending when the proceedings were instituted against him, was received by him, at the earliest time at which he appears to the court to have held it, as a payment or reward in connection with drug trafficking carried on by him;
   (b) that any expenditure of his since the beginning of that period was met out of payments received by him in connection with drug trafficking carried on by him; and
   (c) that, for the purpose of valuing any property received or assumed to have been received by him at any time as such a reward, he received the property free of other interests in it.

For these purposes 'money' includes money and all other property, real or personal, heritable or movable, including things in action and other intangible or incorporeal property. Property may be taken into account whether it is situated in England and Wales or elsewhere. Property is 'held' by a person if he holds any interest in it. For the purpose of assessing the value of the defendant's proceeds of drug trafficking in a case where a confiscation order has previously been made against him, the court must leave out of account any of the proceeds of drug trafficking that are shown to the court to have been taken into account in determining the amount to be recovered under the earlier order (s. 4(6)).

Section 4(2) is couched in mandatory terms, but no particular assumption should be made if it can be shown to be unfounded in the particular case. Thus in *Johnson* (1990) 12 Cr App R (S) 182, the sentencer was entitled to make the prima facie assumption that a particular car was a part of the proceeds of drug trafficking, but was not entitled to make the asumption under (a) above, since the defendant could demonstrate a legitimate source for the funds used to purchase the car. If the court does not apply one or more of the required assumptions, it must give reasons for not doing so (s. 4(4)). Where the prosecution seeks to rely upon the assumptions under s. 2 and if the defendant disputes the assumption which is being made, a prima facie case must be established by the prosecution to support the facts on the basis of which the assumptions are made (*Dickens* (1990) 12 Cr App R (S) 191 and *Comiskey* (1991) 13 Cr App R (S) 227). Once this has been done the defence is then required to rebut any of the assumptions, by showing on a balance of probabilities that the assumption is not justified in respect of that particular item.

9.1.3 Statements relating to drug trafficking

Sections 11 and 12 of the DTA 1994 are concerned with proof of the matters indicated in s. 4. Section 11 provides that, where there is tendered to the Crown Court a statement by the prosecutor as to any matters relevant to the determination of whether the defendant has benefited from drug trafficking, or to the assessment of the value of his proceeds from drug trafficking, and the defendant accepts to any extent any allegation in the statement, the court may, for the purpose of that determination and assessment, treat his acceptance as conclusive of the matters to which it relates (s. 11(7)). Where a statement has been tendered and the court is satisfied that a copy of that statement has been served on the defendant, the court may require the defendant to indicate to what extent he accepts each allegation in the statement and, so far as he does not accept any such allegation, to indicate any matters he proposes to rely on. If the defendant fails in any respect to comply with such a requirement the court may draw such inference from that failure as it considers appropriate (s. 11(8)), and he may be treated for these purposes as accepting the allegations made in the statement.

Where there is tendered to the Crown Court by the defendant a statement as to any matters relevant to determining the amount that might be realised at the time the confiscation order is made, and the prosecutor accepts to any extent any allegation in that statement, the court may, for the purposes of that determination, treat the acceptance by the prosecution as conclusive of the matters to which it relates (s. 11(9)). By s. 12 the court may order the defendant where appropriate to provide such information. In *Emmett* [1997] 3 WLR 1119 the House of Lords considered the meaning of the phrase 'treat his acceptance as conclusive of the matters to which it relates', as used in these sections. It was held that they were procedural provisions designed to facilitate proof, and that the particular phrase should not be construed as ousting the jurisdiction of the Court of Appeal in a case where the defendant had made a fundamental mistake in accepting an allegation in the prosecutor's statement. 'Conclusive' did not deprive the defendant of a right of appeal where that had happened.

9.1.4 The amount to be realised

The amount to be recovered under a confiscation order is the amount the Crown Court assesses to be the value of the defendant's proceeds of drug trafficking (s. 5(1)).

The amount that might be realised under a confiscation order is the total of the values at that time of all the realisable property held by the defendant (less, where there are obligations having priority at that time, the total payments payable in pursuance of such obligations), together with the total of the values at that time of all gifts caught by the DTA 1994 (s. 6(1)).

If the court is satisfied that the amount that might be realised at the time of the confiscation order is made is less than the amount the court assesses to be the value of the defendant's proceeds of drug trafficking, then the order shall be of the amount appearing to the court to be the amount that might be so realised, or a nominal amount if the court concludes that nothing can be recovered (s. 5(3)). It seems that the burden is proof is on the defendant (on a balance of probabilities) to show that the amount which might be realised is less than the value of the proceeds of the drug offending (*Ilsemann* (1990) 12 Cr App R (S) 398 and *Carroll* (1992) 13 Cr App R (S) 99). The determination of the amount to be realised is always a matter, ultimately, for the sentencer. It is, therefore, open to the judge under s. 4(3) to mitigate the severity of the confiscation order if the amount of money available is less than the amount which the court decides was the value of the proceeds of the drug trafficking (*Smith* [1989] 2 All ER 948) or, where appropriate on the evidence received by the court, a sum in excess of that which was originally indicated by the prosecution may be ordered (*Atkinson* (1993) 14 Cr App R (S) 182; *Finch* (1993) 14 Cr App R (S) 226).

9.1.5 Effect of order upon sentence

The seriousness of drug trafficking offences renders it very likely that an immediate custodial sentence will be imposed upon the offender. While the court is obliged to have regard to the general picture of the offender's assets when determining the confiscation order, the sentencer should be careful to relate the length of the custodial sentence only to those offences of which the offender has been convicted (*Bragason* (1988) 10 Cr App R (S) 258). While the offender must not receive a heavier sentence on the basis of what the sentencer has learned during the course of investigation into the offender's involvement in drug trafficking, information received in this way may properly form the basis for rejection of mitigation, such as the offender's claim that he was involved in a 'one-off' transaction (*Harper* (1989) 11 Cr App R (S) 240; approved in *Thompson* [1997] 1 Cr App R (S) 289). It seems that in a case where the offender has failed to cooperate fully with the process of investigation of his assets for the purpose of making a confiscation order, this should not have the effect of reducing his discount for pleading guilty, since the confiscation and sentencing procedures are distinct (*Nicholson* (1990) 12 Cr App R (S) 58).

In *Hedley* (1989) 11 Cr App R (S) 298, the Court of Appeal disapproved the imposition of a fine of £5,000 on an offender, in respect of whom the court had made a confiscation order as well as passing a custodial sentence. The fine was 'not punishment, because that had already been meted out by means of the two years' imprisonment. It was not the removal of ill-gotten gains, because those ill-gotten gains had already been removed by reason of the proceedings under the . . . Act.' In *Hopes* (1988) 11 Cr App R (S) 38 the

Court of Appeal said that it was inappropriate to order the offender (who was made subject to a £12,000 confiscation order and a sentence of 16 years' imprisonment) also to pay prosecution costs of £5,000, unless there was evidence that the offender had means to pay those costs over and above the means required to meet the confiscation order.

9.1.6 Variation of order

If, on application by the defendant or a receiver appointed by the court in respect of a confiscation order, the High Court is satisfied that the realisable property is inadequate for the payment of any amount remaining to be recovered under the order, the court must issue a certificate to that effect, giving its reasons (s. 17(1)). Where such a certificate has been issued, the offender or the receiver must then apply to the Crown Court for the sum specified in the confiscation order to be reduced accordingly (s. 17(3)). The Crown Court must substitute such lesser sum as it thinks just in all the circumstances of the case, and substitute for the term of imprisonment or detention to be served by the offender in default of payment a shorter default term to reflect the lesser sum (s. 17(4)). If the converse situation arises, and it turns out that the amount that might be realised is greater than the amount taken into account in the confiscation order, application may be made to the High Court, by the prosecutor or by the receiver, for the order to be increased, and to the Crown Court for the default term to be increased (s. 16).

9.1.7 Enforcement

Under the current provisions there are two distinct methods of enforcement: through default provisions akin to fine enforcement and through receivership. The former is the province of the Crown Court. The latter must be arranged by application to the High Court, which is given powers to make restraint and charging orders for the better enforcement of confiscation; these are dealt with at **9.1.8**.

Where the Crown Court orders the offender to pay any amount under a confiscation order, the provisions of PCCA 1973 relating to the powers of the Crown Court in relation to fines, and enforcement of Crown Court fines (i.e. PCCA 1973, s. 31), have effect as if that amount were a fine imposed on the offender by the Crown Court (DTA 1994, s. 9(1)). For fine enforcement see **6.5**. Maximum default terms are set out at **6.1.2**. The court may allow time for payment and make arrangements for payment by instalments. If any sum required to be paid is not paid in due time (either forthwith or under any arrangements made for payment), the offender becomes liable to pay interest on the sum for the period for which it remains unpaid (DTA 1994, s. 10(1)). The Crown Court must fix a term in default (*Popple* (1992) 14 Cr App R (S) 60) although it was held in *Ellis* [1996] 2 Cr App R (S) 403 that failure to do so does not invalidate the order itself. If the offender is required to serve the term in default, that term must be served consecutively to any term of imprisonment which was imposed for the offence or offences of which the offender was convicted (DTA 1994, s. 9(2)). In contrast to the legal position in relation to fine default, s. 9(5) provides that the serving of the default term does not expunge the confiscation order.

9.1.8 Restraint and charging orders

In pursuance of the enforcement of confiscation orders made under the DTOA 1986, the High Court has power to make restraint orders (under s. 8(1)) and charging orders (under s. 9(1)).

These powers can be exercised where proceedings have been instituted against the defendant for a drug trafficking offence, those proceedings have not yet been concluded and the court is satisfied that there is reasonable cause to believe that the defendant has benefited from drug trafficking (s. 7(1)). The powers are also exercisable at an earlier stage, where the court is satisfied that a person is to be charged with a drug trafficking offence and there is reasonable cause to believe that he has benefited from drug trafficking (s. 7(2)). The powers must be exercised by the High Court, or by a receiver appointed for that purpose under the DTOA 1986, with a view to making property available for satisfying the confiscation order to the value of any realisable property held by any person (not just the defendant). If the realisable property takes the form of a gift to a third person which is caught by the DTOA 1986, the powers must be exercised in such a way as to realise no more than the value of the gift (s. 13).

A restraint order issued by the High Court prohibits any person from dealing with any realisable property, subject to such conditions and exceptions as may be specified in the order (s. 8(1)). A restraint order may be made only on application by the prosecutor. It may be made on an ex parte application to a judge in chambers, and it must provide for notice to be given to persons affected by the order (s. 8(4)). When a restraint order has been made, the appointed receiver may take possession of any realisable property and manage or otherwise deal with it in accordance with the instructions of the court (s. 8(6)). Under such an order, a constable (or, more likely, a Customs and Excise officer (s. 38(1)) may, in order to prevent realisable property being removed abroad, be empowered to seize such property (s. 8(8)).

A charging order issued by the High Court places a charge on realisable property in order to secure the amount which is payable under a confiscation order (ss. 9(1)) and 38(2)). A charging order may be made only on application by the prosecutor. It may be made on an ex parte application to a judge in chambers, must provide for notice to be given to persons affected by the order and may be made subject to such conditions as the court thinks fit as to the time when the charge is to become effective (s. 9(3)). Under s. 9(4), a charge may be imposed by a charging order only on:

(a) any interest in realisable property, being an interest held beneficially by the defendant (or by a person to whom the defendant has made a gift which is caught by the DTOA 1986), in any asset of a specified kind, or under any trust; or

(b) any interest in realisable property held by a person as trustee of a trust if the interest is in such an asset, or is an interest under another trust and a charge may by virtue of (a) above be imposed by a charging order on the whole beneficial interest under the first-mentioned trust.

The Land Charges Act 1972 and the Land Registration Act 1925 apply in relation to restraint orders or charging orders as they apply in relation to orders and writs affecting land or made by the court for the purpose of enforcing judgments (s. 10(2)). In relation to applications for restraint orders, they apply as they would in relation to other pending land actions (s. 8(10)).

A restraint order or a charging order may be discharged or varied in relation to any property, and must be discharged when proceedings for the offence are concluded (s. 8(5)). A charging order must also be discharged when the amount secured by the charge is paid into court (s. 9(7)). An application for the discharge or variation of a restraint order or a charging order may be made by any person affected by it (ss. 8(5A) and 9(8)).

9.2   CONFISCATION ORDERS: CJA 1988

9.2.1   Outline of powers

Sections 71 to 102 of the CJA 1988 provide the criminal courts with a broad power (and in some cases a duty) to investigate the extent to which an offender has benefited from his offence and/or order confiscation of the proceeds of crime. The arrangements for making confiscation orders under the 1988 Act have been modifed by the CJA 1993 and the PCA 1995, so that they are now broadly parallel to those in relation to drug trafficking contained in the DTA 1994. The 1988 Act scheme, as amended and described below, only applies where all the offences of which the offender has been convicted were committed on or after 1 November 1995. If any of the offences were committed before that date earlier versions of the scheme are applicable, but those earlier versions are not considered here. Formerly, a confiscation order under the CJA 1988 could not be made in a sum less than £10,000. This lower limit was anomalous (there has never been an equivalent rule under the DTA 1994) and it has now been removed. There is no maximum sum which may be seized.

Section 71(1) states that the courts have power (and in some cases a duty) to investigate the extent to which an offender has benefited from his offence (where that is 'an offence of a relevant description'), or more generally from his offending (see 'relevant criminal conduct', explained below). By section 71(1E) an 'offence of a relevant description' means, for the Crown Court, *all* indictable offences. Clearly this is a very broad provision, and may involve the Crown Court in confiscation order proceedings in any case where it appears that the offender has been involved in lucrative offending — perhaps theft, fraud, burglary, blackmail or handling stolen goods. It should be noted, however, that 'offence of a relevant description' does not include drug trafficking offences, where the confiscation order provisions under the DTA 1994 must be used instead. In the magistrates' courts the powers are limited to a group of summary offences listed in sch. 4 to the Act, relating to unlawful supply of videos, use of certain unlicensed premises, copyright offences and certain offences relating to social security. Magistrates cannot use a confiscation order in respect of an either-way offence which was tried summarily.

The court must proceed under s. 71 if the prosecutor has requested the court to proceed, or it may decide itself to do so (s. 71(1)). In either case the court must first decide whether the offender has 'benefited from any relevant criminal conduct' (s. 71(1A)). This term means the offence or offences with which he has been convicted taken together with any offences which the court has taken into consideration (for these, see **3.8**). Section 71 states that a person 'benefits from an offence' if he obtains property or a pecuniary (financial) advantage as a result of that offence. If so, his benefit is the value of the property or pecuniary advantage obtained. Where the court decides that the offender has benefited from any relevant criminal conduct it must assess the extent of that benefit and make a confiscation order requiring the offender to pay that amount (s. 71(1B)), or a lesser sum if it appears to the court that the full benefit cannot be recovered from the offender (s. 71(6)).

The rather oddly named s. 72AA of the CJA 1988 extends confiscation powers to a further group of cases not catered for by s. 71. As has been explained the courts may, under s. 71, make a confiscation order which relates to an offence with which the offender has been convicted or an offence which has been taken into consideration. Section 72AA goes further, and allows the court to confiscate property held by the defendant which is shown (in accordance with the civil standard of proof) to have been the proceeds of other offending. The section can operate only where the prosecutor has so requested and where the offender is convicted on the present occasion of two 'qualifying offences' or is now convicted of one qualifying offence and has a previous conviction for another within a six-year period. A 'qualifying offence' is an offence of a relevant description (see above) committed after 1 November 1995 and in respect of which the court is satisfied that the offender has benefited. One purpose of s. 72AA is, in a case where the prosecution has proceeded against the defendant at trial on the basis that the offences charged represent 'sample counts' (see **3.9**), a confiscation order can be made with respect to all of the alleged offending, not just the offences formally proved or taken into consideration. If these various conditions are made out, the court may make the same assumptions as can be made under the DTA 1994 and which were listed in **9.1.2**, unless the assumption is shown to be incorrect in the defendant's case or there would be a serious risk of injustice to the defendant if the assumption were made.

9.2.2 Making the order

The court must make the confiscation order, and take account of its likely effect upon the offender, before imposing a fine or other financial order, or before making a forfeiture order under the MDA 1971 (see **6.8.1**) or an order under PCCA 1973, s. 43 (see **6.7**). This means that the confiscation order has priority and may well mean, in a case where the confiscation order removes a substantial proportion of the offender's assets, that another financial order cannot be imposed in addition, having regard to the offender's ability to pay. It should be noted, however, that in contrast to the position in respect of confiscation orders under the DTA 1994, a compensation order has priority over a confiscation order made under the CJA 1988. Thus, if the court makes both a compensation order and a confiscation order against the offender, and it appears to the court that the offender will not have sufficient means to pay both the orders in full, it must direct that so much of the compensation as will not be recoverable because of the offender's insufficiency of means shall be paid out of any sums recovered under the confiscation order (CJA 1988, s. 72(7)). The making of a confiscation order should not otherwise affect the sentence passed (e.g. whether a custodial sentence is imposed, or the length of any such sentence) (s. 72(5)).

The CJA 1988, s. 72A, provides for the possibility of a 'postponed determination', whereby the court may decide that it needs further information before determining whether the defendant has benefited from the offending. It may postpone making such a determination for up to six months (s. 72A(3)). In such a case the court may pass sentence immediately but not impose a fine (s. 72A(9)).

9.2.3 Statements relating to orders

The prosecutor, in any case where he has asked the court to proceed, or where the court requests him to do so, must provide a statement of any matters relevant to determining whether, and to what extent, the offender has benefited from the offence. Where the offender accepts to any extent any allegation in the statement, the court may, for the purpose of that determination and assessment, treat his acceptance as conclusive of the matters to which it relates (s. 73(1)). On the meaning of 'conclusive' see *Emmett* [1997] 3 WLR 1119 discussed at **9.1.3**. Where a statement has been so tendered and the court is satisfied that a copy of that statement has been served on the offender, the court may require the offender to indicate to what extent he accepts each allegation in the statement and, so far as he does not accept any such allegation, to indicate any matters he proposes to rely on (s. 73(2)). If the offender fails in any respect to comply with such a requirement, he may be treated as accepting the allegations in the statement. Such failure cannot, however, be treated as an acceptance of a direct allegation that the offender has benefited from the offence or that any property was obtained by him as a result of, or in connection with, the commission of an offence (s. 73(3)).

Section 73A deals with information provided by the offender. Where the prosecutor has asked the court to proceed or where the court requests him to do so, the court may order the defendant to provide it with relevant information. Appropriate inferences may be drawn from a failure to provide the information (s. 73A(5)). Where the prosecutor accepts to any extent any information given in the statement by the defendant, the court may treat that acceptance as conclusive (s. 73A(6)).

If the court is satisfied as to any matter relevant for determining the amount that might be realised at the time the confiscation order is made, whether by an acceptance (under s. 73) or otherwise, the court may issue a certificate giving its opinion as to the matters concerned and the court must do so if it is satisfied that the amount that might be realised at the time the confiscation order is made is less than the amount the court assesses to be the value of the offender's benefit from any relevant criminal conduct (s. 73(6)).

9.2.4 Variation of order

Section 74A allows for later review and revision of a case in which a decision was made by the court not to proceed under these confiscation powers and where the prosecutor now has evidence that such a determination should have been made. Section 74B allows the court to revise its original assessment that the offender had not benefited from the offending but where the prosecutor now has fresh evidence to the contrary. Section 74C allows for an increase to be made in the amount to be recovered from the offender, in the light of fresh information. In each case the further information must come to light not later than six years after the original disposal of the case.

9.2.5 Enforcement

Confiscation orders under the CJA 1988 are enforced by a magistrates' court in the same way as if they were fines. Alternatively the prosecutor may apply to the High Court for a receiver to be appointed. The principal powers of the receiver provided by the Act are restraint and charging orders (see **9.2.6**).

Where the Crown Court orders the offender to pay an amount under a confiscation order, the provisions of PCCA 1973 relating to the powers of the Crown Court in relation to fines and enforcement of Crown Court fines have effect as if that amount were a fine imposed on him by the Crown Court (s. 75(1)). For fine enforcement see **6.5**. The court may allow time for payment, and make arrangements for payment by instalments. Where a magistrates' court made the confiscation order, that amount is to be treated as a fine for the purposes of the provisions of the MCA 1980, s. 31, whereby the general limit on the power of a magistrates' court to impose imprisonment does not apply in the case of imprisonment in default (s. 75(2)). If the offender is required to serve the term in default, that term must be served consecutively to any term of imprisonment which was imposed for the offence or offences with which the offender was convicted (s. 73(3)). The serving of the term of imprisonment in default of payment of the confiscation order does not have the effect of expunging the order (s. 73(5A)).

9.2.6 Restraint and charging orders

In pursuance of the enforcement of confiscation orders made under the CJA 1988, the High Court has power to make restraint orders (s. 77(1)) and charging orders (s. 78(1)).

These powers can be exercised where proceedings have been instituted against the defendant for a specified offence, but the proceedings have not yet been concluded, and either a confiscation order has already been made or the court thinks there are reasonable grounds on which one may be made (s. 76(1)). The powers are also exercisable at any earlier stage, where the court is satisfied that a person is to be charged with a specified offence and it appears that a confiscation order may be made in proceedings for that offence (s. 76(2)). The powers must be exercised by the High Court, or by a receiver appointed for that purpose under the CJA 1988, with a view to making property available for satisfying the confiscation order to the value of any realisable property held by any person (not just the defendant). If the realisable property takes the form of a gift to a third person which is caught by the CJA 1988, the powers must be exercised in such a way as to realise no more than the value of the gift (s. 82(1)).

A restraint order issued by the High Court prohibits any person from dealing with any realisable property, subject to such conditions and exceptions as may be specified in the order (s. 77(1)). A restraint order may be made only on application by the prosecutor. It may be made on an ex parte application to a judge in chambers, and it must provide for notice to be given to persons affected by the order (s. 77(5)). When a restraint order has been made, the appointed receiver may take possession of any realisable property and manage or otherwise deal with it in accordance with the instructions of the court (s. 77(8)). Under such an order, a constable may, in order to prevent realisable property being removed abroad, be empowered to seize such property (s. 77(10)).

A charging order issued by the High Court, places a charge on realisable property, in order to secure the amount which is payable under a confiscation order. A charging order may be made only on application by the prosecutor. It may be made on an ex parte application to a judge in chambers, must provide for notice to be given to persons affected by the order and may be made subject to such conditions as the court thinks fit as to the time when the charge is to become effective (s. 78(3)). Under 78(4), a charge may be imposed by a charging order only on:

(a) any interest in realisable property, being an interest held beneficially by the defendant, or by a person to whom the defendant has made a gift caught by the CJA 1988, in any asset of a specified kind (e.g. land, government stock, unit trusts) or under a trust; or

(b) any interest in realisable property held by a person as trustee of a trust if the interest is in such an asset or is an interest under another trust and a charge may by virtue of (a) above be imposed by a charging order on the whole beneficial interest under the first-mentioned trust.

A restraint order or a charging order may be discharged or varied in relation to any property, and it must be discharged when proceedings for the offence are concluded (s. 78(6)). A charging order must be discharged when the amount secured is paid into court (s. 78(7)). An application for the discharge or variation of a restraint order or a charging order may be made by any person affected by it (s. 78(8)).

10 Disqualification and Exclusion

10.1 DISQUALIFICATION FROM DRIVING AND DRIVING LICENCE ENDORSEMENT

Most motorists who are convicted of road traffic offences are dealt with by way of a fine; 90 per cent of summary traffic offences were dealt with by way of fine in 1996. This high rate of use of the fine also applies to the more serious offences, such as reckless (now dangerous) driving, which in 1996 was dealt with in 43 per cent of cases by the imposition of a fine. Many motoring offenders are less concerned about the financial penalty to be incurred than about endorsement of their driving licence (penalty points) and possible disqualification from driving.

Most road traffic offences are 'endorsable'. This means that particulars of the offence are stamped on the offender's driving licence together with the number of 'penalty points' awarded by the court for the offence. The purpose of the penalty points system is to punish repeated offences, none of which are in themselves sufficiently serious to warrant disqualification, but which taken together indicate a pattern of bad driving or disregard for the law. Sentencing in road traffic cases has traditionally emphasised rather different penal aims than sentencing for what is sometimes referred to as 'real crime'. The main emphasis has been on deterrence (e.g. through the progressive warning and threat inherent in the accumulation of penalty points) and prevention and public protection (through disqualification, sometimes with a requirement that the offender retake the driving test). In recent years, however, the courts have more frequently used the language of punishment in relation to penalty points, making it clear that the number of points awarded should reflect the seriousness of the offence committed. The question of the appropriate length of disqualification, however, seems to be a mix between reductivist and desert considerations (see **1.3** for discussion of these approaches). Lengthy bans following very serious offences have often been reduced on appeal, on the basis that such bans offer no hope to offenders and are counterproductive in tempting them to drive while disqualified.

If an offence is endorsable it also carries with it discretionary or obligatory disqualification from driving. Where an offender is convicted of an offence which carries obligatory disqualification, he will almost certainly be disqualified for at least 12 months under the provisions of RTOA 1988, s. 34. If he is convicted of an offence for which disqualification is discretionary, he is unlikely to lose his licence unless the conviction also results in his total penalty points reaching or exceeding 12, these having been accumulated within a three-year period. In such a case he must normally be disqualified for at least six months, under RTOA 1988, s. 35.

Disqualification from driving debars the offender forthwith from holding or obtaining a driving licence to drive any sort of motor vehicle during the period of the disqualification. Periods of disqualification are not subject to statutory maxima, whether imposed in the Crown Court or by magistrates. Disqualification from driving may occur through four different routes:

(a) in a magistrates' court or the Crown Court under the provisions of RTOA 1988, s. 34, following conviction for an offence carrying obligatory or discretionary disqualification;

(b) in a magistrates' court or the Crown Court following the accumulation of 12 penalty points under RTOA 1988, s. 35;

(c) by order of the Crown Court under PCCA 1973, s. 44; or

(d) in a magistrates' court or the Crown Court under C(S)A 1997, s. 39.

10.1.1 Obligatory and discretionary disqualification under RTOA 1988, s. 34

By RTOA 1988, s. 34(1), where a person is convicted of an offence involving *obligatory* disqualification (or an offence committed by aiding, abetting, counselling or procuring, or inciting the commission of an offence involving *obligatory* disqualification), the court *must* order the offender to be disqualified for such period not less than 12 months as the court thinks fit, unless the court for 'special reasons' thinks fit to order him to be disqualified for a shorter period, or not to order him to be disqualified at all. It will be seen that the word 'obligatory' is, in this context, somewhat misleading. It means 'obligatory in the absence of special reasons'. For some offences (listed below) the minimum period of obligatory disqualification is two years, or three years, rather than 12 months, again in the absence of special reasons. If, however, a person is convicted of an offence involving *discretionary* disqualification, the court *may* order him to be disqualified for such period as the court thinks fit.

Schedule 2 to the RTOA 1988 shows which offences carry obligatory or discretionary disqualification:

(a) *Offences which carry obligatory disqualification.* These are:

(i) causing death by dangerous driving,
(ii) dangerous driving,
(iii) causing death by careless driving while under the influence of drink or drugs,
(iv) driving or attempting to drive when unfit through drink or drugs,
(v) driving or attempting to drive with excess alcohol in blood, breath or urine,
(vi) failing to provide a specimen (but see further **12.9.4**),
(vii) racing or speed trials on public ways,
(viii) manslaughter, and
(ix) aggravated vehicle-taking.

In any case where the offender establishes 'special reasons' (see **10.1.2**), the court is no longer obliged to disqualify but retains a discretion whether or not to disqualify.

By RTOA 1988, s. 34(4), if the offender is convicted of manslaughter, causing death by dangerous driving or causing death by careless driving while under the influence of drink or drugs, the minimum mandatory period of disqualification is *two* years. Further, if the offender has been twice disqualified for 56 days or more in the three years before the commission of the present offence, the minimum period of disqualification is *two* years. By s. 34(3), where a person has been convicted of causing death by careless driving when under the influence of drink or drugs, driving or attempting to drive while unfit, driving or attempting to drive with excess alcohol, or failing to provide a specimen (in circumstances where that is an offence involving obligatory disqualification), and has a previous conviction within the last ten years for any of these offences, the minimum period of disqualification is *three* years.

(b)   *Offences which carry discretionary disqualification.* These are:

(i)   all offences involving obligatory *endorsement* (see **10.1.3**),
(ii)   theft or attempted theft of a motor vehicle,
(iii)   taking a motor vehicle without consent, and
(iv)   going equipped to steal a motor vehicle.

10.1.2   'Special reasons' under RTOA 1988, s. 34

The effect of a finding by a court that there are special reasons for not applying the provisions as to obligatory disqualification is to allow the court a discretion whether or not it disqualifies under RTOA 1988, s. 34(1). In *Whittal* v *Kirby* [1947] KB 194, Lord Goddard CJ stated that:

A special reason within the exception is one which is special to the facts of the particular case, that is, special to the facts which constitute the offence. It is, in other words, a mitigating or extenuating circumstance, not amounting in law to a defence to the charge, yet directly connected with the commission of the offence, and one which the court ought properly to take into consideration when imposing punishment. A circumstance peculiar to the offender as distinguished from the offence is not a special reason within the exception.

The law relating to special reasons was reviewed in *Jackson* [1970] 1 QB 647, where the above principles were confirmed.

Even though special reasons have been established, the court retains a discretion and may still disqualify. In *Taylor* v *Rajan* [1974] QB 424 Lord Widgery CJ said that there 'is a very serious burden on the justices, even when a special reason has been disclosed, to decide whether in their discretion they should decline to disqualify in a particular case'. If the court exercises its discretion not to disqualify, or to disqualify for a shorter period, it should state the grounds for doing so in open court and, if it is a magistrates' court, enter the reasons in the register (RTOA 1988, s. 47(1)). Failure to comply with this requirement does not, however, provide a ground of appeal (*Brown* v *Dyerson* [1969] 1 QB 45). The facts relied upon as constituting 'special reasons' must be established by the defence by evidence on a balance of probabilities, unless the prosecution admits them (*Pugsley* v *Hunter* [1973] 1 WLR 578). Where there has been a trial and the defendant has been convicted of the offence, the defendant may give further evidence to establish whether there are 'special reasons' (*Director of Public Prosecutions* v *Kinnersley* [1993] RTR 105). The court should not find that 'special reasons' exist without allowing counsel to address the court on that matter (*Barnes* v *Gervaux* (1980) 2 Cr App R (S) 258). For sentencing principles applicable to the discretion to disqualify under s. 34 see **10.1.5**.

Examples of matters which have been held *not* to amount to special reasons are listed below; many of the reported cases are concerned specifically with excess alcohol offences (see (h) to (o) below):

(a)   that the offender was a doctor who needed his car to answer calls (*Holroyd* v *Berry* [1973] RTR 145);

(b)   that the offender was disabled and was reliant upon his transport (*Jackson* [1970] 1 QB 647);

(c)   that the offender was a driver in the Army (*Gordon* v *Smith* [1971] RTR 52);

(d)   that the offender had been a professional driver for 29 years with a clean driving record (*Steel* (1968) 52 Cr App R 510);

(e)   that the motorist did not know that a system of street lighting indicated a 30 mph speed limit (*Walker* v *Rawlinson* [1976] RTR 94);

(f)   that the disqualification is a severe penalty in the circumstances (*Williamson* v *Wilson* [1947] 1 All ER 306);

(g)   that the offence was comparatively trivial (*Marks* v *West Midlands Police* [1981] RTR 471);

(h)   the fact that the offender's blood/alcohol level is only just in excess of the permitted level (*Delaroy-Hall* v *Tadman* [1969] 2 QB 208);

(i)   that the alcohol did not apparently affect the offender's driving ability and the accident was not his fault (*Taylor* v *Austin* [1969] 1 WLR 264);

(j)   that the offender's metabolism is such that alcohol is retained in the blood for a longer than average period (*Jackson* [1970] 1 QB 647);

(k)   the fact that no other road user was endangered by the offender's driving (*Milliner* v *Thorne* [1972] RTR 279);

(l)   the fact that the motorist stopped his car as soon as he realised he felt incapacitated through drink (*Duke* v *Peacock* [1949] 1 All ER 318);

(m)   the fact that the offender had been drinking in the evening and was found to have an excess alcohol level the following morning (*Director of Public Prosecutions* v *O'Meara* (1988) 10 Cr App R (S) 56);

(n)   the offender's ignorance that a combination of sleeping tablets and drink would produce a greater impairment to driving ability than drink alone (*Scott* [1970] 1 QB 661);

(o)   the offender's inability to distinguish the respective alcoholic strengths of different drinks (*Beauchamp-Thompson* v *Director of Public Prosecutions* [1988] RTR 54).

Examples of matters which *have* been accepted as constituting a special reason are listed below; again most of the cases relate to drink-driving offences.

(a)   The motorist was anxious about his passenger's health and this caused him to overlook a slight degree of excess speed (*Marks* v *West Midlands Police* [1981] RTR 471).

(b)   The motorist thought he was within a 40 mph limit because nothing other than the street lighting system indicated a change to a 30 mph limit (*Burgess* v *West* [1982] RTR 269).

(c)   In *James* v *Hall* [1972] 2 All ER 59 it was held that the fact that the offender was only trying to drive a few yards from the highway outside a house into the driveway could amount to a special reason, but the authority has been restrictively interpreted in later cases, such as *Haime* v *Walklett* (1983) 5 Cr App R (S) 165. In *Chatters* v *Burke* (1986) 8 Cr App R (S) 222 Taylor J indicated seven matters to be taken into account in a case of this sort:

how far the vehicle was driven, the manner in which it was driven, the state of the vehicle, whether the driver intended to drive any further, the prevailing road and traffic conditions, whether there was any possibility of danger by contact with road users and the reason for the vehicle being driven at all. See also *Director of Public Prosecutions* v *Corcoran* [1991] RTR 329.

(d)   It is open to a court to find special reasons where the offender has consumed laced drinks. In such a case, however, the offender must show that he was misled by a third party, rather than simply failing to inquire about the strength of the drinks and that the added alcohol was responsible for the offence in that, without it, he would have been below the limit (*Director of Public Prosecutions* v *O'Connor* [1992] RTR 66).

(e)   Where an offender had consumed drink not intending to drive, and then drove because of an emergency, this may amount to special reasons only in clear and compelling circumstances (*Director of Public Prosecutions* v *Upchurch* [1994] RTR 366; *Director of Public Prosecutions* v *Whittle* [1996] RTR 154).

10.1.3   Disqualification following endorsement (penalty points): RTOA 1988, s. 35

When a person who is the holder of a licence is convicted of an offence which carries obligatory or discretionary disqualification or endorsement, his licence must be produced to the court (RTOA 1988, s. 27). Failure to produce the licence on request is punishable by a fine up to level 3 on the standard scale, although there is a defence if the offender has recently applied for a new licence which has not yet arrived. The court orders the licence to be endorsed with particulars of the offence and the appropriate penalty points. All endorsable offences involve penalty points and they are always obligatory, but, as with obligatory disqualification, the court is permitted to find special circumstances for not endorsing. The endorsement remains on the licence for four years after the conviction (if disqualification was ordered) or four years after the offence (if no disqualification was ordered) or for 11 years after the conviction (if the offence was for driving under the influence of drink or drugs or driving with an excess blood/alcohol level). A driver who wants to have a 'clean' licence, with no lapsed endorsements on it, must apply to the DVLA and pay for a replacement licence.

The number of penalty points to be attributed to an offence is to be derived from sch. 2 to the RTOA 1988. The court must determine the number of penalty points which are to be attributed to the offence (s. 28(1)). For some offences a range of points is available. The court should determine the appropriate number of points, given the relative degree of seriousness of the offence. Examples of offences carrying penalty points are:

(a)   causing death by dangerous driving (3–11);

(b)   dangerous driving (3–11);

(c)   causing death by careless driving while under the influence of drink or drugs (3–11);

(d)   driving or attempting to drive when unfit through drink or drugs (3–11);

(e)   driving or attempting to drive with excess alcohol in breath, blood or urine (3–11);

(f)   racing or speed trials on public ways (3–11);

(g)   manslaughter (3–11);

(h)   aggravated vehicle-taking (3–11);

(i)   careless driving (3–9);

(j)   speeding (3–6);

(k)   being in charge of vehicle when unfit to drive (10);

(l)   being in charge of vehicle with excess alcohol (10);

(m)   failing to provide breath specimen (4).

In a case involving aiding, abetting, counselling or procuring or inciting the commission of any offence involving obligatory disqualification, the number of penalty points is 10 (s. 28(2)). Where offences are committed on separate occasions but within three years of each other, the number of penalty points applicable to each offence in the period are added together (RTOA 1988, ss. 29 and 35). If a person is convicted of two or more endorsable offences committed on the same occasion then the court has a discretion to aggregate the penalty points imposed (s. 28(4) and (5)). This would probably be done where none of the offences standing alone merited disqualification but where it is seen as justified by the persistence of the offending. 'Same occasion' is not defined in the Act, but it seems that there must be some close physical or temporal link between the offences. In *Johnson* v *Finbow* [1983] 1 WLR 879 the offender was convicted of failing to stop after an accident and of failing to report that same accident to the police. The offences were attributed to the same occasion, Goff LJ stating that 'the lapse of time, although significant, is not sufficiently great to be able to say, as a matter of common sense, that those offences were committed on different occasions'. In *Johnstone* v *Over* (1984) 6 Cr App R (S) 420 it was said that where an offender commits two offences at the same time out of the use of different vehicles, it is a question of fact whether the offences are committed on the same occasion. The offender had parked two vehicles outside his home and had been charged with two offences of using a vehicle without insurance. It was held that the offences were committed on the same occasion.

By RTOA 1988, s. 29, where a person is convicted on one occasion of an offence involving obligatory or discretionary disqualification, the penalty points to be taken into account on that occasion are any that are to be attributed to the offence(s) of which he is convicted, and any ordered on a previous occasion against the offender, unless since such occasion the offender has been disqualified under s. 34 or 35, but if any of the offences was committed more than 3 years before another, the points in respect of that offence are not to be added to those in respect of the other. Where the disqualification is under s. 34, the licence is not wiped clean, and any penalty points which were on the licence at the time of conviction for the offence which resulted in disqualification under s. 34 remain there.

For most offences, the number of penalty points to be awarded is fixed. For some, however, there is a range available. Where the number of penalty points is variable, it seems that the number of points awarded should reflect the seriousness of the offence and, if so, it would seem to be wrong to have regard to the endorsements on the offender's licence before fixing the number of points for the new offence. On the other hand, it can be said that the perceived gravity of the new offence may be affected by the presence or absence of like offences on the offender's record, and thus it is appropriate to consider his record before fixing the number of points.

According to RTOA 1988, s. 35, where a person is convicted of an offence involving obligatory or discretionary disqualification and the penalty points to be taken into account on that occasion number 12 or more, the court *must* order him to be disqualified for not less than the minimum period, unless the court is satisfied, having regard to all the circumstances, that there are *grounds for mitigating* the normal consequences of the conviction, and thinks fit to order him to be disqualified for a shorter period or not to order him to be disqualified. The minimum period is:

(a)   six months if the offender has had no previous disqualification imposed upon him under RTOA 1988, s. 34 or 35 within the last three years; and

(b)   one year if one, and two years if more than one, such disqualification within the last three years is to be taken into account.

Section 35(3) states that, where an offender is convicted on the same occasion of more than one offence involving obligatory or discretionary disqualification, only one disqualification may be imposed, but the court should take into account all the offences when determining the period of the disqualification.

10.1.4   'Mitigating grounds' under RTOA 1988, s. 35

Section 35 speaks of the court being satisfied, 'having regard to all the circumstances, that there are grounds for mitigating the normal consequences of conviction'. Section 35(4) specifically excludes from such consideration any circumstances which are alleged to make the offence or any of the offences not serious, hardship (other than exceptional hardship) or any circumstances which, within the previous three years, have already been taken into account in ordering the offender to be disqualified for a shorter period or not ordering him to be disqualified. Apart from this, it seems that the court may have regard to circumstances relating to the offence, to the offender, or to both. This may be contrasted with the relevant considerations for establishing 'special reasons' for not disqualifying (see **10.1.2**).

It is for the offender to establish, on the balance of probability, the grounds which are relied upon, and it is for him to show that they are different from those put forward on an earlier occasion (*Sandbach Justices, ex parte Pescud* (1983) 5 Cr App R (S) 177). In *Thomas* (1983) 5 Cr App R (S) 354 it was held that the fact that the offender is sentenced to imprisonment may be a mitigating ground for these purposes.

In these cases 'exceptional hardship' is the factor which is most often advanced. The court may take into account hardship caused to the public as well as to the offender (*Cornwall* v *Coke* [1976] Crim LR 519). Exceptional hardship may be advanced in relation to the offender's employment, in which case the court should consider whether a licence to drive is essential to that employment. In *Owen* v *Jones* (1987) 9 Cr App R (S) 34 the Divisional Court said that in most cases the magistrates would need evidence of exceptional hardship but, on the facts of the particular case, where a police officer had acquired a total of 13 points and disqualification would have forced him to resign, thereby losing his job and his home, the magistrates could properly find that this would amount to exceptional hardship without putting the offender to proof.

10.1.5   Disqualification from driving: general principles

Any period of disqualification from driving begins to run from the day on which it is imposed, unless it is suspended by the court pending an appeal. On suspension see **10.1.8**. Consecutive periods of disqualification cannot be ordered (*Johnston* (1972) 56 Cr App R 859), nor may disqualification be ordered to commence at the expiry of a custodial term (*Meese* [1973] 1 WLR 675). Any disqualification must be for a certain period (*Fowler* [1937] 2 All ER 380). Disqualification for life has been held to be disqualification for a certain period, and may thus lawfully be imposed (*Tunde-Olarinde* [1967] 1 WLR 911), but it should be imposed only in very unusual circumstances (*North* [1971] RTR 366). Disqualification for life was appropriate in *Buckley* (1994) 15 Cr App R (S) 695, where the offender had an appalling record, including six convictions for dangerous driving, and constituted a real threat to the public. In a case of obligatory disqualification, the stated statutory period is the minimum that must be imposed and is not the normal period (*Mills* [1974] RTR 215).

In any case where disqualification is discretionary, a sentencer in the Crown Court should not impose disqualification without warning counsel and allowing him to address the court on that matter (*Ireland* (1988) 10 Cr App R (S) 474). In a magistrates' court, by MCA 1980, s. 11(4), whenever the magistrates have disqualification of the offender in mind and the offender is not present in court, they should adjourn in order to give notice of this to the offender.

The policy of the courts has been that very long periods of disqualification should be avoided so far as possible, particularly where the offender does not have a bad driving record (*Dawtrey* [1975] RTR 101), or in cases where a custodial sentence is being imposed for the latest offence. When imposing a disqualification, a sentencer should have regard to the offender's employment prospects (*Weston* (1982) 4 Cr App R (S) 51). For that category of persistent offenders who seem to be incapable of leaving motor vehicles alone, the imposition of a long disqualification, or one which will extend long after the offender's release from custody, may in effect invite the offender to commit further offences and be counterproductive (*Matthews* (1987) 9 Cr App R (S) 1; *Callum* [1995] RTR 248), or handicap the offender in trying to rehabilitate himself (*West* (1986) 8 Cr App R (S) 266). Exceptionally, however, a long disqualification has been upheld as essential to protect the public, and to allow the offender time to mature in the interim (*Gibbons* (1987) 9 Cr App R (S) 21).

In determining the length of the period of disqualification, the court should not have regard to the provisions of RTOA 1988, s. 42, which enable the offender to apply for restoration of his licence before the end of the period of disqualification (*Lobley* (1974) 59 Cr App R 63 and *Lark* (1993) 14 Cr App R (S) 196: see **10.1.8**). Due credit should be given for a timely guilty plea. Indeed in *Harrington-Griffin* [1989] RTR 138 the Court of Appeal declared that 'in no class of case is a plea of guilty of more significance than in the present type, for acknowledgement of blame in driving gives some assurance that the driver will remember what has happened, and will take heed of that lesson'.

10.1.6 Disqualification pending passing of driving test

The RTOA 1988, s. 36 provides that where a person has been disqualified under s. 34 as a result of having been convicted of manslaughter (by the driving of a motor vehicle), causing death by dangerous driving or dangerous driving, the court *must* disqualify him until he passes the appropriate driving test (s. 36(1)). In the case of conviction for any other offence which carries obligatory endorsement, the court *may* order him to be disqualified until he passes the appropriate driving test (s. 36(4)). In any case where the court has a discretion to order disqualification until the test is passed, the court should have regard to the safety of road users (s. 36(6)). An 'appropriate driving test' means an extended driving test, which is more detailed and thorough than a normal test of competence to drive. Once the test has been passed by the offender the period of disqualification comes to an end upon production of evidence that the offender has passed the test. Such evidence must be produced in appropriate form to the Secretary of State (s. 36(8)). The offender must have been disqualified under s. 34. There is no power to order an extended driving test where a person is disqualified under other powers of the court (*Patel* (1995) 16 Cr App R (S) 756).

It is well established that this power should not be used punitively. According to Brooke J in *Buckley* (1988) 10 Cr App R (S) 477:

There is a long line of authorities, which starts with the case of *Donnelly* [1975] 1 WLR 390 which makes it clear that this power of the court is not to be exercised as an additional punishment. It is only appropriate where there is some reason to think that the driver concerned might have difficulty in passing a driving test because of some inability to drive properly. In the case of *Lazzari* (1984) 6 Cr App R (S) 83 the court made it clear that the exercise of this power should only be used where it comes to the court's attention that because of his age or infirmity or the circumstances of the offence a person may not be a competent driver.

In addition to the cases cited by Buckley J, to the same effect is *Peat* (1984) 6 Cr App R (S) 311. In *Hughes* v *Challes* (1983) 5 Cr App R (S) 374 it was held to be inappropriate to make such an order where the offence arose from a temporary, though possibly recurrent, condition of mind due to illness; it was only proper where the offender was 'generally speaking lacking in competence to drive'. Section 36(6) requires the court to have regard to the safety of other road users, and this is an important consideration when deciding whether to make an order under s. 36. An order was upheld in *Miller* (1994) 15 Cr App R (S) 505, where the 23-year-old offender had never passed a driving test and had acquired numerous previous convictions, including 10 for driving while disqualified. See also *Bannister* [1991] RTR 1.

Sections 34A to 34C of the RTOA 1988 provide for driver retraining (on a course approved for that purpose by the Secretary of State) for offenders of or over the age of 17 who are convicted of certain offences. By s. 34A(1), these are:

(a) causing death by careless driving when under the influence of drink or drugs;
(b) driving or being in charge when under the influence of drink or drugs;
(c) driving or being in charge with excess alcohol; or
(d) failing to provide a specimen.

The provisions are also restricted to cases where the court makes an order under s. 34 disqualifying the offender for a period of at least 12 months. These provisions provide an incentive for drivers to attend such a course by allowing a reduction in the period of disqualification for those who do. The reduction must be for not less than three months nor for more than one quarter of the period of disqualification before its reduction. Before it makes such an order, the court must be satisfied that a place on the course specified is available for the offender, the effect of the order must be explained by the court to the offender in ordinary language and the offender must consent (s. 34A(4)). The offender must pay the appropriate fee for the course, before it starts. The retraining course must be completed, at the latest, two months before the period of disqualification comes to an end. If completed successfully, a certificate must be awarded, but the organiser of the retraining course has power not to give a certificate (s. 34B(4)). The order which has the effect of reducing the period of disqualification does not come into effect until the offender's certificate has been received by the clerk of the magistrates' court in the petty sessions area where the offender resides.

10.1.7 Combining orders for disqualification from driving with other sentences or orders

Disqualification from driving is an ancillary order and may be combined with any other sentence or order of the court. Notwithstanding PCCA 1973, s. 1C (see **7.1.4**), a court which convicts a person of an offence involving obligatory or discretionary disqualification may make an order for absolute or conditional discharge as well as disqualifying him under s. 34 or 35 of the RTOA 1988 (RTOA 1988, s. 46). An order for disqualification under PCCA 1973, s. 44 (see **10.1.9**) or under C(S)A 1997, s. 39 (see **10.1.10**) may not be combined with a discharge but the position will change when sch. 8, para. 18 of the CDB is brought into force.

Although a driving disqualification may be combined with immediate custody, care should be taken that a driving ban which continues after the offender's release is not counterproductive since 'if a young man cannot drive a motor vehicle it is a grave handicap when he seeks employment' on leaving prison (*Weston* (1982) 4 Cr App R (S) 51). There is, however, no rule that the end of the period of disqualification should be set so as to coincide with the duration of the custody (*Hansel* (1982) 4 Cr App R (S) 368).

10.1.8 Appeal against, suspension and removal of disqualification

Section 38 of RTOA 1988 provides that a person disqualified by a magistrates' court under s. 34 or s. 35 may appeal against the order as against a conviction and, by CAA 1968, s. 9, a person disqualified by the Crown Court may appeal to the Court of Appeal.

Section 39 of RTOA 1988 states that a magistrates' court or the Crown Court may, if it thinks fit, suspend a disqualification pending an appeal against the order. Section 40 allows the Crown Court or the Court of Appeal to suspend a disqualification pending appeal to that court. Any period of suspension must be disregarded when determining the expiration of the period of disqualification (s. 43).

Section 42 provides for the situation where a person who has been disqualified applies to the court to have that disqualification removed prior to its normal expiry. The court, having regard to the character of the person disqualified and his conduct subsequent to the order, the nature of the offence and any other circumstances of the case, may remove the disqualification as from such date as may be specified in the order. No application can be made to the court under s. 42 before the expiration of the relevant period, namely:

(a)   two years, if the disqualification is for less than four years;

(b)   one half of the period of disqualification, if it is for less than ten years but not less than four years;

(c)   five years in any other case.

If an application is refused, a further application may not be made within three months. A court dealing with an application should be somewhat less ready to remove an obligatory disqualification than a discretionary one (*Damer* v *Davison* [1976] RTR 45). Where a disqualification has been removed after such an application, the court has no power to add a requirement that the offender take a driving test (*Benham* (1981) 3 Cr App R (S) 229).

Sections 44 and 45 deal with the rules relating to endorsement of licences, and are not considered further in this book. Part III of the RTOA 1988 deals with fixed penalty notices, and these too are not considered further in this book.

10.1.9 Disqualification from driving under PCCA 1973, s. 44

Where an offender has been convicted on indictment of an offence punishable with imprisonment for two years or more, or has been convicted summarily of such an offence and is committed to the Crown Court for sentence under MCA 1980, s. 38, the Crown Court may, under PCCA 1973, s. 44, disqualify him from driving if a motor vehicle was used to commit, or to facilitate the commission of, the offence. Power to disqualify under s. 44 does not extend to persons who have been convicted of an offence but discharged absolutely or conditionally (see PCCA 1973, s. 1C and **7.1.4**).

The power in s. 44 is widely drafted. It may be noted in particular that, providing the above conditions are satisfied, the offender may be disqualified from driving by the Crown Court even though the offence with which he has been convicted is non-endorsable. If robbers make their get-away from the scene of crime in a car, they are liable to disqualification under s. 44, notwithstanding that robbery is not an offence attracting mandatory or discretionary disqualification. The fact that the offender did not drive the motor vehicle in the course of the offence does not protect him from disqualification. It is sufficient that the vehicle was used in the circumstances specified in s. 44 (*Matthews* [1975] RTR 32). If one of several joint offenders used a vehicle for the purposes of the joint offence, any or all of the offenders may be disqualified. The phrase 'facilitating the commission of an offence' is defined by PCCA 1973, s. 43(2) as including 'the taking of any steps after [the offence] has been committed for the purpose of disposing of any property to which it relates or of avoiding apprehension or detection'.

No disqualification may be ordered under s. 44 unless the vehicle was actually used to commit the offence of which the offender has been convicted (*Parrington* (1985) 7 Cr App R (S) 18, though see now **10.1.10**). In *Riley* (1983) 5 Cr App R (S) 335, for example, a disqualification under s. 44 was quashed where the offender had been convicted of conspiracy to steal, but the agreement had been reached prior to his use of a motor vehicle to inspect a possible target. In *Patel* (1995) 16 Cr App R (S) 756, the offender had pursued another motorist who had executed a dangerous manoeuvre in front of his car. When both cars stopped at traffic lights the offender got out and seriously assaulted a passenger in the other vehicle. It was held that the use of the car had facilitated the assault, and an order under s. 44 was upheld. Section 44 does not empower the Crown Court to order endorsement of an offender's licence. If an offender is disqualified under s. 44 for a non-endorsable offence he simply surrenders his driving licence to the court (s. 44(3)) and does not regain it until the end of the disqualification period, but particulars of the conviction and disqualification do not go on to the licence.

Where a sentencer is minded to impose a disqualification under s. 44, counsel should be permitted to address the court on that matter (*Powell and Carvell* (1984) 6 Cr App R (S) 354 and *Money* (1988) 10 Cr App R (S) 237). A person disqualified under s. 44 may apply to the court for removal of that disqualification (s. 44(3)(b)).

10.1.10   Disqualification from driving under C(S)A 1997, s. 39

By s. 39 of the C(S)A 1997, which came into effect on 1 January 1998 and introduced on a trial basis, a magistrates' court or the Crown Court may, in addition to dealing with an offender in any other way, order him to be disqualified for such period as the court thinks fit, from holding or obtaining a driving licence. It should be understood that this power is wider than that which exists under PCCA 1973, s. 44, in that it extends to *any* offence (apart from murder and where sentence is imposed under C(S)A 1997, s. 2 or s. 3), not just cases where a motor vehicle was used to commit or facilitate the commission of an offence. Disqualification may be ordered under s. 39 where no motor vehicle has been involved in the offence at all. On the face of it this power is so broad as to render redundant all the powers to disqualify from driving which have been discussed above, but presumably the courts will understand Parliament to have meant that s. 39 confers additional powers to disqualify where the other powers under the RTOA 1988 and the PCCA 1973 are not available. In contrast with the power under the PCCA 1973, s. 44, disqualification under s. 39 is made available to magistrates' courts. In common with s. 44, however, s. 39 does not extend to persons who have been convicted of an offence but discharged absolutely or conditionally (PCCA 1973, s. 1C and **7.1.4**), nor is there power under s. 39 to order the offender to take an extended driving test under the RTOA 1988, s. 36.

By analogy with the power to disqualify under PCCA 1973, s. 44, it may be desirable for the court before disqualifying under s. 39 to give an opportunity to counsel to address that issue.

It is not clear whether an order under s. 39 affects totality of the sentence (by analogy with an order of forfeiture of the offender's property under PCCA 1973, s. 43 (see **6.7**), or whether it should be regarded as an ancillary order like the compensation order, imposition of which should not affect the punishment imposed for the offence. It is suggested that where disqualification is ordered under s. 39 it is imposed as a form of punishment, and so the former view is preferable.

10.2 DISQUALIFICATION OF COMPANY DIRECTORS

10.2.1 Power to make disqualification order

The Company Directors Disqualification Act 1986 specifies certain circumstances in which a court may (or in some cases, must) make an order disqualifying a person from acting as a director of a company. Some, but not all, of these circumstances relate to the commission of criminal offences by the person concerned. Only those provisions of the Act which deal with disqualification after conviction are considered here.

By s. 2(1), the Crown Court or a magistrates' court may make a disqualification order against an offender wherever he is convicted of an indictable offence in connection with the promotion, formation, management or liquidation of a company, or in connection with the receivership or management of a company's property. A disqualification order has the effect that the offender must not, for a specified period beginning with the date of the order, without the leave of the court:

(a)   be a director of a company;
(b)   be a liquidator or administator of a company;
(c)   be a receiver or manager of a company's property; or
(d)   in any way, directly or indirectly, be concerned or take part in the promotion, formation or management of a company (s. 1(1)).

If a magistrates' court makes the order, the maximum period of duration of the order is five years. If the Crown Court makes it, the maximum is 15 years. In *Millard* (1994) 15 Cr App R (S) 445 the Court of Appeal identified an 'upper bracket' of disqualification for more than 10 years, which should be reserved for particularly serious cases (including those where the director has been disqualified before and a 'middle bracket' of six to 10 years.

It has been held that 'management' of a company is a term to be construed widely, and is not limited to the internal affairs of a company. It is sufficient that the offence has some relevant factual connection with the management of a company. In *Goodman* (1993) 14 Cr

App R (S) 148 the offender, who was the chairman of a public company, pleaded guilty to insider dealing. Realising that the company was in trouble, and intending to submit his own resignation, he assigned shares which amounted to a very substantial part of the equity to a lady friend, with instructions for her to sell. He concealed the knowledge which he had about the true state of the company. The sentencer imposed a custodial sentence and disqualified Goodman from being a company director for ten years. This was upheld by the Court of Appeal. In *Georghiou* (1988) 10 Cr App R (S) 137 the offender was convicted by magistrates of carrying on an insurance business without the necessary authorisation from the Secretary of State. He was committed for sentence, and received a prison term of six months and a disqualification for five years. The prison sentence was suspended on appeal, but a challenge to the disqualification order failed. The Court of Appeal, considering the earlier decisions in *Corbin* (1984) 6 Cr App R (S) 17 and *Austen* (1985) 7 Cr App R (S) 214, said that the phrase 'in connection with management' did not confine the use of disqualification orders to offences involving actual misconduct in the handling a company's affairs. Disqualification orders have been upheld by the Court of Appeal in cases where offenders have been convicted of obtaining property by deception and similar offences committed in the course of their trading activities.

It is important to distinguish the criminal courts' powers under s. 2(1) with other powers to disqualify under the 1986 Act, particularly power under s. 6 (where disqualification is mandatory). Disqualification under s. 6 requires a finding that the person concerned has conducted himself in a manner which makes him unfit to be concerned in the management of a company. This limitation does not apply where disqualification is consequent upon conviction, since s. 2 provides the criminal courts with a 'completely general and unfettered power . . . to exercise its powers of disqualification in the very many and varied circumstances in which it may come to exercise those powers' (per Brooke J in *Young* (1990) 12 Cr App R (S) 262).

A disqualification order under the 1986 Act may be imposed in combination with any other sentence or order of the court, except that it cannot be combined when sentencing for a single offence with an absolute or conditional discharge (*Young*). It may well be inappropriate to disqualify an offender at the same time as imposing heavy financial orders upon him, where the disqualification will deprive him of the means to pay. Thus in *Holmes* (1992) 13 Cr App R (S) 29, where the offender pleaded guilty to fraudulent trading and was sentenced to nine months' imprisonment, suspended, together with a disqualification for 12 months, a compensation order for £25,000 and an order for costs of £2,400, the Court of Appeal quashed the compensation order.

10.2.2 Breach of disqualification order

A breach of a disqualification order is itself an offence, punishable with up to two years' imprisonment (1986 Act, s. 13). Where a disqualification order is made against a person who is already subject to such an order, the second period specified runs concurrently with the first (s. 1(3)).

10.3 RECOMMENDATION FOR DEPORTATION

Under the Immigration Act 1971 (IA 1971) the Secretary of State is empowered to order deportation from the UK of persons who are not British citizens. A court, on sentencing an offender aged 17 or over for an offence punishable with imprisonment, may make a recommendation that the offender be deported, by virtue of that Act and the British Nationality Act 1981. The final decision on deportation is taken by the Home Secretary, who is able to take account of a wider range of considerations than the court, such as the political situation in the country to which the offender will go (*Nazari* (1980) 2 Cr App R (S) 84). The fact that the offender has overstayed a limited permission to be in the UK is a matter for the Home Secretary, and is not a ground, in itself, for the court to make a recommendation for deportation (*Miller* v *Lenton* (1981) 3 Cr App R (S) 171). On the other hand, the fact that the offender has refugee status is not a ground, in itself, for not making an order (*Villa* (1992) 14 Cr App R (S) 34).

By IA 1971, s. 6(3), a recommendation may be made in respect of any person who is not a British citizen, who is aged 17 or over and who is convicted of an offence punishable with imprisonment as an adult. A 'British citizen' is, broadly, a person who has a right of abode in the UK. In addition a Commonwealth citizen or a citizen of the Irish Republic must not be recommended for deportation if that person was resident in the UK when the 1971 Act came into force (i.e. 1 January 1973) and has been ordinarily resident in the UK for at least the five years immediately prior to the date of conviction (s. 7(1)). Periods of six months or more spent in prison or detention do not count towards the period of five years mentioned in s. 7(1) (s. 7(3)). Whether continuity of residence has been broken by periods spent abroad is a matter for the sentencer to decide (*Hussain* (1971) 56 Cr App R 165) but temporary absence on holiday is not relevant (*Edgehill* [1963] 1 QB 593).

Whenever an offender's citizenship is questioned for these purposes, IA 1971, s. 3(8) places the onus on the offender to prove citizenship or entitlement to any exemption (see further s. 8 for exemptions in relation to crews of ships and aircraft, military personnel and persons subject to diplomatic immunity).

A recommendation for deportation may be made against a person protected by Art. 48 of the Treaty of Rome (EC Treaty), if the conditions specified in Arts. 3 and 9 of Directive 64/221 are satisfied. These were considered in *Bouchereau* [1978] QB 732 and the principles which emerged have been followed in subsequent cases, particularly *Escauriaza* (1987) 9 Cr App R (S) 542 and *Spura* (1988) 10 Cr App R (S) 376. The main requirement is that a recommendation should be made only if there exists a genuine and sufficiently serious threat to the requirements of public policy affecting one of the fundamental interests of society. The principles applicable here are the same as those which apply in respect of any other non-British subject who does not come within one of the exceptions in IA 1971. In *Escauriaza* it was accepted by the Court of Appeal that EC law 'simply mirrors the law and practice of this country'.

10.3.1 Procedural matters

The court should first determine the sentence which is appropriate for the offence committed and then consider the ancillary issue of deportation of the offender. If an order for deportation is then made, it is wrong to discount the punishment accordingly. It is also wrong to postpone passing sentence to see whether the Secretary of State will give effect to the court's recommendation (*Edgehill* [1963] 1 QB 593).

Section 6(2) of IA 1971 provides that a court shall not make a recommendation for deportation unless the offender has been given at least seven days' written notice of the court's intention. This may well require adjournment after conviction. If the court is considering making a recommendation for deportation, the defence should be given an opportunity to address the court on that matter (*Antypas* (1973) 57 Cr App R 207). No court should make a recommendation for deportation without a full enquiry into the circumstances. Reasons for its decision should always be given (*Nazari* (1980) 2 Cr App R (S) 84, *Compassi* (1987) 9 Cr App R (S) 270), although the Court of Appeal in *Bozat* [1997] 1 Cr App R (S) 270 said that a failure to give reasons might be remedied on appeal.

The Crown Court's common law power to bind over an offender to come up for judgment has on occasion been used as a means of requiring an offender to leave the country and not return (see **7.3**). This power is not restricted by the IA 1971. Bind over to come up for judgment might still be used in respect of British citizens, who are outside the scope of the IA 1971, but it is submitted that in other cases the statutory route should be used rather than common law powers.

10.3.2 Sentencing principles

In *Nazari* (1980) 2 Cr App R (S) 84 Lawton LJ said:

> The country has no use for criminals of other nationalities, particularly if they have committed serious crimes or have long criminal records. That is self-evident. The more serious the crime and the longer the record the more obvious it is that there should be an order recommending deportation. On the other hand a minor offence would not merit an order . . .

In that case Lawton LJ suggested that normally an offence of shoplifting would not justify a recommendation for deportation, but if the offender had been involved in a series of such offences or if he was a member of an organised shoplifting gang, it might be. A case in which the courts have found no evidence of community detriment is *Ariquat* (1981) 3 Cr App R (S) 83, a case of indecent assault, where the 19-year-old offender had sexual intercourse with a girl of 15, believing her to be over 16, and so was not guilty of unlawful sexual intercourse. In *David* (1980) 2 Cr App R (S) 362 the offender was convicted of theft of a passport. Although he had previous convictions, they related to offences committed in other countries, and none had occurred since 1972. The recommendation was quashed. In *Tshuma* (1981) 3 Cr App R (S) 97, notwithstanding 'a very serious offence' of arson causing £3,000 worth of damage, the court took account of the fact that it had been committed under emotional stress and that there was very little chance of reoffending. The case of *Serry* (1980) 2 Cr App R (S) 336 decided that the fact that the offender is living on social security is not in itself to the community's detriment and, accordingly, is not a matter to be taken into account when considering whether to make a recommendation for deportation.

A recommendation for deportation should not be made purely on the basis of an offender's criminal record (*Secretary of State, ex parte Santillo* (1980) 2 Cr App R (S) 274), a principle described by Donaldson LJ as 'not only the law in accordance with Article 3 of the Council Directive [but] also only common sense and fairness'. A recommendation may be made, however, if the court considers that the offender's previous record, in the light of the current offence, renders it likely that he will offend again. In *Kraus* (1982) 4 Cr App R (S) 113 the offender, a West German citizen, pleaded guilty to two offences of theft of a total value of £2,000, in breach of trust. It was argued that a recommendation for deportation was inappropriate since the offender did not constitute a threat to the fundamental interests of society. The court heard, however, that the offender had committed the offences to pay off a blackmailer who had discovered the offender's membership of the Nazi party in Germany, an illegal organisation. Given the offender's membership of that group, together with a reasonable apprehension that he might be subject to further blackmail, the recommendation was upheld.

In *Nazari* Lawton LJ said:

> The courts are not concerned with the political systems which exist in other countries . . . The court has no knowledge of those matters over and above common knowledge; and that may be wrong . . . It is for the Home Secretary to decide in each case whether an offender's return to his country of origin would have consequences which would make his compulsory return unduly harsh.

This principle had been applied in *Antypas* (1972) 57 Cr App R 207 and appears to represent the general rule. A different line was taken in *Thoseby and Krawczyk* (1979) 1 Cr App R (S) 280. In that case the court took account of information from Amnesty International that if the offenders were deported to Poland they would face severe custodial sentences. In the circumstances the Court of Appeal felt that the Home Secretary would have all the relevant information and the question of deportation should be left to his discretion without any recommendation from the court.

A related though distinct point is evidence of special hardship to the offender, or to the offender's family, if he is deported. In most of the decided cases the Court of Appeal has held that it is proper to weigh in the balance the consequences which the making of a recommendation for deportation would have upon third parties. In *Fernandez* (1980) 2 Cr App R (S) 84 the order was quashed where the offender, a Spanish national, had been convicted of conspiracy to rob and aggravated burglary, but where the offender's wife would be forced to choose whether to go with her husband or stay in the UK to look after the interests of her British-born children. See also *David* (1980) 2 Cr App R (S) 362, where a relevant consideration was the impact upon the offender's daughter if the offender was to be deported. In *Shittu* (1992) 14 Cr App R (S) 283 it was said that the court when considering whether to make a recommendation for deportation should always consider the effect of the recommendation on the offender's dependants, and balance that against the potential detriment to the country if he were to remain. The offender in that case was convicted of attempting to obtain property by deception (presentation of a stolen credit card) and handling stolen goods, and was sentenced to 12 months' imprisonment, which included the concurrent activation of a suspended sentence of nine months, and recommended for deportation. The offender was of Nigerian origin but had spent several years in the UK. He was married to a woman born in the UK and they had a child. The offender had been studying at university before receiving the custodial sentence. Since there was no evidence that the sentencer had given proper weight to the likely effect of deportation upon the family, the Court of Appeal quashed the recommendation.

10.3.3 Combining a recommendation for deportation with other sentences or orders

There is no statutory restriction upon combining a recommendation for deportation with any other sentence or order. It may be combined with a sentence of life imprisonment (IA 1971, s. 6(4)). A recommendation for deportation is most commonly combined with a fine or a custodial sentence. In *Akan* [1973] 1 QB 491 the Court of Appeal upheld a recommendation for deportation in conjunction with a conditional discharge. Although a conditional discharge is treated as a conviction for limited purposes only (see **7.1.4**), IA 1971, s. 6(3) states that for the purposes of a recommendation for deportation a person who has been found to have committed an offence 'shall be regarded as a person convicted of the offence'.

10.4 EXCLUSION FROM LICENSED PREMISES

10.4.1 Power to make exclusion order

By s. 1 of the Licensed Premises (Exclusion of Certain Persons) Act 1980, where a person is convicted of an offence committed on licensed premises and the court is satisfied that in committing that offence the offender resorted to violence, or offered or threatened to resort to violence, the court may make an exclusion order, which prohibits the offender from entering those premises, or any other specified premises, without the express consent of the licensee of the premises, or his servant or agent. The court should specify the relevant premises by name and address in the order (s. 4(1)), so that an order which purports to ban an offender from all licensed premises in Norfolk is unlawful (*Grady* (1990) 12 Cr App R (S) 152). An exclusion order takes effect for such period, being not less than three months nor more than two years, as is specified in the order. The expression 'licensed premises' means, in relation to England and Wales, premises in respect of which there is in force a justices' on-licence within the meaning of the Licensing Act 1964, s. 1. When the court makes an exclusion order it should ensure that a copy is sent to the licensee(s) of the establishment(s) listed in the order (s. 4(3)).

An exclusion order may be made in addition to any sentence which is imposed in respect of the offence of which the person is convicted. An exclusion order may be combined with an absolute or conditional discharge, notwithstanding the provisions of PCCA 1973, s. 1C (see **7.1.4**). The order can be made either by the court on its own initiative, or prompted by an application made by the victim or an interested third party to the prosecutor (*Penn* [1996] 2 Cr App R (S) 214).

In *Grady* the offender pleaded guilty to assault occasioning actual bodily harm after she had been involved in an altercation in a public house, during which she had pushed or punched the landlady, causing bruising to her back. The exclusion order had been imposed in addition to a suspended prison sentence. The Court of Appeal said that exclusion orders were appropriate where people had been making a nuisance of themselves in public houses to the annoyance of other customers and so as to create a possible danger to the licensee. It was not suitable in this case, where the offender was a mature woman with a clean record.

10.4.2 Breach of exclusion order

Anyone who enters premises in breach of an exclusion order is guilty of an offence punishable on summary conviction with a fine not exceeding £200 or to imprisonment for one month, or to both (s. 2).

At the time of such conviction, the court must consider whether the exclusion order should continue in force, and it may terminate it, or vary it by deleting the name of any specified premises, if it thinks fit. There is, however, no power on breach to extend the period of the order. A copy of the order which terminates or varies the exclusion order must be sent by the court to the licensee(s) of the premises concerned (s. 4(3)).

10.5 EXCLUSION FROM SPORTING EVENTS

10.5.1 Power to make exclusion order

The Public Order Act 1986, s. 30 provides that where a person is convicted of an offence which fulfils one or more specified conditions in the Act, an exclusion order may be made by the court, in addition to the sentence imposed for the offence. The exclusion order prohibits that person from entering any premises for the purposes of attending any 'prescribed football match'. The conditions (set out in s. 31) are that the offence must have been committed at a time when the offender was entering or leaving a football match, or was travelling to or from such a match, and it must have involved the use or threat of violence by the offender to another person, or the use or threat of violence towards property, or was an offence against the Sporting Events (Control of Alcohol) Act 1980. The court must be satisfied that the making of an exclusion order in the offender's case will help to prevent violence or disorder at or in connection with football matches (s. 30(2)). The exclusion order applies to any football ground. It is not limited to the ground in respect of which the offence took place. A 'prescribed football match' means an associated football match of any description prescribed by order made by the Secretary of State. By the Public Order (Football Exclusion) Order 1987 (SI 1987 No. 853) and the Public Order (Football Exclusion) (Amendment) Order 1992 (SI 1992 No. 1556), such matches include international football matches, matches played by any team in the Premier League or Football League and matches played in the European Champion Clubs Cup, the European Cup Winners Cup or the UEFA Cup.

An exclusion order lasts for the period specified in the order, but the minimum period is three months (s. 32). There is no maximum period. Entering premises in breach of an exclusion order is itself a criminal offence, punishable on summary conviction with imprisonment not exceeding one month or a fine not exceeding level 3 on the standard scale. A person under an exclusion order may apply to the court, after a minimum period of one year, to terminate it (s. 33).

10.5.2 Power to make restriction order

The Football Spectators Act 1989 (FSA 1989) provides the courts with powers to make 'restriction orders'. These are designed to prevent offenders from attending football matches which are to be played within England and Wales, or played abroad, by requiring them to report to a police station in England and Wales at the time of the relevant matches. It was envisaged that this power would supersede the Public Order Act power to make exclusion orders. Section 27(5) of the FSA 1989 provides for the repeal of ss. 30–37 of the 1986 Act. This repeal has not taken place, however, and relevant powers under the 1986 and 1989 Acts exist together.

By FSA, s. 15(1), where a person is convicted of a 'relevant offence' the convicting court, or the Crown Court where the offender is committed to the Crown Court for sentence, may make a restriction order on the offender. No such order should be made unless the court is satisfied that making such an order in the offender's case would help prevent violence or disorder at or in connection with 'designated football matches' (s. 15(2)). The restriction order must specify the police station at which the offender must report (s. 15(5)) and the court must explain the effect of the order to the offender in ordinary language (s. 15(6)). A restriction order will take effect for a period of five years in a case where the offender received an immediate custodial sentence for the relevant offence and, where any other sentence was passed, it will last for two years, beginning with the date of the order (s. 16(1)). The duty imposed by the restriction order is a duty to report, initially to the police station named in the order, within a period of five days of the making of the order and thereafter when required to do so, to any police station in England and Wales at the time or between the times specified in the notice by which the requirement is imposed (s. 16(2)). On making a restriction order, the court must give a copy of the order to the offender, send a copy to the enforcing authority, a copy to the relevant police station and, if the offender has received a custodial sentence, a copy to the governor of the establishment at which he is held (s. 18(1)).

'Designated football matches' are football matches which have been designated by order of the Secretary of State under s. 1(2) of the FSA 1989 (which applies to matches played within England and Wales) or under s. 14(2) (which applies to matches played outside England and Wales). See Football Spectators (Designation of Football Matches in England and Wales) Order 1990 and the Football Spectators (Designation of Football Matches outside England and Wales) Order 1990, as amended by the Sports Grounds and Football (Amendment of Various Orders) Order 1992; by these orders, 'designated football matches' include matches played by the national sides of England or Wales, matches played by any team in the Premier League or Football League, or club matches played under the auspices of UEFA. The Secretary of State may order that, in respect of a particular designated football match, reporting to a police station is obligatory for all persons who are subject to a restriction order, or for a limited class of such persons.

The 'relevant offences' for the purposes of the FSA 1989 are listed in sch. 1 to the Act. A wide range of offences of violence, drunkennness, public disorder, damage to property and road traffic are listed. These fall into two groups. The first group includes certain offences under Part I of the FSA 1989, offences under the Sporting Events (Control of Alcohol etc.) Act 1985, if these were committed at a designated football match, or while entering or leaving such a match, or any offence involving the use or threat of violence towards another person or property during a period relevant to a designated football match, or while entering or leaving such a match. The second group involves offences to which the power to make a restriction order applies only if the prosecutor gives notice, at least five days in advance of the trial, that it is proposed to show that the offence related to a designated football match. If the court finds that the offence was so related, then it may make a 'declaration of relevance'. Offences in the second group are being found drunk (Licensing Act 1872, s. 12), disorderly behaviour while drunk in a public place (CJA 1967, s. 91(1)), possessing alcohol on a coach or train travelling to or from a sporting event (Sporting Events (Control of Alcohol etc.) Act 1985, s. 1), offences under the Public Order Act 1986, s. 5 and Road Traffic Act 1988, ss. 4 and 5, or any offence involving the use or threat of use of violence towards any person or property committed while on a journey to or from a designated football match.

A restriction order may be made in addition to any sentence which is imposed in respect of the offence of which the person is convicted. Where a custodial sentence has been imposed on the offender the duty to report is suspended until such time as the offender is discharged from custody (FSA 1989, s. 16(3)). A restriction order may be combined with an absolute or conditional discharge, notwithstanding the provisions of PCCA 1973, s. 1C (s. 15(3) and (4)).

Failure to comply with the duty to report to the police station is itself an offence, punishable on summary conviction with a term of imprisonment not exceeding one month, a fine not exceeding level 3 on the standard scale, or both (FSA 1989, s. 16(4) and (5)).

A person in relation to whom a restriction order has been in force for at least 12 months may apply to the court by which it was made to terminate it (s. 17(1)). That court, having had regard to the person's character and his conduct since the order was made, the nature of the offence and any other circumstances of the case, may terminate the restriction order or refuse the application (s. 17(2)). If the application is refused, a further application cannot be made within six months of the date of refusal (s. 17(3)). If the court terminates the order, it must ensure that a copy of the terminating order is given to the offender, and that copies are sent to the enforcing authority, the relevant police station and, if the offender is serving a custodial sentence, to the governor of the establishment at which he is held (s. 18(1)).

10.6 OTHER DISQUALIFICATIONS AND EXCLUSIONS

These disqualifications should be distinguished from disqualifications which come into effect automatically upon conviction. See **13.5**.

10.6.1 Licensing and gaming

By the Licensing Act 1964, s. 100, where a person is convicted of an offence under ss. 161, 172, 175, 176 or 177 of the Act, or of an offence under s. 1 of the Betting, Gaming and Lotteries Act 1963, s. 1(1), the court may:

(a) disqualify that person for such period specified in the order, but not exceeding five years, from holding or obtaining a licence under Part IV of the Licensing Act 1964 (an on-licence) or under the Late Night Refreshment Houses Act 1969; and/or
(b) prohibit such licences from being held or granted within such a period to any person in respect of the premises at which the offence in question was committed.

Such an order may be exercised on conviction in addition to any other powers which the court is required to or does exercise on conviction.
A disqualification order under the Licensing Act 1964, s. 100 must not be made unless the person concerned has had an opportunity to be heard by the court (s. 101(2)). Such an order may be suspended pending an appeal (s. 101(1)).
By the Gaming Act 1968, s. 24, where a person is convicted of an offence under s. 23(1) or (2) of the Act (whether or not applied by s. 23(5)), the court may make a disqualification order prohibiting a licence under the Act being held in respect of those premises during such period as may be specified in the order but not exceeding five years.

10.6.2 Corruption

A person convicted of an offence under the Public Bodies Corrupt Practices Act 1889, s. 1, may, at the discretion of the court, be disqualified from any election or appointment to any public office for five years from the date of his conviction and to forfeit any such offence held by him at the time of his conviction (s. 2). If the offender was an officer, or was in the employment of, any public body, he shall be liable to forfeit his claim to any compensation or pension to which he would otherwise have been entitled. In the event of a second conviction for a like offence he shall be liable to be adjudged for ever incapable of holding any public office, and to be disqualified for five years as being registered as an elector and from voting at an election.

10.6.3 Animals

Owners can be disqualified from keeping an animal if they are convicted of cruelty to an animal (Protection of Animals Act 1911, s. 3; Protection of Animals (Amendment) Act 1954, s. 1). Disqualification can be for a specified period in the discretion of the court, or for life, and the disqualification may extend to animals of the species which were involved in the cruelty, or more generally.

11 Mentally Disordered Offenders

11.1 PROBATION ORDERS WITH REQUIREMENT OF TREATMENT

Psychiatric probation orders are the most frequent form of psychiatric disposal in criminal cases, whether in the magistrates' court or the Crown Court. The relevant provision is sch. 1A to PCCA 1973. Paragraph 5 relates to the insertion by the court into a probation order of a condition of treatment for the offender's mental condition.

11.1.1 Power to make probation order with requirement of treatment

This power is only available in circumstances where the court would otherwise have power to make a probation order without such a requirement. It is therefore limited to cases where the offender is aged 16 or over and is convicted of an offence by or before a magistrates' court or the Crown Court. The duration of a probation order may not be for less than six months or more than three years. A probation order is a community order, and no community order can be imposed unless the court is satisfied that the offence (or offences) committed is (or are) serious enough to justify such an order. The court must then be satisfied that a probation order (with the relevant requirement) either standing alone or in combination with other sentences or orders of the court is the most suitable disposal for the offender and that the restrictions on the offender's liberty occasioned by the sentence are not disproportionate to the gravity of the offending behaviour (see **5.2.2**). A pre-sentence report is normally required before a probation order which contains a requirement of this kind can be made (CJA 1991, s. 7(3)).

Paragraph 5(1) provides that where the court is satisfied, on the evidence of a medical practitioner approved for the purposes of MHA 1983, s. 12 as being a person having special experience in the diagnosis and treatment of mental disorder, that the mental condition of an offender is such as requires and may be susceptible to treatment, but is not such as to warrant the making of a hospital order or a guardianship order under the MHA 1983, it may, if it makes a probation order, include in it a requirement that the offender shall submit, during the whole of the probation period or during such part of that period as may be specified in the order, to treatment by or under the direction of a duly qualified medical practitioner or a chartered psychologist, with a view to the improvement of the offender's mental condition. For hospital orders see **11.3**, for guardianship orders see **11.3.4**, and for probation orders generally see **5.2**. A probation order with a condition of psychiatric treatment may be made in a case where the offender is not suffering from one or other of the four forms of mental disorder which justify the making of a hospital order; for these see **11.3.1**. Before the condition of psychiatric treatment can be inserted into the order, the offender must express his willingness to comply with it (para. 5(4), as substituted by the C(S)A 1997).

11.1.2 Forms of treatment

The treatment required by a probation order must be specified in the order and must take one of the following forms (para. 5(10)):

(a) treatment as a resident patient, which may be carried out in a mental hospital (within the meaning of the MHA 1983) or a mental nursing home, but not a special hospital;

(b) treatment as a non-resident patient at such institution or place as may be specified; or

(c) treatment by or under the direction of such duly qualified medical practitioner or chartered psychologist as may be specified.

No other forms of treatment may be specified.

As a precondition of the inclusion of a treatment requirement in a probation order, the court must be satisfied that the necessary arrangements have been made relating to the treatment intended to be specified in the order (including arrangements necessary for the reception of the offender) (para. 5(4)). While the probationer is under treatment as a resident patient, the probation officer must carry out his supervision of the offender 'only as may be necessary for the purpose of discharge or amendment of the order' (para. 5(5)).

Where a probation order with a condition of psychiatric treatment has been made, and the relevant medical practitioner or chartered psychologist takes the view that part of the treatment may more conveniently be given in or at an institution not specified in the original order (even where the institution is not one which could have been specified in that order: para. 5(7)), arrangements may be made, with the consent of the probationer, for this to be done (para. 5(6)). Where such a change is made, the probation officer must be notified in writing (para. 5(8)).

11.1.3 Breach etc. of probation order with requirement of mental treatment

If the probationer fails to comply with any of the conditions specified in the order, including the requirement as to mental treatment and any breach of a condition inserted under para. 5(6) (provided para. 5(8) was complied with), he may be dealt with for breach of the probation order. A probation order is a community order within the meaning of the CJA 1991, s. 6(4). For provisions relating to breach of community orders see **5.6.1**.

If the probationer commits a further offence within the currency of the probation order, he may be dealt with in respect of the original offence in the usual manner. For revocation of community orders see **5.6.2**.

A probation order with a requirement of treatment for a mental condition may be amended on application to the court under CJA 1991, sch. 2, paras. 13 and 14. Paragraph 13(2)(a) permits a court to amend a probation order by inserting into it a mental treatment condition, to deal with the situation where the need for treatment is not discovered until after a probation order has been made, but this power requires the consent of the offender and cannot be exercised later than three months from the date of the original order. Paragraph 14 permits the probation officer, in response to a report in writing from the relevant medical practitioner, to apply to the court for a variation, or cancellation, of the mental treatment requirement.

11.1.4 Sentencing principle

In most cases the courts insert a requirement of treatment into a probation order where, without evidence of the offender's need for treatment, probation would have been an appropriate disposal in any event, being commensurate with the seriousness of the offence. An example might be the compulsive shoplifter whose underlying mental problems need attention. Here the court is simply tailoring the probation order to suit the particular needs of the offender. In the past, however, the Court of Appeal has indicated that a probation order with a requirement of treatment will sometimes be appropriate for an offender who has committed a serious offence, and represents a real risk to the public. If there seems to the court to be a reasonable chance that such an order will have a beneficial effect upon the offender, the court may take the view that the risk to the public is thereby outweighed. An example is *Hoof* (1980) 2 Cr App R (S) 299, where the offender was convicted of arson with intent to endanger life, having set fire to two maisonettes (in one of which a woman was asleep at the time) and a motor car. The Court of Appeal varied a prison sentence of three years to a probation order with a treatment requirement. A requirement of residence at a probation hostel was also inserted into the order (see **5.2.4**). In *McDonald* (1983) 5 Cr App R (S) 419 the Court of Appeal, without any criticism of the trial judge, varied a sentence of two years' imprisonment on an offender who pleaded guilty to an indecent assault on a girl aged 11 to a probation order with a requirement of treatment, on hearing evidence that 'as much has been done as can practically be done to ensure that he will be properly supervised in the community, that he will have a proper place of residence, that the residence will be conveniently sited so that he may attend for treatment and, finally, that treatment will be available over an extended period of time'. A third example is *Jones* (1992) 13 Cr App R (S) 275, where the female offender pleaded guilty to seven counts of robbery, committed at building society branches, when she had pretended to have a gun and obtained £7,000. Sentence was varied from four years' imprisonment to a three-year probation order with a requirement of out-patient mental treatment by the Court of Appeal, which heard that Jones had been severely depressed as a result of family crises and financial problems. She was in need of long-term psychological help and her problems had been made worse by her experience of custody. The Court of Appeal said that the case was 'wholly exceptional'.

Cases decided on the proper use of probation orders with a requirement of treatment which pre-date the CJA 1991 should now be looked at with some care. In the cases cited above, the offences were surely so serious that only a custodial sentence could be justified. The sentencing framework of the CJA 1991 gives primacy to the seriousness of the offence, but under the terms of the Act custody can be avoided if the offender's need for treatment for a mental condition amounts to personal mitigation sufficient to allow selection of a different sentence. This is the principle in *Cox* [1993] 1 WLR 188 and see **4.2.4**.

11.2 SUPERVISION ORDERS WITH REQUIREMENT OF TREATMENT

Power to insert a requirement of treatment for a mental condition into a supervision order may be found in CYPA 1969, s. 12B. The provisions are very similar to those relating to the insertion of a requirement of mental treatment into a probation order (see **11.1**). For supervision orders generally see **5.8**.

This power is available only in circumstances where the court would otherwise have power to make a supervision order without such a requirement. It is therefore limited to cases where the offender is aged 10 to 17 inclusive and is convicted of an offence by or before a youth court or the Crown Court. The maximum duration of a supervision order is three years. A supervision order is a community order, and no community order can be imposed unless the court is satisfied that the offence (or the offence and one or more offences associated with it) is serious enough to justify such an order. The court must then be satisfied that a supervision order (with the relevant requirement), either standing alone or in combination with other sentences or orders of the court, is the most suitable disposal for the offender and that the restrictions on the offender's liberty occasioned by the sentence are not disproportionate to the gravity of the offending behaviour (see **5.2.2**).

By CYPA 1969, s. 12B(1), where a court which proposes to make a supervision order is satisfied, on the evidence of a medical practitioner approved for the purposes of MHA 1983, s. 12, that the mental condition of a supervised person is such as requires and may be susceptible to treatment, but is not such as to warrant his detention under a hospital order, it may include in the supervision order a requirement that the supervised person shall, for a period specified in the order, submit to treatment of one of the following forms:

(a) treatment by or under the direction of a fully registered medical practitioner specified in the order; or

(b) treatment as a resident or non-resident patient at a place specified in the order; or

(c) treatment as a resident patient in a hospital or a mental nursing home, but not a special hospital.

Such a requirement cannot be inserted into a supervision order unless the court is satisfied that arrangements have been made or can be made for the treatment to be carried out and, in the case of treatment as a resident patient, for the reception of the patient (CYPA 1969, s. 12B(2)(a)). A pre-sentence report is normally required before a supervision order which contains a requirement under s. 12B may be ordered (see CJA 1991, s. 7(3)). Since a medical report will generally be required, in most cases the ordering of both reports would constitute good sentencing practice. The supervised person must express a willingness to comply with a requirement under s. 12B, but if the supervised person is under the age of 14 there is an exception and no such expression of a willingness to comply is required (s. 12B(2)(b)). No such requirement shall continue in force after the supervised person has attained the age of 18 (s. 12B(2)(b)).

11.3 HOSPITAL ORDERS

Criminal courts are given powers under MHA 1983 to make a hospital order on a person of any age convicted of an offence which is punishable with imprisonment in the case of an adult. The effect of a hospital order is that a social worker or other suitable person is authorised to take the offender to the mental hospital which is specified in the order. The hospital named in the order may be an ordinary NHS trust hospital, or the psychiatric ward of such a hospital, or it may be one of the secure special hospitals (Broadmoor, Rampton and Ashworth). The latter hospitals are high security institutions and are appropriate only where the patient is thought to represent a serious risk to the safety of the public, including other patients and hospital staff.

An admission to hospital by means of a hospital order has the same effect for most purposes as a compulsory civil commitment under MHA 1983, Part II, with the important exception that the patient's 'nearest relative' does not have the right to order the patient's discharge. The order in principle lapses after six months, but may be (and often is) renewed for a further six months and at yearly intervals thereafter, provided the responsible medical officer (RMO) considers further detention to be 'necessary for the protection of the public or in the interests of the patient's health or safety' (s. 20 and sch. 1). There is no limit to the number of renewals which might subsequently be made, so that a hospital order is in principle an indeterminate sentence, but the patient may be discharged from hospital by way of various powers exercised by the RMO, the hospital managers or a mental health review tribunal (MHRT). Clearly this sentence, while therapeutic in objective, involves a substantial restriction upon the liberty of the offender, or 'patient' as he should after disposal be called. Accordingly, in the case of an offender who is suffering from a degree of mental disorder, the sentencer must always consider whether compulsory hospital detention is appropriate. If not, a probation order with a condition of treatment for the mental condition may be a better alternative (*Birch* (1989) 11 Cr App R (S) 202 and see **11.1**).

Hospital orders are a relatively little-used form of sentence. In 1991 a grand total of 747 orders were made, 404 by the Crown Court (of which 104 also had a restriction order: see **11.5**) and 343 by magistrates' courts. These figures also include guardianship orders (as to which see **11.4**). In the Crown Court, the cases most likely to attract a hospital order on sentence were offences involving violence, followed by offences of criminal damage (including arson), robbery, burglary and sexual offences. It is well known that in a significant number of cases the offender's criminal conduct is clearly associated with his mental problems, but no hospital order is made by the court. Sometimes this is because the degree of restriction of liberty involved in a hospital order cannot be justified by the relative triviality of the offence, in which case a probation order with a requirement of treatment, or simply a lenient disposal, such as a conditional discharge or a bind over, will be used. Sometimes a hospital order is not made because the sentencer thinks that the offender was sufficiently responsible for his conduct to deserve to be punished for it by the passing of a custodial or community sentence in the ordinary way. Whenever the court is considering passing a custodial sentence on a person who is, or who appears to the court to be, mentally disordered, the court must first obtain a medical report (CJA 1991, s. 4(1)). Sometimes a different situation arises, where the court would like to make a hospital order, but the medical reports preclude it. Either the mental problem from which the offender suffers does not come within the categories mentioned in the MHA 1983 (see **11.3.1**) or, if he is suffering from psychopathic disorder or mental impairment, the further requirement of that Act, that the condition must be treatable, may not be satisfied in the offender's case. Sometimes no mental hospital has space to admit the offender, or the only hospital available is not a secure one and the judge is of the view that the offender represents a danger to the public and must be held in the secure environment of a special hospital. Should the secure mental hospitals be unable to admit the patient, the judge would be entitled to pass a determinate custodial sentence or, perhaps, a life sentence if the legal requirements for the passing of that sentence were made out (see **4.3.3**). The undoubted effect of all this is that many offenders who are suffering from various degrees of mental disorder end up serving custodial sentences (where the availability of suitable psychiatric treatment is very limited), rather than receiving proper treatment for their condition in hospital.

It should be noted that the Home Secretary has power, upon receipt of appropriate medical advice, to direct the transfer of an offender who is serving a prison sentence, or a sentence of detention in a young offender institution, from that institution to a mental hospital (MHA 1983, s. 47). This 'transfer direction', as it is called, has the same effect upon the offender as the making of a hospital order in his case (s. 47(3)). A transfer direction lapses after 14 days unless it has been carried out within that time (s. 47(2)).

11.3.1 Power to make hospital order

If a person is convicted before the Crown Court or a magistrates' court of an offence punishable with imprisonment (other than murder or a case which falls to be sentenced under the CJA 1997, s. 2) and certain specified conditions are met, the court may make a hospital order under MHA 1983, s. 37. Only a youth court may make a hospital order or guardianship order on a juvenile (CYPA 1969, s. 7(8)). The specified conditions are as follows:

(a) The court must be satisfied, on the written or oral evidence of two registered medical practitioners, that the offender is suffering from mental illness, psychopathic disorder, severe mental impairment or mental impairment. 'Mental illness' is not defined in the MHA 1983, but see *W* v *L* [1974] QB 711. 'Psychopathic disorder' means a persistent disorder or disability of the mind which results in abnormally aggressive or seriously irresponsible conduct by the person concerned. 'Severe mental impairment' means a state of arrested or incomplete development of the mind, including severe impairment of intelligence and social functioning, which is associated with the kind of conduct mentioned in the definition of psychopathic disorder. 'Mental impairment' is defined in almost the same way as severe mental impairment, save that in the phrase 'severe mental impairment', the word 'significant' is substituted for 'severe'. Thus, both mental impairment and severe mental impairment involve low intelligence, whereas a person suffering from a psychopathic disorder may be of normal, or high, intelligence. These definitions may be found in MHA 1983, s. 1(2).

(b) In addition, the mental disorder from which the offender is suffering must be of a nature or degree which makes it appropriate for him to be detained in a hospital for medical treatment and, in the case of psychopathic disorder or mental impairment, such treatment must be likely to alleviate or prevent a deterioration of his condition (s. 37(2)(i)). There is no need to establish a causal link between the offender's mental disorder and the offence in respect of which the order is made (*McBride* (1972) CSP F2-2A01).

(c) One of the two medical practitioners must be approved for the purposes of MHA 1983, s. 12 as having special experience in the diagnosis or treatment of mental disorder (s. 54(1)). It may seem odd that only one of the doctors must be so qualified; this is explained by the fact that while one of the doctors must be a specialist the other will generally be the offender's own general practitioner. It is desirable in every case that oral evidence should be given by the doctor who will be in charge of the case if the order is made, or by a doctor who is fully informed of his views (*Blackwood* (1974) 59 Cr App R 170). Where the medical evidence is in written form, a copy of the medical report must be given to counsel or solicitor for the defence. If the offender is unrepresented, the gist of the report should be disclosed to him. In *Blackwood* the Court of Appeal said that a court should not normally make a hospital order if the offender was not legally represented. The defence may require the doctors to attend to give oral evidence, and other doctors may be called to give evidence in rebuttal (s. 54(3)). Whenever a hospital order is made the court must specify from which of the forms of mental disorder specified in s. 1(2) the offender is found by the court to be suffering (s. 37(7)). An order cannot be made unless the offender is described by each of the medical practitioners as suffering from the same form of mental disorder, whether or not the offender is also described by either of them as suffering from another of those forms (s. 37(7)).

(d)   A hospital order cannot be made unless the court is satisfied, on the written or oral evidence of the RMO, or of some other person representing the managers of the hospital, that arrangements have been made for the offender's admission to that hospital within 28 days of the date of the order (s. 37(4)). The health authorities are under no legal obligation to accept offenders from the courts, and the court is not empowered to order a hospital to accept an offender (*Parker*, 21 March 1975 (unreported)). Sometimes they are unable to do so, either because no bed is available, or through concern for the safety of staff in the case of a potentially violent or disruptive offender being received from the court. In *Harding* (1983) 5 Cr App R (S) 197, Lawton LJ commented that those who obstruct the court's wish to make such an order might be guilty of contempt of court, but this threat does not appear ever to have been carried out. Hospitals are, however, under a legal obligation to supply information to the court about the availability of beds in their region for the admission of a person under a hospital order (s. 39(1)). In an emergency or other special situation arising within the 28 days following the order, the Secretary of State may give directions for admission of the offender to a different hospital from that specified in the order (s. 37(5)). The court may, pending admission within the 28 days, order the offender's detention in some other 'place of safety' (s. 37(4)). Occasionally it may be appropriate to admit an offender to a hospital not situated locally, with a view to subsequent transfer (*Marsden* (1968) 52 Cr App R 301).

(e)   The court must be of the opinion, having regard to all the circumstances, including the nature of the offence and the character and antecedents of the offender, and to the other available methods of dealing with him, that a hospital order is the most suitable method of disposing of the case (s. 37(2)(b)). The matter is one for the sentencer, who may decide that, notwithstanding the offender's mental disorder, it is proper to pass a custodial sentence on the offender even though a place is available for him at a suitable mental hospital (*Gunnell* (1966) 50 Cr App R 242). Of course such a decision can only be taken after consideration of a medical report (CJA 1991, s. 4(1)).

11.3.2   Consequences of a hospital order

The making of a hospital order authorises the taking of the offender to the specified hospital and his detention there for an initial period of six months. He may be discharged even during that period, by either the RMO or the hospital managers, on the basis of an assessment of whether his continuing detention is 'necessary for the protection of the public or in the interests of the patient's health or safety' (MHA 1983, s. 20 and sch. 1). If he is not, the doctor examines him during the fifth or sixth month of his detention and prepares a report on him. If the report recommends that he should be further detained, that is sufficient authority for the hospital managers to hold him for a further six months. After that the same process may be repeated at yearly intervals (i.e. in the eleventh or twelfth month the doctor examines him and, if the resulting report so recommends, the hospital managers authorise detention for a further year). After the first six months the patient has a right to apply to the MHRT, once during each subsequent period of renewal of the order, for his case to be considered, and his nearest relative has a similar right. A MHRT consists of a legally qualified chairman, a psychiatrist and a lay person. In deciding whether to direct the patient's discharge they have regard to approximately the same considerations as did the RMO, although there are slight differences in the wording of the relevant sections of the MHA 1983.

Where these elaborate procedures fail to result in discharge, there is one very simple remedy which is open to the patient. He may simply abscond, and if he stays at liberty without coming to notice for more than 28 days he may not be taken into custody or returned to the hospital. There is no longer authority to detain him. This 'discharge by operation of law' as it is known is, on the face of it, rather surprising. It applies to patients who are in hospital as a result of a hospital order, unless a restriction order was added to the hospital order and is still in force (see **11.5**). The reason for a patient who avoids 'recapture' by a police officer or local authority social worker for 28 days no longer being liable to detention is that, by coming to no harm during that period, he has shown that he no longer needs to be in hospital.

11.3.3 Interim hospital order

Section 38 of MHA 1983, provides for the making an an 'interim hospital order'. The qualifying conditions are virtually the same as for the making of a hospital order under s. 37, but the interim order is available to the court 'before making a hospital order or dealing with him in some other way' and its purpose is to establish whether the offender is suitable to be the subject of a hospital order. One difference in the powers is that an interim order can be made only where one of the registered medical practitioners who gives evidence is employed at the hospital where the person is to be detained. An interim hospital order is thus not a final disposal of the case but, in a case where there is some doubt, it is an experiment to see if the case can be properly disposed of by way of a full order (*Birch* (1989) 11 Cr App R (S) 202). An interim hospital order can also be used to discover whether a person should be made subject to a hospital direction or a limitation direction under s. 45A of the MHA 1983 (see **11.6**).

An interim hospital order may last for up to 12 weeks, renewable for further periods of not more than 28 days at a time, but in no case to last for more than a total of 12 months (s. 38(5) as amended by the C(S)A 1997). No minimum period is specified. At the end of the interim period the court must make a final disposal of the case, and the interim order comes to an end. In a case where a court renews an interim hospital order, or where it finally disposes of the case by making a hospital order under s. 37, the offender need not appear before the court, provided that he is legally represented and his representative has an opportunity of being heard (s. 38(2) and (6)).

The decision to make an interim hospital order does not commit the court to ultimately disposing of the case by means of a full hospital order. At the end of the interim order the court still has the full range of sentencing options at its disposal, although if it chooses to pass a sentence other than a hospital order the offender must, of course, be present for the hearing.

11.3.4 Combining a hospital order with other sentences or orders

By MHA 1983, s. 37(8), when a hospital order or a guardianship order (see **11.4**) is made the court must not pass a sentence of imprisonment, order for detention, impose a fine, make a probation order or supervision order in respect of the offence or require a parent of a juvenile so dealt with to enter into a recognisance. The court may, however, 'make any other order which the court has power to make apart from this section'. This would permit the making of various ancillary orders, such as a compensation order, though this would always be subject to the offender's means.

11.4 GUARDIANSHIP ORDERS

Where the conditions for making a hospital order are satisfied, the court may, as an alternative, make a guardianship order (MHA 1983, s. 37(1)). The legal conditions for hospital orders and guardianship orders are identical, except that for a guardianship order:

(a)   there is no requirement that the mental disorder from which the offender is suffering is of a nature or degree which requires detention in a hospital; and

(b)   there is no requirement that the mental disorder must be treatable.

It must instead be shown that the mental disorder is of a nature or degree which warrants the offender's reception into guardianship.

The guardian, for the purposes of the order, will be the local authority social services department, or a particular person approved by that department. The order confers on the local authority, or the person who is named as guardian in the order, the same powers as a guardianship application made under MHA 1983, Part II (s. 40(2)). These powers, in outline, are to determine the patient's place of residence, to require the patient's attendance for treatment, occupation, education or training, and to require access to the patient in any place of residence for a doctor, social worker or other specified person (s. 8). A guardianship order cannot be made unless the relevant authority or person is willing to receive the offender into guardianship (s. 37(6)) and s. 39A empowers a court which is minded to make such an order to request the local social services authority to provide the court with information on how it would exercise its powers.

A guardianship order lasts for 12 months, but may be renewed.

11.5   RESTRICTION ORDERS

The Crown Court is given power by MHA 1983, s. 41, when it makes a hospital order under s. 37, to add to it a restriction order. A restriction order has no existence independent of the hospital order to which it relates, but it fundamentally affects the circumstances in which the patient is detained. In 1991 restriction orders were imposed on sentence in 104 cases. The Crown Court should make such an order only where it appears to the court that, given the nature of the offence, the antecedents of the offender and the risk of the offender's committing further offences if set at large, the making of a restriction order is necessary to protect the public from serious harm (s. 41(1) and *Courtney* (1987) 9 Cr App R (S) 404). This entails that the offender will probably require detention and treatment in one of the secure special hospitals rather than in a NHS hospital, and an order under s. 41 affects the arrangements for discharge (see below).

In this context, the protection of the public from 'serious harm' has been held not to be limited to personal injury, nor need it relate to the public in general. It is enough if a specific category of persons, or even one person, is adjudged to be at risk, although the category of persons at risk is taken to exclude the offender himself. The potential harm must be 'serious'. A high possibility of a recurrence of minor offences will not suffice (*Birch* (1989) 11 Cr App R (S) 202). Clearly medical evidence will be of great importance in making this assessment, but it is the court's decision and the court is not bound to accept the medical opinion it receives (*Birch*). In theory the court could reject unanimous medical advice but in practice is unlikely to do so. A sentencer should not add a restriction order to a hospital order simply to mark the gravity of the offence, nor as a means of punishment. It would be a mistake simply to equate the seriousness of the offence with the likelihood of a restriction order being made. It is only one factor, and the court would have to be very sure of its ground to pass a restriction order where the commission of a serious offence was coupled with a very low risk of reoffending. There is no requirement that a causal connection be established between the disorder and the offence (*Hatt* [1962] Crim LR 647, approved in *Birch*).

The main difference between an order under s. 37 and an order under s. 41 is that neither the RMO nor the hospital managers may discharge a restricted patient without the consent of the Secretary of State or a MHRT. Thus, in effect, the restriction order means that the criminal justice system retains a degree of control over the offender once he becomes a 'patient'. The Secretary of State or a MHRT may release a patient who is subject to a restriction order, either with or without the attachment of conditions to the release (s. 42(1) and (2)). If the patient is discharged from hospital conditionally, the restriction order remains in force and the patient may subsequently be recalled to hospital if he comes to notice. Unlike a hospital order under s. 37, a restriction order does not lapse in the ordinary way unless renewed, but continues for as long as the restriction order is in place. If the restriction order is for a fixed period, at the end of that period the restrictions no longer apply but the hospital order continues in effect (s. 41(5)). The restrictions which may thus be added to a hospital order may be declared by the court to be for a period of time which is specified in the order, or without limit of time. Virtually all restriction orders are, in fact, made without limit of time. The Court of Appeal has said that it would be 'imprudent' in any but the most exceptional circumstances to impose a restriction for a fixed rather than an unlimited period (*Haynes* (1981) 3 Cr App R (S) 330). A restriction order cannot be made unless at least one of the two doctors whose evidence is being taken into account by the court has given oral evidence in court (s. 41(2)).

The effect of a restriction order is that for its duration the offender can be discharged from hospital only on the direction of the Secretary of State or a MHRT. The offender may make an application every year to the MHRT for discharge and, if no application is made for three years, the Secretary of State is under a duty to refer the case to the MHRT for their consideration. The MHRT has power to order discharge against the wishes of the Home Secretary. As an alternative to unconditional discharge, the MHRT may direct that the offender shall be released subject to recall for treatment at the discretion of the Home Secretary. It has been held to be a breach of Art. 5 of the European Convention on Human Rights to continue a restriction order if the patient's mental condition does not warrant it (*X* v *United Kingdom* (1981) 4 ECHR 181 and *Kynaston* v *Secretary of State* (1981) 73 Cr App R 281). Thus danger to the public alone cannot be sufficient grounds for the continued detention under a restriction order.

Only the Crown Court may make a restriction order, though magistrates may commit the offender to Crown Court, provided the offender is aged 14 or over, with a view to such a disposal being made (s. 43). The magistrates must commit the offender to Crown Court in custody unless there is a place available for him in a hospital, in which case they can direct that he be detained in the hospital.

If the criteria within s. 41 are established, the sentencer may, but is not obliged to, pass a restriction order. The likely alternative sentences are life imprisonment (see **4.3.3**) and custody for a fixed term. If an offender qualifies for a hospital order with restrictions, and a place is available in a suitable hospital, then the general rule is that a hospital order with restrictions should be made, and it is certainly wrong in principle for the sentencer to impose a life sentence in an attempt to prevent the patient's possible premature release by order of the MHRT (*Mitchell* [1997] 1 Cr App R (S) 90; *Hutchinson* [1997] 2 Cr App R (S) 60). If a sentencer considers that, notwithstanding the offender's mental disorder, there was an element of culpability in the offence which merited punishment, as where there was no connection between the disorder and the offence or where the offender's responsibility was diminished but not extinguished, the imposition of a prison sentence might be correct (*Birch* (1989) 11 Cr App R (S) 202). The cases make it clear that a life sentence is to be preferred to a fixed-term sentence where the offender is subject to a degree of mental instability which makes it probable that he will commit serious offences if not subject to indefinite detention (*Pither* (1979) 1 Cr App R (S) 209).

11.6 HOSPITAL AND LIMITATION DIRECTIONS

Sections 45A and 45B of the MHA 1983 were inserted into that Act by the C(S)A 1997. These new powers are designed to apply in a case where the Crown Court has heard evidence from two registered medical practitioners, at least one of whom must have given oral evidence, that the offender is suffering from psychopathic disorder (for the definition of this condition see **11.3.1**), that his condition is of a nature and degree which makes it appropriate for him to be detained in hospital for treatment, and that such treatment is likely to alleviate his condition. The Crown Court may intend to pass a hospital order in that case rather than to impose a sentence of imprisonment, but may be anxious to ensure that when the offender's treatment is completed (or if it turns out that the offender is not, after all, capable of responding to treatment) he will be transferred to prison, rather than being released from hospital into the community. The court may make a 'hospital direction' under s. 45A to ensure that this will happen. Before making a hospital direction the court must be satisfied on the written or oral evidence of the RMO who would be in charge of the offender's treatment, or of some other person representing the managers of the relevant hospital, that arrangements have been made for the offender's admission to that hospital, and for his admission within 28 days of making the order. The court may also make a 'limitation direction', which ensures that the offender is made subject to the restrictions set out in MHA 1983, s. 41.

There is power in s. 45A(10) for the Secretary of State by order to provide that offenders suffering from other forms of mental disorder than psychopathic disorder may be made subject to hospital and limitation directions, but no such order has been made.

11.7 ORDERS CONSEQUENT UPON A FINDING OF INSANITY, UNFITNESS TO PLEAD, ETC.

The Criminal Procedure (Insanity) Act 1964, s. 5 (as substituted by the Criminal Procedure (Insanity and Unfitness to Plead) Act 1991) introduces new powers of disposal after the Crown Court has either (a) returned a special verdict that the accused is not guilty by reason of insanity, or (b) recorded a finding that the defendant is under a disability (he is 'unfit to plead') and that he did the act or made the omission charged against him. In neither of these situations, of course, has the defendant been convicted of the offence charged, but provision is made for a range of disposals in such cases which are so closely similar to the sentencing options discussed elsewhere in this book that it is appropriate to consider them here.

The 1964 Act, by s. 5 and sch. 1, formerly stated that, on a finding that the defendant was not guilty by reason of insanity or was unfit to plead, the Crown Court judge was required to impose an order upon the defendant equivalent to an order under MHA 1983, s. 37 imposed upon a person convicted, together with a restriction order under MHA 1983, s. 41. Thus a person who was found not guilty by reason of insanity faced mandatory commitment to a mental hospital, with restrictions upon release. These provisions attracted much criticism, particularly in the context of the courts' expansion of the reach of the insanity defence in recent years, to include offenders afflicted with conditions such as epilepsy (*Sullivan* [1984] AC 156), diabetes (*Hennessy* [1989] 1 WLR 287) and somnambulism

(*Burgess* [1991] 1 QB 92). The 1991 Act broadens the options available to the Crown Court judge dealing with such cases so that the following options are available:

(a)   To make an order for admission to hospital. By sch. 1 to the 1991 Act, such order shall be equivalent to a hospital order made under MHA 1983, s. 37, to which there *may* be added a restriction under MHA 1983, s. 41, with or without limit of time. A restriction order without limit of time is, however, mandatory in cases where the charge brought against the defendant was murder.

(b)   To make a guardianship order (see **11.4**).

(c)   To make a supervision and treatment order. This order is very similar to a probation order with a requirement of treatment for a mental condition (see **11.1**) though there are minor differences. A supervision and treatment order may be made only on the evidence of two doctors (rather than one, in the case of a probation order) that the defendant's mental condition is such that it requires and may be susceptible to treatment but does not warrant the making of a hospital or guardianship order. The order requires the defendant to be under supervision for a period specified in the order of not more than two years (the maximum duration of a probation order is three years) and, during that period or a specific part of it, to submit to medical treatment, whether as a resident patient, a non-resident patient, or otherwise, with a view to the improvement of his mental condition. Such an order may also include residence requirements.

(d)   To make an order for the defendant's absolute discharge (see **7.1.1**). In *Bromley* 15 January 1992 (unreported) the defendant suffered from brain damage which could induce him to act violently after consuming a small amount of alcohol. On a charge of attempted rape, he was found not guilty by reason of insanity and was given an absolute discharge.

Section 37(3) of MHA 1983 gives power to magistrates' courts to make a hospital order (or guardianship order) in a case where such a court is satisfied that a person charged before it with an offence is suffering from mental illness or severe mental impairment and the court is satisfied that the person did the act or made the omission charged, without proceeding to conviction. This provision gives magistrates' courts a power which is rather similar to the Crown Court's powers to return a special verdict of not guilty by reason of insanity, or to make a finding that the accused is unfit to plead. Neither of these powers is available in the magistrates' courts, although it was confirmed in *Horseferry Road Magistrates' Court, ex parte K* [1996] 2 Cr App R 574 that a defence of insanity, leading to a clear acquittal rather than a special verdict, is available in the summary courts. The power in s. 37(3) should be very sparingly used (see *Lincoln (Kesteven) Justices, ex parte O'Connor* [1983] 1 WLR 335 and *Ramsgate Justices, ex parte Kazmarek* (1984) 80 Cr App R 366). If a magistrates' court makes such an order, the person so dealt with has the same right of appeal to the Crown Court as if he was appealing against conviction and sentence (MHA 1983, s. 45(1)). In 1991 magistrates' courts exercised their powers under MHA 1983, s. 37(3) in 64 cases. In 52 of those a hospital order was made and in the remainder a guardianship order was made; 11 defendants were placed under the guardianship of a relative or other named individual and in one case the guardian was the local authority.

12   Sentencing for a Range of Offences

'What sentence will I get if I am convicted of this offence?' asks the defendant before the trial. 'Is it worth appealing against this?' asks the offender after he has been sentenced. These commonly asked and very natural questions prompt a third: to what extent can the general principles of sentencing (discussed in Chapter 2 of this book) and Court of Appeal decisions be used to predict either the sentence which will be imposed on an offender or his chances of appealing successfully against whatever sentence has been imposed upon him?

The great majority of Court of Appeal sentencing decisions do *not* generate binding precedents since they turn, not upon a point of law, but upon an assessment by the Court of Appeal of the proper exercise of sentencing discretion in the particular circumstances of the offender and the offence which were before the court. These circumstances will not be precisely duplicated in any later case. The fact that few sentencing cases involve a point of law explains why for all practical purposes the Court of Appeal sits at the apex of the sentencing appeal hierarchy. Leave to appeal to the House of Lords is given only where there is a point of law of general public importance. Even in the bulk of Court of Appeal decisions that turn on their particular facts, however, the Court of Appeal will be influenced by what it has done in comparable cases in the past. While the maxim that 'all cases are different' is a truism, it is an unhelpful one in this context, and can turn out merely to be an excuse for a lack of principle in sentence decision-making.

The main approach is to point to sentencing principles and sentencing brackets which have a coherent rationale and which help to identify important common features amongst sentencing cases. Not without some resistance, the sentencing courts are coming to appreciate the importance of a common approach to sentencing which, if followed through, may help to tackle the pervasive problems of sentencing disparity. Two important developments in recent years have been the introduction of a more consistent rationale in sentencing decision-making, through the implementation of the CJA 1991 and the production by the Court of Appeal of 'guideline judgments' which take the opportunity of a particular sentencing appeal to travel well beyond the facts of the instant case and give guidance to sentencers on the proper general approach to sentencing in, for example, rape cases, robbery cases, or burglary cases. As was explained above, however, most Court of Appeal sentencing decisions are *not* guideline judgments. They are decisions made on particular facts, given in extempore form by appeal judges working under great pressure of time. Even in these cases, however, senior judges for the most part now recognise the importance of consistency of approach and therefore welcome reference being made by lawyers to earlier Court of Appeal cases. Taking these earlier cases into account, therefore, one may advise on the likely outcome of an appeal, with a reasonable measure of confidence.

The purpose of this chapter is to indicate the approach which has been approved by the Court of Appeal to sentencing in a wide variety of commonly encountered criminal offences. Where a guideline judgement has been issued in respect of a particular offence, prominence is given to that judgment. Whether or not there has been a guideline judgment, reference is then made to a sample of Court of Appeal decisions in relation to the particular offence. These decisions, taken together, often suggest a 'sentencing bracket', within which most examples of sentencing for a particular offence should fall, or suggest different brackets for different forms of that offence. The range within these sentencing brackets is not, and cannot be, a matter of precise formulation. Indeed the Court of Appeal will usually intervene and change a sentence on appeal only if it regards it as being wrong in principle, manifestly excessive or manifestly lenient. The normal upper and lower limits to the sentencing bracket can often, however, be gleaned from these decisions, as can important aggravating and mitigating factors which should be borne in mind by the sentencer when dealing with the offence.

When reading the material in this chapter, however, a number of very important considerations must be borne in mind:

(a)   Until changes were made by the CJA 1988, the offender, but not the prosecution, had a right to appeal to the Court of Appeal against a sentence imposed by the Crown Court. A limited right of prosecution appeal was introduced in 1988 (see **13.8**). It remains the fact, however, that most appeals against sentence are brought by offenders, and that most Court of Appeal decisions involve offences at the very serious end of the spectrum of criminal offending. In consequence there is plenty of Court of Appeal guidance on sentencing for offences like manslaughter, rape, and robbery, but hardly any guidance on the proper sentencing bracket for offences like careless driving, taking vehicles without the owner's authority, the less serious assaults and criminal damage. Of course most of these offences are normally dealt with in magistrates' courts, where there is a right of appeal by the offender (but not the prosecution) to the Crown Court. Unfortunately appellate advice to magistrates from the Crown Court is rarely very detailed, is not reported in the law reports and so cannot be included in a book like this one. Important advice and guidance on sentencing matters is available to magistrates, however, in the form of the Magistrates' Association Guidelines, the latest version of which was published in 1997. Reference is made to these Guidelines where appropriate in what follows.

(b)   The coming into force of the CJA 1991 in October 1992 had a significant impact on the proper approach to sentencing for a number of the offences covered in this chapter. Any earlier decisions which are referred to should, therefore, always be read in the light of the statutory sentencing structure and sentencing principles put in place by that Act (see further Chapter 2). In particular, it should be remembered that:

(i)   the imposition of a custodial sentence now requires justification in accordance with the terms of CJA 1991, s. 1(2), its length requires justification in terms of CJA 1991, s. 2(2), and the imposition of any community order requires justification in terms of CJA 1991, s. 6(1); and

(ii)   the length of custodial sentences indicated in all earlier cases, including the guideline judgments, will require adjustment in the light of the Lord Chief Justice's *Practice Statement (Crime: Sentencing)* [1992] 1 WLR 948 on early release and custodial sentence length (see **4.5.3**); and

(iii)   where sentence imposed by the Crown Court judge has been increased by the Court of Appeal following an Attorney-General's reference, it cannot be assumed that the sentence substituted by the appellate court is the sentence which it was right for the Crown Court judge to have passed, since the Court of Appeal reduces the new sentence by an (often unspecified) amount, to take into account the fact that the offender has had to suffer the anguish of being sentenced twice (see further **13.3**).

(c)   Since Court of Appeal guidance tends to relate mainly to the most serious offences, and often to rather untypical cases, reference is made in numerous places in this chapter to material from the *Criminal Statistics for England and Wales* which, in their Supplementary Volumes, provide an overview of the actual sentencing practice of Crown Courts and magistrates' courts. It will be seen that the generality of sentencing is often at a more lenient level than that which is indicated by the Court of Appeal. This may be to some extent because the Court of Appeal is simply 'out of touch', but it should be remembered that the Court of Appeal will reduce a sentence only where it is regarded as manifestly excessive. This often leads to appellate approval of a broad sentencing bracket, with the upper end considerably above the level of sentence the average Crown Court judge is likely to impose.

12.1   SENTENCING FOR HOMICIDE AND RELATED OFFENCES

12.1.1   Murder

Murder carries a mandatory penalty of life imprisonment (Murder (Abolition of Death Penalty) Act 1965, s. 1(1)). Where the murder is committed by a person aged 18 but less than 21, the mandatory sentence is custody for life (CJA 1982, s. 8(1)). If murder is committed by a person aged under 18, the mandatory sentence is detention during Her Majesty's Pleasure (CYPA 1933, s. 53(1)). In 1996 257 offenders were sentenced for murder, of whom 251 were men and 6 were women. Of this total, 201 received the mandatory life sentence, 24 received custody for life and 26 were dealt with under the CYPA 1933. The offence of attempted murder carries a discretionary life sentence; 56 people were sentenced for attempted murder in 1996, of whom 48 received immediate custody, three received hospital orders, there was one suspended sentence, three probation orders and one community service order.

For the procedures which determine the date of the release of an offender convicted of murder see **4.5.2**.

12.1.2   Manslaughter: diminished responsibility

By the Offences against the Person Act 1861 (OAPA 1861), the maximum penalty for manslaughter is life imprisonment (s. 5). The offence is triable only on indictment. The Crown Court sentenced 22 cases of manslaughter by diminished responsibility in 1996. Fourteen offenders received hospital orders (eight with restrictions) and seven received immediate custody. One case was otherwise dealt with.

In *Chambers* (1983) 5 Cr App R (S) 190 Leonard J explained that in diminished responsibility cases there are various courses open to a judge. If the psychiatric reports recommend and justify it and there are no contrary indications, a hospital order may well be the right sentence. Where a hospital order is not recommended, or is not appropriate, and the defendant constitutes a danger to the public for an unpredictable period of time, the right sentence will, in all probability, be one of life imprisonment. In cases where the evidence indicates that the accused's responsibility for his acts was so grossly impaired that his degree of responsibility for them was minimal, then a lenient course will be open. Provided there is no danger of repetition of violence, it will usually be possible to make such an order as will give the accused his freedom, such as a probation order. There will however be cases where there is no proper basis for a hospital order, but in which the accused's degree of responsibility is not minimal. Then the judge should pass a determinate sentence of imprisonment, the length of which will depend on two factors: the degree of the accused's responsibility and the period of time, if any, for which the accused will continue to be a danger to the public.

An example of a case falling within the first category in *Chambers* is *Courtney* (1987) 9 Cr App R (S) 404. In that case the offender pleaded guilty to the manslaughter of his wife, whom he had strangled after a domestic argument. He immediately tried to revive her and to summon help. The offender had been undergoing treatment for depression and the medical witnesses agreed that the offender was suffering from depression to a degree which warranted his detention in hospital for treatment. The Court of Appeal, taking account of the medical advice that the offender did not represent a risk to other members of the public and that his depression could be cured within a year, varied a restriction order under s. 41 of the MHA 1983 to a hospital order under s. 37 of that Act. See further the decision in *Birch* (1989) 11 Cr App R (S) 202, where the criteria for deciding between a hospital order, a life sentence and a determinate custodial sentence were discussed. A life sentence was upheld in *Sanderson* (1994) 15 Cr App R (S) 263, where the offender was a man with a long history of drug addiction and violence towards women. He had battered his girlfriend to death. The period specified under s. 34 of the Criminal Justice Act 1991 was eight years (see **4.5.2**).

In the second category of case is *Sangha* [1997] 1 Cr App R (S) 262 where the offender had suffered physical and mental cruelty and abuse from her husband over a period of 22 years. She had made several attempts at suicide. Following discovery that the husband had been having an affair she took an overdose, but subsequently discharged herself from hospital and the following day stabbed her husband. He died four days later during which time the offender stabbed herself, causing minor injury. The medical evidence was that she was suffering from depressive illness and was subject to acute stress reaction. A sentence of 18 months' imprisonment was varied by the Court of Appeal to a probation order for three years, although by that time the offender had served five months of her sentence.

An example of the third type of case is *Leggett* [1996] 2 Cr App R (S) 77, where the appellant pleaded guilty to the manslaughter of her 14-month-old child. Psychiatric reports indicated that the offender had an immature personality disorder and that at the time of the killing she was in a state of emotional turmoil brought about by her separation from the child's father and her irrational fear that the child would be taken from her, together with the fact that the child would not stop crying. The medical advice was that the offender was unlikely to reoffend and that detention in a psychiatric institution might not alleviate her condition. The Court of Appeal regretted that a hospital order could not be made, but said that since the offender retained a degree of responsibility for the killing there had to be an element of retribution and deterrence. A prison sentence of four years was upheld. See also *Yeomans* (1988) 10 Cr App R (S) 63 (eight years' imprisonment reduced to five where a man drowned his 18-month-old daughter in the sea while suffering from acute reactive depression), *Michael* (1993) 15 Cr App R (S) 265 and *Bourne* (1994) 16 Cr App R (S) 237.

12.1.3 Manslaughter: provocation

The maximum penalty for manslaughter is life imprisonment (OAPA 1861, s. 5). The offence is triable only on indictment. The *Criminal Statistics* do not provide separate figures for sentences imposed for manslaughter under provocation. For manslaughter due to diminished responsibility see **12.1.2** and for other forms of manslaughter see **12.1.5**.

The usual sentencing bracket is three to seven years, but longer sentences are sometimes upheld. In *Attorney-General's Reference (No. 33 of 1996)* [1997] 2 Cr App R (S) 10 the Court of Appeal said that when an offender went out armed with a weapon and used it to cause death, even where there had been provocation, seven years was too low. Much shorter sentences may be appropriate in exceptional cases (e.g. *Dimasi* (1981) 3 Cr App R (S) 146, where a man of exemplary character killed his daughter after intervening in a domestic argument and under severe provocation). What is the appropriate punishment in these cases seems to turn upon the amount of provocation present, any opportunity there was for 'cooling off' before the fatal injury was caused, the extent to which the offender was at fault in bringing about the situation in the first place and the means used to kill the victim. According to Shaw LJ in *Bancroft*:

> notwithstanding that a man's reason might be unseated on the basis that the reasonable man would have found himself out of control, there is still in every human being a residual capacity for self-control which the exigencies of a given situation may call for; that must be the justification for passing a sentence of imprisonment, to recognise that there is still some degree of culpability.

Lord Lane CJ commented in *Taylor* (1987) 9 Cr App R (S) 175 that sentencing in provocation cases was 'an almost impossible task' but that the sentencer should have two objects in view. These were 'to ensure that the criminal expiates his offence' (almost always requiring immediate custody) and to 'provide a lesson to other people that they should keep their tempers and not be provoked'. The task of the judge then is to determine what the least period is which will reflect those two matters.

A situation giving rise to particular difficulty in sentencing is that of so-called 'cumulative' provocation, where the offender has killed the victim after a prolonged period of violence or abuse. In *Gardner* (1993) 14 Cr App R (S) 364 the offender had lived together with the victim for five years, during which time the victim had subjected her to violence on many occasions. The offender had stabbed the deceased with a kitchen knife, after both of them had consumed a good deal of drink. There had been an argument and the deceased had assaulted her by banging her head on a door. Psychiatric evidence was received that the offender was in a 'cumulative state of exhaustion, hopelessness, helplessness and depression, these features being charactertic of what has been described as battered-woman syndrome'. In the light of this evidence, the Court of Appeal substituted a probation order for the original sentence of five years' imprisonment. By the time of the hearing of the appeal the offender had served the equivalent of 18 months in custody, and the case should not be taken as saying that a probation order would have been the correct original sentence for the offence. The case may be contrasted with *Harrison* (1992) 13 Cr App R (S) 40 where the offender and the victim had lived together for ten years, during which time the victim had 'taken control' of the offender's life, dictating how she should dress and not allowing her to leave the house on her own. She had been subjected to violent sexual acts, some of which were carried out in front of the children. The offender paid a man £15,000 to kill her husband and this was planned and carried out, with the offender present when the victim was strangled. The Court of Appeal upheld a sentence of seven years, stating that 'considerable though the provocation undoubtedly was . . . no-one, however desperate their plight, is entitled deliberately to plan the execution of another human being'.

12.1.4 Manslaughter: suicide pact

The maximum penalty for manslaughter is life imprisonment (OAPA 1861, s. 5). The offence is triable only on indictment.

The offender in *Sweeney* (1986) 8 Cr App R (S) 419 pleaded guilty to the manslaughter of his wife. He was prone to depression and had married the deceased when she was suffering from advanced muscular dystrophy. They decided to commit suicide together by taking tablets and then setting fire to their car when they were inside it. Once the fire started both tried to escape, but the wife was killed. The offender suffered serious burns. The Court of Appeal reduced a four-year prison term to one of two years, that being 'sufficient, in our judgment, to mark the seriousness of this matter'.

12.1.5 Involuntary manslaughter

The maximum penalty for manslaughter is life imprisonment (OAPA 1861, s. 5). The offence is triable only on indictment. The *Criminal Statistics* show that the Crown Court passed sentence in cases of manslaughter (other than manslaughter due to diminished responsibility) in 232 cases in 1996. Of those, 211 received immediate custodial sentences and there were three suspended sentences. Thirteen hospital orders were imposed (five with restrictions), and the remaining five cases were dealt with by probation order or supervision order.

These offences vary very widely in culpability and circumstances, since they cover the full range of homicide between murder and accidental death. Unless there are 'outstandingly serious features' a sentence in excess of ten years is rare (*Barrell* (1992) 13 Cr App R (S) 646). The main difficulty in sentencing for manslaughter is to gain an appropriate balance between a sentence which is properly reflective of the offender's culpability (which in some cases may be low) but which also marks the fact that a life has been taken. The Court of Appeal authorities are not consistent, but the general approach seems to be to assess the sentence which would have been appropriate if death had not occurred, and then to add on something to reflect the fact that a person was killed (see *Paget* (1982) 4 Cr App R (S) 399).

In manslaughter arising from fights, according to Cumming-Bruce LJ in *Stuart* (1979) 1 Cr App R (S) 228, 'English law has always regarded the causing of the death of a man as an offence of great gravity, although the circumstances in which death is caused are manifestly relevant to assessing the degree of criminal responsibility and wickedness.' A sentence of four years was reduced to two years in that case, where the offender, in the course of a fight, had pushed the victim down some steps where he had fallen and fractured his skull. In *Cenci* (1989) 11 Cr App R (S) 199, following an incident of domestic violence between a man and a woman living together, the woman climbed out of a window to escape, but fell to her death. Ten years' imprisonment was reduced to five. Some general indications of sentencing in this type of case, following a review of the earlier authorities, were given in *Coleman* (1991) 11 Cr App R (S) 159. Lord Lane CJ said that, in a case of involuntary manslaughter where the victim was felled by a blow, cracked his head on the floor or pavement, suffered a skull fracture and died, the starting point for sentence on a plea of guilty was 12 months. Relevant mitigating factors would be absence of premeditation, the fact that the injury resulted from a single blow of moderate force, remorse, and an immediate admission of guilt. Aggravating factors would include a history of violent behaviour, the fact that the assault was gratuitous or unprovoked, and the fact that more than one blow had been struck. Another example is *Bryant* (1993) 14 Cr App R (S) 621.

Cases where there had been an accidental fall resulting in a fracture of the skull had to be distinguished from more serious cases where a victim on the ground had been kicked about the head or where a weapon had been used. An example is *Silver* (1994) 15 Cr App R (S) 836. In *Shelton* (1979) 1 Cr App R (S) 202, an exceptional case, the Court of Appeal said that a custodial sentence should not have been imposed where two brothers, both in their sixties had fought following a family quarrel. The offender had fallen on the victim, injuring him with his knee. The victim failed to take medical advice and died three days later.

In cases of manslaughter involving firearms, again much depends on the circumstances, particularly the degree of planning in the use of the firearm. In *O'Mahoney* (1980) 2 Cr App R (S) 57 a sentence of fifteen years was upheld. The offender and two other men had set out to find a fourth man to give him a beating, having first obtained a pistol and some ammunition. Although they did not find the man they were looking for, the pistol was subsequently fired on two occasions on that same day and then a completely innocent man was shot in the chest at close range and killed after an argument at a club. Eveleigh J said that it was proper to take account of the whole day's events in fixing the sentence: 'This is not the case of a man who, having taken drink, is suddenly in possession of a firearm and then carelessly, because of drink, fires it.' This may be compared with *Wesson* (1989) 11 Cr App R (S) 161, a case of reckless manslaughter, where a sentence of seven years was reduced to two years. The offender had been cleaning his shotgun, waving it about but saying that it was unloaded, and it had gone off, killing his wife.

In cases where manslaughter is committed in the course of the commission of another offence, such as burglary, robbery or arson, the Court of Appeal has held that the sentence should not be the same as would have been imposed for the lesser offence and according to Russell LJ in *Daly* (1994) 16 Cr App R (S) 777, 'loss of life, however unintended, is a very serious aggravating feature of dangerous and unlawful behaviour'. In *Tominey* (1986) 8 Cr App R (S) 161, a case of manslaughter of a security guard in the course of an armed robbery, it was said that the proper approach was to determine 'in relation to each of these appellants what is the proper sentence for the enterprise taken as a whole'. Sentences of 22 years, 18 years and 17 years were, however, each reduced by four years. Again, a great deal depends on the precise circumstances of the killing. In *Cook* (1982) 4 Cr App R (S) 237, where a manslaughter by stabbing in the course of a burglary was described as 'close to being accidental', six years' was appropriate, while ten years' was proper in *Wood* (1984) 6 Cr App R (S) 139, where the offenders had broken into the home of an elderly lady and had left her with her eyes and mouth covered with sticking plaster and had tied her to the bed. In *Palma* (1986) 8 Cr App R (S) 148 the offender pleaded guilty to manslaughter, arson being reckless whether life was endangered and theft. He had been dismissed from his employment and sought revenge by pouring petrol through the letterbox of the person who had caused his dismissal and starting a fire. The son of his intended victim died in the fire. A sentence of 12 years was upheld, Lawton LJ saying that 'this was as bad a case of manslaughter as it is possible to have, short of murder'.

Manslaughter of a young child normally attracts a custodial sentence between two and eight years, depending upon the degree of culpability. A sentence at the top end of the range was upheld in *Ali* (1988) 10 Cr App R (S) 59, where the victim was a four-year-old child who had been maltreated over a lengthy period and died of a fractured skull; the child was found to have had a number of other fractures caused on various other occasions. In *Bashford* (1988) 10 Cr App R (S) 359 the child died from being shaken violently after persistent crying, and there was no evidence of violence used on any other occasion. Stocker LJ commented that 'it is not really disputed that a custodial sentence, and an immediate one, was the only course open . . . the sentence [of two years] appears to be, if anything, at the bottom limit'. See also *Staynor* [1996] 1 Cr App R (S) 376, where the offender struck his baby daughter twice, fracturing her skull. Three years' imprisonment was upheld.

There are few appellate cases dealing with reckless manslaughter, as opposed to manslaughter by unlawful act. One example is *Morgan* (1990) 12 Cr App R (S) 504. The offender, an engine driver, inexplicably ignored yellow and red track warning signals with the result that his train crashed into another. Five people were killed and 87 were injured. He pleaded guilty and was a person of good character, and there was no suggestion that he had been drinking. The Court of Appeal reduced a sentence of 18 months (with six months immediate and the balance suspended) to one of four months, saying that prison could achieve nothing in this case and that the crime would trouble the offender's conscience for the rest of his life. Another is *Kite* [1996] 2 Cr App R (S) 295, where two years' imprisonment was appropriate for the manager of a company which organised canoeing trips for young people. As a result of poor safety standards, four youngsters were drowned.

12.1.6 Child destruction, infanticide and abortion

The maximum penalty for child destruction, infanticide and procuring an illegal abortion is, in each case, life imprisonment (Infant Life (Preservation) Act 1929, s. 1, Infanticide Act 1938, s. 1 and OAPA 1861, s. 58). These offences are triable only on indictment.

The proper approach for sentencing in cases of infanticide was considered by the Court of Appeal in *Sainsbury* (1989) 11 Cr App R (S) 533. The offender had become pregnant at the age of 15. She did not tell anyone about this, and gave birth to the baby without medical assistance in the bathroom of her boyfriend's flat. The baby was then wrapped in a blanket, taken some distance away and drowned in a river. The sentencer accepted that the balance of the offender's mind was disturbed by the effect of giving birth and that she was very immature, but did not accept that her responsibility was removed altogether. He imposed a sentence of 12 months' detention in a young offender institution. The Court of Appeal, however, having regard to statistics which indicated that of 59 cases of infanticide dealt with between 1979 and 1988 there had been no custodial sentences (all offenders having been dealt with by way of probation, supervision or hospital orders), decided that although the offence was serious the mitigating factors were overwhelming, and varied the sentence to probation. See also *Lewis* (1989) 11 Cr App R (S) 457. The 1996 statistics confirm this sentencing pattern. Of the four offenders dealt with for infanticide, all were given probation orders.

12.1.7 Complicity in suicide

The maximum penalty for aiding suicide is 14 years' imprisonment (Suicide Act 1961, s. 2).

In *Hough* (1984) 6 Cr App R (S) 406 Lord Lane CJ commented that this crime could vary 'from the borders of cold-blooded murder down to the shadowy area of mercy killing or common humanity'. In that case a prison term of nine months was upheld on a 60-year-old woman of unblemished character who had been a regular visitor to an 84-year-old woman who was partly blind, partly deaf and suffered from arthritis. The old lady had persisted in various statements to the effect that she intended to take her own life and the offender eventually supplied her with tablets. When she became unconscious, the offender placed a plastic bag over her head. In *Wallis* (1983) 5 Cr App R (S) 342 a sentence of 12 months' imprisonment was described by the Court of Appeal as 'at the extreme of leniency' in a case where the offender pleaded guilty to aiding the suicide of a 17-year-old flatmate by buying her tablets and alcohol, sitting with her while she took the tablets and not calling an ambulance until she was dead. The case of *McGranaghan* (1987) 9 Cr App R (S) 447 was dealt with much more severely. The offender, who was serving a prison sentence and sharing a cell with another prisoner who suffered from physical disabilities, persuaded the other prisoner to attempt suicide. The offender made a noose from a sheet and helped the victim to climb onto a cupboard and jump with the noose round his neck. The victim survived. Despite a guilty plea, and evidence of remorse, a sentence of eight years was upheld for aiding and abetting attempted suicide. The Crown Court sentenced just one case of aiding suicide in 1996, for which a probation order was imposed.

12.1.8 Causing death by dangerous driving

The maximum penalty for causing death by dangerous driving is ten years (RTA 1988, s. 1 and sch. 2). It carries a one-year minimum disqualification from driving (RTA 1988, s. 34 and sch. 2). It is triable only on indictment. In 1996, 215 offenders were sentenced for causing death by dangerous driving; of those, 163 received immediate custody, 26 were given community service, 15 were fined, there were eight suspended sentences, two combination orders and one probation order.

The Guideline case on this offence is *Boswell* (1984) 6 Cr App R (S) 257 (although at the time of that decision the offence was causing death by 'reckless driving' and the maximum penalty was only five years). According to Lord Lane CJ, the following matters, among others, may be regarded as aggravating features:

(a) the consumption of alcohol or drugs, which may range from a couple of drinks to what was described by the Court of Appeal in *Wheatley* (1982) 4 Cr App R (S) 371 as a 'motorised pub crawl';

(b) competitive driving against another vehicle on the public highway, and/or grossly excessive speed and/or showing off;

(c) the driver having disregarded warnings from his passengers;

(d) a prolonged, persistent and deliberate course of very bad driving;

(e) committing other offences at the same time, including related offences, such as driving without ever having had any licence, driving while disqualified, driving whilst a learner driver without a supervising driver;

(f) previous convictions for motoring offences, particularly offences which involve bad driving or offences involving the consumption of excessive alcohol before driving;

(g) several people having been killed as a result of the particular incident of reckless driving;

(h) aggravating behaviour at the time of the offence, for example, failing to stop or, even more reprehensible, trying to throw off the victim from the bonnet of the car by swerving in order to escape;

(i) causing death in the course of reckless driving carried out in an attempt to avoid detection or apprehension.

According to *Boswell* the mitigating features may be numbered as follows:

(a) where the piece of reckless driving might be described as a 'one-off', i.e. a momentary reckless error of judgment, such as briefly dozing off at the wheel or failing to notice a pedestrian on a crossing;

(b)   a good driving record;

(c)   good character;

(d)   a plea of guilty;

(e)   sometimes the effect on the defendant, if he is genuinely remorseful and/or if he is genuinely shocked;

(f)   where the victim was either a close relative of the defendant or a close friend and the consequent emotional shock is great.

If there are no aggravating features present, a non-custodial penalty may well be appropriate, but where aggravating features are, or an aggravating feature is, present then a custodial sentence is generally necessary. Drivers who indulge in racing on the highway and/or drive with reckless disregard for the safety of others after taking alcohol, should, according to Lord Lane, lose their liberty for five years or more (the figure in the original case was 'two years or more', but this has since been adjusted because of the increase in the maximum penalty: see *Attorney-General's Reference (Nos. 12 and 24 of 1993)* (1993) 15 Cr App R (S) 640). It will seldom be that a community service order or a suspended sentence will be appropriate in a serious case. That type of driver should, according to Lord Lane, be removed from the road for a long period of disqualification. *Boswell* states that there is a distinction to be drawn, so far as disqualification is concerned, between cases of driving while disqualified and similar offences where there is no question of bad driving, and cases where the essence of the crime is the manner of the driving on the occasion in question. In the latter case, where the driver has shown himself to be a menace to others using the highway, he should be debarred from driving for a substantial length of time; in a bad case, seven to ten years will not be too long.

Examples where the offence was committed by a driver affected by alcohol are *Attorney-General's Reference (No. 22 of 1994)* (1994) 16 Cr App R (S) 670 (where the custodial sentence was increased from 15 months to five years in a case where the amount of drink taken was very high and two people were killed), and *Attorney-General's Reference (No. 48 of 1996)* [1997] 2 Cr App R (S) 46 (two years' imprisonment increased to four years where the offender drank seven pints of stout and was driving his car with five passengers when he struck another car killing one of the passengers; disqualification increased to four years). Examples where the offence was committed after the offender drove at excessive speed are *Attorney-General's Reference (No. 67 of 1995)* [1996] 2 Cr Ap R (S) 373 (where the offender, on bail at the time for an offence of aggravated vehicle taking, stole a car from a car park and raced it on the highway, colliding with another car and killing the driver, five years was increased to seven years after a contested case) and *Attorney-General's Reference (No. 6 of 1996)* [1997] 1 Cr App R (S) 79 (where the offender, who admitted driving at 45 m.p.h. in a built-up area in the early hours of the morning, had struck a woman on a crossing and killed her, a nine-month sentence was increased to 21 months; four-year disqualification unchanged). Other cases involve drivers who have fallen asleep at the wheel (*de Meersman* [1997] 1 Cr App R (S) 106: three years' imprisonment and four years' disqualification upheld) and offenders using vehicles which they know to be in a dangerous condition (*Kang* [1997] 1 Cr App R (S) 306: lorry with seriously defective brakes went out of control and killed a person sitting in a stationary car, where 30 months' imprisonment together with disqualification for four years was upheld). Finally, *Moore* [1997] 2 Cr App R (S) 239 was a case of momentary inattention by the driver, who was looking at a road map on the dashboard when he ran into the back of a stationary car, killing the driver. Six months' imprisonment was reduced to two months.

12.1.9 Threats to kill

The maximum penalty for making threats to kill is ten years (CLA 1977, sch. 12, replacing OAPA 1861, s. 16). The maximum penalty for solicitation of murder is life imprisonment (OAPA 1861, s. 4). The offences are triable only on indictment. The 1996 statistics indicate that 241 offenders were dealt with for making threats to kill or for conspiracy to murder in that year. Of that total, 146 received immediate custody, 17 received suspended sentences, 44 received probation orders, nine received hospital orders and there were a number of other disposals, including two conditional discharges.

Sentences approved by the Court of Appeal for making threats to kill range downwards from the five years' imprisonment upheld in *Bowden* (1986) 8 Cr App R (S) 155, where the offender, who was receiving treatment for alcoholism, went to the home of a woman with whom he had formerly lived and threatened her with a sword. The woman barricaded herself in the bedroom and the police had to force their way into the house to arrest the offender. The court heard evidence that the offender had a large collection of weapons which he intended to use against a list of people, headed by his ex-girlfriend. In *Martin* (1993) 14 Cr App R (S) 645 four years' imprisonment was reduced to three years where the offender sent two anonymous notes stained with blood to the victim.

As far as solicitation of murder is concerned, in *Raw* (1983) 5 Cr App R (S) 229, where the offender attempted to contact someone who would murder his wife for a fee of £2,000, the Court of Appeal said that a prison sentence of seven years was 'the minimum sentence, regardless of the fact of the personality and circumstances of the appellant, that would constitute a proper deterrent'. This case was followed in *Peatfield* (1985) 7 Cr App R (S) 132, where a prison sentence of ten years was upheld on an offender who offered to pay a man £5,000 to murder his wife and ten-year-old daughter. Where a man solicited another to murder a political opponent, a 12-year term was held to be correct (*Gill* (1988) 10 Cr App R (S) 373).

12.2 SENTENCING FOR NON-FATAL OFFENCES AGAINST THE PERSON

The following table shows the types of sentence which were imposed on offenders sentenced for indictable offences involving violence against the person in 1996:

absolute or conditional discharge:	16 per cent
probation order:	10 per cent
supervision order:	3 per cent
fine:	13 per cent
community service order:	14 per cent
combination order:	5 per cent
attendance centre order:	3 per cent
detention in YOI:	8 per cent
immediate imprisonment:	23 per cent
suspended imprisonment:	2 per cent
other:	3 per cent

12.2.1 Assault and battery

The maximum penalty for common assault and battery is six months' imprisonment, a fine not exceeding level 5 on the standard scale, or both (CJA 1988, s. 39). Assault and battery are triable only summarily. In 1996, 18,762 cases of common assault were sentenced by magistrates. Of those, 1,506 received custody. The most frequent disposals were the discharge (6,687) and the fine (4,598). Just over 900 cases were otherwise dealt with (mainly bind over, or compensation order alone).

The Magistrates' Association Guidelines (1997) state the following:

Aggravating Factors +
racial motivation, group action, offender in position of authority, premeditated, injury, weapon, victim particularly vulnerable, victim public servant, offence committed on bail, previous convictions and failures to respond to previous sentences, if relevant.

Mitigating Factors −
impulsive, minor injury, provocation, single blow.

The Guidelines state that magistrates should consider whether the offence is serious enough for a community penalty.

In *Fenton* (1994) 15 Cr App R (S) 682 the offender had pushed another motorist in the chest in the course of an altercation on the road. The Court of Appeal said that the appropriate sentence was 7 days' imprisonment.

12.2.2 Assault on a police officer

The maximum penalty for assault on a constable in the execution of his duty is six months' imprisonment, a fine not exceeding level 5, or both (Police Act 1996, s. 89). The offence is triable only summarily. In 1996, 10,643 cases of assault on a police officer were sentenced by magistrates. Of those, 1,254 received custody. The most frequent other disposals were fine (4,277), community service (1,182) and probation (1,040).

The Magistrates' Association Guidelines (1997) indicate the following:

Aggravating Factors +
any injuries caused, gross disregard for police authority, group action, premeditated, offence committed on bail, previous convictions and failures to respond to previous sentences, if relevant.

Mitigating Factors −
impulsive action, unaware that victim was PC.

The Guidelines state that magistrates should consider whether the offence is so serious that only custody is appropriate.

See also the sentencing considerations for assault occasioning actual bodily harm at **12.2.3**.

12.2.3 Assault occasioning actual bodily harm

The maximum penalty for assault occasioning actual bodily harm on indictment is five years' imprisonment (OAPA 1861, s. 47): on summary conviction, the maximum penalty is six months, a fine not exceeding level 5, or both.

The *Practice Note* (*Mode of Trial: Guidelines*) (1995) indicate that the following matters are relevant to determining mode of trial:

(1) The use of weapon of a kind likely to cause serious injury.

(2) A weapon is used and serious injury is caused.

(3) More than minor injury is caused by kicking, head-butting or similar forms of assault.

(4) Serious violence is caused to those whose work has to be done in contact with the public (e.g. police officers, bus drivers, taxi drivers, publicans and shopkeepers).

(5) Violence to vulnerable people (e.g., the elderly and infirm).

The same considerations apply to cases of domestic violence.

The Magistrates' Association Guidelines (1997) indicate the following:

Aggravating Factors +
    racial motivation, deliberate kicking or biting, extensive injuries (may be psychiatric), group action, offender in position of authority, premeditated, victim particularly vulnerable, victim public servant, weapon, offence committed on bail, previous convictions and failures to respond to previous sentences, if relevant.

Mitigating Factors −
    impulsive action, minor injury, provocation, single blow.

The Guidelines state that magistrates should consider whether the offence is so serious that only custody is appropriate.

Only a minority of sentences for assault occasioning actual bodily harm are custodial and, of those, most are for three months or less. Sentences of up to three years for this offence have, however, been upheld by the Court of Appeal where aggravating factors have been present or where the offence has been close to the borderline with the offence of wounding with intent. Heavier sentences will be imposed where the assault was committed against a police officer. In *McKenlay* (1979) 1 Cr App R (S) 161, when upholding a six-month prison term on the offender, a man of good character, who had punched and butted a police officer in the face in the course of an industrial dispute, Watkins J commented that a custodial sentence for 'an attack deliberately made upon a police officer inflicting upon him harm, no matter how slight it be, is never wrong in principle'. Two years' imprisonment was upheld in *Moore* (1993) 14 Cr App R (S) 273, where the offender misbehaved in a public house and, when two police officers arrived, one male and one female, he verbally abused and attacked them, causing numerous minor injuries by kicking and punching, and a custodial sentence of eight months was upheld in *Leather* (1993) 14 Cr App R (S) 736, where a 17-year-old woman had seized a police officer by the testicles, in order to prevent her boyfriend from being arrested. If it is not proved that the offender knew that the victim was a police officer, then the heavier sentence will not be appropriate (*Stosiek* (1982) 4 Cr App R (S) 205).

Other examples of cases where custodial sentences of more than three months may be proper are where a weapon is used by the offender and where the assault is committed upon a public servant (*Foster* (1982) 4 Cr App R (S) 101, where six months' detention was ordered for an assault by a youth on a bus conductor who had been cut on the head: see also *Tremlett* (1983) 5 Cr App R (S) 199). It will be an aggravating feature of the offence where the assault is committed at a football match, particularly against someone who was not involved in violence (*Birkin* (1988) 10 Cr App R (S) 303). In *Hassan* (1989) 11 Cr App R (S) 8 the Court of Appeal reduced a sentence of four months' imprisonment to two months on an offender who had punched another man after a dispute over who had priority to a car parking space. Lord Lane CJ said that normally such incidents could be dealt with by way of a fine, but that incidents involving drivers losing their tempers, getting out of their cars and striking other drivers or pedestrians were becoming too frequent. In *Arnold* [1996] 1 Cr App R (S) 115 it was said that an assault committed by one motorist on another was just as serious as an assault committed in other circumstances.

Examples of assaults committed in the course of competitive sporting matches are *Birkin* (1988) 10 Cr App R (S) 303, where the offender, after a late tackle by an opponent in a football match struck the victim and broke his jaw in two places (eight months' imprisonment reduced to six months on appeal) and *Davies* (1990) 12 Cr App R (S) 308 where the offender struck an opponent in the face and fractured his cheekbone, when tempers became frayed in a football match (six months' imprisonment upheld).

Assaults between spouses should not be treated more leniently than other assaults (*Nicholas* (1994) 15 Cr App R (S) 381). An offender convicted of assault committed by 'stalking' the victim over a four-year period received a custodial term of 21 months in *Smith* [1998] 1 Cr App R (S) 138.

12.2.4 Malicious wounding or inflicting grievous bodily harm

The maximum penalty for unlawfully and maliciously wounding or inflicting grievous bodily harm on indictment is five years (OAPA 1861, s. 20); on summary conviction, the maximum penalty is six months, a fine not exceeding level 5, or both.

The *Practice Note* (*Mode of Trial: Guidelines*) (1995) are the same for this offence as for assault occasioning actual bodily harm (see **12.2.3**). The Magistrates' Association Guidelines (1997) are also virtually identical.

Only a minority of sentences for malicious wounding are custodial but sentences of up to three years for this offence have been upheld by the Court of Appeal where aggravating factors have been present, or where the offence is close to the borderline with wounding with intent, or where it was committed against a police officer or other public servant, or a child. In *Fox* (1980) 2 Cr App R (S) 188 the offender, a bouncer at a club, lost his temper with a man who refused to leave and struck him in the face causing 'considerable injury'. Sentence was reduced from three years to 12 months. An unprovoked assault in a public house, by a man of previous good character on a man wearing glasses, thereby causing severe cuts in the region of his eye, merited six months' imprisonment in *Martin* (1981) 3 Cr App R (S) 39. In *Rogers* (1993) 15 Cr App R (S) 393 the offender head-butted an opposing player during an amateur soccer match, causing a displaced fracture of the cheekbone. Nine months' imprisonment was reduced to four months on appeal.

The use of a weapon is an important aggravating feature. In *Lachtay* (1982) 4 Cr App R (S) 229 the offender grabbed the victim at a party, accused him of insulting the offender's girlfriend, and struck him on the forehead with a bottle, causing a one inch cut. In the Court of Appeal Michael Davies J described the six-month sentence imposed as 'lenient; some would say it was very lenient'. In other cases of 'glassing', where more severe injury has been caused, longer sentences have been imposed. In *Jones* (1984) 6 Cr App R (S) 55, where the victim was struck in the face with a beer glass which, when it broke, was pushed into the victim's face, causing grave injury including the probable loss of sight in one eye, a sentence of two years was upheld. See also *Marsden* (1993) 15 Cr App R (S) 177. In *Bayes* (1994) 16 Cr App R (S) 290, after a driving incident, the offender attacked the other driver, punching him and striking him on the back with a hammer. Fifteen months' imprisonment was reduced to nine months to take account of personal mitigation and remorse.

A sentence of three years' imprisonment was upheld in *Moore* (1991) 13 Cr App R (S) 130, where the offender, after a disagreement with another man over the use of a telephone box, struck the victim and then kicked him about the head and body as he lay on the ground. The victim suffered serious facial injuries and was detained in hospital for two weeks.

12.2.5 Wounding with intent to do grievous bodily harm

The maximum penalty for wounding or causing grievous bodily harm with intent to do grievous bodily harm is life imprisonment (OAPA 1861, s. 18). Closely related offences, all punishable with a maximum of life, are attempting to choke, suffocate or strangle with intent (OAPA 1861, s. 21) and throwing corrosive fluid (OAPA 1861, s. 29). All are triable only on indictment.

The normal sentencing bracket is three to eight years, although sentences over eight years have been upheld in particularly grave cases. Relevant aggravating factors include extensive injuries, premeditation, use of a weapon and kicking or stamping on the victim. Relevant mitigating factors are a plea of guilty and previous good character of the offender, though these may be of little weight in very serious cases. Substantial provocation is also to be taken into account.

In a case involving stabbing, the Court of Appeal upheld a nine-year sentence in *Polley* [1997] 2 Cr App R (S) 356, where, after a disagreement over rent to be paid, the offender stabbed the victim several times with a kitchen knife, severing an artery in his arm. A term of seven-years was upheld on a 19-year-old in *Robinson* (1980) 2 Cr App R (S) 193, where the offender had accosted an older man and threatened him with a knife. When he refused to hand over any money, he was stabbed twice and could have died as a result of his injuries. In *Dunning* (1984) 6 Cr App R (S) 337, three years was upheld as 'the lowest sentence which could be passed' on an offender who called on his ex-wife and found her in the company of another man. He returned to the house later and stabbed the ex-wife in the stomach. The offender had a history of violence towards his ex-wife.

The use of other weapons will attract comparable sentences, depending upon the extent of the injuries, taken together with relevant mitigating and aggravating factors. In *Chesterman* (1984) 6 Cr App R (S) 151 a 12-year sentence was upheld on an offender who fired a shotgun twice at a police officer. The officer was permanently blinded and suffered other injuries. The offender was acquitted of attempted murder, but the case was described as 'at the very top of the scale for offences of causing grievous bodily harm with intent'. In *Craney* [1996] 2 Cr App R (S) 336 sentences of 11 years were proper for an unprovoked and racially motivated attack by two youths using a torch and iron bar, leaving the victim with severe head injuries and a badly broken leg. An axe was the weapon used in *Reilly* (1982) 4 Cr App R (S) 288. Six years was held to be proper in that case where a man, previously of good character, inflicted grave head injuries on his wife.

The Court of Appeal has considered cases of 'glassing' on several occasions. A sentence of five years was upheld in *James* (1981) 3 Cr App R (S) 223, where the offender attacked a shopkeeper with two broken milk bottles, pushing them into his face and cutting him very badly. The court described this as 'about as bad a case of . . . glassing as it is possible to imagine'. In *Harwood* (1979) 1 Cr App R (S) 354 Lord Lane CJ said that 'one cannot really recognise anything less than three years as being right for deliberate glassing', and exactly that sentence was upheld in the case of an 18-year-old who had been involved in a fight in a public house and had pushed a broken bottle into the victim's face. In *Attorney-General's Reference (No. 23 of 1990)* (1990) 12 Cr App R (S) 575 the offender, who was at a New Year's Eve party at a public house, struck the victim on the back of the head with a bottle, and then pushed the broken bottle into his cheek and towards his neck. A sentence of 18 months' imprisonment was said by the Court of Appeal to be 'undoubtedly excessively lenient'. The minimum appropriate sentence on the facts was said to be four years, and the sentence was so increased, though Lord Lane CJ noted that something less than four years might have been proper if the offender had pleaded guilty.

It is clear that an offender who causes grievous bodily harm by kicking or stamping on the victim's head while the latter is on the ground should receive a substantial custodial term. In *Ivey* (1981) 3 Cr App R (S) 185 a man of previous good character became caught up in a fracas in a club, during the course of which he knocked a man to the ground and stamped on his head, inflicting grave injuries to his face and skull. A four-year sentence was upheld, Griffiths LJ commenting that 'The degree of injury likely to be caused by kicking a man when he is down is of a wholly different degree to that which is likely to be suffered in the course of a fist fight.' Those comments have been approved in several later cases, including *Attorney-General's Reference (No. 59 of 1996)* [1997] 2 Cr App R (S) 250. In *Legge* (1988) 10 Cr App R (S) 208 the victim was stripped and subjected to various indignities, as well as being severely beaten and kicked: seven years upheld. Eighteen months' imprisonment was upheld in *Lloyd* (1989) 11 Cr App R (S) 36, where the deliberate kicking was inflicted by a rugby player on a member of the opposition during a match, the victim suffering a fractured cheekbone.

In cases where corrosive fluid is thrown, lengthy terms will be appropriate. In *Radford* (1986) 8 Cr App R (S) 61 five years was upheld where the offender squirted a corrosive substance into the victim's face, causing substantial loss of vision in one eye.

12.2.6 Administering poison

The maximum penalty for administering any poison or noxious thing with intent to injure etc. is five years (OAPA 1861, s. 24). Where the act is done with intent to endanger life or inflict grievous bodily harm, the maximum penalty is ten years (OAPA 1861, s. 23). These offences are triable only on indictment. In *Jones* (1990) 12 Cr App R (S) 233, the sentence bracket for the s. 24 offence was said to be the same as for malicious wounding (see **12.2.4**). Nine months was the correct sentence in *Hogan* (1994) 15 Cr App R (S) 834, where the offender gave to a woman a drink which contained a large quantity of a Class C drug. It caused her to fall into a deep sleep for a day.

12.2.7 False imprisonment and kidnapping

These are both common law offences and the penalties are at large. Both are triable only on indictment.

According to Lord Lane CJ in *Spence* (1983) 5 Cr App R (S) 413, such offences vary widely, from carefully planned abductions where the victim is used as a hostage or where ransom money is demanded (seldom less than eight years' imprisonment and more, perhaps much more, if violence or firearms are used) to incidents more akin to family tiffs or lovers' disputes (18 months or less, sometimes a great deal less). The Crown Court dealt with 378 cases of kidnapping in 1996, 264 of which were dealt with by custodial sentences. There were also 25 probation orders and 23 community service orders.

Brown (1985) 7 Cr App R (S) 15 was a case of unpremeditated kidnapping and false imprisonment of a young woman by forcing her into her car and causing her minor injuries in an ensuing struggle. Sentences of five years concurrent imposed on the kidnapping and false imprisonment counts were upheld. In *Karunaratne* (1983) 5 Cr App R (S) 2, an

11-year-old child was abducted and ransom demands made. Sentences of 12 years and 10 years were imposed on the offenders for offences of kidnapping, false imprisonment and blackmail. Kidnapping was for a political motive in *Barak* (1985) 7 Cr App R (S) 404, where sentences varying between 10 and 14 years were imposed on the offenders involved.

12.3 SENTENCING FOR SEXUAL OFFENCES

The following table shows the types of sentence which were imposed on offenders sentenced for indictable sexual offences in 1996:

absolute or conditional discharge:	6 per cent
probation order:	17 per cent
supervision order:	4 per cent
fine:	8 per cent
community service order:	3 per cent
combination order:	1 per cent
attendance centre order:	0 per cent
detention in YOI:	3 per cent
immediate imprisonment:	52 per cent
suspended imprisonment:	2 per cent
other:	2 per cent

12.3.1 Rape

The maximum penalty for rape is life imprisonment (SOA 1956, s. 37). The maximum penalty for attempted rape is also life (SOA 1985, sch. 2). Rape and attempted rape are triable only on indictment. In 1996 the Crown Court sentenced 575 cases of rape. Of those the overwhelming majority, 554, received immediate custody or detention under CYPA 1933, s. 53(2); of the remaining 21 cases two were dealt with by suspended sentence, eight by hospital order, six by probation, three by supervision order, one by absolute discharge and one case was otherwise dealt with.

The Guideline case for this offence is *Billam* (1986) 8 Cr App R (S) 48. The case states that 'rape is always a serious crime which calls for an immediate custodial sentence other than in wholly exceptional circumstances'. Lord Lane CJ went on to say:

For rape committed by an adult without any aggravating or mitigating features, a figure of five years should be taken as the starting point in a contested case. Where a rape is committed by two or more men acting together, or by a man who has broken into or otherwise gained access to a place where the victim is living, or by a person who is in a position of responsibility towards the victim, or by a person who abducts the victim and holds her captive, the starting point should be eight years.

At the top of the scale comes the defendant who has carried out what might be described as a campaign of rape, committing the crime upon a number of different women or girls. He represents a more than ordinary danger and a sentence of fifteen years or more may be appropriate.

Where the defendant's behaviour has manifested perverted or psychopathic tendencies or gross personality disorder, and where he is likely, if at large, to remain a danger to women for an indefinite time, a life sentence will not be inappropriate.

Lord Lane CJ then indicated that the crime should in any event be treated as aggravated by any of the following factors:

(a) violence is used over and above the force necessary to commit the rape;

(b) a weapon is used to frighten or wound the victim;

(c) the rape is repeated;

(d) the rape has been carefully planned;

(e) the defendant has previous convictions for rape or other serious offences of a violent or sexual kind;

(f) the woman is subjected to further sexual indignities or perversions;

(g) the victim is either very old or very young;

(h) the effect upon the victim, whether physical or mental, is of special seriousness.

Where 'any one or more' of these aggravating features are present, the sentence should be 'substantially higher' than the figure suggested as the starting point.

As far as mitigation is concerned, *Billam* indicates that the extra distress which giving evidence can cause to a rape victim means that a plea of guilty, perhaps more so than in other cases, should normally result in some reduction from what would otherwise be the appropriate sentence. The amount of such reduction will of course depend on all the circumstances, including the likelihood of a finding of not guilty had the matter been contested. The fact that the victim may be considered to have exposed herself to danger by acting imprudently (as for instance by accepting a lift in a car from a stranger) is *not* a mitigating factor, and the victim's previous sexual experience is equally irrelevant. But if the victim has behaved in a manner which was calculated to lead the defendant to believe that she would consent to sexual intercourse, then there should be some mitigation of sentence. Previous good character is of only minor relevance.

About one third of those convicted of rape are under the age of 21. In the ordinary case the appropriate sentence would be one of detention in a young offender institution, following the terms suggested as terms of imprisonment for an adult, but making some reduction to reflect the youth of the offender. In the case of a juvenile, the court will in most cases exercise the power to order detention under the Children and Young Persons Act 1933, s. 53(2).

Life sentences for rape were approved in *Fox* (1995) 16 Cr App R (S) 688, where the offender, a man described as of 'dull intellect' but not mentally disordered, had committed several offences of rape on mentally deficient women resident in a hospital where the offender worked as a nursing assistant, and in *Attorney-General's Reference (No. 6 of 1993)* (1994) 15 Cr App R (S) 375, where a 20-year-old offender with a previous conviction for rape was convicted of rape and robbery, the carefully planned offences having been committed within seven days of his release from prison. Psychiatric reports in the latter case indicated that the offender was suffering from a form of psychopathic disorder. In *Thomas* (1994) 16 Cr App R (S) 686, 15 years' imprisonment was upheld for the rape of a 78-year-old woman. The offender, who had numerous previous convictions for burglary and was on parole at the time of the offence, broke into the victim's home, assaulted her with his fists and with a piece of wood and then raped her. The Court of Appeal heard that the victim's life had been completely ruined by what had happened and that she was too frightened to return to her home where she had lived for many years. In *Farmer* (1993) 14 Cr App R (S) 664 the Court of Appeal upheld a 'severe' but 'warranted' sentence of 13 years in a case where the offender had lured a young woman into his car, assaulted her, tied her up and then raped her twice with considerable violence. The defendant contested the case and the victim was required to give evidence and relive the circumstances of the offence in detail. A number of the aggravating features referred to in *Billam* were also present in *Malcolm* (1987) 9 Cr App R (S) 487. There the offender pleaded guilty to false imprisonment and rape. The victim was dragged to the offender's flat, threatened with a knife, forced to participate in oral sex and raped twice. The sentencer imposed a sentence of 12 years for the rape, with five years concurrent for the false imprisonment. He also stated that he regarded public awareness that a rape victim may contact AIDS as being a general aggravating feature in rape cases. The Court of Appeal reduced the sentence to 10 years, taking 12 years from *Billam* as the starting point and reducing it by two years for the guilty plea. It was also said that fear of contacting AIDS would justify a heavier sentence if the victim had a valid reason for believing that she had contacted it from the offender, or where that had actually happened. In *Attorney-General's Reference (No. 1 of 1991)* [1992] 3 WLR 432 the victim, a woman in her mid-sixties, worked as a bereavement counsellor and had invited the offender, who had posed as a distressed widower, to her home. He made sexual advances to her and, when these were resisted, he pushed her into the bedroom and raped her several times. The sentence of five years' imprisonment was said by the Court of Appeal to be 'inordinately low' in the light of the *Billam* guidelines. The aggravating features present, and the absence of mitigation to be derived from a guilty plea, required a minimum sentence of eight years.

A case without some of the aggravating features present in the preceding paragraph is *Harvey* (1987) 9 Cr App R (S) 124, where the victim had known the offender for about a year. She went to his home looking for her friend, the offender's cousin. When the victim rejected his sexual advances, the offender raped her. He had previous convictions for indecent assault on a young boy and for incest. Lord Lane CJ described the case as 'a typical *Billam* case' where five years was the appropriate starting point. The sentence of seven years was reduced to six, one year in addition to the baseline of five being sufficient to take account of the related previous convictions. In *Attorney-General's Reference (No. 7 of 1989)* (1990) 12 Cr App R (S) 1 the offender was convicted of raping a woman with whom he had lived for about 18 months and with whom he had had regular sexual intercourse. The offence took place three months after the relationship had ended. The offender invited the complainant to visit his flat, which she did; he then pushed her across the room, removed her clothes and raped her. A sentence of two years was increased on appeal to four and a half years, Lord Lane CJ observing that previous cohabitation did not license a man to have sexual intercourse with the woman whenever he wished, but it was said that 'some weight' should be given to the previous relationship. The main reason for increasing the sentence in this case was that the defendant, in contesting the matter, had deprived himself of 'one of the most powerful points in mitigation which he has'.

The appropriate sentence for rape committed by a man upon his wife was considered in *Stephen W* (1993) 14 Cr App R (S) 256. The offender and his wife had been married and living together for three years. After an argument, the offender forced his wife to have sexual intercourse, threatening her with a knife. A sentence of five years was upheld. The Court of Appeal said it should not be thought that a lower scale of sentencing than that set out in *Billam* applied to rape by a husband. All would depend on the circumstances of the case. The existence of a previous consensual sexual relationship would be a mitigating factor in a case where the parties were cohabiting normally and the husband insisted on intercourse against the wife's will but without using violence or threats, but where there had been violence or threats the previous relationship was of little relevance. The instant case fell at the grave end of the scale and the offender had contested the case.

In *Attorney-General's Reference (No. 12 of 1992)* (1993) 14 Cr App R (S) 233 the offender pleaded guilty to the rape of a prostitute, with whom he had previously had sexual relations. When the woman requested payment in advance, the offender threatened her with a knife and forced her to have oral sex and sexual intercourse. He also said that he would kill her if she reported the incident. The Court of Appeal said that the original sentence of two years' imprisonment was too lenient and that, bearing in mind that the offender had now been sentenced twice over, the 'least sentence that could properly be imposed' was three years. While the fact that the victim behaved in a manner calculated to lead the defendant to believe that she would consent to intercourse could be taken into consideration, according to *Billam*, in this case the basis upon which the woman was prepared to have intercourse was quite different from that on which the offender, armed with a knife, sought to have it. In *Masood* [1997] 2 Cr App R (S) 137, where the 16-year-old victim was held captive in the offender's car for four hours, was subjected to a series of violent attacks and was forced to have unprotected sexual intercourse, the Court of Appeal said that the fact that the victim was a prostitute was largely irrelevant to the sentence.

In *Taylor* (1983) 5 Cr App R (S) 241 a sentence of three years was varied to a probation order where the offender, who was mentally retarded, pleaded guilty to rape of a 19-year-old girl suffering from Down's syndrome who attended the same special school as the offender. The Court of Appeal justified the exceptional sentence on the ground of the nature of the sexual act itself (some degree of sexual penetration, but in the nature of sexual exploration with no real understanding), the mental deficiency of the offender (described as on the borderline between low intelligence and mental handicap) and the inability of the victim to communicate any effective protest at the conduct. Following changes to the law on rape brought about by the CJPOA 1994, cases of non-consensual anal intercourse, whether committed on a woman or on a man, are now charged as rape rather than buggery. Although dating from before the statutory change, in *Mendez* (1992) 13 Cr App R (S) 9, a case where the offender had attacked the female victim while she was walking home, pushed her into an alleyway and twice committed buggery. Glidewell LJ referred to the *Billam* guidelines on rape and said that 'in our view forcible buggery of a woman is equivalent to rape but worse than normal vaginal rape'. A prison sentence of five years was upheld. This comment has been relied upon in later cases, including *Attorney-General's Reference (No. 25 of 1994)* (1995) 16 Cr App R (S) 562.

The *Criminal Statistics* indicate that of the 575 cases of rape sentenced by the Crown Court in 1996, the victim was female in 551 cases and male in 24 cases.

12.3.2 Unlawful sexual intercourse

The maximum penalty for unlawful sexual intercourse with a girl aged under 13 is life imprisonment (SOA 1956, sch. 2). The maximum for attempted unlawful sexual intercourse with a girl under 13 is seven years (SOA 1956, sch. 2). The maximum for unlawful sexual intercourse with a girl under 16 is two years on indictment (SOA 1956, sch. 2); six months, a fine not exceeding the statutory maximum, or both, summarily.

Unlawful sexual intercourse with a girl under 13 is triable only on indictment. In 1996, 50 offenders were sentenced for this offence. Of these 35 received immediate custody, three received a suspended sentence, five received probation, four supervision orders, one hospital order, one community service order and one combination order.

Unlawful sexual intercourse with a girl under 16 is triable either way. In 1996, 136 offenders were dealt with for this offence in the Crown Court. Of these 78 received immediate custody, 6 received suspended sentences, 10 community service, 16 probation, 10 supervision orders, four combination orders, four fines and six discharges. Two were otherwise dealt with. In the magistrates' courts, 74 offenders were sentenced for this offence, of whom eight received a custodial sentence. Probation, fine and conditional discharge were the preferred disposals.

Where an offence of unlawful sexual intercourse is triable either way, *Practice Note (Mode of Trial: Guidelines)* (1995) indicate that the following matters are relevant to determining mode of trial:

(a)   wide disparity of age;
(b)   breach of position of trust;
(c)   victim particularly vulnerable.

A number of cases illustrate the sentencing bracket for the offence of unlawful sexual intercourse with a girl aged under 13. In *Upfield* (1984) 6 Cr App R (S) 63 the offender pleaded guilty to one offence of unlawful sexual intercourse with a girl of 12. The offender had a long-standing relationship with the girl's mother and often acted as a baby-sitter for the daughter. The Court of Appeal said that the offence was 'a gross breach of trust' and a three-year sentence was upheld. Thirty months' imprisonment was appropriate in *Polley* [1997] 2 Cr App R (S) 144, where a 45-year-old man with no previous convictions pleaded guilty to having sexual intercourse with a girl of 12 who was described as 'alert, precocious and sexually experienced'. In *Luff* (1986) 8 Cr App R (S) 318 the offender committed a series of indecent assaults and unlawful sexual intercourse on his step daughter, starting when she was aged nine. The Court of Appeal said that there was no error in principle in a sentence of six years' imprisonment for the unlawful sexual intercourse and three years concurrent for the indecent assault, though it was a 'sentence at the top of the appropriate range, perhaps very near the top of it'. In *Robertson* (1988) 10 Cr App R (S) 183, however, a total of ten years' imprisonment was upheld on an offender who was convicted, after a trial, of four counts of indecent assault and one of unlawful sexual intercourse committed on his two stepdaughters, with whom the offender had sexual intercourse on several occasions over a period of years, threatening them with being taken into a home if they told their mother. Hazan J in the Court of Appeal, said that:

> This court approaches its task in this case only too conscious of the increase of sexual child abuse, especially within the home and the concern that is felt about that matter and the need to protect children not only from physical injury but from appalling psychological damage which may blight their lives as they grow from adolescence into adulthood.

In *Attorney-General's Reference (No. 4 of 1991)* (1992) 13 Cr App R (S) 182 the Court of Appeal said that the most useful guide for sentencing in a case of unlawful sexual intercourse on a girl aged under 13 committed by her stepfather were the guidelines for cases of incest given in *Attorney-General's Reference (No. 1 of 1989)* [1989] 1 WLR 1117 (see **12.3.5**).

The guideline case on sentencing for unlawful sexual intercourse with a girl aged under 16 is *Taylor* (1977) 64 Cr App R 183. According to Lawton LJ:

> At one end of [the] spectrum is the youth who stands in the dock, maybe 16, 17 or 18, who has had what started off as a virtuous friendship with a girl under the age of 16. That

virtuous friendship has ended with them having sexual intercourse with one another. At the other end of the spectrum is the man in a supervisory capacity, a schoolmaster or social worker, who sets out deliberately to seduce a girl under the age of 16 who is in his charge. The penalties appropriate for the two types of case to which I have just referred are very different indeed.

In the former type of case, Lawton LJ said that there was no need to pass a punitive sentence. In the latter type, he said that a man in a supervisory capacity who abuses his position of trust for sexual gratification ought to get a sentence somewhere near the maximum of two years. He took the view that in between there come many degrees of guilt.

Court of Appeal decisions illustrate cases in the upper reaches of the tariff for this offence. In *Goy* (1986) 8 Cr App R (S) 40 the offender pleaded guilty to two counts of unlawful sexual intercourse and admitted having sexual intercourse with his stepdaughter on four occasions. A sentence of two years' imprisonment was upheld. A sentence of 15 months was upheld in *Dewar* (1986) 8 Cr App R (S) 311, where the victim was the 14-year-old stepsister of the offender's wife and was spending the night at the offender's house. The victim had been drinking during the evening, and the offender, aged 30, went to her room in the night and had sexual intercourse with her. In *Kalkan* (1992) 13 Cr App R (S) 547 the offender pleaded guilty to unlawful sexual intercourse with a girl aged 14, the daughter of the woman with whom he was living at the time. A sentence of 21 months' imprisonment was reduced to nine months by the Court of Appeal, on the basis that the girl was sexually experienced and was at the time of the offence acting as a prostitute. In *Carter* [1997] 1 Cr App R (S) 434 a 32-year-old man pleaded guilty to having sexual intercourse on one occasion with a 14-year-old girl, who was the daughter of a neighbour. She became pregnant and gave birth to a child. A sentence of six months' imprisonment was appropriate.

12.3.3 Indecent assault

The maximum penalty for indecent assault, whether committed on a male or on a female, is ten years on indictment; six months, a fine not exceeding the statutory maximum, or both, summarily (SOA 1956, sch. 2).

When dealt with summarily, the Magistrates' Association Guidelines (1997) indicate the following:

Aggravating Factors +
vulnerable victim, breach of trust, age differential, injury (may be psychiatric), very young victim, offence committed on bail, previous convictions and failure to respond to previous sentences, if relevant.

Mitigating Factors −
slight contact.

The Guidelines state that the magistrates should consider whether the offence is so serious that only custody is appropriate.

In the Crown Court in 1996, there were 1,752 offenders sentenced for indecent assault on a female. Of those 1,192 received immediate custody and 70 received a suspended sentence. Of the remaining cases 318 received probation, 44 received community service, 29 were discharged, 27 were fined, 27 received hospital orders, 19 supervision orders and 17 combination orders. Nine were otherwise dealt with. By comparison, 378 cases of indecent assault on a male were sentenced, of which 263 received immediate custody and 81 received a probation or supervision order. In the magistrates' courts in 1996, 650 offenders were sentenced for indecent assault on a female. Of those 73 received immediate custody. The most frequently used disposals were probation orders (173), supervision orders (108), discharge (107), fine (86), community service (40), combination order (21) and attendance centre (16). For indecent assault on a man, magistrates dealt with 97 cases, of which 17 received custody. The most frequently used sentences were probation or supervision orders (54) and conditional discharge (17).

For very serious cases of indecent assault, a sentence approaching the maximum will be approved. In *Sheen* (1987) 9 Cr App R (S) 164 the offender pleaded guilty to false imprisonment, indecent assault and assault occasioning actual bodily harm. The offender accosted a young woman, grabbed her by the hair and forced her into his car. He then indecently assaulted her in various ways, including ejaculating into her mouth. She eventually escaped. The offender had previous convictions for indecent assault. A sentence of eight years was upheld. Many of the worse cases concern indecent assaults committed on children by offenders who were in a position of authority, such offences often being repeated regularly over periods of time. In *Cook* (1988) 10 Cr App R (S) 42 the offender pleaded guilty to eight counts of indecent assault and one of buggery, committed against his four stepchildren, as part of a pattern of offending which took place over a period of nine years. The offences did not come to light until the children had become adults. Sentences totalling 11 years were upheld in this 'dreadful case' by the Court of Appeal, which took account of 'the number of children, their ages, the period of the offending, the breach of trust, the nature and variety of the acts, the number of the acts, their regularity, the distress they caused, their persistence nevertheless, the threats, the violence and the lasting effect on at least some of the children'.

In *Attorney-General's Reference (No. 12 of 1994)* (1995) 16 Cr App R (S) 559 the offender was convicted of six offences of indecent assault, one of abduction of a girl and one of attempted rape. He persistently assaulted very young girls who were the daughters of his neighbours, or friends of his own children, at intervals over 10 years. The Court of Appeal held that the original sentence of four and a half years was unduly lenient, and increased it to seven years.

Other examples of indecent assault which fall into a bracket somewhat below those cases are *Knibbs* (1991) 12 Cr App R (S) 655, where the offender accosted a woman who was walking home, pretended that he had a knife and attempted to force her into some bushes — three years' imprisonment upheld; *Taylor* [1997] 1 Cr App R (S) 36, where the offender was a volunteer worker who indecently assaulted four disabled women while escorting them from one railway station to another — four years upheld; *Pike* [1996] 1 Cr App R (S) 4, where the offender pretended to be a hypnotherapist and conducted vaginal examinations on patients — four years upheld. In *Edwards* (1993) 14 Cr App R (S) 79 sentences of nine months for indecently assaulting two young women in the street by grabbing at their breasts, so that their clothes were torn and one of the women fell to the ground, were reduced to six months, on compassionate grounds and in the light of a psychiatric report prepared on the offender. In *Drysdale* (1992) 14 Cr App R (S) 15, a sentence of six months' imprisonment was upheld on the offender, a male nurse, who under the pretext of showing a female student how to deal with a patient, told her to lean over a bath and inserted his finger into her vagina.

General guidance on the less serious offences of indecent assault may be derived from *Bibi* [1980] 1 WLR 1193, where Lord Lane CJ said that 'Many offenders can be dealt with equally justly and effectively by a sentence of six or nine months' imprisonment as by one of 18 months or three years. We have in mind . . . the minor cases of sexual indecency.' In *Freeman* (1980) 2 Cr App R (S) 194, a case decided on the same day and intended to illustrate the category suggested, the Court of Appeal reduced a four-year prison sentence to 12 months, where the offender pleaded guilty to five counts of indecently assaulting a number of girls aged between eight and 13 by kissing and cuddling them.

A case where a non-custodial sentence was approved was *Ariquat* (1981) 3 Cr App R (S) 83, where the offender had sexual intercourse with a 15-year-old girl with her consent. As he believed her to be over 16, he did not commit the offence of unlawful sexual intercourse. A conditional discharge was regarded as being the proper sentence. A custodial sentence was held to be 'wrong in principle' in *Neem* (1993) 14 Cr App R (S) 18, where the offender, who was convicted of indecent assault, had pressed against a young woman in an underground train in an indecent manner. Noting that 'cases of this kind are usually dealt with in the magistrates' courts', the Court of Appeal substituted a fine of £300, together with a compensation order for £250, and costs.

12.3.4 Indecency with children

The maximum penalty for gross indecency with or towards a child aged under 14 (or inciting a child under 14 to commit an act of gross indecency) is 10 years on indictment; six months, a fine not exceeding the statutory maximum, or both, summarily (Indecency with Children Act 1960, s. 1) as amended by the C(S)A 1997, s. 52. In the Crown Court in 1996, 123 offenders were sentenced for this offence. Seventy-one received immediate custody and there were six suspended prison sentences, with 41 offenders receiving probation orders. Magistrates' courts dealt with 39 such offences in 1996. Seven offenders received custody and 25 were dealt with by probation or supervision orders.

12.3.5 Incest

The maximum penalty for incest by a man with a girl aged under 13 is life imprisonment (SOA 1956, sch. 2). The maximum for incest by a man with a female over 13 is seven years (SOA 1956, sch. 2). The maximum for incest by a woman is seven years (SOA 1956, sch. 2). The maxima for attempts to commit the offence in these three circumstances are seven years, two years and two years, respectively. The maximum for incitement by a man of a girl under 16, whom he knows to be his granddaughter, daughter or sister to have sexual intercourse with him is two years on indictment; six months or a fine not exceeding the statutory maximum, or both, summarily (CLA 1977, s. 54). There were 49 incest cases sentenced in the Crown Court in 1996; 46 received immediate custody. There were two probation orders and one supervision order. In the magistrates' courts incest cases were all committed for trial to the Crown Court.

The guideline case is *Attorney-General's Reference (No. 1 of 1989)* [1989] 1 WLR 1117. According to Lord Lane CJ, the gravity of incest varies greatly according to the age of the victim and the degree of coercion or corruption. At one end of the scale, he said, is incest committed by a father with a daughter in her later teens, or older, who is a willing participant and indeed may be the instigator. In such a case, little if any punishment is required. The most difficult area is that involving girls under the age of 13. As in the case of those between 13 and 16, sexual intercourse is an offence, quite apart from the parental relationship. For victims under the age of 13, however, a further factor comes into play.

Although the girl may 'consent' to the act of intercourse in such a way as to render a charge of rape inappropriate, the girl is in a particularly vulnerable position, which the father is in a position to exploit. The following guide was suggested, on the assumption that there has been no plea of guilty:

(a) *Where the girl is over 16.* A range from three years down to a nominal penalty will be appropriate depending on whether force was used, the degree of harm, if any, to the girl, and the desirability, where appropriate, of keeping family disruption to a minimum. The lower the degree of corruption, the lower the penalty.

(b) *Where the girl is aged from 13 to 16.* Terms of custody of between about five years and three years will be appropriate. Much the same principles will apply as in (a), though the likelihood of corruption is greater here.

(c) *Where the girl is aged under 13.* It is here that the widest range of sentence is likely to be found. If one can properly describe any case of incest as the 'ordinary' type of case, it will be one where the sexual relationship between husband and wife has broken down, the father has probably resorted to excessive drinking and the eldest daughter is gradually, by way of familiarities, indecent acts and suggestions, made the object of the father's frustrated sexual inclinations. If the girl is not far short of her thirteenth birthday and there are no particularly adverse or unfavourable features on a not guilty plea, a term of about six years would seem to be appropriate. The younger the girl when the sexual approach is started, the more likely it will be that the girl's will was overborne and accordingly the more serious would be the crime.

Other aggravating factors, whatever the age of the girl may be, include the following:

(a) If the girl has suffered physically or psychologically from the incest.
(b) If the incest has continued at frequent intervals over a long period of time.
(c) If the girl has been threatened or treated violently by, or was terrified of, the father.
(d) If the incest has been accompanied by perversions abhorrent to the girl, e.g. buggery or fellatio.
(e) If the girl has become pregnant by reason of the father failing to take contraceptive measures.
(f) If the defendant has committed similar offences against more than one girl.

Possible mitigating features include the following.

(a) A plea of guilty, which should be met by an appropriate discount, depending on how promptly the offender confessed, his degree of contrition etc.
(b) If it seems that there was genuine affection on the offender's part, rather than the mere use of the girl as an outlet for his sexual inclinations.
(c) Where the girl has had previous sexual experience.
(d) Where the girl has made deliberate attempts at seduction.
(e) Where, as very occasionally is the case, a shorter term of imprisonment for the father may be of benefit to the victim and the family.

12.3.6 Buggery

The maximum penalty for buggery committed with a boy under the age of 16, or with an animal is life imprisonment (SOA 1956, sch. 2). If the offender is aged 21 or over and the other person is under the age of 18, the maximum is five years, but otherwise two years. Where buggery of a male or female victim is committed without consent, the offence committed is rape, not buggery (see **12.3.1**). The Crown Court sentenced 112 cases of buggery in 1996, 99 of which received custodial sentences.

The Guideline case is *Willis* (1974) 60 Cr App R 146, which deals with buggery committed between an adult and a male partner under the age of 16. Lawton LJ said that in the absence of strong mitigating factors the offence should result in immediate custody. Should there be neither aggravating nor mitigating factors, the correct bracket is three to five years, with placement in the bracket depending on the age, intelligence and education of the offender.

Aggravating factors include:

(a) physical injury to the boy, whether by the penetration itself or by the use of force to overcome his resistance;

(b) emotional and psychological damage to the victim;

(c) moral corruption (e.g. use of gifts to corrupt boys);

(d) abuse of authority or trust.

Mitigating factors include the offender having been in a state of emotional stress or suffering from mental illness. Where the offender is suffering from a personality disorder which does not justify a hospital order, Lawton LJ advised that a probation order with a condition of psychiatric treatment might be appropriate, but if the offender represents a danger to boys if at liberty a lengthy custodial sentence will be necessary to protect other victims.

In *Malloy* [1997] 1 Cr App R (S) 189 the offender was convicted of buggery and indecent assault on a boy aged 15. They both worked at a café and the offender took advantage of a relationship which had developed between them. The victim went in the offender's car to a car park where the offences took place. Five years' imprisonment was the appropriate sentence for the buggery, with three years concurrent for the indecent assault. In *Attorney-General's Reference (No. 31 of 1996)* [1997] 1 Cr App R (S) 308 the offender, a man with no convictions, pleaded guilty to one count of buggery with a boy of 13, a count of rape not having been proceeded with. Payment of £10 was made. The Court of Appeal said that the sentence was unduly lenient and increased it from two years to three and a half years.

In a case of buggery of a dog, *Higson* (1984) 6 Cr App R (S) 20, a probation order was substituted for a two-year prison term by the Court of Appeal, on the basis that 'it is the appellant, and indeed his wife, and not the dog, who need help'.

Where consenting parties to a homosexual act are both over 18, but the act is still a criminal offence because of its taking place in a cubicle in a public lavatory, a custodial sentence is wrong in principle (*Tosland* (1981) 3 Cr App R (S) 265). The case was followed in *Bedborough* (1984) 6 Cr App R (S) 98. In these cases the Court of Appeal said that the proper sentence would have been a fine.

12.3.7 Gross indecency between men

The maximum penalty for gross indecency beween men, if by a man of or over the age of 21 with a man under the age of 18, is five years. Otherwise the maximum is two years, on indictment; six months, a fine not exceeding the statutory maximum, or both, summarily (SOA 1956, sch. 2). In the Crown Court there were 17 such cases in 1996; immediate custody was given in four cases. The most frequent disposals were the probation order and the conditional discharge. In magistrates' courts 202 cases were sentenced; the great majority (155) were fined and 41 received conditional discharges.

The guideline case on the offence of gross indecency between men is *Morgan* (1978) CSP B4-9.2B, where the offenders, aged 61 and 39, had been seen committing an act of gross indecency in a public lavatory. Lawton LJ said that:

> In general first offenders using public lavatories and behaving in this sort of way in them do not get sent to prison. They are generally fined. On occasions they may be put on probation or some other non-custodial order is made . . . Occasionally those who are convicted persist in this kind of behaviour and when they do, prison sentences may be appropriate.

See also *Clayton* (1981) 3 Cr App R (S) 67. In a case of importuning for an immoral purpose, *Gray* (1981) 3 Cr App R (S) 363, a fine was also held to be the appropriate sentence.

12.3.8   Offences related to prostitution

The maximum penalty for living on the earnings of prostitution is seven years on indictment; six months, a fine not exceeding the statutory maximum, or both, summarily (SOA 1956, sch. 2). The maximum for loitering or soliciting for the purposes of prostitution is (for an offence committed after conviction for a similar offence), a fine not exceeding level 3 on the standard scale; otherwise a fine not exceeding level 2 on the standard scale (Street Offences Act 1959, s. 1); this offence is triable only summarily. The maximum for 'kerb-crawling' is a fine not exceeding level 3 on the standard scale (SOA 1985, s. 1(2)); this offence is triable only summarily. Cases of prostitution and kerb crawling are dealt with in the magistrates' courts, and are usually dealt with by way of fine. Sentencing patterns for the offences in 1996 were as follows:

(a)   soliciting by a woman: 5,441 cases, of which 4,698 were fined, 679 discharged, and 35 placed on probation or supervision orders;

(b)   soliciting by a man: 66 cases, of which 55 were fined, 10 discharged and one probation order;

(c)   kerb crawling: 1,162 cases, of which 1,224 were fined and 25 discharged;

(d)   brothel keeping: 33 cases, of which 17 were fined and 12 discharged.

In the case of *Farrugia* (1979) 69 Cr App R 108, Lawton LJ said that the crucial factor in sentencing in cases of living on immoral earnings is whether there is any evidence of coercion, whether physical or mental, of the prostitutes involved or of corruption. A sentence exceeding two years should, he said, be reserved for cases where there is such coercion or corruption. In *Thomas* (1983) 5 Cr App R (S) 138 the Court of Appeal said that three years was proper, despite exceeding Lawton LJ's guidelines, since the offender had a history of similar offending. In *Kirk* (1995) 16 Cr App R (S) 895, where there were no relevant aggravating factors, a nine months' sentence was upheld.

Other cases concern the running of 'escort agencies' or 'massage parlours'. In *El-Gazzar* (1986) 8 Cr App R (S) 182, a sentence of 12 months for living on the earnings of prostitution was upheld on an offender who operated an escort agency.

Martin (1988) 10 Cr App R (S) 339 was a case where the offender was convicted of keeping a disorderly house where various sexual activities were offered for payment. No other prostitute was involved but the offender had previously been fined for a similar offence. Nine months was reduced to three months, to take account of the much smaller scale of the activites involved, as compared with *Payne* (1980) 2 Cr App R (S) 161, where the custodial sentence had been reduced to six months.

12.4 SENTENCING FOR THEFT AND RELATED OFFENCES

12.4.1 Theft

The maximum penalty for theft is seven years (Theft Act 1968, s. 1(7)) on indictment; six months or a fine not exceeding the statutory maximum, or both, summarily. Where triable either way, the *Practice Note* (*Mode of Trial: Guidelines*) (1995) state that theft should, in general, be tried summarily, unless the court considers that one or more of the following features is present in the case and that its sentencing powers are insufficient:

(a)   breach of trust by a person in a position of substantial authority, or in whom a high degree of trust is placed;
(b)   theft which has been committed or disguised in a sophisticated manner;
(c)   theft committed by an organised gang;
(d)   the victim is particularly vulnerable to theft (e.g. the elderly or infirm);
(e)   the unrecovered property is of high value (at least £10,000).

Theft is such a wide offence that there is little which can be said by way of general sentencing guidance. In *Upton* (1980) 2 Cr App R (S) 132, where the offender was convicted of theft of goods worth £5 from the supermarket of which he was deputy manager, Lord Lane CJ said:

This was petty theft and in ordinary circumstances it would, and should, not have attracted any immediate sentence of imprisonment . . . non-violent petty offenders should not be allowed to take up what has become valuable space in prison. If there really is no alternative . . . to an immediate prison sentence, then it should be as short as possible . . . a prison sentence, however short, is a very unpleasant experience indeed for the inmates.

When dealt with summarily, the Magistrates' Association Guidelines (1997) indicate the following guideline for theft:

Aggravating Factors +
   high value, planned, sophisticated, adult involving children; organised team, related damage, vulnerable victim, offence committed on bail, previous convictions and failures to respond to previous sentences, if relevant.

Mitigating Factors −
   impulsive action, low value.

The Guidelines indicate that magistrates should consider whether compensation, discharge or a fine is appropriate. The guideline fine is £135 (low income), £340 (average income) or £810 (high income).
   For practical sentencing purposes the offence of theft is subdivided into several specific forms of the offence:

(a) theft from shops;
(b) theft from vehicles;
(c) theft from the person;
(d) theft in breach of trust.

(a) *Theft from shops.* In 1996, the Crown Court sentenced 1,801 offenders for shoplifting; of these 730 received custodial sentences (around 40 per cent) and 41 suspended sentences. The most frequently used other disposals were probation (351), conditional discharge (194), fine (149) and community service (236). In the magistrates' courts in 1996, 52,192 offenders were sentenced for shoplifting; less than 4,000 received immediate custody. Overwhelmingly the most frequent disposals were the fine (18,290) and the discharge (16,395). Probation orders accounted for 7,514, and community service 2,175.

Court of Appeal decisions indicate that shoplifting should not attract a custodial sentence, unless the offender has a record of similar offending, the shoplifting was carefully planned and executed or there were other aggravating features. In *Ball* (1981) 3 Cr App R (S) 283 a suspended sentence for shoplifting a small quantity of children's clothes was quashed. The offender was a single woman aged 18 with one child, lived on social security benefit and was in breach of a conditional discharge imposed for handling stolen goods. That was her only previous conviction. Holding that 'this was not the sort of case which merited imprisonment at all, whether immediate or suspended', and accepting advice from the social enquiry report that the offender was not in need of supervision, the Court of Appeal substituted a small fine with six months in which to pay as being 'the least wrong course which is open to us'.

Where a custodial sentence is imposed for shoplifting, it will generally be very short. In *Roth* (1980) 2 Cr App R (S) 65 a one-month prison sentence was regarded as being a proper disposal for a man aged 58 who, together with his wife, committed a carefully planned theft from a shop involving goods to the value of £91; see also *MacLeod* (1981) 3 Cr App R (S) 247 (planned shoplifting of £100 worth of drink from supermarket; six weeks' imprisonment upheld). Much longer custodial sentences will be upheld in shoplifting cases where the offender has a serious record of similar offending (e.g. *Reeves* (1980) 2 Cr App R (S) 36: three-year sentence on offender sentenced for 40 shoplifting offences with 20 previous convictions for similar offences) or where 'professional' shoplifters are at work (e.g. *Jones* (1979) 1 Cr App R (S) 136: four years upheld on offenders with 'lamentable' criminal histories who stole £300 worth of records by use of a specially made box for concealing them). Taking young children along when shoplifting is regarded by the courts as a serious aggravating feature (*Moss* (1986) 8 Cr App R (S) 276).

(b) *Theft from vehicles.* In 1996 the Crown Court sentenced 115 offenders for theft from vehicles; of these 51 received custodial sentences. In magistrates' courts in 1996, 4,768 offenders were sentenced for theft from vehicles; only 537 received immediate custody (11 per cent). The most frequent disposals were the fine (1,176) and the discharge (1,028).

(c) *Theft from the person.* This category covers the taking of articles from handbags, shopping bags and the activities of pickpockets. In 1996 the Crown Court sentenced 2,416 offenders for theft from the person; of these 1,253 received custodial sentences (around 52 per cent). The most frequently used other disposals were community service (348), probation (282), fine (125), and conditional discharge (166). In magistrates' courts in 1996, 3,184 offenders were sentenced for theft from the person; 523 received immediate custody (16 per cent). The most frequent disposals were the fine (717) and the discharge (797).

While recognising that the majority of cases involving theft from the person are dealt with by non-custodial sentences, custodial sentences have sometimes been upheld by the

Court of Appeal, particularly in cases where the offender has a record of similar offending. One example is *Benon* (1982) 4 Cr App R (S) 45, where two years' imprisonment was upheld on an offender who had been 'at the pickpocketing game' since 1975. Another, said to be a case of 'professional' pickpocketing, is *Wilson* (1979) 1 Cr App R (S) 102, where three years' imprisonment was upheld on offenders who worked as a team, one distracting the victims while the other stole from the victim's bag; they had numerous previous convictions for similar offences. In *Masagh* (1990) 12 Cr App R (S) 568 Lloyd LJ stressed that while heavy custodial sentences were appropriate for systematic pickpocketing they were quite wrong for isolated offences committed by an individual.

(d) *Theft in breach of trust.* While this category of theft is well recognised in the case-law, it does not appear separately in the criminal statistics. The figures given below are derived by adding together the categories of 'theft by employee' and 'theft or unauthorised taking from mail' from the 1996 statistics. It is thought that this will give a good impresssion of the sentencing range used by the courts. In 1996, the Crown Court sentenced 616 offenders for theft in breach of trust; of these 344 received custodial sentences (56 per cent) and there were 49 suspended sentences. The other disposal most frequently used was community service (115). In magistrates' courts in 1996, 1,834 offenders were sentenced for theft in breach of trust; only 151 received immediate custody (8 per cent). The most frequent disposals were community service (554), the fine (400) and the discharge (343).

When this category of offence is dealt with summarily, the Magistrates' Association Guidelines (1997) note the following:

Aggravating Factors +
   casting suspicion on others, committed over a period, large amount, high value, organised team, planned, senior employee, sophisticated, vulnerable victim, offence committed on bail, previous convictions and failures to respond to previous sentences, if relevant.

Mitigating Factors −
   impulsive action, low value, previous inconsistent attitude by employer, single item, unsupported junior.

The Guidelines indicate that magistrates should consider whether the offence is so serious that only custody is appropriate.

The Guideline case of *Barrick* (1985) 7 Cr App R (S) 142 is concerned with cases towards the top end of the range of this offending normally dealt with in the Crown Court, where:

a person in a position of trust, for example, an accountant, solicitor, bank employee or postman, has used that privileged and trusted position to defraud his partners or clients or employers or the general public of sizeable sums of money. He will usually, as in this case, be a person of impeccable character. It is practically certain, again as in this case, that he will never offend again and, in the nature of things, he will never again in his life be able to secure similar employment with all that that means in the shape of disgrace for himself and hardship for himself and his family.

The *Barrick* guidelines indicate that such a case will attract immediate custody, save in very exceptional circumstances, or where the sum involved is small. Where the sum is less than £17,500, sentences ranging from the very short up to 21 months are appropriate. Where the sum is between, £17,500 and £100,000 the appropriate range is two to three years. For thefts totalling between £100,000 and £250,000 the range is three to four years, where the theft is between £250,000 and £1 million the range is five to nine years, and in cases where the theft is over £1 million the custodial sentence length will be 10 years or more. It should be noted that these figures are taken not from *Barrick* itself, but from the case of *Clark (1997) The Times*, 4 December 1997; [1998] Crim LR 227, which updated the sentencing brackets accordingly to take account of the effect of inflation, the reduction in the maximum penalty for theft from 10 years to seven years by the CJA 1991 and the effect of the *Practice Statement (Crime: Sentencing)* [1992] 1 WLR 948 (see **4.5.3**). These figures assume that the case is contested; in the event of a guilty plea, an appropriate discount should be given. Other matters to be taken into account by the court, apart from the size of the sum involved, are:

(a) the quality and degree of trust reposed in the offender;
(b) the period over which the thefts were committed;
(c) the use to which the money was put;
(d) the effect upon the victim;
(e) the impact on the public and public confidence;
(f) the effect upon fellow employees or partners;
(g) the effect on the offender;
(h) the offender's own history;
(i) matters of mitigation special to the offender; and
(j) any help given by the offender to the police.

The offender in *Clark* was employed as a bursar of the Royal Academy and he also acted as treasurer of his local church. The prosecution case was that in respect of both of these he had abused his position of trust in order to steal just under £400,000 from his employers and £29,000 from the church. It was significant for the purposes of sentence that the offender had been dishonest in two different directions and this would have entitled the trial judge to have passed consecutive sentences on the two counts. The offences were aggravated by the degree of trust reposed in the offender, the period of four years over which the offences took place and the fact that the money was spent on personal expenditure which was partly of an extravagant kind. The offender's good character, his frankness and co-operation, and pleas of guilty at the first available opportunity were among the factors mitigating the sentence in this case. It was also significant that he had repaid some £120,000. The total sentence of five years imposed by the trial judge was excessive, and the court quashed that and substituted a sentence of three years' imprisonment on count 1 and one year's imprisonment on count 2, the sentences to run consecutively.

Examples of cases where custody has been avoided are *Kirk* (1984) 6 Cr App R (S) 231, a case decided before *Barrick* but followed in *Boggs* (1990) 12 Cr App R (S) 39, where a hotel cashier stole £316 in small amounts over a period of six weeks. A sentence of two months' imprisonment suspended for twelve months was approved by the Court of Appeal, and the same sentence was upheld in *Boggs* in respect of theft of £439 by a person employed in a kiosk. In both cases, compensation orders in the sum taken were also made.

12.4.2 Handling stolen goods

The maximum penalty for handling is 14 years (Theft Act 1968, s. 22(2)) on indictment; six months or a fine not exceeding the statutory maximum, or both, summarily. The *Practice*

Note (*Mode of Trial: Guidelines*) (1995) state that handling stolen goods should, in general, be tried summarily unless the court considers that one or more of the following features is present in the case and that its sentencing powers are insufficient:

(a)   dishonest handling of stolen property by a receiver who has commissioned the theft;
(b)   the offence has professional hallmarks;
(c)   the property is of high value (at least £10,000).

When tried summarily, the Magistrates' Association Guidelines (1997) indicate the following:

Aggravating Factors +
   adult involving children, high value, organiser or distributor, offence committed on bail, previous convictions and failures to respond to previous sentences, if relevant.

Mitigating Factors −
   for personal use, impulsive action, low value, no financial gain, not part of a sophisticated operation, single item.

The Guidelines indicate that magistrates should consider whether the offence is serious enough for a community penalty.

In 1996 the Crown Court sentenced 4,717 offenders for handling stolen goods. Those receiving immediate custody totalled 2,080, and there were 115 suspended sentences. The most frequently used other disposals were community service (1,039), probation (688), conditional discharge (289), combination order (241) and fine (218). In magistrates' courts in 1996, 14,780 offenders were sentenced for handling stolen goods. Only 1,173 received custodial sentences. The most frequent disposals were the fine (3,778), the conditional discharge (3,301), probation (2,470), community service (2,138) and combination order (623).

The maximum penalty available for handling stolen goods is significantly higher than that available for theft, reflecting the view that some cases of handling may be more serious than any case of theft. Long custodial sentences are, however, rare, being reserved for cases where the handler was closely involved in a large-scale criminal enterprise. In *Patel* (1984) 6 Cr App R (S) 191 a sentence of four years was upheld on a man who received 660 cartons of cigarettes, worth £160,000, part of a larger consignment worth £1 million which had been stolen from a manufacturer's depot. The offender had previously served a six-year term for importing drugs. Lord Lane CJ said that:

Proper penalties for cases of handling will vary enormously according to the circumstances. At the top end of the scale come the cases where the handler provides an outlet for the proceeds of very substantial thefts or robberies, where the advantages to the thief of having such an outlet are very great and where accordingly the receiver or handler is indirectly encouraging the thefts to take place, and where also the profits to the handler are likewise very great, as plainly they were going to be here . . .

See also *Hutchings* (1994) 15 Cr App R (S) 498. Where a 'fence' deals directly with thieves or burglars, and provides a regular outlet for whatever property they may steal, sentences in a bracket of two to four years will be appropriate. In *Byrne* (1994) 15 Cr App R (S) 34 a sentence of 15 months was upheld for handling stolen computers worth £48,000 and in *Amlani* (1995) 16 Cr App R (S) 339 the appropriate sentence for handling a large number of stolen mobile phones was 21 months. Most handlers receive non-custodial sentences. For the 'one-off', opportunistic offence, the Court of Appeal has indicated that a fine will often be the correct penalty. In *Khemlani* (1981) 3 Cr App R (S) 208 the offender was a young businessman running a cash and carry store. He bought 350 watches, which were part of a stolen consignment, at an undervalue from an unnamed person. He was of previous good character and pleaded guilty. A sentence of three months' imprisonment was quashed and a fine of £1,000 substituted. A suspended sentence was varied to a fine in *Murray* [1983] Crim LR 203, where the offender, who had no previous convictions, assisted a motor cycle thief to change parts on the cycle so as to disguise it. The Court of Appeal said that the case was properly dealt with by way of a £60 fine.

12.4.3 Robbery

The maximum penalty for robbery is life imprisonment (Theft Act 1968, s. 8(2)). This offence is triable only on indictment. In 1996 the Crown Court sentenced 4,480 offenders for robbery. Those receiving immediate custody, including detention under CYPA 1933, s. 53(2), totalled 3,962 (over 88 per cent) and there were 23 suspended sentences. The other disposals used were mainly probation and supervision orders (281), community service (78), combination order (69) and hospital order (40).

The combination of violence and theft makes robbery the most serious of the common offences of dishonesty. The great majority of offenders convicted of robbery receive custodial sentences. In *Turner* (1975) 61 Cr App R 67 there were 19 appellants, members of a gang which over a period of four years had carried out 20 armed robberies on banks and security vans, netting over £1 million at 1975 values. Firearms and ammonia were carried, but used only to frighten, and injuries inflicted were slight. Lawton LJ said that the normal starting point for sentence for anyone taking part in a bank robbery, or in the hold-up of a security vehicle or a Post Office van, should be 15 years, if firearms were carried and no serious injury done. The lack of a previous criminal record is not, he said, to be regarded as a powerful mitigating matter. In *Daly* (1981) 3 Cr App R (S) 340 Lord Lane CJ indicated that in a bank robbery type of case the most serious features calling for heavy sentences:

> are detailed planning, use of loaded firearms or ammonia, where a number of men execute a planned attack on a bank or similar target in the hope of stealing substantial sums of money, where the participants are masked and armed either with guns, handguns or sawn-off shotguns, or sometimes with ammonia, and squirt ammonia into the faces of clients or staff of the bank in order to overpower resistance. In such cases, as Lawton LJ in *Turner* . . . has rightly said, a starting point of 15 years is correct. It may be, and no doubt will in nearly every case where there has been a plea of guilty, possible to reduce that term in the light of the plea and in the light of assistance given to the police and other mitigating factors. It may be necessary on the other hand in some cases to increase the starting number of years because of the number of offences which the particular defendant has committed during the course of his depredation.

In *Gould* (1983) 5 Cr App R (S) 72 Lord Lane CJ confirmed that the *Turner* guidelines remained the basis for sentencing in armed robbery offences. He also added that some of the features likely to mitigate an offence are:

(a)   a plea of guilty;
(b)   the youth of the offender;
(c)   a previously clean record;
(d)   the fact that the defendant had no companion when committing the offence; and
(e)   the fact that no one was injured.

Against these matters must be weighed, amongst other things:

(a)   that a real, rather than an imitation, weapon was used;
(b)   that the weapon was discharged;
(c)   that violence was used upon the victim;
(d)   that a number of men took part in the attack;
(e)   that careful reconaissance and planning were involved; and
(f)   that there was more than one offence committed by the offender.

For robberies in the so-called 'first division', which are the subject of the guideline cases described above, the normal starting point is 15 years. Sentences of 18 years and 17 years were imposed in *Knight* (1981) 3 Cr App R (S) 211 and *Reed* (1988) 10 Cr App R (S) 243 respectively. Wholly abnormal crimes, such as the Great Train Robbery, will attract sentences in excess of 18 years (*Wilson* (1964) 48 Cr App R 329). The 'irreducible minimum' in such cases is said to be 11 years (*Davis* (1980) 2 Cr App R (S) 168).

Robberies at sub-post offices, shops and similar premises will also attract substantial custodial sentences, though generally in a bracket below the 'first division' for the offence. The relevant aggravating and mitigating factors appear to be very similar to those cited in that context. In *Stanford* (1988) 10 Cr App R (S) 222 the offenders, aged between 20 and 22, pleaded guilty to two counts of robbery, two of attempted robbery and two of taking a conveyance. In the robberies, they had entered post offices, threatened the owners with an imitation firearm and demanded money. A sentence of seven years was upheld on the offender who 'was the front man with the gun'. Sentences on the others were reduced to five years to take account of the fact that no actual violence was used and that the offenders gave up their attempts very easily when meeting any resistance, their guilty pleas, previous good character and ages. In *Attorney-General's Reference (Nos. 26 and 27 of 1996)* [1997] 1 Cr App R (S) 243 sentences of four and a half years' detention in a young offender institution for robberies at building society branches in which imitation firearms were brandished were increased to seven and a half years. In *Attorney-General's Reference (No. 3 of 1990)* (1991) 92 Cr App R 166 the Court of Appeal dealt with four separate references and increased custodial sentences on seven offenders involved in robberies of small shops, off-licences and similar premises; in each case the sentences were increased to ranges between three and a half and six years.

A third category of robbery is street robbery or 'mugging'. The Court of Appeal's approved tariff seems to be in a bracket of two to five years, although the criminal statistics indicate that some less serious cases of mugging are dealt with by shorter terms or non-custodial sentences. Custodial terms of five years were reduced to three years in *Brennan* (1980) 2 Cr App R (S) 250, 'a typical case of mugging', where the offenders, both with substantial records, had jostled and punched a man in a public lavatory and stolen his wallet containing £63. The victim did not require medical attention. In *Attorney-General's Reference (No. 6 of 1994)* (1994) 16 Cr App R (S) 343 a community service order was held to be an unduly lenient sentence on an offender who accosted an 18-year-old victim and made him hand over his pay packet. A female mugger received 30 months in *Williams* (1982) 4 Cr App R (S) 156. A case at the lower end of seriousness is *Golding* (1992) 13 Cr App R (S) 142, where a sentence of six months' detention in a young offender institution was upheld on an 18-year-old youth who had accosted a 16-year-old and threatened to beat him up if he did not hand over his bicycle. Despite a guilty plea and the offender's good record, it was held that the offence was so serious that a non-custodial sentence could not be justified. See also *Pretty* (1992) 13 Cr App R (S) 280.

Finally, where victims are attacked in their own homes, sentence varies according to the degree of violence used and the value of the property taken. In *Clark* (1994) 16 Cr App R (S) 546 the offender, together with two others, attacked a 69-year-old woman and beat her about the head, fracturing her cheekbone. A sentence of 11 years' imprisonment was correct. In *Skilton* (1982) 4 Cr App R (S) 339 a sentence of three and a half years was held to be proper where the offenders tricked their way into the home of a blind man, tied him up and then made off with his £28 social security payment.

12.4.4 Blackmail

The maximum penalty for blackmail is 14 years (Theft Act 1968, s. 21(3)). It is triable only on indictment. In 1996 the Crown Court sentenced 154 offenders for blackmail; of those 130 received immediate custody and 8 suspended sentences. Other disposals included probation (7), community service (4) and combination order (3).

Sentences of six years and five years were reduced to four years and three years in *Cox* (1979) 1 Cr App R (S) 190, where the offenders removed valuable computer discs and tapes from their employer and demanded £275,000 as the price for returning them. In *Read* [1996] 2 Cr App R (S) 240 the offender wrote to a clergyman and threatened to make fake allegations of homosexual behaviour unless £7,000 was paid. The proper sentence was 21 months' imprisonment. *Riolfo* [1997] 1 Cr App R (S) 57 is a case where the offender telephoned a supermarket to say that food on the shelves had been contaminated with the AIDS virus. He demanded £250,000 and received £7,500. Eight years' imprisonment was reduced to six on appeal. In a 'wholly exceptional' case, where the claim which was made was on the face of it warranted, but improper means were used to enforce the claim (threat to publish nude photographs of the victim) a sentence of six months' imprisonment, suspended for two years was imposed (*Helal* (1980) 2 Cr App R (S) 383). See also *West* (1985) 7 Cr App R (S) 46, where the offender kidnapped the victim's dog and demanded money for its safe return.

12.4.5 Burglary

When sentencing for this offence, a distinction is drawn between burglaries from dwellings and burglaries from buildings other than dwellings, such as shops, offices, commercial premises and schools.

(a) *Burglary from a dwelling.* The maximum penalty for burglary, when committed in a dwelling is 14 years on indictment; six months or a fine not exceeding the statutory maximum, or both, summarily (Theft Act 1968, s. 9(4)). The offence is triable either way. The *Practice Note* (*Mode of Trial: Guidelines*) (1995) indicate that, in general, cases of burglary committed in a dwelling should be tried summarily unless the magistrates' court considers that one or more of the following features is present and that its sentencing powers are insufficient:

(a)   entry in the daytime when the occupier or another person is present;

(b)   entry at night of a house which is normally occupied, whether or not occupied at that time;

(c)   the offence is alleged to be one of a series of similar offences;

(d)   soiling, damage or vandalism has occurred;

(e)   the offence has professional hallmarks;

(f)   the unrecovered property is of high value (at least £10,000).

If the offence is dealt with summarily, the Magistrates' Association Guidelines (1997) indicate the following:

Aggravating Factors +
   racial motivation, deliberately frightening occupants, group offence, people in house, professional operation, forceable entry, soiling, ransacking, damage, offence committed on bail, previous convictions and failures to respond to previous sentences, if relevant.

Mitigating Factors −
   low value, nobody frightened, no damage or disturbance, no forcible entry, opportunist.

The Guidelines suggest that magistrates should consider whether the offence is so serious that only custody can be justified.

In 1996 the Crown Court sentenced 9,267 offenders for burglary in a dwelling (excluding aggravated burglary). Those receiving immediate custody totalled 7,152, and there were 90 suspended sentences. The most frequently used other disposals were probation (876) community service (518), combination order (366), supervision order (134), discharge (54), hospital order (33), and fine (18). In magistrates' courts in 1996, 7,820 offenders were sentenced for burglary in a dwelling. Of those, 2,024 received custodial sentences. The most frequent other disposals were the supervision order (1,174), probation (1,147), community service (946), the discharge (921), combination order (577), attendance centre order (510) and fine (420).

In respect of burglaries from dwellings, in *Brewster* [1998] 1 Cr App R (S) 181 Lord Bingham of Cornhill CJ issued the following sentencing guidance.

Domestic burglary is, and always has been, regarded as a very serious offence. It may involve considerable loss to the victim. Even where it does not, the victim may lose possessions of particular value to him or her. To those who are insured, the receipt of financial compensation does not replace what is lost. But many victims are uninsured: because they may have fewer possessions, they are the more seriously injured by the loss of those they do have.

The loss of material possessions is, however, only part (and often a minor part) of the reason why domestic burglary is a serious offence. Most people, perfectly legitimately, attach importance to the privacy and security of their own homes. That an intruder should break in or enter, for his own dishonest purposes, leaves the victim with a sense of violation and insecurity. Even where the victim is unaware, at the time, that a burglar is in the house, it can be a frightening experience to learn that a burglary has taken place; and it is all the more frightening if the victim confronts or hears the burglar. Generally speaking it is more frightening if the victim is in the house when the burglary takes place, and if the intrusion takes place at night; but that does not mean that the offence is not serious if the victim returns to an empty house during the daytime to find that it has been burgled.

The seriousness of the offence can vary almost infinitely from case to case. It may involve an impulsive act involving an object of little value (reaching through a window to take a bottle of milk, or stealing a can of petrol from an outhouse). At the other end of the spectrum it may involve a professional, planned organisation, directed at objects of high value. Or the offence may be deliberately directed at the elderly, the disabled or the sick, and it may involve repeated burglaries of the same premises. It may sometimes be accompanied by acts of wanton vandalism.

The record of the offender is of more significance in the case of domestic burglary than in the case of some other crimes. There are some professional burglars whose records show that from an early age they have behaved as predators preying on their fellow citizens, returning to their trade almost as soon as each prison sentence has been served. Such defendants must continue to receive substantial terms of imprisonment. There are, however, other domestic burglars whose activities are of a different character, and whose careers may lack any element of persistence or deliberation. They are entitled to more lenient treatment.

It is common knowledge that many domestic burglars are drug addicts who burgle and steal in order to raise money to satisfy their craving for drugs. This is often an expensive craving, and it is not uncommon to learn that addicts commit a burglary, or even several burglaries, each day, often preying on houses in less affluent areas of the country. But to the victim of burglary the motivation of the burglar may well be of secondary interest. Self-induced addiction cannot be relied on as mitigation. The courts will not be readily persuaded that an addicted offender is genuinely determined and able to conquer his addiction.

Generally speaking, domestic burglaries are the more serious if they are of occupied houses at night; if they are the result of professional planning, organisation or execution; if they are targeted at the elderly, the disabled and the sick; if there are repeated visits to the same premises; if they are committed by persistent offenders; if they are accompanied by vandalism or any wanton injury to the victim; if they are shown to have a seriously traumatic effect on the victim; if the offender operates as one of a group; if goods of high value (whether actual or sentimental) are targeted or taken; if force is used or threatened; if there is a pattern of repeat offending. It mitigates the seriousness of an offence if the offender pleads guilty, particularly if the plea is indicated at an early stage and there is hard evidence of genuine regret and remorse.

Lord Bingham CJ stated that, overall, the cases showed that:

(a)   burglary of a dwelling house, occupied or unoccupied, is not necessarily and in all cases an offence of such seriousness that a non-custodial sentence cannot be justified;

(b)   the decision whether a custodial sentence is required, and if so the length of such sentence, is heavily dependent on the aggravating and mitigating features mentioned above and, usually to a lesser extent, the personal circumstances of the offender;

(c)   the courts, particularly the higher courts, have generally reflected in their sentences the abhorrence with which the public regard those who burgle the houses of others.

This guidance may be regarded as superseding that which had earlier been provided by the Court of Appeal in *Mussell* [1991] 1 WLR 187 and in *Edwards* (1996) *The Times*,

1 July 1996. In respect of the latter case, Lord Bingham CJ commented that the decision had sought to establish clear sentencing brackets for the offence where it was not possible or desirable to do so, and that it had placed too much emphasis upon a distinction between burglary of occupied and unoccupied houses.

Decisions on house burglary reflect the balance of considerations outlined by Lord Bingham. At the top end of the sentencing scale are cases of 'professional burglars'. In *Brewster* (1980) 2 Cr App R (S) 191 a sentence of ten years was approved in the case of such an offender, who had convictions for 57 burglaries in the previous ten years and had committed two more burglaries while on parole, involving property worth £60,000. A more typical case is *Harvey* (1990) 12 Cr App R (S) 165, where 21 months was upheld in respect of a single offence of burglary of a house involving property worth £1,400, committed by day while the occupiers were on holiday. A so-called 'obituary burglary', where the offence took place at the home of a person whose recent death had been announced in the newspaper, was regarded as a very serious offence and merited an immediate custodial term of 18 months in *Lewis* (1993) 14 Cr App R (S) 744. The offender pleaded guilty to the burglary and to eight counts of handling stolen goods from other such burglaries, for which he received two years' imprisonment, consecutive to the 18 months. In *Herridge* (1994) 15 Cr App R (S) 648 the offender pleaded guilty to two counts of burglary, having gained access to the homes of two elderly women by pretending to be a council official, and stealing £130 and other items from one victim and £55 from the other. The Court of Appeal said that three and a half years was the appropriate sentence.

Notwithstanding the emphasis on custodial sentencing, it is clear from the criminal statistics that sentencing practice in the Crown Court, and more especially magistrates' courts, is somewhat more lenient. In some Court of Appeal cases, there has been a willingness to substitute a community sentence for a custodial term. In *Coulston* (1990) 12 Cr App R (S) 286 a 16-year-old offender pleaded guilty to two counts of burglary and asked for two others to be taken into consideration. The offences, which all occurred within a period of 11 days, were committed in the company of an 18-year-old who played the major role in the offences and received 21 months' detention in a young offender institution. The sentence on Coulston was varied to a community service order. Custody was also held to be inappropriate in *Suker* (1990) 12 Cr App R (S) 290, where a 19-year-old offender, affected by drink and looking for money to pay his taxi fare home, attempted to climb through the bathroom window of a house in the early hours of the morning and was detained by the householder.

(b) *Burglary from buildings other than dwellings.* When committed elsewhere than a dwelling the maximum penalty for burglary is ten years (Theft Act 1968, s. 9(4)). Burglary is triable either way and, when dealt with summarily, the maximum penalty is six months or a fine not exceeding the statutory maximum, or both, summarily. The *Practice Note (Mode of Trial: Guidelines)* (1995) indicate that, in general, cases of burglary committed in premises other than a dwelling should be tried summarily unless the magistrates' court considers that one or more of the following features is present and that its sentencing powers are insufficient:

(a) entry of a pharmacy or doctor's surgery;
(b) fear is caused or violence is done to anyone lawfully on the premises, such as a nightwatchman or a security guard;
(c) the offence has professional hallmarks;

(d)   there has been vandalism on a substantial scale;
(e)   the unrecovered property is of high value (at least £10,000).

If the offence is dealt with summarily, the Magistrates' Association Guidelines (1997) indicate the following:

Aggravating Factors +
   racial motivation, deliberately frightening occupants, group offence, night time, professional operation, forceable entry, soiling, ransacking, damage, serious harm to business, offence committed on bail, previous convictions and failures to respond to previous sentences, if relevant.

Mitigating Factors −
   low value, nobody frightened, no damage or disturbance, no forcible entry.

The Guidelines indicate that magistrates should consider whether the offence is serious enough for a community penalty.

In 1996 the Crown Court sentenced 2,185 offenders for burglary not in a dwelling (excluding aggravated burglary). Those receiving immediate custody totalled 1,482, and there were 30 suspended sentences. The most frequently used other disposals were probation (251) community service (231), combination order (117), discharge (39) and fine (14). In magistrates' courts in 1996, 12,818 offenders were sentenced for burglary not in a dwelling. Of those, 2,590 received custodial sentences. The most frequent other disposals were probation (2,202), discharge (2,039), community service (2,000), combination order (849), supervision order (877), attendance centre order (672) and fine (1,389).

Burglary from commercial premises, such as factories and offices, has always been considered as somewhat less serious than burglary of someone's home. Ordinarily, the victim will be in a better position to recover from the loss, and commercial burglary does not usually involve the same kind of emotional impact as burglary of the home. Otherwise, the appropriate sentence will reflect the value of the property taken, the level of associated damage and the degree of planning involved in the offence, as well as matters relating to the offender, such as degree of involvement in the offence, previous record and mitigating matters. In *Dorries* (1993) 14 Cr App R (S) 609 the offenders pleaded guilty to burglary of a shop. They had been seen in the vicinity of the shop and, when the police arrived, they drove away. Entry had been effected by removing bricks from a wall, and property worth £600 had been taken. A hammer, crowbar and radio scanner were found in their car. The Court of Appeal agreed with the trial judge that the offence was so serious that only custody could be justified, but reduced the sentence from 10 months to six months. In contrast, the Court of Appeal held in *Tetteh* (1994) 15 Cr App R (S) 46 that the offence did not pass the custody threshold. The offender had forced open the spirits store at a YMCA club and the drayman's entry cover had been opened to give access to the street. Nothing had been taken, however, and it had been an opportunistic rather than a planned offence.

Some other specific types of non-domestic burglary have been the subject of comment by the Court of Appeal. In *Larcher* (1979) 1 Cr App R (S) 137 the offender admitted a series of burglaries of doctors' premises and chemists' shops in order to obtain drugs. Although he had not served a custodial sentence before, five years was imposed by the Court of Appeal. In *Percy* (1992) 14 Cr App R (S) 10 a sentence of five years' imprisonment was upheld on 25-year-old offenders for a 'ram-raid' on a shop carried out by a group of men using stolen cars to break through a security fence and a window. They stole £2,000 worth of clothing from the shop, and did £,6000 worth of damage to the premises and the vehicles.

Sentences of five years were approved in two cases of burglary with intent to rape. In *Bolland* (1988) 10 Cr App R (S) 129 the offender entered at night the house of a woman known to him, assaulted her and threatened her with a knife. In *Palmer* (1990) 12 Cr App R (S) 550 the offender broke into a woman's home at night and made sexual advances to her. Concurrent sentences for indecent assault were approved in both cases.

12.4.6 Aggravated burglary

The maximum penalty for aggravated burglary, whether committed in a dwelling or not, is life imprisonment (Theft Act 1968, s. 10(2)). In 1996, the Crown Court sentenced 266 offenders for aggravated burglary in a dwelling; of those 242 received immediate custody (91 per cent) and 5 received suspended sentences. Other disposals were probation (4), community service (5), supervision order (2), combination order (7) and hospital order (1). The Crown Court also sentenced 15 offenders for aggravated burglary not in a dwelling; 11 received immediate custody and the other 4 received probation.

In *Attorney-General's Reference (No. 16 of 1994)* (1995) 16 Cr App R (S) 629 the offender, a man with a record of violent offences, went to the flat of a man he knew, armed with a baseball bat. He used the bat to smash property in the flat, thereby frightening the occupant. A sentence of 18 months' imprisonment was increased to three years. In *Funnell* (1986) 8 Cr App R (S) 143 nine years' imprisonment was reduced to six on two men who burgled the home of a man aged 84, armed with an imitation firearm, and then tied up the victim. Towards the top of the scale of seriousness is *O'Driscoll* (1986) 8 Cr App R (S) 121, where the offender gained access to the home of an elderly man and struck him a number of blows with a hammer. The victim was also threatened with a lighted gas poker, tied up with wire and gagged. A sentence of 15 years was upheld. Subsequent decisions which treat *O'Driscoll* as a guideline case include *Attorney-General's Reference (Nos. 32 and 33 of 1995)* [1996] 2 Cr App R (S) 345 and *Eastap* [1997] 2 Cr App R (S) 55.

12.4.7 Abstracting electricity

The maximum penalty is five years (Theft Act 1968, s. 13) on indictment; six months or a fine not exceeding the statutory maximum, or both, summarily. In 1996, 26 cases of abstracting electricity were sentenced at Crown Court; three received immediate custody and there were three suspended sentences. In magistrates' courts in 1996, 674 offenders were sentenced for this offence; only 27 received immediate custody. Other disposals were fine (285), conditional discharge (253), probation order (54) and community service (28); 20 offenders were otherwise dealt with.

In *Hodkinson* (1980) 2 Cr App R (S) 331 the offender pleaded guilty to abstracting electricity, in that he had fitted a device to the electricity meter at his home, which caused the meter to give a false reading. Bristow J commented that: 'In the judgment of this Court deliberately stealing electricity in this way is an offence which calls for deterrent treatment when caught. In the circumstances of this case the Court has come to the view that the necessary deterrent element would be sufficiently dealt with by a sentence of one month's imprisonment, accompanied by a fine of £750.' See also *Western* (1987) 9 Cr App R (S) 6.

12.4.8 Obtaining property by deception

The maximum penalty for obtaining property by deception is ten years (Theft Act 1968, s. 15(1)) on indictment; six months, or a fine not exceeding the statutory maximum, or both, summarily. The maximum penalty looks somewhat anomalous, given the very substantial overlap between theft and deception offences (see *Gomez* [1993] AC 442) and the reduction in the maximum sentence for the former offence to seven years by the CJA 1991.

The *Practice Note* (*Mode of Trial: Guidelines*) (1995) indicate that, in general, cases of fraud should be tried summarily unless the court considers that one or more of the following features is present and that its sentencing powers are insufficient:

(a) breach of trust by a person in a position of substantial authority, or in whom a high degree of trust has been placed;
(b) fraud which has been committed or disguised in a sophisticated manner;
(c) fraud committed by an organised gang;
(d) the victim is particularly vulnerable to fraud (e.g. the elderly or infirm);
(e) the unrecovered property is of high value (at least £10,000).

If the offence is dealt with summarily, the Magistrates' Association Guidelines (1997) indicate the following:

Aggravating Factors +
committed over lengthy period, large sums or valuable goods, two or more involved, victim particularly vulnerable, offence committed on bail, previous convictions and failures to respond to previous sentences, if relevant.

Mitigating Factors −
impulsive action, short period, small sum.

The Guidelines indicate that magistrates should consider whether the offence is serious enough for a community penalty.

In 1996, the Crown Court sentenced 3,109 offenders for the offence category 'other fraud', which includes the offence of obtaining property by deception. Of those sentenced, 1,600 received custodial sentences (51 per cent) and there were 218 suspended sentences. The main other disposals were community service (552), probation order (183), combination order (154), discharge (148) and fine (132). In the magistrates' courts in 1996, 10,108 offenders were sentenced for 'other fraud', of whom 1,024 received custodial sentences. The main other disposals were discharge (2,504), fine (2,320), probation (1,860), community service (1,495) and combination order (492). A further 202 cases were otherwise dealt with, presumably by way of compensation order.

The sentencing pattern for this and related offences of deception overlaps substantially with that for theft (see **12.4.1**). Since the offence varies so widely, there is no guideline judgment. The appropriate sentencing bracket for frauds committed by professional persons was reconsidered in *Barrick* (1985) 7 Cr App R (S) 142, which was discussed at **12.4.1**.

Large-scale commercial frauds will attract lengthy custodial sentences. In *Copeland* (1982) 4 Cr App R (S) 110 the offender was involved in a well organised scheme by which cheque books and cheque cards were stolen in Britain, passports were obtained in the names of the losers, and teams of two went to the continent, using the passports, and obtained money by means of the stolen cheque books and cards. Each trip netted about £15,000 and the scheme had been operational for a considerable time. The offender had several previous convictions for dishonesty resulting in prison terms of up to three years. The Court of Appeal reduced the sentence from six years to four and a half years. In *Griffiths* (1989) 11

Cr App R (S) 216 the offender, an 'intelligent and resourceful man', pleaded guilty to 23 counts of deception relating to a total of 93 multiple applications for shares. He made a profit of £5,000, but if all the applications had been successful he would have made £64,000. The Court of Appeal said that an immediate custodial sentence was appropriate, varying the original sentence of 12 months, with six to serve and six suspended, to an immediate term of six months. In one of a series of recent decisions on sentencing for 'mortgage frauds', the Court of Appeal upheld a custodial term of three and a half years together with a confiscation order of £142,000 in *Judge* (1992) 13 Cr App R (S) 685, where a total of £1 million had been procured by separate mortgage advances on 12 properties. See also *Stevens* (1993) 14 Cr App R (S) 372, where the Court of Appeal said that relevant matters in this type of case are the degree of involvement of the offender, the scale and duration of the fraud, the personal benefit derived and whether the offender is a professional person.

In contrast to the large-scale frauds are what may be described as the activities of 'con men'. Non-custodial sentences will often be appropriate but, once again, much turns on the sum involved. Also relevant is the method of deception (callous deception of the elderly, for example, will attract a more severe sentence) and the previous record of the offender. In *Pashby* (1982) 4 Cr App R (S) 382 the offender pleaded guilty to five counts of obtaining property by deception, by calling at the homes of elderly people, telling them that their roofs required repair and obtaining various sums by pretending that he would do, or had done, the necessary work. A sentence of five years was reduced to three years. In *Williams* (1983) 5 Cr App R (S) 244 the offender, 'a confidence trickster, especially of gullible women', who had a record of dishonesty over 15 years, had obtained £300 and £175 from different women by telling false hard-luck stories. A sentence of 15 months was reduced to nine months.

12.4.9 Social security and benefit fraud

Serious offending involving large-scale benefit fraud will usually be dealt with as an obtaining of property by deception (see **12.4.8**). A large number of social security and other benefit frauds have reached the Court of Appeal. In *Livingstone Stewart* (1987) 9 Cr App R (S) 135 Lord Lane CJ provided the following guidance for sentencers:

> only a small proportion of offences of this nature . . . are dealt with in the Crown Court. It will only be the apparently more serious cases which will come before the Crown Court. These offences involve the dishonest abstraction of honest taxpayers' money and are not to be treated lightly. They are easy to commit and difficult and expensive to track down. However it must be remembered that they are non-violent, non-sexual and non-frightening crimes.

Lord Lane CJ indicated that immediate custody was required at the top of the range of offenders, where there had been carefully organised frauds on a large scale. As to the remainder, who form the great majority, it may well be advisable for the court to enquire what steps the DSS proposes to take to recover their loss from the offender. Other considerations which may affect the sentence are:

(a) a guilty plea;

(b) the amount involved and the length of time over which the defalcations were persisted in (bearing in mind that a large total may in fact represent a very small amount weekly);

(c) the circumstances in which the offence began (e.g. there is a plain difference between a legitimate claim which becomes false owing to a change of situation and on the other hand a claim which is false from the very beginning);

(d) the use to which the money is put (the provision of household necessities is more venial than spending the money on unnecessary luxury);

(e) previous character of the offender;

(f) matters special to the offender, such as illness, disability, family difficulties, etc;

(g) any voluntary repayment of the amounts overpaid.

If immediate custody is necessary, Lord Lane suggested that a term of up to about nine or 12 months will usually be sufficient in a contested case where the overpayment is less than £10,000. If no immediate custodial sentence is imposed, and the amount of overpayment is below £1,000, a compensation order is often of value. This will usually only be the case where the defendant is in work. Lord Lane concluded by saying that '... we do not think that the element of deterrence should play a large part in the sentencing of this sort of case'.

The guidelines in *Livingstone Stewart* have been applied in numerous later cases. Recent examples are *Breeze* (1993) 15 Cr App R (S) 94, where the offender, a 'foot soldier' in a larger fraudulent enterprise who obtained £264 by deception, should not have received a custodial sentence despite having relevant previous convictions; *Tucker* (1993) 15 Cr App R (S) 349, where a sentence of six months' imprisonment for an offender who had been claiming supplementary benefit to which he was not entitled for about 18 months, obtaining £8,500, was upheld in light of considerable personal mitigation; and *Adewuyi* [1997] 1 Cr App R (S) 254, a case of 'exceptional seriousness', where more than £100,000 had been obtained over four years, and four years' imprisonment was upheld on appeal.

As indicated above, the great majority of social security benefit frauds are dealt with in magistrates' courts, and most are prosecuted by use of the summary offence in the Social Security Administration Act 1992, s. 112. The maximum penalty available for this offence is three months' imprisonment, a fine not exceeding £5,000, or both (s. 112(2)). In respect of this offence the Magistrates' Association Guidelines (1997) provide:

Aggravating Factors +
    fraudulent claims over a long period, large amount, organised group offence, planned deception, offence committed on bail, previous convictions and failures to respond to previous sentences, if relevant.

Mitigating Factors −
    misunderstanding of regulations, pressurised by others, small amount.

The Guidelines indicate that magistrates should consider whether the offence is serious enough for a community penalty. In the magistrates' courts in 1996, 10,585 offenders were sentenced for this offence. Most offenders were fined (3,598) or discharged (3,596). There were 2,056 community service orders and 142 custodial sentences (1 per cent).

12.4.10 Other deception offences

The maximum penalty for the offences of obtaining a pecuniary advantage by deception, for obtaining services by deception, and for evasion of liability by deception is, on conviction or indictment, five years (Theft Act 1978, s. 4(2)(a) and Theft Act 1968, s. 16(1)) and on summary conviction, six months, a fine not exceeding the statutory maximum, or both. The maximum for false accounting is seven years (Theft Act 1968, s. 17(1)) on indictment; six months, a fine not exceeding the statutory maximum, or both, summarily. The maximum for making off without payment is two years (Theft Act 1978, s. 4(2)(b)) on indictment; six months, a fine not exceeding the statutory maximum, or both, summarily.

12.5 SENTENCING FOR CRIMINAL DAMAGE AND ARSON

12.5.1 Criminal damage

The maximum penalty for criminal damage, committed with intent to endanger life or with recklessness whether life is endangered, is life imprisonment (Criminal Damage Act 1971, s. 4(1)). This offence is triable only on indictment. The maximum penalty for any other form of criminal damage is ten years (Criminal Damage Act 1971, s. 4(2)) on indictment; six months or a fine not exceeding the statutory maximum, or both, summarily. If, however, the damage is quantified at not more than £5,000 (unless it was caused by fire and thus constitutes arson: see **12.5.2**), criminal damage is triable summarily only: the maximum penalty is then three months, a fine not exceeding level 4 on the standard scale, or both.

Even if the value involved is more than £5,000 the offence should, in general, be tried summarily unless the court considers that one or more of the following features is present and that its sentencing powers are insufficient:

(a) deliberate fire-raising;
(b) committed by a group;
(c) damage of a high value (at least £10,000);
(d) the offence has a clear racial motivation.

Where tried summarily, the Magistrates' Association Guidelines (1997) indicate the following:

Aggravating Factors +
racial motivation, deliberate, group offence, serious damage, offence committed on bail, previous convictions and failures to respond to previous sentences, if relevant.

Mitigating Factors −
impulsive action, minor damage, provocation.

The Guidelines indicate that magistrates should consider whether compensation, discharge or a fine is appropriate. The guideline fine is £135 (low income), £340 (average income) and £810 (high income).

In 1996, the Crown Court sentenced 69 cases of criminal damage endangering life; of which 43 offenders received immediate custody, eight were given probation, eight were given community service and there were five hospital orders.

For 'ordinary' criminal damage, the Crown Court sentenced 509 offenders in 1996. The disposals were probation (112), immediate custody (106), community service (92), discharge (59), fine (50), hospital order (16), 17 cases were otherwise dealt with. In 1996, magistrates' courts sentenced 7,596 such cases. Disposals were fine (1,689), discharge (2,543), probation (1,027), community service (460), immediate custody (347, which is five per cent of the total), attendance centre order (253), supervision order (406), combination order (259); 595 cases were otherwise dealt with.

As can be seen from these statistics, most cases of minor criminal damage are dealt with by non-custodial means, particularly fines and discharges. Compensation should be ordered wherever possible. In *Fenton* (1988) 10 Cr App R (S) 250 and *Ferreira* (1988) 10 Cr App R (S) 343, community service was regarded as an appropriate penalty for criminal damage.

There are few Court of Appeal decisions relating to criminal damage. In *Bowles* (1988) 10 Cr App R (S) 146, a sentence of 14 days' imprisonment was upheld in a case where the offender daubed paint over the door and surrounding walls of South Africa House, as a political protest. In *Toomey* (1993) 14 Cr App R (S) 42 the offenders smashed the windows and door of a restaurant after an argument with the owner, causing £2,000 worth of damage. Eighteen months' imprisonment was reduced to 12 months on appeal. In *Dodd* [1997] 1 Cr App R (S) 127 the offender drove his car at 40 m.p.h. through the glass-fronted doors of Plymouth magistrates' court, causing £34,000 worth of damage. Four years' imprisonment was upheld by the Court of Appeal.

12.5.2 Arson

The maximum penalty for arson (i.e. where either form of criminal damage dealt with at **12.5.1** is committed by fire) is life imprisonment (Criminal Damage Act 1971, s. 4(1)) on indictment. If the criminal damage has been caused by fire but it does not amount to criminal damage with intent or recklessness whether life is endangered, the arson is triable either way and, on summary conviction, is punishable with six months or a fine not exceeding the statutory maximum, or both. The £5,000 rule (see **12.5.1**) does not apply where criminal damage amounts to arson. CJA 1991, s. 31(1) states that any offence which is required to be charged as arson is included within the meaning of 'violent offence' (see **4.2.7**), whether or not it would fall within the definition having effect for Part I of that Act.

In 1996, the Crown Court sentenced 753 cases of arson. Sixty four per cent of these offenders received immediate custody (479), and a further 12 received suspended sentences. The main other disposals were probation (127), supervision order (36), hospital order (35), community service (29) and combination order (28). In 1996, magistrates' courts sentenced 527 cases of arson. The main sentence disposals were discharge (143), supervision order (97), custody (63) and probation (60).

According to Donaldson LJ in *Priest* (1980) 2 Cr App R (S) 68, '(a)rson is a very odd offence in the sense that it covers a very wide range of circumstances. There can be very simple arson cases — simple in terms of sentencing — and there can be very difficult ones.' The Court of Appeal cases taken together indicate that there should be a psychiatric report available on the offender in cases of arson, and that, where there is appropriate psychiatric evidence, a medical disposal, such as a probation order with a condition of psychiatric treatment or a hospital order, may be passed. Minor cases can be dealt with by non-custodial sentences. Otherwise, in the absence of mitigation, a custodial sentence will generally be appropriate. Longer custodial sentences are appropriate where substantial damage has been caused or where death or serious injury has been risked by the offender. In *Hartley* (1993) 14 Cr App R (S) 198 Roch J, upholding sentences of three years custody imposed on offenders who pleaded guilty to setting fire to their employer's factory, causing losses of £690,000, said that:

Arson cases are difficult. Sentences passed must reflect the grave consequences which can flow, and in this case did flow, from the fire. It has to be remembered that firemen called to large fires are always in danger, and that commercial companies whose premises are damaged by fire can also face serious consequences. Sentences passed on arsonists must contain an element of deterrence . . .

In *Blunsden* (1988) 10 Cr App R (S) 139 the offender set fire to a pile of furniture in his flat. When arrested he claimed that he had given no thought to other residents living nearby. He had 18 previous convictions, including two for arson and eight for criminal damage. He was put on probation with a condition that he reside in a clinic to undergo treatment for a mental condition. Within a few months he left the clinic and was returned to court in breach of the order. He was then sentenced to five years' imprisonment. Reports indicated that he was a man of low intelligence, subject to schizophrenic episodes. He was likely to set further fires in future. He was deemed unsuitable for a normal mental hospital and no space was available in a special hospital. The custodial sentence was upheld by the Court of Appeal. In *Smith* (1993) 15 Cr App R (S) 594 the offender was an animal rights activist, who placed incendiary devices under a number of tractor units at the victim's farm. They were removed before any damage was done, but it was estimated that loss to the value of £200,000 would have been incurred if they had gone off. The offender had served a previous custodial sentence for a similar offence, and six years' imprisonment was upheld on this occasion as a deterrent sentence to the offender and to others. In *Attorney-General's Reference (No. 35 of 1996)* [1997] 1 Cr App R (S) 350 the offender pleaded guilty to arson being reckless whether life was endangered. In arrears with his rent and following a number of letters from the landlord, the offender started a fire in his own flat. It was quickly discovered, but £2,000 worth of damage was done. The Court of Appeal held that the combination order imposed by the trial judge had been unduly lenient, and substituted a custodial sentence of 18 months.

12.6 SENTENCING FOR OFFENCES RELATED TO PUBLIC ORDER

12.6.1 Firearms offences

The maximum penalty for possessing a firearm, shotgun or ammunition without a certificate is five years' imprisonment, a fine, or both, on indictment; six months, a fine not exceeding the statutory maximum, or both, summarily. Where the firearm is a shortened shotgun, the maximum penalty on indictment is seven years, a fine, or both. The maximum penalty for shortening a shotgun is seven years, a fine, or both, on indictment; six months, a fine not exceeding the statutory maximum, or both, summarily.

The maximum penalty for each of the following offences is life imprisonment: possession of a firearm with intent to endanger life or damage property, the use of a firearm to resist arrest, possessing a firearm while committing an offence specified in the Firearms Act 1968, sch. 1 (currently offences under Criminal Damage Act 1971, s. 1; OAPA 1861, ss. 20, 21, 22, 30, 32, 38 and 47; Child Abduction Act 1984, Part I; Police Act 1964, s. 51(1); SOA 1956, ss. 1, 17, 18 and 20; theft, burglary, blackmail and any offence under s. 12(1) of the Theft Act 1968), or for carrying a firearm or an imitation firearm with intent to commit an indictable offence.

The maximum penalty for carrying a loaded firearm in a public place is seven years' imprisonment, a fine, or both, on indictment; six months, a fine not exceeding the statutory maximum, or both, summarily. The maximum penalty for the summary offence of a person aged under 17 acquiring a firearm is six months, a fine not exceeding level 5 on the standard scale, or both.

All the above penalties are listed in Firearms Act 1968, sch. 6 and many of them were increased by the CJPOA 1994.

The Crown Court sentenced 528 offenders for offences under the Firearms Act 1968 during 1996. Of these, 306 received immediate custody (60 per cent) and there were 28 suspended sentences. The other disposals were fine (47), discharge (45), community service (44), probation (39), combination order (13), hospital order (2). Four cases were otherwise dealt with. In the magistrates' courts in 1996, 1,193 Firearms Act 1968 cases were sentenced. Of those, 67 received immediate custody (5 per cent). Other significant disposals were fine (595), discharge (292), community service (108) and probation (85).

Following revision in recent years of the maximum penalties for firearms offences, the Court of Appeal has indicated in recent cases that the appropriate level of sentencing, particularly for serious offences, has been revised upwards. In *Ashman* [1997] 1 Cr App R (S) 241 the Court of Appeal dealt with an offender who pleaded guilty to possession of a sawn-off shotgun. A sentence of 30 months' imprisonment was upheld, with the court noting that Parliament had increased the maximum penalty for the offence in 1994 and that higher sentences were appropriate for the offence, even where the offender was just acting as a 'minder' for the weapon. In *Clarke* [1997] 1 Cr App R (S) 323 the Court of Appeal confirmed that it was no longer appropriate to follow the sentencing levels prescribed in cases before the 1994 Act. In *Avis* [1998] 1 Cr App R 420, Lord Bingham of Cornhill CJ said that the criminal statistics indicated that there had been a sharp increase in the number of certain firearms offences coming before the courts, a fact which had confirmed the subjective impression of the judges. The unlawful possession and use of firearms was generally regarded as a grave source of danger to society. Firearms could be used to take life, to cause serious injury, or to further the commission of other serious crime. Often the victims would be those charged with the enforcement of the law or the protection of persons or property. In the conflicts which arose between competing criminal gangs, often related to the supply of drugs, the use and possession of firearms provoked an escalating spiral of violence. Where imitation firearms were used, the risk to life and limb was absent but such weapons could be and often were used to frighten victims in order to enforce unlawful demands, and such weapons were often difficult to distinguish from the real thing. His lordship commented that, although the Court of Appeal would not lay down precise guidelines for firearms offences, sentencers dealing with such cases should ask themselves:

(a) What sort of weapon was used? Genuine weapons were more dangerous than imitation ones, loaded than unloaded, unloaded for which ammunition was available than where it was not. Possession of a firearm which had no lawful use, such as a sawn-off shotgun, would be viewed even more seriously than possession of a firearm which could have a legitimate use.

(b) What use had been made of the weapon? The more prolonged and violent the use of the weapon the more serious the offence was likely to be.

(c) With what intention was the weapon possessed or used? Generally the most serious offences under the Act were those requiring proof of an intention to endanger life, cause fear of violence, resist arrest etc. The more serious the act intended, the more serious the offence.

(d) What was the defendant's record? Inevitably the offence was worse if the offender had a record of firearms offences or crimes of violence.

His lordship stated that some of the sentences passed for firearms offences in the past had failed to reflect their true degree of seriousness and the justifiable public concern which they aroused. Save for minor infringements which could properly be dealt with by magistrates, offences against these provisions would almost invariably merit terms of custody, even on a plea of guilty and where the offender had no previous record.

12.6.2 Offensive weapons

The maximum penalty for carrying an offensive weapon without lawful authority or reasonable excuse is four years, a fine, or both, on indictment (Prevention of Crime Act 1953, s. 1); six months, a fine not exceeding the statutory maximum, or both, summarily. The maximum penalty was increased from two years in 1996.

When dealt with summarily the Magistrates' Association Guidelines (1997) indicate:

Aggravating Factors +
   location of offence, group action or joint possession, people put in fear/weapon brandished, planned use, offence committed on bail, previous convictions and failures to respond to previous sentences, if relevant

Mitigating Factors −
   acting out of genuine fear, not premeditated

The Guidelines indicate that magistrates should consider whether the offence is so serious that only custody can be justified.

No separate sentencing statistics are provided for this offence in the *Criminal Statistics*.

The Court of Appeal has considered the appropriate sentencing bracket for the offence of possessing an offensive weapon in a number of reported cases. In *Webster* (1985) 7 Cr App R (S) 359 the offender, aged 27, after having been arrested for urinating against a wall, was found to be in possession of a Stanley knife, which he claimed to carry in case he was attacked. He had 11 previous convictions for violence and one previous conviction, two years earlier, for possession of an offensive weapon for which he had received three months' imprisonment. The Court of Appeal noted that a Stanley knife was capable of inflicting a very serious injury, and in light of the fact that the offender had contested the case and had a poor record, no mitigation was available from either of those sources; 12 months' imprisonment was upheld. In *Shorter* (1988) 10 Cr App R (S) 4, where the offender had two similar previous convictions, six months' imprisonment was upheld on an offender found in possession of a vegetable knife. Nine months was appropriate in *Simpson* (1992) 13 Cr App R (S) 665, where the offender had a flick knife, and in *Norman* (1995) 16 Cr App R (S) 848, 15 months was upheld for an offender with a previous conviction for the offence who was found in possession of a broken pool cue and a nasal spray containing ammonia.

12.6.3 Riot

The maximum penalty for riot is ten years (Public Order Act 1986, s. 1(6)). The offence is triable on indictment only. In 1996 there were seven cases of riot sentenced by the Crown Court. Oddly enough for what is regarded as the most serious of public order offences, six offenders received community service and one got a probation order.

Some general guidance on the gravity of public order offences, including riot, is to be found in *Caird* (1970) 54 Cr App R 499, although that case was decided in respect of common law offences of public order which were replaced by the statutory scheme in 1986. Sachs LJ said that where there had been 'wanton and vicious violence of gross degree' the court is not concerned with whether it originates from gang rivalry or from political motives. It is the degree of mob violence which matters and the extent to which the public peace is being broken. He also said that it was wrong to deal leniently with those who had been caught because others had not been. Individual acts of the perpetrators should not be seen in isolation, since they were not committed in isolation and it is that very fact that constitutes the gravity of the offence.

In *Pilgrim* (1983) 5 Cr App R (S) 140 three offenders had been involved in a riot in which 100 youths, equipped with various weapons, had attacked a public house frequented by members of an opposing group, and subsequently attacked a number of people who were unconnected with the event, one of whom was killed. The first offender was convicted of manslaughter in respect of that, and received sentences totalling eight years. The other two received sentences of five years and three years respectively. The Court of Appeal upheld the sentences, Lord Lane CJ noting that factors of particular importance in fixing sentence in such cases are:

(a)   the level of violence used;
(b)   the scale of the riot or affray, as described by the witnesses;
(c)   the extent to which it is premeditated, or arises spontaneously; and
(d)   the number of people involved.

The case of *Sallis* (1994) 15 Cr App R (S) 281, concerning prisoners who took part in a riot at a remand centre, confirms the continuing relevance of the above principles. Sentences of four and a half and five years were imposed on two of those involved.

12.6.4   Violent disorder

The maximum penalty for violent disorder is five years, a fine, or both, on indictment (Public Order Act 1986, s. 2(5)); six months, a fine not exceeding the statutory maximum, or both, summarily.

The *Practice Note* (*Mode of Trial: Guidelines*) (1995) indicate that cases of violent disorder should generally be committed for trial. When dealt with summarily, the Magistrates' Association Guidelines (1997) indicate that:

Aggravating Factors +
racial motivation, busy public place, large group, fighting between rival groups, large group, people put in fear, planned, vulnerable victims, weapon, offence committed on bail, previous convictions and failures to respond to previous sentences, if relevant.

Mitigating Factors −
impulsive, nobody actually afraid, provocation.

The Guidelines indicate that magistrates should consider whether the offence is so serious that only custody can be justified.

In 1996 the Crown Court sentenced 740 offenders for violent disorder. Of those, 476 received a custodial sentence (64 per cent). Other significant disposals were community service (133), combination order (43) and probation (24). In the magistrates' courts in 1996,

123 cases of violent disorder were sentenced. Of those, 20 received immediate custody. Other sentences included community service (26), supervision order (22), fine (17) and attendance centre order (14).

There are a few examples of Court of Appeal decisions in relation to sentencing for violent disorder. In *Vanes* (1989) 11 Cr App R (S) 147 the offenders pleaded guilty to violent disorder. They took part in a fight between members of two families. Between 15 and 20 people were involved. Various implements were used as weapons and there was £800 worth of damage done to a public house. Although no serious injury resulted the disorder was premeditated. Sentences of two years' and 12 months' imprisonment were upheld, the offenders being distinguished on grounds of the degree of their involvement and their records. Another example is *Alderson* (1989) 11 Cr App R (S) 301, where the offender and others created a disturbance in a restaurant which was directed at a party of Jordanian students. The victims were kicked, punched and hit with furniture and £500 worth of damage was done to the restaurant. A sentence of 30 months' imprisonment was upheld, the court taking account of the aggravating racial element in the offence. A third is *Coote* (1992) 14 Cr App R (S) 40, where the offender and a number of friends were celebrating his birthday in a nightclub. A fight broke out after a doorman warned one of the group about his behaviour. A police officer who tried to restrain one of the group was held by the offender in an attempt to prevent arrest. A sentence of 12 months' imprisonment was upheld. Finally, in *Green* [1997] 2 Cr App R (S) 191 four years' imprisonment was upheld in a case where the offender took part in a violent revenge attack on the home of a man believed to have assaulted a relative of one of the offenders. Two people in the house were attacked and baseball bats were used to smash windows. The court noted that all the offenders had records and had armed themselves in advance.

12.6.5 Affray

The maximum penalty for affray is three years, a fine, or both, on indictment (Public Order Act 1986, s. 3(7)); six months, a fine not exceeding the statutory maximum, or both, summarily.

The *Practice Note* (*Mode of Trial: Guidelines*) (1995) indicate that cases of affray should be tried summarily unless the court considers that one or more of the following features is present in the case and that its sentencing powers are insufficient:

(a) organised violence or use of weapons;
(b) significant injury or substantial damage;
(c) the attack has clear racial motivation;
(d) an attack upon police officers, ambulancemen, firemen etc.

When dealt with summarily, the Magistrates' Association Guidelines (1997) indicate that:

Aggravating Factors +
    racial motivation, busy public place, group action, large group, people put in fear, vulnerable victims, offence committed on bail, previous convictions and failures to respond to previous sentences, if relevant.

Mitigating Factors −
    offender acting alone, provocation, did not start the trouble, stopped as soon as police arrived.

A number of Court of Appeal decisions on this offence relate to affray prior to the Public Order Act 1986. They are misleading, since they commonly deal with cases of very serious violence which attracted sentences in excess of three years, and which would more appropriately be charged now as riot or violent disorder. A more representative case, however, is *Charles* (1989) 11 Cr App R (S) 125, where offenders in their thirties, both previously of good character and described as 'ordinary, decent, hard working members of society', pleaded guilty to affray. They had been eating in a restaurant when a member of another party made an offensive remark to one of the offenders and a fight broke out, during which chairs were broken and used as weapons. Several of the participants sustained minor injuries. Sentences of 12 months' imprisonment were reduced to three months in each case to take account of substantial mitigation. Another example is *Williams* [1997] 2 Cr App R (S) 67, where the offender was one of about 35 men involved in a racially motivated incident in which bottles were thrown in the vicinity of a corner shop in the early hours of the morning. A sentence of 21 months' imprisonment was reduced to 12 months on appeal.

12.6.6   Minor public order offences

The maximum penalty for the offence of causing fear or provoking violence is six months, a fine not exceeding level 5 on the standard scale, or both (Public Order Act 1986, s. 4(4)). For the offence of *intentionally* causing harassment, alarm or distress the maximum penalty is six months, a fine not exceeding level 5 on the standard scale, or both (Public Order Act 1986, s. 4A). The maximum penalty for causing harassment, alarm or distress is a fine not exceeding level 3 on the standard scale (Public Order Act 1986, s. 5(6)). The maximum penalty for the offence of wasting police time is six months, a fine not exceeding level 4 on the standard scale, or both (CLA 1967, s. 5(2)). All these offences are triable only summarily.

There were 26,364 summary offences under the 1986 Act sentenced in 1996. The disposals used most were fine (15,132) and discharge (7,978) but 667 offenders received immediate custody.

12.6.7   Bomb hoaxes

The maximum penalty is seven years on indictment (CLA 1977, s. 51(4)); six months, a fine not exceeding the statutory maximum, or both, summarily.

In *Browne* (1984) 6 Cr App R (S) 5 a codefendant had made two hoax telephone calls to a bank saying that he and the offender were members of the IRA and that there was a bomb in the building which would explode in 40 minutes. Both were sentenced to two years' imprisonment. The Court of Appeal varied the sentence on the offender to bring about his immediate release (he had already served just over 12 months) in the light of his lesser participation in the offence and personal mitigation, but said that this should not encourage the codefendant to appeal. In *Dunbar* (1987) 9 Cr App R (S) 393 the offenders pleaded guilty to communicating a bomb hoax. They telephoned the police to say that incendiary devices had been placed in various stores, apparently in order to cause financial loss to the stores. Sentences of 12 months' imprisonment were upheld by the Court of Appeal, Leggatt J commenting that: '[a] bomb hoax of this kind, as this Court has had occasion to say in the past, is a public nuisance, and it is important not to underrate the anxiety and apprehension that this kind of offence engenders. The public rightly expects judges to pass severe sentences as a mark of public disapprobation'. Imprisonment for 12 months was also upheld in *Rung-Ruangap* (1993) 15 Cr App R (S) 326, where the offender made a call to the police to say that there was a bomb outside a Wimpy bar. The offender later admitted she had rung up for a 'dare'.

12.6.8 Official secrets

The maximum penalty for spying, contrary to the Official Secrets Act 1911, s. 1, is 14 years (Official Secrets Act 1920, s. 8(1)). The maximum for wrongful communication of information, contrary to the Official Secrets Act 1989, s. 1, is two years on indictment (Official Secrets Act 1920, s. 8(2)); three months, a fine not exceeding the statutory maximum, or both, summarily.

Offences committed under the Official Secrets Act 1911, s. 1 (spying) will inevitably attract a lengthy custodial sentence. In *Prime* (1983) 5 Cr App R (S) 127 the offender pleaded guilty to two indictments. On the first, he admitted seven offences against the Official Secrets Acts. The offender had been employed for nine years in the Government Communications Service, where he had access to highly sensitive intelligence information of importance to national security. During that period he passed on information to the Soviet Union. On the second indictment, he pleaded guilty to counts of indecent assault against young girls. For the espionage offences, he received consecutive terms of 14, 14 and seven years' imprisonment. For the indecent assault offences he received a further three years, consecutive, a total of 38 years. These sentences were upheld on appeal. In *Schulze* (1986) 8 Cr App R (S) 463 the offenders' home was found to contain spying equipment, forged documents and radio-receiving equipment. They were convicted of doing acts preparatory to the commission of an offence under s. 1 of the 1911 Act. Sentences of 10 years were upheld in each case.

Where the offence is committed under the Official Secrets Act 1989, much will depend upon the precise nature of the offence. Few appellate decisions are reported and all precede the 1989 Act. In *Tisdall* (1984) 6 Cr App R (S) 155 the offender was a civil servant who made additional copies of Foreign Office documents and sent them anonymously to a national newspaper. She was sentenced to six months' imprisonment, which was upheld on appeal, Lord Lane CJ commenting that because:

> an individual disapproves of the law, or thinks that it is unreasonable for him or her to have to obey it in any particular circumstance, does not mean that that individual will escape prosecution or, if convicted, will escape punishment . . . in the circumstances of this case an immediate custodial sentence was unavoidable.

Twelve months' immediate custody was upheld in *Jackson* (1987) 9 Cr App R (S) 315 where an ex-soldier had retained confidential documents after leaving the army.

12.6.9 Racial hatred

The maximum penalty for using words or behaviour or displaying written material intended to stir up racial hatred, contrary to the Public Order Act 1986, s. 18, is two years, a fine, or both, on indictment (Public Order Act 1986, s. 27(3)); six months, a fine not exceeding the statutory maximum, or both, summarily.

In *Relf* (1979) 1 Cr App R (S) 111 the offenders were convicted of publishing leaflets containing derogatory remarks about West Indians, the leaflets being displayed in public places. The conduct did not lead to disorder. The Court of Appeal agreed with the trial judge that an immediate custodial penalty was necessary for Relf, but reduced the sentence from 15 months to nine. Cole, more peripherally involved in the offence, received a nine-month prison sentence, suspended, together with a fine of £250. In *Edwards* (1983) 5 Cr App R (S) 145, where the offender had drawn up a comic strip to be published in a magazine intended to stir up racial hatred, he received a 12-month sentence. Lawton LJ, in the Court of Appeal, said that the sentence 'was not a day too long', since the offender's conduct had been 'intended to prejudice children against Jews, Asians and people of coloured blood'.

12.7 SENTENCING FOR OFFENCES AGAINST THE ADMINISTRATION OF JUSTICE

12.7.1 Perjury

The maximum penalty for perjury in judicial proceedings is seven years (Perjury Act 1911, s. 1). The offence is triable only on indictment. In the Crown Court in 1996, 75 offenders were sentenced for perjury. Immediate custody was imposed in 43 cases (57 per cent) and there were 11 suspended sentences. Other disposals for perjury were fine (4), conditional discharge (3), probation (2) and community service (8).

There are several Court of Appeal decisions dealing with sentencing for this offence. They stress that a custodial sentence is almost always necessary where perjury has been committed in judicial proceedings. This may not appear to be borne out by the statistics given above, but those figures contain an (unknown) number of cases where perjury was committed in other, perhaps less serious, circumstances (e.g. making a false statement to a registrar of births, marriages or deaths).

The reason for insistence upon custody is, according to Roskill LJ in *Davies* (1974) 59 Cr App R 311 that:

> there is too much perjury committed in courts . . . But it is one thing to suspect that perjury has been committed and another thing to prove it. Perjury is not always easy to prove. Perjurers are not easily brought to justice. When they are they must be punished.

In *Rothwell* (1980) 2 Cr App R (S) 338 the offender was a passenger in a car of which he was the owner when it was involved in a collision. He gave false evidence to the effect that he had been the driver. The perjury was believed in the magistrates' court but the other driver's conviction was overturned when the perjury came to light. A sentence of three years was reduced to a 'richly deserved' 18 months on appeal. In *Hall* (1982) 4 Cr App R (S) 153 Talbot J said that 'it is almost inconceivable that a sentence of less than three months would be given for a deliberate perjury in the face of the court', since 'such false evidence strikes at the whole basis of the administration of the law'. In that case a three-month sentence was upheld on a 62-year-old woman who had given false alibi evidence at a magistrates' court in respect of a man charged with assault occasioning actual bodily harm. Exceptionally, in *Stanley* (1981) 3 Cr App R (S) 373, where the offenders pleaded guilty to perjury in the course of summary proceedings against the first offender for driving a car while unfit through drink, custodial sentences of three months were reduced to conditional discharges, to take account of mitigating factors, in particular their impending discharge from the Army should their custodial sentences stand.

In *Lewins* (1979) 1 Cr App R (S) 246 the offender, a police officer, was sentenced to four years for perjury and subornation. He had persuaded witnesses to testify that he had taken drink between the time of a road accident he had been involved in and the administration of a breath test. The sentence was reduced to two years to take account of personal mitigation including loss of his employment, the fact that the perjury was not committed in his capacity as a police officer and the fact that a custodial sentence 'for an ex-police officer is a great deal more unpleasant than it is for other members of the community'. It seems that where the original charge in relation to which the perjury was committed was one of very serious crime, the penalty for the perjury should be proportionally higher. Six months' imprisonment was upheld in *Healey* (1990) 12 Cr App R (S) 297, where the offender committed perjury in the course of a means inquiry in a magistrates' court.

12.7.2 Perverting the course of justice

This is a common law offence, so the penalty is at large. It is triable only on indictment. The Crown Court sentenced 1,518 offenders for this offence in 1996. Immediate custody was imposed in 768 cases (50 per cent) and there were 78 suspended sentences. Other disposals were community service (299), probation (182), discharge (46), fine (63), and combination order (63).

A number of Court of Appeal authorities give guidance on the appropriate sentencing bracket for this offence. In *Hill* (1980) 2 Cr App R (S) 110 a sentence of 18 months' imprisonment was upheld where the offender, awaiting trial on a charge of attempted theft of a battery, threatened to kill an intending prosecution witness. The attempt to pervert the course of justice was committed on the spur of the moment. If, according to the Court of Appeal, there had been an element of premeditation the sentence would have been longer. The relative triviality of the attempted theft charge was, apparently, irrelevant. See also *McFarlane* (1984) 6 Cr App R (S) 49, where 18 months was upheld on an offender who threatened a potential witness with violence if he did not change his statement. In *Bilby* (1987) 9 Cr App R (S) 185 a young woman aged 17, of previous good character, pleaded guilty to doing an act tending to pervert the course of justice. Her father and brother were due to appear for trial at a magistrates' court and the offender approached an intending prosecution witness and threatened to kill her if she gave evidence. A sentence of three months' youth custody was upheld, Ian Kennedy J saying that: 'In very few cases will threats to witnesses not be followed by immediate sentences of custody. A feeling of family loyalty will be of no avail. This is not one of the exceptional cases. The sentence passed by the learned judge was correct in principle and its length was not excessive.' See also *Kelly* (1993) 14 Cr App R (S) 170.

Comparable sentences would appear to be appropriate where the offence takes the form of a false allegation of crime. In *Goodwin* (1989) 11 Cr App R (S) 194 a 20-year-old woman made a false complaint of rape, naming a particular man. The man was arrested and held in custody for 14 days, but released subsequently when the woman admitted what she had done. A sentence of three years' detention in a young offender institution was reduced on appeal to 18 months. Lord Lane CJ said that: 'It is necessary to make people understand that this sort of lie will be met by severe punishment. But we have to balance against that the age of this young woman and the circumstances in which she saw fit to tell these lies'. A comparable case is *Gregson* (1993) 14 Cr App R (S) 85, where the false allegation was withdrawn after the man had been in custody for 20 hours. A sentence of four months was appropriate. Another example is *Nutbrown* (1994) 15 Cr App R (S) 269, where the offender, who was stopped by the police when driving while disqualified gave the name of another man. The other man was subsequently arrested before the deception was discovered.

A sentence of 12 months for perverting the course of justice was reduced to six months on appeal.

12.8 SENTENCING FOR OFFENCES INVOLVING DANGEROUS DRUGS

In the Crown Court in 1996, 9,900 offenders were sentenced for drug-related offences. For sentencing purposes it is necessary to draw a distinction between three different types of drugs:

(a)   Class A Drugs (such as heroin, morphine, cocaine, LSD, Ecstasy, opium and mescaline);

(b)   Class B Drugs (such as amphetamine, cannabis, cannabis resin and codeine); and

(c)   Class C Drugs (such as benzphetamine and permoline).

For powers to confiscate drugs and drug-related equipment from offenders see **6.7.1** and for powers to deprive drug traffickers of the proceeds of their offending under the DTA 1994, see **9.1**.

12.8.1   Class A drug offences

The maximum penalty for producing heroin or another Class A drug, supplying such a drug, or possessing such a drug with intent to supply is life imprisonment (MDA 1971, sch. 4) on indictment; six months, a fine not exceeding £5,000, or both, summarily. The maximum for possessing such a drug is seven years (MDA 1971, sch. 4) on indictment; six months, a fine not exceeding £5,000, or both, summarily. The maximum, for being concerned in the management of premises etc. is 14 years (MDA 1971, sch. 4) on indictment; six months, a fine not exceeding £5,000, or both, summarily, and the maximum for fraudulently evading prohibition on importation or exportation of a Class A drug is life (Customs and Excise Management Act 1979, s. 170) on indictment; six months, a fine not exceeding £5,000, or both, summarily.

In the Crown Court in 1996, 953 offenders were sentenced for unlawful importation of drugs. No breakdown is given in the *Statistics* between unlawful importation of different kinds of drugs. Of those, 914 received immediate custodial sentences, 96 per cent of offenders dealt with. In the Crown Court in 1996, there were 2,781 offenders sentenced for production, supply, or possession with intent to supply a Class A drug. Of those, 2,289 received immediate custodial sentences, 82 per cent of offenders dealt with. There were 730 offenders sentenced for possession of a Class A drug, 236 of whom received custody. Other significant disposals for possession were fine (101), probation (156) and community service (118).

The starting point for sentencing for these offences is the guideline case of *Aramah* (1982) 4 Cr App R (S) 407, modified in later cases to take account of the alteration in maximum penalties for these offences and other matters. The following guidelines from *Aramah* (Lord Lane CJ at pp. 408–9) have, therefore, been amended to incorporate those changes:

> Class A Drugs and particularly heroin and morphine: It is common knowledge that these are the most dangerous of all the addictive drugs . . .
>
> I turn to the importation of heroin, morphine and so on: Large scale importation, that is where [the weight of the drugs at 100 per cent purity is of the order of 500 g] or more, sentences of [ten years] and upwards are appropriate. There will be cases where the

[weight at 100 per cent purity is of the order of 5 kg] or more, in which case the offence should be visited by sentences of [14 years] and upwards. It will be seldom that an importer of any appreciable amount of the drug will deserve less than four years. This, however, is one area in which it is particularly important that offenders should be encouraged to give information to the police, and a confession of guilt, coupled with considerable assistance to the police can properly be marked by a substantial reduction in what would otherwise be the proper sentence.

Next, supplying heroin, morphine and so on: It goes without saying that the sentence will largely depend on the degree of involvement, the amount of trafficking and the value of the drug handled. It is seldom that a sentence of less than [five] years will be justified and the nearer the source of supply the defendant is shown to be, the heavier will be the sentence. There may well be cases where sentences similar to those appropriate to large scale importers may be necessary. It is however unhappily all too seldom that those big fish amongst the suppliers get caught.

Possession of heroin, morphine etc. (simple possession): It is at this level that the circumstances of the individual offender become of much greater importance. Indeed the possible variety of considerations is so wide, including often those of a medical nature, that we feel it impossible to lay down any practical guidelines. On the other hand the maximum penalty for simple possession of Class A drugs is seven years' imprisonment and/or a fine, and there will be very many cases where deprivation of liberty is both proper and expedient.

In *Martinez* (1984) 6 Cr App R (S) 364, Lord Lane CJ confirmed that the *Aramah* guidelines were not confined to heroin, but applied equally to other Class A drugs such as cocaine and LSD. In *Hurley* [1998] 1 Cr App R (S) 299, the Court of Appeal issued guidance on sentencing levels for importation of LSD. In the case of 25,000 or more quarter-inch squares or dosage units the sentence should in the ordinary case be 10 years plus. For 250,000 or more dosage units the sentence should ordinarily be 14 years plus. In each case their lordships were assuming that the dosage unit was of approximately 50 micrograms content pure LSD. Adjustment might be needed when it was shown to vary significantly from that figure. Where the seizure was of tablets or of crystals in a form which enabled a precise weight to be ascertained readily there should be no problem in calculating the number of 50 microgram doses. The Court of Appeal appreciated that cases might arise where, to do justice in individual cases, the sentence level could vary from the guidelines indicated.

The Court of Appeal has also rejected arguments that Ecstasy is to be treated as a drug less dangerous than other Class A drugs such as heroin or cocaine. In *Warren* [1996] 1 Cr App R (S) 233 the Court of Appeal tied this drug into the *Aramah* guideline framework by stating that in cases involving importation of 5,000 or more Ecstasy tablets the appropriate sentence would be in the order of 10 years and upwards, while for 50,000 or more tablets it would be 14 years and upwards. These figures were based on the assumption that the tablets were of average, or near average, quality. If analysis showed a substantially different content, the weight of the constituent would be the determinative factor. The Court again stressed that other matters were also of importance, such as the role of the offender in the offence, his plea, and whether he had provided assistance to the authorities.

The *Aramah* guidelines show that most offences relating to Class A drugs are not suitable for summary trial. The only exceptions seem to be cases of simple possession of a small amount of Class A drugs. In such cases, the Magistrates' Association Guidelines (1997) indicate the following:

Aggravating Factors +

an amount other than a very small quantity, offence committed on bail, previous convictions and failures to respond to previous sentences, if relevant.

Mitigating Factors −

very small quantity.

The Guidelines indicate that magistrates should consider whether the offence is serious enough for a community penalty. Forfeiture of all drugs and equipment should be considered in every case.

Magistrates tried 4,516 such cases in 1996, of which 210 were dealt with by immediate custody. Most offenders were fined (2,335), discharged (786) or placed on probation (740).

There are many Court of Appeal decisions which apply the *Aramah* guidelines to Class A drug offences. The first group is concerned with importation. An example is *Latif* [1995] 1 Cr App R (S) 270, where 20 kg of heroin had been imported by a 'principal organiser'. A sentence of 20 years' imprisonment was upheld on appeal. In *Bayley* (1995) 16 Cr App R (S) 605, 15 years was upheld for the importation of 58 kg of Ecstasy. In *Bilinski* (1987) 9 Cr App R (S) 360 the offender pleaded guilty to importing over 3 kg of heroin. The Court of Appeal said that a sentence of eight years was appropriate, bearing in mind the guilty plea and the offender's assistance given to the authorities. The case also establishes that an offender's belief that the drugs were in fact Class B and not Class A drugs is relevant to sentence (see, to the same effect, *Ghandi* (1986) 8 Cr App R (S) 391). If this matter is in dispute, a *Newton* hearing may be appropriate to determine it (see **3.3.2**). In *Bilinski*, it seems, a cursory enquiry would have revealed the true nature of the drug and, accordingly, the appropriate reduction was small. Other recent cases are *Daniel* (1995) 16 Cr App R (S) 892 (offender stopped at Gatwick Airport and found to be in possession of 1.43 kg of heroin of 45 per cent purity; nine years' imprisonment upheld) and *Mouzulukwe* [1996] 2 Cr App R (S) 48 (offender concealed within his body 31 packets containing 231 g of powder, including 38 g of pure heroin; six years' imprisonment upheld). A sentence of eight years was upheld in *Gerami* (1980) 2 Cr App R (S) 291, where the offender and his codefendant had been involved in the importation of 8.87 kg of prepared opium. The sentence on the codefendant was reduced to six years to reflect his lesser role in the offence.

As far as distribution of Class A drugs is concerned, in *France* (1984) 6 Cr App R (S) 283 the offender had been dealing in heroin and other Class A drugs for a few weeks, on a small scale, in order to finance his own consumption of heroin; four years' imprisonment was upheld. See also *Eliot* (1988) 10 Cr App R (S) 454, where the offender was a heroin addict who also supplied heroin to others to service his own addiction. It was argued that the offender was on the bottom rung of suppliers, that he supplied only addicts and hence had corrupted no one, had been frank with the police and had pleaded guilty. The Court of Appeal, having referred to the availability of a maximum penalty of life imprisonment for the offence, approved a custodial sentence of 30 months, commenting that the sentencer had given a proper discount for the mitigation. In *Singh* (1988) 10 Cr App R (S) 402 the offender, a medical practitioner who was 'a regular dealer in heroin', was convicted of possessing heroin with intent to supply and pleaded guilty to a range of other drug offences including supplying cannabis, being in possession of amphetamines and being found in possession of heroin when in prison. A total of eight years' imprisonment was approved by the Court of Appeal, in a case where 'there is no mitigating feature at all'. In *Bowman-Powell* (1985) 7 Cr App R (S) 85 the offender pleaded guilty to possession of 92 doses of

LSD and admitted that he intended to sell about half of the LSD to a regular set of friends and customers. He had a number of drug-related convictions over the previous nine years, including two previous convictions for possession of LSD. A sentence of four years' imprisonment was upheld. The same sentence was upheld in *Jones* (1994) 15 Cr App R (S) 856, where the offender was in possession of 27 Ecstasy tablets (worth about £400) with intent to supply.

As far as sentencing for possession of Class A drugs is concerned, the *Aramah* guidelines indicate that sentence may differ widely according to the circumstances, but that 'there will be very many cases where deprivation of liberty is both proper and expedient'. In *Omashebi* (1981) 3 Cr App R (S) 271 it was said that possession of cocaine for personal consumption should be dealt with by a short, sharp prison sentence; 12 months was reduced to six months in that case for possession of 3.5 gm of the drug. In *Layton* (1988) 10 Cr App R (S) 109 the offender, who had a bad criminal record but no previous drug-related convictions, pleaded guilty to possession of 5.6 gm of cocaine. A sentence of three months' imprisonment was substituted for the 30 months imposed by the sentencer. Three-month sentences were also appropriate in *Long* (1984) 6 Cr App R (S) 115, where the offenders pleaded guilty to possession of heroin for personal use and each had a previous conviction for possession of cannabis and in *Cox* (1994) 15 Cr App R (S) 216, where the offender was in possession of 16 Ecstacy tablets and 1.5 g of crack cocaine.

12.8.2 Class B drug offences

The maximum penalty for producing cannabis or another Class B drug, supplying such a drug, or possession of such a drug with intent to supply, is 14 years' on indictment (MDA 1971, sch. 4); six months, a fine not exceeding £5,000, or both, summarily. The maximum for possession of such a drug is five years on indictment (MDA 1971, sch. 4); three months, a fine not exceeding £5,000, or both, summarily. The maximum penalty for being concerned in the management of premises etc. is 14 years on indictment (MDA 1971, sch. 4); six months, a fine not exceeding £5,000 or both, summarily. The maximum for fraudulently evading prohibition on importation or exportation of such a drug is 14 years on indictment (Customs and Excise Management Act 1979, s. 170); six months, a fine not exceeding £5,000, or both, summarily. The maximum for cultivation of cannabis plants is 14 years on indictment (MDA 1971, sch. 4); six months, a fine not exceeding £5,000, or both, summarily.

In the Crown Court in 1996, there were 4,086 offenders sentenced for production, supply, or possession with intent to supply a Class B drug, of whom 2,322 received immediate custody, 57 per cent of offenders dealt with. There were 1,030 offenders sentenced for possession of a Class B drug, 148 of whom received immediate custody. Other significant disposals were fine (321), probation (167) and community service (116).

The Court of Appeal guideline case for these offences is, again, *Aramah* (1982) 4 Cr App R (S) 407, where Lord Lane CJ distinguished importation, supply and possession of cannabis. The passage is set out as amended by later decisions, including *Ronchetti* (1997) *The Times*, 9 December 1997.

Class B Drugs, particularly cannabis:
Importation of cannabis: Importation of very small amounts for personal use can be dealt with as if it were simple possession, with which we will deal later. Otherwise importations of amounts up to about 20 kg of [cannabis resin and cannabis, or the

equivalent in cannabis oil] will, save in the most exceptional circumstances, attract sentences of between 18 months and three years, with the lowest ranges reserved for pleas of guilty where there has been small profit to the offender. The good character of the courier (as he usually is) is of less importance than the good character of the defendant in other cases. The reason for this is, it is well known that the large scale operator looks for couriers of good character and for people of a sort which are likely to exercise the sympathy of the court if they are detected and arrested. Consequently one will frequently find that students and sick and elderly people are used as couriers for two reasons: first of all they are vulnerable to suggestion and vulnerable to the offer of quick profit, and secondly it is felt that the courts may be moved to misplaced sympathy in their case. There are few, if any, occasions when anything other than an immediate custodial sentence is proper in this type of importation. Medium quantities, over 20 kg, will attract sentences of three to six years' imprisonment, depending upon the amount involved, and all the other circumstances of the case. [Importation of 100 kg by persons playing more than a subordinate role should attract a sentence of seven to eight years.] Large scale or wholesale importation [500 kg or more] will justify sentences in the region of 10 years' imprisonment for those playing other than a subordinate role. [Larger importations would attract a higher starting point, which should rise according to the roles played, the weight involved and all the other circumstances of the case, up to the statutory maximum of 14 years provided by Parliament.]

Supply of cannabis: Here again the supply of massive quantities will justify sentences in the region of 10 years for those playing anything more than a subordinate role. Otherwise the bracket should be between one to four years' imprisonment, depending on the scale of the operation. Supplying a number of small sellers — wholesaling if you like — comes at the top of the bracket. At the lower end will be the retailer of a small amount to a consumer. Where there is no commercial motive (for example, where cannabis is supplied at a party), the offence may well be serious enough to justify a custodial sentence.

Possession of cannabis: When only small amounts are involved being for personal use, the offence can often be met by a fine. If the history shows however a persistent flouting of the law, imprisonment may become necessary.

As far as supply, and possession with intent to supply, a Class B drug is concerned, when tried summarily, the Magistrates' Association Guidelines (1997) indicate the following:

Aggravating Factors +
commercial production, large amount, venue (e.g., prisons, educational establishments, deliberate adulteration, offence committed on bail, previous convictions and failures to respond to previous sentences, if relevant.

Mitigating Factors −
not commercial, small amount.

The Guidelines suggest that magistrates should consider whether the offence is so serious that only custody can be justified. Other cases should be committed for trial. In all cases forfeiture of drugs and equipment should be considered.

When cases of simple possession of Class B drugs are dealt with summarily the Magistrates' Association Guidelines (1997) indicate the following:

Aggravating Factors +
for example large amount, offence committed on bail, previous convictions and failures to respond to previous sentences, if relevant.

Mitigating Factors −
for example small amount.

Guideline level of sentence: Is compensation, discharge or a fine appropriate? The guideline fine is £90 (low income), £225 (average income) and £540 (high income). In all cases forfeiture of all drugs and equipment should be considered.

The Association Guidelines relating to cultivation of cannabis are similar. Specific factors indicating a lesser degree of seriousness are where the cultivation was for personal use rather than commercial, and where the offender was not responsible for the planting.

In 1996 magistrates' courts sentenced 2,783 cases of possession of Class B drugs with intent to supply. Of those, 159 received custodial sentences. More frequent disposals were fine (1,330), discharge (459), community service (405) and probation (249). There were 15,825 cases of simple possession of Class B drugs. The great majority (10,960) were fined. Other disposals included discharge (3,122), probation (712) and custody (172).

There are several Court of Appeal decisions following and applying the guidelines in *Aramah* and dealing with the appropriate sentences for offences in connection with Class B drug offences, mainly cannabis. The first group is concerned with importation. At the top end of the scale, the offenders in *Fishleigh* [1996] 2 Cr App R (S) 283 imported four tonnes of cannabis, worth £13 million, in a fishing boat. Sentences of 12½ years were reduced to nine years on appeal. In *Klitkze* (1994) 16 Cr App R (S) 445 the offender imported over 15 kg of herbal cannabis concealed in a crate containing machinery. A prison sentence of four years was reduced to three years on appeal. Towards the lower end of the importation scale, in *Watson* (1988) 10 Cr App R (S) 256 the offender and another woman imported 12 kg of cannabis, the offender's suitcase containing 7.4 kg. She was convicted after a trial and sentenced to four years. This was reduced to two years, in line with the *Aramah* guidelines. In *Harris* (1989) 11 Cr App R (S) 169, where the amount involved was just over 6 kg and the offender pleaded guilty, a three-year sentence was reduced to 18 months.

In *Morgan* (1985) 7 Cr App R (S) 443 sentences of six years, seven years and eight years were upheld on offenders convicted after a trial of conspiring to manufacture amphetamine sulphate and who had already successfully marketed 2.5 kg of the drug with a street value of £40,000 to £50,000. See also *Shaw* (1986) 8 Cr App R (S) 16, where a sentence of ten years was upheld in respect of a carefully planned operation to produce amphetamine, albeit that 'some of the arrangements were ill-concealed, and even inept'.

The second group of cases involves distribution of Class B drugs, mainly cannabis. Again, a scale of sentences may be ascertained, following the *Aramah* guidelines. Distribution on a large scale was involved in *Netts* [1997] 2 Cr App R (S) 117, where the offender was stopped while driving his car and found to be in possession of 90 kg of cannabis resin in 24 packages. It was accepted that he was acting as a courier for the drugs. Taking account of the fact that the offender had no previous convictions, a sentence of seven years was reduced to five years on appeal. In *Chatfield* (1983) 5 Cr App R (S) 289 the offenders pleaded guilty to possession of 2 kg of cannabis with intent to supply. Sentences of 30 months were upheld by the Court of Appeal, Watkins LJ commenting that: 'They came somewhere between about half-way towards and the end of the bracket, allowance being made for the fact that they pleaded guilty and for their characters.' In *Hill* (1988) 10 Cr App

R (S) 150 the offender had been dealing in cannabis from his home on a regular basis for some time, earning £100 per week from this activity. A 30-month sentence, described by the Court of Appeal as 'near the top end of the bracket for offences of this sort' was reduced to 21 months, since 'although the supply was on a regular basis to a large number of people, the amounts involved were comparatively small' and greater recognition should have been given to the offender's guilty plea. Thirty months was reduced to 15 months in *Barton* [1997] 1 Cr App R (S) 140, where the amount of the drug was relatively small (7.2 kg) but the offence was aggravated by the fact that the offender had supplied a serving prisoner.

For cases of simple possession of small amounts of cannabis for personal use, the guidelines in *Aramah* indicate that a fine will often be an appropriate penalty, unless there is repetition involving 'flouting of the law'. In *Jones* (1981) 3 Cr App R (S) 51 the offender was convicted of possession of 3.2 g of cannabis. Five years earlier he had been convicted of cultivating and possessing cannabis and fined £30. This time he was sentenced to three months' imprisonment, suspended, plus a £50 fine. The Court of Appeal said that the prison sentence was inappropriate, and quashed it, leaving the fine in place. See also *Aldred* (1983) 5 Cr App R (S) 393.

In cases involving the cultivation of cannabis, a crucial matter is whether the cannabis was for personal use or for supply. In *Stearn* (1982) 4 Cr App R (S) 195 the Court of Appeal said that an immediate custodial sentence was necessary where the offender grew 44 cannabis plants and admitted selling cannabis at about £20 an ounce, earning £1,500 from a crop of plants. A sentence of three and a half years was reduced to two years, taking account of the offender's previous good character, cooperation with the police and guilty plea. Other cases involving commercial cultivation of plants are *Challis* [1997] 1 Cr App R (S) 425 and *Mineham* [1997] 1 Cr App R (S) 268. Custodial sentences of two years and three years respectively were correct. Few cases are reported on the appropriate sentencing pattern for the offence of permitting premises to be used for smoking cannabis. In *Morrison* [1996] 1 Cr App R (S) 263 the offender allowed young people aged 14 or 15 to visit his home and smoke cannabis, but he did not supply them with the drug. Twelve months' imprisonment was upheld. In *Pusser* (1983) 5 Cr App R (S) 225, however, the offender was the licensee of a public house at which cannabis was smoked, though there was no evidence that he used cannabis himself. After a warning, the police searched the premises and found cannabis in several forms. The Court of Appeal described this as 'a bad case' and upheld the sentence of six months' imprisonment.

12.8.3 Class C drug offences

The maximum penalty for producing, supplying, or possession with intent to supply a Class C drug is five years on indictment (MDA 1971, sch. 4); three months, a fine not exceeding £500, or both, summarily. The maximum penalty for possession of a Class C drug is two years on indictment (MDA 1971, sch. 4); three months, a fine not exceeding £200, or both, summarily.

In the Crown Court in 1996, there were 68 offenders sentenced for production, supply, or possession with intent to supply a Class C drug, of whom 46 received immediate custody. There were five offenders sentenced for possession of a Class C drug, one of whom received custody. In the magistrates' courts in 1996, 41 offenders were sentenced for production, supply, or possession with intent to supply a Class C drug, of whom six received immediate custody. There were 89 offenders sentenced for possession of a Class C drug, three of whom received custody.

12.9 SENTENCING FOR ROAD TRAFFIC OFFENCES

It should be noted that where the power to endorse is specified in relation to the offences below, the court must endorse, unless special reasons are established. The court has discretion to disqualify in every case where it endorses a licence. Where mandatory disqualification is indicated, the court must disqualify for at least 12 months, unless special reasons are established (see **10.1**). The power to order disqualification until the offender passes the driving test is considered at **10.1.7**. For causing death by dangerous driving, see **12.1.8**.

12.9.1 Dangerous driving

The maximum penalty for dangerous driving is two years on indictment; six months, a fine not exceeding £5,000, or both, summarily (RTA 1988, s. 2). The court must disqualify for at least 12 months and must endorse the licence (3–11 points) if not disqualified. An extended re-test must be ordered.

When tried summarily, the Magistrates' Association Guidelines (1997) indicate the following:

Aggravating Factors +
avoiding detection or apprehension; competitive driving; racing, showing off; disregard of warnings e.g. from passengers or others in vicinity; evidence of alcohol or drugs; excessive speed; prolonged, persistent, deliberate, bad driving; serious risk, offence committed on bail, previous convictions and failures to respond to previous sentences, if relevant.

Mitigating Factors −
momentary risk not fully appreciated; no alcohol or drugs involved; single incident; speed not excessive.

The Guidelines state that 'injury or damage cannot be *equated* with the degree of danger but may *indicate* it'. The Guidelines advise that magistrates should consider whether the offence is serious enough for a community penalty; the offender's licence must be endorsed and he should be disqualified for at least the compulsory minimum and required to re-test.

In the Crown Court in 1996, there were 1,685 offenders for dangerous driving, of whom 978 received immediate custody, 58 per cent of offenders dealt with. Other significant disposals were community service (255) and fine (161). In the magistrates' courts, there were 2,667 offenders sentenced for the offence, of whom 505 received immediate custody, 19 per cent of offenders dealt with. Other significant disposals were fine (902) and community service (603).

There is no guideline judgment on the offence of dangerous driving, though some of the observations of the Court of Appeal in the guideline case of *Boswell* (1984) 6 Cr App R (S) 257, which relates to the offence of causing death by reckless driving, are relevant (see **12.2.8**). There are several helpful Court of Appeal decisions dealing with sentencing for the most serious instances of dangerous driving. In *Steel* (1993) 14 Cr App R (S) 218 Tudor Evans J said 'when sentencing in cases of [dangerous] driving where personal injury has been caused the judge must consider and give full weight to all the facts and circumstances, including the gravity of the consequences of the driving to members of the public. It seems to us that if a driver drives recklessly he takes his chance as to the consequences of his driving.' In that case the offender, who had a blood alcohol level of 146 mg per 100 ml of blood (the legal limit is 80 mg) was driving at an excessive speed and executed a dangerous overtaking manoevre on a dual carriageway. His car hit the central verge and landed in the other carriageway, where it collided with a motor-cyclist. The motor-cyclist was severely injured, part of his leg being severed in the impact. The Court of Appeal reduced a sentence of 15 months' imprisonment to 12 months, having regard to the fact that the maximum sentence was two years and giving proper weight to mitigation in 'what was a bad case of reckless driving but not at the top of the scale'. Disqualification for five years was upheld. The weight given in this case to the results of the bad driving may be contrasted with the approach taken in *Krawec* (1984) 6 Cr App R (S) 367 (see **12.9.2**).

In *Modeste* (1984) 6 Cr App R (S) 221 the offender, at about 5 am one morning had driven his car at high speed through a series of traffic lights, pursued by an unmarked police car. Nine months' imprisonment was reduced to four months since, although the offender had contested the case, he had no record of bad driving. The disqualification for two years was not altered. In *Garraway* (1988) 10 Cr App R (S) 316 the offender had been seen by police officers driving at an excessive speed in a restricted area. When they pursued him, he drove past a second police car which attempted to stop him, mounting the pavement to do so, and drove away with no lights at high speed, crossing traffic lights at red in a 'deliberate and determined attempt to avoid the police'. Three months' imprisonment was upheld. Another example is *Moore* (1994) 16 Cr App R (S) 536, where the offender had been driving a heavy goods vehicle in patchy fog. He approached roadworks and was unable to stop in time, colliding with a van and injuring the driver. A sentence of nine months' imprisonment was upheld, together with disqualification for five years with an order to retake the driving test thereafter. In *Offer* [1996] 1 Cr App R (S) 143 the offender was seen driving on the motorway at speeds in excess of 100 m.p.h. while using a mobile telephone and with a map draped over the steering wheel. While driving at this speed he narrowly missed a workman who was putting out cones and who was forced to jump out of the way. The offender had an exemplary character and clean record. A prison sentence of three months was reduced to 28 days, and disqualification for 18 months was upheld. In *Bull* [1997] 2 Cr App R (S) 178 the offender drove very close behind another car with his lights full on, and twice overtook the car and slowed down in front of it. The Court of Appeal accepted that this was 'a dreadful exhibition of a course of driving which was intended to terrify' the other driver, who eventually got out and hid in a garden. A sentence of six months' imprisonment was upheld but the term of disqualification was reduced from three years to two.

12.9.2 Careless driving

The maximum penalty for careless driving is a fine not exceeding level 4. The court must endorse (3–9 penalty points) and may disqualify (RTA 1988, s. 3). The offence is triable only summarily.

The Magistrates' Association Guidelines (1997) indicate that:

Aggravating Factors +
    excessive speed, serious risk, high degree of carelessness, offence committed on bail, previous convictions and failures to respond to previous sentences, if relevant.

Mitigating Factors −
    sudden change in weather conditions, minor risk, momentary lapse, negligible/parking damage.

The Guidelines state that 'injury or damage cannot be *equated* with the degree of carelessness but may *indicate* it'. The Guidelines indicate that magistrates should consider whether discharge or a fine is appropriate.

In straightforward cases of careless driving, the appropriate penalty is almost invariably a fine, together with the imposition of penalty points, with the possibility of disqualification in a very bad case. Where the careless driving results in unforeseen and tragic results, a difficult sentencing problem arises. Since the offence is summary only, few opportunities arise for Court of Appeal guidance. In *Krawec* (1984) 6 Cr App R (S) 367, however, the offender had been convicted of careless driving on an indictment for causing death by reckless driving. While riding his motor-cycle he had collided with an elderly pedestrian, who was killed. The offender said that at the time of the collision he had been concentrating on a car in front of him which was turning right at traffic lights and he failed to see the pedestrian until it was too late. The offender was fined £350 and his licence was endorsed with five penalty points. According to Lord Lane CJ, on appeal, 'In our judgment the unforeseen and unexpected results of the carelessness are not in themselves relevant to penalty. The primary considerations are the quality of the driving, the extent to which the appellant on the particular occasion fell below the standard of the reasonably competent driver; in other words, the degree of carelessness and culpability. The unforeseen circumstances may sometimes be relevant to those considerations. In the present case the fact that the appellant failed to see the pedestrian until it was too late and therefore collided with him was plainly a relevant factor. We do not think that the fact that the unfortunate man died was relevant to this charge.' The fine was reduced to £250. *Krawec* was followed in subsequent cases, including *Soutar* (1993) 15 Cr App R (S) 432.

In *Sanders* (1987) 9 Cr App R (S) 312 the offender, aged 44, pleaded guilty to careless driving on an indictment for reckless driving. He had driven at an excessive speed, lost control of his car on a bridge and collided with a car coming in the opposite direction, severely injuring the other driver. The offender was fined £750 and disqualified for 12 months. The Court of Appeal noted the mitigating factors of the offender's guilty plea and his completely clean record. The fine was approved, but the period of disqualification was reduced to six months. Another example is *Soutar* (1993) 15 Cr App R (S) 432, where the offender was driving at 50 mph in a 40 mph limit late at night and failed to see a pedestrian who was crossing the road. The pedestrian was gravely injured. The Court of Appeal adjusted the penalty to a fine of £750 and disqualification for 18 months. In *Downing* [1996] 1 Cr App R (S) 419 the offender, driving a car with four passengers, crossed to the opposite carriageway at a bend, swerved to avoid an oncoming car and collided with a pub sign. Three of the passengers were killed. There was no suggestion that the offender had been drinking. The penalty was a £500 fine together with disqualification for six months.

12.9.3 Drunken driving

The maximum penalty for drunken driving or driving with excess alcohol is six months, a fine not exceeding £5,000, or both. Disqualification (at least 12 months) and endorsement (3–11 penalty points) are obligatory. The offence is triable only summarily.

The level of penalty is closely related to the extent by which the offender exceeds the legal limit. The legal limits are:

(a)   breath: 35 mcg per 100 ml;
(b)   blood: 80 mg per 100 ml;
(c)   urine: 107 mg per 100 ml.

The Magistrates' Association Guidelines (1997) indicate:

Aggravating Factors +
police chase, caused injury/fear/damage, type of vehicle e.g. carrying passengers for reward/large goods vehicle, evidence of nature of the driving, high reading (and in combination with above) ability to drive seriously impaired.

Mitigating Factors −
spiked drinks, moving a vehicle a very short distance.

The following table indicates the suggested level of sentence:

Breath	Blood	Urine	Disqualify	Guide-line	Low income	Average income	High income
36–55	80–125	107–170	12 months	Fine	£180	£450	£1,080
56–70	126–160	171–214	18 months	Fine	£240	£600	£1,440
71–85	161–195	215–260	24 months	Fine	£300	£750	£1,800
86–100	196–229	261–308	24 months	Consider community penalty			
101–115	230–264	309–354	30 months				
116–130	265–300	355–400	30 months	Consider custody			
131 +	301 +	401 +	36 months				

In *Tupa* (1973) 58 Cr App R 234 Roskill LJ commented in respect of an offender who was found to have 289 mg of alcohol per 100 ml of blood (equivalent to 125 mcg of alcohol in breath) that 'this court wishes to make it as clear as it can that, in many cases of this kind where the amount of alcohol imbibed and found in a person's blood after he had been breathalysed is anything like the quantity in the present case, a custodial sentence is entirely proper and ought not to be interfered with on appeal'. In *Shoult* [1996] 2 Cr App R (S) 234 Lord Taylor of Gosforth CJ said that 'We consider that the guidelines as to penalties set out by the Magistrates' Association are sound and appropriate although, of course, each case has to be considered individually on its own merits.'

12.9.4 Refusal to provide a specimen

The maximum penalty for refusing to provide an evidential specimen after driving is six months, a fine not exceeding £5,000, or both. Disqualification (at least 12 months) and endorsement (3–11 penalty points) are obligatory. The offence is triable only summarily. The Magistrates' Association Guidelines (1997) suggest a fine of £600 (average income) and disqualification for 18 months.

The maximum penalty for being drunk in charge of a vehicle or refusing to provide an evidential specimen is three months, a fine not exceeding level 4, or both. Endorsement (10 penalty points) is obligatory. The offence is triable only summarily. The Magistrates' Association Guidelines (1997) suggest a fine of £360 (average income).

The maximum penalty for refusing a roadside breath test is a fine not exceeding level 3. Endorsement (4 penalty points) is obligatory; disqualification is discretionary. The offence is triable only summarily. The Magistrates' Association Guidelines (1997) suggest a fine of £180 (average income).

12.9.5 Failing to stop

The maximum penalty for failing to stop after an accident (or failing to report it) is six months' imprisonment, or a fine not exceeding level 5, or both. Endorsement (5–10 penalty points) is obligatory; disqualification is discretionary. The offence is triable only summarily. The Magistrates' Association Guidelines (1997) suggest a fine of £360 (average income) for either of these offence, and disqualification in serious cases.

12.9.6 Exceeding speed limit

The maximum penalty for exceeding the speed limit is a fine not exceeding level 3 (or level 4 if on the motorway). Endorsement (3–6 penalty points) is obligatory; disqualification is discretionary. The offence is triable only summarily. The Magistrates' Association Guidelines (1997) suggest the following table of penalties for speeding:

			Guideline fines		
Guideline penalty points	*Legal speed limits*	*Excess speed*	*Low income*	*Average income*	*High income*
3	20–30 m.p.h. 40–50 m.p.h. 60–70 m.p.h.	Up to 10 m.p.h. Up to 15 m.p.h. Up to 20 m.p.h.	£60	£150	£360
4 or 5	20–30 m.p.h. 40–50 m.p.h. 60–70 m.p.h.	From 11–20 From 16–25 From 21–30	£90	£225	£540
6 or disqualify (14–56 days)	20–30 m.p.h. 40–50 m.p.h. 60–70 m.p.h.	From 21–30 From 26–35 From 31–40	£135	£335	£810

Relevant aggravating features of the offence are where the vehicle was an LGV, HGV, PCV, or minicab, depending on the location, time of day, and whether the vehicle was drawing a caravan. Relevant mitigating factors are where there was a genuine emergency or where there was a sudden charge of speed limit (e.g., from 40 m.p.h. to 30 m.p.h.).

12.9.7 Driving while disqualified

The maximum penalty for driving while disqualified is six months, a fine not exceeding £5,000, or both (RTA 1988, s. 103). Endorsement (6 penalty points) is obligatory; disqualification is discretionary. The offence is triable only summarily.

The Magistrates' Association Guidelines (1997) indicate that:

Aggravating Factors +
    efforts to avoid detection; long distance driven; planned, long term evasion; recent disqualification, offence committed on bail, previous convictions and failures to respond to previous sentences, if relevant.

Mitigating Factors −
    emergency established; short distance driven, single breach.

The Guidelines suggest that magistrates should consider whether the offence is so serious that only custody can be justified.

12.9.8 Taking vehicle without consent

The maximum penalty for taking a conveyance, usually a motor vehicle, without the owner's consent (known colloquially as TWOC) is six months, a fine not exceeding £5,000, or both (Theft Act 1968, s. 12). The court may disqualify. The offence is triable only summarily.

Magistrates' courts sentenced 6,443 cases of TWOC in 1996, and imposed custodial sentences in 1,231 of those cases (19 per cent). The most frequent disposals were discharge (1,347), fine (930), community service (837), probation (698), attendance centre (490), supervision (494) and combination order (318). The Crown Court also sentenced 185 offenders for this offence where the matter was committed there under CJA 1988, s. 40 or 41. Custody was imposed in 88 of those cases (47 per cent).

The Magistrates' Association Guidelines (1997) indicate:

Aggravating Factors +
    group action, premeditated, related damage, professional hallmarks, vulnerable victim, offence committed on bail, previous convictions and failures to respond to previous sentences, if relevant.

Mitigating Factors −
    misunderstanding with owner, soon returned, vehicle belonged to family or friend.

The Guidelines indicate that magistrates should consider whether the offence is serious enough for a community penalty.

This offence was formerly triable either way. Hence there is some Court of Appeal guidance as to the more serious examples of this offence, though such cases might now be charged as aggravated vehicle-taking (see **12.9.9**). In *Bushell* (1987) 9 Cr App R (S) 537 the offender, aged 17 and with no previous convictions, took a friend's car without permission and subsequently crashed it, damaging it beyond repair. A sentence of 180 hours' community service, together with a disqualification for one year, was upheld by the Court of Appeal. Where the offence is combined with other offences arising out of the same circumstances, an immediate custodial sentence may be appropriate. Thus in *Jeary* (1986) 8 Cr App R (S) 491 the offender, who was aged 18 and had one previous finding of guilt for assault occasioning actual bodily harm, pleaded guilty to two counts of taking a conveyance, two counts of theft and asked for two other offences to be taken into consideration. He was involved with others in taking several cars in the course of an evening and driving them at high speed in a city centre 'just as a bit of fun'. Three cars were damaged, one beyond repair. The offender also admitted taking property from the cars, though most of that was recovered. The Court of Appeal agreed with the sentencer's view that the offences were so serious that a non-custodial sentence could not be justified because, in addition to the unlawful taking, the cars had been deliberately damaged. Four months' detention was upheld.

12.9.9 Aggravated vehicle-taking

The maximum penalty for this offence is two years on indictment (or five years where it is proved that the accident caused the death of the person concerned); six months, a fine not exceeding £5,000 or both, summarily (Theft Act 1968, s. 12A). Disqualification and endorsement (3–11 penalty points) are obligatory.

Magistrates' courts sentenced 1,119 cases of summary aggravated vehicle-taking in 1996, and imposed custodial sentences in 251 of those cases (22 per cent). The Crown Court sentenced 1,574 offenders for aggravated vehicle-taking in 1996, imposing custody in 1,129 cases (72 per cent).

When dealt with summarily, the Magistrates' Association Guidelines (1997) indicate:

Aggravating Factors +
   avoiding detection or apprehension, competitive driving, racing, showing off, disregard of warnings, e.g. from passengers or others in vicinity, group action, pre-meditated, serious injury/damage, serious risk, offence committed on bail, previous convictions and failures to respond to previous sentences, if relevant.

Mitigating Factors −
   impulsive, no competitiveness/racing, passenger only, single incident of bad driving, speed not excessive, very minor injury/damage.

The Guidelines suggest that magistrates should consider whether the offence is so serious that only custody can be justified.

In *Bird* (1993) 14 Cr App R (S) 343 the Court of Appeal said that when sentencing for this offence, relevant aggravating features would be related to the overall culpability of the driver: how bad the driving was and for how long it had lasted and, to a lesser extent, how much injury or damage had been caused. Drink would affect the assessment of culpability, but where drink was a major factor in the case it would be the subject of a separate charge. Mitigation might be found in a guilty plea showing contrition, but the youth of the offender would be of less significance in this type of case than in others, since the offence was committed primarily by young offenders. Subsequent cases include *Evans* (1993) 15 Cr App R (S) 13, where the offender, after spending the afternoon drinking, so that he had a blood alcohol level of 142 mg per 100 ml of blood, took a car which had the keys left in it. He drove for a mile or so and then hit a tree, killing one of the passengers. Nine months' detention in a young offender institution was upheld. Another example is *Robinson* (1993) 15 Cr App R (S) 342, where the offender and an accomplice took the car, used it in connection with a burglary and then drove it at over 100 mph until colliding with another car and injuring its occupants. Twenty-one months' detention in a young offender institution was appropriate for the offender who drove the car, and 18 months for his accomplice passenger. In *Sealey* (1993) 15 Cr App R (S) 189 the offender was a passenger in a car which had been taken unlawfully and then driven at excessive speed and dangerously when chased by the police. Nine months' imprisonment plus disqualification for two years was upheld.

12.9.10   Interference with motor vehicles

The maximum penalty is three months' imprisonment, a fine not exceeding level 4 on the standard scale, or both (Criminal Attempts Act 1981, s. 9). The offence is triable only summarily. In 1996 magistrates sentenced 2,671 offenders for this offence. The main disposals were discharge (736), fine (635), custody (295) and community service (286).

13 Appeals, Rehabilitation and Pardon

The courts which hear appeals against sentence have, it is suggested, two vital tasks to perform in addition to the obvious one of ensuring that any injustice done to an individual appellant when sentenced at first instance is corrected. The first of these tasks is to establish, explain and develop a coherent body of sentencing principles which can be applied by all sentencers. The second is to encourage consistency in sentencing practice, within the appropriate statutory framework and sentencing guideline cases, so that there are not wild fluctuations from one court to another in the way in which similar cases are dealt with. This chapter considers the arrangements for appeal against sentences passed by magistrates' courts and by the Crown Court.

13.1 APPEAL AGAINST SENTENCE PASSED BY A MAGISTRATES' COURT

Most appeals against sentence passed by a magistrates' court are heard by the Crown Court. A small minority are heard by a Divisional Court of the Queen's Bench Division. These methods of appeal are the same whether the sentence was passed for a summary offence or for an offence triable either way, and irrespective of whether the sentence was passed in the youth court or in the adult magistrates' court.

13.1.1 Appeals to the Crown Court

Only the offender may appeal (and of course he may be appealing solely against sentence or, if he pleaded not guilty at his trial, he may appeal against conviction and sentence). There is no right of prosecution appeal against a sentence which is considered to be too lenient (in contrast to the position on appeal from some sentences passed in the Crown Court). The offender's right of appeal is automatic, and lies without any requirement of leave (MCA 1980, s. 108). Notice merely has to be given to the clerk of the magistrates' court which passed the sentence, within 21 days of being sentenced, that the offender intends to appeal. The appellant can appeal against any sentence or order made by the magistrates, apart from:

(a) an order to pay prosecution costs; or
(b) an order under the Protection of Animals Act 1911, s. 2, ordering the destruction of an animal; or
(c) an order connected with the contribution which he should make to his own legal aid costs (*Hayden* [1975] 1 WLR 852).

For avoidance of any doubt, appeal does lie against a magistrates' court's decision to pass an absolute or conditional discharge upon an offender (MCA 1980, s. 108(1A)), though it is unlikely that an offender would wish to appeal against such a sentence. Appeal does lie against an order disqualifying the offender from driving, ordering his deportation, making a hospital order or a compensation order against him or binding him over to keep the peace. On this last, see Magistrates' Courts (Appeals from Binding Over Orders) Act 1956, s. 1(1).

One other possibility, apart from the offender bringing an appeal, is that the Criminal Cases Review Commission (established by the CAA 1995) may choose to refer a case decided in a magistrates' court to the Crown Court if, according to the test in s. 13 of the CAA 1995, there is a real possibility that the conviction or sentence will not be upheld if the reference is made. If such a reference is made, it is to be treated for all purposes as an appeal under MCA 1980, s. 108, except that in these circumstances the Crown Court cannot increase the sentence (CAA 1995, s. 11(6)).

The appeal is heard by a Crown Court judge, probably a circuit judge or a recorder, who sits for this purpose with at least two lay justices. The involvement of lay justices in the appeal process is to ensure that the judge is fully aware of magistrates' sentencing practice. The appeal takes the form of a rehearing of the stage between conviction and sentence. There may be additional material before the court, such as an updated pre-sentence report. Whenever a Crown Court judge sits with lay justices, the latter should take a full part in the proceedings. In the event of disagreement, the majority view prevails. Thus, at least in theory, the magistrates can outvote the judge. The justices must, however, accept any directions from the judge on any point of law relevant to the appeal (*Orpin* [1975] QB 283). The Crown Court may confirm the sentence which was passed by the magistrates and dismiss the appeal, it may reduce the sentence or it may increase it up to the maximum which the magistrates could have imposed. Thus, unlike the Court of Appeal (see **13.2**), the Crown Court does have a limited power to increase sentence on appeal. In fact it is unusual for the Crown Court to increase sentence but, bearing in mind that leave is not required for appeal to the Crown Court, the possibility of increasing sentence may act as a deterrent against unmeritorious appeals. Further, whenever an appeal fails, the appellant may be ordered to pay the prosecution costs (POA 1985, s. 18(1)(b)). The Crown Court can increase any part of the original sentence, even if the appellant is not appealing against that part (SCA 1981, s. 48(2)).

In announcing its decision on an appeal from a magistrates' court, the Crown Court will give only brief oral reasons, which are not reported. Thus, appeal to the Crown Court provides a quick and convenient way of correcting sentencing errors made by the magistrates in individual cases, but this procedure has not developed into a means for Crown Court judges to provide general sentencing guidance for magistrates. A note of the Crown Court's decision, and a short summary of reasons, is sent from the Crown Court to the clerk of the magistrates' court concerned. The clerk may wish to show this to the magistrates who made the original decision.

A decision of the Crown Court on an appeal from a magistrates' court may be appealed by way of case stated (see **13.1.2**) in the same circumstances as a decision by magistrates may be appealed (SCA 1981, s. 28). Judicial review may also be available (SCA 1981, s. 29).

13.1.2   Appeal to the Divisional Court: case stated

Either the offender or the prosecution may appeal to the Divisional Court against a sentencing decision made by a magistrates' court. The appeal must either be on the grounds that the sentence was wrong in law or that the sentence was in excess of jurisdiction (MCA 1980, s. 111). Appeals to the Divisional Court are relatively rare because, whilst many offenders might claim that they were sentenced by magistrates more severely than they should have been, only a handful can claim that the magistrates demonstrably approached their sentencing task on the wrong legal basis or passed a sentence which was beyond their powers. If the offender's complaint is simply that he was sentenced too severely, his recourse must (subject to one exception considered below) be to the Crown Court. Indeed, if an appellant chooses to appeal to the Divisional Court, he loses his right of appeal to the Crown Court (MCA 1980, s. 111(4)). An offender will succeed in such an application only where the sentence imposed by the magistrates was 'truly astonishing' (*Tucker* v *Director of Public Prosecutions* [1992] 4 All ER 901). The imposition of such a sentence shows that the magistrates must have made an error of law.

This method of appeal is known as appeal by case stated. The magistrates, on application by the appellant made within 21 days, are required to draw up a document listing the facts which they found proved, the question of law or jurisdiction upon which the view of the Divisional Court is sought and their own ruling on the matter. The 21-day period is strict, and cannot be varied, even by the High Court (MCA 1980, s. 111(2); *Michael* v *Gowland* [1977] 1 WLR 296). The hearing in the Divisional Court generally takes the form of legal argument based on the facts set out in the case which the magistrates have stated (rather than being a rehearing). The Divisional Court must consist of at least two High Court judges (SCA 1981, s. 66(3)). Often three judges sit, including the Lord Chief Justice and, at his request, Lords Justices of Appeal may also sit. Thus, there is a considerable overlap of personnel between the Divisional Court and the Court of Appeal. Full, reasoned judgments are given, which are reported in the same way as judgments of the Court of Appeal. If a two-judge court is evenly divided, the appeal fails (*Flannagan* v *Shaw* [1920] 3 KB 96). Section 111 of the MCA 1980 states that, in addition to the offender and the prosecution, 'Any person who . . . is aggrieved by the conviction, order, determination, or other proceeding of the court' may state a case for the Divisional Court. It is thus possible that, say, the victim of an offence who feels aggrieved by the failure of the magistrates to make a compensation order in a clear case or, perhaps, by the imposition upon the offender of what the victim regards as an unduly lenient sentence, might take the complaint to the Divisional Court in this way.

In disposing of an appeal, the Divisional Court may 'reverse, affirm or amend' the magistrates' decision, remit the matter to them with their opinion thereon or make any other order it thinks fit (Summary Jurisdiction Act 1857, s. 6). Thus, to take an example encountered frequently in practice, if the prosecution appeals against the magistrates' refusal to disqualify for an offence carrying obligatory disqualification, the Divisional Court could send the case back to the magistrates with its opinion that the facts relied on by the motorist concerned were not capable in law of amounting to special reasons. The magistrates would then have to disqualify for at least 12 months. In other cases, where it is plain what the proper sentence should be, the Divisional Court may simply substitute the correct sentence for the original one.

A decision of the Crown Court on an appeal from a magistrates' court may be appealed by way of case stated in the same circumstances as a decision by the magistrates may be appealed (SCA 1981, s. 28). An application for judicial review might also be made (SCA 1981, s. 29).

13.1.3 Application to the Divisional Court: judicial review

One of the High Court's tasks is to supervise the work of inferior tribunals. In doing so, the High Court exercises its powers of judicial review (principally the issuing of prerogative orders) to control the way in which a wide variety of courts and tribunals, and other persons who are under a duty to act judicially, exercise their powers. Judicial review is available in respect of all decisions taken by magistrates, including sentencing decisions. It is also available with respect to decisions of the Crown Court, when that court is not exercising its jurisdiction in matters relating to trial on indictment. As an alternative to appealing by case stated, a person having 'sufficient interest' in the matter (which certainly includes the offender and the prosecution) who considers that a sentence passed (whether by a magistrates' court, or by the Crown Court on appeal from magistrates) was outside the scope of the court's powers, that person may apply for judicial review of the decision which was made. While the offender and the prosecution clearly have 'sufficient interest' to make an application, it seems clear that other persons, such as the victim of an offence, might have such an interest. The application is to the Divisional Court, which may quash the sentence by means of an order of *certiorari* and replace it with whatever sentence it considers best (SCA 1981, ss. 31(5) and 43). As with case stated, the normal appeal process should have been exhausted before such an application is made.

On the face of it, the case stated and judicial review procedures are available in very similar circumstances and are likely to produce the same result. It was held in *St Albans Crown Court, ex parte Cinnamond* [1981] QB 480 that if magistrates pass a sentence which is far above the normal level of sentence for the offence in question, so that it may fairly be described as 'harsh and oppressive', they thereby err in law or act in excess of jurisdiction, and consequently the Divisional Court has power to reduce that sentence, even though the sentence passed was within the magistrates' statutory powers. The Divisional Court stated in *Universal Salvage* v *Boothby* (1983) 5 Cr App R (S) 428, that the Court is entitled to assume, either on a case stated or on an application for judicial review, that magistrates must have erred in law in a case where they have passed a sentence grossly out of line with good sentencing practice.

It seems that, where both case stated and judicial review might be available to an applicant, the former is the preferable course to choose because it enables the facts found by the magistrates, or by the Crown Court, to be placed more clearly before the Divisional Court. See further *Morpeth Justices, ex parte Ward* (1992) 95 Cr App R 215.

13.2 APPEAL BY OFFENDER AGAINST SENTENCE PASSED BY THE CROWN COURT

Appeals against sentences passed by the Crown Court are heard by the Court of Appeal (Criminal Division). This is so whether the sentence was passed following the offender's conviction on indictment or following his summary conviction and committal for sentence. This has been the case since 1907, when the Court of Criminal Appeal (as it was then called) was created.

All the Lords Justices of Appeal are members of the Court of Appeal (Criminal Division) (SCA 1981, s. 2(2)). In addition, the Division has certain ex officio members, notably the Lord Chief Justice, who is its president (SCA 1981, s. 3(2)). Although all the Lords Justices are entitled to sit in the Criminal Division, in practice only a minority do so, chiefly those who have had experience of the criminal courts either at the Bar or as a judge at first instance. The Lords Justices are assisted by High Court judges who may be requested (in effect, required) by the Lord Chief Justice to act as judges of the Criminal Division (s. 9(1)). Much of the Division's work is, in fact, carried out by High Court judges although, as one would expect, a judge is not allowed to be involved in any way in the disposal of an appeal against sentence which he imposed when sitting as a Crown Court judge (s. 56(2)). Any number of courts of the Criminal Divison may sit at any one time (s. 3(5)). For the purposes of determining an appeal against sentence, or granting or refusing any application connected with an appeal against sentence, a court is validly constituted if it comprises at least two judges qualified to sit in that Division (s. 55(4)). Decisions may be taken by a majority, but if a two-judge court is divided the case must be reassigned and re-argued before three judges (s. 55(5)). Only one judgment is given, that being pronounced either by the senior judge or such other member of the court as he directs to pronounce it (s. 59). Typically, a court hearing appeals against sentence might consist of the Lord Chief Justice plus two High Court judges or a Lord Justice plus one or two High Court judges, or even just two High Court judges. It should be noted that many ancillary decisions connected with an appeal (e.g. granting leave to appeal) do not have to go before a court but may be taken by a single judge, either a Lord Justice or a High Court judge requested by the Lord Chief Justice to act as a judge of the Criminal Division (see CAA 1968, s. 31). It should also be noted that the administration of the Division's work is in the hands of an official, the Registrar of Criminal Appeals, and his staff. In addition, the Registrar has certain quasi-judicial powers (e.g. in respect of granting legal aid).

As a result of the broad definition of 'sentence' contained in CAA 1968, s. 50(1), almost any order made by a Crown Court judge in respect of a convicted offender is capable of being the subject of an appeal to the Crown Court against sentence. This is so whether the order is a punishment or an ancillary order. The exceptional orders against which there is no possibility of an appeal are:

(a)   the mandatory sentence of life imprisonment, custody for life or detention during Her Majesty's pleasure which, depending on the offender's age, must be passed on an offender convicted of murder;

(b)   a recommendation that an offender sentenced to life for murder should serve a minimum term in prison before being considered for early release on licence (*Aitken* [1966] 1 WLR 1076);

(c)   an order concerning the contribution which the offender should make to his own legal aid costs, since even an acquitted defendant may be ordered to make such a contribution (*Raeburn* (1982) 74 Cr App R 21).

Subject to obtaining the Court of Appeal's leave, an offender convicted on indictment may appeal to the Court of Appeal against any sentence passed on him for the offence (CAA 1968, s. 9). Again, subject to obtaining leave, an offender summarily convicted and then committed by the magistrates to the Crown Court to be sentenced may appeal to the Court of Appeal against the Crown Court's sentence, but only if:

(a)   it was one of custody for six months or more;
(b)   a suspended sentence was brought into effect;
(c)   the offender was disqualified from driving, or an order was made for his deportation; or
(d)   the sentence is one which the convicting court had no power to pass (CAA 1968, s. 10).

Where the Crown Court has passed two or more sentences on the offender, an application for leave to appeal against any one of the sentences is treated as an application in respect of all of them (s. 11(2)).

Another possibility, apart from the offender bringing an appeal, is that the Criminal Cases Review Commission (established by the CAA 1995) may choose to refer a case decided in the Crown Court to the Court of Appeal if, according to the test in s. 13 of the CAA 1995, there is a real possibility that the conviction or sentence will not be upheld if the reference is made. If such a reference is made it is treated for all purposes as an appeal under the CAA 1968.

Appeals to the Court of Appeal against sentence normally lie only with leave of the court itself (CAA 1968, s. 11). It seems that leave is needed even where the trial court did not have power to pass the sentence it did (*Briggs* (1909) 1 Cr App R 192). The only exception is where the Crown Court judge who has just passed the sentence then grants a certificate that the case is fit for an appeal against sentence without the leave of the Court of Appeal (s. 11(1) and (1A)). This occurs very infrequently (an exceptional case is *Grant* (1990) 12 Cr App R (S) 441). So, for all practical purposes, leave of the Court of Appeal is always required. The granting of leave to appeal is customarily considered by a single judge. In summary, the procedure is that the appellant's solicitors serve on the Registrar of Criminal Appeals a Notice of Appeal and Grounds of Appeal. Notice should be served within 28 days of the date on which sentence was passed or order made (s. 18). If sentence was subsequently varied under SCA 1981, s. 47, then notice should be served within 28 days of that variation (SCA 1981, s. 47(5)). The Court of Appeal has power to extend the time-limit for giving notice (CAA 1968, s. 18(3)), but an application for an extension of time should be accompanied with an explanation for the delay (*Cullum* (1942) 28 Cr App R 150). The grounds are usually settled by counsel, and must identify with reasonable detail the matters relied on by the appellant to justify a reduction in sentence.

The Registrar of Criminal Appeals then obtains all the relevant documents, such as a transcript of the proceedings in the Crown Court at the sentencing stage, together with copies of any reports which were put before the Crown Court judge. These documents, plus the Notice and Grounds of Appeal, are handed to the single judge who considers them privately and without hearing legal argument (CAA 1968, s. 31(1)). If the judge thinks that there is a reasonable possibility that an appeal might succeed, leave to appeal is granted; otherwise it is refused. In the latter event the would-be appellant may renew the application for leave to a full court of the Criminal Division, provided that the Registrar is served with notice within 14 days from the date of refusal. There are a number of variations on the above procedure. In particular, it is always open to an appellant to settle his own Grounds of Appeal. Also, to save time, an application for leave to appeal is occasionally referred at once to a court of the Criminal Division (rather than going to a single judge first) and that court may then treat the application for leave as the hearing of the appeal and reduce the appellant's sentence forthwith.

At the hearing of the appeal, the Court of Appeal will have before it the documents considered by the single judge, plus possible additional documents, such as an up-to-date pre-sentence report or, if the offender was given a custodial sentence, a report on his progress at the institution at which he has been detained. Counsel for the appellant will then present the arguments in favour of reducing the sentence. The prosecution are unlikely to be represented, this being in keeping with their generally neutral attitude to sentence.

In disposing of an appeal their lordships may quash the sentence or order appealed against and replace it with whatever they consider appropriate, provided that:

(a) the replacement sentence or order is one which the Crown Court had power to make when dealing with the appellant; and

(b)   the appellant, taking the case as a whole, is not dealt with more severely on appeal than he was at the Crown Court (CAA 1968, s. 11(3)).

In other words the Court of Appeal may reduce but not increase sentence on an appeal by the offender against sentence. This may be contrasted with the powers of the Crown Court when dealing with an appeal against sentence imposed by magistrates (see **13.1.1**). The Court of Appeal formerly had power to increase sentence on appeal, but this power was removed in 1966. However, provided that the total effect of what the Court of Appeal does is not to increase the aggregate sentence, their lordships may make the sentence for one of several offences for which the appellant was dealt with at Crown Court more severe. Or, where two orders were imposed on sentence for a single offence, they can both be adjusted so as to achieve no more severe a result (*McLaren* (1983) 5 Cr App R (S) 332, where the offender's fine was increased but his driving disqualification reduced). There are several cases which have considered what does or does not amount to being 'more severely dealt with on appeal'. In *Socratous* (1984) 6 Cr App R (S) 33 the offender was put on probation for shoplifting and imprisoned for three months for contempt of court which consisted of intimidating a witness. The Court of Appeal held that it was wrong in principle to make a probation order at the same time as passing an immediate custodial sentence, and so the Court varied the probation order to three months' imprisonment, to be served concurrently with the three months for contempt. Although the sentence for shoplifting was clearly more severe, the Court was acting within its powers because the sentence's overall effect was to the appellant's advantage in that he would not serve any longer in prison and, when he was released, he would not be subject to probation supervision. It was held in *Whittaker* [1967] Crim LR 431 that a sentence of imprisonment for a fixed term of years could not be varied to a life sentence on appeal, and this is still true after the CJA 1991, since s. 2(4) of that Act states that a life sentence is to be regarded as a custodial sentence 'for a term longer than any actual term'. An immediate term of imprisonment is more severe than a suspended sentence, even where the immediate term is much shorter than the suspended term (*Thompson* (1977) 66 Cr App R 130).

It may appear that the lack of any general power in the Court of Appeal to increase sentence on appeal means that there is no bar to unmeritorious appeals. There is one way, however, in which the Court of Appeal may penalise an appellant for commencing such an appeal. That is to direct that some or all of the time the offender has spent in custody between the submission of the Grounds of Appeal and the dismissal of his application for leave to appeal shall not (as it normally would) count towards service of any custodial sentence imposed on him by the Crown Court (CAA 1968, s. 29). This is known as a direction for loss of time. Such a direction cannot, however, be made in a case where counsel (rather the appellant himself) settled the Grounds of Appeal, unless the appellant insists on renewing the application for leave to appeal after it has been turned down by the single judge (see *Practice Direction* (*Crime: Sentence: Loss of Time*) [1980] 1 WLR 270). This is because counsel is under a duty not to settle Grounds of Appeal unless they are reasonable and there is a genuine prospect of success. It would therefore be unfair to penalise an appellant who had merely pursued his appeal to the single judge stage in reliance on counsel's advice that there were reasonable grounds upon which an appeal could be based.

Where an appellant is appealing against a custodial sentence, the single judge has power to grant bail pending determination of the appeal (CAA 1968, ss. 19(1) and 13). If the single judge refuses bail, an application may be made to a court of the Criminal Division. Unless the sentence appealed against is very short, there is a marked reluctance to grant bail. In *Watton* (1979) 68 Cr App R 293 Geoffrey Lane LJ commented that the circumstances in which bail would be appropriate are 'exceptional'. Consequently the majority of appellants have spent several weeks, if not months, in custody before their appeals are heard. It quite often happens then that the Court of Appeal will reduce the term of the sentence appealed against to one which will permit the appellant's immediate release. Such cases are somewhat unreliable guides to the level of sentence the court considers appropriate for the type of case in question. It may be that their lordships really think the original sentence should not have been a custodial one at all, but prefer not to say so; they may genuinely consider that the time the appellant has already served in custody represents about the proper penalty; or they may even approve of what the Crown Court judge did but feel, perhaps in the light of a report from the custodial institution where he has been held thus far, that the offender has learned his lesson and should, as an act of clemency, be released.

At the outset of this chapter it was said that there were two vital tasks which the appellate system should perform in sentencing in addition to ensuring the correction of injustice done to an individual offender on sentence. These are to establish, explain and develop sentencing principles and to encourage sentencing consistency. How well does the body of Court of Appeal sentencing decisions measure up to these objectives? The Court of Criminal Appeal soon after its creation in 1907 accepted that these objectives were part of its remit, but took the line, which the Court of Appeal has adhered to ever since, that it should only alter a sentence where that sentence was 'wrong in principle' (*Gumbs* (1926) 19 Cr App R 74). The principle that the maximum sentence should be reserved for the most grave cases was developed early on; other principles have evolved gradually over the years, on a case-by-case basis. The principled development of a jurisprudence of sentencing was hampered by a number of factors, such as the lack of systematic reporting of appellate sentencing decisions, the failure to regard sentencing decisions as in any sense precedents and the prevailing orthodoxy of substantial sentencing discretion. The development of useful guidance for lower courts was hampered by the fact that the Court of Appeal only had the opportunity to see an atypical selection of cases, generally appeals brought by offenders against long custodial sentences for very serious offences.

There have been a number of important developments in this area over the last 30 years:

(a)   The first change has been that reporting of sentencing decisions has become more widespread and systematic. This trend began with the reports and commentaries by Dr Thomas in the *Criminal Law Review* and has continued with the introduction in 1979 of a set of law reports, the *Criminal Appeal Reports (Sentencing)*, dedicated to Court of Appeal and Divisional Court sentencing decisions and, from 1982, the publication of a looseleaf sentencing encyclopaedia *Current Sentencing Practice*, which is also edited by Dr Thomas. While in the past there was a reluctance amongst judges to accept the citation to them by counsel of previous sentencing decisions, on the ground that sentencing decisions turned on their own particular facts, such citation is now the norm in sentencing appeals.

(b)   The second development has been the gradual appreciation amongst practitioners of the importance of more formal legal principles in sentencing. One of the most important areas has been the development of improved procedural arrangements at the sentencing stage, arising from a large number of cases clustered around the decision in *Newton* (1982) 4 Cr App R (S) 388. These cases were considered in Chapter 3. This has also been reflected in sentence selection. The importance of giving reasons for sentence is now well accepted and is formally required by statute in a range of situations. There has been considerable development in the shaping of sentence decision-making, partly through legislative change and partly through judicial development. Section 1(4A) of the CJA 1982 was a milestone in this area, requiring sentencers for the first time to articulate clearly their reason for imposing a custodial sentence on a young offender, and requiring them to select that reason from a limited statutory menu. This kind of approach led to the more general statutory framework of the CJA 1991 (see Chapter 2).

(c)   Thirdly, the Court of Appeal, under Lawton LJ, Lord Lane CJ, Lord Taylor CJ, and now Lord Bingham CJ, have taken the opportunity, when dealing with a particular sentencing appeal or a batch of sentencing appeals gathered together to illustrate a particular point, to develop more general and principled sentencing guidance. The so-called 'guideline judgments' are of greater significance as precedents than other sentencing appeals, and they form the basis for the sentencing pattern for a particular type of offending. Some of the most important of the guideline judgments are *Aramah* (1982) 4 Cr App R (S) 407 on drug offences, *Barrick* (1985) 7 Cr App R (S) 143 on theft in breach of trust, *Billam* (1986) 8 Cr App R (S) 48 on rape, *Attorney-General's Reference (No. 1 of 1989)* [1989] 1 WLR 1117 on incest, and *Brewster* [1998] 1 Cr App R (S) 181 on house burglary, and the guideline judgments are set out, or referred to, where appropriate, in Chapter 12 of this book. These judgments acquire special authority by virtue of their being given by the Lord Chief Justice. While it could in theory be argued that much of what is contained in them is not directly relevant to the case or cases in hand and is obiter, it is quite clear that they are intended to be, and are accepted as being, binding on the lower courts. The judgments typically indicate a normal sentencing bracket for a particular offence, or sometimes several sentencing brackets for different forms of the offence. Then a series of significant aggravating and mitigating factors, which may often accompany such cases, are identified. It is rare for the Court of Appeal to go further and to attempt to quantify the relative weight of such factors, or to suggest how the sentencer should deal with a case in which several aggravating factors appear, or where there appear both aggravating and mitigating factors. These adjustments are left largely to the sentencer's discretion, though examples of comparable cases involving sentencing for the same offence might be considered at this point. The main function of the guideline judgment is to direct the sentencer towards the correct sentencing bracket or 'starting point', and to identify relevant aggravating and mitigating factors. Sometimes the Court of Appeal will also point out a factor which should not be taken into account, but which a sentencer might be misled into thinking is relevant (e.g. the victim's 'contributory negligence' in a rape case: *Billam*).

Despite these changes, the body of sentencing principles generated by the Court of Appeal is still of limited help to the lower courts. This is because it remains true that the majority of cases before the Court of Appeal lie at the top end of the range of seriousness. This means that, in general, those offences and those sentencing measures which are most frequently encountered in the courts are subject to the least amount of helpful guidance. While there are numerous Court of Appeal decisions on manslaughter, rape and armed robbery, for example, there is relatively little guidance on some of the most commonly encountered offences, such as theft, deception, and handling stolen goods. The Crime and Disorder Bill, by cl. 75, for the first time places a statutory duty on the Court of Appeal to produce new sentencing guidelines for criminal offences, and to revise existing ones. Clause 76 further requires the Lord Chancellor, after consultation, to establish a Sentencing Advisory Panel to act as an advisory body to the Court of Appeal in framing those guidelines. The Court of Appeal's power to produce the guidelines will arise either where a case of the relevant type is before it on appeal (and the guidelines will be issued as part of the Court's judgment in that case), or where the Sentencing Advisory Panel refers a category of case to the Court for the framing of new guidelines or the revising of old ones, in which case the guidelines will be published separately.

As we have seen, one of the principal limitations on the usefulness of Court of Appeal guidance has been the restricted class of cases which come before it. This, in turn, is because until 1988 it was only the offender who had the opportunity to bring an appeal against sentence and so, in practice, appeals were confined to cases where the sentence was thought to be much too severe. The procedure, introduced by the CJA 1988, allows the Attorney-General to refer a Crown Court sentence which is thought to be unduly lenient, to the Court of Appeal. This is considered next.

13.3   REFERENCE BY ATTORNEY-GENERAL IN RESPECT OF SENTENCE PASSED BY THE CROWN COURT

The effect of ss. 35 and 36 of the CJA 1988 is that where the Attorney-General considers that an offender's sentence was unduly lenient in proceedings in the Crown Court he may refer the matter to the Court of Appeal (Criminal Division) for a review of that sentence (s. 36(1)). This is subject to:

(a)   the Court of Appeal giving leave; and

(b)   the offence for which sentence was passed being either one which is triable only on indictment or one which is triable either way and specified in an order made by the Home Secretary by statutory instrument (CJA 1988, s. 35(3)).

The reference procedure has been extended by the Criminal Justice Act 1988 (Reviews of Sentencing) Order 1994 (SI 1994/19) to cover offences of indecent assault, threats to kill, cruelty to a person under 16 and attempting to commit or inciting the commission of those offences. It was further extended by the Criminal Justice Act 1988 (Reviews of Sentencing) Order 1995 (SI 1995/10) to include some cases of serious fraud.

In *Attorney-General's Reference (Nos. 3, 4 and 5 of 1992)* (1993) 14 Cr App R (S) 191 the offenders had pleaded guilty to conspiracy to evade the prohibition on the importation of a Class A drug (LSD). They also pleaded guilty to certain offences triable either way, which were charged on a separate indictment. The Court of Appeal increased the sentence for conspiracy from two and a half years to five years in the case of two of the offenders and four years in the case of the other. It was accepted that the Court had no power to review the sentences for the offences triable either way, but the Court regarded the fact that the conspiracy had been committed while the offenders were on bail for those offences as an aggravating feature of the conspiracy, in part justifying the increase in sentence. For the purposes of a sentencing reference by the Attorney-General, 'sentence' has the same wide meaning as it has under CAA 1968, s. 50(1), except that it does not extend to an interim hospital order (CJA 1988, s. 35(6)). It extends to a decision by the Crown Court to grant a conditional discharge (*Attorney-General's Reference (No. 57 of 1995)* [1996] 2 Cr App R (S) 159 and to a decision by the Crown Court to defer sentence (*Attorney-General's Reference (No. 22 of 1992)* [1994] 1 All ER 105).

If the Court of Appeal does give leave for reference, in disposing of the appeal it will, in contrast to appeals against sentence brought by offenders, hear argument from both sides. Upon an Attorney-General's sentencing reference the Court of Appeal may quash the sentence passed by the Crown Court and replace it with the sentence which it thinks is appropriate. It is specifically provided in s. 36(2) that the Attorney-General may refer a sentence to the Court of Appeal if he considers that the judge has erred in law, but the powers of the Court of Appeal to review the sentence go much wider than that. In the majority of cases the judge has understood his powers correctly but has chosen, in his discretion, to pass a sentence that appears to the Attorney-General to be too lenient in all the circumstances of the case. The replacement sentence must be one which the Crown Court would have had power to pass on the offender (s. 36(1)). Of course, the judge whose sentence is under consideration cannot sit in the appeal (s. 36(4)).

In *Attorney-General's Reference (No. 4. of 1989)* (1989) 11 Cr App R (S) 517 the Court of Appeal set out its approach to the disposition of references under s. 36. According to that case, two main considerations must be borne in mind in all such cases.

(a) The Court of Appeal should only increase a sentence which is unduly lenient. It is not enough that the members of the Court of Appeal would themselves have imposed a more severe sentence. To be 'unduly lenient' a sentence must fall outside the range of sentences which the judge, applying his mind to all the relevant factors, could reasonably consider appropriate. In that connection regard must be had, of course, to reported cases and, in particular, to guideline judgments of the Court of Appeal. Nevertheless, it must be remembered that the trial judge is particularly well placed to assess the weight to be given to various competing considerations, and that leniency in sentencing is, in itself, not a vice. In *Attorney-General's Reference (No. 5 of 1989)* (1990) 90 Cr App R 358 the Court of Appeal said that it would not intervene unless it had been shown that there was some error of principle in the judge's sentence, so that public confidence would be damaged if the sentence was not altered. This test has been mentioned in several subsequent cases. In *Attorney-General's Reference (No. 16 of 1992)* (1993) 14 Cr App R (S) 319 a sentence of four years for a particular case of rape was 'as lenient as it possibly could be, without this Court interfering with it'.

(b) The second point was that, even where a sentence is considered to be unduly lenient, the Court of Appeal has a discretion whether to exercise its powers. It may be, for instance, that in the light of events which have occurred since the trial, the sentence now turns out to be an appropriate one, or that it would be unfair to the offender or detrimental to others to increase it. An example is *Attorney-General's Reference (No. 8 of 1992)* (1993) 14 Cr App R (S) 130. A youth aged 17 was convicted of manslaughter on an indictment for murder. Following an argument in a park and a degree of provocation, he stabbed the unarmed deceased in the chest with a lock-knife which he had been carrying for his own protection. After the incident, the offender was attacked in his own home by friends of the deceased seeking revenge. The trial judge imposed a probation order for two years. The Court of Appeal was clear that the sentence was unduly lenient, but considered whether it should, in the exercise of its discretion, vary it. The Court gave weight to the fact that the jury at the trial had added a rider to the verdict saying that they had 'great sympathy' for the offender and asking the judge to pass a lenient sentence, that the offender was a young man of 'excellent reputation' who was training for a professional career, that since the trial the offender's family had moved to another area and that the offender 'has become as a result of this matter a religious young man'. The sentence was, nonetheless, increased to two years' detention in a young offender institution.

(c) The Court of Appeal has said on several occasions that in cases where it does increase the sentence it will bear in mind that the offender has undergone the additional stess of having to be sentenced twice over. This may be especially the case where the Court of Appeal, in the event, varies a non-custodial sentence to a custodial one. Some discount from the properly justified sentence would, then, often be appropriate. In *Attorney-General's Reference (No. 15 of 1992)* (1993) 14 Cr App R (S) 324, a case where a sentence of nine months' imprisonment suspended for 18 months for buggery committed by a man on his wife without her consent was increased to four years' immediate imprisonment, Lord Taylor CJ said that 'allowance should be made for the fact that the offender has to be sentenced on a second occasion, that he will have had a second period of suspense awaiting the decision of the court, and . . . that he is a man who, having been allowed his liberty after his trial, now finds himself called upon to serve a sentence of imprisonment'.

It will be appreciated that points (a) and (b) above, while designed to ensure fairness for the appellant, tend to rob the procedure of much of its potential usefulness as a source of guidance. They entail that a decision of the Court of Appeal not to interfere with a sentence does not mean that the original sentence is viewed by the Court as being correct; merely that it is not so far wrong as to justify correction. In *Attorney-General's Reference (No. 16 of 1992)* (1993) 14 Cr App R (S) 319 Lord Taylor CJ said that it should not be thought that 'leaving this sentence of four years unaltered is to be regarded as a guideline . . . the level of sentencing which ought to be applied at first instance cannot be translated directly from the decision in this case'. While a similar principle against 'tinkering' with sentence also operates where the Court is dealing with offender appeals against sentence, there is even greater reluctance to vary a sentence to the offender's detriment unless the case for doing so is very clear indeed. Requirement (c), that the Court should have regard to 'double jeopardy' (that the offender has had to undergo the strain of being sentenced twice) also tends to dilute the guidance value of these cases. Typically, where the Court does increase the sentence, it states that it has made such an allowance but does not make it clear what discount has been allowed the offender. When no figure is given for the discount, the sentence selected by the Court of Appeal may well be a misleading guide. Thus in *Attorney-General's Reference (No. 8 of 1992)* (see above) the Court of Appeal varied the sentence upwards to two years' detention, commenting that this was 'a much shorter sentence than would otherwise have been the case'. It would be helpful in all cases for the Court to indicate clearly what the proper sentence should have been, and then either to dismiss the appeal on the basis that the difference between that sentence and the one actually imposed is not sufficient to justify any variation, or to increase the sentence, making it clear what discount has been allowed the offender in all the circumstances.

13.4   APPEAL TO HOUSE OF LORDS AGAINST SENTENCE

Appeal lies to the House of Lords against the decisions of both the Court of Appeal (Criminal Division) and the Divisional Court (CAA 1968, s. 33 and Administration of Justice Act 1960, s. 1(1)(a), respectively). In the case of the Divisional Court, a direct appeal to the House of Lords is possible only if the decision in question was taken in a criminal cause or matter, but that obviously will be so where the decision relates to sentencing. The right of appeal to the House of Lords is not restricted to the offender. In particular, if the offender in the Crown Court successfully appealed to the Court of Appeal, the prosecution could in theory then appeal to the House of Lords to have the original Crown Court decision reinstated. An appeal to the House of Lords is restricted to cases where:

(a)   the lower court certifies that there is a point of law of general public importance; and

(b)   either the lower court or the House of Lords gives leave to appeal.

It is the first restriction which makes appeals to the House of Lords on sentencing matters so rare. Sentencing rarely raises points of law, let alone points of law of general public importance. Moreover the argument that an exceedingly harsh sentence necessarily raises a point of law was rejected in *Ashdown* [1974] 1 WLR 270. It was said in that case that, provided the sentence was within the sentencing court's powers, the propriety of the sentence could never raise a point of law of general public importance. The rarity value of sentencing appeals which reach the House of Lords is neatly illustrated by the remarks of Lord Diplock in *Courtie* [1984] AC 463, in which he said that the case came before the House in the guise of an appeal against sentence only, but in fact raised questions of substantive law. He then continued: 'I cannot myself recall any criminal appeal confined to sentence only having come before this House since I started to sit here in 1968.'

Where a sentencing matter has gone to the Court of Appeal on a reference by the Attorney-General (see **13.3**) and the Court of Appeal has concluded its review and either upheld an allegedly lenient sentence or varied it, the Attorney-General or the person to whose sentence the reference relates may refer a point of law involved in the sentence to the House of Lords for their opinion. The House of Lords may either deal with the matter themselves or remit the case to the Court of Appeal to be dealt with there (CJA 1988, s. 36(5)). Such a reference to the House of Lords can only be made with the leave of the House of Lords or the Court of Appeal, and leave requires that there is a point of law of general public importance involved in the case (s. 36(6)). No such cases have yet been reported.

Although not an appeal against sentence as such, a recent decision of the House of Lords which is closely related to sentencing is *Secretary of State for the Home Department, ex parte Venables* [1997] 3 WLR 23. This was a case involving judicial review of the powers of the Home Secretary with respect to the sentence of detention during Her Majesty's pleasure, the mandatory sentence for offenders convicted of murder who were aged under 18 at the time of the offence. The House of Lords held that the welfare of the child or young person was of great importance, and had to be balanced against the gravity of the crime committed when determining the date at which he should be considered for early release. Their lordships also held that it was wrong for the Home Secretary to take into account an orchestrated campaign by a popular newspaper when fixing the appropriate period to be served. Another example is *Secretary of State for the Home Department, ex parte Doody* [1994] 1 AC 531, which is concerned with the Home Secretary's powers when setting the 'tariff period' of mandatory life sentence to be served by adult murderers.

13.5 DISQUALIFICATIONS UPON CONVICTION

While detained in custody following conviction for any offence, an offender is legally incapable of voting at any parliamentary or local government election (Representation of the People Act 1983, s. 3(1)). Any person who has been convicted of an offence and had imposed upon them a custodial sentence of three months or more, whether suspended or not, is disqualified from being, or being elected, a member of a local authority for a period of five years from the date of the conviction (Local Government Act 1972, s. 80(1)(d)). A person convicted of an offence for which he has received a custodial sentence of three years or more is prohibited from possessing or acquiring any firearm or ammunition for life (Firearms Act 1968, s. 21). Where the sentence was for three months or more but for less than three years, the ban lasts for five years. An offender who has served at any time a custodial sentence of five years or more, or within the last ten years has served a custodial sentence of any length, or within the last ten years has had imposed on them a suspended prison sentence or a community service order, or within the last five years have been placed on probation, is disqualified from jury service (Juries Act 1974, sch I, Part II).

On conviction for treason (a rare event), a person is rendered incapable of holding any military or related office, being an MP or, indeed, voting (Forfeiture Act 1870, s. 2).

By the Sex Offenders Act 1997, where a person has been convicted of a sexual offence to which the Act applies, or where he has been found not guilty of a sexual offence by reason of insanity, or has been found to be under a disability (unfit to plead) and to have done the act charged against him, he is required to register his name, address and date of birth, and any subsequent changes, with the police. These come into effect automatically upon conviction. The duration of the notification period varies with the sentence passed for the sexual offence. In the case of a custodial sentence for life, or for a fixed term of 30 months or more, or a hospital order with restrictions, the period is indefinite. If the custodial sentence was for more than six months but less than 30 months the period is 10 years, and for a custodial sentence for six months or less the period is seven years. If the offender received a hospital order without restrictions, the period is seven years, and for any other sentence the period is five years. For offenders aged under 18 the fixed periods are reduced by half. Offenders who have been formally cautioned after admitting the offence, as well as those convicted, are subject to the requirements of the Act (see the Sex Offenders (Certificate of Caution) Order 1997 (SI 1997/1921)).

The definition of 'sexual offence' for the purposes of the 1997 Act (listed in sch. 1) is slightly different from that in the CJA 1991, s. 31(1) (see **4.2.7**). In particular, the offence of burglary with intent to commit rape under the Theft Act 1968, s. 9 and the offence under MHA 1959, s. 128 are included in s. 31(1) of the CJA 1991 but not in sch. 1 to the 1997 Act, and the offences under s. 160 of the CJA 1988 (possession of indecent photographs of a child) and s. 170 of the Customs and Excise Management Act 1979 (penalty for fraudulent evasion of duty on certain goods) are included in sch. 1 but are not listed in s. 31.

None of these disqualifications are affected by the operation of the ROA 1974 (see **13.6**).

13.6 REHABILITATION OF OFFENDERS

Under the ROA 1974, after the passage of time convictions may become 'spent', and a convicted person may consider himself legally 'rehabilitated'. When a conviction is spent, the offender is treated for a range of purposes as if he had never been convicted of the offence concerned. While ROA 1974, s. 7(2) excludes from its scope the operation of criminal proceedings, *Practice Direction (Crime: Spent Convictions)* [1975] 1 WLR 1065 none the less requires that spent convictions which appear on an offender's record should be marked as such, and that nobody should refer in open court to such spent convictions without the authority of judge. This matter was considered at **3.4.4**.

13.6.1 Main provisions of the ROA 1974

The protection of the ROA 1974 applies to all convictions, except those which result in an excluded sentence (see below). The term 'conviction' is given a broad meaning in the Act, but would not extend to cover the imposition of a bind over to keep the peace which is imposed at any time except at sentence (see **7.2**). It is unclear whether the Act applies to a recommendation for deportation. An offence for which an order for absolute or conditional discharge is made does not count as a conviction for a variety of purposes (see **7.1.4**), but s. 1(4) of the Act provides that these are convictions which may be the subject of rehabilitation. Certain sentences fall outside the scope of the Act and an offender who has received such a sentence can never become rehabilitated with respect to that conviction. Those excluded sentences are:

(a) life imprisonment;
(b) imprisonment or detention in a young offender institution (or youth custody) for a term exceeding 30 months;
(c) detention during Her Majesty's pleasure;
(d) detention under CYPA 1933, s. 53 for a term exceeding 30 months; and
(e) custody for life.

The commission of an offence resulting in one of these excluded sentences also acts so as to prevent any earlier unspent conviction from becoming spent.

Rehabilitation periods in respect of other sentences are set out in the table below. Some sentences mentioned in the table appear in square brackets; these have been abolished by statute and are no longer available to sentencers, but will still appear on criminal records. The relevant period runs from the date of conviction, even where sentence is deferred. Some of the rehabilitation periods are, as indicated, reduced where the offender was under 18 years of age at the date of conviction.

Sentence	*Rehabilitation period*
A sentence of imprisonment or detention in a young offender institution [or youth custody] for more than 6 months but not more than 30 months	10 years for an adult, 5 years for a juvenile
A sentence of imprisonment or detention in a young offender institution [or youth custody] of 6 months or less	7 years for an adult, $3\frac{1}{2}$ years for a juvenile
[A sentence of detention in a detention centre]	3 years
A fine	5 years for an adult, $2\frac{1}{2}$ years for a juvenile
A community service order	5 years for an adult, $2\frac{1}{2}$ years for a juvenile
Probation, (offender placed on probation before 3 February 1995) bind over to keep the peace or be of good behaviour, conditional discharge	The date the order or bind over ceases or 1 year, whichever is the longer
Probation (offender placed on probation on or after 3 February 1995)	5 years for an adult, $2\frac{1}{2}$ years for a juvenile

Sentence	*Rehabilitation period*
Supervision order [or care order]	The date the order ceases or 1 year, whichever is the longer
Attendance centre order	1 year after the order expires
Hospital orders	5 years from the date of conviction or 2 years after the order expires, whichever is the longer
Disqualification and other orders imposing disability, prohibition, or other penalty	The date the order ceases to have effect
Absolute discharge	6 months

Some sentences or orders do not appear in this table. For the purposes of the ROA 1974, a suspended sentence of imprisonment counts as a sentence of immediate imprisonment of the same length. The relevant length of a partly suspended sentence (a sentence now abolished by the CJA 1991) is the length of the served and suspended parts of the sentence added together. Two consecutive custodial sentences are aggregated for the purposes of the ROA 1974 (s. 5(9)(b)). Where an offender receives more than one sentence or order in respect of a single offence, the relevant rehabilitation period is the longest of those applicable (s. 6(2)).

A person who has been convicted can only become rehabilitated under the Act if that person is not reconvicted within the relevant rehabilitation period (s. 6(4)). If an offender is reconvicted of anything other than a summary offence (s. 6(6)), the rehabilitation period for the first offence continues to run until the expiry of the period for the second offence. This is a very important rule, and has the practical effect that persistent offenders are unlikely to have any spent convictions, even if the earliest of these may have been committed many years before. An exception to the subsequent offence rule is that periods arising from orders of disqualification, disability, prohibition or other penalty are to be disregarded (s. 6(5)), whether such disqualification etc. relates to the first or the second conviction. If an excluded sentence (see above) is passed for the second offence, then this excludes both convictions permanently from the possibility of rehabilitation.

13.6.2 Exceptions to the scope of the ROA 1974

The practical operation of the ROA 1974 is affected by the far-reaching exceptions which apply to it. The relevant law can be found in the Rehabilitation of Offenders Act 1974 (Exceptions) Order 1975, as amended.

The exceptions have the effect that none of the provisions of s. 4(2) of the Act apply (and hence details of spent convictions must be revealed) in relation to any questions asked by a person, in the course of their office or employment, in order to assess the suitability of a person for the following:

(a) *professions*: doctor, lawyer, accountant, dentist, vet, nurse, midwife, optician or pharmacist;

(b) *offices or employments*: judges, prosecutors, justices' clerks, police, prison staff, traffic wardens, probation officers, employees of local authorities who have access in their normal duties to vulnerable persons (including those over 65 years of age, persons suffering from serious illness or mental disorder, persons addicted to drink or drugs, persons who are blind, deaf or dumb and persons who are substantially and permanently handicapped by illness or injury), any employment concerned with the provision of health services where the person employed has access to persons in receipt of such services in the normal course of their duties, any employment concerned with the provision to persons under 18 of accommodation, care, leisure and recreational facilities, schooling, social services, supervision or training, where the person has access in the normal course of their duties to persons under 18;

(c) *regulated occupations*: firearms dealer, occupations requiring a betting or gaming licence, senior officials in insurance companies, management of any place approval of which is required by the Secretary of State under the Abortion Act 1967, or management of a nursing home requiring registration under statute, or any occupation involving the supervision of explosives under the Explosives Act 1875;

(d) *licences*: firearm certificate or shotgun certificate issued under the Firearms Act 1968, licence to keep explosives issued under the Explosives Act 1875.

The ROA 1974 does not affect the operation of any of the statutory provisions mentioned in **13.5** by which, in consequence of conviction, a person is subject to a disqualification or prohibition (s. 7(1)(d)).

13.7 PARDON AND RELEASE ON COMPASSIONATE GROUNDS

As an act of grace, the Sovereign may either grant a free (or conditional) pardon or remit the rest of an offender's sentence (the royal prerogative of mercy: CAA 1968, s. 49). In practice, of course, these powers are not exercised personally by the Sovereign, but are administered on her behalf by Home Office officials.

A pardon is normally granted only where it has been established that the original conviction was unjustified, such as where a miscarriage of justice is shown to have occurred. An example encountered not infrequently is where an offender has been convicted and fined for speeding, only for it to emerge later that the stretch of road concerned was not subject to a speed limit. Although it was once thought that the pardon 'wipes out not only the sentence for the offence but the conviction and all its consequences' (*Hay* v *Tower Division of London Justices* (1890) 24 QBD 561), it is now clear that the pardon 'does not in any sense eliminate the conviction', although it relieves the subject of the effect of any penalties as a result of conviction (*Foster* [1985] QB 115). In that case the Court of Appeal held that a person who had been pardoned in respect of an offence of rape, following later confession to that offence by another man, might properly still bring an appeal against conviction. See also *Bolton Justices, ex parte Scally* [1991] 1 QB 537. A pardon may have great symbolic importance to those concerned, so that pardons are sometimes sought by an offender's relatives long after the offender's death. See, for example, *Secretary of State for the Home Department, ex parte Bentley* [1994] QB 439. In that case the court indicated that the prerogative was a 'flexible power', and that the grant of a conditional, rather than a free, pardon was appropriate where 'a mistake had been made' and the offender should not have been executed. There are about 200 pardons granted every year. A person pardoned may receive compensation under CJA 1988, s. 133.

In contrast to the grant of a pardon, remission of an offender's sentence by executive authorities certainly does not imply that the original conviction was unjustified: it means merely that the rest of the sentence need not be served. Remission is generally used for one of two reasons. The first is where a prisoner has given particular help to the authorities in the detection of other offences or the apprehension of other offenders. The second is in cases where the offender is discovered to be suffering from a terminal disease and has a short time left to live. Sentence is remitted so that the person need not die in custody (see **2.2.4(i)**). Sentence is remitted by executive authority under statutory provisions such as CJA 1991, s. 36, in about 150 cases each year. In such cases the matter may be drawn to the attention of the Home Office by a member of staff of the prison, the offender or the offender's family or by any other interested party. There is also the possibility of remission of other sentences. For the circumstances in which fines may be remitted see **6.5**.

Appendix

SECURE TRAINING ORDERS

The Criminal Justice and Public Order Act 1994 contained powers by which the Crown Court and the youth courts would be able to impose a new custodial sentence on young offenders — the secure training order. The measure was designed by the Conservative administration at a time when there was particular public concern about persistent serious offending by young offenders, some of whom were under the age of 15 and hence too young be eligible for the sentence of detention in a young offender institution. The secure training order was intended to provide an appropriate custodial sentence for 12, 13 or 14 year-olds in cases where they had not committed an offence serious enough to qualify them for a sentence of detention under s. 53(2) of the CYPA 1933. Implementation of the powers to impose secure training orders was deferred by the government until such time as secure training centres had been built and put into service under the privatisation initiative. For further discussion of the background to these orders see M. Wasik and R. Taylor (1995).

In the event, by the time of the change of government in 1997 only one of the five planned secure training centre was nearing completion. The new government had its own ideas about custodial sentences for young offenders, which are set out in the Crime and Disorder Bill. These involve the introduction of detention and training orders, which in principle are to be available for offenders aged between 10 and 17, but subject to certain restrictions for those aged under 15 (see further on detention and training orders **4.3.10**). It was widely assumed that the detention and training order would simply supersede the secure training order, with the latter sentence never being brought into force, and indeed the CDB contains provision for the repeal of the relevant powers in the CJPOA 1994. Early in 1998, however, the Labour government announced that it would, after all, implement the secure training order provisions, so as to allow the courts to make use of the solitary secure training centre which, by that time, had been completed. The upshot is that from April 1998 the secure training order is made available to the courts, until such time as the detention and training order powers in the CDB are brought into force and it is repealed. At present the government anticipates that the detention and training order will not be implemented before the summer of 1999. It is therefore appropriate to say something here about the secure training order.

The secure training order is available where an offender aged under 15 but not less than 12 is convicted of an imprisonable offence and the court is satisfied that the offender

(a)   was not aged under 12 when the offence was committed; and
(b)   has been convicted of three or more imprisonable offences; and

(c)   either on this or a previous occasion has been found by a court to be in breach of a supervision order, or has been convicted of an imprisonable offence while subject to a supervision order (s. 1(5)).

When the court passes a secure training order it must specify that the above three conditions are satisfied. The secure training order also qualifies as a custodial sentence for the purposes of the CJA 1991, ss. 1 to 4 so that, in addition to the above conditions, the general statutory criteria for determining the imposition and length of a custodial sentence, and the obtaining of a pre-sentence report, will apply. The CJA 1982, s. 3 (prohibition of imposition of custodial sentence on unrepresented offender) will also apply. It is not clear from the wording whether the 'three or more imprisonable offences' are offences for which the offender is being sentenced on the present occasion, or include his previous convictions. Time spent in custody or in secure accommodation on remand will count towards a secure training order sentence (CJA 1967, s. 67(5)).

The order itself comprises two parts, the first half being a period of detention and the second half a period of supervision. The total length of the secure training order must be specified by the court which imposes it, and must be for not less than six months and not more than two years (s. 1(3)). The normal restrictions on the imposition of custodial sentences by magistrates' courts entail that the passing of a secure training order will be a sentence at the top end of the sentencing range for the lower courts. During the supervision part of the order the offender will be supervised by a probation officer, a social worker or such order person as the Secretary of State shall designate (s. 3). As explained above, it is envisaged that the secure training order will be served by the offender in a secure training centre. Section 2(2) of the 1994 Act states that where accommodation in a secure training centre 'is not immediately available' the court may commit the offender to such place and on such conditions as the Secretary of State may direct or as the Secretary of State may arrange with a local authority, voluntary organisation, or a person carrying on a registered children's home. Committal to such alternative premises can be for a period not exceeding 28 days which, on application, can be extended for further periods of up to 28 days. Home Office Circular No 2/1998 explains that such accommodation is intended to be temporary and should not be used to hold trainees indefinitely. This Circular is reprinted at (1998) 162 *Justice of the Peace* 226–228. It states that the purpose of the secure training centre regime is to provide

. . . high standards of education and training tailored to individuals' needs and with programmes specifically designed to tackling trainees' offending behaviour and to force them to face up to the consequences of their actions. Although the centres will be secure they will accommodate trainees in a safe environment with a domestic, not institutional, atmosphere. Continuity throughout the entire sentence will be provided by appointing a supervising officer at the start who will help to draw up training plans and follow these through after release . . . As a minimum, programmes will include the following:

(a)   25 hours every week conventional education appropriate to their academic level and based on the national curriculum;
(b)   a one-hour daily programme for tackling offending behaviour and crime avoidance;
(c)   regular practical tuition in social skills and domestic training;

(d)   the opportunity through award schemes and constructive use of leisure time in the evenings and at weekends to acquire and develop interests to occupy leisure time while in custody and after release.

See further the Secure Training Centre Rules (SI 472/1998)

Power to make a secure training order came into effect on March 1, 1998, but only in relation to offences committed on or after that date, by virtue of the Criminal Justice and Public Order Act 1994 (Commencement Order No 12 and Transitional Provision) Order 1998. The only available secure training centre is at Cookham Wood near Rochester in Kent, and it opened in April 1998. The Home Office Circular makes the point that courts will wish to take account of the distance of that training centre from the offender's home before making an order. Plans to complete four further secure training centres are at various stages of completion. A centre at Onley in Northamptonshire is due to open early in 1999 and a third, in Consett, Durham, will open later that year.

If an offender who has been subject to a secure training order fails to comply with, or contravenes any requirement in, the supervision part of the order, the offender may be arrested and brought before the youth court. That court may order the offender to be detained in a secure training centre for the remainder of the order or for three months (whichever is the shorter period) or impose a fine on the offender not exceeding level 3 on the standard scale.

References and Bibliography

Advisory Council on the Penal System (1978), *Sentences of Imprisonment: A Review of Maximum Penalties* (HMSO).

Ashworth, A.J. (1995), *Sentencing and Criminal Justice*, 2nd ed. (Butterworths).

Ashworth, A.J. and von Hirsch, A. (1997), 'Recognizing elephants: the problem of the custody threshold' [1997] *Criminal Law Review* 187.

Bottoms, A. *et al.* (1990), *Intermediate Treatment and Juvenile Justice* (HMSO).

Brody, S.R. (1975), *The Effectiveness of Sentencing* (Home Office Research Study No. 35) (HMSO).

Clarkson, C. and Morgan, R. (1995), *The Politics of Sentencing Reform* (Oxford).

Floud, J. and Young, W. (1981), *Dangerousness and Criminal Justice* (Heinemann).

Glidewell, Rt Hon. Lord Justice (1992), 'The Judicial Studies Board' in Munro, C. and Wasik, M., *Sentencing, Judicial Discretion and Training* (Sweet and Maxwell).

H.M. Inspectorate of Probation (1993), *The CJA 1991 Inspection* (Home Office).

Hodgson Committee (1984), *Profits of Crime and their Recovery* (Cambridge Studies in Criminology, 52) (Heinemann).

Home Office (1990), *Crime, Justice and Protecting the Public* (HMSO).

Home Office (1995b), *National Standards for the Supervision of Offenders in the Community*, 2nd ed. (HMSO).

Home Office (1996a), *Protecting the Public* (Cm 3190) (HMSO).

Home Office (1996b), *Sentencing and Supervision of Sex Offenders* (Cm 3304) (HMSO).

Home Office (1997a), *No More Excuses — A New Approach to Tackling Youth Crime in England and Wales* (Cm 3809) (HMSO).

Home Office (1997b), *Criminal Statistics for England and Wales 1996* (Cm 3764) (HMSO).

Home Office (1997c), *Criminal Statistics for England and Wales, Supplementary Tables 1996*, (Home Office).

Law Commission (1987), *Binding Over: the Issues* (Working Paper No. 103) (HMSO).

Law Commission (1994), *Binding Over* (Law Com No. 222) (HMSO)

Magistrates' Association (1997), *Sentencing Guidelines* (Magistrates' Association).

Mair, G. (1988), *Probation Day Centres* (Home Office Research Study No. 100) (HMSO).

Mair, G. and McNee, C. (1990) *Electronic Monitoring: the Trials and Their Results* (Home Office Research Study No. 120) (HMSO)

Martinson, R. 'What works: questions and answers about prison reform' *Public Interest* (Spring) 22.

McGuire, J. (1995), *What Works: Reducing Reoffending* (John Wiley).

Moxon, D. (1988), *Sentencing Practice in the Crown Court* (Home Office Research Study No. 103) (HMSO).

Sallon, C. and Bedingfield, D. (1993), 'Drugs, money and the law' [1993] *Criminal Law Review* 165.

Schichor, D. and Sechrest, D. (1996) *Three Strikes and You're Out* (Sage).

Sprack, J. (1997), *Emmins on Criminal Procedure*, 7th ed. (Blackstone Press).

Stone, N. (1994), *A Companion Guide to Enforcement* (Owen Wells).

Thomas, D.A. (1979), *Principles of Sentencing* (Heinemann).

Thomas, D.A. (1982), *Current Sentencing Practice* (Sweet and Maxwell, loose-leaf).

Thomas, D.A. (1997), 'Sentencing legislation: the case for consolidation' [1997] *Criminal Law Review* 406.

von Hirsch, A. (1976), *Doing Justice* (Hill and Wang).

Walker, N. and Padfield, N. (1996), *Sentencing Theory, Law and Practice,* 2nd ed. (Butterworths).

Wasik, M. and von Hirsch, A. (1994), 'Section 29 revised: previous convictions in sentencing' [1994] *Criminal Law Review* 409.

Wasik, M. and Taylor, R. (1995), *Blackstone's Guide to the Criminal Justice and Public Order Act 1994* (Blackstone Press).

Index